An Introduction to Programming with C++

Third Edition

Diane Zak

THOMSON
COURSE TECHNOLOGY™

Australia • Canada • Mexico • Singapore • Spain • United Kingdom • United States

An Introduction to Programming with C++, Third Edition,
by Diane Zak

Managing Editor:
Jennifer Muroff

Product Manager:
Alyssa Pratt

Associate Product Manager:
Janet Aras

Editorial Assistant:
Christy Urban

Product Marketing Manager:
Angie Laughlin

Production Editor:
Melissa Panagos

Cover Designer:
Steve Deschene

Text Designer:
Julie Malone

Compositor:
GEX Publishing Services

Manufacturing Coordinator:
Laura Burns

Printed in the United States of America.

1 2 3 4 5 6 7 8 9 QWT 07 06 05 04 03

For more information, contact Course Technology, 25 Thomson Place, Boston, Massachusetts, 02210.

Or find us on the World Wide Web at: www.course.com

ISBN 0-619-06473-0

Contents

Tutorial 2

Tutorial 3

Tutorial 4

Tutorial 5

Tutorial 6

Tutorial 7

Tutorial 8

The Repetition Structure 331

Tutorial 9

More on the Repetition Structure 377

Tutorial 10

Tutorial 11

Tutorial 12

Tutorial 13

More on Arrays 539

Tutorial 14

Database Access 565

Appendix A

Appendix B

Appendix C

Appendix D

Preface

An Introduction to Programming with C++, Third Edition is designed for a beginning programming course. This book uses the Microsoft Visual C++ .NET programming language to teach programming concepts.

Organization and Coverage

An Introduction to Programming with C++, Third Edition contains 14 tutorials that present hands-on instruction, and 4 appendixes. In the tutorials, students with no previous programming experience learn how to plan and create well-structured programs. By the end of the book, students will have learned how to write programs using the sequence, selection, and repetition structures, as well as how to create and manipulate functions, classes, objects, sequential access files, and arrays.

Approach

An Introduction to Programming with C++, Third Edition is distinguished from other textbooks because of its unique approach, which motivates students by demonstrating why they need to learn the concepts and skills presented. This book teaches programming concepts using a task-driven, rather than a command-driven, approach. By working through the tutorials—which are each motivated by a realistic case—students learn how to create programs that solve problems they are likely to encounter in the workplace. This is much more effective than memorizing a list of commands out of context.

Features

An Introduction to Programming with C++, Third Edition is an exceptional textbook because it also includes the following features:

- **"Read This Before You Begin" Section** This section is consistent with Course Technology's unequaled commitment to helping instructors introduce technology into the classroom. Technical considerations and assumptions about hardware, software, and default settings are listed in one place to help instructors save time and eliminate unnecessary aggravation.
- **Lessons** Each tutorial is divided into two lessons—Concept and Application. The Concept Lesson introduces various programming concepts, including programming syntax and code examples. The Application Lesson begins with a case, or business-related problem, which the student could reasonably expect to encounter in business. In the remainder of the Application Lesson, the student creates the program that solves the case problem. Concepts are combined in later Application Lessons so that the student has the opportunity to use multiple programming features to efficiently solve programming tasks.

- **Step-by-Step Methodology** The unique Course Technology methodology keeps students on track. They click or press keys always within the context of solving a specific problem or the Application Lesson case. The text constantly guides students, letting them know where they are in the process of solving the problem. The numerous illustrations include labels that direct students' attention to what they should look at on the screen.
- **Help?** Help? notes anticipate problems that students might encounter and help them resolve these problems on their own. This feature facilitates independent learning and frees the instructor to focus on substantive conceptual issues, rather than on common procedural errors.
- **TIP** Tip notes provide additional information about a procedure—for example, an alternative method of performing the procedure. They also relate the OOP terminology learned in the Overview to applications created in Visual C++ .NET.
- **Mini-Quizzes** Mini-quizzes are strategically placed to test the student's knowledge at various points in each tutorial. Answers to the quiz questions are provided in the tutorials, allowing the student to determine whether he or she has mastered the material covered thus far before continuing with the lesson.
- **Summary** Following each Concept Lesson is a Summary, which recaps the programming concepts and commands covered in the lesson.
- **Questions and Exercises** Each Concept Lesson concludes with meaningful, conceptual Questions that test students' understanding of what they learned in the lesson. The Questions are followed by Exercises, which provide students with additional practice of the skills and concepts they learned in the lesson. Each Application Lesson also includes Exercises, many of which provide practice in applying cumulative programming knowledge or allow the student to explore alternative solutions to programming tasks. The answers to the even-numbered Exercises (except Discovery and Debugging Exercises) can be found at **www.course.com** in the "Downloads" section.
- **Discovery Exercises** are designated by the icon in the margin, and encourage students to challenge and independently develop their own programming skills.
- **Debugging Exercises** One of the most important programming skills a student can learn is the ability to correct problems, called "bugs", in an existing program. The Debugging Exercises, which are designated by the icon, provide an opportunity for students to detect and correct errors in an existing program.
- **Microsoft Visual Studio .NET Professional Edition 60-Day Trial Edition**

Teaching Tools

The following supplemental materials are available when this book is used in a classroom setting. All of the teaching tools available with this book are provided to the instructor on a single CD-ROM.

Electronic Instructor's Manual The Instructor's Manual that accompanies this textbook includes:

- Additional instructional material to assist in class preparation, including suggestions for lecture topics.
- Solutions to all end-of-lesson Questions and Exercises.

ExamView® This textbook is accompanied by ExamView, a powerful testing software package that allows instructors to create and administer printed, computer (LAN-based), and Internet exams. ExamView includes hundreds of questions that correspond to the topics covered in this text, enabling students to generate detailed study guides that include page references for further review. The computer-based and Internet testing components allow students to take exams at their computers, and also save the instructor time by grading each exam automatically.

PowerPoint Presentations This book comes with Microsoft PowerPoint slides for each tutorial. These are included as a teaching aid for classroom presentation, to make available to students on the network for tutorial review, or to be printed for classroom distribution. Instructors can add their own slides for additional topics they introduce to the class.

Data Files Data Files, containing all of the data necessary for steps within the tutorials and the end-of-lesson Exercises, are provided through the Course Technology Web site at **www.course.com**, and are also available on the Teaching Tools CD-ROM.

Solutions Files Solutions to end-of-lesson Questions and Exercises are provided on the Teaching Tools CD-ROM and may also be found on the Course Technology Web site at **www.course.com**. The solutions are password protected.

Distance Learning Course Technology is proud to present online courses in WebCT and Blackboard, to provide the most complete and dynamic learning experience possible. When you add online content to one of your courses, you're adding a lot: self tests, links, glossaries, and, most of all, a gateway to the 21st century's most important information resource. We hope you will make the most of your course, both online and offline. For more information on how to bring distance learning to your course, contact your local Course Technology sales representative.

Acknowledgments

I would like to thank all of the people who helped to make this book a reality, especially Jennifer Muroff and Alyssa Pratt (Product Managers), Melissa Panagos (Production Editor), and Shawn Day (Quality Assurance Manuscript Reviewer). I am grateful to the many reviewers who provided invaluable comments on the manuscript, in particular: James Chegwidden, Tarrant County College; Steven Gramlich, Pasco Hernando Community College; Sally Sullivan, Prince George's Community College; John Humphrey, Asheville–Buncombe Technical Community College; and Mark Shellman, Gaston College.

Finally, I dedicate this book to the loving memory of Mary Clare Karnick. We all loved you more.

Diane Zak

Read This Before You Begin

To the User

Data Files

To complete the steps and exercises in this book, you will need data files that have been created for this book. Your instructor will provide the data files to you. You also can obtain the files electronically from the Course Technology Web site by connecting to **www.course.com**, and then searching for this book title.

Each tutorial in this book has its own set of data files, which are stored in a separate folder within the CppNet folder. For example, the files for Tutorial 3 are stored in the CppNet\Tut03 folder. Similarly, the files for Tutorial 4 are stored in the CppNet\Tut04 folder. Throughout this book, you will be instructed to open files from or save files to these folders.

You can use a computer in your school lab or your own computer to complete the tutorials and exercises in this book.

Using Your Own Computer

To use your own computer to complete the tutorials and exercises in this book, you will need the following:

- **A 486-level or higher personal computer running Microsoft Windows XP.**
- **Microsoft Visual Studio.NET Professional Edition, or Enterprise Edition, installed on your computer.**
- **Data files.** You will not be able to complete the tutorials and exercises in this book using your own computer unless you have the data files. You can get the data files from your instructor, or you can obtain the data files electronically from the Course Technology Web site by connecting to **www.course.com**, and then searching for this book title.

Visit Our World Wide Web Site

Additional materials designed especially for you might be available for your course on the World Wide Web. Go to **www.course.com**. Periodically search this site for more details.

To the Instructor

To complete the tutorials in this book, your students must use a set of data files. These files are included in the Instructor's Resource Kit. They may also be obtained electronically through the Course Technology Web site at **www.course.com**. Follow the instructions in the Help file to copy the data files to your server or standalone computer. You can view the Help file using a text editor such as WordPad or Notepad. Once the files are copied, you should instruct your users how to copy the files to their own computers or workstations.

The tutorials and exercises in this book were tested using the final version of Visual Studio .NET on a Microsoft Windows XP system.

Course Technology Data Files

You are granted a license to copy the data files to any computer or computer network used by individuals who have purchased this book.

Overview

An Overview of a Microcomputer System

Objectives

After completing this overview, you will be able to:

- Describe the components of a microcomputer system
- Explain the relationship between hardware and software
- Explain the history of programming languages

An Introduction to a Microcomputer System

In 1975, the first **microcomputers**, also called **personal computers**, appeared in the marketplace. Since then, the microcomputer has become so popular that it is difficult to imagine what a person ever did without one. Imagine typing a letter on a typewriter, or keeping track of your investments manually, or drawing the blueprints for a house without the aid of a computer!

Since the introduction of the microcomputer, situations and tasks that once were considered impossible are now commonplace. For example, **telecommuting**, where an employee works from home and uses a microcomputer to communicate with his or her office, is now an option available to many business professionals. Microcomputers also allow you to access information from around the world, via the Internet and the World Wide Web, from the comfort of your home, office, or school.

Figure 1 shows a typical microcomputer system found in most businesses and homes.

Figure 1: A typical microcomputer system

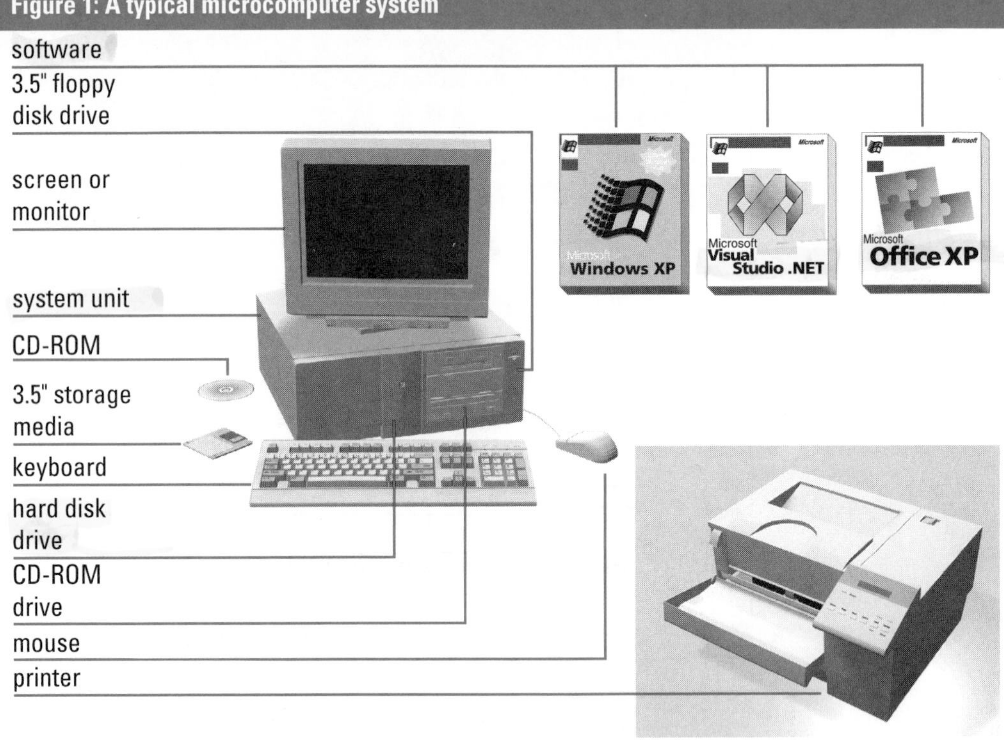

Notice that a **microcomputer system** is composed of both hardware and software. **Hardware** refers to the physical components of the microcomputer system. **Software** refers to the programs (step-by-step instructions) that tell the hardware how to perform a task. In the next section, you learn about the hardware and software found in a microcomputer system and how they interact.

An Overview of Hardware and Software

As Figure 1 shows, the hardware in a microcomputer system consists of a **system unit**, which is the case or box that contains the main circuit boards and storage devices, and other devices, called peripheral devices.

Peripherals

A **peripheral device** is a device that is attached to the system unit. Peripheral devices extend the capabilities of the computer system, and they provide the user a means by which he or she can communicate with the computer. The three categories of peripheral devices are input devices, output devices, and auxiliary storage devices.

An **input device** allows you to communicate with the computer by entering data into it. Examples of commonly used input devices are a keyboard, mouse, and scanner. As you are working through the lessons and exercises in this book, you will use an input device—the keyboard—to enter your C++ program instructions into the computer.

An **output device** allows the computer to communicate with you by displaying or printing information. Examples of commonly used output devices are a monitor and printer. You will use a monitor to display the C++ instructions you enter into the computer, and you will use a printer to print the instructions. You also will use a monitor and printer to display and print the results of your C++ programs.

Auxiliary storage devices, the third category of peripheral devices, allow you to permanently store information. Floppy disk drives, CD-ROM drives, and hard disk drives are the most common auxiliary storage devices. These storage devices use an auxiliary storage media—a floppy disk, a CD-ROM disk, or a hard disk—to store the information. You will use an auxiliary storage device to save your C++ program instructions. By doing so, you will be able to use the program again without having to retype it.

tip

Auxiliary (which means "additional" or "secondary") storage devices and auxiliary storage media are so named because they provide storage capability in addition to that available in the internal memory of the computer.

Internal Memory

Now look inside the system unit to see what it contains. See Figure 2.

Figure 2: The inside of the system unit

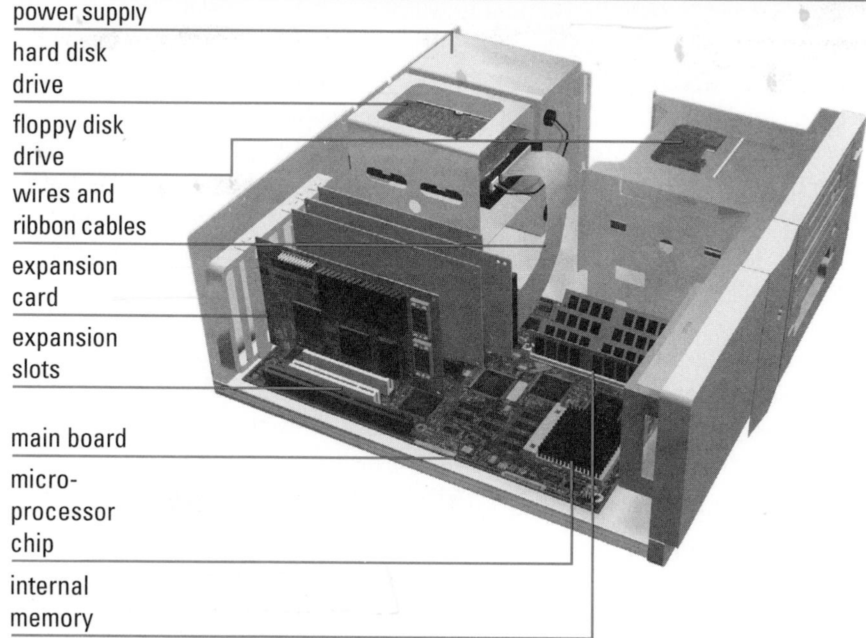

The system unit houses an area called **internal memory**, which is simply an ordered sequence of memory cells contained on chips—integrated circuits residing on silicon. Internal memory is like a large post office, where each memory cell, like each post office box, has a unique address, and each can contain mail. Figure 3 illustrates this comparison.

Figure 3: Comparison of post office boxes to internal memory

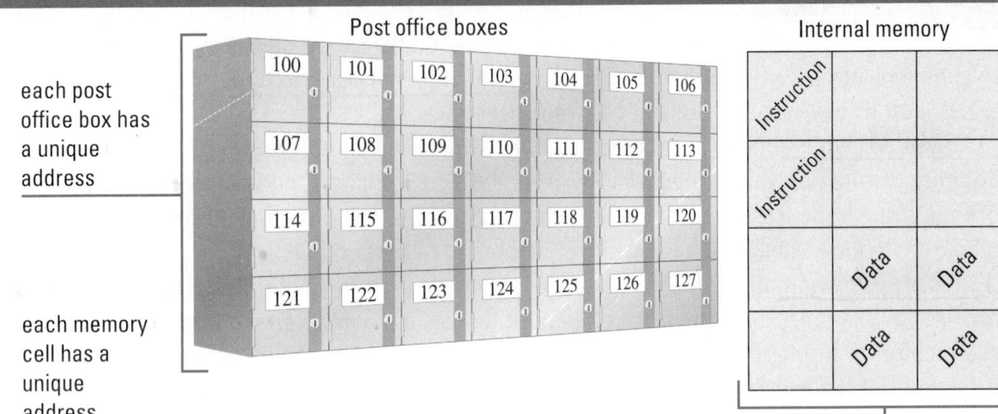

Unlike a post office box, which can contain many pieces of mail at the same time, a memory cell can store only one piece of mail at any time. The mail found in a memory cell is typically either a program instruction or an item of data. **Data** refers to the information processed by a program. The data may be input by the user, such as the number of hours an employee worked, or it may be the result of a calculation made by the computer, such as an employee's gross pay.

Some of the chips in internal memory are **Random-Access Memory (RAM)** chips; others are **Read-Only Memory (ROM)** chips. There are two major differences between a RAM chip and a ROM chip. First, while the computer is on, the user can both write information to and read information from the memory cells located on a RAM chip. In contrast, a user can only read information from a ROM chip's cells; he or she cannot write information to the memory cells on a ROM chip. Second, a RAM chip is volatile, which means that any information stored on the chip is temporary. The information contained on a RAM chip is lost when the computer is turned off or loses power unexpectedly. A ROM chip, on the other hand, is non-volatile; instructions remain on a ROM chip even when the computer is off.

The memory cells located on ROM chips contain instructions written there by the manufacturer. When you turn a computer on, these instructions perform an automatic self-test of the computer. The self-test makes sure that the different components of the computer are working properly. If all is well, the instructions contained on the ROM chips search either the computer's hard drive or a floppy drive for a set of instructions known as the operating system, which is discussed in the Types of Software section later in this Overview.

The instructions on the ROM chips direct the computer to read the operating system instructions from either the hard disk or a floppy disk. As the instructions are read, they are written to the RAM chips in internal memory, where they are stored until the computer is turned off (or loses power). In addition to the operating system instructions, the RAM chips also store program instructions and data entered from the keyboard or read from a file previously saved on a disk.

The Central Processing Unit

Besides internal memory, the system unit also houses the **Central Processing Unit (CPU)**, which is the brain of the computer. The CPU resides on a microprocessor chip, which is a single integrated circuit, and it contains two principal components—the control unit and the Arithmetic/Logic Unit (ALU). It also contains special high-speed storage locations called **registers**.

The **control unit** in the CPU directs the flow of information from one part of the computer to another. The control unit is responsible for making sure that the computer correctly processes the program instructions and data stored in internal memory.

The second component of the CPU, the **Arithmetic/Logic Unit** (**ALU**), performs the arithmetic calculations and comparison operations for the computer. If the control unit instructs the computer to add two numbers, it is the ALU that performs the addition. The ALU also would be responsible for comparing the number of hours an employee worked with the number 40 to determine whether the employee should receive overtime pay.

The ALU uses the registers in the CPU to hold the data that is being processed. It uses a special register, called an **accumulator**, to temporarily store the result of an arithmetic or comparison operation. Figure 4 illustrates how the CPU processes an instruction to add the numbers 4 and 5.

Figure 4: Diagram of how the CPU processes an instruction to add two numbers

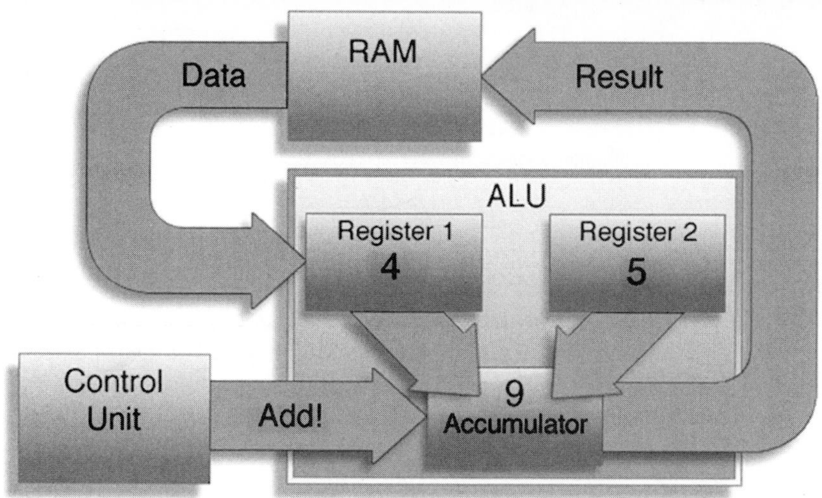

First, the control unit sends the data to be processed—in this case, the numbers 4 and 5—from RAM to the ALU, where it is held in registers. The control unit then sends a signal to the ALU, directing it to add both numbers. After performing the necessary operation, the ALU stores the result—in this case, the number 9—in the accumulator. The control unit then sends the contents of the accumulator to RAM so it can be output, saved on a disk, or used for further processing.

Types of Software

The hardware component of a computer system isn't of much use without software. Recall that the term *software* refers to the instructions that tell the computer how to perform a task. Software typically is divided into two general categories: system software and application software. Each of these categories contains various types of software, as shown in Figure 5 (on the next page).

The purpose of **system software** is to manage the computer and its peripheral devices. As Figure 5 indicates, included in the system software category are operating systems, device drivers, utilities, and programming languages. **Operating systems** are programs that coordinate the activities within the computer and allow both you and the computer to communicate with each other. Windows, Mac OS, UNIX, and Linux are popular operating systems. **Device drivers** are programs that help the computer control a peripheral device, and **utilities** are programs that allow the user to perform tasks such as formatting a disk, copying data from one disk to another, and protecting the computer from viruses. **Programming languages** are programs that allow a user to control how the computer processes data to produce the information that he or she wants. You learn more about programming languages in the next section.

Unlike system software, **application software** allows a user to computerize a task that he or she might otherwise perform manually, such as writing a letter, preparing a budget, or playing a game. Included in the application software category are productivity software (such as word processors, spreadsheets, databases, and graphics programs), entertainment software (such as computer games), and educational software (such as math tutors and encyclopedias).

Figure 5: Types of software included in the system and application software categories

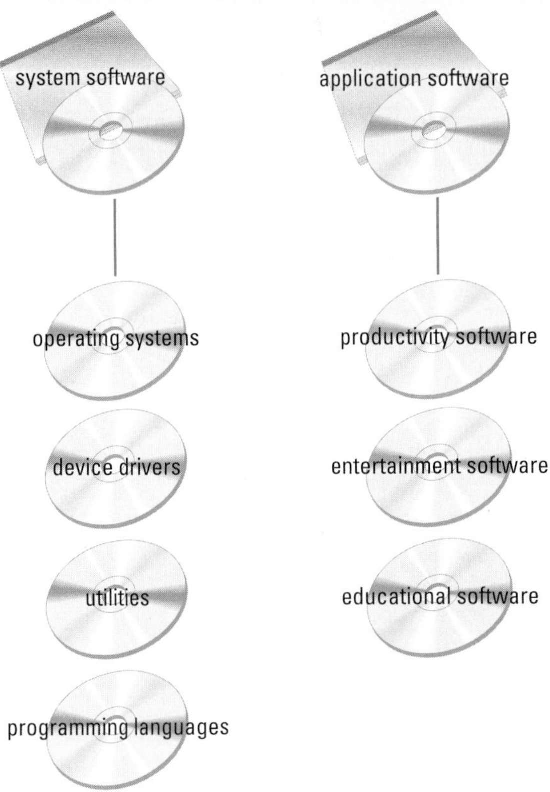

In the next section, you learn more about the programming language component of system software.

MINI-QUIZ

Mini Quiz 1

1) The two components of a microcomputer system are ________________ and ________________.
2) The three categories of peripheral devices are ________________, ________________, and ________________.
3) The information processed by a program is called ________________.
4) When you enter a program into the computer, the program is stored on ________________ chips in internal memory.
5) The CPU contains the ________________, ________________, and special high-speed storage locations called ________________.
6) Word processors belong to a category of software called ________________ software.
7) Programming languages belong to a category of software called ________________ software.
8) The data to be processed is stored in ________________ in the ALU.

A Brief History of Programming Languages

Although computers appear to be amazingly intelligent machines, they cannot yet think on their own. Computers still rely on human beings to give them directions. These directions are called **programs**, and the people who write the programs are called **programmers**.

Just as human beings communicate with each other through the use of languages such as English, Spanish, Hindi, or Chinese, programmers use a variety of special languages, called **programming languages**, to communicate with the computer. Some popular programming languages are C++, C#, Java, Visual Basic, Perl (Practical Extraction and Report Language), C, and COBOL (Common Business Oriented Language). In the next sections, you follow the progression of programming languages from machine languages to assembly languages, then to procedure-oriented high-level languages, and finally to object-oriented high-level languages.

Machine Languages

A computer represents each character in its **character set**—the letters, numerals, and special symbols that can be entered into the computer—by a series of microscopic electronic switches. Like the light switches in your house, each electronic switch can be either on or off. Computers use the binary number system to represent the two switch states. Unlike the decimal number system, with which you are familiar, the **binary number system** uses only the digits 0 and 1, rather than the digits 0 through 9. A 0 in the binary number system indicates that the switch is off; a 1 indicates that it is on. Each character in the computer's character set is represented by a series of these off and on switches—in other words, by a series of 0s and 1s.

Each switch—each 0 or 1—is called a **bit**, which is short for *binary digit*. Most computers use eight switches—in other words, eight bits or binary digits—to represent each number, letter, or symbol. Which of the eight switches are on and which are off is determined both by the character being represented and by the coding scheme used by the computer. Microcomputers typically use a coding scheme called **ASCII** (pronounced *ASK-ee*), which stands for American Standard Code for Information Interchange. The letter X, for example, is represented in the ASCII coding scheme by the eight bits 01011000. The collection of eight bits used to represent a character is called a **byte**. Appendix A in this book shows the ASCII codes for the letters, numerals, and special symbols included in your computer's character set.

Because computers can understand only these on and off switches, the first programmers had to write the program instructions using nothing but combinations of 0s and 1s. Instructions written in 0s and 1s are called **machine language** or **machine code**. The machine languages (each type of machine has its own language) represent the only way to communicate directly with the computer. Figure 6 shows a segment of a program written in a machine language.

Figure 6: A segment of a program written in a machine language

```
0100
001101 100000 001101 110001
00101 10001 10000
01110
111001
111001 001 11000 001
11000
0011100
100010 00110
```

As you can imagine, programming in machine language is very tedious and error-prone and requires highly trained programmers.

Assembly Languages

Slightly more advanced programming languages are called **assembly languages**. Figure 7 shows a segment of a program written in an assembly language.

Figure 7: A segment of a program written in an assembly language

```
main proc pay
        mov ax, dseg
        mov ax, 0b00h
        add ax, dx
        mov al, bl
        mul bl, ax
        mov bl, 04h
```

The assembly languages simplify the programmer's job by allowing the programmer to use mnemonics in place of the 0s and 1s in the program. **Mnemonics** are memory aids—in this case, alphabetic abbreviations for instructions. For example, most assembly languages use the mnemonic ADD to represent an add operation and the mnemonic MUL to represent a multiply operation. The mnemonic MOV is used to move data from one area of memory to another. Programs written in an assembly language require an **assembler**, which also is a program, to convert the assembly instructions into machine code—the 0s and 1s the computer can understand. Although it is much easier to write programs in assembly language than in machine language, programming in assembly language still is tedious and requires highly trained programmers.

The next major development in programming languages was the introduction of the high-level languages.

High-Level Languages

tip

Some high-level languages—for example, some versions of the BASIC language—use a program called an interpreter, instead of a compiler, to convert the English-like instructions into machine code. Unlike a compiler, an interpreter translates the high-level instructions into machine code, line-by-line, as the program is running.

High-level languages, which allow the programmer to use instructions that more closely resemble the English language, represent the next major development in programming languages. Programs written in a high-level language require a compiler to convert the English-like instructions into the 0s and 1s the computer can understand. Like assemblers, compilers are separate programs. A **compiler** translates the entire program into machine code before running the program.

Like their predecessors, the first high-level languages were procedure-oriented.

Procedure-Oriented High-Level Languages

In **procedure-oriented high-level languages**, the emphasis of a program is on *how* to accomplish a task. The programmer must instruct the computer every step of the way, from the start of the task to its completion. The programmer determines and controls the order in which the computer processes the instructions. Examples of procedure-oriented high-level languages include COBOL, BASIC (Beginner's All-Purpose Symbolic Instruction Code), and C.

Figure 8 shows a segment of a program written in BASIC. Notice how closely most of the instructions resemble the English language. Even if you do not know the BASIC language, it is easy to see that the program shown in Figure 8 tells the computer, step by step, *how* to compute and display an employee's net pay.

- view a solution as a set of ordered tasks.

Figure 8: A program written in BASIC—a procedure-oriented high-level language

```
input "Enter name";names$
input "Enter hours worked";hours
input "Enter pay rate";rate
grossPay = hours * rate
federalTax = .2 * grossPay
socSecTax = .07 * grossPay
stateTax = .06 * grossPay
netPay = grossPay – federalTax – socSecTax – stateTax
print names$, netPay
end
```

In all procedure-oriented programs, the order of the instructions is extremely important. For example, in the program shown in Figure 8, you could not put the instruction to display the net pay before the instruction to calculate the net pay, and then expect the computer to display the correct results. When writing programs in a procedure-oriented language, the programmer must determine not only the proper instructions to give the computer, but the correct sequence of those instructions as well. A programmer typically uses a design methodology called **top-down design** to assist him or her in planning a procedure-oriented program.

When using top-down design to create a procedure-oriented program, the programmer begins with a statement that describes the overall purpose or goal of the program—in other words, it describes what the program is supposed to do. The purpose of the program shown in Figure 8, for example, is to determine the amount an employee should be paid. The program's purpose states *what* needs to be done, but it does not tell *how* to get it done. The programmer tells *how* to accomplish the program's purpose by dividing the solution into small, manageable tasks. The payroll program shown in Figure 8, for example, is broken up into small tasks that input the employee name, hours worked, and pay rate; calculate the gross pay, taxes, and net pay; and display the employee name and net pay. These tasks describe how to reach the program's goal—in this case, determining how much to pay the employee. You learn more about top-down design in Tutorial 2.

tip

Almost everyone, at one time or another, has used top-down design to create a solution to a problem. You probably used top-down design when you planned your last vacation. Your overall goal was to "take a vacation." To accomplish that goal, you divided the solution into small tasks, such as "choose vacation spot," "make hotel reservations," "make airline reservations," and "call kennel."

Procedure-oriented high-level languages are a vast improvement over machine and assembly languages. Some of the procedure-oriented high-level languages—for example, the BASIC language—do not require a great amount of technical expertise to write simple programs.

Object-Oriented High-Level Languages

Recently, more advanced high-level languages, referred to as object-oriented languages, have become popular. Examples of popular object-oriented languages include C++, C#, Java, Smalltalk, and Visual Basic. Unlike procedure-oriented languages, which view a problem solution simply as a set of ordered tasks, **object-oriented languages** view a problem solution as a set of interacting objects. A programmer typically uses a design methodology called **object-oriented design** (**OOD**) to assist him or her in planning an object-oriented program. As with top-down design, the programmer begins with a statement that describes the purpose of the program. However, rather than breaking up the program into one or more tasks, the programmer divides the program into one or more objects, resulting in programs whose code is very different from those created using the procedure-oriented approach.

The objects in an object-oriented program can take on many different forms. For example, the menus, option buttons, and command buttons included in many Windows programs are objects. An object also can represent something encountered in real life. For example, a payroll program may include objects that represent a time card, an employee, and a date. The partial program shown in Figure 9 shows how you can use the C++ language to create a Date object named payDay.

Figure 9: A partial program written in C++—an object-oriented high-level language

```
class Date                                          //defines what a Date object looks like
{
public:
        void changeDate(int month, int day, int year);  //changes the month, day, and year
        void displayDate( );                        //displays the month, day, and year
private:
        int month;                                  //a Date object contains a month,
        int day;                                    //a day, and a year
        int year;
};

Date payDay;                                        //creates a Date object named payDay
```

All but the last instruction shown in Figure 9 simply describe what a Date object looks like. You describe an object by specifying its characteristics and behaviors. In this case, a Date object is composed of a month, day, and year. The Date object's month, day, and year can be both changed and displayed. The last instruction shown in Figure 9—`Date payDay;`—uses the object's description to create the object named payDay.

tip

Languages that can be used to create both procedure-oriented and object-oriented programs are often referred to as hybrid languages.

The object-oriented languages offer two advantages over the procedure-oriented languages. First, object-oriented languages allow a programmer to use familiar objects to solve problems. The ability to use objects that model things found in the real world makes problem solving much easier. Assume, for example, that your task is to create a program that handles the checking account transactions for a bank. Thinking in terms of the objects used by the bank—checking accounts, withdrawal slips, deposit slips, and so on—will make this task easier to accomplish. Second, because each object is viewed as an independent unit, an object can be used in more than one application, with either little or no modification; this saves programming time and money. For example, you can use the Date object shown in Figure 9 in any program that requires a date. In a personnel program, for instance, you could use a Date object to represent a hire date. In an airline reservation program, on the other hand, a Date object might represent a departure date.

Many object-oriented languages, such as C++ and Visual Basic, are direct descendants of existing procedure-oriented languages. The C++ language, for example, is a superset of the procedure-oriented C language; the procedure-oriented predecessor of Visual Basic is the QBasic language. Because both C++ and Visual Basic are based on procedure-oriented languages, you can use either C++ or Visual Basic to create not only object-oriented programs, but procedure-oriented programs as well.

Like procedure-oriented high-level languages, object-oriented high-level languages need a compiler to translate the high-level instructions into machine code.

MINI-QUIZ

Mini Quiz 2

1) The collection of letters, numerals, and symbols that you can enter into a computer is called the computer's ______________.
2) Instructions written in 0s and 1s are called ______________ language.
3) ______________ languages allow a programmer to use mnemonics in place of the 0s and 1s in a program.
4) In ______________ languages, the emphasis of a program is on *how* to accomplish a task.
5) In ______________ languages, the programmer breaks up a problem into interacting objects.
6) When designing programs, procedure-oriented languages use a design methodology called ______________, whereas object-oriented languages use a design methodology called ______________.

As you can see, programming languages have come a long way since the first machine languages. What hasn't changed about programming languages, however, are the three basic control structures used by programmers: sequence, selection, and repetition. These structures are referred to as **control structures** because they control the flow of the program; in other words, they control the order in which the program instructions are processed. You learn about these three structures in Tutorial 1.

You now have completed the Overview. You can either take a break or complete the end-of-lesson questions and exercises.

SUMMARY

A microcomputer system contains both hardware and software. Hardware refers to the physical components of the system, and consists of the system unit, input devices, output devices, and peripheral devices. The system unit houses internal memory, which is composed of both RAM and ROM chips, and the Central Processing Unit (CPU), which is the brain of the computer.

The CPU contains two principle components—the control unit and the Arithmetic/Logic Unit (ALU)—and special high-speed storage locations called registers. The control unit is responsible for making sure that the computer correctly processes the program instructions and data stored in internal memory. The ALU performs the arithmetic calculations and comparison operations for the computer. The data to be processed is stored in registers in the CPU. The result of arithmetic or comparison operations is stored in a special register, called the accumulator.

Software refers to the step-by-step instructions, called programs, that tell the hardware how to perform a task. Software typically is divided into two categories: system software and application software. System software includes operating systems, device drivers, utilities, and programming languages. Application software includes productivity software, entertainment software, and educational software.

A computer represents each character in its character set—the letters, numerals, and special symbols that can be entered into the computer—by a series of microscopic electronic switches that can be either on or off. Computers use the binary number system to represent the two switch states. The binary number system uses the digit 0 to indicate that a switch is off; it uses a 1 to indicate that the switch is on.

Each switch—each 0 or 1—is called a bit, which is short for *binary digit*. Most computers use eight bits, referred to as a byte, to represent each number, letter, or symbol. Which of the eight bits are on and which are off is determined both by the character being represented and by the coding scheme used by the computer. Microcomputers typically use a coding scheme called ASCII (pronounced ASK-ee), which stands for American Standard Code for Information Interchange.

Programs are the step-by-step instructions that tell a computer how to perform a task. Programmers, the people who write computer programs, use various programming languages to communicate with the computer. The first programming languages were machine languages, also called machine code. The assembly languages came next, followed by the procedure-oriented high-level languages and then the object-oriented high-level languages.

ANSWERS TO MINI-QUIZZES

Mini-Quiz 1

1) hardware, software

2) input devices, output devices, auxiliary storage devices

3) data

4) RAM

5) ALU, control unit, registers

6) application (or productivity)

7) system

8) registers

Mini-Quiz 2

1) character set

2) machine

3) Assembly

4) procedure-oriented high-level

5) object-oriented high-level

6) top-down design, object-oriented design

QUESTIONS

1) Which of the following is not a peripheral device?

A. auxiliary storage device

B. input device

C. output device

D. system unit

2) A computer's system unit contains ______________.
   A. the ALU
   B. the control unit
   C. internal memory
   D. all of the above

3) A storage cell in the internal memory of a computer can store ______________ at a time.
   A. one instruction
   B. one piece of data
   C. two or more pieces of data
   D. either a or b

4) While the computer is on, you can both write information to and read information from a storage cell located on ______________.
   A. a RAM chip
   B. a ROM chip
   C. either a RAM chip or a ROM chip

5) Which of the following is responsible for making sure that the program instructions stored in internal memory are processed correctly?
   A. ALU
   B. control unit
   C. internal memory unit
   D. RAM chip

6) Which of the following performs the arithmetic calculations and logic operations for the computer?
   A. ALU
   B. control unit
   C. internal memory unit
   D. ROM chip

7) Where is the result of an arithmetic or comparison operation stored?
   A. accumulator
   B. adder
   C. compiler
   D. control unit

8) The set of step-by-step directions given to a computer is called ______________.
   A. computerese
   B. a command
   C. a collection
   D. a program

9) Using the binary number system, which of the following indicates that a switch is off?
   A. 0
   B. 1
   C. 2
   D. 3

10) Which of the following is a program that translates high-level instructions into machine code?
   A. assembler
   B. compiler
   C. source program
   D. translator

Look For These Symbols

Debugging

Discovery

EXERCISES

1) Briefly explain the history of programming languages as outlined in the Overview.

2) Make a list of your computer system's input devices, output devices, and auxiliary storage devices. Which operating system is your computer using?

3) Appendix A in this book lists the ASCII codes for the letters, numerals, and special symbols included in a computer's character set. What are the ASCII codes for the ampersand (&), the letter S, and the letter s?

4) Explain the difference between top-down design and object-oriented design.

5) List and explain two advantages of using object-oriented languages.

Exercises 6 and 7 are Discovery Exercises. Discovery Exercises, which may include topics that are not covered in the lesson, allow you to "discover" the solutions to problems on your own.

6) Research the C++ programming language. Where did it originate? Who developed it? What is the meaning of the two plus signs in the C++ name? (You can use either the Internet or the library to do your research.)

7) Research both the decimal number system and the binary number system. Explain how both systems work. For example, why do the digits 10100 represent a different number in each system? What number do those digits represent in each system? How can you convert a binary number to its decimal equivalent? How can you convert a decimal number to its binary equivalent?

Tutorial 1

An Introduction to Control Structures

Objectives

After completing this tutorial, you will be able to:

- Explain the sequence, selection, and repetition structures
- Write simple algorithms using the sequence, selection, and repetition structures

Concept Lesson

Defining Control Structures

All computer programs, no matter how simple or how complex, are written using one or more of three basic structures: sequence, selection, and repetition. These structures are called **control structures** or **logic structures**, because they control the flow of a program's logic. You will use the sequence structure in every program you write. In most programs, you also will use both the selection and repetition structures.

This tutorial gives you an introduction to the three control structures used in computer programs. It also introduces you to a computerized mechanical man named Rob, who will help illustrate the control structures. More detailed information about each structure, as well as how to implement these structures using the C++ language, is provided in subsequent tutorials. Begin by learning about the sequence structure.

The Sequence Structure

You already are familiar with the sequence structure—you use it each time you follow a set of directions, in order, from beginning to end. A cookie recipe, for example, provides a good example of the sequence structure. To get to the finished product—edible cookies—you need to follow each recipe instruction in order, beginning with the first instruction and ending with the last. Likewise, the **sequence structure** in a computer program directs the computer to process the program instructions, one after another, in the order listed in the program. You will find the sequence structure in every program.

You can observe how the sequence structure works by programming a mechanical man named Rob. Like a computer, Rob has a limited instruction set—in other words, Rob can understand only a specific number of instructions, also called commands. Rob's instruction set includes the following three commands: `walk`, `turn`, and `sit`. When told to `walk`, Rob takes one complete step forward; in other words, Rob moves his right foot forward one step, then moves his left foot to meet his right foot. When told to `turn`, Rob turns 180 degrees, which is half of a full turn of 360 degrees. When told to `sit`, Rob simply sits down.

For this first example, assume that Rob is facing a chair that is two steps away from him. Your task is to write the instructions, using only the commands that Rob understands, that direct Rob to sit in the chair. Figure 1-1 shows Rob, the chair, and the instructions that will get Rob seated in the chair.

Figure 1-1: An example of the sequence structure

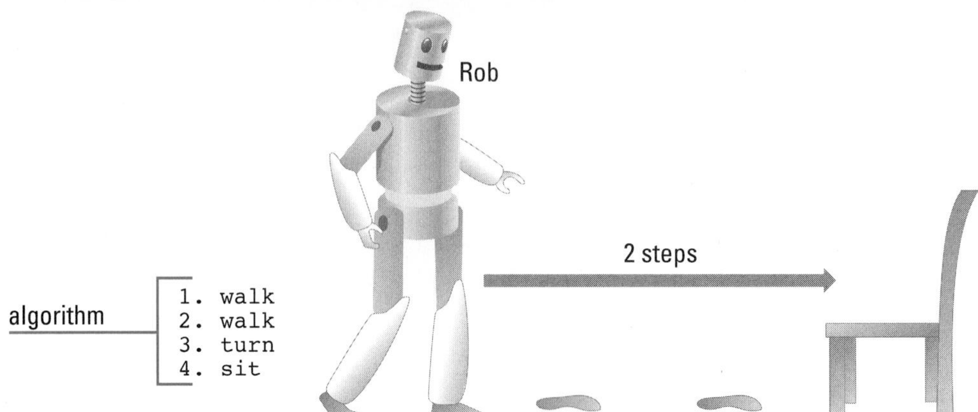

The four instructions shown in Figure 1-1 are called an algorithm. An **algorithm** is simply the set of step-by-step instructions that accomplish a task. Figure 1-1's algorithm, for example, contains the instructions that are necessary to get Rob seated in the chair. Notice that it is important that Rob follow the instructions in the list in order—in other words, in sequence. Rob first must walk two times, then turn, and then sit. He cannot turn first, then walk two times, and then sit.

Learn about the repetition structure next.

MINI-QUIZ

Mini-Quiz 1

1) The three basic control structures are ______________, ______________, and ______________.
2) All programs contain the ______________ structure.
3) When using the ______________ structure, instructions are followed in the order that they appear in the program.
4) The step-by-step instructions that accomplish a task are called a(n) ______________.

The Repetition Structure

As with the sequence structure, you already are familiar with the repetition structure. For example, shampoo bottles typically include the repetition structure in the directions for washing your hair. Those directions usually tell you to repeat the "apply shampoo to hair," "lather," and "rinse" steps until your hair is clean. When used in a program, the **repetition structure**, also referred to as a **loop**, directs the computer to repeat one or more instructions until some condition is met, at which time the computer should stop repeating the instructions.

tip
The repetition structure also is referred to as **iteration**.

You can observe how the repetition structure works by programming Rob, the mechanical man. In this example, Rob is facing a chair that is 50 steps away from him. Your task is to write the algorithm that sits Rob in the chair. If the sequence structure was the only control structure available to you, you would need to write the `walk` instruction 50 times, followed by `turn`, then `sit`. Although that algorithm would work, it is quite cumbersome to write. Imagine if Rob were 500 steps away from the chair! The best way to write the algorithm to get Rob seated in a chair that is 50 steps away from him is to use the repetition structure. To do so, however, you need to add another instruction to Rob's instruction set: in addition to `walk`, `turn`, and `sit`, Rob now can understand the command `repeat x times:`, where `x` is the number of times you want him to repeat something. The illustration of Rob and the chair, along with the correct algorithm, is shown in Figure 1-2 (on the next page). Notice that the algorithm contains both the sequence and repetition structures.

Rather than writing the `walk` instruction 50 times, the algorithm shown in Figure 1-2 uses the `repeat 50 times:` instruction to direct Rob to walk 50 times before he turns and then sits. Notice that the instruction to be repeated—in this case, `walk`—is indented below the `repeat 50 times:` instruction. Indenting in this manner indicates the instructions that are part of the repetition structure and, therefore, are to be repeated. Because the `turn` and `sit` instructions are not part of the repetition structure—in other words, they are to be followed only once, not 50 times—they are not indented. The algorithm shown in Figure 1-2 is both easier to write and much clearer than one containing 50 `walk` instructions.

Figure 1-2: An example of the repetition structure

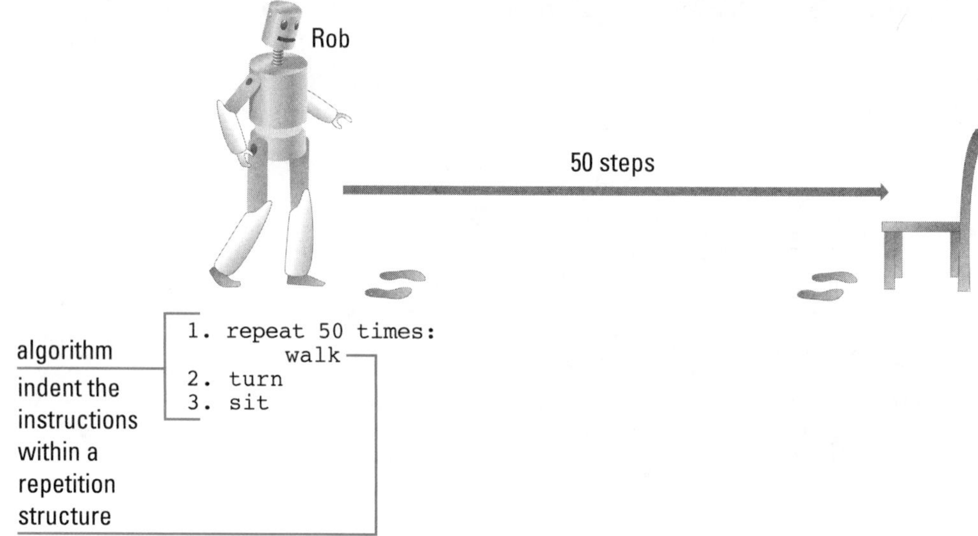

tip

Although the repetition structure shown in Figure 1-2 includes only one instruction, a repetition structure can include many instructions.

Recall that the repetition structure repeats one or more instructions until some condition is met, at which time the repetition structure ends. In the example shown in Figure 1-2, the repetition structure ends after Rob walks 50 times. Rob is then free to continue to the next instruction in the algorithm—in this case, `turn`, followed by `sit`. But what if you don't know precisely how many steps there are between Rob and the chair? In that case, you need simply to change the repetition structure's condition.

In the next example, assume that Rob is facing a chair and you don't know how far away from the chair he is. As before, your task is to write the algorithm that gets Rob seated in the chair. To accomplish this task, you need to add another instruction to Rob's instruction set: Rob now can understand the instruction `repeat until you are directly in front of the chair:`. The new algorithm is shown in Figure 1-3.

Figure 1-3: Another example of the repetition structure

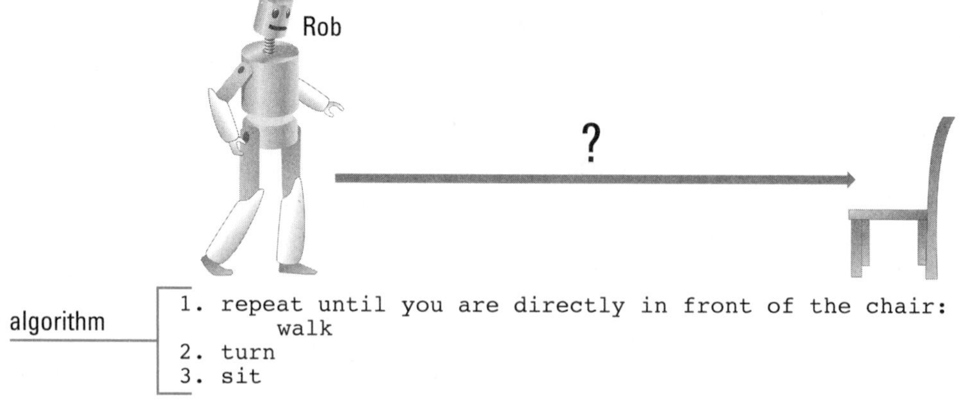

The repetition structure shown in Figure 1-3's algorithm ends when Rob is standing directly in front of the chair. If Rob is 10 steps away from the chair, the repetition structure directs him to walk 10 times before he turns and then sits. If Rob is 500 steps away from the chair, the repetition structure directs him to walk 500 times before he turns and then sits. If Rob is directly in front of the chair, the repetition structure is bypassed, and Rob simply turns and then sits.

The last of the three control structures is the selection structure.

The Selection Structure

Like the sequence and repetition structures, you already are familiar with the **selection structure**, also called the **decision structure**. The selection structure makes a decision, and then takes an appropriate action based on that decision. You use the selection structure every time you drive your car and approach an intersection. Your decision, as well as the appropriate action, is based on whether the intersection has a stop sign. If the intersection has a stop sign, then you stop your car; otherwise, you proceed with caution through the intersection. When used in a computer program, the selection structure alerts the computer that a decision needs to be made. The selection structure also provides the appropriate action to take based on the result of that decision.

As before, Rob can demonstrate the selection structure, although you need to add to his instruction set to do so. In this example, assume that Rob is holding either a red or yellow balloon, and that he is facing two boxes. One of the boxes is colored yellow and the other is colored red. The two boxes are located 20 steps away from Rob. Your task is to have Rob drop the balloon into the appropriate box—the yellow balloon belongs in the yellow box, and the red balloon belongs in the red box. After Rob drops the balloon, you then should return him to his original position. To write an algorithm to accomplish the current task, you need to add four additional instructions to Rob's instruction set. The new instructions allow Rob to make a decision about the color of the balloon he is holding, and then take the appropriate action based on that decision. Rob's new instruction set is shown in Figure 1-4.

Figure 1-4: Rob's new instruction set

```
walk
turn
sit
repeat x times:
repeat until you are directly in front of the chair:
if the balloon is red, do this:
otherwise, do this: (this instruction can be used only in combination with
   an if instruction)
drop the balloon in the red box
drop the balloon in the yellow box
```

four new instructions (callout marking the last four instructions: if the balloon is red, do this:; otherwise, do this:; drop the balloon in the red box; drop the balloon in the yellow box)

Figure 1-5 (on the next page) shows an illustration of this example, along with the correct algorithm.

Figure 1-5: An example of the selection structure

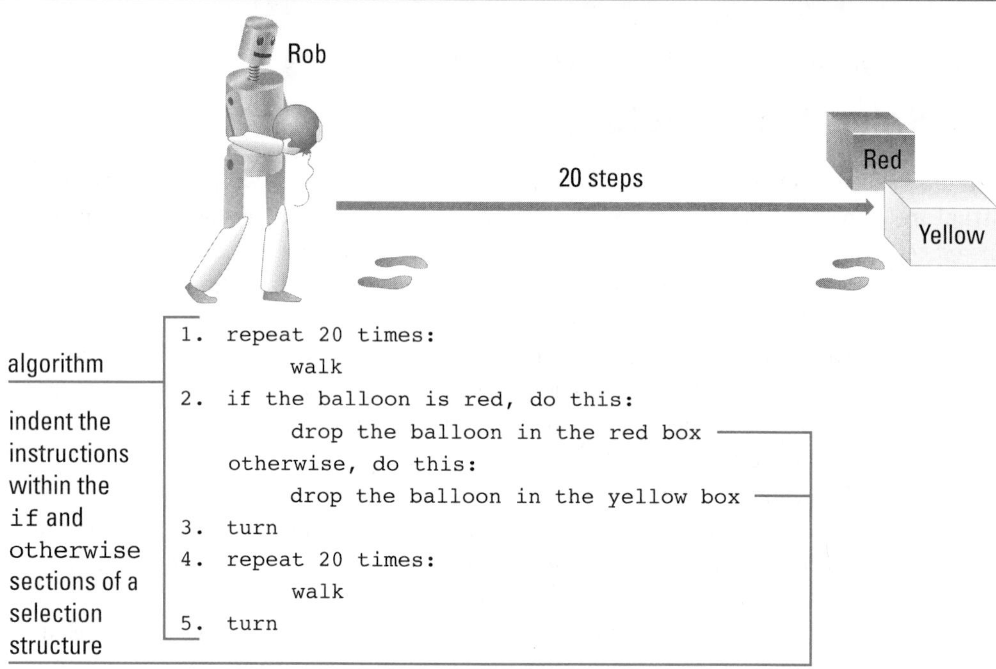
Rob
20 steps
Red
Yellow
algorithm
indent the instructions within the if and otherwise sections of a selection structure
1. repeat 20 times:
walk
2. if the balloon is red, do this:
drop the balloon in the red box
otherwise, do this:
drop the balloon in the yellow box
3. turn
4. repeat 20 times:
walk
5. turn

Notice that the instruction to be followed when the balloon is red—in this case, `drop the balloon in the red box`—and the instruction to be followed when the balloon is not red—in this case, `drop the balloon in the yellow box`—are indented. As you do with the instructions contained in a repetition structure, you also indent the instructions contained within the `if` and `otherwise` sections of a selection structure. Indenting in this manner makes it clear which instructions are to be followed when the balloon is red and which should be followed when the balloon is not red. Also indented in Figure 1-5 is the `walk` instruction contained in both repetition structures.

Notice that the algorithm shown in Figure 1-5 contains all three control structures: sequence, selection, and repetition. The repetition structure, which directs Rob to walk 20 times, is processed first. After Rob walks the 20 steps, the repetition structure ends and Rob proceeds, sequentially, to the next instruction listed in the algorithm; that instruction involves a decision. If the balloon Rob is holding is red, then Rob should drop it into the red box; otherwise, he should drop it into the yellow box. Once the decision is made and the proper action is taken, the selection structure ends and Rob proceeds to the next instruction listed in the algorithm—`turn`. After turning 180 degrees, the second repetition structure, which directs Rob to walk 20 times, and the last instruction, which turns Rob 180 degrees, returns Rob to his original position.

MINI-QUIZ

Mini-Quiz 2

1) You use the ________________ structure to repeat one or more instructions in a program.

2) The ________________ structure ends when its condition has been met.

3) The ________________ structure, also called the decision structure, instructs the computer to make a decision, and then take some action based on the result of the decision.

You now have completed Tutorial 1's Concept lesson. You can either take a break or complete the end-of-lesson questions and exercises before moving on to the Application lesson.

SUMMARY

An algorithm is the set of step-by-step instructions that solve a problem. The algorithms for all computer programs contain one or more of the following three control structures: sequence, selection, and repetition. The control structures, also called logic structures, are so named because they control the flow of a program's logic.

The sequence structure directs the computer to process the program instructions, one after another, in the order listed in the program. The repetition structure directs the computer to repeat one or more program instructions until some condition is met. The selection structure, also called the decision structure, directs the computer to make a decision, and then selects an appropriate action to take based on that decision. The sequence structure is used in all programs. Most programs also contain both the selection and repetition structures.

ANSWERS TO MINI-QUIZZES

Mini-Quiz 1

1) sequence, selection, repetition

2) sequence

3) sequence

4) algorithm

Mini-Quiz 2

1) repetition

2) repetition

3) selection

QUESTIONS

1) Which of the following is not a programming control structure?
A. repetition
B. selection
C. sequence
D. sorting

2) Which of the following control structures is used in every program?
A. repetition
B. selection
C. sequence
D. switching

3) The set of instructions for how to add two numbers is an example of the ______________ structure.

A. control

B. repetition

C. selection

D. sequence

4) The set of step-by-step instructions that solve a problem is called ______________.

A. an algorithm

B. a list

C. a plan

D. a sequential structure

5) The recipe instruction "Beat until smooth" is an example of the ______________ structure.

A. control

B. repetition

C. selection

D. sequence

6) The instruction "If it's raining outside, then take an umbrella to work" is an example of the ______________ structure.

A. control

B. repetition

C. selection

D. sequence

7) Which control structure would an algorithm use to determine whether a credit card holder is over his or her credit limit?

A. repetition

B. selection

C. both repetition and selection

8) Which control structure would an algorithm use to calculate a 5% commission for each of a company's salespeople?

A. repetition

B. selection

C. both repetition and selection

9) Assume a company pays a 3% annual bonus to employees who have been with the company over 5 years; other employees receive a 1% bonus. Which control structure would an algorithm use to calculate each employee's bonus?

A. repetition

B. selection

C. both repetition and selection

Look For These Symbols

Debugging

Discovery

EXERCISES

You use Rob, the mechanical man, to complete Exercises 1 and 2. Rob's instruction set is shown in Figure 1-6.

Figure 1-6

walk (Rob moves his right foot forward one step, then moves his left foot to meet his right foot)
sit
turn (180-degree turn)
jump (allows Rob to jump over anything in his path)
throw the box out of the way
if the box is red, do this:
otherwise, do this: (this instruction can be used only in combination with an `if` instruction)
repeat x times:

1) Rob is five steps away from a box, and the box is 10 steps away from a chair, as illustrated in Figure 1-7. Create an algorithm, using only the instructions shown in Figure 1-6, that sit Rob in the chair. Assume that Rob must jump over the box before he can continue toward the chair.

Figure 1-7

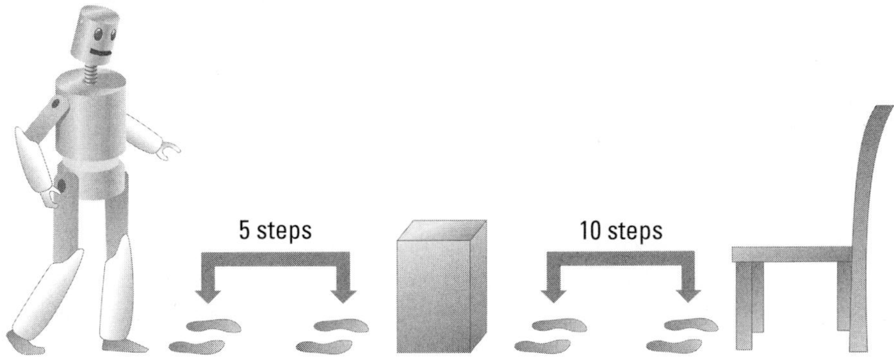

2) Rob is five steps away from a box, and the box is 10 steps away from a chair, as illustrated in Figure 1-7. Create an algorithm, using only the instructions shown in Figure 1-6, that sit Rob in the chair. Assume that Rob must jump over the box if the box is red; otherwise he must throw the box out of the way.

3) Assume a company pays an annual bonus to its employees. The bonus is based on the number of years the employee has been with the company. Employees working at the company for less than 5 years receive a 1% bonus; all others receive a 2% bonus. Write two versions of an algorithm that prints each employee's bonus; use only the instructions shown in Figure 1-8 (on the next page) to do so. Be sure to indent the instructions appropriately.

Figure 1-8

calculate the bonus by multiplying the salary by 1%
calculate the bonus by multiplying the salary by 2%
if the years employed are greater than or equal to 5, do this:
if the years employed are less than 5, do this:
otherwise, do this:
print the bonus
read the salary and years employed
repeat for each employee:

4) Assume a store gives a 10% discount to customers who are at least 65 years old. Write two versions of an algorithm that prints the amount of money a customer owes. Use only the instructions shown in Figure 1-9 to do so. Be sure to indent the instructions appropriately.

Figure 1-9

assign 10% as the discount rate
assign 0 as the discount rate
calculate the amount due by multiplying the item price by (1 minus the discount rate)
if the customer's age is greater than or equal to 65, do this:
if the customer's age is less than 65, do this:
otherwise, do this:
print the amount due
read the customer's age and item price

Exercise 5 is a Discovery Exercise. Discovery Exercises, which may include topics that are not covered in the lesson, allow you to "discover" the solutions to problems on your own.

5) Create an algorithm that tells someone how to evaluate the following expression (the / operator means division and the * operator means multiplication). (*Hint*: As you may remember from your math courses, division and multiplication are performed before addition and subtraction.)

12 / 2 + 3 * 2 – 3

A computer program is good only if it works. Errors in either an algorithm or programming code can cause a program to run incorrectly. Therefore, a programmer needs to know how to locate and fix these errors. Exercise 6 is a Debugging Exercise. Debugging Exercises allow you to practice recognizing and solving errors in a program.

6) The algorithm shown in Figure 1-10 should evaluate the expression x + y / z * 3, but it is not working correctly. Correct the algorithm.

Figure 1-10

1. add x to y
2. divide the result of step 1 by z
3. multiply the result of step 2 by 3

Application Lesson

Using the Control Structures

CASE Rob, the mechanical man, is standing in front of a flower bed that contains six flowers. Your task in this lesson is to create an algorithm that directs Rob to pick the flowers as he walks to the other side of the flower bed. Rob should pick all red flowers with his right hand. Flowers that are not red should be picked with his left hand.

Programming Rob the Mechanical Man

Before you can complete this lesson, the Rob the Mechanical Man files must be installed on your computer's hard disk; the installation process is described in the following eight steps.

Important note: If you are working on a computer in your school's computer lab, the files may already be installed on the computer. If they are installed, you can skip the following eight steps. If you are unsure whether the files are installed, ask your instructor or technical support person before completing the eight steps.

To install the Rob the Mechanical Man files on your computer's hard disk:

1. Click the **Start** button on the taskbar, and then click **Run** to open the Run dialog box.
2. Click the **Browse** button to open the Browse dialog box. Open the **Rob Installation Files** folder, which is located in the CppNet folder on your computer's hard disk.
3. Click **Setup** (Setup.exe) in the list of filenames, and then click the **Open** button to return to the Run dialog box.
4. Click the **OK** button in the Run dialog box. A message box appears and indicates that seven files are being copied to your computer's hard disk. After the files are copied, the Rob the Mechanical Man Setup dialog box opens.
5. Read the message in the dialog box. If necessary, close any open files, then click the **OK** button in the dialog box. A message concerning installation appears in the dialog box, as shown in Figure 1-11.

Figure 1-11: Installation message shown in the Rob the Mechanical Man Setup dialog box

As the dialog box indicates, the files will be installed in the Program Files\Rob directory (folder) on your computer's hard disk. You can use the Change Directory button to install the files in another directory.

6. If desired, change the default installation directory to one of your choosing.
7. Click the **Click here to begin setup** button in the dialog box. The Rob the Mechanical Man – Choose Program Group dialog box opens and shows Rob the Mechanical Man selected in the list of groups.
8. Click the **Continue** button. When the message "Rob the Mechanical Man Setup was completed successfully" appears, click the **OK** button.

Figure 1-12 shows an illustration of Rob and the flower bed.

Figure 1-12: Illustration of Rob and the flower bed

Rob should end up on the other side of the flower bed

Your computer's hard disk contains an application that you can use to create the algorithm that directs Rob to pick the flowers as he walks to the other side of the flower bed.

To run the application that you will use to create Rob's algorithm:

1. Click the **Start** button on the taskbar, and then point to **All Programs** on the Start menu.
2. Point to **Rob the Mechanical Man** on the All Programs menu, and then click **Application Lesson**. The Rob the Mechanical Man application shown in Figure 1-13 appears on your screen.

Figure 1-13: Rob the Mechanical Man application

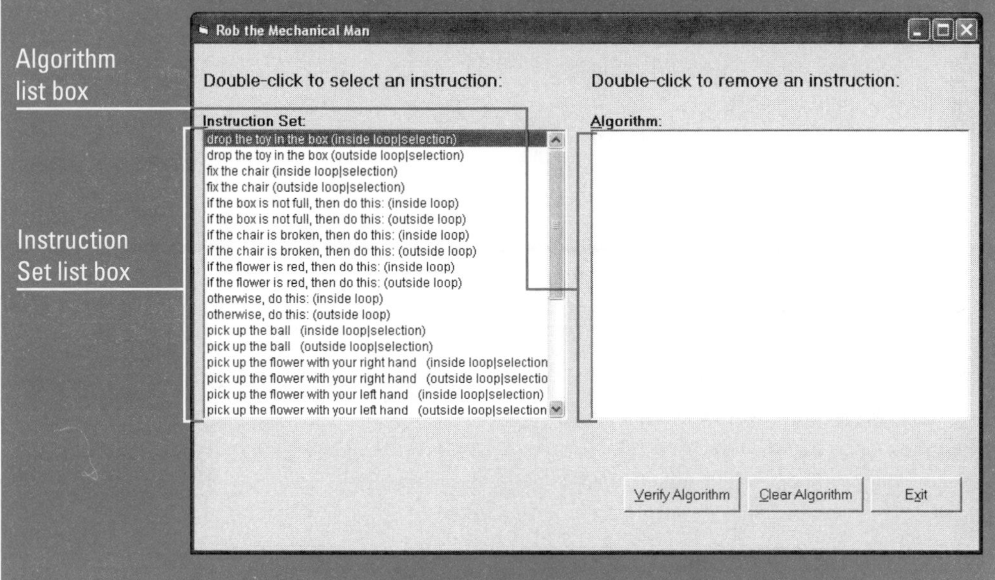

The application shown in Figure 1-13 contains two list boxes, identified by the labels Instruction Set and Algorithm. The Instruction Set list box displays the set of instructions that Rob can understand. Double-clicking an instruction in the Instruction Set list box copies the instruction to the Algorithm list box, which currently is empty. If you make a mistake and want to remove an instruction from the Algorithm list box, you do so simply by double-clicking the instruction in the Algorithm list box. When you are finished adding the appropriate instructions to the Algorithm list box, you can click the Verify Algorithm button to verify that the algorithm is correct. Clicking the Clear Algorithm button removes all of the instructions from the Algorithm list box, and clicking the Exit button ends the application.

As Figure 1-12 indicates, Rob is standing in front of a flower bed that contains six flowers. If the first flower is red, Rob should pick the flower with his right hand; otherwise, he should pick it with his left hand. He then should walk one step forward to position himself in front of the second flower. If the second flower is red, Rob should pick it with his right hand; otherwise, he should use his left hand. He then should walk one step forward to position himself in front of the third flower. Rob needs to follow the same procedure for each flower in the flower bed. After picking the last flower, Rob must walk two steps forward, rather than one step, to end up on the other side of the flower bed. Figure 1-14 shows the initial algorithm for Rob.

Figure 1-14: Initial algorithm for Rob

1. if the flower is red, then do this:
   pick up the flower with your right hand
   otherwise, do this:
   pick up the flower with your left hand
2. walk
3. if the flower is red, then do this:
   pick up the flower with your right hand
   otherwise, do this:
   pick up the flower with your left hand
4. walk

Figure 1-14: Initial algorithm for Rob (continued)

5. if the flower is red, then do this:
        pick up the flower with your right hand
    otherwise, do this:
        pick up the flower with your left hand
6. walk
7. if the flower is red, then do this:
        pick up the flower with your right hand
    otherwise, do this:
        pick up the flower with your left hand
8. walk
9. if the flower is red, then do this:
        pick up the flower with your right hand
    otherwise, do this:
        pick up the flower with your left hand
10. walk
11. if the flower is red, then do this:
        pick up the flower with your right hand
    otherwise, do this:
        pick up the flower with your left hand
12. walk
13. walk

Although the algorithm shown in Figure 1-14 works correctly, notice that it is quite long. Imagine if Rob had 50 flowers to pick—you would need to repeat the selection structure and the `walk` instruction 50 times! Figure 1-15 shows a more efficient and convenient way of writing this algorithm.

Figure 1-15: Final algorithm for Rob

1. repeat 6 times:
        if the flower is red, then do this:
            pick up the flower with your right hand
        otherwise, do this:
            pick up the flower with your left hand
        walk
2. walk

You can remove an instruction from the Algorithm list box by double-clicking the instruction in the list box.

Rather than listing the instructions to determine the color, pick the flower, and then walk for each of the six flowers, the algorithm shown in Figure 1-15 uses the repetition structure to direct Rob to repeat those instructions six times.

Now use the application on your screen to enter the algorithm shown in Figure 1-15 and verify that it works correctly.

To enter the algorithm shown in Figure 1-15, and then verify that it works correctly:

1. Scroll down the Instruction Set list box until you see the `repeat 6 times:` instruction. Double-click **repeat 6 times:** in the Instruction Set list box. The instruction appears in the Algorithm list box, as shown in Figure 1-16.

Figure 1-16: First instruction shown in the Algorithm list box

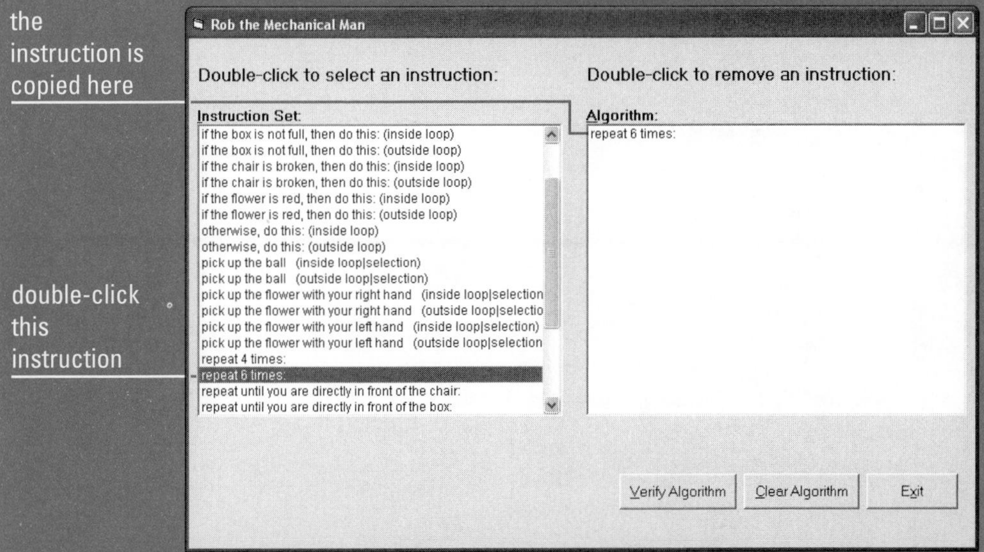

HELP? If you inadvertently selected the wrong instruction, double-click the incorrect instruction in the Algorithm list box to remove the instruction, then repeat Step 1.

According to the algorithm shown in Figure 1-15, Rob needs to use a selection structure to determine whether the color of the current flower is red. The Instruction Set list box contains two instructions that can be used to determine this: `if the flower is red, then do this: (inside loop)` and `if the flower is red, then do this: (outside loop)`. The instruction you use depends on whether you want the instruction to be part of a repetition structure (loop). If the instruction should be included in a repetition structure, you choose `if the flower is red, then do this: (inside loop)`; otherwise, you choose `if the flower is red, then do this: (outside loop)`. In this case, you want the instruction that determines the flower's color to be included in the loop.

2. Double-click **if the flower is red, then do this: (inside loop)** to copy this instruction to the Algorithm list box. Notice that the instruction appears indented below the `repeat 6 times:` instruction. The indentation indicates that the `if the flower is red, then do this: (inside loop)` instruction is included in the repetition structure.

   If the flower is red, then Rob must pick it with his right hand. The instruction to pick the flower should be included in the selection structure. You can do so using the `pick up the flower with your right hand (inside loop|selection)` instruction. (The `loop|selection` in an instruction means that you can use the instruction within either a loop or a selection structure.)

3. Double-click **pick up the flower with your right hand (inside loop|selection)** to copy this instruction to the Algorithm list box. Because this instruction is part of the selection structure, it appears indented below the `if the flower is red, then do this: (inside loop)` instruction.

tip

As you learned in the Concept Lesson, the repetition structure also is referred to as a loop.

tip
Technically, the `pick up the flower with your right hand (inside loop|selection)` instruction also is inside the `repeat 6 times:` loop. This is because the selection structure that contains the instruction is inside the loop.

If the flower is not red, then Rob must pick it with his left hand.

4. Double-click **otherwise, do this: (inside loop)**, then double-click **pick up the flower with your left hand (inside loop|selection)**.

   After picking a flower, Rob must walk one step forward. This instruction should be part of the `repeat 6 times:` repetition structure, because it needs to be done after picking each of the six flowers.

5. Scroll down the Instruction Set list box, if necessary, until you locate the `walk (inside loop|selection)` instruction, then double-click **walk (inside loop|selection)**.

   The last instruction in the algorithm shown in Figure 1-15 is to have Rob walk one step forward, which positions him at the end of the flower bed. Because this instruction should be followed only once, after Rob has picked the six flowers, you place the instruction outside of the `repeat 6 times:` repetition structure.

6. Double-click **walk (outside loop|selection)**. Figure 1-17 shows the completed algorithm in the Algorithm list box.

Figure 1-17: Completed algorithm shown in the Algorithm list box

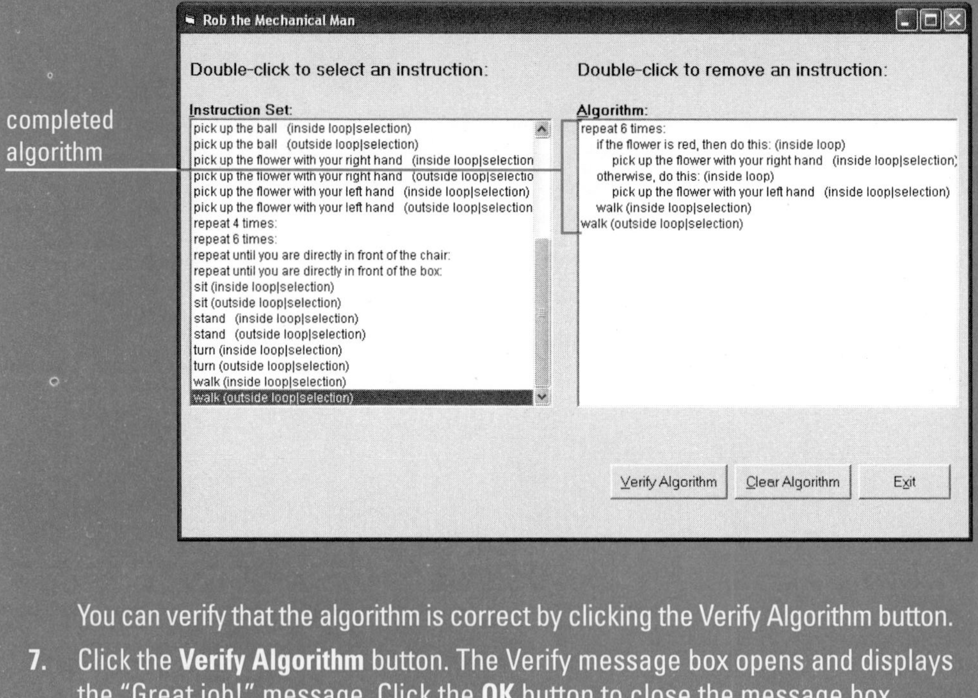

You can verify that the algorithm is correct by clicking the Verify Algorithm button.

7. Click the **Verify Algorithm** button. The Verify message box opens and displays the "Great job!" message. Click the **OK** button to close the message box.
8. Click the **Exit** button to close the application.

You now have completed Tutorial 1's Application lesson. You can either take a break or complete the end-of-lesson exercises.

Important note: Rob, the mechanical man, is used only in this tutorial. When you have completed this lesson's Exercises, you can remove the Rob the Mechanical Man files from your computer's hard disk. However, if you are working on a computer in your school's computer lab, check with your instructor or technical support person before removing the files.

To uninstall the Rob the Mechanical Man program:

1. Click the **Start** button, and then click **Control Panel** on the Start menu.
2. Click **Add or Remove Programs** to open the Add or Remove Programs window.
3. Scroll down the list of currently installed programs, if necessary, then click **Rob the Mechanical Man** in the list. Click the **Change/Remove** button. When you are asked if you are sure you want to remove Rob the Mechanical Man and all of its components, click the **Yes** button.
4. When the "Program installation removed" message appears, click the **OK** button.
5. Click the **Close** button to close the Add or Remove Programs window, then close the Control Panel window.

EXERCISES

Look For These Symbols

Debugging

Discovery

1) In this exercise, you create an algorithm that directs Rob, the mechanical man, to perform a set of tasks.

A. Click the Start button, and then point to All Programs on the Start menu. Point to Rob the Mechanical Man on the All Programs menu, and then click Application Exercises.

B. Rob is facing a box that is located zero or more steps away from him. Rob is carrying a toy in his right hand. Create an algorithm, using only the instructions shown in the Instruction Set list box, that directs Rob to drop the toy in the box.

C. When you have completed the algorithm, click the Exercise 1 button to verify that the algorithm is correct.

D. When the algorithm is working correctly, click the Exit button to end the application.

2) In this exercise, you create an algorithm that directs Rob, the mechanical man, to perform a set of tasks.

A. Click the Start button, and then point to All Programs on the Start menu. Point to Rob the Mechanical Man on the All Programs menu, and then click Application Exercises.

B. Rob is seated in a chair and is four steps away from a table. A ball is resting on the top of the table, as illustrated in Figure 1-18 (on the next page). Create an algorithm, using only the instructions shown in the Instruction Set list box, that directs Rob to pick up the ball, and then return him to his original position.

C. When you have completed the algorithm, click the Exercise 2 button to verify that the algorithm is correct.

D. When the algorithm is working correctly, click the Exit button to end the application.

Figure 1-18

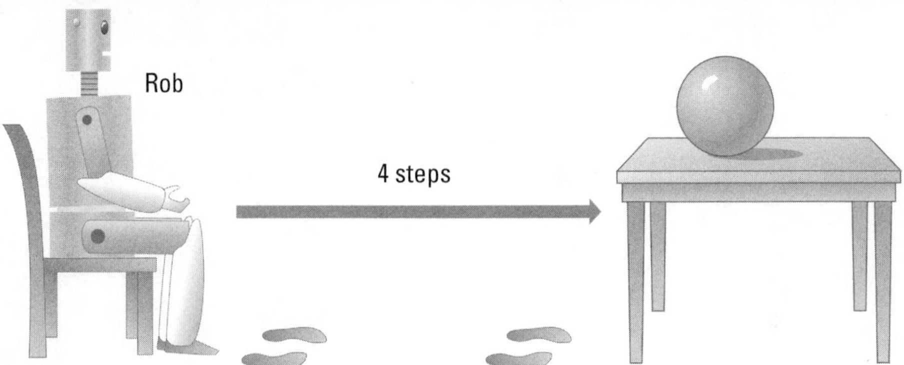

3) In this exercise, you create an algorithm that directs Rob, the mechanical man, to perform a set of tasks.

   A. Click the Start button, and then point to All Programs on the Start menu. Point to Rob the Mechanical Man on the All Programs menu, and then click Application Exercises.

   B. Rob is facing a chair that is located zero or more steps away from him. Create an algorithm, using only the instructions shown in the Instruction Set list box, that sits Rob in the chair, but only if the chair is not broken. If the chair is broken, the algorithm should instruct Rob to fix the chair.

   C. When you have completed the algorithm, click the Exercise 3 button to verify that the algorithm is correct.

   D. When the algorithm is working correctly, click the Exit button to end the application.

4) In this exercise, you create an algorithm that directs Rob, the mechanical man, to perform a set of tasks.

   A. Click the Start button, and then point to All Programs on the Start menu. Point to Rob the Mechanical Man on the All Programs menu, and then click Application Exercises.

   B. Rob is seated in a chair, facing a box that is zero or more steps away from him. Rob is holding a toy in his left hand. Create an algorithm, using only the instructions shown in the Instruction Set list box, that directs Rob to drop the toy in the box—but only if the box is not full. The algorithm also should return Rob to his original position.

   C. When you have completed the algorithm, click the Exercise 4 button to verify that the algorithm is correct.

   D. When the algorithm is working correctly, click the Exit button to end the application.

5) Using only the instructions shown in Figure 1-19, create an algorithm that shows the steps an instructor takes when grading a test that contains 25 questions.

Figure 1-19

if the student's answer is not the same as the correct answer, do this:
repeat 25 times:
read the student's answer and the correct answer
mark the student's answer incorrect

6) You have just purchased a new personal computer system. Before putting the system components together, you read the instruction booklet that came with the system. The booklet contains a list of the components that you should have received. The booklet advises you to verify that you received all of the components by matching those that you received with those on the list. If a component was received, you should cross its name off the list; otherwise, you should draw a circle around the component's name in the list. Using only the instructions shown in Figure 1-20, create an algorithm that shows the steps you should take to verify that the package contains the correct components.

Figure 1-20

cross the component name off the list
read the component name from the list
circle the component's name on the list
search the package for the component
if the component was received, do this:
otherwise, do this: **(this instruction can be used only in combination with an `if` instruction)**
repeat for each component name on the list:

Exercises 7 and 8 are Discovery Exercises. Discovery Exercises, which may include topics that are not covered in the lesson, allow you to "discover" the solutions to problems on your own.

7) Complete the algorithm shown in Figure 1-21. The algorithm should show a payroll clerk how to calculate and print the gross pay for five workers. If an employee works more than 40 hours, he or she should receive time and one-half for the hours worked over 40.

Figure 1-21

1.____
    read the employee's name, hours worked, and pay rate
    ____
        calculate the gross pay by multiplying the hours worked by the pay rate
    otherwise, do this:
        calculate the overtime hours by subtracting 40 from the number of hours worked
        calculate the overtime pay by multiplying the overtime hours by the pay rate divided by 2
        calculate the gross pay by ______________________________
    print the employee's name and gross pay

8) Create an algorithm that tells someone how to evaluate the following expression (the / operator means division and the * operator means multiplication):

12 / 2 + 3 * (4 – 2) + 1

A computer program is good only if it works. Errors in either an algorithm or programming code can cause a program to run incorrectly. Therefore, a programmer needs to know how to locate and fix these errors. Exercises 9 and 10 are Debugging Exercises. Debugging Exercises allow you to practice recognizing and solving errors in a program.

9) The algorithm shown in Figure 1-22 is not working correctly, because it does not get Rob seated in the chair. Correct the algorithm.

Figure 1-22

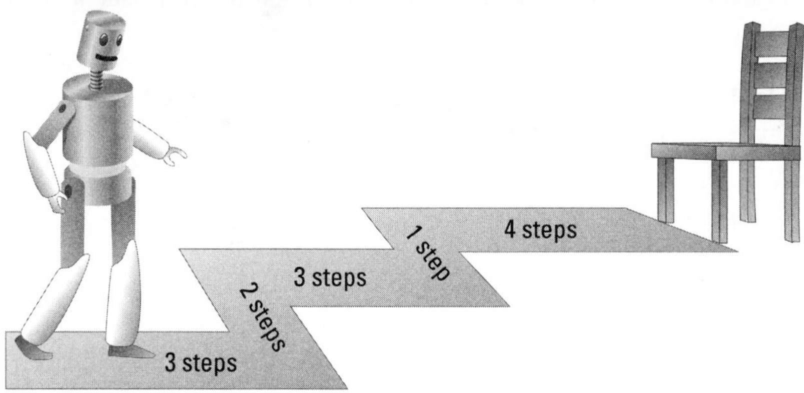

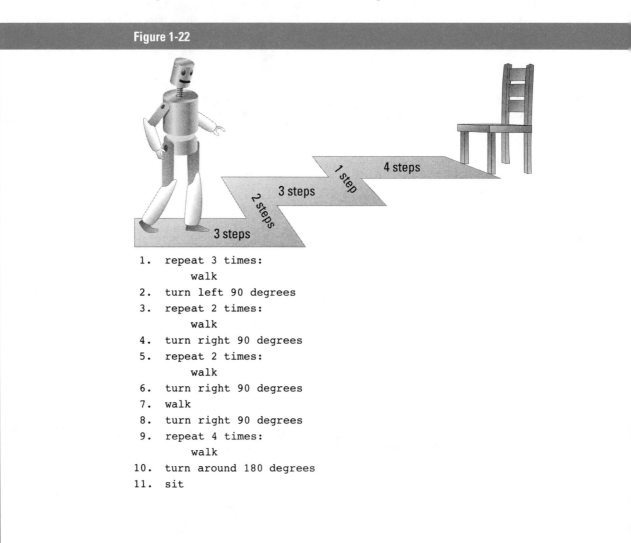

```
1.  repeat 3 times:
        walk
2.  turn left 90 degrees
3.  repeat 2 times:
        walk
4.  turn right 90 degrees
5.  repeat 2 times:
        walk
6.  turn right 90 degrees
7.  walk
8.  turn right 90 degrees
9.  repeat 4 times:
        walk
10. turn around 180 degrees
11. sit
```

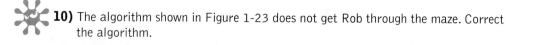

10) The algorithm shown in Figure 1-23 does not get Rob through the maze. Correct the algorithm.

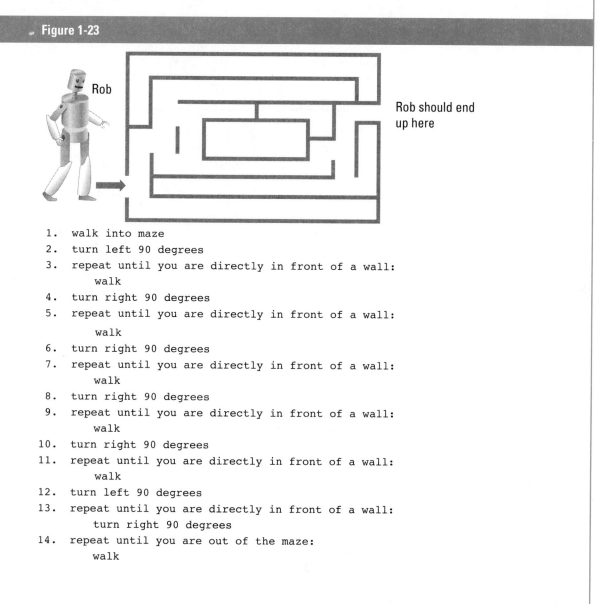

Figure 1-23

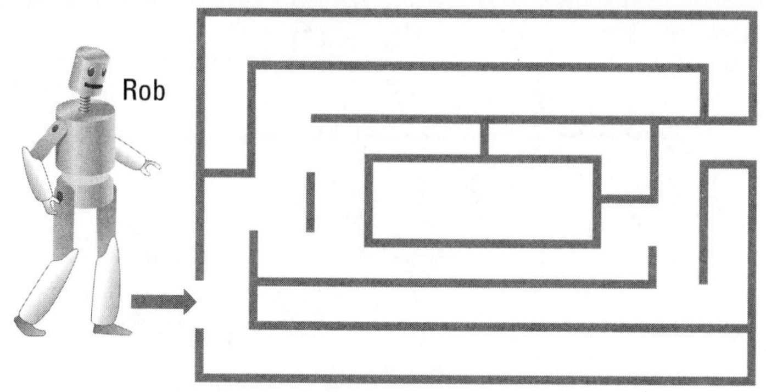

Rob should end up here

```
1.  walk into maze
2.  turn left 90 degrees
3.  repeat until you are directly in front of a wall:
        walk
4.  turn right 90 degrees
5.  repeat until you are directly in front of a wall:
        walk
6.  turn right 90 degrees
7.  repeat until you are directly in front of a wall:
        walk
8.  turn right 90 degrees
9.  repeat until you are directly in front of a wall:
        walk
10. turn right 90 degrees
11. repeat until you are directly in front of a wall:
        walk
12. turn left 90 degrees
13. repeat until you are directly in front of a wall:
        turn right 90 degrees
14. repeat until you are out of the maze:
        walk
```

Tutorial 2

Beginning the Problem-Solving Process

Objectives

After completing this tutorial, you will be able to:

- Explain the problem-solving process used to create a computer program
- Analyze a problem
- Complete an IPO chart
- Plan an algorithm using pseudocode and flowcharts
- Desk-check an algorithm

Concept Lesson

Problem Solving

In this tutorial, you learn the process that programmers follow to solve problems using a computer. Although you may not realize it, you use a similar process to solve hundreds of small problems every day, such as how to get to school and what to do when you are hungry. Because most of these problems occur so often, however, you typically solve them almost automatically, without giving much thought to the process your brain goes through to arrive at the solutions. Unfortunately, problems that are either complex or unfamiliar usually cannot be solved so easily; most require extensive analysis and planning. Understanding the thought process involved in solving simple and familiar problems will make solving complex or unfamiliar ones easier.

tip

In Tutorials 6 and 7, you learn how to include the selection structure in a program. Then, in Tutorial 8, you learn how to include the repetition structure.

First, you explore the thought process that you follow when solving common, daily problems. Then, you learn how to use a similar process to create a computer solution to a problem—in other words, to create a computer program. The computer solutions you create in this tutorial contain the sequence control structure only, where each instruction is processed in order, from beginning to end.

Solving Everyday Problems

The first step in solving a familiar problem is to analyze the problem. You then plan, review, implement, evaluate, and modify (if necessary) the solution. Consider, for example, how you solve the everyday problem of being hungry. First, your mind analyzes the problem to identify its important components. One very important component of any problem is the goal of solving the problem. In this case, the goal is to stop the hunger pangs. Other important components of a problem are the things that you can use to accomplish the goal. For example, you can use the lettuce, tomato, cucumber, and salad dressing that are in your refrigerator to relieve your hunger pangs.

After analyzing the problem, your mind plans an algorithm. Recall from Tutorial 1 that an algorithm is the set of step-by-step instructions that describe how to accomplish a task. In other words, an algorithm is a solution to a problem. The hunger problem's algorithm, for example, describes how to use the lettuce, tomato, cucumber, and salad dressing to stop your hunger pangs. Figure 2-1 shows a summary of the analysis and planning steps for the hunger problem.

After planning the algorithm, you review it (in your mind) to verify that it works as intended. When you are satisfied that the algorithm is correct, you implement the algorithm by following each of its instructions in the order indicated. In this case, for example, you rinse the lettuce, tomato, and cucumber, and then cut them up, place them in a salad bowl, pour salad dressing on the salad, and then eat the salad.

Figure 2-1: Summary of the analysis and planning steps for the hunger problem

result of analysis step

Items used to accomplish the goal	Algorithm	Goal
lettuce tomato cucumber salad dressing	1. rinse the lettuce, tomato, and cucumber 2. cut up the lettuce, tomato, and cucumber 3. place the lettuce, tomato, and cucumber in a salad bowl 4. pour the salad dressing on the salad 5. eat the salad	stop the hunger pangs

result of planning step

Finally, after implementing the algorithm, you evaluate it and, if necessary, you modify it. In this case, if your hunger pangs are gone after eating the salad, then your algorithm is correct because it accomplishes its goal. If, on the other hand, you still are hungry, then you know that you need to modify the algorithm for the next time. An example of a modified algorithm for the hunger problem is shown in Figure 2-2.

Figure 2-2: Modified algorithm for the hunger problem

Items used to accomplish the goal	Algorithm	Goal
lettuce tomato cucumber salad dressing apple	1. rinse the lettuce, tomato, and cucumber 2. cut up the lettuce, tomato, and cucumber 3. place the lettuce, tomato, and cucumber in a salad bowl 4. pour the salad dressing on the salad 5. eat the salad 6. rinse the apple 7. eat the apple	stop the hunger pangs

modifications made to original algorithm

In the next section, you learn that a similar thought process is used to create computer solutions to problems.

Creating Computer Solutions to Problems

In the previous section, you learned how you create a solution to a problem that occurs every day. A similar problem-solving process is used to create a computer program. A computer program also is a solution, but one that is implemented with a computer. The problem-solving process that computer programmers use when creating a computer program is shown in Figure 2-3.

Figure 2-3: The problem-solving process for creating a computer program

1. Analyze the problem.
2. Plan the algorithm.
3. Desk-check the algorithm.
4. Code the algorithm into a program.
5. Desk-check the program.
6. Evaluate and modify (if necessary) the program.

tip

The term *desk-checking* refers to the fact that the programmer is seated at his or her desk, rather than in front of the computer, when reviewing the algorithm. The term *hand-tracing* refers to the fact that the programmer uses a pencil and paper to follow each of the steps in the algorithm by hand.

Just like you do, a computer programmer also first analyzes the problem. He or she then plans the algorithm—the steps that tell the computer how to solve the problem. Programmers use tools such as IPO (Input, Processing, Output) charts, pseudocode, and flowcharts to help them analyze problems and develop algorithms. You learn about these tools in this lesson.

After the analysis and planning steps, the programmer then desk-checks the algorithm. **Desk-checking**, also called **hand-tracing**, means that you use pencil and paper, along with sample data, to walk through each of the steps in the algorithm manually, just as if you were the computer. Programmers desk-check the algorithm to verify that it works as intended. If any errors are found in the algorithm, the errors are corrected before the programmer continues to the next step in the problem-solving process. Eliminating errors at this pencil and paper stage makes it much easier to produce a correct program in the later steps of the problem-solving process.

tip

The importance of the first three steps in the problem-solving process cannot be emphasized enough. If a programmer does not take the time to analyze the problem, then plan and desk-check the algorithm, the computer program he or she creates typically will contain errors that are difficult to find and expensive to correct.

When the programmer is satisfied that the algorithm is correct, he or she then translates the algorithm into a language that the computer can understand. Programmers refer to this step as **coding** the algorithm. You begin learning how to code an algorithm in Tutorial 3. A coded algorithm is called a **program**. In this book, you use the C++ programming language to code your algorithms.

After creating the program—the coded version of the algorithm—the programmer desk-checks the program to make sure that he or she translated each of the algorithm's steps correctly. If any errors are found in the program, the errors are corrected before the programmer continues to the final step in the problem-solving process.

The final step in the problem-solving process is to evaluate and modify (if necessary) the program. A programmer evaluates a program by running it, along with sample data, on the computer. If the program does not work as intended, then the programmer makes the necessary modifications until the program works correctly.

In this tutorial, you learn how to use the first three problem-solving steps to create a computer program; you explore the last three steps in Tutorial 3. Begin with the first step in the problem-solving process, which is to analyze the problem.

Analyzing the Problem

You cannot solve a problem unless you understand it, and you cannot understand a problem unless you analyze it—in other words, unless you identify its important components. The purpose of analyzing a problem is to determine the goal of solving the problem, and the items that are needed to achieve that goal. Programmers refer to the goal as the **output**, and the items needed to achieve the goal as the **input**. When analyzing a problem, you always search first for the output, and then for the input. Many times you will need to consult with the program's user—the person for whom you are creating the program—to determine the output and the input. This is especially true if the problem specification provided by the user is unclear or incomplete. Analyze the problem specification shown in Figure 2-4.

Figure 2-4: Problem specification

Sarah Martin has been working for Quality Builders for four years. Last year, Sarah received a 4% raise, which brought her current weekly pay to $250. Sarah is scheduled to receive a 3% raise next week. She wants you to write a program that will display, on the computer screen, the amount of her new weekly pay.

When analyzing a problem, you always determine the output first. A helpful way to identify the output is to search the problem specification for an answer to the following question: *What does the user want to see printed on paper, displayed on the screen, or stored in a file?* The answer to this question typically is stated as nouns and adjectives in the problem specification. The problem specification shown in Figure 2-4, for instance, indicates that Sarah (the program's user) wants to see her new weekly pay displayed on the screen; the output, therefore, is the new weekly pay. Notice that the words *new* and *weekly* are adjectives, and that the word *pay* is a noun.

IPO Charts

Programmers use an **IPO (Input, Processing, Output)** chart to organize and summarize the results of a problem analysis. Figure 2-5 shows a partially completed IPO chart for Sarah's problem. Notice that you list the output items in the Output column of the IPO chart.

Figure 2-5: Partially completed IPO chart showing the output

Input	Processing	Output
	Processing items: Algorithm:	new weekly pay

You can draw an IPO chart by hand, or you can use the table feature in a word processor (such as Microsoft Word) to draw one.

After determining the output, you then determine the input. A helpful way to identify the input is to search the problem specification for an answer to the following question: *What information will the computer need to know to print, display, or store the output items?* As with the output, the input typically is stated as nouns and adjectives in the problem specification. When determining the input, it helps to think about the information that you would need to solve the problem manually, because the computer will need to know the same information. For example, to determine Sarah's new weekly pay, both you and the computer need to know Sarah's current weekly pay, as well as her raise rate; both of these items, therefore, are the input. Here again, notice that *current*, *weekly*, and *raise* are adjectives, and *pay* and *rate* are nouns. Figure 2-6 shows the partially completed IPO chart listing the problem's input and output. Notice that you list the input items in the Input column of the IPO chart.

Figure 2-6: Partially completed IPO chart showing the input and output items

result of analysis step

Input	Processing	Output
current weekly pay raise rate	Processing items: Algorithm:	new weekly pay

You now have completed the analysis step for the current problem. Keep in mind that analyzing real-world problems will not always be as easy as analyzing the ones found in a textbook. You will find that the analysis step is the most difficult of the problem-solving steps, primarily because most problem specifications contain either too much information or too little information.

A problem specification that contains too much information—more than is necessary to solve the problem—can be confusing to analyze. If you are not sure if an item of information is important, ask yourself this question: *If I didn't know this information, could I still solve the problem?* If your answer is "Yes," then the information is superfluous and you can ignore it. The current problem specification, for example, tells you that Sarah works for Quality Builders. Now ask yourself the following question: *If I didn't know that Sarah worked for Quality Builders, could I still solve the problem?* The answer is "Yes," so you can ignore this information.

When reading a problem specification, it helps to use a pencil to lightly cross out the information that you feel is unimportant to the solution, thereby reducing the amount of information you need to consider in your analysis. If you later find that the information is important, you can always erase the pencil line. In the current problem, for example, you can cross out the unimportant information as shown in Figure 2-7.

Figure 2-7: Problem specification with unimportant information crossed out

~~Sarah Martin has been working for Quality Builders for four years. Last year, Sarah received a 4% raise, which brought her~~ current weekly pay to $250. Sarah is scheduled to receive a 3% raise next week. ~~She wants you to~~ write a program that will display, on the computer screen, the amount of her new weekly pay.

Even worse than having too much information in a problem specification is not having enough information to solve a problem. Consider, for example, the problem specification shown in Figure 2-8.

Figure 2-8: Problem specification that does not contain enough information

Jack Osaki, one of the shipping clerks at Quality Builders, earns $7 per hour. Last week, Jack worked 40 hours. He wants you to write a program that will display his weekly net pay.

It is clear from reading the problem specification that the output is the weekly net pay. The input appears to be both the hourly pay and the number of hours worked during the week. However, is that the only information the computer needs to know to display Jack's net pay? Although you can display a person's gross pay if you know only the hours worked and the hourly pay, a net pay calculation typically involves deducting federal and state taxes, as well as insurance, from the gross pay. What taxes and insurance, if any, will you need to deduct from Jack's gross pay to calculate his net pay? You cannot tell because the problem specification does not contain enough information. Before you can solve this problem, you will need to ask Jack to be more specific about how his net pay is to be calculated.

As a programmer, it is important to distinguish between information that truly is missing in the problem specification, and information that simply is not stated, explicitly, in the problem specification—that is, information that is implied. For example, consider the problem specification shown in Figure 2-9.

Figure 2-9: Problem specification in which the input is not explicitly stated

Sharon Begay, who works for Quality Builders, needs a program that will display the area of any rectangle. The dimensions of the rectangle will be given in feet.

As you may remember from your math courses, you calculate the area of a rectangle by multiplying its length by its width. Therefore, the length and width of the rectangle are the input items for this problem. Notice, however, that the words *length* and *width* do not appear in the problem specification. Although both items are not stated explicitly in the problem specification, both are not considered missing information, because the formula for calculating the area of a rectangle is common knowledge—or, at least, the formula can be found in any math book. With practice, you will be able to "fill in the gaps" in a problem specification also.

If you are having trouble analyzing a problem, try reading the problem specification several times, as it is easy to miss information during the first reading. If the problem still is not clear to you, do not be shy about asking the user for more information. Remember, the greater your understanding of a problem, the easier it will be for you to write a correct and efficient solution to the problem.

MINI-QUIZ

Mini-Quiz 1

For each problem specification that follows, identify the output and the input. Also identify what information, if any, is missing from the problem specification.

1) Paul Eisenstein lives in a state that charges a 3% state income tax on his yearly taxable wages. He wants you to write a program that displays the amount of state income tax he must pay at the end of the year.
2) Deepa Charna belongs to a CD (compact disc) club. The club requires Deepa to purchase 10 CDs each year, at a reduced cost of $8 per CD. Deepa wants to know how much she saves each year by buying the CDs through the club rather than through a store.
3) Penny Long saves $1.25 per day. Penny would like to know the total amount she saved during the month of January.
4) If Jerry Rides saves $1.45 per day, how much will he save in one year?

After analyzing a problem, you then plan its algorithm—its solution.

Planning the Algorithm

The second step in the problem-solving process is to plan the algorithm—the step-by-step instructions that the computer must follow to transform the problem's input into its output. You record the algorithm in the Processing column of the IPO chart.

Most algorithms begin with an instruction that enters the input items into the computer. The input items are the items listed in the Input column of the IPO chart. To determine Sarah Martin's new weekly pay, for example, you will record the instruction "enter the current weekly pay and raise rate" as the first step in the algorithm. You will record this instruction in the Processing column of the IPO chart, below the word "Algorithm."

After the instruction to enter the input items, you usually record instructions to process those items, typically by performing some calculations on them, to achieve the problem's required results. The required results are listed in the Output column of the IPO chart. In Sarah's problem specification, consider how you can use the input items (current weekly pay and raise rate) to achieve the output item (new weekly pay).

Before you can display the new weekly pay, you must compute it. To compute the new weekly pay, you first calculate the weekly raise by multiplying the current weekly pay by the raise rate; you then add the weekly raise to the current weekly pay. You will record the instructions, "calculate the weekly raise by multiplying the current weekly pay by the raise rate" and "calculate the new weekly pay by adding the weekly raise to the current weekly pay," as Steps 2 and 3 in the IPO chart. Notice that both calculation instructions state both *what* is to be calculated and *how* to calculate it.

Unlike the current weekly pay, raise rate, and new weekly pay, the weekly raise amount calculated within the algorithm is neither an input item nor an output item; rather, it is a special item, commonly referred to as a processing item. A **processing item** represents an intermediate value that the algorithm uses when processing the input into the output. In this case, the algorithm uses the two input items (current weekly pay and raise rate) to calculate the intermediate value—weekly raise—which the algorithm then uses to compute the new weekly pay. Not all algorithms require a processing item. If one or more processing items are required, they are listed in the Processing column of the IPO chart, below the words "Processing items." You will enter "weekly raise" as a processing item used in the current algorithm.

Most algorithms end with an instruction either to print, display, or store the output items, which are listed in the Output column of the IPO chart. (*Display*, *print*, and *store* refer to the computer screen, the printer, and a file on a disk, respectively.) In this case, you need to display Sarah's new weekly pay, so you will record the instruction "display the new weekly pay" as the last step in the IPO chart. The completed IPO chart is shown in Figure 2-10. Notice that the algorithm begins by entering some data (the input items), then processing that data (the two calculations), and then displaying some data (the output item). Most algorithms follow this same format.

Notice that the algorithm shown in Figure 2-10 is composed of short English statements. The statements represent the steps the computer must follow to display the new weekly pay. In programming terms, the list of steps shown in Figure 2-10 is called pseudocode. **Pseudocode** is a tool programmers use to help them plan an algorithm. Pseudocode is not standardized—every programmer has his or her own version—but you will find some similarities among the various versions.

Figure 2-10: Completed IPO chart

Input	Processing	Output
current weekly pay raise rate	Processing items: weekly raise Algorithm: 1. enter the current weekly pay and raise rate 2. calculate the weekly raise by multiplying the current weekly pay by the raise rate 3. calculate the new weekly pay by adding the weekly raise to the current weekly pay 4. display the new weekly pay	new weekly pay

Although the word *pseudocode* might be unfamiliar to you, you already have written pseudocode without even realizing it. Think about the last time you gave directions to someone. You wrote down each direction on paper, in your own words. These directions were a form of pseudocode. As you will learn in Tutorial 3, a programmer uses the pseudocode as a guide when coding the algorithm.

To avoid confusion, it is important to be consistent when referring to the input, output, and processing items in the IPO chart. For example, if the input item is called "current weekly pay" in the Input column, then the algorithm should refer to the item as "current weekly pay", rather than using a different name, such as "weekly pay" or "current pay".

In addition to using pseudocode, programmers also use flowcharts to help them plan the algorithm for a problem. Unlike pseudocode, which consists of short English statements, a **flowchart** uses standardized symbols to show the steps the computer needs to take to accomplish the program's goal. Figure 2-11 shows the current problem's algorithm in flowchart form.

tip

You can draw the flowchart symbols by hand, or you can use the drawing feature in a word processor. You also can use a flowcharting program, such as SmartDraw.

Figure 2-11: IPO chart shown with a flowchart in the Processing column

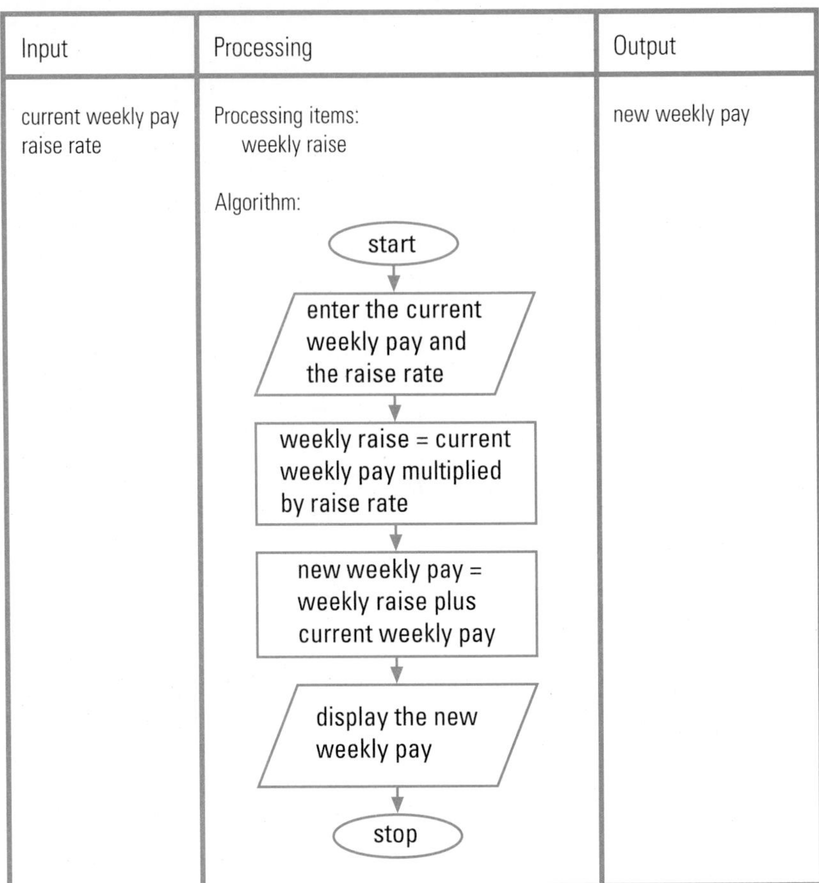
Input
Processing
Output
current weekly pay
raise rate
Processing items:
weekly raise
Algorithm:
start
enter the current weekly pay and the raise rate
weekly raise = current weekly pay multiplied by raise rate
new weekly pay = weekly raise plus current weekly pay
display the new weekly pay
stop
new weekly pay

Notice that the flowchart shown in Figure 2-11 contains three different symbols: an oval, a rectangle, and a parallelogram. The symbols are connected with lines, called **flowlines.** The oval symbol is called the **start/stop symbol.** The start oval indicates the beginning of the flowchart, and the stop oval indicates the end of the flowchart. Between the start and the stop ovals are two rectangles, called **process symbols.** You use the process symbol to represent tasks such as calculations.

The parallelogram is called the **input/output symbol** and is used to represent input tasks, such as getting information from the user, and output tasks, such as displaying or printing information. The first parallelogram shown in Figure 2-11 represents an input task. The last parallelogram represents an output task.

When planning the algorithm, you do not need to create both a flowchart and pseudocode; you need to use only one of these planning tools. The tool you use is really a matter of personal preference. For simple algorithms, pseudocode works just fine. When an algorithm becomes more complex, however, the program's logic may be easier to see in a flowchart. In this book, you usually will use pseudocode in planning algorithms.

Keep in mind that a problem can have more than one solution. For example, you could have solved Sarah's problem without using a processing item, as shown in Figure 2-12.

tip

Many programmers prefer flowcharts to pseudocode, since a picture is sometimes worth a thousand words.

Figure 2-12: Another way of solving Sarah's problem

Input	Processing	Output
current weekly pay raise rate	Processing items: none Algorithm: 1. enter the current weekly pay and raise rate 2. calculate the new weekly pay by multiplying the current weekly pay by the raise rate, and then adding the result to the current weekly pay 3. display the new weekly pay	new weekly pay

Rather than calculating the weekly raise separately, the algorithm shown in Figure 2-12 includes the calculation in the one that computes the new weekly pay.

In the next section, you learn some hints for writing algorithms.

Hints for Writing Algorithms

It is important to remember that you don't need to "reinvent the wheel" each time you create a solution to a problem. Before you write an algorithm, consider whether the problem you are solving is similar to one you have already solved. If it is, you then can use that problem's algorithm to solve the current problem, often with very little modification. For example, consider the problem specification shown in Figure 2-13.

Figure 2-13: Problem specification similar to one you worked with in this lesson

Quality Builders is increasing each of its prices by 3%. The owner of the company wants you to write a program that will display the amount of the increase and the new price.

Although it may not be obvious at first glance, the problem specification shown in Figure 2-13 is almost identical to the one shown earlier in Figure 2-4—only the terminology is different. As you may remember, the problem specification shown in Figure 2-4 required you to calculate and display both the increase in Sarah's pay and her new pay. That is no different than calculating and displaying both an increase in an item's price and a new price, which Figure 2-13's problem specification requires you to do. The IPO chart for Figure 2-13's problem is shown in Figure 2-14 (on the next page). If you compare this IPO chart to the one shown earlier in Figure 2-10, you will notice the similarity between both solutions.

Figure 2-14: IPO chart for the problem specification shown in Figure 2-13

Input	Processing	Output
current price increase rate	Processing items: none Algorithm: 1. enter the current price and increase rate 2. calculate the increase amount by multiplying the current price by the increase rate 3. calculate the new price by adding the increase amount to the current price 4. display the increase amount and new price	increase amount new price

Even if the problem you are trying to solve is not identical to one that you already solved, you may be able to use a portion of a previous solution to solve the current problem. Consider, for example, the problem specification shown in Figure 2-15.

Figure 2-15: Problem specification that contains a portion that is similar to one you worked with in this lesson

At the end of every year, Quality Builders gives each of its employees a bonus. This year the bonus rate is 6% of the employee's current yearly salary. Mary Vasko wants you to write a program that will display her bonus.

Although the problem specified in Figure 2-15 is not identical to any that you solved in this lesson, you can use a part of a previous algorithm to solve it; more specifically, you can use the raise calculation part of Figure 2-10's algorithm. Calculating a bonus, which you need to do now, is no different than calculating a raise. Both calculations require you to take an amount and multiply it by a percentage rate. Recall that you calculated Sarah's raise by multiplying her current weekly pay by her raise rate. Similarly, in Figure 2-15's problem, you calculate Mary's bonus by multiplying her yearly salary by her bonus rate. The IPO chart for the current problem is shown in Figure 2-16.

Figure 2-16: IPO chart for the problem specification shown in Figure 2-15

Input	Processing	Output
current yearly salary bonus rate	Processing items: none Algorithm: 1. enter the current yearly salary and bonus rate 2. calculate the bonus by multiplying the current yearly salary by the bonus rate 3. display the bonus	bonus

If you have not solved a similar problem, and you cannot find a portion of an existing algorithm that you can use, try solving the problem manually, writing down on paper every step you take to do so. If you were to solve Figure 2-15's problem manually, for example, you would need first to read Mary's yearly salary and her bonus rate into your mind. You then would calculate her bonus by multiplying the bonus rate by the yearly salary. Lastly, you would write down the bonus amount on a piece of paper. You can use the steps that you wrote down as a guide when creating your algorithm.

Figure 2-17 summarizes what you learned in this section about planning algorithms.

Figure 2-17: Hints for planning algorithms

1. Before writing an algorithm, consider whether you have already solved a similar problem. If you have, you can use the same solution, often with little modification, to solve the current problem.
2. If you have not solved a similar problem, consider whether you can use a portion of an existing algorithm to solve the current problem.
3. If you have not solved a similar problem, and if you cannot use a portion of an existing algorithm, solve the problem manually, noting each step you take to do so.

Mini-Quiz 2

1) The input/output symbol in a flowchart is represented by a(n) _______________.

2) Calculation tasks are placed in a processing symbol, which is represented in a flowchart by a(n) _______________.

3) Paul Eisenstein lives in a state that charges a 3% state income tax on his yearly taxable wages. He wants you to create a program that displays the state income tax he would need to pay at the end of the year. The output is the annual state income tax. The input is the yearly taxable wages and the state income tax rate. Complete the Processing section of the IPO chart. (Use pseudocode to show the steps.)

4) Deepa Charna belongs to a CD (compact disc) club. The club requires Deepa to purchase 10 CDs each year, at a reduced cost of $8 per CD. Deepa wants to know how much she saves each year by buying the CDs through the club rather than through a store that charges $12 for each CD. The output is the annual savings. The input is the number of CDs purchased each year, the club's CD price, and the store's CD price. Complete the Processing section of the IPO chart. (Use pseudocode to show the steps.)

After analyzing a problem and planning its algorithm, you then desk-check the algorithm, using either the flowchart or the pseudocode, along with sample data.

Desk-Checking the Algorithm

A programmer reviews an algorithm by desk-checking, or hand-tracing, it—in other words, by completing each step in the algorithm manually. You desk-check an algorithm to verify that it is not missing any steps, and that the existing steps are correct and in the proper order. Before you begin the desk-check, you first choose a set of sample data for the input values, which you then use to manually compute the expected output values. For example, you will use input values of $250 and .03 (3%) as Sarah Martin's current weekly pay and raise rate, respectively. Sarah's new weekly pay should be $257.50, which is her current weekly pay of $250 plus her weekly raise of $7.50 (250 multiplied by .03); the 257.50 is the expected output value. You now use the sample input values (250 and .03) to desk-check the algorithm. If the algorithm produces the expected output value of 257.50, then the algorithm appears to be correct.

You can use a desk-check table to help you desk-check an algorithm. The table should contain one column for each input item shown in the IPO chart, as well as one column for each output item and one column for each processing item. Figure 2-18 shows a partially completed desk-check table for Sarah Martin's problem.

Figure 2-18: Desk-check table showing columns for the input, processing, and output items from the IPO chart

current weekly pay	raise rate	weekly raise	new weekly pay

You can desk-check an algorithm using either its pseudocode or its flowchart. The pseudocode for Sarah Martin's problem is shown in Figure 2-10, and the flowchart is shown in Figure 2-11. In both figures, the first step is to enter the input values—in this case, the current weekly pay of 250 and the raise rate of .03. You record the results of this step by writing 250 and .03 in the current weekly pay and raise rate columns, respectively, in the desk-check table, as shown in Figure 2-19.

Figure 2-19: Desk-check table showing input values entered in the appropriate columns

current weekly pay	raise rate	weekly raise	new weekly pay
250	.03		

The second step in the algorithm is to calculate the weekly raise by multiplying the current weekly pay by the raise rate. The desk-check table shows that the current weekly pay is 250 and the raise rate is .03. Notice that you use the table to determine the current weekly pay and raise rate values; this helps to verify the accuracy of the algorithm. If, for example, the table did not show any amount in the raise rate column, you would know that your algorithm missed a step—in this case, it would have missed entering the raise rate.

Multiplying the current weekly pay of 250 by the raise rate of .03 results in a 7.50 raise. You record the number 7.50 in the weekly raise column, as shown in Figure 2-20.

Figure 2-20: Weekly raise entry included in the desk-check table

current weekly pay	raise rate	weekly raise	new weekly pay
250	.03	7.50	

The next step in the algorithm is to calculate the new weekly pay by adding the weekly raise to the current weekly pay. According to the desk-check table, the weekly raise is 7.50 and the current weekly pay is 250. Added together, those amounts result in a new weekly pay of 257.50. You write the 257.50 in the new weekly pay column, as shown in Figure 2-21.

Figure 2-21: New weekly pay entry included in the desk-check table

current weekly pay	raise rate	weekly raise	new weekly pay
250	.03	7.50	257.50

The last instruction in the algorithm is to display the new weekly pay on the screen. In this case, 257.50 will be displayed, because that is what appears in the table's new weekly pay column. Notice that this amount agrees with the manual calculation you performed prior to desk-checking the algorithm, so the algorithm appears to be correct. The only way to know for sure, however, is to test the algorithm a few more times with different input values. For example, you will test the algorithm with a current weekly pay of $100 and a raise rate of .10 (10%). The new weekly pay should be $110, which is the current weekly pay of $100 plus the weekly raise of $10 (100 multiplied by .10).

Recall that the first instruction in the algorithm is to enter the current weekly pay and the raise rate. Therefore, you write 100 in the current weekly pay column and .10 in the raise rate column, as shown in Figure 2-22.

Figure 2-22: Desk-check table for the second set of input values

cross out the previous values

current weekly pay	raise rate	weekly raise	new weekly pay
~~250~~ 100	~~.03~~ .10	7.50	257.50

Notice that you cross out the previous values of these two items in the table before recording the new values; this is because each column should contain only one value at any time.

The next step in the algorithm is to calculate the weekly raise. Multiplying the current weekly pay, which is listed in the table as 100, by the raise rate, which is listed as .10, results in a weekly raise of 10. So you cross out the 7.50 that appears in the weekly raise column in the table and write 10 immediately below it.

The next step is to calculate the new weekly pay. Adding the raise, which is listed in the table as 10, to the current weekly pay, which is listed in the table as 100, results in a new weekly pay of 110. Therefore, you cross out the 257.50 that appears in the new weekly pay column in the table and write 110 immediately below it. The completed desk-check table is shown in Figure 2-23.

Figure 2-23: Desk-check table showing the results of the second desk-check

current weekly pay	raise rate	weekly raise	new weekly pay
~~250~~ 100	~~.03~~ .10	~~7.50~~ 10	~~257.50~~ 110

The last step in the algorithm is to display the new weekly pay. In this case, the algorithm will display 110, because that is what appears in the table's new weekly pay column. The amount in the table agrees with the manual calculation you performed earlier, so the algorithm still appears to be correct. To be sure, however, you should desk-check it a few more times.

In addition to desk-checking the algorithm using valid data, you also should desk-check it using invalid data, because users sometimes make mistakes when entering data. **Valid data** is data that the programmer is expecting the user to enter. For example, in the algorithm that you just finished desk-checking, the programmer expects the user to provide positive numbers for the input values (current weekly pay and raise rate). **Invalid data** is data that the programmer is not expecting the user to enter. In this case, the programmer is not expecting the user to enter a negative value as the current weekly pay. A negative weekly pay is obviously an input error, because an employee cannot earn a negative amount for the week. Beginning in Tutorial 6, you learn how to create algorithms that correctly handle input errors. For now, however, you can assume that the user of the program will always enter valid data.

As a way of summarizing what you learned in this lesson, you will use the first three steps in the problem-solving process to solve another problem.

The Gas Mileage Problem

Figure 2-24 shows the problem specification for the gas mileage problem, which you solve next.

Figure 2-24: Problem specification for the gas mileage problem

When Jacob Steinberg began his trip from California to Vermont, he filled his car's tank with gas and reset its trip meter to zero. After traveling 324 miles, Jacob stopped at a gas station to refuel; the gas tank required 17 gallons. Create a program that Jacob can use to display his car's gas mileage—the number of miles his car can be driven per gallon of gas—at anytime during the trip.

First, analyze the problem, looking for nouns and adjectives that represent both the output and the input. The output should answer the question *What does the user want to see printed on paper, displayed on the screen, or stored in a file?* The input should answer the question *What information will the computer need to know to print, display, or store the output items?* In the gas mileage problem, the output is the miles per gallon, and the input is the number of miles driven and the number of gallons used.

Next, plan the algorithm. Recall that most algorithms begin with an instruction that enters the input items into the computer, followed by instructions that process the input items and then print, display, or store the output items. Figure 2-25 shows the completed IPO chart for the gas mileage problem.

Figure 2-25: Completed IPO chart for the gas mileage problem

Input	Processing	Output
number of miles driven number of gallons used	Processing items: none Algorithm: 1. enter the number of miles driven and the number of gallons used 2. calculate the miles per gallon by dividing the number of miles driven by the number of gallons used 3. display the miles per gallon	miles per gallon

After planning the algorithm, you then desk-check it, which is the third step in the problem-solving process. You will desk-check the algorithm twice, first using 324 and 17 as the miles driven and number of gallons, respectively, and then using 200 and 12. Figure 2-26 shows the completed desk-check table for the gas mileage problem.

Figure 2-26: Completed desk-check table for the gas mileage problem

number of miles driven	number of gallons used	miles per gallon
~~324~~ 200	~~17~~ 12	~~19.06~~ 16.67

MINI-QUIZ

Mini-Quiz 3

1) Desk-check the following algorithm. Use a yearly taxable wage of $20,000 and a 3% state income tax rate, and then use a yearly taxable wage of $10,000 and a 2% state income tax.

Input	Processing	Output
yearly taxable wages state income tax rate	Processing items: none Algorithm: 1. enter the yearly taxable wages and the state income tax rate 2. calculate the annual state income tax by multiplying the yearly taxable wages by the state income tax rate 3. display the annual state income tax	annual state income tax

2) Desk-check the following algorithm. Use 5 and 7 as the first set of input values, then use 6 and 8 as the second set of input values.

Input	Processing	Output
first number second number	Processing items: sum Algorithm: 1. enter the first number and the second number 2. calculate the sum by adding together the first number and the second number 3. calculate the average by dividing the sum by 2 4. display the average	average

You now have completed Tutorial 2's Concept lesson, which covered the first three of the six steps required to create a computer program. Recall that the first three steps are to analyze the problem, plan the algorithm, and desk-check the algorithm. You complete the last three steps—code the algorithm into a program, desk-check the program, and evaluate and modify (if necessary) the program—in Tutorial 3. You can either take a break or complete the end-of-lesson questions and exercises before moving on to the Application lesson.

SUMMARY

If you are like most people, you probably do not pay much attention to the problem-solving process that you use when solving everyday problems. This process typically involves analyzing the problem, and then planning, reviewing, implementing, evaluating, and modifying (if necessary) the solution. You can use a similar problem-solving process to create a computer program, which also is a solution to a problem.

Programmers use tools such as IPO (Input, Processing, Output) charts, pseudocode, and flowcharts to help them analyze problems and develop algorithms. During the analysis step, the programmer first determines the output, which is the goal or purpose of solving the problem. The programmer then determines the input, which is the information he or she needs to reach the goal. During the planning step, programmers write the steps that will transform the input into the output. Most algorithms begin by entering some data (the input items), then processing that data (usually by doing some calculations), and then displaying some data (the output items).

After the analysis and planning steps, a programmer then desk-checks the algorithm to determine whether it will work as intended. Desk-checking means that the programmer follows each of the steps in the algorithm by hand, just as if he or she were the computer. When the programmer is satisfied that the algorithm is correct, he or she then codes the algorithm. Coding refers to translating the algorithm into a language that the computer can understand. A coded algorithm is called a program. After coding the algorithm, the programmer then desk-checks the program to be sure that he or she translated each of the steps in the algorithm correctly. The programmer then evaluates and modifies (if necessary) the program by executing it, along with sample data, using the computer. If the program does not work as intended, then the programmer makes the necessary modifications until it does.

Before writing an algorithm, you should consider whether you have already solved a similar problem. If you have, you can use that solution, often with little modification, to solve the current problem. If you have not solved a similar problem, consider whether a portion of an existing algorithm is similar enough to use in the current problem. If no existing algorithms help, try solving the problem manually, being sure to write down every step you take to do so, because the computer will need to follow the same steps.

ANSWERS TO MINI-QUIZZES

Mini-Quiz 1

1) Output: annual state income tax
Input: yearly taxable wages, state income tax rate
Missing information: none

2) Output: annual savings
Input: number of CDs purchased each year, CD cost when purchased through the club, CD cost when purchased through the store
Missing information: CD cost when purchased through the store

3) Output: total amount saved in January
Input: amount saved per day, number of days in January
Missing information: none (Although the number of days in January is not specified in the problem specification, that information can be found in any calendar.)

4) Output: yearly savings
Input: amount saved per day, number of days in the year
Missing information: number of days in the year (Because some years are leap years, you would need to know the number of days in the year.)

Mini-Quiz 2

1) parallelogram ▱

2) rectangle ▭

3)

Input	Processing	Output
yearly taxable wages state income tax rate	Processing items: none Algorithm: 1. enter the yearly taxable wages and the state income tax rate 2. calculate the annual state income tax by multiplying the yearly taxable wages by the state income tax rate 3. display the annual state income tax	annual state income tax

4)

Input	Processing	Output
number of CDs purchased each year club's CD price store's CD price	Processing items: amount spent through the club amount spent at the store Algorithm: 1. enter the number of CDs purchased each year, the club's CD price, and the store's CD price 2. calculate the amount spent through the club by multiplying the number of CDs purchased each year by the club's CD price 3. calculate the amount spent at the store by multiplying the number of CDs purchased each year by the store's CD price 4. calculate the annual savings by subtracting the amount spent through the club from the amount spent at the store 5. display the annual savings	annual savings

Mini-Quiz 3

1)

yearly taxable wages	state income tax rate	annual state income tax
~~20000~~ 10000	~~.03~~ .02	~~600~~ 200

2)

first number	second number	sum	average
~~5~~ 6	~~7~~ 8	~~12~~ 14	~~6~~ 7

QUESTIONS

1) The first step in the problem-solving process is to ______________.

A. plan the algorithm
B. analyze the problem
C. desk-check the algorithm
D. code the algorithm

2) Programmers refer to the goal of solving a problem as the ______________.

A. input
B. output
C. processing
D. purpose

3) Programmers refer to the items needed to reach a problem's goal as the ______________.

A. input
B. output
C. processing
D. purpose

4) A problem's ______________ will answer the question *What does the user want to see printed on the printer, displayed on the screen, or stored in a file?*

A. input
B. output
C. processing
D. purpose

5) Programmers use ______________ to organize and summarize the results of their problem analysis.

A. input charts

B. IPO charts

C. output charts

D. processing charts

6) A problem's ______________ will answer the question *What information will the computer need to know to print, display, or store the output items?*

A. input

B. output

C. processing

D. purpose

7) Most algorithms begin by ______________.

A. displaying the input items

B. entering the input items into the computer

C. entering the output items into the computer

D. processing the input items by doing some calculations on them

8) You record the algorithm in the ______________ column of the IPO chart.

A. Input

B. Output

C. Processing

D. Purpose

9) The calculation instructions in an algorithm should state ______________.

A. only *what* is to be calculated

B. only *how* to calculate something

C. both *what* is to be calculated and *how* to calculate it

D. both *what* is to be calculated and *why* it is calculated

10) Most algorithms follow the format of ______________.

A. entering the input items, then displaying, printing, or storing the input items, and then processing the output items

B. entering the input items, then processing the output items, and then displaying, printing, or storing the output items

C. entering the input items, then processing the input items, and then displaying, printing, or storing the output items

D. entering the output items, then processing the output items, and then displaying, printing, or storing the output items

11) The short statements that represent the steps the computer must follow to solve a problem are called ______________.

A. flow diagrams

B. IPO charts

C. pseudocharts

D. pseudocode

12) ______________ use standardized symbols to represent an algorithm.

A. Flowcharts

B. Flow diagrams

C. IPO charts

D. Pseudocharts

13) The ______________ symbol is used in a flowchart to represent a calculation task.

A. input

B. output

C. process

D. start

14) The ______________ symbol is used in a flowchart to represent a step that gets information from the user.

A. input/output

B. process

C. selection/repetition

D. start/stop

15) The process symbol in a flowchart is the ______________.

A. ◇

B. ⬭

C. ▱

D. ▭

16) The input/output symbol in a flowchart is the ______________.

A. ◇

B. ⬭

C. ▱

D. ▭

17) The start/stop symbol, which marks both the beginning and ending of a flowchart, is a(n) ______________.

A. ◇

B. ⬭

C. ▱

D. ▭

18) After planning an algorithm, you should ______________ to verify that it will work correctly.

A. analyze the algorithm

B. code the algorithm

C. desk-check the algorithm

D. evaluate and modify (if necessary) the program

19) When desk-checking an algorithm, you should set up a table that contains ________________.

A. one column for each input item
B. one column for each output item
C. one column for each processing item
D. all of the above

Look For These Symbols

Debugging

Discovery

EXERCISES

1) Hai Chang needs a program that calculates and displays the square of a number. Complete an IPO chart for this problem. Use pseudocode in the Processing column. Also complete a desk-check table for your algorithm. Use the number 4 for the first desk-check, then use the number 6.

2) Mingo Sales needs a program that the company can use to enter the sales made in each of two states. The program should display the commission, which is 5% of the total sales. (In other words, if you have sales totaling $3,000, your commission is $150.) The commission rate may change in the future, so you should treat it as an input item. Complete an IPO chart for this problem. Use pseudocode in the Processing column. Also complete a desk-check table for your algorithm. For the first desk-check, use 1000 and 2000 as the two state sales, and use .05 (the decimal equivalent of 5%) as the commission rate. Then use 3000 and 2500 as the two state sales, and use .06 as the commission rate.

3) Joan Brimley is the accountant at Paper Products. The salespeople at Paper Products are paid a commission, which is a percentage of the sales they make. The current commission rate is 10%, but that rate may change in the future. (In other words, if you have sales totaling $2,000, your commission is $200.) Joan wants you to create a program that displays the commission after she enters the salesperson's sales and commission rate. Complete an IPO chart for this problem. Use a flowchart in the Processing column. Also complete a desk-check table for your algorithm. Use 2000 and .1 (the decimal equivalent of 10%) as the salesperson's sales amount and commission rate, respectively. Then use 5000 and .06.

4) RM Sales divides its sales territory into three regions: 1, 2, and 3. Robert Gonzales, the sales manager, wants a program in which he can enter the current year's sales for each region and the projected increase (expressed as a percentage) in sales for each region. He then wants the program to display the following year's projected sales for each region. (For example, if Robert enters 10,000 as the current sales for region 1, and then enters a 10% projected increase, the program should display 11,000 as next year's projected sales.) Complete an IPO chart for this problem. Use pseudocode in the Processing column. Also complete a desk-check table for your algorithm.

Use the following information for the first desk-check:

Region	Sales	Increase rate
1	10000	.1
2	3000	.09
3	6000	.1

Use the following information for the second desk-check:

Region	Sales	Increase rate
1	5000	.02
2	2000	.03
3	1000	.02

5) Modify the algorithm that you created in Exercise 1 so that it calculates and displays the square of positive numbers only. If the number entered by the user is either zero or less than zero, the algorithm should display an error message. Desk-check the algorithm using the numbers 10 and –3.

6) Etola Systems wants a program that displays the ending inventory amount, given the beginning inventory amount, the amount sold, and the amount returned. The algorithm shown in Figure 2-27 is supposed to solve this problem, but it is not working correctly. First calculate the expected results using a beginning inventory of 50, an amount sold of 10, and an amount returned of 2. Then use these values to desk-check the algorithm. Rewrite the algorithm correctly, then desk-check it again.

Figure 2-27

Input	Processing	Output
beginning inventory amount sold amount returned	Processing items: none Algorithm: 1. enter the beginning inventory, amount sold, and amount returned 2. calculate the ending inventory by adding the amount sold to the beginning inventory, then subtracting the amount returned from the result 3. display the ending inventory	ending inventory

7) The algorithm shown in Figure 2-28 should calculate an employee's gross pay. Correct any errors in the algorithm. (You do not have to worry about overtime pay.)

Figure 2-28

Input	Processing	Output
hours worked rate of pay	Processing items: none Algorithm: 1. enter the hours worked and pay rate 2. calculate the gross pay by multiplying the hours by the rate of pay 3. display the gross pay	gross pay

Application Lesson

Using the First Steps in the Problem-Solving Process

CASE Last year, Mark Williams opened a new wallpaper store named The Paper Tree. Business is booming at the store, and Mark and his salesclerks are always busy. Recently, however, Mark has received several complaints from customers about the store's slow service, and he has decided to ask his salesclerks for suggestions on how the service can be improved. The overwhelming response from the salesclerks is that they need a more convenient way to calculate the number of single rolls of wallpaper required to cover a room. Currently, the salesclerks perform this calculation manually, using pencil and paper. Doing this for so many customers, however, takes a great deal of time, and service has begun to suffer. Mark has asked for your assistance in this matter. He would like you to create a program that the salesclerks can use to quickly calculate and display the required number of rolls.

The Problem Specification

Before you begin the problem-solving process, you meet with Mark to develop an appropriate problem specification—one that contains all of the information needed to solve the problem. You also ask Mark to show you how the clerks currently calculate the required number of rolls. As you learned in the Concept lesson, the computer needs to make the same calculations as you do. Figure 2-29 shows the final problem specification and a sample calculation.

Figure 2-29: Problem specification and sample calculation

Problem specification:

Create a program that calculates and displays the number of single rolls of wallpaper needed to cover a room. The salesclerk will provide the length, width, and ceiling height of the room, in feet. He or she also will provide the number of square feet a single roll will cover.

Sample calculation:

Room size: 10 feet by 12 feet, with a ceiling height of 8 feet
Single roll coverage: 30 square feet

1. Calculate the perimeter of the room by adding together its length and width, and then multiplying the sum by 2: (10 feet + 12 feet) * 2 = 44 feet
2. Calculate the wall area by multiplying the room's perimeter by its height: 44 feet * 8 feet = 352 square feet
3. Calculate the required number of single rolls by dividing the wall area by the number of square feet a single roll provides: 352 square feet / 30 square feet = 11.73 (rounded to two decimal places), or approximately 12 single rolls

Armed with this information, you now can begin the problem-solving process.

Analyze the Problem

As you learned in the Concept lesson, the first step in the problem-solving process is to analyze the problem. You do so to determine the goal of solving the problem (output), and the items that are needed to achieve the goal (input). Recall that you always search the problem specification first for the output, and then for the input. The input and output typically are stated as nouns and adjectives in the problem specification.

Asking yourself the question *What does the user want to see printed on the printer, displayed on the screen, or stored in a file?* will help you determine the output. In this case, the user wants to see the number of single rolls of wallpaper needed to cover a room, so you record "number of single rolls" in the Output column of this problem's IPO chart.

The question *What information will the computer need to know to print, display, or store the output items?* will help you determine the input. In this case, the input is the length, width, and ceiling height of the room, as well as the coverage provided by a single roll of wallpaper. Figure 2-30 shows the IPO chart with the Input and Output columns completed.

Figure 2-30: IPO chart showing input and output items

Input	Processing	Output
room length room width ceiling height single roll coverage	Processing items: Algorithm:	number of single rolls

The next step in the problem-solving process is to plan the algorithm.

Planning the Algorithm

After determining a problem's input and output, you then plan its algorithm, which is the step-by-step instructions that will transform the input into the output. Recall that most algorithms begin by entering the input items into the computer. In the current problem's algorithm, for example, the first step will be "enter the room length, room width, ceiling height, and single roll coverage". Notice that the instruction refers to the input items using the same names listed in the Input column of the IPO chart.

After the instruction to enter the input items, you usually record instructions to process those items, typically by performing some calculations on them. According to the sample calculation shown in Figure 2-29, first you calculate the room's perimeter. You do so by adding together the room's length and width, and then multiplying that sum by two. Notice that the room perimeter does not appear in either the Input or Output column in the IPO chart. This is because the room perimeter is neither an input item nor an output item; rather, it is a processing item. As you learned in the Concept lesson, a processing item represents an intermediate value that the algorithm uses when processing the input into the output. For this problem, you enter "room perimeter" in the Processing items section of the IPO chart, and "calculate the room perimeter by adding together the room length and room width, and then multiplying the sum by 2" in the Algorithm section, as shown in Figure 2-31 (on the next page).

Next, you calculate the wall area by multiplying the room's perimeter by the height of its ceiling. This calculation gives you the total number of square feet to be covered. Like the perimeter, the wall area is a processing item. Therefore, you enter "wall area" in the Processing items section of the IPO chart, and "calculate the wall area by multiplying the room perimeter by the ceiling height" in the Algorithm section.

Figure 2-31: IPO chart showing the partially completed algorithm

Input	Processing	Output
room length room width ceiling height single roll coverage	Processing items: room perimeter Algorithm: 1. enter the room length, room width, ceiling height, and single roll coverage 2. calculate the room perimeter by adding together the room length and room width, and then multiplying the sum by 2	number of single rolls

The last calculation you make is to divide the wall area by the coverage provided by a single roll. This calculation gives you the required number of single rolls. You enter "calculate the number of single rolls by dividing the wall area by the single roll coverage" in the Algorithm section of the IPO chart.

Recall that most algorithms end with an instruction to print, display, or store the output items. In this case, you need simply to display the number of single rolls. You record "display the number of single rolls" in the Algorithm section of the IPO chart. The completed IPO chart is shown in Figure 2-32.

Figure 2-32: Completed IPO chart for the wallpaper store problem

Input	Processing	Output
room length room width ceiling height single roll coverage	Processing items: room perimeter wall area Algorithm: 1. enter the room length, room width, ceiling height, and single roll coverage 2. calculate the room perimeter by adding together the room length and room width, and then multiplying the sum by 2 3. calculate the wall area by multiplying the room perimeter by the ceiling height 4. calculate the number of single rolls by dividing the wall area by the single roll coverage 5. display the number of single rolls	number of single rolls

After completing the IPO chart, you then move on to the third step in the problem-solving process, which is to desk-check the algorithm that appears in the chart.

Desk-Checking the Algorithm

You desk-check an algorithm to verify that it is not missing any steps, and that the existing steps are correct and in the proper order. Recall that, before you begin the desk-check, you first choose a set of sample data for the input values, which you then use to manually compute the expected output values. In this case, you will use the input values shown earlier in Figure 2-29. In that figure, the values 10 feet, 12 feet, 8 feet, and 30 square feet are specified as the room length, room width, ceiling height, and single roll coverage, respectively. The sample calculation provided in Figure 2-29 shows that the required number of single rolls, using those input values, is 11.73 (rounded to two decimal places), or approximately 12 single rolls. Now see whether the algorithm shown in Figure 2-32 results in the same amount.

First, create a desk-check table that contains a column for each input, processing, and output item, as shown in Figure 2-33.

Figure 2-33: Desk-check table for the wallpaper store problem

room length	room width	ceiling height	single roll coverage	room perimeter	wall area	number of single rolls

Now you can begin desk-checking the algorithm. The first instruction in the algorithm is to enter the room length, room width, ceiling height, and single roll coverage. Figure 2-34 shows these values entered in the desk-check table.

Figure 2-34: Input values entered in the desk-check table

room length	room width	ceiling height	single roll coverage	room perimeter	wall area	number of single rolls
10	12	8	30			

The next instruction is to calculate the room perimeter by adding together the room length and room width, and then multiplying the sum by 2. The room length column in the desk-check table contains the number 10, and the room width column contains the number 12. When you add together the numbers 10 and 12, you get 22. And when you multiply the 22 by 2, you get 44, which you enter in the room perimeter column in the table, as shown in Figure 2-35.

Figure 2-35: Room perimeter value entered in the desk-check table

room length	room width	ceiling height	single roll coverage	room perimeter	wall area	number of single rolls
10	12	8	30	44		

The third instruction in the algorithm is to calculate the wall area by multiplying the room perimeter by the ceiling height. The room perimeter column in the table contains the number 44, and the ceiling height column contains the number 8. When you multiply 44 by 8, you get 352, which you enter in the wall area column in the table, as shown in Figure 2-36.

Figure 2-36: Wall area value entered in the desk-check table

room length	room width	ceiling height	single roll coverage	room perimeter	wall area	number of single rolls
10	12	8	30	44	352	

The fourth instruction in the algorithm is to calculate the number of single rolls by dividing the wall area by the single roll coverage. The wall area column in the table contains the number 352, and the single roll coverage column contains the number 30. When you divide 352 by 30, you get 11.73 (rounded to two decimal places), which you enter in the number of single rolls column in the table. The completed desk-check table is shown in Figure 2-37.

Figure 2-37: Desk-check table showing the results of the first desk-check

room length	room width	ceiling height	single roll coverage	room perimeter	wall area	number of single rolls
10	12	8	30	44	352	11.73

The last instruction in the algorithm is to display the number of single rolls. According to the desk-check table, the number of single rolls is 11.73, which agrees with the manual calculation shown earlier in Figure 2-29. Although the algorithm appears to be correct, recall that you should test it several times using different data to be sure. Figure 2-38 shows the desk-check table using input values of 12 feet, 14 feet, 10 feet, and 37 square feet as the room length, room width, ceiling height, and single roll coverage, respectively.

Figure 2-38: Desk-check table showing the results of the second desk-check

room length	room width	ceiling height	single roll coverage	room perimeter	wall area	number of single rolls
~~10~~ 12	~~12~~ 14	~~8~~ 10	~~30~~ 37	~~44~~ 52	~~352~~ 520	~~11.73~~ 14.05

Almost every problem—no matter how simple it is—can be solved in more than one way. For example, rather than using the algorithm shown in Figure 2-32 to solve the wallpaper problem, you also can use the algorithm shown in Figure 2-39.

Figure 2-39: Another correct algorithm for the wallpaper store problem

Input	Processing	Output
room length room width ceiling height single roll coverage	Processing items: room perimeter Algorithm: 1. enter the room length, room width, ceiling height, and single roll coverage 2. calculate the room perimeter by adding together the room length and room width, and then multiplying the sum by 2 3. calculate the number of single rolls by multiplying the room perimeter by the ceiling height, and then dividing the result by the single roll coverage 4. display the number of single rolls	number of single rolls

You now have completed Tutorial 2's Application lesson. You can either take a break or complete the end-of-lesson exercises.

EXERCISES

Look For These Symbols

Debugging

Discovery

1) Rewrite the IPO chart shown in Figure 2-32 using a flowchart in the Algorithm section.

2) John Lee wants a program that allows him to enter the following three pieces of information: his savings account balance at the beginning of the month, the amount of money he deposited during the month, and the amount of money he withdrew during the month. He wants the program to display his balance at the end of the month. Complete an IPO chart for this problem, using pseudocode in the Processing column. Also complete a desk-check table for your algorithm.

Use the following information for the first desk-check:

savings account balance at the beginning of the month:	2000
money deposited during the month:	775
money withdrawn during the month:	1200

Use the following information for the second desk-check:

savings account balance at the beginning of the month:	500
money deposited during the month:	100
money withdrawn during the month:	610

3) Lana Jones wants a program that displays the average of any three numbers she enters. Complete an IPO chart for this problem, using pseudocode in the Processing column. Also complete a desk-check table for your algorithm. Use the following three numbers for the first desk-check: 25, 76, and 33. Use the following three numbers for the second desk-check: 10, 15, and 20.

4) Jackets Unlimited is having a sale on all of its merchandise. The store manager asks you to create a program that requires the clerk to enter the original price of a jacket and the discount rate. The program should then display both the sales discount and the new sales price. Complete an IPO chart for this problem, using pseudocode in the Processing column. Also complete a desk-check table for your algorithm. For the first desk-check, use 100 as the jacket price and .25 (the decimal equivalent of 25%) as the discount rate. For the second desk-check, use 50 as the jacket price and .1 as the discount rate.

5) Typing Salon currently charges $.10 per typed envelope and $.25 per typed page, although those prices may change in the future. The company accountant wants a program that will help her prepare the customer bills. She will enter the number of typed envelopes and the number of typed pages, as well as the current charges per typed envelope and per typed page. The program should display the total amount due from the customer. Complete an IPO chart for this problem, using pseudocode in the Processing column. Also complete a desk-check table for your algorithm.

Use the following information for the first desk-check:

number of typed envelopes:	100
number of typed pages:	100
charge per typed envelope:	.10
charge per typed page:	.25

Use the following information for the second desk-check:

number of typed envelopes:	10
number of typed pages:	15
charge per typed envelope:	.20
charge per typed page:	.30

6) Management USA, a small training center, plans to run two full-day seminars on December 1. (Because each seminar lasts the entire day, a person can register for only one of the two seminars at a time.) The current seminar price is $200, but that price could change in the future. Registration for the seminars will be taken by telephone. When a company calls to register its employees, the Management USA telephone representative will ask for the following two items of information: the number of employees registering for the first seminar and the number registering for the second seminar. Claire Jenkowski, the owner of Management USA, wants a program that displays the total number of employees the company is registering and the total cost. Complete an IPO chart for this problem, using pseudocode in the Processing column. Also complete a desk-check table for your algorithm.

Use the following information for the first desk-check:

number registering for the first seminar:	10
number registering for the second seminar:	10
seminar price:	200

Use the following information for the second desk-check:

number registering for the first seminar:	30
number registering for the second seminar:	10
seminar price:	100

7) Suman Gadhari, the payroll clerk at Sun Projects, wants a program that computes an employee's net pay. Suman will enter the hours worked, the hourly rate of pay, the federal withholding tax (FWT) rate, the Social Security (FICA) tax rate, and the state income tax rate. For this program, you do not have to worry about overtime, as this company does not allow anyone to work more than 40 hours. Suman wants the program to display the employee's gross pay, FWT, FICA, state income tax, and net pay. Complete an IPO chart for this problem, using pseudocode in the Processing column. Also complete a desk-check table for your algorithm.

Use the following information for the first desk-check:

hours worked:	20
hourly pay rate:	6
FWT rate:	.2
FICA rate:	.08
state income tax rate:	.02

Use the following information for the second desk-check:

hours worked:	30
hourly pay rate:	10
FWT rate:	.2
FICA rate:	.08
state income tax rate:	.04

8) Perry Brown needs a program that allows him to enter the length of four sides of a polygon. The program should display the perimeter of the polygon. Complete an IPO chart for this problem, using pseudocode in the Processing column. Also complete a desk-check table. Desk-check the algorithm twice, using your own sample data.

9) Builders Inc. needs a program that allows its salesclerks to enter the diameter of a circle and the price of railing material per foot. The program should display the circumference of the circle and the total price of the railing material. (Use 3.14 as the value of pi.) Complete an IPO chart for this problem, using a flowchart in the Processing column. Also complete a desk-check table for your algorithm. Desk-check the algorithm twice, using your own sample data.

10) Tile Limited wants a program that allows its salesclerks to enter the length and width (in feet) of a rectangle and the price of a square foot of tile. The program should display the area of the rectangle and the total price of the tile. Complete an IPO chart for this problem, using pseudocode in the Processing column. Also complete a desk-check table for your algorithm. Desk-check the algorithm twice, using your own sample data.

11) Willow Pools wants a program that allows its salespeople to enter the dimensions of a rectangle in feet. The program should display the volume of the rectangle. Complete an IPO chart for this problem, using pseudocode in the Processing column. Also complete a desk-check table for your algorithm. Desk-check the algorithm twice, using your own sample data.

12) IMY Industries needs a program that its personnel clerks can use to display the new hourly pay, given both the current hourly pay for each of three job codes (1, 2, and 3) and the raise rate (entered as a decimal). Complete an IPO chart for this problem, using pseudocode in the Processing column. Also complete a desk-check table for your algorithm.

Use the following information for the first desk-check:

current hourly pay for job code 1:	7.55
current hourly pay for job code 2:	10.00
current hourly pay for job code 3:	10.30
raise rate:	.02

Use the following information for the second desk-check:

current hourly pay for job code 1:	8.00
current hourly pay for job code 2:	6.50
current hourly pay for job code 3:	7.25
raise rate:	.02

13) Sue Chen attends Jefferson University in Kentucky. Students attending Jefferson University are considered full-time students if they are registered for at least 15 semester hours. Students registered for less than 15 hours are considered part-time students. Sue would like you to create a program that displays the total cost per semester. Tuition is $100 per semester hour. Room and board is $3000. (Assume that all students live on campus and will have room and board charges.) Complete an IPO chart for this problem, using a flowchart in the Processing column. Also complete a desk-check table for your algorithm. Desk-check the algorithm twice. Use 20 semester hours for the first desk-check, and use 14 hours for the second desk-check.

14) George Markos, the payroll clerk at Microstep Company, wants a program that computes an employee's gross pay. George will enter the hours worked and the hourly rate of pay. Employees working over 40 hours receive time and one-half on the hours over 40. George wants the program to display the employee's gross pay. Complete an IPO chart for this problem, using pseudocode in the Processing column. Also complete a desk-check table for your algorithm. For the first desk-check, use 20 as the hours worked and 6 as the hourly pay rate. For the second desk-check, use 43 as the hours worked and 10 as the hourly pay rate.

15) Jean Marie wants a program that displays the cube of a number. The algorithm shown in Figure 2-40 is supposed to solve this problem, but it is not working correctly. Rewrite the algorithm correctly, then desk-check it using the number 4.

Figure 2-40

Input	Processing	Output
number	Processing items: none Algorithm: 1. calculate the cube of the number by multiplying the number by itself three times	cube of the number

16) GeeBees Clothiers is having a sale. The manager of the store wants a program that allows the clerk to enter the original price of an item and the discount rate. The program should display the discount and the sale price. The algorithm shown in Figure 2-41 is supposed to solve this problem, but it is not working correctly. Rewrite the algorithm correctly, then desk-check it using an original price of $100 and a discount rate of 25%.

Figure 2-41

Input	Processing	Output
original price discount rate	Processing items: none Algorithm: 1. enter the original price and the discount rate 2. calculate the sale price by subtracting the discount from the original price 3. display the discount and the sale price	discount sale price

Tutorial 3

Completing the Problem-Solving Process and Getting Started with C++

Objectives

After completing this tutorial, you will be able to:

- Distinguish between a variable, a named constant, and a literal constant
- Select an appropriate name, data type, and initial value for a memory location
- Explain how data is stored in memory
- Reserve and initialize a memory location
- Type cast data
- Use an assignment statement to assign data to a variable
- Include arithmetic operators in an expression

- Display information on the computer screen using the `Console::Write()` and `Console::WriteLine()` methods
- Get string input using the `Console::ReadLine()` method
- Code an algorithm into a program
- Desk-check a program
- Evaluate and modify a program
- Differentiate between source code, object code, and executable code
- Start and customize Visual Studio .NET
- Create a console application
- Understand the components of a C++ program
- Save, close, and open a solution
- Build, execute, and print a C++ program
- Locate an error in a C++ program
- Make a backup copy of a C++ solution

Concept Lesson

More on the Problem-Solving Process

In Tutorial 2, you learned how to analyze a problem, as well as how to plan and desk-check an algorithm designed to solve the problem. Recall that analyzing, planning, and desk-checking are the first three steps in the problem-solving process used to create a computer program. The entire process is shown in Figure 3-1.

Only after the programmer is satisfied that an algorithm is correct does he or she then move on to the fourth step in the problem-solving process. As Figure 3-1 indicates, Step 4 is to code the algorithm—in other words, to translate the algorithm into a language that the computer can understand. As you may remember from Tutorial 2, a coded algorithm is called a program. In this book, you use the C++ programming language to translate your algorithms into programs.

After completing the coding step, the programmer then desk-checks the program to make sure that the algorithm was translated correctly—this is Step 5 in the problem-solving process. Programmers typically desk-check the program using the same sample data used to desk-check the algorithm. If the program does not produce the same results as the algorithm, the programmer corrects the errors in the program before continuing to the final step in the problem-solving process.

Figure 3-1: The problem-solving process for creating a computer program

1. Analyze the problem.
2. Plan the algorithm.
3. Desk-check the algorithm.
4. Code the algorithm into a program.
5. Desk-check the program.
6. Evaluate and modify (if necessary) the program.

The final step in the problem-solving process is to evaluate and modify (if necessary) the program. A programmer evaluates a program by running (executing) it on the computer. While the program is running, the programmer enters the same sample data he or she used when desk-checking the program. If the executed program does not work as intended, the programmer makes the necessary modifications until it does.

In this tutorial, you learn how to complete the problem-solving process by performing Steps 4 through 6. Before you can do so, however, you need to learn about variables, named constants, assignment statements, and arithmetic operators. Additionally, you need to learn how to get data from the user at the keyboard and also display information on the computer screen. This knowledge is necessary to code the algorithms you create in this book. Begin by learning about variables and named constants.

Variables and Named Constants

Variables and named constants are locations (within the computer's internal memory) where a program can temporarily store data. The data may be entered by the user at the keyboard, or it may be read in from a file, or it may be the result of a calculation made by the computer. It may be helpful to picture a memory location as a small box inside the computer. You can enter and store data in the box, but you cannot actually see the box.

Two types of memory locations (boxes) are available for your program to use: variable memory locations and named constant memory locations. The difference between the two types is that the contents of a variable memory location can change (vary) as the program is running, whereas the contents of a named constant memory location cannot.

You need to reserve a memory location for each unique input, processing, and output item listed in a problem's IPO chart. But how do you determine which type of memory location to reserve—variable or named constant? If an item's value will change each time a program is executed, you need to store the value in a variable memory location, referred to simply as a **variable**, because that is the only type of memory location whose contents can change while a program is running. In a payroll program, for example, you would store the employee name, hours worked, and rate of pay in variables, because the value of those items will be different for each employee. On the other hand, you use a named constant memory location, referred to simply as a **named constant**, for any item whose value will remain the same each time the program is executed. The FICA (Federal Insurance Contributions Act) tax rate in a payroll program would be stored in a named constant, because its value will be the same for each employee.

The problem specification and IPO chart shown in Figure 3-2 provide another example of using variables and named constants.

Figure 3-2: Problem specification and IPO chart for the circle area problem

Problem specification:

Mr. Johnson needs a program that he can use to calculate and display the area of a circle, based on the circle radius he enters. Use 3.141593 as the value for pi.

Input	Processing	Output
radius pi (3.141593)	Processing items: radius squared Algorithm: 1. enter the radius 2. calculate the radius squared by multiplying the radius by itself 3. calculate the area by multiplying pi by the radius squared 4. display the area	area

The IPO chart indicates that the program, which calculates and displays the area of a circle, requires four memory locations: two for the input items (radius and pi), one for the processing item (radius squared), and one for the output item (area). The values of the radius, radius squared, and area items should be stored in variables, because those values will change each time the program is executed. The value of the pi item, however, will remain constant at 3.141593, and should be stored in a named constant.

The method of creating variables and named constants—in other words, the method of reserving memory locations in a program—differs in each programming language. However, most programming languages require the programmer to assign both a name and data type to each variable and named constant the program uses. The programmer also must assign a beginning value to each named constant. Although assigning a beginning value to a variable is optional in most programming languages, it is considered a good programming practice to do so and is highly recommended.

Before learning how to reserve variables and named constants in a C++ program, you learn how to select an appropriate name, data type, and initial value for the memory location.

Selecting a Name for a Memory Location

You should assign a descriptive name to each variable and named constant used in a program. The name, also called the **identifier**, should help you remember the purpose of the memory location—in other words, the meaning of the value stored therein. For example, the names `length` and `width` are much more meaningful than are the names `x` and `y`, because `length` and `width` remind you that the amounts stored in the memory locations represent a length and width measurement, respectively.

In addition to being descriptive, the name that a programmer assigns to a memory location must follow several specific rules. The C++ naming rules, along with examples of valid and invalid names in C++, are listed in Figure 3-3. Figure 3-3 also lists the keywords in C++. A **keyword**—often referred to as a **reserved word**—is a word that has a special meaning in a programming language. You cannot use a keyword—for example, the word `double`—as the name of a variable or named constant in a C++ program, as indicated in the fourth rule shown in the figure.

Figure 3-3: Naming rules, examples of valid and invalid names, and C++ keywords

Rules for names (identifiers) in a C++ program

1. The name must begin with a letter.
2. The name must contain only letters, numbers, and the underscore. No punctuation characters or spaces are allowed in the name.
3. The C++ compiler you are using determines the maximum number of characters in a name. In Microsoft Visual C++ .NET, a name cannot be longer than 2048 characters.
4. The name cannot be a keyword, such as `double`, because a keyword has a special meaning in C++. The C++ keywords, also called reserved words, are listed below.
5. Names in C++ are case sensitive.

Valid names	Invalid names	
`deposit`	`98deposit`	(the name must begin with a letter)
`end_Balance`	`end Balance`	(the name cannot contain a space)
`withdrawal`	`withdrawal.amt`	(the name cannot contain punctuation)
`privateLocation`	`private`	(the name cannot be a keyword)

C++ Keywords

asm	else	operator	throw
auto	enum	private	true
bool	explicit	protected	try
break	extern	public	typedef
case	false	register	typeid
catch	float	reinterpret_cast	typename
char	for	return	union
class	friend	short	unsigned
const	goto	signed	using
const_cast	if	sizeof	virtual
continue	inline	static	void
default	int	static_cast	volatile
delete	long	struct	wchar_t
do	mutable	switch	while
double	namespace	template	
dynamic_cast	new	this	

tip
The practice of capitalizing only the first letter in the second and subsequent words in a memory location's name is referred to as "camel casing." Because the uppercase letters in the name are taller than the lowercase letters, the uppercase letters appear as "humps" in the name.

Notice that a memory location's name must begin with a letter and include only letters, numbers, and the underscore; no punctuation characters or spaces are allowed in the name. Many C++ programmers use uppercase letters when naming named constants, and lowercase letters when naming variables; this allows them to distinguish between the named constants and variables in a program. If a variable's name contains two or more words, however, most C++ programmers capitalize the first letter in the second and subsequent words, as shown in the names `grossPay` and `juneInventoryAmount`. In this book, you will follow the naming convention used by most C++ programmers.

Figure 3-4 lists possible names that you could use in a C++ program to identify the circle area problem's input, processing, and output items (shown earlier in Figure 3-2's IPO chart).

Figure 3-4: Names of memory locations for the circle area problem

Memory location type	Name

variable
variable
variable
named constant
	`radius`
	`radiusSquared`
	`area`
	`PI`

tip

Some programmers pronounce `char` as "care" because it is short for *character*, while others pronounce `char` as in the first syllable of the word *charcoal*.

In addition to selecting an appropriate name for each variable and named constant the program uses, you also must determine the appropriate data type for each.

Selecting a Data Type for a Memory Location

Each variable and named constant must be assigned a **data type**, which controls the type of data the memory location can store. Figure 3-5 shows some of the data types available in C++.

Figure 3-5: Some of the data types available in C++

Data type	Stores	Memory required	Values
`char`	one character	1 byte	one character
`short`	integer	2 bytes	-32,768 to 32,767
`int`	integer	4 bytes	-2,147,483,648 to 2,147,483,647
`float`	single precision floating point number	4 bytes	-3.4e38 to 3.4e38
`double`	double precision floating point number	8 bytes	-1.7e308 to 1.7e308
`String`	zero or more characters	1 byte per character	zero or more characters
`bool`	Boolean value	1 byte	`true`, `false`

tip

C++ uses the keywords `true` and `false` to represent the Boolean values True and False. These values are called Boolean values in honor of the English mathematician George Boole (1815-1864), who invented Boolean algebra. You would use a `bool` variable to keep track of whether a bill has been paid—for example, either it has been paid (`true`) or it has not been paid (`false`).

All of the data types listed in Figure 3-5, except the `String` data type, belong to a category of data types called fundamental data types. The **fundamental data types** are the basic data types built into the C++ language, and must be typed using lowercase letters.

Unlike the other data types listed in Figure 3-5, the `String` data type is not a fundamental data type; rather, it is a data type that is added to the C++ language through the use of a class. A **class** is a group of instructions used to create an object. The `String` class (data type), for example, creates a string, which is considered an object. Some classes, like the `String` class, come with Visual C++ .NET. However, you also can create your own classes; you learn how to do so in Tutorial 10. It is a common practice to begin class names with an uppercase letter.

As Figure 3-5 indicates, the C++ programming language contains one or more data types for storing **integers** (whole numbers), **floating-point numbers** (numbers with a decimal place), **characters** (letters, symbols, and numbers that will not be used in calculations), and **Boolean** values (`true` and `false`). The appropriate data type to use for a memory location depends on the values the memory location will store. For example, memory locations assigned either the `short` or `int` data type can store integers only. The differences between the two data types are in the range of integers each type can store and the amount of memory each type needs to store the integer. You can reduce the amount of internal memory that a program consumes, thereby improving the program's efficiency, by using memory locations with smaller memory requirements wherever possible. For example, although an `int` memory location can store numbers in the `short` range of -32,768 to 32,767, the `int` data type takes twice as much memory as the `short` data type to do so. Therefore, you can conserve internal memory by storing a person's age in a `short` variable rather than in an `int` variable.

Keep in mind, however, that memory usage is not the only important factor in determining a program's efficiency; the speed at which a program executes also is important. Although a `short` memory location uses less internal memory than does an `int` memory location, a calculation containing `int` memory locations takes less time to process than the equivalent equation containing `short` memory locations. This is because the computer must convert `short` memory locations to the `int` data type while the calculation is being performed. Similarly, the computer converts `float` memory locations to the `double` data type when performing calculations. Therefore, a calculation containing `double` variables takes less time to process than the same calculation containing `float` variables.

tip
The `String` class instructions are contained in a file named Mscorlib.dll, which comes with Visual C++ .NET.

Important note: In most of the programs you create in this book, you will use the `int` data type to store integers, and the `double` data type to store numbers with a decimal place.

As Figure 3-6 shows, the data type selected for each of the circle area problem's memory locations is `double`. The `double` data type allows each memory location to store a floating-point number.

tip
In the past, the amount of storage space consumed by a program was much more of a concern than it is now. This is because computers can now store vast amounts of data.

Figure 3-6: Data type assigned to the memory locations for the circle area problem

Memory location	Name	Data type
variable	`radius`	`double`
variable	`radiusSquared`	`double`
variable	`area`	`double`
named constant	`PI`	`double`

Knowing how data is stored in the computer's internal memory will help you understand the importance of a memory location's data type.

How Data is Stored in Internal Memory

Numeric data—data assigned to memory locations that can store only numbers—is represented in internal memory using the binary (or *base 2*) number system. Recall from the Overview that the binary number system uses only the two digits 0 and 1. Although the binary number system may not be as familiar to you as the decimal (or *base 10*) number system, which uses the ten digits 0 through 9, it is just as easy to understand. Figure 3-7 compares both number systems.

Figure 3-7: Comparison of the decimal and binary number systems

Decimal number system (base 10)		**Decimal number**	**10^7**	**10^6**	**10^5**	**10^4**	**10^3**	**10^2**	**10^1**	**10^0**
		110						1	1	0
		342						3	4	2
		31509				3	1	5	0	9
Binary number system (base 2)	**Binary number**	**Decimal equivalent of binary number**	**2^7**	**2^6**	**2^5**	**2^4**	**2^3**	**2^2**	**2^1**	**2^0**
	110	6						1	1	0
	11010	26				1	1	0	1	0
	1001						1	0	0	1

As Figure 3-7 illustrates, the position of each digit in the decimal number system is associated with the system's base number, 10, raised to a power. Starting with the right-most position, for example, the positions represent the number 10 raised to a power of 0, 1, 2, 3, and so on. The decimal number 110, therefore, means zero 1s (10^0), one 10 (10^1), and one 100 (10^2), and the decimal number 342 means two 1s (10^0), four 10s (10^1), and three 100s (10^2). The decimal number 31509 means nine 1s (10^0), zero 10s (10^1), five 100s (10^2), one 1000 (10^3), and three 10000s (10^4).

tip

As you may remember from your math courses, when you raise any number to the 0th power, the result is 1. When you raise a number to the 1st power, the result is the number itself.

The position of each digit in the binary number system also is associated with the system's base number—in this case, 2—raised to a power. Starting with the right-most position, the positions represent 2 raised to a power of 0, 1, 2, 3, and so on. The binary number 110, therefore, means zero 1s (2^0), one 2 (2^1), and one 4 (2^2). The decimal equivalent of the binary number 110 is 6, which is calculated by adding together 0 + 2 + 4 (zero 1s + one 2 + one 4). The binary number 11010 means zero 1s (2^0), one 2 (2^1), zero 4s (2^2), one 8 (2^3), and one 16 (2^4). The decimal equivalent of the binary number 11010 is 26, which is calculated by adding together 0 + 2 + 0 + 8 + 16. On your own, calculate the decimal equivalent of the last binary number (1001) shown in Figure 3-7. If your answer is the decimal number 9 (one 1 + zero 2s + zero 4s + one 8), you are correct.

Unlike numeric data, character data—data assigned to memory locations that can store characters—is represented in internal memory using ASCII codes. ASCII (pronounced *ASK-ee*) stands for American Standard Code for Information Interchange. The ASCII coding scheme assigns a specific code to each character (letter, number, and symbol) on your keyboard. The ASCII codes for the letters, numbers, colon, and semicolon, along with the binary representation of these codes, are shown in Figure 3-8.

As Figure 3-8 shows, the uppercase letter A is assigned the ASCII code 65, which is stored in internal memory using the eight bits ("binary digits") 01000001 (one 64 and one 1). Notice that the lowercase version of each letter on your keyboard is assigned a different ASCII code than the letter's uppercase version. The lowercase letter a, for example, is assigned the ASCII code 97, which is stored in internal memory using the eight bits 01100001. This fact indicates that the computer does not consider both cases of a letter to be equivalent; in other words, the uppercase letter A is not the same as the lowercase letter a. This concept will become important when you compare characters and strings in later tutorials.

Figure 3-8: Partial ASCII chart

Character	ASCII	Binary	Character	ASCII	Binary	Character	ASCII	Binary
0	48	00110000	K	75	01001011	g	103	01100111
1	49	00110001	L	76	01001100	h	104	01101000
2	50	00110010	M	77	01001101	i	105	01101001
3	51	00110011	N	78	01001110	j	106	01101010
4	52	00110100	O	79	01001111	k	107	01101011
5	53	00110101	P	80	01010000	l	108	01101100
6	54	00110110	Q	81	01010001	m	109	01101101
7	55	00110111	R	82	01010010	n	110	01101110
8	56	00111000	S	83	01010011	o	111	01101111
9	57	00111001	T	84	01010100	p	112	01110000
:	58	00111010	U	85	01010101	q	113	01110001
;	59	00111011	V	86	01010110	r	114	01110010
A	65	01000001	W	87	01010111	s	115	01110011
B	66	01000010	X	88	01011000	t	116	01110100
C	67	01000011	Y	89	01011001	u	117	01110101
D	68	01000100	Z	90	01011010	v	118	01110110
E	69	01000101	a	97	01100001	w	119	01110111
F	70	01000110	b	98	01100010	x	120	01111000
G	71	01000111	c	99	01100011	y	121	01111001
H	72	01001000	d	100	01100100	z	122	01111010
I	73	01001001	e	101	01100101			
J	74	01001010	f	102	01100110			

tip
The full ASCII chart is shown in Appendix A.

At this point, you may be wondering why the numeric characters on your keyboard are assigned an ASCII code. Aren't they supposed to be stored using the binary number system, as you learned earlier? The answer is this: the computer uses the binary number system to store the *number* 9, but it uses the ASCII coding scheme to store the *character* 9. But how does the computer know whether the 9 is a number or a character? The answer to this question is simple: by the memory location's data type. For example, assume that a program displays the message "Enter the age of your pet:" on the computer screen. Also assume that the program stores your response in a variable named `age`. When you press the 9 key on your keyboard in response to the message, the computer uses the `age` variable's data type to determine whether to store the 9 as a number (using the binary number system) or as a character (using the ASCII coding scheme). If the variable's data type is `int`, the 9 is stored as the binary number `1001` (one `1` + one 8). If the variable's data type is `char`, on the other hand, the 9 is stored as a character using the ASCII code 57, which is represented in internal memory as `00111001` (one `1` + one 8 + one `16` + one 32).

The memory location's data type also determines how the computer interprets the data already stored in a memory location. For example, if a program instruction needs to access the value stored in a memory location—perhaps to display the value on the screen—the computer uses the memory location's data type to determine the value's data type. For instance, assume that a memory location named `inputItem` contains the eight bits `01000001`. If the memory location's data type is `char`, the computer displays the uppercase letter A on the screen. This is because the computer interprets the `01000001` as the ASCII code 65, which is equivalent to the uppercase letter A. However, if the memory location's data type is `int`, the computer displays the number 65 on the screen, because the `01000001` is interpreted as the binary code for the decimal number 65.

tip

Exponential notation, often referred to as *e notation*, provides a convenient way of writing very large and very small numbers by expressing the number as a multiple of some power of 10. For example, the large number 3,200,000,000 written using e notation is 3.2e9. The positive number after the e indicates how many places to the right to move the decimal point. In this case, e9 says to move the decimal point nine places to the right, which is the same as multiplying the number by 10 to the ninth power. Numbers written using e notation also can have a negative number after the e; the negative number indicates how many places to the left to move the decimal point. For example, 3.2e–9 says to move the decimal point nine places to the left (.0000000032), which is the same as dividing the number by 10 to the ninth power.

As you can see, the data type of the memory location is important, because it determines how the data is stored when first entered into the memory location. It also determines how the data is interpreted when the memory location is used in an instruction later in the program.

In addition to assigning an appropriate name and data type to each variable and named constant, recall that you also should assign an initial value to each.

Selecting an Initial Value for a Memory Location

Assigning an initial, or beginning, value to a memory location is referred to as **initializing**. You typically initialize a memory location by assigning a literal constant to it. Unlike variables and named constants, literal constants are not memory locations. Rather, a **literal constant** is an item of data that can appear in a program instruction, and that can be stored in a memory location. Literal constants can have a data type that is numeric, character, or string.

A **numeric literal constant** is simply a number. The numbers 0.0, -2.5, and 146 are examples of numeric literal constants. Numeric literal constants can consist only of numbers, the plus sign (+), the minus sign (-), the decimal point (.), and the letter e in uppercase or lowercase (for exponential notation). Numeric literal constants cannot contain a space, a comma, or a special character, such as the dollar sign ($) or the percent sign (%).

A **character literal constant** is one character enclosed in single quotation marks. The letter 'X' is a character literal constant, and so are the dollar sign '$' and a space ' ' (two single quotation marks with a space between). A **string literal constant**, on the other hand, is zero or more characters enclosed in double quotation marks, such as the word "Hello", the message "Enter room length: ", and the empty string "" (two double quotation marks with no space between). Figure 3-9 shows examples of numeric, character, and string literal constants.

Figure 3-9: Examples of numeric, character, and string literal constants

Numeric literal constants	Character literal constants	String literal constants
2 3.14 3.2e6 -2300 0	'X' '$' 'b' '2' ' ' (a space enclosed in single quotation marks)	"Hello" "Enter room length: " "450" "345AB" "" (two double quotation marks with no space between)

Important note: Notice that character literal constants are enclosed in single quotation marks and string literal constants are enclosed in double quotation marks. Numeric literal constants, however, are not enclosed in any quotation marks.

When using a literal constant to initialize a memory location in a program, the data type of the literal constant should match the data type of the memory location to which it is assigned. In other words, you should use only integers to initialize memory locations having the `short` or `int` data type, and only floating-point numbers to initialize memory locations having the `float` or `double` data type. Character literal constants should be used to initialize `char` memory locations, and string literal constants to initialize `String` memory locations. Memory locations having the `bool` data type typically are initialized using either the C++ keyword `true` or the C++ keyword `false`, which stand for the Boolean values True and False, respectively.

When a program instructs the computer to initialize a memory location, the computer first compares the data type of the value assigned to the memory location with the data type of the memory location itself to verify that the value is appropriate for the memory location. If the value's data type does not match the memory location's data type, the computer uses a process called **implicit type conversion** to convert the value to fit the memory location. For example, if you assign the integer 9 to a memory location that can store floating-point numbers, the computer converts the integer to a floating-point number before storing the value in the memory location; it does so by appending a decimal point and the number 0 to the end of the integer. In this case, for example, the integer 9 is converted to the floating-point number 9.0, and it is the floating-point number 9.0 that is assigned to the memory location. Similarly, if you use a floating-point number—such as 3.7—to initialize a memory location that can store only integers, the computer converts the floating-point number to an integer before storing the value in the memory location; it does so by truncating (dropping off) the decimal portion of the number. In this case, the computer will convert the floating-point number 3.7 to the integer 3. As a result, the number 3, rather than the number 3.7, is assigned to the memory location.

It is not always possible to convert a value to match the memory location's data type. For example, using a string literal constant to initialize a memory location that can store only integers produces an error, because the computer cannot convert a string literal constant to an integer.

If a memory location is a named constant, the problem description and/or IPO chart will provide the appropriate initial value to use. For example, the problem description and IPO chart shown earlier in Figure 3-2 indicate that the PI named constant should be initialized to 3.141593 (the value of pi rounded to six decimal places). The initial value for a variable, on the other hand, typically is not stated in a problem description or IPO chart, because the value is supplied by the user while the program is running. As a result, `short` and `int` variables generally are initialized to the integer 0. Variables of the `float` and `double` data types typically are initialized to the floating-point number 0.0. `String` variables usually are initialized to the empty string (""), and `char` variables to a space (' '). As mentioned earlier, the C++ keywords `true` and `false` are used to initialize `bool` variables.

Be aware that the Visual C++ compiler will display the warning message *'initializing' : truncation from 'double' to 'float'* when you initialize a `float` memory location to a number other than 0.0—for example, a number such as 3.1. This warning message appears because the Visual C++ compiler treats all numeric literal constants containing a decimal place as a `double` data type. When you assign a `double` number (which requires eight bytes of memory) to a `float` memory location (which can store only four bytes), the compiler warns you that it may need to truncate part of the number before it can store the number in the memory location. Some programmers simply ignore the warning message—although this practice is not recommended. Other programmers use a process called *type casting* to prevent the compiler from displaying the warning message; type casting is the preferred approach.

Type Casting

Type casting, also known as **explicit type conversion**, is the explicit conversion of data from one data type to another. You type cast, or explicitly convert, an item of data by using the methods defined in the **`Convert` class**. As you learned earlier, a class is a group of instructions used to create an object. The `Convert` class, for example, creates an object that is either a number or a string, depending on the method used. A **method** is a specific portion of the class instructions, and its purpose is to perform a task for the class. The methods in the `Convert` class, for instance, convert a value to a specified data type, and then return the result of doing so. Figure 3-10 shows the most commonly used methods contained in the `Convert` class.

tip

You can learn more about initializing `bool` variables by completing Exercise 16 at the end of the Application lesson.

tip

The Visual C++ compiler displays a warning message when data is truncated as a result of an implicit type conversion. The warning message is displayed when you build the program. You learn how to build a Visual C++ program in this tutorial's Application lesson.

tip

When you distinguish between a literal constant, a named constant, and a variable, it is helpful to remember that a literal constant is simply an item of data. Variables and named constants, on the other hand, are memory locations where literal constants are stored. Unlike the contents of a variable, the contents of a named constant cannot change while the program is running.

tip
The .NET Framework, upon which Visual Studio .NET is based, is Microsoft's newest computing platform. The .NET Framework allows programmers to write applications in their development language of choice (such as the C++, C#, or Visual Basic languages), yet use the components and code from other .NET-compatible languages. Each of the fundamental data types in the .NET-compatible languages is an alias, or other name for, a base data type in the .NET Framework. For example, the C++ `double`, `short`, `int`, and `float` data types are aliases for the .NET Framework's `Double`, `Int16`, `Int32` and `Single` data types, respectively. Notice that the Convert methods listed in Figure 3-10 refer to the .NET Framework base types rather than to their C++ aliases.

Figure 3-10: Most commonly used methods contained in the `Convert` class

Method	Purpose
`Convert::ToDouble(`*`value`*`)`	convert *value* to the `double` data type
`Convert::ToInt16(`*`value`*`)`	convert *value* to the `short` data type
`Convert::ToInt32(`*`value`*`)`	convert *value* to the `int` data type
`Convert::ToSingle(`*`value`*`)`	convert *value* to the `float` data type
`Convert::ToString(`*`value`*`)`	convert *value* to the `String` data type

The two colons (`::`) that appear between the class name and method name in Figure 3-10 are called the **scope resolution operator** and indicate that the method to the right of the operator is contained in the class whose name appears to the left of the operator. In other words, the `ToDouble()` method is contained in the `Convert` class, and so is the `ToInt16()` method.

Notice that each method name shown in Figure 3-10 is followed by a set of parentheses; all methods in C++ have parentheses after their name. Some methods require you to enter one or more items of data between the parentheses. Each item is called an **actual argument** and represents information that the method needs to perform its task. The `Convert` methods, for example, require you to enter one actual argument: the value that you want to convert to another data type. Other methods, like the `Console::ReadLine()` method that you learn about later in this tutorial, require only an empty set of parentheses after the method name.

As Figure 3-10 indicates, you would use `Convert::ToSingle(3.7)` to convert (type cast) the `double` number 3.7 to a `float` data type. Similarly, you would use `Convert::ToString(3.7)` to type cast the `double` number 3.7 to a `String` data type.

Figure 3-11 shows the initial values appropriate for the circle area problem's memory locations. In each case, the data type of the initial value matches the data type of the memory location, so no type casting is necessary.

Figure 3-11: Initial values assigned to memory locations for the circle area problem

Memory location	Name	Data type	Initial value
variable	`radius`	`double`	0.0
variable	`radiusSquared`	`double`	0.0
variable	`area`	`double`	0.0
named constant	`PI`	`double`	3.141593

Now that you know how to select an appropriate name, data type, and initial value for a memory location, you learn how to use that information to reserve a memory location in a C++ program. Begin by learning how to reserve a named constant.

MINI-QUIZ

Mini-Quiz 1

1) Which of the following is an invalid name for a variable?
   a. `class2003`
   b. `gallons`
   c. `88TaxAmt`
   d. `tuition`

2) The letter 'w' is a ______________.
   a. character literal constant
   b. named constant
   c. numeric literal constant
   d. string literal constant

3) "Jacob Motors" is a ______________.
   a. character literal constant
   b. named constant
   c. numeric literal constant
   d. string literal constant

4) In the binary number system, the decimal number 23 is represented as ______________.
   a. 10111
   b. 10011
   c. 11000
   d. 10001

5) The lowercase letter b is stored in internal memory using the eight bits ______________.
   a. 01100010
   b. 01100011
   c. 01100000
   d. 01010001

6) Which of the following converts the number 75.46 to the `float` data type?
   a. `Convert.ToFloat(75.46)`
   b. `Convert.ToSingle(75.46)`
   c. `Convert::ToFloat(75.46)`
   d. `Convert::ToSingle(75.46)`

Reserving a Named Constant

The instruction you use to reserve, or declare, a named constant allows you to specify the named constant's name, data type, and initial value. Figure 3-12 (on the next page) shows the syntax and examples of instructions used to reserve named constants in C++.

In the syntax, *datatype* is the type of data the named constant will store, *constantname* is the name of the named constant, and *value* is a literal constant that represents the value you want stored in the named constant. Words and symbols in **bold** in an instruction's syntax are required parts of the syntax. In this case, for example, the word `const` and the = sign and `;` (semicolon) are required. Items in square brackets ([]), on the other hand, are optional parts of the syntax. For instance, in the syntax for declaring a named constant, the * (asterisk) is required only when the named constant's data type is `String`. Items in *italics* in an instruction's syntax represent places where the programmer must supply information relative to the program. In this case, the programmer must supply the named constant's data type and name, as well as its initial value.

Figure 3-12: Syntax and examples of instructions that reserve named constants in C++

Syntax
const *datatype* [*]*constantname* = *value*;
Examples

`const double PI = 3.141593;`
`const float MAXPAY = Convert::ToSingle(15.75);`
`const int AGE = 65;`
`const bool PAID = true;`
`const char YES = 'Y';`
`const String *TITLE = "IMG";` (Note the asterisk before the `String` constant's name.)

tip

The * (asterisk) indicates that a memory location is a pointer. Rather than storing a value, a pointer stores the address of an object in the computer's internal memory. A `String` named constant, for example, stores the address of a string, and so does a `String` variable. For now, you do not have to worry about the term *pointer*; just remember to include the asterisk when you declare a `String` memory location (named constant and variable). You learn more about pointers later in this book.

Notice that the instruction to declare a named constant ends with a semicolon. This is because the instruction is considered a statement in C++. A **statement** is simply an instruction that causes the computer to perform some action after it is executed, or processed, by the computer. All statements in C++ must end with a semicolon.

The first example shown in Figure 3-12, `const double PI = 3.141593;`, creates a named constant whose name is `PI` and whose value is 3.141593. This statement tells the computer to set aside a small box in internal memory, and to name the box `PI`. The `PI` box (memory location) will have a data type of `double` and an initial value of 3.141593. The keyword `const` at the beginning of the statement indicates that the `PI` memory location is a named constant, which means that its value cannot be changed later in the program. If the program contains a statement that attempts to change the value stored in the `PI` named constant, the C++ compiler will display an error message.

The second example shown in Figure 3-12, `const float MAXPAY = Convert::ToSingle(15.75);`, first converts the `double` number 15.75 to a `float` data type. It then creates the `MAXPAY` named constant and initializes it to 15.75. (Recall that the `float` data type consumes less memory than the `double` data type.)

The third example shown in Figure 3-12, `const int AGE = 65;`, creates a named constant named `AGE` and initializes it to the number 65. The fourth example, `const bool PAID = true;`, creates a `bool` named constant named `PAID` and uses the C++ keyword `true` to initialize the constant. The fifth example, `const char YES = 'Y';`, creates a `char` named constant named `YES` and initializes it to the letter Y. The last example, `const String *TITLE = "IMG";`, creates a String named constant whose name is `TITLE` and whose value is "IMG". Notice the asterisk (*) that appears before the named constant's name. Recall that the asterisk is required when the named constant's data type is `String`.

After you reserve, or declare, a named constant, you then can use its name, instead of its value, in another statement. For example, you can use the C++ statement `Console::WriteLine(PI);` to display the contents of the `PI` named constant on the screen; this instruction will display the value 3.141593. You also can use the `PI` named constant in a C++ statement that calculates the area of a circle, like this: `area = radiusSquared * PI;`. The computer will use the value stored in the `PI` named constant (3.141593) to calculate the area.

Named constants make a program more self-documenting and, therefore, easier to modify because they allow you to use meaningful words in place of values that may be less clear. For example, the named constant `PI` is much more meaningful than is the number 3.141593.

Additionally, typing `PI`, rather than typing 3.141593, in a statement that calculates the area of a circle is easier and less prone to typing errors. If you do mistype `PI` in the area calculation statement—for example, if you type `Pi` rather than `PI`—the C++ compiler will display an error message. Mistyping 3.141593 in the area calculation statement, however, will not trigger an error message and will result in an incorrect answer.

Next, learn how to reserve a variable in a C++ program.

Reserving a Variable

The instruction you use to reserve, or declare, a variable in C++ allows you to specify the variable's name, data type, and initial value. Figure 3-13 shows the syntax and examples of instructions used to declare and initialize variables in C++. Notice that a variable declaration ends with a semicolon; this is because it is considered a statement in C++.

Figure 3-13: Syntax and examples of instructions that reserve and initialize variables in C++

Syntax	
datatype [*]*variablename* [= *initialvalue*];	
Examples	**Initial value**
`int age = 0;`	0
`float rate = 0.0;`	0.0
`float rate = Convert::ToSingle(3.5);`	3.5
`double sale = 0.0;`	0.0
`bool insured = false;`	false
`char grade = ' ';`	one space
`String *company = "";` (Note the asterisk before the `String` variable's name.)	empty string

tip

If you do not supply an initial value for a variable in a C++ program, the variable may contain a meaningless value, referred to by programmers as garbage. The garbage is the remains of what was last stored at the memory location that the variable now occupies.

In the syntax, *datatype* designates the type of data the variable can store, *variablename* is the name of the variable, and *initialvalue* is usually a literal constant that represents the beginning (initial) value for the variable. Recall that items in *italics* in an instruction's syntax represent places where the programmer supplies information relative to the program. When declaring a variable, the programmer supplies the variable's data type, name, and initial value.

Notice that the * (asterisk), = sign, and *initialvalue* appear in square brackets in the variable declaration's syntax. Recall that items appearing in square brackets in an instruction's syntax are optional parts of the syntax. In this case, the asterisk is required only when you are declaring a `String` variable. Although the = sign and *initialvalue* are optional in the syntax, recall that it is a good programming practice to initialize the variables that a program uses. A variable can be initialized to any value, as long as the value's data type matches the variable's data type. However, recall that `short` and `int` variables generally are initialized to the integer 0. Variables of the `float` and `double` data types typically are initialized to the floating-point number 0.0. `String` variables usually are initialized to the empty string (""), and `char` variables to a space (' '). The C++ keywords `true` and `false` are used to initialize `bool` variables.

tip

Recall that the * (asterisk) indicates that a memory location is a pointer, which stores an address of an object rather than a value. Also recall that, for now, you do not have to worry about the term *pointer*; just remember to include the asterisk when you declare a `String` memory location (named constant and variable).

The first statement shown in Figure 3-13 creates an `int` variable named `age` and initializes it to the number 0. The second statement creates a `float` variable named `rate` and initializes it to the number 0.0. The third statement shows how you initialize a `float` variable to a number other than 0.0. Notice that you use the `Convert::ToSingle()` method to convert the `double` number—in this case, the number 3.5—to the `float` data type before storing it in the `rate` variable.

The fourth statement shown in Figure 3-13 creates a `double` variable named `sale` and initializes it to the number 0.0. The fifth statement creates a `bool` variable named `insured` and initializes it using the C++ keyword `false`. The sixth statement creates a `char` variable named `grade` and initializes it to a space. The last statement, `String *company = "";`, creates a `String` variable named `company` and initializes it to the empty string. Notice the asterisk (`*`) that appears before the variable name. Recall that the asterisk is required when the variable's data type is `String`.

Figure 3-14 shows the statements that you would use in a C++ program to reserve the `radius`, `radiusSquared`, and `area` variables.

Figure 3-14: C++ statements reserving the `radius`, `radiusSquared`, and `area` variables

```
double radius = 0.0;
double radiusSquared = 0.0;
double area = 0.0;
```

The C++ statements shown in Figure 3-14 tell the computer to set aside three memory locations that can store floating-point numbers. The memory locations will be named `radius`, `radiusSquared`, and `area`, and each will be initialized to the numeric literal constant 0.0.

MINI-QUIZ

Mini-Quiz 2

1) Write a C++ instruction that reserves a named constant named `CITY`. Use the string literal constant "Chicago" to initialize the memory location.
2) Write a C++ instruction that reserves a variable named `numberOfPeople`. Assign the data type `int` to the variable, and initialize it appropriately.
3) Write a C++ instruction that reserves a variable named `studentName`. Assign the data type `String` to the variable, and initialize it appropriately.
4) Write a C++ instruction that reserves a variable named `interestRate`. Assign the data type `double` to the variable, and initialize it appropriately.
5) Write a C++ instruction that reserves a `float` variable named `rate`. Initialize the variable to the number 5.6.

In the next section, you learn how to write an assignment statement, which you can use to change the contents of a variable while a program is running.

Using an Assignment Statement to Store Data in a Variable

You can use an assignment statement to change the contents of a variable while a program is running. Figure 3-15 shows the syntax and examples of assignment statements written in the C++ language. Notice that C++ requires a semicolon at the end of an assignment statement.

Figure 3-15: Syntax and examples of assignment statements in C++

Syntax

variablename = *expression*;

Examples

Note: `hoursWkd`, `overtime`, and `age` are `int` variables, `cost` is a `float` variable, and `bonus` and `sales` are `double` variables. `RATE` is a `double` named constant, `name` is a `String` variable, `middleInitial` is a `char` variable, and `paid` is a `bool` variable.

```
hoursWkd = 50;
overtime = hoursWkd – 40;
age = age + 1;
cost = Convert::ToSingle(6300.75);
bonus = sales * RATE;
name = "Jackie";
middleInitial = 'P';
paid = true;
```

tip

You cannot use an assignment statement to assign a value to a named constant, because the contents of a named constant cannot be changed while a program is running.

tip

It is easy to confuse an assignment statement (`hoursWkd = 50;`) with a variable declaration statement (`int hoursWkd = 50;`) in C++. You use a variable declaration statement, which must begin with a data type, to create and initialize a new variable. You use an assignment statement to change the value stored in an existing variable. An assignment statement does not reserve a variable in memory.

When an assignment statement is encountered in a program, the computer assigns the value of the *expression* appearing on the right side of the **assignment operator** (=) to the variable whose *variablename* appears on the left side of the assignment operator (=). The data type of the *expression*—which can include items such as literal constants, named constants, variables, and arithmetic operators (you learn more about these in the next section)—must match the data type of the variable to which it is assigned. For example, you should assign only *expressions* that represent integers to memory locations declared using the `int` data type, and only *expressions* that represent strings to memory locations declared using the `String` data type. As you learned earlier, if the data type of the *expression*'s value does not match the data type of the memory location to which the value is assigned, the computer uses a process called implicit type conversion to convert the value to fit the memory location. Also recall that it is not always possible for the computer to convert a value to match the memory location's data type.

The first assignment statement shown in Figure 3-15, `hoursWkd = 50;`, stores the integer 50 (a numeric literal constant) in an `int` variable named `hoursWkd`. The second assignment statement `overtime = hoursWkd - 40;`—whose *expression* contains a variable (`hoursWkd`), an arithmetic operator (-), and a numeric literal constant (40)—first subtracts the integer 40 from the contents of the `int` variable named `hoursWkd`, and then assigns the result to the `int` variable named `overtime`. Assuming the `hoursWkd` variable contains the number 50, the second assignment statement assigns the number 10 to the `overtime` variable.

The third assignment statement shown in Figure 3-15, `age = age + 1;`, uses an arithmetic operator (+) to add the integer 1 to the value stored in the `int` variable named `age`; it then assigns the sum to the `age` variable. If the `age` variable contains the value 16 before the computer processes this statement, it contains the value 17 after it is processed.

The fourth assignment statement, `cost = Convert::ToSingle(6300.75);`, uses the `Convert::ToSingle()` method to convert the `double` number 6300.75 to a `float` number, and then assigns the result to the `float` variable named `cost`. The

tip

Recall that C++ treats all numbers with a decimal place as a `double` data type.

`Convert::ToSingle()` method tells the computer to treat the number 6300.75 as a `float` rather than as a `double`.

The fifth assignment statement, `bonus = sales * RATE;`, contains two `double` variables (`bonus` and `sales`), a `double` named constant (`RATE`), and an arithmetic operator (`*`). This assignment statement tells the computer to multiply the contents of the `sales` variable by the contents of the `RATE` named constant, and then assign the result to the `bonus` variable.

The sixth assignment statement shown in Figure 3-15, `name = "Jackie";`, simply stores the string literal constant "Jackie" in a `String` variable named `name`. The seventh assignment statement, `middleInitial = 'P';`, stores the character literal constant 'P' in a `char` variable named `middleInitial`. The last assignment statement, `paid = true;`, assigns the C++ keyword `true` to a `bool` variable named `paid`.

It is important to remember that a variable can store only one value at a time. When you assign another value to the variable, the new value replaces the existing value. For example, assume that a C++ program contains the following statements:

```
int temp = 3;
temp = temp + 1;
temp = temp * 2;
```

When you run the program containing these statements, the three lines of code are processed as follows:

- The declaration statement `int temp = 3;` creates the `temp` variable in the computer's internal memory and initializes the variable to the integer 3. Here again, you may want to picture the `temp` variable as a small box inside the computer. This statement tells the computer to place the numeric literal constant 3 inside the box.
- The assignment statement `temp = temp + 1;` adds the number 1 to the contents of the `temp` variable, giving 4. It then replaces the 3 currently stored in the `temp` variable with the number 4. Notice that C++ evaluates the *expression* appearing on the right side of the assignment operator before assigning the result to the variable whose name appears on the left side. (All programming languages process assignment statements in the same manner.)
- The assignment statement `temp = temp * 2;` first multiplies the contents of the `temp` variable (4) by 2, giving 8. It then removes the number 4 from the `temp` variable and stores the number 8 there instead.

Several of the examples shown in this lesson contain arithmetic operators, which are used to perform calculations in a program. The next section provides a more thorough discussion of arithmetic operators.

Arithmetic Operators

Most programs require the computer to perform one or more calculations. You instruct the computer to perform a calculation by writing an arithmetic expression that contains one or more arithmetic operators. Figure 3-16 lists the standard arithmetic operators in C++, along with their precedence numbers. The precedence numbers indicate the order in which a programming language performs the arithmetic operations in an expression. Operations with a precedence number of 1 are performed before operations with a precedence number of 2, which are performed before operations with a precedence number of 3, and so on. However, you can use parentheses to override the order of precedence, because operations within parentheses always are performed before operations outside of parentheses.

Figure 3-16: Standard arithmetic operators and their order of precedence

Operator	Operation	Precedence number
()	override normal precedence rules	1
-	negation	2
*, /, %	multiplication, division, and modulus arithmetic	3
+, -	addition and subtraction	4

Notice that some operators shown in Figure 3-16 have the same precedence number. For example, both the addition and subtraction operator have a precedence number of 4. If an expression contains more than one operator having the same priority, those operators are evaluated from left to right. In the expression 3 + 12 / 3 - 1, for instance, the division (/) is performed first, then the addition (+), and then the subtraction (-). In other words, the computer first divides 12 by 3, then adds the result of the division (4) to 3, and then subtracts 1 from the result of the addition (7). The expression evaluates to 6.

You can use parentheses to change the order in which the operators in an expression are evaluated. For example, the expression 3 + 12 / (3 - 1) evaluates to 9, not 6. This is because the parentheses tell the computer to subtract 1 from 3 first, then divide the result of the subtraction (2) into 12, and then add the result of the division (6) to 3.

One of the arithmetic operators listed in Figure 3-16, the modulus arithmetic operator (%), might be less familiar to you. The modulus arithmetic operator is used to divide two integers, and results in the remainder of the division. For example, 211 % 4 (read 211 mod 4) equals 3, which is the remainder of 211 divided by 4. One use for the modulus operator is to determine whether a year is a leap year—one that has 366 days rather than 365 days. As you may know, if a year is a leap year, then its year number is evenly divisible by the number 4. In other words, if you divide the year number by 4 and the remainder is 0 (zero), then the year is a leap year. You can determine whether the year 2004 is a leap year by using the expression 2004 % 4. This expression evaluates to 0 (the remainder of 2004 divided by 4), so the year 2004 is a leap year. Similarly, you can determine whether the year 2005 is a leap year by using the expression 2005 % 4. This expression evaluates to 1 (the remainder of 2005 divided by 4), so the year 2005 is not a leap year.

tip

The difference between the negation and subtraction operators shown in Figure 3-16 is that the negation operator is unary, whereas the subtraction operator is binary. *Unary* and *binary* refer to the number of operands required by the operator. Unary operators require one operand. For example, the negative number -3 contains the negation operator (-), which is unary, and one operand—the number 3. Unlike unary operators, binary operators require two operands. For example, the expression 4 - 3 contains the subtraction operator (-), which is binary, and two operands: the number 4 and the number 3.

tip

Years ending in 00 are not leap years unless they also are evenly divisible by 400.

MINI-QUIZ

Mini-Quiz 3

1) Write a C++ assignment statement that assigns the value 23.25 to a `float` variable named `price`.
2) Write a C++ assignment statement that assigns the letter T to a `char` variable named `insured`.
3) Write a C++ assignment statement that multiplies the number 10.75 by the contents of a `double` variable named `hours`, and then assigns the result to a `double` variable named `grossPay`.
4) The assignment statement `answer = 8 / 4 * 3 – 5 % 2;` assigns the value ______________ to the `answer` variable. (The `answer` variable is an `int` variable.)
5) What value will be assigned to the `answer` variable in Question 4 if the variable is a `double` variable?

Next, learn how a program communicates with the user by displaying information on the computer screen.

The `Console::Write()` and `Console::WriteLine()` Methods

You can use either the **`Console::Write()` method** or the **`Console::WriteLine()` method** to display a message on the computer screen. The difference between the two methods is the location of the cursor after the message is displayed. The `Console::Write()` method positions the cursor at the end of the last character it displays on the computer screen. The `Console::WriteLine()` method, on the other hand, positions the cursor at the beginning of the next line on the computer screen; it does so by appending a **line terminator character**, which is simply a carriage return followed by a line feed, to the end of the message. Figure 3-17 shows examples of using both methods. The figure also indicates the placement of the cursor, designated by an underscore in the figure, after the computer processes the method.

tip

The scope resolution operator (`::`) indicates that the `Write()` and `WriteLine()` methods are contained in the `Console` class.

The `Console::Write("Enter your name:");` statement in Example 1 displays the message "Enter your name:" on the computer screen and then positions the cursor immediately after the colon, which is the last character in the message. (You can tell that this line is a statement because it ends with a semicolon.) The `Console::WriteLine("Enter your name:");` statement in Example 2 also displays the message "Enter your name:" on the computer screen, but it appends a line terminator character to the end of the message. The line terminator character positions the cursor at the beginning of the next line on the computer screen, as indicated in the example.

The `Console::WriteLine(name);` statement in Example 3 in Figure 3-17 displays the contents of the `name` variable on the computer screen. If the variable contains the string "Phyllis", the statement displays the variable's contents and then positions the cursor at the beginning of the next line on the computer screen.

Many times, you will want a program to display a message along with the contents of a variable. You can accomplish this task by using the syntax *writemethod***(***formatstring***,** *variablelist***);**, where *writemethod* is either the `Console::Write()` or `Console::WriteLine()` method. As you learned earlier, the items of data that appear within the parentheses following a method's name are called actual arguments and represent information that the method needs to perform its task. In this case, the *formatstring* argument is a string of characters that contains the message you want to display and one or more place holders for variable values. A **place holder** consists of a pair of curly braces containing a number, like this: {0}. The number indicates the position of the desired variable in the *variablelist* argument, which is a comma-separated list of variables. The first variable in the *variablelist* is always in position zero, the second is in position one, and so on. The *variablelist* can contain one or more `String` variables; it also can contain variables of other data types, but you must use the `Convert::ToString()` method to convert the contents of the variable to a string.

Figure 3-17: Examples of using the Console::Write() and Console::WriteLine() methods

Examples and results

Example 1
```
Console::Write("Enter your name:");
```
Result
Enter your name: _
cursor

Example 2
```
Console::WriteLine("Enter your name:");
```
Result
Enter your name:
_
cursor

Example 3
```
Console::WriteLine(name);
```
Result (assuming that the `name` variable contains the string "Phyllis")
Phyllis
_
cursor

Example 4
```
Console::Write("Her name is {0}.", name);
```
Result (assuming that the `name` variable contains the string "Phyllis")
Her name is Phyllis. _
cursor

Example 5
```
Console::WriteLine("He is {0} years old.",
Convert::ToString(age));
```
Result (assuming that the `age` variable contains the number 21)
He is 21 years old.
_
cursor

Example 6
```
Console::Write("He is {0} and she is {1}.",
Convert::ToString(age1), Convert::ToString(age2));
```
Result (assuming that the `age1` and `age2` variables contain the numbers 30 and 28, respectively)
He is 30 and she is 28. _
cursor

tip
The "Enter your name:" message, which is displayed by the code shown in Examples 1 and 2 in Figure 3-17, is often referred to as a prompt, because the message prompts the user to enter the appropriate information.

tip
The `Convert::ToString(age)` method in Example 5 does not change the value stored in the `age` variable. Rather, it first makes a temporary copy of the value in internal memory, and then converts the copied value to a string.

tip
You also can write Example 5's code without converting the `age` variable's value to a string; but to do so, you need to use three statements rather than one. The three statements are `Console::Write("He is ");`, `Console::Write(age);`, and `Console::WriteLine(" years old.");`.

In Example 4 in Figure 3-17, the `Console::Write("Her name is {0}.", name);` statement contains a *formatstring* ("Her name is {0}.") and a *variablelist* that lists one variable: a `String` variable named `name`. If the `name` variable contains the string "Phyllis", the statement displays the message "Her name is Phyllis." on the computer screen.

tip
You can use the statement `Console::WriteLine();` to display a blank line on the computer screen.

In Example 5, the `Console::WriteLine("He is {0} years old.", Convert::ToString(age));` statement also contains a *formatstring* ("He is {0} years old.") and a *variablelist* that lists one variable; however, in this example, the variable is an `int` variable named `age`. Notice that the statement uses the `Convert::ToString()` method to convert the contents of the `int` variable to a string. If the `age` variable contains the number 21, the statement displays the message "He is 21 years old." on the computer screen.

The last example shown in Figure 3-17, `Console::Write("He is {0} and she is {1}.", Convert::ToString(age1), Convert::ToString(age2));`, contains two place holders in its *formatstring* and two `int` variables in its *variablelist*. Notice that the statement uses the `Convert::ToString()` method to convert the contents of both `int` variables to a string. If the `age1` and `age2` variables contain the numbers 30 and 28, respectively, the statement displays the message "He is 30 and she is 28." on the computer screen.

Now learn how to use the `Console::ReadLine()` method to accept user input.

The `Console::ReadLine()` Method

You can use the **`Console::ReadLine()`** method to accept user input from the keyboard. The `Console::ReadLine()` method accepts all the characters a user enters until the user presses the Enter key; the characters are treated as a string. In most cases, you assign the input string to a variable. If you want to keep the input as a string—for example, if the input is a word—then you assign the input to a variable whose data type is `String`. However, if you want to use the input as a number, then you must use a `Convert` method (shown earlier in Figure 3-10) to convert the input string to the proper type. Figure 3-18 shows examples of using the `Console::ReadLine()` method to accept keyboard input. Notice that the `Console::ReadLine()` method does not require any actual arguments.

Figure 3-18: Examples of using the `Console::ReadLine()` method

Examples

Example 1
```
String *state = "";
Console::Write("Enter a state name: ");
state = Console::ReadLine();
Console::WriteLine("You entered {0}.", state);
```

Example 2
```
String *inputNumber = "";
int number = 0;
Console::Write("Enter a number: ");
inputNumber = Console::ReadLine();
number = Convert::ToInt32(inputNumber);
number = number * 2;
```

Example 3
```
int number = 0;
Console::Write("Enter a number: ");
number = Convert::ToInt32(Console::ReadLine());
number = number * 2;
```

The `String *state = "";` statement shown in Example 1 in Figure 3-18 creates a `String` variable named `state` and initializes it to the empty string. The `Console::Write("Enter a state name: ");` statement then displays the message "Enter a state name: " on the computer screen. A message such as this is often referred to as a **prompt**, because it prompts the user to enter the appropriate data. The `state = Console::ReadLine();` statement pauses computer processing and waits for the user to enter some data at the keyboard. When the user presses the Enter key, which indicates that he or she has finished entering the data, the statement stores the user's input in the `state` variable. The `Console::WriteLine("You entered {0}.", state);` statement then displays a message along with the contents of the `state` variable on the computer screen.

The first two statements shown in Example 2 in Figure 3-18 create and initialize a `String` variable named `inputNumber` and an `int` variable named `number`. The `Console::Write("Enter a number: ");` statement then displays a message that prompts the user to enter a number. The `inputNumber = Console::ReadLine();` statement allows the user to enter the number, and assigns the number (treated as a string) to the `String` variable named `inputNumber`. The `number = Convert::ToInt32(inputNumber);` statement converts the string stored in the `inputNumber` variable to an integer, and assigns the result to the `int` variable named `number`. The `number = number * 2;` statement multiplies the integer stored in the `number` variable by two, and then assigns the result to the `number` variable.

Example 3 in Figure 3-18 shows another way of writing the logic from Example 2. Comparing the code shown in both examples, you will notice that the code in Example 3 uses only the `int` variable named `number`; it does not use the `String` variable named `inputNumber`. Rather than assigning the string returned by the `Console::ReadLine()` method to a `String` variable, as Example 2's code does, Example 3's code first uses the `Convert::ToInt32()` method to convert the string to an integer; it then assigns the integer to the `number` variable.

Mini-Quiz 4

1) Write a C++ statement that displays the message "Hello" on the computer screen. After displaying the message, position the cursor on the next line.
2) Write a C++ statement that displays the message "I live in *city*." on the computer screen, where *city* is the contents of a `String` variable named `city`. After displaying the message, position the cursor after the period.
3) Write a C++ statement that displays the contents of a `double` variable named `grossPay` on the computer screen. After displaying the variable's contents, position the cursor on the next line.
4) Write a C++ statement that allows the user to enter a number at the keyboard. Assign the number to a `String` variable named `input`.
5) Write a C++ statement that allows the user to enter a number at the keyboard. Assign the number to a `double` variable named `input`.

Now that you know how to create variables and named constants, as well as how to use assignment statements, arithmetic operators, and the `Console::Write()`, `Console::WriteLine()`, and `Console::ReadLine()` methods, you can begin coding the algorithm for The Paper Tree wallpaper store. Recall that coding the algorithm into a program is the fourth step in the problem-solving process for creating a computer program.

Coding the Algorithm into a Program

In Tutorial 2's Application lesson, you analyzed the problem specification shown in Figure 3-19 for The Paper Tree wallpaper store. You then created and desk-checked an appropriate algorithm.

Figure 3-19: Problem specification for The Paper Tree wallpaper store

Problem specification:
Create a program that calculates and displays the number of single rolls of wallpaper needed to cover a room. The salesclerk will provide the length, width, and ceiling height of the room, in feet. He or she also will provide the number of square feet a single roll will cover.
Sample calculation:
Room size: 10 feet by 12 feet, with a ceiling height of 8 feet
Single roll coverage: 30 square feet

1. Calculate the perimeter of the room by adding together its length and width, and then multiplying the sum by 2: (10 feet + 12 feet) * 2 = 44 feet
2. Calculate the wall area by multiplying the room's perimeter by its height: 44 feet * 8 feet = 352 square feet
3. Calculate the required number of single rolls by dividing the wall area by the number of square feet a single roll provides: 352 square feet / 30 square feet = 11.73 (rounded to two decimal places), or approximately 12 single rolls.

Figure 3-20 shows the IPO chart that you created for this problem.

Figure 3-20: IPO chart for The Paper Tree wallpaper store problem

Input	Processing	Output
room length room width ceiling height single roll coverage	Processing items: room perimeter wall area Algorithm: 1. enter the room length, room width, ceiling height, and single roll coverage 2. calculate the room perimeter by adding together the room length and room width, and then multiplying the sum by 2 3. calculate the wall area by multiplying the room perimeter by the ceiling height 4. calculate the number of single rolls by dividing the wall area by the single roll coverage 5. display the number of single rolls	number of single rolls

Recall that the IPO chart shows the problem's input, processing, and output items, as well as the algorithm needed to solve the problem. The algorithm shown in Figure 3-20, for example, shows the steps the computer must follow to calculate and display the number of single rolls of paper required to wallpaper a room. The calculation is based on the values of the room length, room width, ceiling height, and single roll coverage entered by the user. Notice that the algorithm also calculates two intermediate values: room perimeter and wall area. As you learned in Tutorial 2, an intermediate value, referred to as a processing item, is one that the algorithm uses when processing the input into the output.

Programmers use the information in the IPO chart to code the algorithm. First, the programmer assigns a descriptive name to each unique input, processing, and output item listed in the IPO chart. You will assign the names **length**, **width**, **height**, and **rollCoverage** to the four input items; **perimeter** and **area** to the two processing items; and **rolls** to the output item.

The programmer also assigns a data type and initial value to each unique input, processing, and output item. The data type specifies the type of data the item can store. In this case, because the input, processing, and output items could contain decimal numbers, you will assign the **double** data type to each item. Recall that **double** variables typically are initialized to zero using the value 0.0, as shown in Figure 3-21.

Figure 3-21: C++ instructions corresponding to the wallpaper store problem's input, processing, and output items

IPO chart information	C++ instructions
Input	
room length	`double length = 0.0;`
room width	`double width = 0.0;`
ceiling height	`double height = 0.0;`
single roll coverage	`double rollCoverage = 0.0;`
Processing	
room perimeter	`double perimeter = 0.0;`
wall area	`double area = 0.0;`
Output	
number of single rolls	`double rolls = 0.0;`
Algorithm	
1. enter the room length, room width, ceiling height, and single roll coverage	
2. calculate the room perimeter by adding together the room length and room width, and then multiplying the sum by 2	
3. calculate the wall area by multiplying the room perimeter by the ceiling height	
4. calculate the number of single rolls by dividing the wall area by the single roll coverage	
5. display the number of single rolls	

After assigning a name, data type, and initial value to each unique input, processing, and output item, the programmer then translates each step in the algorithm into one or more C++ instructions. For example, the first step in the algorithm is to enter the input items—room length, room width, ceiling height, and single roll coverage. You will have the user enter the input items at the keyboard. To do so, you first use the `Console::Write()` method to display an appropriate message, or prompt, on the computer screen. The message should clearly indicate the information that you want the user to enter. You then use the `Console::ReadLine()` method to accept the input items from the user, and (in this case) the `Convert::ToDouble()` method to convert the input items to `double` numbers. The C++ code that corresponds to the first step in the algorithm is shown in Figure 3-22.

tip

Recall that if you want to use the data returned by the `Console::ReadLine()` method as a number, then you must use a `Convert` method to convert the input string to the proper type.

Figure 3-22: C++ instructions corresponding to the first step in the algorithm

IPO chart information	C++ instructions
Input	
room length	`double length = 0.0;`
room width	`double width = 0.0;`
ceiling height	`double height = 0.0;`
single roll coverage	`double rollCoverage = 0.0;`
Processing	
room perimeter	`double perimeter = 0.0;`
wall area	`double area = 0.0;`
Output	
number of single rolls	`double rolls = 0.0;`
Algorithm	

1. enter the room length, room width, ceiling height, and single roll coverage	`Console::Write("Enter room length: ");`
	`length = Convert::ToDouble(Console::ReadLine());`
	`Console::Write("Enter room width: ");`
	`width = Convert::ToDouble(Console::ReadLine());`
	`Console::Write("Enter ceiling height: ");`
	`height = Convert::ToDouble(Console::ReadLine());`
	`Console::Write("Enter single roll coverage: ");`
	`rollCoverage = Convert::ToDouble(Console::ReadLine());`

2. calculate the room perimeter by adding together the room length and room width, and then multiplying the sum by 2	
3. calculate the wall area by multiplying the room perimeter by the ceiling height	
4. calculate the number of single rolls by dividing the wall area by the single roll coverage	
5. display the number of single rolls	

Step 2 in the algorithm is to calculate the perimeter of the room by adding together the room's length and width, and then multiplying that sum by 2. The C++ statement `perimeter = (length + width) * 2;` accomplishes this task by adding the value stored in the `length` variable to the value stored in the `width` variable, and then multiplying that sum by 2. The statement stores the result of the calculation in the `perimeter` variable. Recall that the `perimeter` variable is one of the two processing items.

The third step in the algorithm is to calculate the wall area by multiplying the perimeter of the room by the height of the ceiling. This task is handled by the C++ statement `area = perimeter * height;`, which multiplies the contents of the `perimeter` variable by the contents of the `height` variable, and then stores the result in the `area` variable. Recall that the `area` variable is the second processing item.

Step 4 in the algorithm is to calculate the number of single rolls of wallpaper by dividing the wall area by the single roll coverage, which is the area that a single roll can cover. The C++ statement `rolls = area / rollCoverage;` accomplishes this by dividing the value stored in the `area` variable by the value stored in the `rollCoverage` variable. The quotient will be stored in the `rolls` variable.

The last step in the algorithm is to display the required number of single rolls of wallpaper, which was calculated in the previous step. You can do so using the C++ statement `Console::WriteLine("Single rolls: {0}", Convert::ToString (rolls));`. This statement will display the message "Single rolls: " along with the contents of the `rolls` variable. Figure 3-23 shows the code corresponding to the wallpaper store problem's algorithm. Notice how each instruction corresponds to a step in the algorithm. Also notice that some steps require more than one instruction.

Figure 3-23: C++ instructions corresponding to the wallpaper store problem's algorithm

IPO chart information	C++ instructions
Input	
room length	`double length = 0.0;`
room width	`double width = 0.0;`
ceiling height	`double height = 0.0;`
single roll coverage	`double rollCoverage = 0.0;`
Processing	
room perimeter	`double perimeter = 0.0;`
wall area	`double area = 0.0;`
Output	
number of single rolls	`double rolls = 0.0;`
Algorithm	

1. enter the room length, room width, ceiling height, and single roll coverage	`Console::Write("Enter room length: ");`
	`length = Convert::ToDouble(Console::ReadLine());`
	`Console::Write("Enter room width: ");`
	`width = Convert::ToDouble(Console::ReadLine());`
	`Console::Write("Enter ceiling height: ");`
	`height = Convert::ToDouble(Console::ReadLine());`
	`Console::Write("Enter single roll coverage: ");`
	`rollCoverage = Convert::ToDouble(Console::`
	`ReadLine());`

Figure 3-23: C++ instructions corresponding to the wallpaper store problem's algorithm (continued)

IPO chart information	C++ instructions
2. calculate the room perimeter by adding together the room length and room width, and then multiplying the sum by 2	`perimeter = (length + width) * 2;`
3. calculate the wall area by multiplying the room perimeter by the ceiling height	`area = perimeter * height;`
4. calculate the number of single rolls by dividing the wall area by the single roll coverage	`rolls = area / rollCoverage;`
5. display the number of single rolls	`Console::WriteLine("Single rolls: {0}",` `Convert::ToString(rolls));`

After the programmer finishes coding the algorithm into a program, he or she then moves on to the fifth step in the problem-solving process, which is to desk-check the program.

Desk-checking the Program

The fifth step in the problem-solving process is to desk-check the program to make sure that each step in the algorithm was translated correctly. You should desk-check the program using the same sample data that you used to desk-check the algorithm. The results obtained when desk-checking the program should be identical to the results obtained when desk-checking the algorithm. For your convenience in comparing the results of both desk-checks later in this lesson, Figure 3-24 shows the desk-check table that you completed for the wallpaper store algorithm in Tutorial 2's Application lesson.

Figure 3-24: Completed desk-check table for the wallpaper store algorithm

room length	room width	ceiling height	single roll coverage	room perimeter	wall area	number of single rolls
~~10~~ 12	~~12~~ 14	~~8~~ 10	~~30~~ 37	~~44~~ 52	~~352~~ 520	~~11.73~~ 14.05

As Figure 3-24 indicates, you desk-checked the algorithm twice, using two sets of data. The first set of data used 10 as the room length, 12 as the room width, 8 as the ceiling height, and 30 as the single roll coverage. The second set of data used 12 as the room length, 14 as the room width, 10 as the ceiling height, and 37 as the single roll coverage. You will use both sets of data to desk-check the program.

When desk-checking the program, you first place the names of the unique input, processing, and output variables in a new desk-check table, along with each variable's initial value, as shown in Figure 3-25.

Figure 3-25: Variable names and initial values shown in the program's desk-check table

variable names — initial values

length	width	height	rollCoverage	perimeter	area	rolls
0.0	0.0	0.0	0.0	0.0	0.0	0.0

Next, you complete each of the C++ instructions in order, recording in the desk-check table any changes made to the variables. For example, the statement `Console::Write ("Enter room length: ");` prompts the user to enter the length of the room. The statement does not make any changes to the program's variables, so no entry is necessary in the desk-check table as a result of the statement. However, recall that the next statement, `length = Convert::ToDouble(Console::ReadLine());`, allows the user to enter the length, and it stores the user's response in the `length` variable. If the user enters the number 10 as the room length, for example, the statement stores the number 10 in the `length` variable. You record the result of the statement by crossing out the 0.0 that appears as the initial value in the `length` column, and entering the number 10.0 there instead.

The statement `Console::Write("Enter room width: ");` prompts the user to enter the width of the room, and the statement `width = Convert::ToDouble (Console::ReadLine());` stores the user's response in the `width` variable. Assuming the user enters the number 12, you cross out the 0.0 that appears in the desk-check table's `width` column, and record the number 12.0 there instead.

The statement `Console::Write("Enter ceiling height: ");` prompts the user to enter the ceiling height, and the statement `height = Convert::ToDouble (Console::ReadLine());` stores the user's response in the `height` variable. Assuming the user enters the number 8, you cross out the 0.0 that appears in the desk-check table's `height` column, and record the number 8.0 there instead.

The statement `Console::Write("Enter single roll coverage: ");` prompts the user to enter the area covered by a single roll of wallpaper, and the statement `rollCoverage = Convert::ToDouble(Console::ReadLine());` stores the user's response in the `rollCoverage` variable. Assuming the user enters the number 30, you cross out the 0.0 that appears in the desk-check table's `rollCoverage` column, and record the number 30.0 there instead, as shown in Figure 3-26.

tip

As you learned in Tutorial 2, each column in a desk-check table should contain only one value at any time.

Figure 3-26: Current status of the desk-check table

length	width	height	rollCoverage	perimeter	area	rolls
~~0.0~~ 10.0	~~0.0~~ 12.0	~~0.0~~ 8.0	~~0.0~~ 30.0	0.0	0.0	0.0

The next statement, `perimeter = (length + width) * 2;`, first adds the contents of the `length` variable (10.0 according to the desk-check table) to the contents of the `width` variable (12.0 according to the desk-check table), giving 22.0. It then multiplies that sum by 2, giving 44.0. The statement stores the number 44.0 in the `perimeter` variable. Notice that the calculation that appears on the right side of the assignment operator in the statement is performed first, and then the result is stored in the variable whose name appears on the left side of the assignment operator. As a result of this statement, you cross out the number 0.0 that appears in the desk-check table's `perimeter` column, and record the number 44.0 there instead, as shown in Figure 3-27.

Figure 3-27: Desk-check table showing the result of the perimeter calculation

length	width	height	rollCoverage	perimeter	area	rolls
~~0.0~~ 10.0	~~0.0~~ 12.0	~~0.0~~ 8.0	~~0.0~~ 30.0	~~0.0~~ 44.0	0.0	0.0

The next statement, `area = perimeter * height;`, first multiplies the contents of the `perimeter` variable (44.0) by the contents of the `height` variable (8.0), and then stores the result (352.0) in the `area` variable. In the desk-check table, you cross out the 0.0 that appears in the `area` column, and record the number 352.0 there instead, as shown in Figure 3-28.

Figure 3-28: Desk-check table showing the result of the area calculation

length	width	height	rollCoverage	perimeter	area	rolls
~~0.0~~ 10.0	~~0.0~~ 12.0	~~0.0~~ 8.0	~~0.0~~ 30.0	~~0.0~~ 44.0	~~0.0~~ 352.0	0.0

The next statement, `rolls = area / rollCoverage;`, first divides the contents of the `area` variable (352.0) by the contents of the `rollCoverage` variable (30.0), and then stores the result (approximately 11.73) in the `rolls` variable. In the desk-check table, you cross out the 0.0 that appears in the `rolls` column, and record the number 11.73 there instead, as shown in Figure 3-29.

Figure 3-29: Desk-check table showing the result of the rolls calculation

length	width	height	rollCoverage	perimeter	area	rolls
~~0.0~~ 10.0	~~0.0~~ 12.0	~~0.0~~ 8.0	~~0.0~~ 30.0	~~0.0~~ 44.0	~~0.0~~ 352.0	~~0.0~~ 11.73

The last statement, `Console::WriteLine("Single rolls: {0}", Convert::ToString(rolls));`, displays the message "Single rolls: ", along with the contents of the `rolls` variable (11.73), on the screen.

If you compare the second row of values shown in Figure 3-29 with the first row of values shown earlier in Figure 3-24, you will notice that the results obtained when desk-checking the program are identical to the results obtained when desk-checking the algorithm. Recall, however, that you should perform several desk-checks, using different data, to make sure that the program is correct.

Next, desk-check the program using 12 as the room length, 14 as the room width, 10 as the ceiling height, and 37 as the single roll coverage; this is the same data used in the second desk-check shown in Figure 3-24. Each time you desk-check a program, keep in mind that you must complete all of the program's instructions, beginning with the first instruction. In this case, the first instruction initializes the `length` variable. The completed desk-check table is shown in Figure 3-30.

Figure 3-30: Desk-check table showing the results of the second desk-check

length	width	height	rollCoverage	perimeter	area	rolls
~~0.0~~ ~~10.0~~ ~~0.0~~ 12.0	~~0.0~~ ~~12.0~~ ~~0.0~~ 14.0	~~0.0~~ ~~8.0~~ ~~0.0~~ 10.0	~~0.0~~ ~~30.0~~ ~~0.0~~ 37.0	~~0.0~~ ~~44.0~~ ~~0.0~~ 52.0	~~0.0~~ ~~352.0~~ ~~0.0~~ 520.0	~~0.0~~ ~~11.73~~ ~~0.0~~ 14.05

Here again, if you compare the fourth row of values shown in Figure 3-30 with the second row of values shown earlier in Figure 3-24, you will notice that the program produced the same results as did the algorithm.

After desk-checking the program, the programmer then evaluates and modifies (if necessary) the program.

Evaluating and Modifying the Program

The final step in the problem-solving process is to evaluate and modify (if necessary) the program. You do so by entering the program instructions into the computer, and then running (executing) the program. In this tutorial's Application lesson, you learn how to enter the C++ instructions listed in Figure 3-23 into the computer. You also learn how to run a C++ program.

Programmers often refer to the final step in the problem-solving process as the "testing and debugging" step. **Testing** refers to running the program, along with sample data, on the computer. The results obtained when the program is run on the computer should agree with those shown in the program's desk-check table. If the results of running the program differ from those of the desk-check, then the program contains errors that must be corrected.

Debugging refers to the process of locating and removing any errors, called **bugs**, in a program. Program errors can be either syntax errors or logic errors. You create a **syntax error** when you enter an instruction that violates the programming language's **syntax**, which is the set of rules that you must follow when using the language. Typing the statement `Console::Writeline("Hello");`, rather than the statement `Console::WriteLine ("Hello");`, is an example of a syntax error. (Notice that `WriteLine` is spelled incorrectly as `Writeline`.) Most syntax errors occur as a result of mistyping a keyword or variable name, or forgetting to enter a semicolon at the end of a statement. In most cases, syntax errors are easy to both locate and correct, because they trigger an error message from the compiler. The error message indicates the general vicinity of the error and includes a brief explanation of the error.

Logic errors, on the other hand, are much more difficult to find, because they can occur for a variety of reasons and do not trigger an error message from the compiler. The instruction `perimeter = length + width * 2;`, which is supposed to calculate the perimeter, is an example of a logic error. Although the instruction is syntactically correct, it is logically incorrect, because it tells the computer first to multiply the contents of the `width` variable by 2, then add that product to the contents of the `length` variable, and then assign the sum to the `perimeter` variable. This error occurs because multiplication is performed before addition in an arithmetic expression. The instruction to calculate the perimeter, written correctly, is `perimeter = (length + width) * 2;`. Adding the parentheses to this instruction tells the computer first to add the contents of the `length` variable to the contents of the `width` variable, then multiply that sum by 2, and then assign the product to the `perimeter` variable. Other logic errors occur typically as a result of neglecting to enter a program instruction or entering the program instructions in the wrong order.

If a program contains an error, the programmer must locate and then correct the error. The programmer's job is not finished until the program runs without errors and produces the expected results.

MINI-QUIZ

Mini-Quiz 5

1) How many values can a variable contain at any time?
2) Errors in a program are also called ______________.
3) Program errors can be either ______________ errors or ______________ errors.

You now have completed five of the six steps needed to create a computer program for The Paper Tree wallpaper store. Recall that you analyzed the wallpaper store's problem in Tutorial 2's Application lesson. You also planned an appropriate algorithm, and then desk-checked the algorithm. In this lesson, you coded the algorithm into a program, and then desk-checked the program. You complete the final step—evaluate and modify (if necessary) the program—in the Application lesson. For now, you can either take a break or complete the end-of-lesson questions and exercises before moving on to the Application lesson.

SUMMARY

Most programs include variables, constants (named and literal), and arithmetic operators (which are used to perform calculations). Variables and named constants are memory locations (inside the computer) where you can temporarily store data. The contents of a variable can change as the program is running, but the contents of a named constant cannot change. You must assign a name, data type, and initial value to each named constant you create. You also must assign a name and data type to each variable you create. Although assigning an initial value to a variable is optional in most programming languages, it is considered a good programming practice to do so to ensure that the variable does not contain garbage.

In C++, you declare and initialize a named constant using the syntax **const** *datatype* [*]*constantname* = *value*;. You declare and initialize a variable in C++ using the syntax *datatype* [*]*variablename* [= *initialvalue*];. You typically use a literal constant, which simply is an item of data, to initialize named constants and variables. C++ has three types of literal constants: numeric, character, and string. A numeric literal constant is a number. A character literal constant is one letter, number, or symbol enclosed in single quotation marks (' '). A string literal constant is zero or more characters enclosed in double quotation marks ("").

You can use an assignment statement, which must conform to the C++ syntax *variablename* = *expression*;, to store data in a variable. The data type of the *expression* must match the data type of the variable. When C++ encounters an assignment statement in a program, it assigns the value of the *expression* appearing on the right side of the assignment operator (=) to the variable whose *variablename* appears on the left side of the assignment operator. A variable can store only one item of data at any time. When you assign another item to the variable, the new data replaces the existing data.

When assigning a value to a memory location, it is important that the value fit the memory location's data type. If you assign a value that does not match the data type of the memory location, the computer uses a process called implicit type conversion to convert the value to fit the memory location. However, it is not always possible for the computer to make the conversion. You can use the methods contained in the `Convert` class to type cast—in other words, to explicitly convert—data from one data type to another.

Most programs require the computer to perform one or more calculations. You instruct the computer to perform a calculation by writing an arithmetic expression that contains one or more arithmetic operators. Each arithmetic operator is associated with a precedence number, which controls the order in which the operation is performed in an expression. You can use parentheses to override the normal order of precedence, because operations within parentheses always are performed before operations outside of parentheses.

You can use either the `Console::Write()` method or the `Console::WriteLine()` method to display a message on the computer screen. You can use the `Console::ReadLine()` method to get input from the user at the keyboard.

After analyzing a problem, and then planning and desk-checking an appropriate algorithm, the programmer continues to the fourth step in the problem-solving process, which is to code the algorithm into a program, using the information in the IPO chart. First the programmer assigns a name, data type, and initial value to each unique input, processing, and output item listed in the IPO chart. He or she then translates each step in the algorithm into one or more C++ instructions.

After coding the algorithm, the programmer then desk-checks the program to make sure that the algorithm was translated correctly. You should desk-check the program using the same sample data that you used to desk-check the algorithm. The results obtained when desk-checking the program should be identical to the results obtained when desk-checking the algorithm.

The final step in the problem-solving process is to evaluate and modify (if necessary) the program. A programmer evaluates, or tests, a program by running (executing) it, along with sample data, on the computer. If the executed program does not work as intended, the programmer makes the necessary modifications until it does.

Some programs have errors, called bugs. Program errors can be either syntax errors or logic errors. A syntax error occurs when you violate one of the rules of the programming language, referred to as the language's syntax. Examples of syntax errors include mistyping a keyword or variable name and forgetting to enter a semicolon at the end of a statement. A logic error can occur for a variety of reasons—such as neglecting to enter an instruction or entering the program instructions in the wrong order. Debugging refers to the process of locating and removing the errors in a program.

ANSWERS TO MINI-QUIZZES

Mini-Quiz 1

1) c. `88TaxAmt`
2) a. character literal constant
3) d. string literal constant
4) a. `10111`
5) a. `01100010`
6) d. `Convert::ToSingle(75.46)`

Mini-Quiz 2

1) `const *String CITY = "Chicago";`
2) `int numberOfPeople = 0;`
3) `String *studentName = "";`
4) `double interestRate = 0.0;`
5) `float rate = Convert::ToSingle(5.6);`

Mini-Quiz 3

1) `price = Convert::ToSingle(23.25);`
2) `insured = 'T';`
3) `grossPay = 10.75 * hours;`
4) 5
5) 5.0

Mini-Quiz 4

1) `Console::WriteLine("Hello");`

2) `Console::Write("I live in {0}", city);`

3) `Console::WriteLine(grossPay);`

4) `input = Console::ReadLine();`

5) `input = Convert::ToDouble(Console::ReadLine());`

Mini-Quiz 5

1) one

2) bugs

3) syntax, logic

QUESTIONS

1) A variable is ______________.

A. an item of data

B. a literal constant

C. a memory location whose value can change while the program is running

D. a memory location whose value cannot change while the program is running

2) To create a named constant, you must assign ______________ to it.

A. a data type

B. a name

C. an initial value

D. all of the above

3) Which of the following declares and initializes a C++ variable that can store whole numbers only?

A. `int numItems = 0;`

B. `int numItems = '0';`

C. `int numItems = "0";`

D. `numItems = 0;`

4) Which of the following is a valid name for a variable?

A. `amt-Sold`

B. `amt   Sold`

C. `amt_Sold`

D. `98SoldAmt`

5) Which of the following is not a valid name for a C++ variable?

A. `float`

B. `payRate`

C. `total`

D. `winnings`

6) The number 4.5e3 is a ______________ literal constant.

A. character

B. named

C. numeric

D. string

7) Which of the following stores the letter H in a `char` variable named `initial`?

A. `initial = 'H'`

B. `initial = 'H';`

C. `initial = "H"`

D. `initial = "H";`

8) You typically initialize `int` variables in a C++ program to ______________.

A. the number 0 enclosed in double quotation marks

B. the number 0 enclosed in single quotation marks

C. the number 0

D. the number 0.0

9) You typically initialize `char` variables in a C++ program to ______________.

A. a space enclosed in double quotation marks

B. a space enclosed in single quotation marks

C. the number 0

D. the number 0.0

10) Which of the following C++ statements declares and initializes a `float` variable named `rate`?

A. `float rate = 0.0`

B. `float rate = '0.0';`

C. `float rate = 0.0;`

D. `rate = 0.0;`

11) Which of the following are valid characters for a numeric literal constant?

A. a decimal point

B. the letter e

C. a minus sign

D. all of the above

12) Which of the following are valid characters for a numeric literal constant?

A. a comma

B. a dollar sign ($)

C. a percent sign (%)

D. none of the above

13) Which of the following C++ statements creates a named constant called `RATE` whose value is 16.5?

A. `const RATE = 16.5;`

B. `const double RATE = 16.5;`

C. `double RATE = 16.5;`

D. `RATE const = 16.5;`

14) Assume that the following instructions are part of a valid C++ program. What is the value contained in the `number` variable after the instructions are processed?

```
int number = 0;
number = 10;
number = number + 5;
```

A. 0

B. 5

C. 10

D. 15

15) What value will be assigned to the `answer` variable as a result of the `answer = 3 + 2 * 9 % (10 – 6);` statement? (The `answer` variable is an `int` variable.)

A. 1

B. 5

C. 6

D. 11

16) Which of the following displays the contents of the `String` variable named `state` on the computer screen?

A. `Console::Write(state);`

B. `Console::WriteLine(state);`

C. `Console::Write("{0}", state);`

D. all of the above

17) Which of the following displays the message "Her gross pay is *gross*, and her net pay is *net*." on the computer screen, where *gross* and *net* are the contents of two `double` variables named `grossPay` and `netPay`?

A. `Console::WriteLine("Her gross pay is grossPay, and her net pay is netPay.");`

B. `Console::WriteLine("Her gross pay is (0), and her net pay is (1).", grossPay, netPay);`

C. `Console::WriteLine("Her gross pay is {0}, and her net pay is {1}.", grossPay, netPay);`

D. `Console::WriteLine("Her gross pay is {0}, and her net pay is {1}.", Convert::ToString(grossPay), Convert::ToString(netPay));`

18) Which of the following assigns the user's input to the `int` variable named `quantity`?

A. `Console::Read(quantity);`

B. `Console::ReadLine(quantity);`

C. `quantity = Console::ReadLine();`

D. none of the above

19) Which of the following is the fourth step in the problem-solving process?

A. Evaluate and modify (if necessary) the program.

B. Code the algorithm into a program.

C. Plan the algorithm.

D. Desk-check the program.

20) The rules of a programming language are called its ________.
   A. guidelines
   B. procedures
   C. regulations
   D. syntax

21) A C++ statement must end with a ________.
   A. : (colon)
   B. , (comma)
   C. ; (semicolon)
   D. none of the above

22) The final step in the problem-solving process is to ________.
   A. evaluate and modify (if necessary) the program
   B. code the algorithm into a program
   C. plan the algorithm
   D. desk-check the program

23) The process of locating and removing the errors in a program is called ________.
   A. analyzing
   B. correcting
   C. debugging
   D. tracking

24) Misspelling an instruction is an example of ________.
   A. an entry error
   B. a function error
   C. a logic error
   D. a syntax error

25) Typing the instruction `grossPay = hoursWorked – hourlyPay;` is an example of ________.
   A. an entry error
   B. a function error
   C. a logic error
   D. a syntax error

Look For These Symbols

Debugging

Discovery

EXERCISES

1) Write the statement to declare and initialize a variable that can store an item's price, which can contain decimal places. Name the variable `price` and assign the `double` data type to it. Then write an assignment statement that assigns the value 16.23 to the variable.

2) Write the statements to declare and initialize two variables: one to store an item's height and the other to store an item's width. Both dimensions can contain decimal places. Name the variables **height** and **width**, and assign the **float** data type to each. Then write an assignment statement that assigns the value 4.5 to the **height** variable. Also write an assignment statement that assigns the value 6.9 to the **width** variable.

3) Write the statement to declare and initialize a variable that can store the population of a city. Name the variable **population**, and assign the **int** data type to it. Then write an assignment statement that assigns the value 60,000 to the variable.

4) Write the statement to declare and initialize a variable that can store a letter of the alphabet. Name the variable **letter**, and assign the **char** data type to it. Then write an assignment statement that assigns the letter A to the variable.

5) Write a C++ statement to declare and initialize a **double** named constant called **TAXRATE** whose value is .15.

6) Write a C++ statement to declare and initialize an **int** named constant called **MAXPAY** whose value is 20.

7) Write a C++ statement to declare and initialize a **char** named constant called **INSURED** whose value is the letter Y.

8) Write a C++ statement to declare and initialize a **String** named constant called **PROMPT** whose value is the string "Press any key to continue".

9) Assume a program needs to store the number of units in stock at the beginning of the current month, the number of units purchased during the current month, the number of units sold during the current month, and the number of units in stock at the end of the current month. (The number of units is always an integer.) Write the appropriate C++ statements to declare and initialize the necessary variables. Name the variables **beginStock**, **purchased**, **sold**, and **endStock**. Use the **int** data type to declare each variable. Then write an assignment statement that calculates the number of units in stock at the end of the current month.

10) Assume a program needs to calculate a bonus, which is always 5% of the sales. Write the appropriate C++ statements to declare and initialize the necessary memory locations. Be sure to assign a descriptive name to each memory location. Use the **double** data type for all memory locations. Then write an assignment statement that calculates the bonus.

11) Assume a program needs to calculate an employee's gross pay. The input items will be the employee's name, hours worked, and pay rate. Write the appropriate C++ statements to declare and initialize the necessary memory locations. The hours worked and pay rate will always be integers. Then write an assignment statement that calculates the gross pay. You do not need to worry about overtime pay, because no employees work more than 40 hours.

12) Three C++ instructions are missing from the code shown in Figure 3-31. First study the algorithm, then complete the C++ code by entering the three missing instructions.

Figure 3-31

IPO chart information	C++ instructions

Input
first number
second number
	
	`double num1 = 0.0;`
	`double num2 = 0.0;`

Processing	
Output sum	 `double sum = 0.0;`

Algorithm
1. enter the first number and the second number
	`Console::Write("Enter first number: ");`
	`num1 = Convert::ToDouble(Console::ReadLine());`
	____________________
	____________________

2. calculate the sum by adding the first number to the second number	____________________
3. display the sum	`Console::WriteLine("The sum is {0}.",` `Convert::ToString(sum));`

13) Desk-check the program you completed in Exercise 12 two times, using the numbers 3 and 5 first, and then using the numbers 50.5 and 31.3. Use the desk-check table shown in Figure 3-32.

Figure 3-32

num1	num2	sum

14) Study the algorithm shown in Figure 3-33, then complete the C++ code shown in the figure.

Figure 3-33

IPO chart information	C++ instructions

Input
current weekly pay
raise rate
	
	`double currentPay = 0.0;`
	`double rate = 0.0;`

Processing weekly raise	______________________
Output new weekly pay	______________________

Algorithm
1. enter the current weekly pay and raise rate
	`Console::Write("Enter current weekly pay: ");`
	`currentPay =`
	`Convert::ToDouble(Console::ReadLine());`
	`Console::Write("Enter raise rate: ");`
	______________________

2. calculate the weekly raise by multiplying the current weekly pay by the raise rate	`raise =` ______________________
3. calculate the new weekly pay by adding the weekly raise to the current weekly pay	`newPay =` ______________________
4. display the new weekly pay	______________________

15) Create a desk-check table for the program you completed in Exercise 14. Desk-check the program twice. For the first desk-check, use 250 as the current weekly pay and .03 as the raise rate. For the second desk-check, use 100 as the current weekly pay and .10 as the raise rate. When you are finished desk-checking, compare your desk-check table with the one shown in Tutorial 2's Figure 2-23; the results (other than the initialization rows) should be the same.

16) Study the algorithm shown in Figure 3-34, then write the appropriate C++ code. Use the `int` data type to declare the appropriate variables.

Figure 3-34

IPO chart information	C++ instructions
Input	
first number	______________________
second number	______________________
third number	______________________
Processing	
Output	
sum	______________________
Algorithm	
1. enter the first number, second number, and third number	______________________ ______________________ ______________________ ______________________ ______________________ ______________________
2. calculate the sum by adding together the first number, second number, and third number	______________________
3. display the sum	______________________

17) Create an appropriate desk-check table for the program you completed in Exercise 16. Desk-check the program twice. For the first desk-check, use the numbers 25, 76, and 33. For the second desk-check, use the numbers 10, 15, and 20.

18) In this exercise, you learn about the arithmetic assignment operators available in C++.

A. In addition to the standard arithmetic operators, the C++ programming language also has an addition assignment operator (+=), a subtraction assignment operator (-=), a multiplication assignment operator (*=), a division assignment operator (/=), and a modulus assignment operator (%=). What is the purpose of these operators?

B. Write a C++ statement that uses the addition assignment operator to add the number 10 to the contents of an `int` variable named `quantity`.

19) In this exercise, you learn about the increment and decrement operators in C++.

A. The C++ programming language has an increment operator (++) and a decrement operator (--). What is the purpose of these operators?

B. Write a C++ statement that uses the increment operator to increment the `quantity` variable by 1.

20) In this exercise, you debug C++ code.

A. Study the algorithm and C++ code shown in Figure 3-35. Desk-check the code using an original price of 100 and a discount rate of 25%.

B. Make the necessary changes to the code, then desk-check the code again, using the same sample data.

Figure 3-35

IPO chart information	C++ instructions
Input original price discount rate	`double original = 0.0;` `double rate = 0.0;`
Processing discount	`double discount = 0.0;`
Output sale price	`double sale = 0.0;`

Algorithm
1. enter the original price and the discount rate
	`Console::Write("Original price: ");`
	`original = Convert::ToDouble(Console::ReadLine());`
	`Console::Write("Discount rate: ");`
	`rate = Convert::ToDouble(Console::ReadLine());`

2. calculate the discount by multiplying the original price by the discount rate	`discount = original * discRate;`
3. calculate the sale price by subtracting the discount from the original price	`sale = discount – original;`
4. display the sale price	`Console::WriteLine("Sale price: {0}",` `Convert::ToString(sale));`

Application Lesson

Creating a C++ Program

CASE In Tutorial 2, you analyzed a problem description for Mark Williams and The Paper Tree wallpaper store. You also planned an appropriate algorithm and then desk-checked the algorithm. You coded the algorithm into a C++ program in Tutorial 3's Concept lesson, and also desk-checked the program. In this lesson, you complete the final step in the problem-solving process: evaluate and modify (if necessary) the program. Recall that the final step involves entering the C++ program instructions into the computer and then running the program.

The C++ Programming Language

C++ evolved from the procedure-oriented C programming language, which was developed in 1972 at Bell Laboratories by Dennis Ritchie. In 1985, Bjarne Stroustrup, also of Bell Laboratories, added, among other things, object-oriented features to the C language. This enhanced version of the C language was named C++.

C++ is a superset of C, which means that, with few exceptions, everything available in C also is available in C++. This means that you can use C++ as a procedural, as well as an object-oriented, language. Before using the object-oriented features of C++, you learn how to use C++ to create procedure-oriented programs. The techniques you learn from procedural programming will help you create object-oriented programs later.

To create and execute a C++ program, you need to have access to a text editor, often simply called an editor, and a C++ compiler. You use the editor to enter the C++ instructions, called **source code**, into the computer. You then save the source code in a file on a disk, using the filename extension .cpp. (The *cpp* stands for *C plus plus*.) The file containing the source code is called the **source file**.

As you learned in the Overview, the computer cannot understand instructions written in a high-level language. Rather, a compiler is necessary to translate the high-level instructions into machine code—the 0s and 1s that the computer *can* understand. Machine code is usually called **object code**. When you compile a C++ program, the compiler generates the appropriate object code, saving it automatically in a file whose filename extension is .obj. (The *obj* stands for *object*.) The file containing the object code is called the **object file**.

After the compiler creates the object file, it then invokes another program called a linker. The **linker** combines the object file with other machine code necessary for your C++ program to run correctly—such as machine code that allows your program to communicate with input and output devices. The linker produces an **executable file**, which is a file that contains all of the machine code necessary to run your C++ program as many times as desired without the need for translating the program again. The executable file has an extension of .exe on its filename. (The *exe* stands for *executable*.)

Figure 3-36 illustrates the process the C++ compiler follows when translating your source code into executable code.

Figure 3-36: Process by which source code is translated into executable code

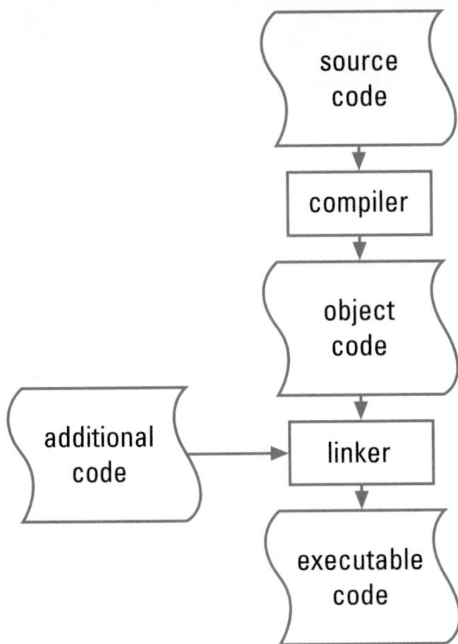

Many C++ systems, such as Microsoft Visual C++ and Borland C++Builder, contain both the editor and compiler in one integrated environment, referred to as an **IDE** (**Integrated Development Environment**). Other C++ systems, called command-line compilers, contain only the compiler and require you to use a general-purpose editor (such as Notepad and WordPad) to enter the program instructions into the computer. In this book, you use Microsoft Visual C++ .NET to enter and run your C++ programs.

Starting and Customizing Visual Studio .NET

Before you can use Visual C++ .NET to create a C++ program, you must start Visual Studio .NET. Visual Studio .NET is Microsoft's newest IDE and includes programming languages such as Visual C++ .NET, Visual Basic .NET, and Visual C# .NET.

tip

Microsoft licenses the Visual Studio .NET IDE to other vendors, who also can add languages to the IDE.

To start Visual Studio .NET:

1. Click the **Start** button on the Windows XP taskbar to open the Start menu.
2. Point to **All Programs**, then point to **Microsoft Visual Studio .NET**, and then click **Microsoft Visual Studio .NET**. The Microsoft Visual Studio .NET copyright screen appears momentarily, and then the Microsoft Development Environment window opens.
3. If necessary, maximize the Microsoft Development Environment window.
4. If necessary, click the **My Profile** link on the Start Page. The My Profile pane appears in the Start Page window, as shown in Figure 3-37. (Your screen might not look identical to Figure 3-37, but it should show the Start Page.)

Figure 3-37: Microsoft Development Environment window

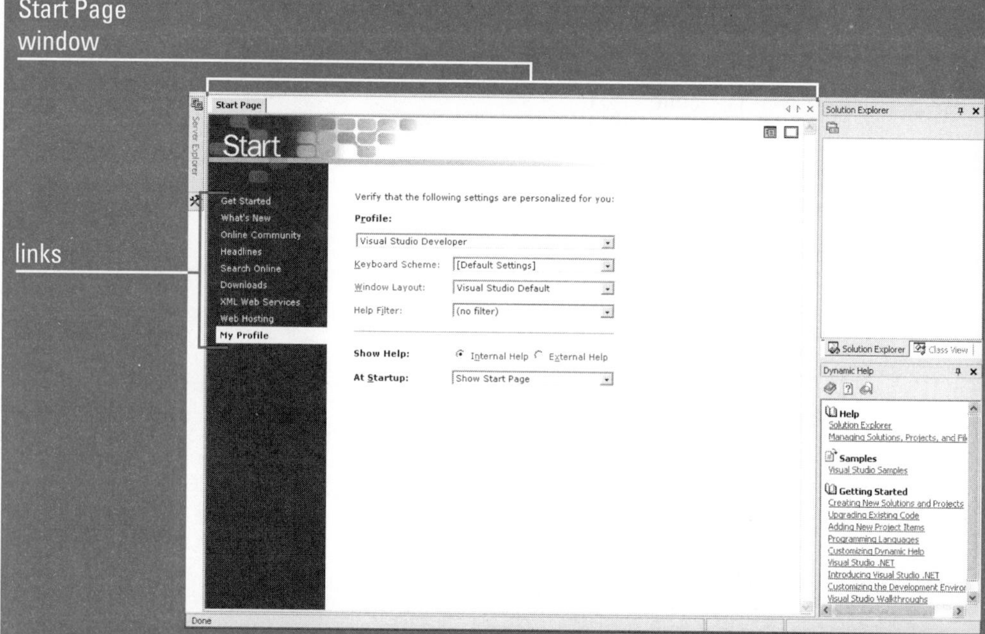

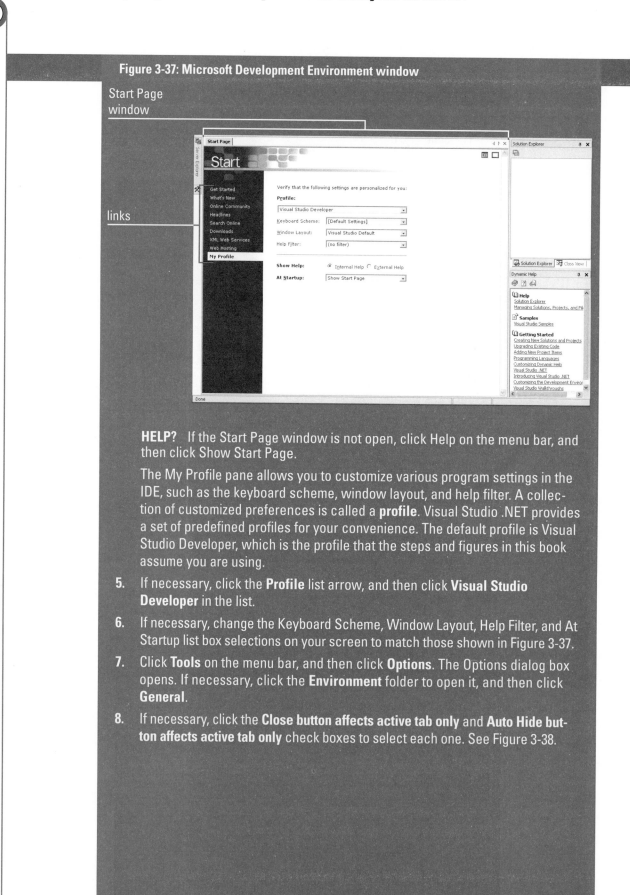

HELP? If the Start Page window is not open, click Help on the menu bar, and then click Show Start Page.

The My Profile pane allows you to customize various program settings in the IDE, such as the keyboard scheme, window layout, and help filter. A collection of customized preferences is called a **profile**. Visual Studio .NET provides a set of predefined profiles for your convenience. The default profile is Visual Studio Developer, which is the profile that the steps and figures in this book assume you are using.

5. If necessary, click the **Profile** list arrow, and then click **Visual Studio Developer** in the list.
6. If necessary, change the Keyboard Scheme, Window Layout, Help Filter, and At Startup list box selections on your screen to match those shown in Figure 3-37.
7. Click **Tools** on the menu bar, and then click **Options**. The Options dialog box opens. If necessary, click the **Environment** folder to open it, and then click **General**.
8. If necessary, click the **Close button affects active tab only** and **Auto Hide button affects active tab only** check boxes to select each one. See Figure 3-38.

Figure 3-38: Options dialog box

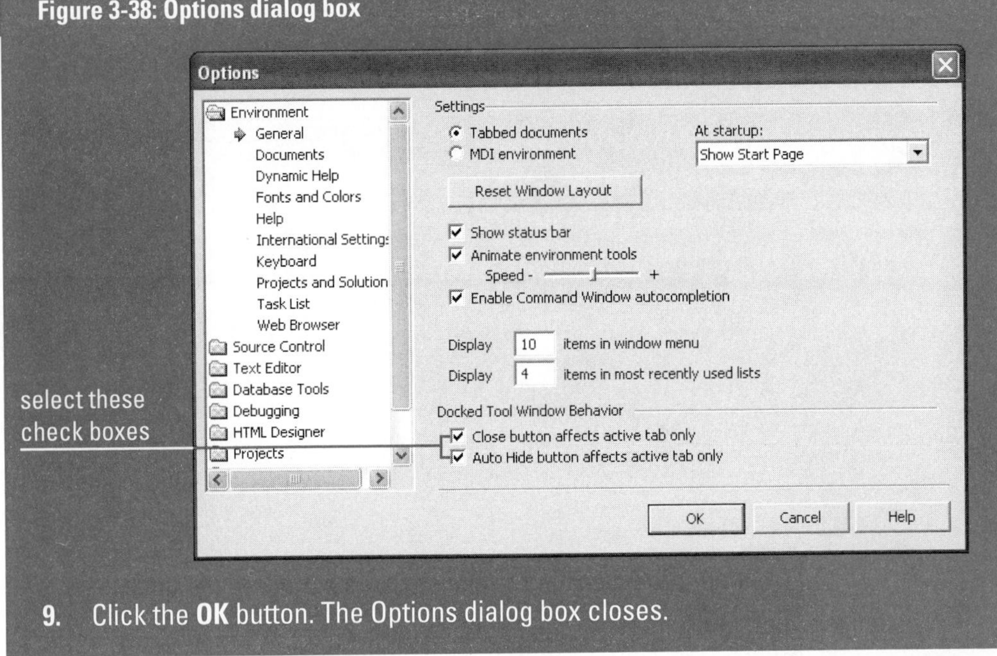

9. Click the **OK** button. The Options dialog box closes.

tip

You can use the Reset Window Layout button in the Options dialog box to return the layout of the windows in the IDE to the default layout that was provided during the initial setup of Visual Studio .NET.

In addition to the My Profile link, the Start Page window contains eight other links. Each link displays information in a pane in the Start Page window. Figure 3-39 describes the purpose of each link.

Figure 3-39: Purpose of the links included on the Start Page

Link	Purpose
Get Started	create new projects and open existing projects
What's New	access information about the new features in Visual Studio .NET and check for Visual Studio .NET updates
Online Community	contact fellow developers online
Headlines	view links to the latest news from the MSDN Online Library, including information on seminars, trade shows, and conferences, as well as training opportunities offered by Microsoft
Search Online	search the MSDN Online Library
Downloads	access the latest product updates and sample code available for download
XML Web Services	search for XML Web services to include in your applications, and publish your own XML Web services
Web Hosting	post Web applications, for a fee, on servers provided by third-party Internet service providers
My Profile	customize various program settings in the IDE

Notice that the What's New, Headlines, Search Online, and Downloads links allow you to access the most current information about Visual Studio .NET. You can use the Online Community link to contact fellow developers online, and the Web Hosting link to post Web applications on a server. The XML Web Services link allows you to search for and publish

XML Web services. The My Profile link allows you to customize the IDE, and the Get Started link provides options for creating and opening projects. View the pane displayed by the Get Started link.

To view the pane displayed by the Get Started link:

1. Click the **Get Started** link on the Start Page. The Get Started pane appears in the Start Page window, as shown in Figure 3-40. (Do not be concerned if your Get Started pane shows project names and dates.)

Figure 3-40: Get Started pane shown in the Start Page window

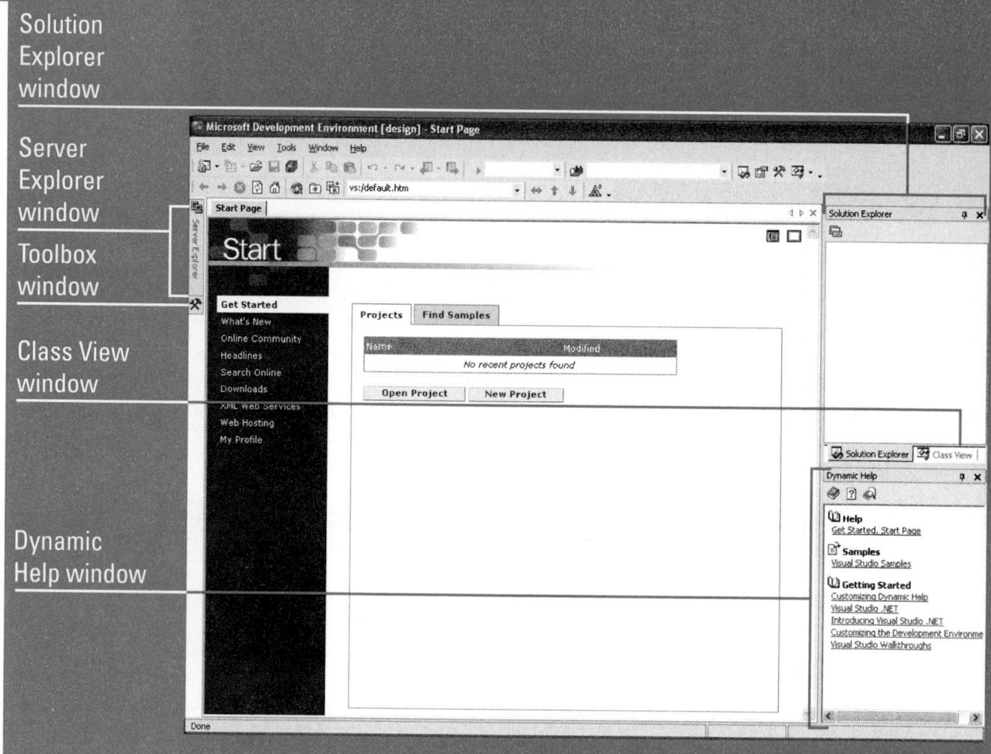

As Figure 3-40 indicates, the IDE contains five windows in addition to the Start Page window: Server Explorer, Toolbox, Solution Explorer, Class View, and Dynamic Help. Figure 3-41 briefly describes the purpose of each window.

Figure 3-41: Purpose of the windows included in the IDE

Window	Purpose
Class View	display the classes, methods, and properties included in a solution
Dynamic Help	display links to context-sensitive help
Server Explorer	display data connections and servers
Solution Explorer	display the names of projects and files included in a solution
Start Page	display the panes associated with the Start Page links
Toolbox	display items that you can use when creating a project

After starting Visual Studio .NET, you then can use Visual C++ .NET to enter your C++ program instructions into the computer.

Creating a Console Application in Visual C++ .NET

Although you can create many different types of applications in Visual C++ .NET, most of the applications you create in this book are console applications. A **console application** is a program that runs in a Command Prompt window.

You create an application by first creating a blank Visual Studio .NET solution, and then you add one or more projects to the solution, and one or more files to a project. A **solution** is simply a container that stores the projects and files for an entire application. A **project** also is a container, but it stores files associated with only a specific piece of the application. Although the idea of solutions, projects, and files may sound confusing, the concept of placing things in containers is nothing new to you. Think of a solution as being similar to a drawer in a filing cabinet. A project then is similar to a file folder that you store in the drawer, and a file is similar to a document that you store in the file folder. You can place many file folders in a filing cabinet drawer, just as you can place many projects in a solution. You also can store many documents in a file folder, similar to the way you can store many files in a project. Figure 3-42 illustrates this analogy

Figure 3-42: Illustration of a solution, project, and file

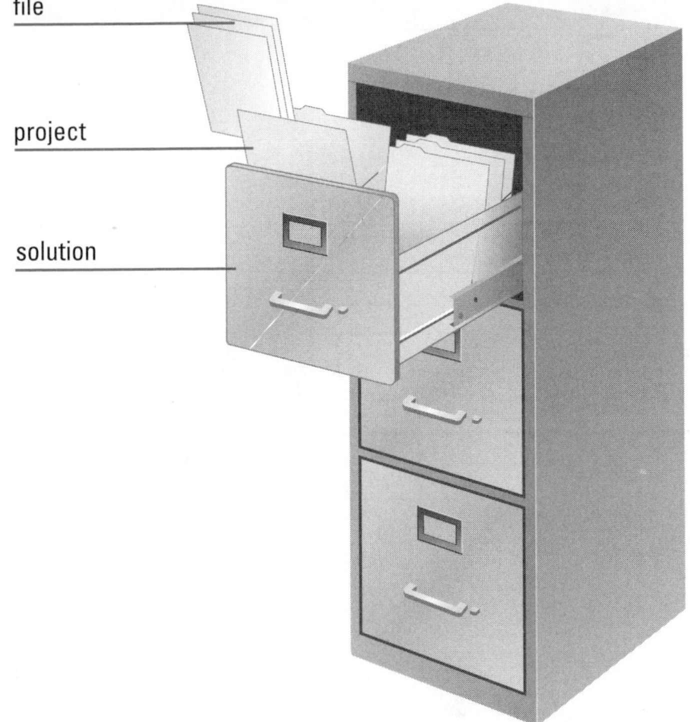

You can create a blank Visual Studio .NET solution by clicking File on the menu bar, pointing to New, and then clicking Blank Solution. You also can create a blank solution by clicking the New Blank Solution button on the Standard toolbar.

tip

If the New Blank Solution button is not displayed on the Standard toolbar, click the list arrow on the New Project button, which also is located on the Standard toolbar, and then click New Blank Solution in the list.

To create a blank Visual Studio .NET solution:

1. Click **File** on the menu bar, point to **New**, and then click **Blank Solution**. The New Project dialog box opens with Visual Studio Solutions selected in the Project Types list box, and Blank Solution selected in the Templates list box. The message located below the Project Types list box indicates that the Blank Solution template creates an empty solution containing no projects.

   A **template** is a pattern that Visual Studio .NET uses to create solutions and projects. Each template listed in the Templates list box includes a set of standard folders and files appropriate for the solution or project. The Blank Solution template, for example, contains one folder and two files. The folder and files are automatically created on your computer's hard disk when you click the OK button in the New Project dialog box.

2. Change the name entered in the Name text box to **T3App Solution**. (The *T3App* in the filename stands for *Tutorial 3, Application lesson.*) If necessary, use the Browse button, which appears to the right of the Location text box, to open the **CppNet\Tut03** folder on your computer's hard disk. See Figure 3-43.

Figure 3-43: New Project dialog box used to create a blank solution

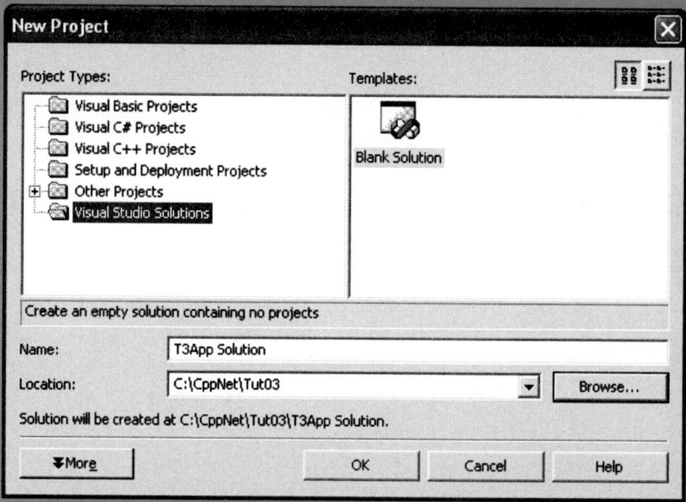

HELP? If the More button is not displayed, click the Less button.

Notice that the message "Solution will be created at C:\CppNet\Tut03\T3App Solution." appears above the More button in the dialog box.

3. Click the **OK** button to close the New Project dialog box. Visual Studio .NET creates a blank solution on your computer's hard disk. It also records in the Solution Explorer window the solution's name (T3App Solution) and the number of projects contained in the solution (0 projects). See Figure 3-44.

Figure 3-44: Solution Explorer window showing the name of a blank solution

When a solution's name appears in the Solution Explorer window, it indicates that the solution is open and ready for you to add information to it. (You also can delete information from a solution.)

Recall that when you use the Blank Solution template to create a solution, Visual Studio .NET automatically creates one folder and two files on your computer's hard disk. The folder has the same name as the solution; in this case, the folder is named T3App Solution. The two files, which are stored in the folder, also bear the solution's name. However, one file has .sln (which stands for "solution") as its filename extension, and the other has .suo (which stands for "solution user options"). The T3App Solution.sln file keeps track of the projects and files included in the solution. The T3App Solution.suo file, which is a hidden file, records the options associated with your solution so that each time you open the solution, it includes any customizations you made.

After you create a blank solution, you then add one or more projects to it. The number of projects in a solution depends on the application you are creating. Most simple applications require one project only, while complex applications usually involve several projects. The wallpaper store application you are working on is a simple application and requires just one project, which you will create using Visual C++ .NET.

You can add a new project to the current solution by clicking File on the menu bar, pointing to Add Project, and then clicking New Project. You also can right-click the solution's name in the Solution Explorer window, point to Add, and then click New Project. Additionally, you can click either the New Project button on the Get Started pane in the Start Page window, or the New Project button on the Standard toolbar.

tip

To view the names of hidden files, click Start on the Windows XP taskbar, then click My Computer. The My Computer window opens. Click Tools on the menu bar, and then click Folder Options. When the Folder Options dialog box opens, click the View tab, then click the Show hidden files and folders radio button, and then click the OK button.

tip

If the New Project button is not displayed on the Standard toolbar, click the list arrow on the New Blank Solution button, which also is located on the Standard toolbar, and then click New Project in the list.

To add a new Visual C++ .NET project to the current solution:

1. Click **File** on the menu bar. Point to **Add Project** and then click **New Project**. The Add New Project dialog box opens.

   The Project Types list box lists the various types of projects you can add to a solution.

2. Click **Visual C++ Projects** in the Project Types list box.

   The Templates list box lists the project templates available in Visual C++.

3. Scroll the Templates list box until you see Managed C++ Empty Project, then click **Managed C++ Empty Project**.
4. Change the name in the Name text box to **T3App Project**.
5. Verify that the Location text box contains the location of the T3App Solution folder. The completed Add New Project dialog box is shown in Figure 3-45. Notice that the message "Project will be created at C:\CppNet\Tut03\T3App Solution\T3App Project." appears below the Location text box in the dialog box.

Figure 3-45: Completed Add New Project dialog box

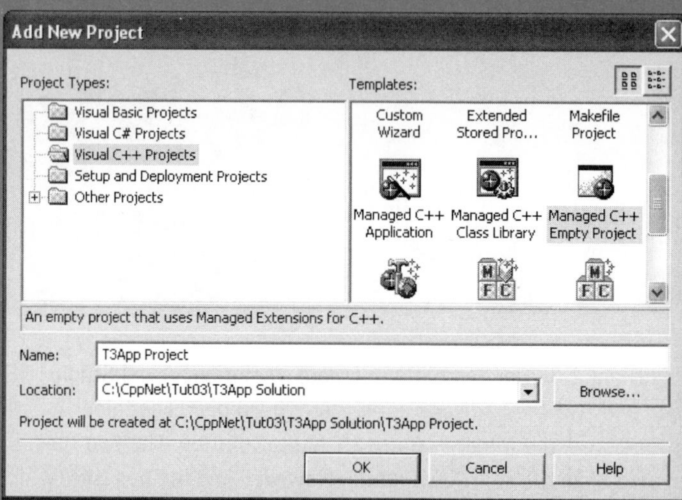

As you learned earlier, a template contains a set of standard folders and files. The folders and files included in the Managed C++ Empty Project template are automatically created on your computer's hard disk when you click the OK button in the Add New Project dialog box.

6. Click the **OK** button to close the Add New Project dialog box. Visual Studio .NET adds a new managed C++ empty project to the current solution. It also records the project's name (T3App Project), as well as other information pertaining to the project, in the Solution Explorer window. See Figure 3-46.

   HELP? If the Properties window does not appear in the IDE, click View on the menu bar, and then click Properties Window.

Figure 3-46: New managed C++ empty project added to the solution

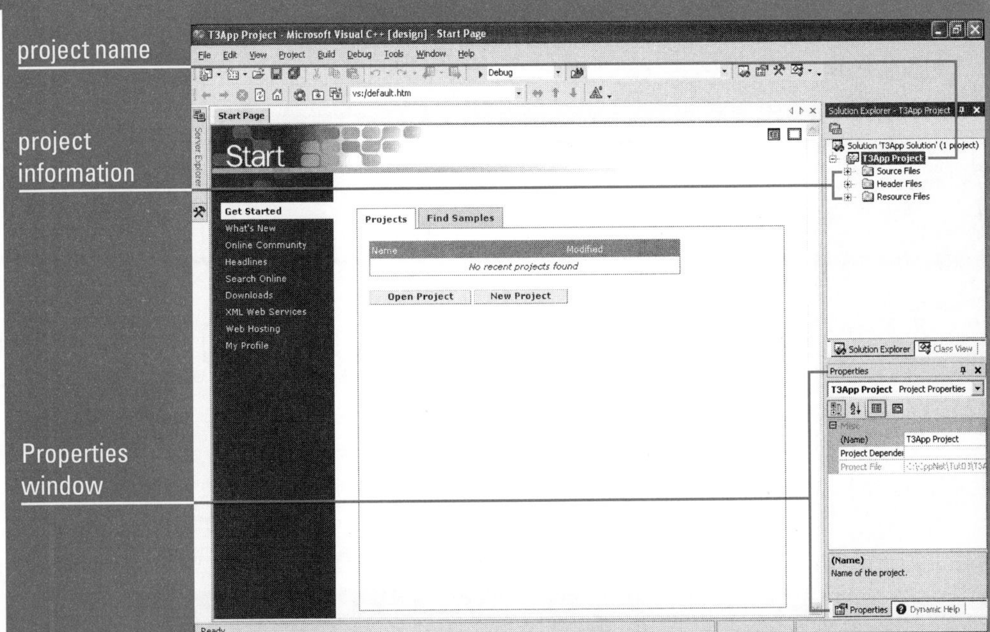

Notice that, in addition to the six windows discussed earlier, a new window appears in the development environment: the Properties window. Having seven windows open at the same time can be confusing, especially when you are first learning the IDE. In most cases, you will find it easier to work in the IDE if you either close or auto-hide the windows you are not currently using. In the next section, you learn how to manage the windows in the IDE.

After adding a managed C++ empty project to the solution, you then add a C++ source file to the project. You can do so by clicking File on the menu bar, and then clicking Add New Item. You also can right-click the project name in the Solution Explorer window, point to Add, and then click Add New Item.

tip

Recall that a source file is the file containing the source code—in this case, the C++ program instructions.

To add a C++ source file to the project:

1. Click **File** on the menu bar, and then click **Add New Item**. The Add New Item dialog box opens.
2. Click **C++ File (.cpp)** in the Templates list box.
3. Change the name in the Name text box to **T3App**.
4. Verify that the Location text box contains the location of the T3App Project folder. The completed Add New Item dialog box is shown in Figure 3-47.

Figure 3-47: Completed Add New Item dialog box

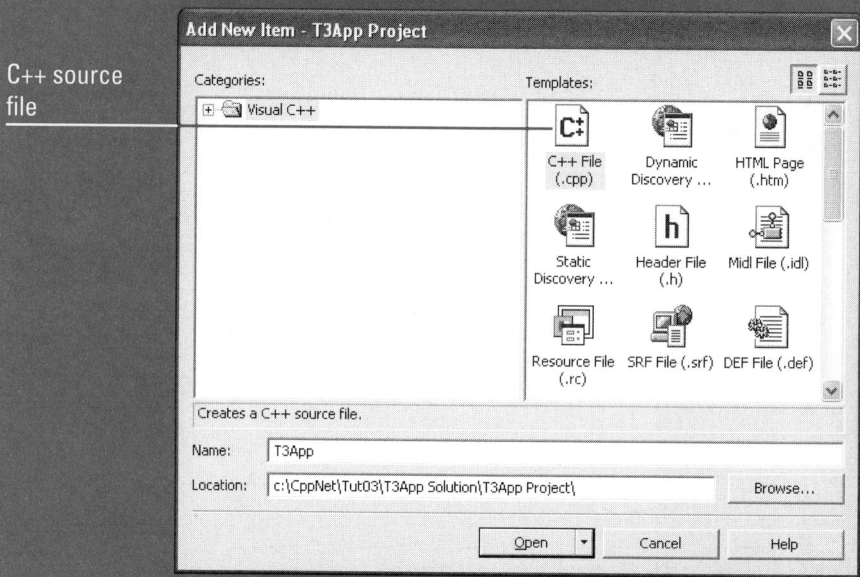

5. Click the **Open** button to close the Add New Item dialog box. Visual Studio .NET adds an empty C++ source file to the project. It also records the file's name (T3App.cpp) in the Solution Explorer window. See Figure 3-48.

Figure 3-48: Source file added to the project

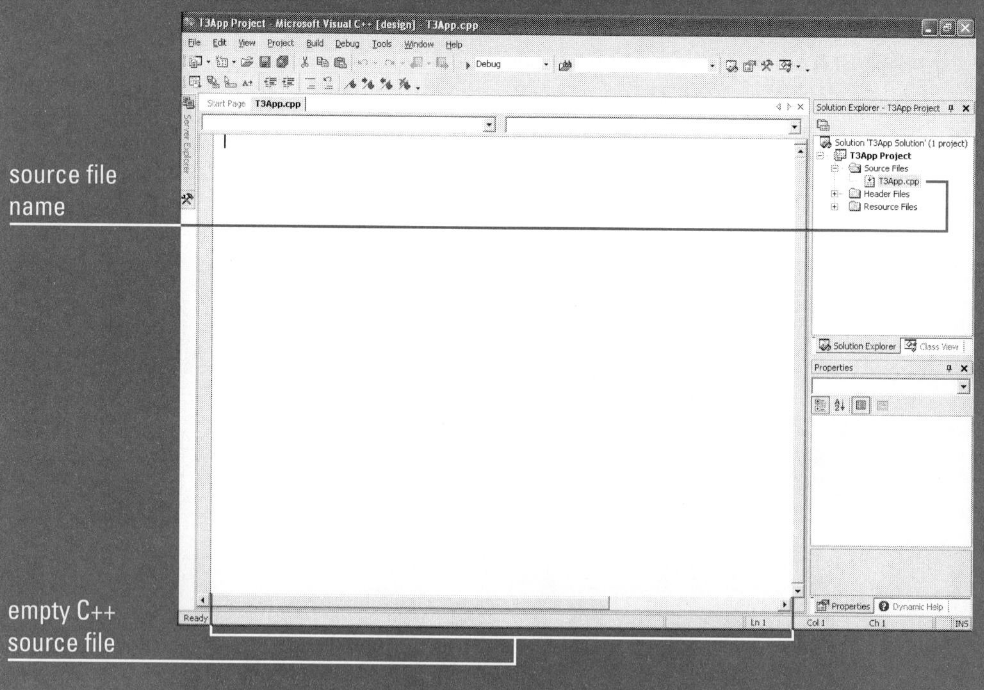

As mentioned earlier, you will find it easier to work in the Visual Studio .NET IDE if you either close or auto-hide the windows you are not currently using.

Managing the Windows in the IDE

The easiest way to close an open window in the IDE is to click the Close button on the window's title bar. You also can close a window by right-clicking its title bar and then clicking Hide on the context menu. Or, you can click the window's title bar, then click Window on the menu bar, and then click Hide on the menu. In most cases, the View menu provides an appropriate option for opening a closed window. To open the Toolbox window, for instance, you click View on the menu bar, and then click Toolbox on the menu. The options for opening the Start Page and Dynamic Help windows, however, are located on the Help menu rather than on the View menu.

You can use the Auto Hide button on a window's title bar to auto-hide a window. You also can auto-hide a window by right-clicking its title bar, and then clicking Auto Hide on the context menu. Or, you can click the window's title bar, then click Window on the menu bar, and then click Auto Hide on the menu. When you **auto-hide** a window and then move the mouse pointer away from the window, the window is minimized and appears as a tab on the edge of the IDE. Additionally, the button on the window's title bar is replaced with the button, which indicates that the window is auto-hidden. The Server Explorer and Toolbox windows shown in Figure 3-48 are examples of an auto-hidden window.

To temporarily display a window that has been auto-hidden, you simply place your mouse pointer on the window's tab; doing so slides the window into view. You can permanently display an auto-hidden window by clicking the button on the window's title bar. When you click the button, the button is replaced by the button, which indicates that the window is not auto-hidden.

In the next set of steps, you close all of the windows except the Solution Explorer window, because you will not need these windows to create the wallpaper store program.

To close most of the windows in the IDE:

1. Place your mouse pointer on the **Server Explorer** tab. (The Server Explorer tab usually is located on the left edge of the IDE.) When the Server Explorer window slides into view, which may take several moments, click the **Close** button on its title bar.

   Now close the Toolbox, Start Page, Class View, and Properties windows.

2. Place your mouse pointer on the **Toolbox** tab. (The Toolbox tab usually is located on the left edge of the IDE.) When the Toolbox window slides into view, click the **Close** button on its title bar.
3. Click the **Start Page** tab to make the Start Page window the active window, then click the **Close** button on its title bar.
4. Click the **Class View** tab to make the Class View window the active window, then click the **Close** button on its title bar.
5. Click the **Properties** tab to make the Properties window the active window, then click the **Close** button on its title bar.

   You close the Dynamic Help window next. The **Dynamic Help window** is a context-sensitive system. As you are working in the IDE, the window is constantly being updated with links pertaining to whatever is appropriate at the time. An advantage of keeping the Dynamic Help window open is that it allows you to conveniently access help as you are working in the IDE. A disadvantage is that an open Dynamic Help window consumes computer memory and processor time, both of which are required to keep the window updated.

6. Click the **Close** button on the Dynamic Help window's title bar.

Next, you practice auto-hiding and displaying the Solution Explorer window.

To practice auto-hiding and displaying the Solution Explorer window:

1. Click the **Auto Hide** button on the Solution Explorer window's title bar, then move the mouse pointer away from the window. The Solution Explorer window is minimized and appears as a tab on the right edge of the IDE.

   HELP? If the Solution Explorer window remains on the screen when you move your mouse pointer away from the window, click another window's title bar.

   Now temporarily display the Solution Explorer window.
2. Place your mouse pointer on the **Solution Explorer** tab. The Solution Explorer window slides into view.

   Now hide the window.
3. Move your mouse pointer away from the Solution Explorer window. The window is minimized and appears as a tab again.

   Next, remove the Auto Hide feature from the Solution Explorer window; this will permanently display the window on the screen.
4. Place your mouse pointer on the **Solution Explorer** tab. When the Solution Explorer window slides into view, click the **Auto Hide** button on its title bar. The button is replaced with the button.
5. Move your mouse pointer away from the Solution Explorer window. The window remains displayed on the screen.

   Now auto-hide the Solution Explorer window again.
6. Click the **Auto Hide** button on the Solution Explorer window's title bar, then move the mouse pointer away from the window.

Now you can begin entering the C++ instructions for the wallpaper store's program.

Creating a C++ Program

Figure 3-49 shows the basic structure of the C++ programs that you will create in this book. Items in square brackets ([]) in the structure are optional. Items in **bold**, on the other hand, are required. Items in *italics* represent places where the programmer must supply information relative to the program.

As Figure 3-49 indicates, a C++ program begins with comments that identify the program's name and purpose. A **comment** is a message to the person reading the program and is referred to as **internal documentation**. It is a good programming practice to include comments in a program—not only to identify the program's name and purpose, but also to explain various sections of the program code. Comments make the program instructions more readable and easier to understand by anyone viewing the program.

tip

Like most programming languages, the C++ language follows a specific format, referred to as its syntax. The syntax of a language, whether it is C++ or English, is the set of rules that you must follow to use the language. The syntax of the C++ language, like the syntax of the English language, will take some time and effort to learn.

Figure 3-49: Basic structure of a C++ program

```
[comments that identify the program's name and purpose]

#using <mscorlib.dll>
using namespace System;

int main()
{
        [named constant declarations]
        [variable declarations]

        [input statements]
        [calculation statements]
        [output statements]

        return 0;
} //end of main function
```

tip

It is a good programming practice to declare the named constants first so they are easier to locate if you need to change their values in the future.

You create a comment by typing two forward slashes (//) before the text you want treated as a comment, like this: `//T3App.cpp`. The compiler does not process the comments in a program; rather, the compiler ignores the comments when it translates the source code into object code.

tip

Most programmers also include comments that identify their name and the date the program was either written or revised.

The second and third lines of code in the program structure are called directives. C++ programs typically include at least one directive, and most include many directives. The `#using <mscorlib.dll>` directive tells the C++ compiler to include the contents of the mscorlib.dll file, which contains the core components of Visual Studio .NET, in the current program. The `using namespace System;` directive, on the other hand, tells the compiler that the definition of standard C++ keywords and classes—such as `double` and `Console::ReadLine()`—can be found in a namespace (a special area in the computer's internal memory) named `System`.

tip

"Mscorlib" stands for "Microsoft Core Library".

The fourth line of code in the program structure shown in Figure 3-49 is `int main()`. The word `main()`, which must be typed using lowercase letters, is the name of a function. Similar to a method, a **function** is a block of code that performs a task. Functions, like methods, have parentheses following their names. Some functions require you to enter information between the parentheses; other functions, like `main()`, do not. The difference between a function and a method is that a method is part of a class, whereas a function is not.

tip

The `#using <mscorlib.dll>` directive does not end with a semicolon, because it is not a C++ statement. The `using namespace System;` directive, on the other hand, does end with a semicolon, because it is a C++ statement.

Every C++ program must have a `main()` function, because this is where the execution of a C++ program always begins. Most C++ programs contain many more functions in addition to `main()`. Some functions return a value after completing their assigned task, while others, referred to as **void functions**, do not. If a function returns a value, the data type of the value it returns appears to the left of the function name; otherwise, the keyword `void` appears to the left of the name. Notice that the data type `int` precedes `main()` in the program structure shown in Figure 3-49. The `int` indicates that the `main()` function returns a value of the integer data type—in other words, the function returns a number that does not contain a decimal place. The entire line of code, `int main()`, is referred to as a **function header**, because it marks the beginning of the function.

After the function header, you enter the code that directs the function on how to perform its assigned task. Examples of such code include statements that declare named constants and variables, and statements that input, calculate, and output data.

In C++, you enclose a function's code within a set of braces ({}). The braces mark the beginning and the end of the code block that comprises the function. As the program structure indicates, you enter the opening brace ({)immediately below the `int main()` function header in the program, and you enter the closing brace (}) at the end of the function. Everything between the opening and closing braces is included, in this case, in the `main()` function, and is referred to as the **function body**. Notice that you can include a comment—in this case, `//end of main function`—on the same line with any C++ instruction. However you must be sure to enter the comment *after* the instruction, and not before it. Only the text appearing after the // on a line is interpreted as a comment.

Above the closing brace in the program structure shown in Figure 3-49 is the statement `return 0;`. As mentioned earlier, the `main()` function returns an integer value. In this case, it returns the number 0 to the operating system to indicate that the program ended normally.

You will follow the basic structure shown in Figure 3-49 when entering the C++ instructions for The Paper Tree wallpaper store. Figure 3-50 shows the information from the IPO chart that you created in Tutorial 2's Application lesson. The figure also shows the corresponding C++ instructions, which you learned about in this tutorial's Concept lesson.

Figure 3-50: IPO chart information and the corresponding C++ instructions for The Paper Tree wallpaper store

IPO chart information	C++ instructions
Input	
room length	`double length = 0.0;`
room width	`double width = 0.0;`
ceiling height	`double height = 0.0;`
single roll coverage	`double rollCoverage = 0.0;`
Processing	
room perimeter	`double perimeter = 0.0;`
wall area	`double area = 0.0;`
Output	
number of single rolls	`double rolls = 0.0;`
Algorithm	

1. enter the room length, room width, ceiling height, and single roll coverage	`Console::Write("Enter room length: ");`
	`length = Convert::ToDouble(Console::ReadLine());`
	`Console::Write("Enter room width: ");`
	`width = Convert::ToDouble(Console::ReadLine());`
	`Console::Write("Enter ceiling height: ");`
	`height = Convert::ToDouble(Console::ReadLine());`
	`Console::Write("Enter single roll coverage: ");`
	`rollCoverage = Convert::ToDouble(Console::`
	`ReadLine());`

Figure 3-50: IPO chart information and the corresponding C++ instructions for The Paper Tree wallpaper store (continued)

IPO chart information	C++ instructions
2. calculate the room perimeter by adding together the room length and room width, and then multiplying the sum by 2	`perimeter = (length + width) * 2;`
3. calculate the wall area by multiplying the room perimeter by the ceiling height	`area = perimeter * height;`
4. calculate the number of single rolls by dividing the wall area by the single roll coverage	`rolls = area / rollCoverage;`
5. display the number of single rolls	`Console::WriteLine("Single rolls: {0}", Convert::ToString(rolls));`

To begin entering the C++ instructions into the T3App.cpp source file:

1. Type **// T3App.cpp** and press **Enter**, then type **//calculates and displays required number of single rolls of wallpaper** and press **Enter** twice.

   Next, enter the two directives; when doing so, keep in mind that the C++ language is case sensitive. Typing `#Using`, rather than `#using`, will create a syntax error, because the compiler will not recognize the word `Using`. In other words, in the C++ programming language, `using` is not the same as `Using` or `USING`.

2. Type **#using <mscorlib.dll>** and press **Enter**, then type **using namespace System;** and press **Enter** twice.

   If you are using a color monitor, you will notice that the Visual C++ .NET editor displays the comments, keywords, and symbols (`using`, `namespace`, and `#`) in a different color from the rest of the code. The colors help you quickly identify the various elements in the code.

   Next, enter the `main()` function header.

3. Type **int main()** and press **Enter**. (Do not include a space between the opening and closing parentheses.)

   Recall that the `main()` function's instructions must be enclosed in a set of braces, and the last statement in the function should be `return 0;`. It is a good practice to type the opening and closing braces and the `return 0;` statement right away, so that you don't forget to do it.

4. Type **{** (the opening brace) and press **Enter** twice. Notice that the Visual C++ editor indents the next line in the T3App.cpp window.
5. Type **return 0;** and press **Enter**, then type **}** (the closing brace). Notice that the Visual C++ editor enters the closing brace at the window's left margin to align it with the opening brace.
6. Press **Tab**, then type **//end of main function** and press **Enter**. Figure 3-51 shows the current status of the T3App program.

Figure 3-51: Current status of the T3App program

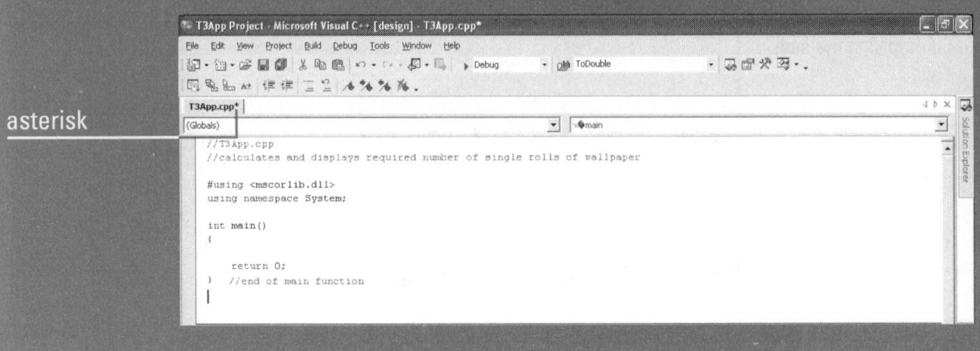

The asterisk that appears on the T3App.cpp tab indicates that the T3App.cpp file contains changes that have not been saved. You learn how to save the changes in the next section.

Saving a Solution

It is a good practice to save the current solution every 10 or 15 minutes so that you will not lose a lot of work if the computer loses power. The easiest way to save the solution is to click the Save All button on the Standard toolbar. Doing so saves any changes made to the files included in the solution. You also can click File on the menu bar, and then click Save All.

tip

You also can save the solution by right-clicking its name in the Solution Explorer window, and then clicking Save *<solution filename>* on the context menu. Or, you can click the solution's name in the Solution Explorer window, click File on the menu bar, and then click Save *<solution filename>* on the menu.

To save the current solution:

1. Click the **Save All** button on the Standard toolbar. The asterisk disappears from the T3App.cpp tab, indicating that the file does not contain any unsaved changes.

You also can use the Save button on the Standard toolbar to save the solution, but you first must select the solution's name in the Solution Explorer window, because the Save button saves only the changes made to the selected item. For example, if the source filename is selected in the Solution Explorer window, then the Save button saves only the changes made to the source file. Similarly, if the project name is selected, then only changes made to the files included in the project are saved. The tooltip box that appears when you rest your mouse pointer on the Save button indicates which files will be saved. In this case, the tooltip box will say "Save T3App.cpp" if the source file's name is selected, "Save T3App Project" if the project name is selected, and "Save T3App Solution.sln" if the solution name is selected.

Next, you learn how to close the current solution, and how to open an existing solution. Both of these skills will help you complete the end-of-lesson exercises.

Closing the Current Solution

You close a solution using the Close Solution option on the File menu. When you close a solution, all projects and files contained in the solution also are closed. If unsaved changes were made to the solution, project, or source file, a dialog box opens and prompts you to save the appropriate files. The dialog box contains Yes, No, Cancel, and Help buttons. You click the Yes button to save the files before the solution is closed. You click the No button to close the solution without saving the files. You click the Cancel button to leave the solution open, and you click the Help button to display Help pertaining to the dialog box.

tip

The Close button ✖ on the T3App.cpp window's title bar closes the window only; it does not close the solution.

To close the current solution:

1. Click **File** on the menu bar, and then click **Close Solution**.
2. Temporarily display the Solution Explorer window to verify that the entire T3App Solution is closed.

Next, you learn how to open a solution that was saved previously.

Opening an Existing Solution

To open an existing solution, you click File on the menu bar, and then click Open Solution. You then select the appropriate solution file in the Open Solution dialog box. (Solution filenames have an .sln filename extension.) If a solution is already open in the IDE, it is closed before another solution is opened. In other words, only one solution can be open in the IDE at any one time.

To open the T3App Solution:

1. Click **File** on the menu bar, and then click **Open Solution**. The Open Solution dialog box opens.
2. Locate and then open the **CppNet\Tut03\T3App Solution** folder.
3. Click **T3App Solution** (T3App Solution.sln) in the list of filenames, and then click the **Open** button.
4. If the T3App.cpp source file is not displayed, right-click **T3App.cpp** in the Solution Explorer window, and then click **Open**.

Now complete the T3App program by entering the `main()` function's instructions.

To complete the T3App program:

1. Type the variable declaration statements shown in Figure 3-52, then position the insertion point as shown in the figure. Although the C++ programming language does not require you to align the assignment operators (=) in a list of declaration statements, doing so helps to make the program easier to read.

Figure 3-52: Variable declaration statements

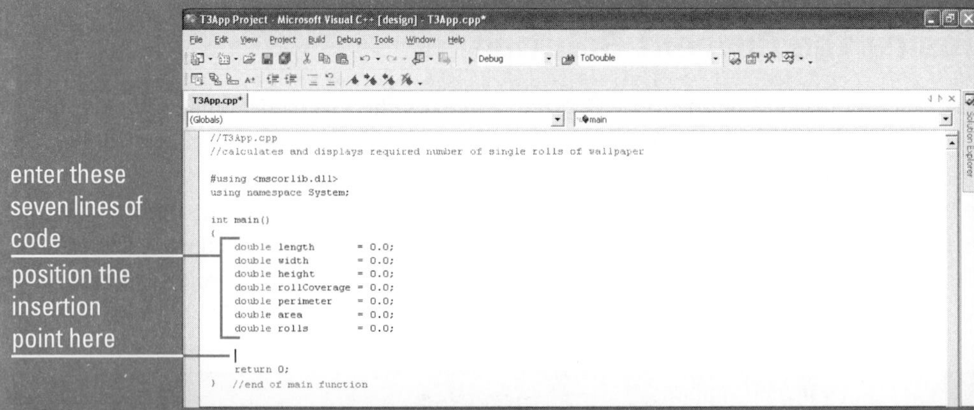

Now enter the instructions that get the room length, room width, ceiling height, and roll coverage.

2. Type the comment and additional statements shown in Figure 3-53, then position the insertion point as shown in the figure. (Do not be concerned about the box that might appear when you type the second colon in the `Console::Write()`, `Convert::ToDouble()`, and `Console::ReadLine()` methods.)

Figure 3-53: Instructions to enter the input items

enter these nine lines of code

position the insertion point here

```
//T3App.cpp
//calculates and displays required number of single rolls of wallpaper

#using <mscorlib.dll>
using namespace System;

int main()
{
    double length       = 0.0;
    double width        = 0.0;
    double height       = 0.0;
    double rollCoverage = 0.0;
    double perimeter    = 0.0;
    double area         = 0.0;
    double rolls        = 0.0;

    //enter input items
    Console::Write("Enter room length: ");
    length = Convert::ToDouble(Console::ReadLine());
    Console::Write("Enter room width: ");
    width = Convert::ToDouble(Console::ReadLine());
    Console::Write("Enter ceiling height: ");
    height = Convert::ToDouble(Console::ReadLine());
    Console::Write("Enter single roll coverage: ");
    rollCoverage = Convert::ToDouble(Console::ReadLine());

    return 0;
}   //end of main function
```

Next, enter the instructions to calculate the perimeter, area, and number of single rolls. Also enter the instruction to display the number of single rolls.

3. Type the comments and additional statements shown in Figure 3-54, which shows the completed T3App program. (The size of the font used in the editor was changed so that you can view all of the program instructions in the figure. It is not necessary for you to change the font size. However, to do so, click Tools on the menu bar, then click Options to open the Options dialog box. Open the Environment folder, and then click Fonts and Colors. Change the font size to 9, then click the OK button to close the Options dialog box.)

Figure 3-54: Completed T3App program

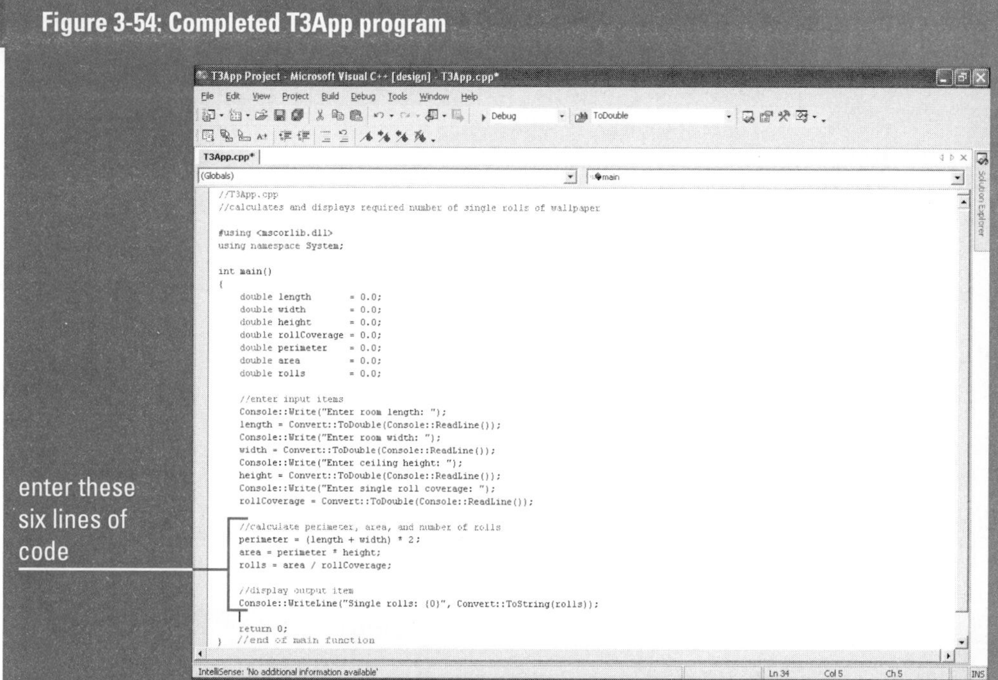

Next, you learn how to build and execute a C++ program.

Building and Executing a C++ Program

Before you can execute a C++ program, you need to save it and then build it. Building a C++ program involves compiling the source code into object code, and then invoking the linker program to link the object code to other machine code necessary for the program to run.

tip

You always should save a program before compiling the program. That way, if a fatal error occurs in the program, you will not lose the instructions you entered; you can simply reopen the file.

To save, build, and then execute the T3App.cpp program:

1. Click the **Save All** button on the Standard toolbar.
2. Click **Build** on the menu bar, then click **Build Solution**. The compiler translates the source code into object code, and the linker links the object code with other machine code. The message "Build: 1 succeeded, 0 failed, 0 skipped" appears in the Output window, as shown in Figure 3-55. This message indicates that the program was built (compiled and linked) successfully.

Figure 3-55: Build message displayed in the Output window

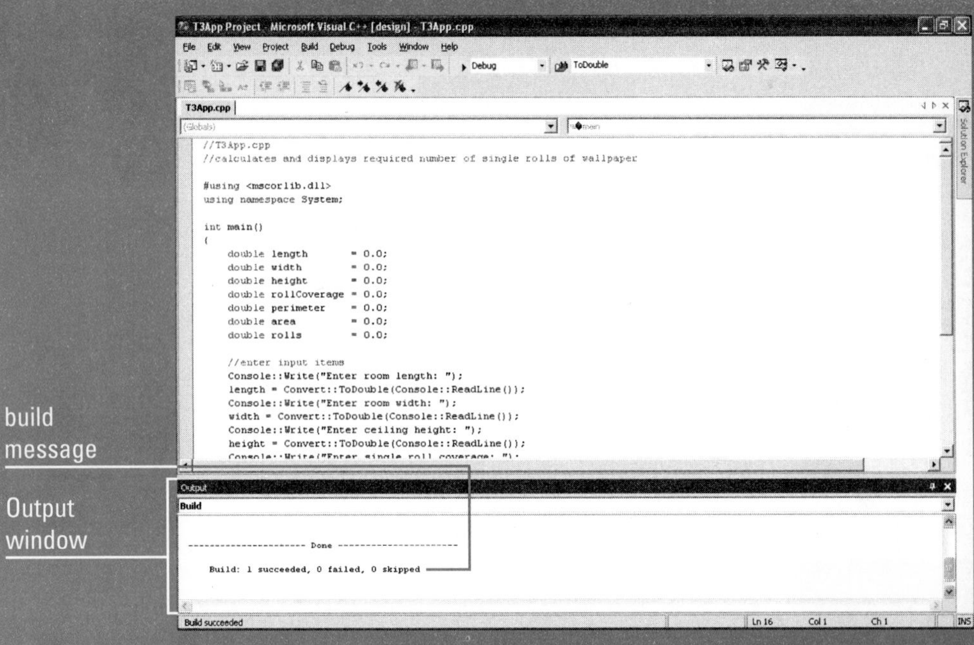

Other messages also are displayed in the Output window while the program is being built. It is a good practice to view those messages to be sure that the program generated no warnings. (An error in a program results in an unsuccessful build; however, a warning does not.)

3. Scroll up the Output window, as shown in Figure 3-56.

Figure 3-56: Status messages displayed in the Output window

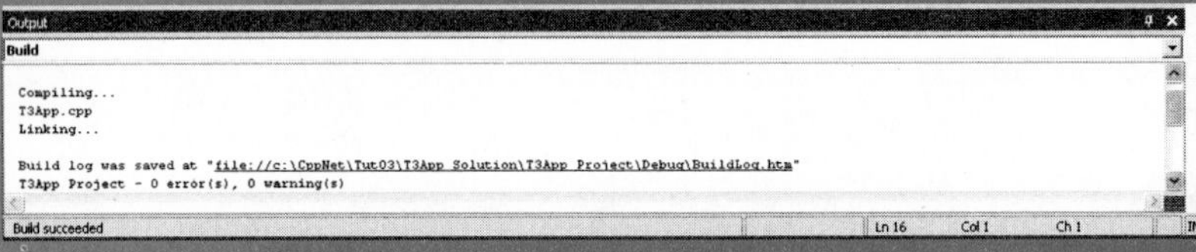

The messages in the Output window indicate that the program was compiled and linked, and that no errors or warnings occurred during the build process. The program is now ready to execute.

4. Click **Debug** on the menu bar, and then click **Start Without Debugging**. The "Enter room length: " prompt appears in a Command Prompt window, as shown in Figure 3-57.

Figure 3-57: Prompt appears in a Command Prompt window

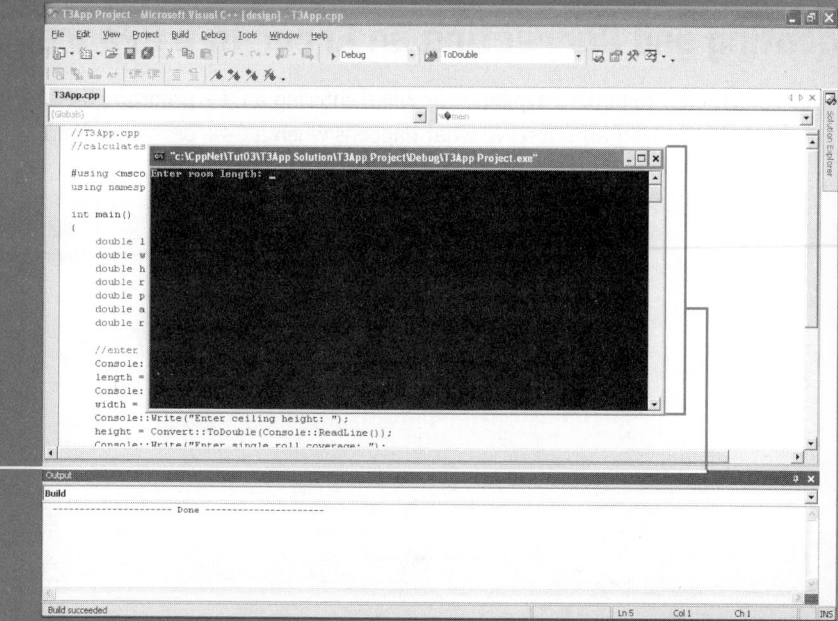

You will test the program using 10 as the room length, 12 as the room width, 8 as the ceiling height, and 30 as the roll coverage. According to the desk-check table shown in the Concept lesson's Figure 3-29, the required number of single rolls should be 11.73.

5. Type **10** as the room length, and then press **Enter**. When the prompt to enter the room width appears, type **12** and then press **Enter**. When the prompt to enter the ceiling height appears, type **8** and then press **Enter**. When the prompt to enter the single roll coverage appears, type **30** and then press **Enter**. The required number of single rolls, 11.7333333333333 (notice that the computer carries the answer out to 13 decimal places), appears on the screen, along with the "Press any key to continue" message. The Visual C++ .NET editor automatically displays the "Press any key to continue" message on the screen when your program ends. See Figure 3-58.

Figure 3-58: Command Prompt window showing the results of executing the program

HELP? If your result is different, you probably made an error when entering the program instructions. You learn how to correct errors in C++ code in the next section.

6. Press **Enter** to close the Command Prompt window, then close the Output window by clicking the **Close** button on its title bar.

Next, you introduce a syntax error into the current program. You then learn how to locate and correct the error; in other words, you learn how to debug and modify the program.

Locating and Correcting an Error in a Program

It is extremely easy to make a typing error when entering a C++ program, thereby producing a syntax error in the program. Observe what happens when a C++ program contains a syntax error.

To introduce a syntax error, then locate and correct the error:

1. Delete the semicolon that appears at the end of the `double length = 0.0;` statement in the program.
2. Click the **Save All** button on the Standard toolbar.
3. Click **Build** on the menu bar, and then click **Build Solution**. The Task List window opens and indicates that line 10 in the program contains a syntax error. See Figure 3-59.

Figure 3-59: Error message displayed in the Task List window

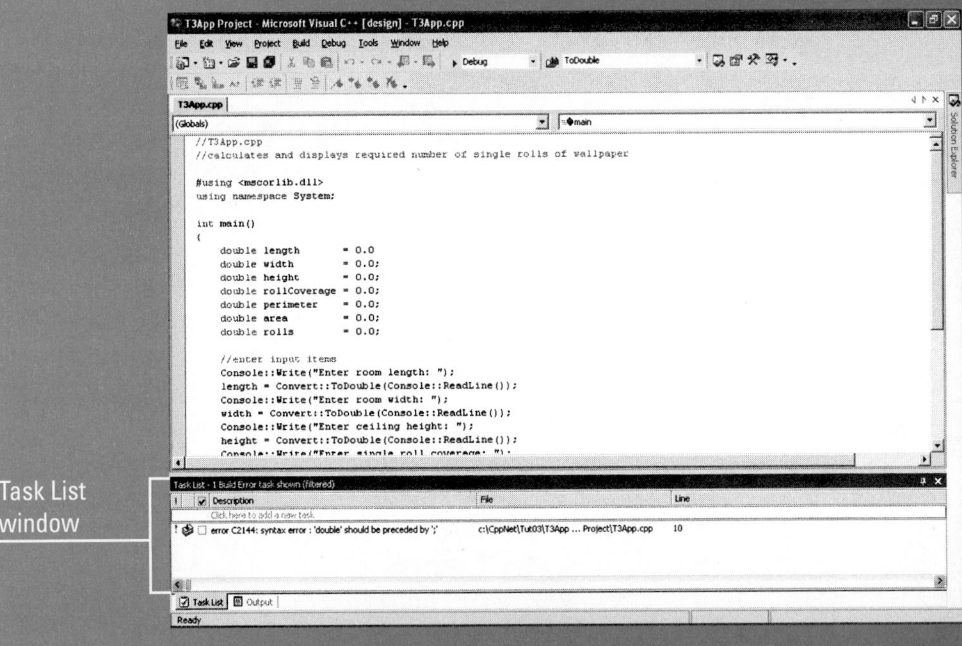

4. Double-click the **error message in the Task List window**. See Figure 3-60.

   The editor displays an arrow at the location where the error was encountered in the program. In this case, the arrow is pointing to the statement `double width = 0.0;`. Although that is the statement where the compiler discovered the error, it is not the statement that actually caused the error. Rather, the error occurred as a result of the previous statement, `double length = 0.0`. Notice that the semicolon is missing from that statement.

Figure 3-60: Screen showing the description and location of the syntax error

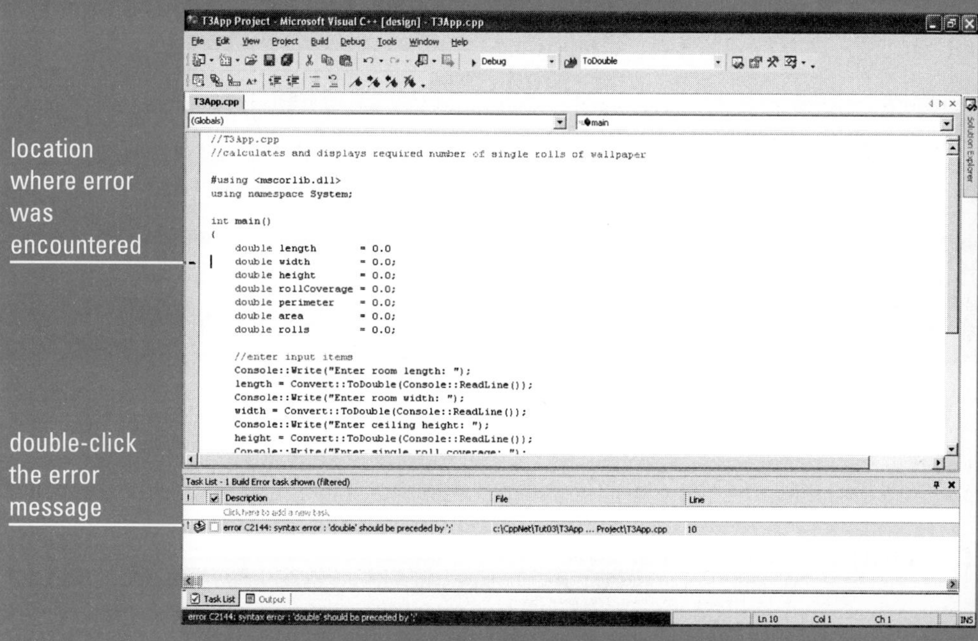

5. Type a semicolon at the end of the `double length = 0.0` statement.

   Now save, build, and execute the program to verify that it is working correctly.

6. Save and then build the solution. The message "Build: 1 succeeded, 0 failed, 0 skipped" appears in the Output window.
7. Scroll up the Output window to view all of the messages generated during the build process. Verify that the process generated no warnings.

   Now use the program to display the required number of single rolls of wallpaper for a room with a length of 12 feet, a width of 14 feet, and a ceiling height of 10 feet. In this case, a single roll covers 37 square feet. According to the desk-check table shown in Figure 3-30 in the Concept lesson, the required number of single rolls should be 14.05.

8. Execute the program by clicking **Debug** on the menu bar, and then clicking **Start Without Debugging**. Type **12** as the room length, **14** as the room width, **10** as the ceiling height, and **37** as the single roll coverage. The required number of single rolls (14.0540540540541) appears in the Command Prompt window, along with the "Press any key to continue" message.
9. Press **Enter** to close the Command Prompt window.

Although the program is not designed currently to handle invalid data correctly, you will test it with invalid data simply to see the results. You will do so using a negative number as the room length. Because you did not make any changes to the program since the last time it was saved and built, you simply can execute the program; you do not need to save and build it again.

To test the program using invalid data:

1. Execute the program by clicking **Debug** on the menu bar, and then clicking **Start Without Debugging**.

2. When the "Enter room length: " prompt appears, type **-10** (be sure to type the hyphen before the number 10) and press **Enter**.

   Because the room length should not be a negative number, the program should respond at this point by prompting the user to enter a positive number, rather than by prompting the user to enter the room width; you learn how to design a program that does so in a later tutorial.
3. Type **10** as the room width, **10** as the ceiling height, and **30** as the single roll coverage. The number 0 appears as the number of single rolls.
4. Press **Enter** to close the Command Prompt window.
5. Close the Output and Task List windows.

When you are sure that a program works correctly, you should keep your IPO chart and a printout of the program in a safe place, so you can refer to them if you need to change the program in the future. The IPO chart and printout are referred to as **external documentation.**

Printing a C++ Program

The File menu on the menu bar contains a Print command, which you can use to print the program.

To print the current program, and then close the program's solution and exit Visual Studio .NET:

1. Click **File** on the menu bar, and then click **Print**. When the Print dialog box appears, click the **OK** button. The program prints on your printer.
2. Click **File** on the menu bar, and then click **Close Solution** to close the current solution. This removes the solution from the computer's internal memory. You now can open either a new or an existing solution.
3. Click **File** on the menu bar, and then click **Exit** to exit Visual Studio .NET.

Finally, learn how to make a backup copy of a C++ solution.

Making a Backup Copy of a C++ Solution

It is a good idea to make a backup copy of your C++ solutions so that you don't lose a lot of work if your computer stops working.

To make a backup copy of a C++ solution:

1. Click the **Start** button on the Windows XP taskbar to open the Start menu, then click **My Computer** on the Start menu.
2. Right-click **the drive that contains the CppNet folder** (in most cases, this will be the C: drive), and then click **Open** on the context menu.
3. Open the **CppNet** folder, and then open the **Tut03** folder.
4. Open the **T3App Solution** folder, and then delete the **T3App Solution.ncb** file.
5. Open the **T3App Project** folder, and then delete the **Debug** folder.

6. Click the **Back** button twice to return to the T3App Solution folder.
7. Right-click the **T3App Solution** folder. Point to **Send To** on the context menu, and then click **3½ Floppy (A:)**.

You now have completed Tutorial 3's Application lesson. You can either take a break or complete the end-of-lesson exercises.

Look For These Symbols

Debugging

Discovery

EXERCISES

1) In this exercise, you complete an existing program that calculates and displays the sum of two numbers. The IPO chart information, C++ code, and desk-check for this problem are shown in Figures 3-31 and 3-32 in the Concept lesson.

A. If necessary, start Visual Studio .NET. Open the T3AppE01 Solution (T3AppE01 Solution.sln) file, which is contained in the CppNet\Tut03\T3AppE01 Solution folder. The program calculates and displays the sum of two numbers. Review the IPO chart and code shown in Figure 3-31. Notice that three instructions are missing from the program: the instruction that prompts the user to enter the second number, the instruction that allows the user to enter the number, and the instruction that calculates the sum. Enter the missing statements in the appropriate areas of the program.

B. Save and then build the solution. If necessary, correct any syntax errors, and then save and build the solution again.

C. Execute the program. Test the program twice, using the numbers 3 and 5 first, and then using the numbers 50.5 and 31.3. Compare your results to the desk-check table shown in Figure 3-32.

D. When the program is working correctly, close the Output window, and then use the File menu to close the solution.

2) In this exercise, you complete an existing program that calculates and displays the new weekly pay based on the current weekly pay and raise rate entered by the user. The IPO chart information and C++ code for this problem are shown in Figure 3-33 in the Concept lesson. You completed the desk-check in Exercise 15 in the Concept lesson.

A. If necessary, start Visual Studio .NET. Open the T3AppE02 Solution (T3AppE02 Solution.sln) file, which is contained in the CppNet\Tut03\T3AppE02 Solution folder. The program calculates and displays the new weekly pay based on the current weekly pay and raise rate entered by the user. Review the IPO chart and code shown in Figure 3-33. Notice that six statements are missing from the program. Enter the missing statements in the appropriate areas of the program.

B. Save and then build the solution. If necessary, correct any syntax errors, and then save and build the solution again.

C. Execute the program. Test the program twice. For the first test, use 250 as the current weekly pay and .03 as the raise rate. For the second test, use 100 as the current weekly pay and .10 as the raise rate. Compare your results to the desk-check table that you created in Exercise 15 in the Concept lesson.

D. When the program is working correctly, close the Output window, and then use the File menu to close the solution.

3) In this exercise, you complete an existing program that calculates and displays a commission amount based on the sales and commission rate entered by the user.

A. If necessary, start Visual Studio .NET. Open the T3AppE03 Solution (T3AppE03 Solution.sln) file, which is contained in the CppNet\Tut03\T3AppE03 Solution folder. The program calculates and displays a commission amount.

B. Study the existing code. Notice that the statements to calculate and display the commission are missing from the program. Enter the missing statements in the appropriate areas of the program. The statement that displays the commission amount should display the message "Your commission is $*commission*.", where *commission* is the commission amount.

C. Create an appropriate desk-check table, then desk-check the program twice. For the first desk-check, use 2000 as the sales and .10 as the commission rate. For the second desk-check, use 5000 as the sales and .06 as the commission rate.

D. Save and then build the solution. If necessary, correct any syntax errors, and then save and build the solution again.

E. Execute the program. Test the program twice, using the same data used in Step C. Compare your results to the desk-check table that you created in Step C.

F. When the program is working correctly, close the Output window, and then use the File menu to close the solution.

4) In this exercise, you complete an existing program that calculates and displays an ending balance amount based on the beginning balance, deposit, and withdrawal amounts entered by the user.

A. If necessary, start Visual Studio .NET. Open the T3AppE04 Solution (T3AppE04 Solution.sln) file, which is contained in the CppNet\Tut03\T3AppE04 Solution folder. The program calculates and displays the ending balance amount.

B. Study the existing code. Notice that the statements to prompt the user to enter the beginning balance, deposit, and withdrawal amounts are missing from the program. The statements that allow the user to enter that data also are missing from the program. Enter the missing statements in the appropriate areas of the program.

C. Create an appropriate desk-check table, then desk-check the program twice. For the first desk-check, use 2000 as the beginning balance amount, 775 as the deposit amount, and 1200 as the withdrawal amount. For the second desk-check, use 500 as the beginning balance amount, 100 as the deposit amount, and 610 as the withdrawal amount.

D. Save and then build the solution. If necessary, correct any syntax errors, and then save and build the solution again.

E. Execute the program. Test the program twice, using the same data used in Step C. Compare your results to the desk-check table that you created in Step C.

F. When the program is working correctly, close the Output window, and then use the File menu to close the solution.

5) In this exercise, you complete an existing program that calculates and displays the average of three numbers.

A. If necessary, start Visual Studio .NET. Open the T3AppE05 Solution (T3AppE05 Solution.sln) file, which is contained in the CppNet\Tut03\T3AppE05 Solution folder. The program calculates and displays the average of three numbers.

B. Complete the program by entering the missing statements.

C. Create an appropriate desk-check table, then desk-check the program twice. For the first desk-check, use the numbers 25, 76, and 33. For the second desk-check, use the numbers 10, 15, and 20.

D. Save and then build the solution. If necessary, correct any syntax errors, and then save and build the solution again.

E. Execute the program. Test the program twice, using the same data used in Step C. Compare your results to the desk-check table that you created in Step C.

F. When the program is working correctly, close the Output window, and then use the File menu to close the solution.

6) Acme Appliances needs a program to calculate a bonus, which is always 5% of the sales.

A. Complete an IPO chart for this problem.

B. Desk-check the algorithm. Use 330.50 as the sales.

C. Use the IPO chart to code the program.

D. Desk-check the program using the data specified in Step B.

E. If necessary, start Visual Studio .NET. Create a blank solution named T3AppE06 Solution. Save the solution in the CppNet\Tut03 folder.

F. Add a new managed C++ empty project to the solution. Name the project T3AppE06 Project.

G. Add a new C++ source file to the project. Name the source file T3AppE06.

H. Enter the appropriate C++ instructions into the source file.

I. Save and then build the solution. Execute the program. Test the program using the data specified in Step B.

J. When the program is working correctly, close the Output window, and then use the File menu to close the solution.

7) Write a program to calculate the square of a number. The number will always be an integer.

A. Complete an IPO chart for this problem.

B. Desk-check the algorithm. Use 10 as the number.

C. Use the IPO chart to code the program.

D. Desk-check the program using the data specified in Step B.

E. If necessary, start Visual Studio .NET. Create a blank solution named T3AppE07 Solution. Save the solution in the CppNet\Tut03 folder.

F. Add a new managed C++ empty project to the solution. Name the project T3AppE07 Project.

G. Add a new C++ source file to the project. Name the source file T3AppE07.

H. Enter the appropriate C++ instructions into the source file.

I. Save and then build the solution. Execute the program. Test the program using the data specified in Step B.

J. When the program is working correctly, close the Output window, and then use the File menu to close the solution.

8) Builders Inc. needs a program that allows the company's salesclerks to enter both the diameter of a circle (in feet) and the price of railing material per foot. The diameter and the price may contain decimal places. The program should display both the circumference of the circle and the total price of the railing material. Use 3.141593 as the value of pi.

A. Complete an IPO chart for this problem.

B. Desk-check the algorithm. Use 36.5 feet as the diameter, and $2.35 as the price per foot of railing material.

C. Use the IPO chart to code the program.

D. Desk-check the program using the data specified in Step B.

E. If necessary, start Visual Studio .NET. Create a blank solution named T3AppE08 Solution. Save the solution in the CppNet\Tut03 folder.

F. Add a new managed C++ empty project to the solution. Name the project T3AppE08 Project.

G. Add a new C++ source file to the project. Name the source file T3AppE08.

H. Enter the appropriate C++ instructions into the source file.

I. Save and then build the solution. Execute the program. Test the program using the data specified in Step B.

J. When the program is working correctly, close the Output window, and then use the File menu to close the solution.

9) A-1 Appliances needs a program that allows the store clerks to enter the number of dishwashers in stock at the beginning of the current month, the number of dishwashers purchased during the current month, and the number of dishwashers sold during the current month. The program should calculate and display the number of dishwashers in stock at the end of the current month.

A. Complete an IPO chart for this problem.

B. Desk-check the algorithm, using 5000 as the number of dishwashers at the beginning of the month, 1000 as the number of dishwashers purchased during the month, and 3500 as the number of dishwashers sold during the month.

C. Use the IPO chart to code the program.

D. Desk-check the program using the data specified in Step B.

E. If necessary, start Visual Studio .NET. Create a blank solution named T3AppE09 Solution. Save the solution in the CppNet\Tut03 folder.

F. Add a new managed C++ empty project to the solution. Name the project T3AppE09 Project.

G. Add a new C++ source file to the project. Name the source file T3AppE09.

H. Enter the appropriate C++ instructions into the source file.

I. Save and then build the solution. Execute the program. Test the program using the data specified in Step B.

J. When the program is working correctly, close the Output window, and then use the File menu to close the solution.

10) Tile Limited wants a program that allows the company's salesclerks to enter the length and width (in feet) of a rectangle, and the price of a square foot of tile. The length, width, and price may contain decimal places. The program should display the area of the rectangle and the total price of the tile.

A. Complete an IPO chart for this problem.

B. Desk-check the algorithm. Use 12.5 feet as the length, 14.5 feet as the width, and $3.10 as the price per square foot of tile.

C. Use the IPO chart to code the program.

D. Desk-check the program using the data specified in Step B.

E. If necessary, start Visual Studio .NET. Create a blank solution named T3AppE10 Solution. Save the solution in the CppNet\Tut03 folder.

F. Add a new managed C++ empty project to the solution. Name the project T3AppE10 Project.

G. Add a new C++ source file to the project. Name the source file T3AppE10.

H. Enter the appropriate C++ instructions into the source file.

I. Save and then build the solution. Execute the program. Test the program using the data specified in Step B.

J. When the program is working correctly, close the Output window, and then use the File menu to close the solution.

11) Jerome Symanski wants a program that he can use to display the number of cubic feet of water contained in a rectangular pool. (*Hint*: Find the volume of the rectangle.)

A. Complete an IPO chart for this problem.

B. Desk-check the algorithm, using 100 feet as the length, 30.5 feet as the width, and 4 feet as the depth.

C. Use the IPO chart to code the program. Use `double` variables for the length, width, depth, and volume.

D. Desk-check the program using the data specified in Step B.

E. If necessary, start Visual Studio .NET. Create a blank solution named T3AppE11 Solution. Save the solution in the CppNet\Tut03 folder.

F. Add a new managed C++ empty project to the solution. Name the project T3AppE11 Project.

G. Add a new C++ source file to the project. Name the source file T3AppE11.

H. Enter the appropriate C++ instructions into the source file.

I. Save and then build the solution. Execute the program. Test the program using the data specified in Step B.

J. When the program is working correctly, close the Output window, and then use the File menu to close the solution.

12) Temp Employers wants a program that allows the company's clerks to enter an employee's name and the number of hours the employee worked during the month. (The number of hours worked will always be an integer.) The program should display the name, number of weeks (assume a 40-hour week), days (assume an eight-hour day), and hours worked. For example, if the employee worked 70 hours during the month, the program should display 1 week, 3 days, and 6 hours.

A. Complete an IPO chart for this problem.

B. Desk-check the algorithm three times, using the following data:

Mary Claire, 88 hours worked
Jackie Smith, 111 hours worked
Sue Jones, 12 hours worked

C. Use the IPO chart to code the program.

D. Desk-check the program using the data specified in Step B.

E. If necessary, start Visual Studio .NET. Create a blank solution named T3AppE12 Solution. Save the solution in the CppNet\Tut03 folder.

F. Add a new managed C++ empty project to the solution. Name the project T3AppE12 Project.

G. Add a new C++ source file to the project. Name the source file T3AppE12.

H. Enter the appropriate C++ instructions into the source file.

I. Save and then build the solution. Execute the program. Test the program using the data specified in Step B.

J. When the program is working correctly, close the Output window, and then use the File menu to close the solution.

13) Colfax Industries needs a program that allows the shipping clerk to enter an item's name, the quantity of the item in inventory, and how many units of the item can be packed in a box for shipping. The program should display the item's name, the number of full boxes that can be packed from the quantity on hand, and how many of the item are left over.

A. Complete an IPO chart for this problem.

B. Desk-check the algorithm three times, using the following data:

Cleanser, 45 in inventory, six can be packed in a box
Hair Spray, 100 in inventory, three can be packed in a box
Comb, 78 in inventory, five can be packed in a box

C. Use the IPO chart to code the program.

D. Desk-check the program using the data specified in Step B.

E. If necessary, start Visual Studio .NET. Create a blank solution named T3AppE13 Solution. Save the solution in the CppNet\Tut03 folder.

F. Add a new managed C++ empty project to the solution. Name the project T3AppE13 Project.

G. Add a new C++ source file to the project. Name the source file T3AppE13.

H. Enter the appropriate C++ instructions into the source file.

I. Save and then build the solution. Execute the program. Test the program using the data specified in Step B.

J. When the program is working correctly, close the Output window, and then use the File menu to close the solution.

14) Your friend Joe saves pennies in a jar, which he empties every month when he goes to the bank. You are to create a program that allows him to enter the number of pennies, and then calculates and displays the number of dollars, quarters, dimes, nickels, and pennies he will receive when he trades in the pennies at the bank.

A. Complete an IPO chart for this problem.

B. Desk-check the algorithm two times, using the following data: 2311 pennies and 7333 pennies.

C. Use the IPO chart to code the program.

D. Desk-check the program using the data specified in Step B.

E. If necessary, start Visual Studio .NET. Create a blank solution named T3AppE14 Solution. Save the solution in the CppNet\Tut03 folder.

F. Add a new managed C++ empty project to the solution. Name the project T3AppE14 Project.

G. Add a new C++ source file to the project. Name the source file T3AppE14.

H. Enter the appropriate C++ instructions into the source file.

I. Save and then build the solution. Execute the program. Test the program using the data specified in Step B.

J. When the program is working correctly, close the Output window, and then use the File menu to close the solution.

15) A third-grade teacher at Hinsbrook Elementary School would like you to create a program that will help her students learn how to make change. The program should allow the student to enter the amount of money the customer owes and the amount of money the customer paid. The program should calculate and display the amount of change, as well as how many dollars, quarters, dimes, nickels, and pennies to return to the customer. For now, you do not have to worry about the situation where the price is greater than what the customer pays. You can always assume that the customer paid either the exact amount or more than the exact amount.

A. Complete an IPO chart for this problem.

B. Desk-check the algorithm three times, using the following data:

75.34 as the amount due and 80.00 as the amount paid
39.67 as the amount due and 50.00 as the amount paid
45.55 as the amount due and 45.55 as the amount paid

C. Use the IPO chart to code the program.

D. Desk-check the program using the data specified in Step B.

E. If necessary, start Visual Studio .NET. Create a blank solution named T3AppE15 Solution. Save the solution in the CppNet\Tut03 folder.

F. Add a new managed C++ empty project to the solution. Name the project T3AppE15 Project.

G. Add a new C++ source file to the project. Name the source file T3AppE15.

H. Enter the appropriate C++ instructions into the source file.

I. Save and then build the solution. Execute the program. Test the program using the data specified in Step B.

J. When the program is working correctly, close the Output window, and then use the File menu to close the solution.

16) As you learned in the Concept lesson, you can initialize a `bool` variable in C++ using either the keyword `false` or the keyword `true`. You also can use an integer—either 0 or 1—to initialize a `bool` variable. Initializing a `bool` variable to the number 0 is the same as initializing it using the keyword `false`. Initializing a `bool` variable to the number 1 is the same as initializing it using the keyword `true`. Although you can use an integer to initialize a `bool` variable, the keywords make your program more self-documenting.

A. If necessary, start Visual Studio .NET. Open the T3AppE16 Solution (T3AppE16 Solution.sln) file, which is contained in the CppNet\Tut03\T3AppE16 Solution folder. The program initializes a `bool` variable named `insured` and then displays its value. Build the solution, and then execute the program. What does the program display in the Command Prompt window? Close the Command Prompt window.

B. Change the `bool insured = false;` statement to `bool insured = true;`. Save and then build the solution. Execute the program. What does the program display in the Command Prompt window? Close the Command Prompt window.

C. Change the `bool insured = true;` statement to `bool insured = 0;`. Save and then build the solution. Execute the program. What does the program display in the Command Prompt window? Close the Command Prompt window.

D. Change the `bool insured = 0;` statement to `bool insured = 1;`. Save and then build the solution. Execute the program. What does the program display in the Command Prompt window? Close the Command Prompt window.

E. Close the Output window, then use the File menu to close the solution.

17) In this exercise, you debug a C++ program.

A. If necessary, start Visual Studio .NET. Open the T3AppE17 Solution (T3AppE17 Solution.sln) file, which is contained in the CppNet\Tut03\T3AppE17 Solution folder. The program first initializes the `temp` variable. It then adds 1.5 to the variable before displaying its value.

B. Build the solution. Correct any errors, then save and build the solution again. Execute the program. When the program is working correctly, close the Output window, and then use the File menu to close the solution.

18) In this exercise, you debug a C++ program.

A. If necessary, start Visual Studio .NET. Open the T3AppE18 Solution (T3AppE18 Solution.sln) file, which is contained in the CppNet\Tut03\T3AppE18 Solution folder. The program should calculate the average of the three sales amounts entered by the user.

B. Build the solution. Correct any errors, then save and build the solution again. Execute the program. Use the following sales amounts to test the program: 110.55, 203.45, and 100.68. Correct the program so that it produces the proper output.

C. When the program is working correctly, close the Output window, and then use the File menu to close the solution.

19) In this exercise, you debug a C++ program.

A. If necessary, start Visual Studio .NET. Open the T3AppE19 Solution (T3AppE19 Solution.sln) file, which is contained in the CppNet\Tut03\T3AppE19 Solution folder. The program should calculate and display the sales discount and the new sales price.

B. Create an appropriate desk-check table, then desk-check the program using 100 as the original price and .25 as the discount rate.

C. Correct any errors in the program, then desk-check the program twice. For the first desk-check, use 100 as the original price and .25 as the discount rate. For the second desk-check, use 50 as the original price and .1 as the discount rate.

D. Save and then build the solution. If necessary, correct any errors, and then save and build the solution again. Execute the program. Test the program twice, using the data supplied in Step C. Compare your results to the desk-check table that you created in Step C.

E. When the program is working correctly, close the Output window, and then use the File menu to close the solution.

20) In this exercise, you debug a C++ program.

A. If necessary, start Visual Studio .NET. Open the T3AppE20 Solution (T3AppE20 Solution.sln) file, which is contained in the CppNet\Tut03\T3AppE20 Solution folder. The program should display the total price of CDs purchased at a store.

B. Study the program's code, then build the solution and execute the program. Correct any errors in the program, and then save and build the solution again. Execute the program. Use the program to calculate the total price for the purchase of three CDs at a price of $10.99 per CD. (The answer should be 32.97.)

C. When the program is working correctly, close the Output window, and then use the File menu to close the solution.

Tutorial 4

Value-Returning Functions

Objectives

After completing this tutorial, you will be able to:

- Create and invoke a function that returns a value
- Pass information, *by value*, to a function
- Understand a variable's scope and lifetime
- Raise a number to a power using the `Math::Pow()` method
- Write a function prototype
- Format the numeric output in a C++ program

Concept Lesson

tip
Like a function, a method also is a block of code that performs a task. The difference between a function and a method is that a method is part of a class, whereas a function is not.

tip
The ability to create functions within a program allows more than one programmer to work on a program at the same time, decreasing the time it takes to write the program.

tip
Any function, not just `main()`, can call another function.

tip
Recall that the items of information that appear within the parentheses following a method's name are called actual arguments.

Functions

As you learned in Tutorial 3, a function is a block of code that performs a task. Every C++ program contains at least one function—`main()`—and most contain many more. Programmers use functions for two reasons. First, functions allow the programmer to avoid duplicating code in different parts of a program. If a program needs to perform the same task several times, it is more efficient to enter the appropriate code once, in a function, and then simply call the function to perform its task when needed. Second, functions allow large and complex programs, which typically are written by a team of programmers, to be broken into small and manageable tasks; each member of the team can be assigned one of the tasks to code as a function. When each programmer has completed his or her function, all of the functions then are gathered together into one program. Typically, the `main()` function in the program is responsible for calling (or invoking) each of the other functions when needed. You call a function in exactly the same way as you call a method—by including its name and actual arguments (if any) in a statement.

All functions are categorized as either value-returning functions or void functions. Value-returning functions return a value to the statement that called the function, whereas void functions do not return a value. You learn how to create value-returning functions in this tutorial, and how to create void functions in Tutorial 5.

Creating Value-Returning Functions

A **value-returning function** is a function that returns a value after completing its assigned task. The `main()` function in a C++ program is an example of a value-returning function. All value-returning functions return precisely one value to the statement that called the function. The only exception to this rule is the `main()` function, which returns its one value to the operating system. Value-returning functions typically are called from statements that display the function's return value, use the return value in a calculation, or assign the return value to a variable.

Figure 4-1 shows the syntax used to create (or define) a value-returning function in C++. The figure also shows an example of a value-returning function whose task is to cube a number and then return the result.

Figure 4-1: Syntax and an example of a value-returning function in C++

Syntax

returnDataType functionName(**[***parameterList***]**)
{
one or more statements ending with a semicolon
return *expression*;
}

function header

function body

Note: Items within square brackets ([]) in the syntax are optional. Items in **bold**, however, are essential components of the syntax. Items in *italics* indicate where the programmer must supply information pertaining to the current program.

Example

```
int calcCube(int num)
{
      return num * num * num;
}
```

function definition

tip You do not have to call the `main()` function in a C++ program, as this is handled by the operating system when you execute the program. When the `main()` function completes its task, the statement `return 0;` returns the number 0 to the operating system to indicate that the program ended normally.

As Figure 4-1 indicates, a function is composed of a function header and a function body.

Function Header

The **function header** is the first line in a function definition and is so named because it appears at the top (head) of the function. The function header specifies the type of data the function returns (if any), as well as the function's name and an optional *parameterList*. The *parameterList* lists the data type and name of memory locations used by the function to store information passed to it. Notice that a function header does not end with a semicolon. This is because a function header is not considered a statement in C++.

tip As you will learn in Tutorial 5, you use the keyword `void` as the *returnDataType* for functions that do not return a value.

The function header for a value-returning function begins with *returnDataType*, where *returnDataType* indicates the data type of the value returned by the function. If the function returns an integer, as does the `calcCube()` function shown in Figure 4-1, *returnDataType* will be `int`; however, it will be `char` if the function returns a character.

tip You can use any of the C++ data types listed in Tutorial 3's Figure 3-5 as the *returnDataType* for a value-returning function.

The function header also specifies the name of the function. The rules for naming functions are the same as for naming variables. To make your programs more self-documenting and easier to understand, you should use meaningful names that describe the task the function performs. In the example shown in Figure 4-1, the name `calcCube()` indicates that the function calculates the cube of a number.

tip The rules for naming variables in C++, which also should be followed for naming C++ functions, are shown in Tutorial 3's Figure 3-3.

In Tutorial 3, you learned how to send (pass) information, called actual arguments, to a method; you also can pass actual arguments to a function. The actual arguments, referred to as the *argumentList*, can be one or more variables, named constants, literal constants, or keywords. When the actual argument is a variable, the variable can be passed either *by value* or *by reference*. When a variable is passed **by value**, only the value stored in the variable is passed to the function. When a variable is passed **by reference**, on the other hand, the address of the variable in the computer's internal memory is passed. Unless you specify otherwise, variables in C++ are automatically passed *by value*. For now, you do not need to concern yourself with passing *by reference*, because all variables passed to functions in this tutorial are passed *by value*. You learn how to pass variables *by reference* in Tutorial 5.

You pass information to a function when you want the function to process the information in some way. In the case of the `calcCube()` function shown in Figure 4-1, you pass the number you want the function to cube. To cube the number three, for example, you use the expression `calcCube(3)` in a C++ statement. The `calcCube(3)` expression calls (invokes) the `calcCube()` function, passing it the literal constant 3. Similarly, to cube the number stored in the `number` variable, you use the expression `calcCube(number)` in a C++ statement. The `calcCube(number)` expression calls the `calcCube()` function, passing it the value stored in the `number` variable.

When you pass a literal constant, a keyword, a named constant, or a variable's value to a function, the function stores the value it receives in a memory location. The name and data type of the memory locations that a function uses to store the values passed to it are listed in the function's *parameterList*, which appears within parentheses in the function header. The `calcCube()` function's *parameterList* in Figure 4-1, for example, indicates that the function uses an `int` variable named `num` to store the value passed to it.

Each memory location listed in the *parameterList* is referred to as a **formal parameter**. The number of formal parameters included in the *parameterList* should agree with the number of actual arguments passed to the function. If you pass one actual argument, then the function needs only one formal parameter to store the value of that argument. Similarly, a function that is passed three actual arguments when called requires three formal parameters in its *parameterList*. Each formal parameter must be assigned a data type and name. If a *parameterList* contains more than one formal parameter, you use a comma to separate one parameter from another.

tip

You also can define a default value for one or more of the formal parameters listed in the function header. If a formal parameter has a default value, then you do not need to provide an actual argument for it when you call the function. Defining default values for formal parameters is beyond the scope of this book.

In addition to having the same number of formal parameters as actual arguments, the data type and position of each formal parameter in the *parameterList* must agree with the data type and position of its corresponding actual argument in the *argumentList*. For instance, if the actual argument is a variable whose data type is `int`, then the formal parameter that will store the variable's value should have a data type of `int`. Likewise, if two actual arguments are passed to a function—the first one being a character and the second one being a number with a decimal place—the first formal parameter should have a data type of `char`, and the second formal parameter should have a data type of either `float` or `double`.

Not every function requires information to be passed to it, so not every function has formal parameters listed in its function header. Functions that do not require a *parameterList* have an empty set of parentheses after the function's name.

In addition to a function header, a function definition also includes a function body.

Function Body

tip

Rather than using an empty set of parentheses to indicate that a function does not receive any information, some C++ programmers enter the C++ keyword `void` within the parentheses.

The **function body** contains the instructions the function must follow to perform its assigned task. The function body begins with the opening brace ({) and ends with the closing brace (}). Although only one statement appears in the function body shown in Figure 4-1, a function body typically contains many statements.

In most cases, the last statement in the function body of a value-returning function is **return** *expression*;, where *expression* represents the value the function returns to the statement that called it. The `return` statement alerts the computer that the function has completed its task, and it ends the function. The data type of the *expression* in the `return` statement must agree with the *returnDataType* specified in the function header.

MINI-QUIZ

Mini-Quiz 1

1) Assume a program uses the statement `discount = calcDisc(300.45);` to call the `calcDisc()` function. The function returns a number having a decimal place. Which of the following is a valid function header for the `calcDisc()` function?
   a. calcDisc(double sales)
   b. double calcDisc(sales);
   c. double calcDisc(double sales)
   d. double calcDisc(double sales);
2) Write a function header for a function named `calcTotal()`. The function will be passed two integers when it is called. Use the variable names `sale1` and `sale2` as the formal parameters. The function will return an integer.
3) Assume a program uses the statement `Console::Write(calcGross (hours, rate));` to call the `calcGross()` function. Also assume that `hours` is an `int` variable, and `rate` is a `double` variable. The function header used in the program is `double calcGross(double hoursWkd, payRate)`, which is incorrect. Correct the function header.
4) Write the C++ statement that instructs the `calcGross()` function to return the contents of the `grossPay` variable.

In the next section, you learn how the computer processes a function when a statement within the program calls the function.

Processing a Function

As mentioned earlier, you call a function in exactly the same way as you call a method—by including its name and actual arguments (if any) in a statement. When the computer processes a statement containing a function, the computer first locates the function's code in the program; in a C++ program, this code typically is located after the `main()` function. If the function call contains an *argumentList*, the computer passes the values of the actual arguments (assuming the variables included in the *argumentList* are passed *by value*) to the called function. The function receives these values and stores them in the memory locations listed in the function's *parameterList*. Then the computer processes the function's code and, in the case of a value-returning function, the computer returns the appropriate value to the statement that called the function. This is the same process the computer uses when processing a statement containing a built-in method, such as the `name = Console:: ReadLine()` statement. The only difference is that the computer locates a function's code in the current program rather than in a library file. (Recall that the `Console::ReadLine()` method's code is contained in the Mscorlib.dll file. "Mscorlib" stands for "Microsoft Core Library.")

Figure 4-2 shows examples of calling and defining value-returning functions in C++. The function calls, which appear in the `main()` function in both examples, are shaded in the figure.

Figure 4-2: Examples of calling and defining value-returning functions in C++

typically located below the `main()` function in a C++ program

one actual argument, one formal parameter

no actual arguments, no formal parameters

two actual arguments, two formal parameters

Function call	Function definition

`//Example 1`
`int main()`
`{`
`   int number = 0;`
`   Console::Write`
`   ("Enter an integer: ");`
`   number =`
`      Convert::ToInt32`
`      (Console::ReadLine());`
`   Console::WriteLine`
`   (calcCube(number));`
`   return 0;`
`}  //end of main function`
	`//*****function definitions*****`
	
	`int calcCube(int num)`
	`{`
	`    return num * num * num;`
	`}   //end of calcCube function`

`//Example 2`
`int main()`
`{`
`   int salesAmt     = 0;`
`   double bonusAmt = 0.0;`
`   salesAmt = getSales();`
 	
`   bonusAmt = bonus(salesAmt, .05);`
`   Console::WriteLine(bonusAmt);`
`   return 0;`
`}  //end of main function`
	`//*****function definitions*****`
	
	`int getSales()`
	`{`
	`    int sales = 0;`
	`    Console::Write("Enter sales: ");`
	`    sales =`
	`    Convert::ToInt32 (Console::`
	`    ReadLine());`
	`    return sales;`
	`}   //end of getSales function`
	
	`double bonus(int dollars, double rate)`
	`{`
	`    double bonusAmt = 0.0;`
	`    bonusAmt = dollars * rate;`
	`    return bonusAmt;`
	`}   //end of bonus function`

tip

Recall that most C++ programmers enter the function definitions below the `main()` function in a C++ program. Many programmers also use a comment (such as `//***** function definitions *****`) to separate the `main()` function's code from the code for the function definitions.

Notice that the quantity and data type of the actual arguments match the quantity and data type of the corresponding formal parameters. Also notice that the names of the formal parameters do not need to be identical to the names of their corresponding actual arguments. In the first example, for instance, the function call contains one actual argument named number, and the corresponding function header contains one formal parameter named num. Both the actual argument and the formal parameter are of data type int.

In the second example, the call to the getSales() function contains no actual arguments, and the corresponding function header contains no formal parameters. In that same example, the call to the bonus() function contains two actual arguments: an int variable and a number with a decimal place. The bonus() function header correctly contains two formal parameters to receive the information passed to the function: an int variable named dollars and a double variable named rate.

Desk-checking the two programs shown in Figure 4-2 will help you understand how the computer processes a function when it appears in a statement. Begin with the first program shown in the figure.

Desk-checking Example 1

The first statement in Example 1's main() function creates and initializes an int variable named number. The next two statements prompt the user to enter an integer, and then store the user's response in the number variable. Assume that the user enters the number four. Figure 4-3 shows the contents of memory after the first three statements in the main() function are processed.

Figure 4-3: Contents of memory after the first three statements in the main() function are processed

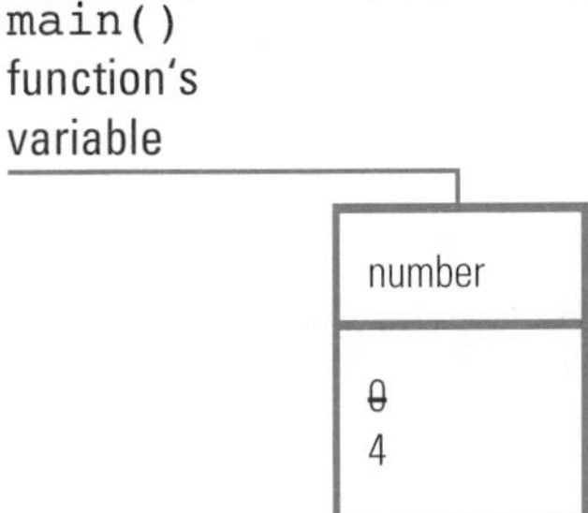

The fourth statement, `Console::WriteLine(calcCube(number));`, calls the calcCube() function, passing it one actual argument: an int variable named number. Recall that unless specified otherwise, variables in C++ are passed *by value*, which means that only the contents of the variables are passed to the function. In this case, the computer passes the number four to the calcCube() function.

At this point, the computer temporarily leaves the main() function to process the code contained in the calcCube() function, beginning with the function header. In this case, the *parameterList* in the calcCube() function header tells the computer to reserve one memory location—an int variable named num. After reserving the num variable, the computer stores the value passed to the function—in this case, the number four—in the variable, as shown in Figure 4-4.

Figure 4-4: Contents of memory after the `calcCube()` function header is processed

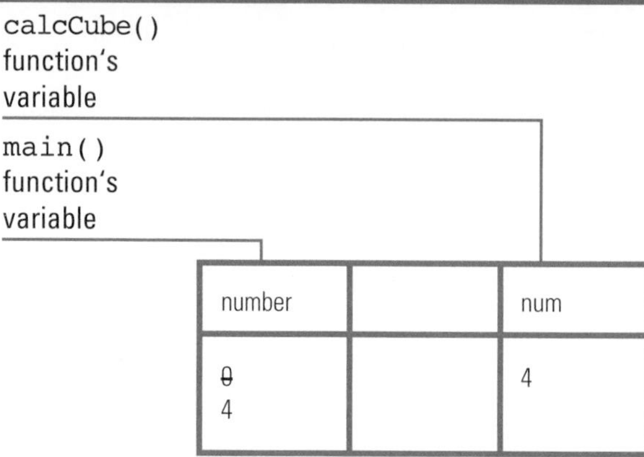

Next, the computer processes the `return num * num * num;` statement contained in the `calcCube()` function body. This statement cubes the value stored in the `num` variable (4), and returns the result (64) to the statement that called the function—the `Console::WriteLine(calcCube(number));` statement in the `main()` function. After processing the `calcCube()` function's `return` statement, the computer removes the `num` variable from memory, and then the `calcCube()` function ends. Figure 4-5 shows the contents of memory after the `calcCube()` function has completed its task and returned its value. Notice that only the `main()` function's `number` variable is still in the computer's memory.

Figure 4-5: Contents of memory after the `calcCube()` function completes its task and returns its value

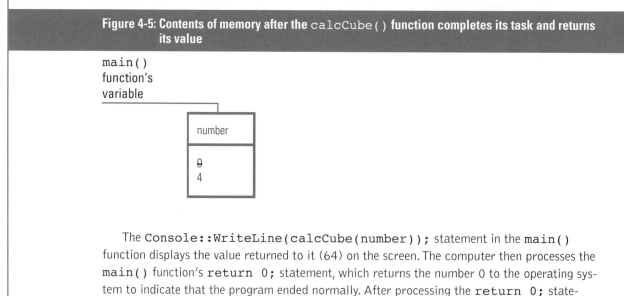

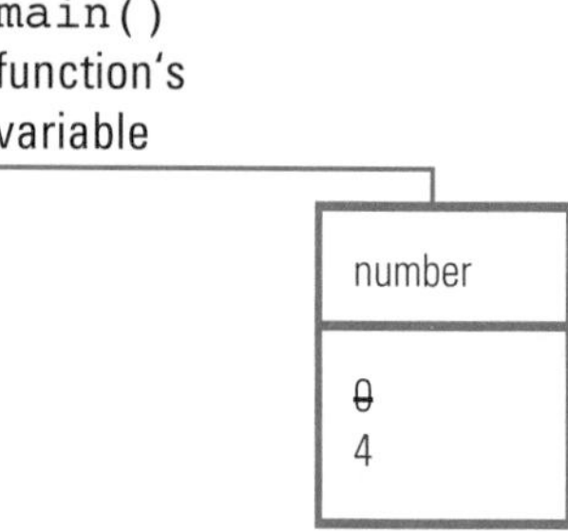

The `Console::WriteLine(calcCube(number));` statement in the `main()` function displays the value returned to it (64) on the screen. The computer then processes the `main()` function's `return 0;` statement, which returns the number 0 to the operating system to indicate that the program ended normally. After processing the `return 0;` statement, the computer removes the `number` variable from memory, and then the program ends.

At this point, you may be wondering why the program needs to pass the contents of the `number` variable to the `calcCube()` function. Why can't the function just use the `number` variable in its `return` statement, like this: `return number * number * number;`? You also may be wondering why the computer removes the `num` variable from memory after it processes the `calcCube()` function's `return` statement, but waits until after it processes the `main()` function's `return` statement before it removes the `number` variable. Why are the variables removed from memory at different times? To answer these questions, you need to learn about the scope and lifetime of a variable.

The Scope and Lifetime of a Variable

A variable's **scope**, which can be either local or global, indicates which portions of a program can use the variable. A variable's **lifetime**, on the other hand, indicates how long the variable remains in the computer's memory. The scope and lifetime typically are determined by where you declare the variable in the program. Variables declared within a function, and those that appear in a function's *parameterList*, have a local scope and are referred to as **local variables**. Local variables can be used only by the function in which they are declared or in whose *parameterList* they appear. Local variables remain in memory until the function ends. In the case of a value-returning function, the function ends after the computer processes the function's `return` statement.

Unlike local variables, **global variables** are declared outside of any function in the program, and they remain in memory until the program ends. Also unlike a local variable, a global variable can be used by any statement in the program. Declaring a variable as global rather than local allows unintentional errors to occur when a function that should not have access to the variable inadvertently changes the variable's contents. Because of this, you should avoid using global variables in your programs. If more than one function needs access to the same variable, it is better to create a local variable in one of the functions and then pass that variable only to the other functions that need it.

In the Example 1 program shown earlier in Figure 4-2, the `number` variable is local to the `main()` function, because `main()` is the function in which the variable is declared. Therefore, only the `main()` function can use the `number` variable; the `calcCube()` function is not even aware of the variable's existence in memory. If you want the `calcCube()` function to cube the value stored in the `number` variable, you must pass the variable's value to the function.

The `num` variable, which appears in the `calcCube()` function's *parameterList* in Example 1, is local to the `calcCube()` function. Therefore, only the `calcCube()` function can use the `num` variable.

As mentioned earlier, local variables remain in memory until the function in which they are created ends. This explains why the `num` variable is removed from memory after the computer processes the `calcCube()` function's `return` statement, and why the computer waits until after it processes the `main()` function's `return` statement before it removes the `number` variable from memory.

Now that you understand the concepts of scope and lifetime, you will desk-check the second example shown earlier in Figure 4-2.

Desk-checking Example 2

Figure 4-6 shows the program that you will desk-check in this section. This program appeared earlier as Example 2 in Figure 4-2.

tip

As you will learn in future tutorials, any variable that is declared in a statement block in a C++ program is considered a local variable. A statement block is a group of instructions enclosed in braces; a function, for example, is a statement block. C++ also allows you to create statement blocks that are not functions. Variables declared within these statement blocks can be used only by the statement block, and they are removed from memory when the statement block ends, which is when the computer encounters the statement block's closing brace. Later in this book, you will learn more about statement blocks that are not functions.

tip

You can experiment with the concepts of scope and lifetime by completing Discovery Exercise 7 at the end of this lesson.

Figure 4-6: Code from Example 2

no actual arguments, no formal parameters

two actual arguments, two formal parameters

Function call	Function definition

`//Example 2`
`int main()`
`{`
`int salesAmt = 0;`
`double bonusAmt = 0.0;`
`salesAmt = getSales();`
	`//*****function definitions*****`
	
	`int getSales()`
	`{`
	`int sales = 0;`
	`Console::Write("Enter sales: ");`
	`sales =`
	`Convert::ToInt32(Console::`
	`ReadLine());`
	`return sales;`
	`} //end of getSales function`

`bonusAmt = bonus(salesAmt, .05);`
`Console::WriteLine(bonusAmt);`
`return 0;`
`} //end of main function`
	`double bonus(int dollars, double rate)`
	`{`
	`double bonusAmt = 0.0;`
	`bonusAmt = dollars * rate;`
	`return bonusAmt;`
	`} //end of bonus function`

The first two statements in the `main()` function create and initialize two local variables: an `int` variable named `salesAmt` and a `double` variable named `bonusAmt`. Both variables can be used only by the `main()` function, and both remain in memory until the `main()` function's `return` statement is processed. Figure 4-7 shows the contents of memory after the first two statements in the `main()` function are processed.

Figure 4-7: Contents of memory after the first two statements in the `main()` function are processed

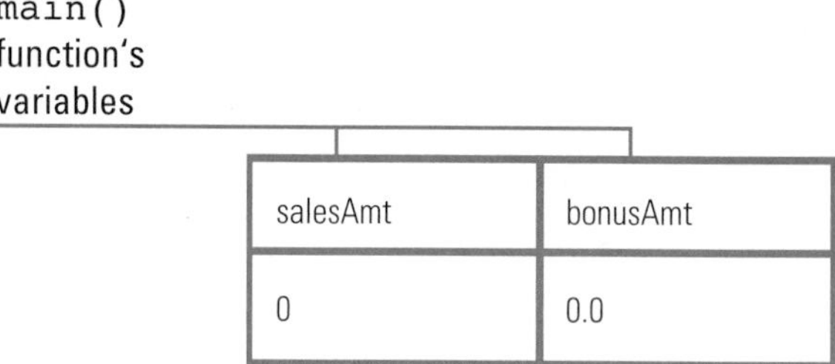

`main()` function's variables

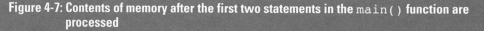

salesAmt	bonusAmt
0	0.0

When the computer encounters the third statement, `salesAmt = getSales();`, it temporarily leaves the `main()` function to process the instructions in the `getSales()` function, beginning with the function header. The `getSales()` function header does not contain any formal parameters, which indicates that the function will not receive any information when it is called.

The first statement in the `getSales()` function body creates and initializes a local `int` variable named `sales`. The `sales` variable can be used only by the `getSales()` function, and it remains in memory until the `getSales()` function's `return` statement is processed.

The next two statements in the `getSales()` function body prompt the user to enter a sales amount, and then store the user's response in the `sales` variable. Figure 4-8 shows the contents of memory at this point, assuming the user entered the number 1575 as the sales amount.

Figure 4-8: Contents of memory after the user enters the sales amount

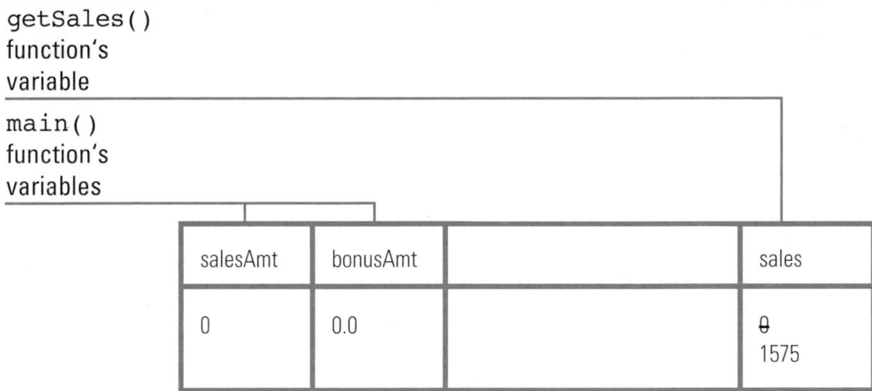

Next, the computer processes the `return sales;` statement contained in the `getSales()` function body. The statement returns the contents of the `sales` variable (1575) to the statement that called the function—the `salesAmt = getSales();` statement in the `main()` function—which assigns the return value (1575) to the `salesAmt` variable, as shown in Figure 4-9.

Figure 4-9: Contents of memory after the `return sales;` statement is processed

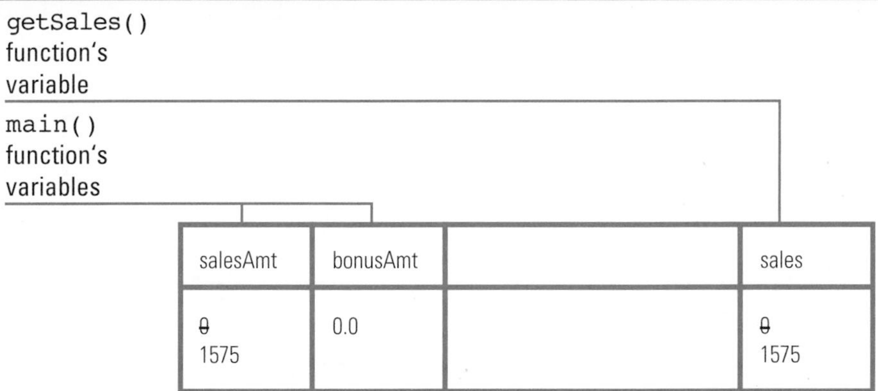

After processing the `getSales()` function's `return` statement, the computer removes the `sales` variable from memory, and then the `getSales()` function ends. Figure 4-10 shows the contents of memory after the `getSales()` function has completed its task and returned its value. Notice that only the `main()` function's variables are still in memory.

Figure 4-10: Contents of memory after the `getSales()` function completes its task and returns its value

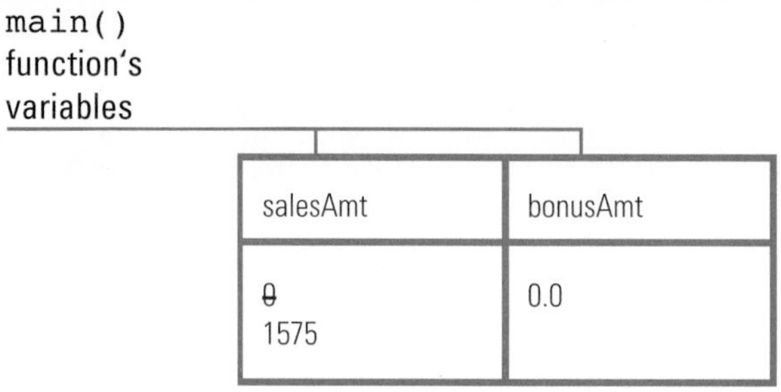

main() function's variables

salesAmt	bonusAmt
~~0~~ 1575	0.0

The next statement to be processed is the **`main()`** function's **`bonusAmt = bonus(salesAmt, .05);`** statement. Here again, the computer temporarily leaves the **`main()`** function; in this case, it does so to process the code in the **`bonus()`** function. The *parameterList* in the **`bonus()`** function header tells the computer to create two local variables—an **`int`** variable named **`dollars`** and a **`double`** variable named **`rate`**. After creating both variables, the computer stores the first value passed to the function (the contents of the **`salesAmt`** variable) in the first formal parameter (the **`dollars`** variable). It then stores the second value passed to the function (the number .05) in the second formal parameter (the **`rate`** variable), as shown in Figure 4-11.

Figure 4-11: Contents of memory after the `bonus()` function header is processed

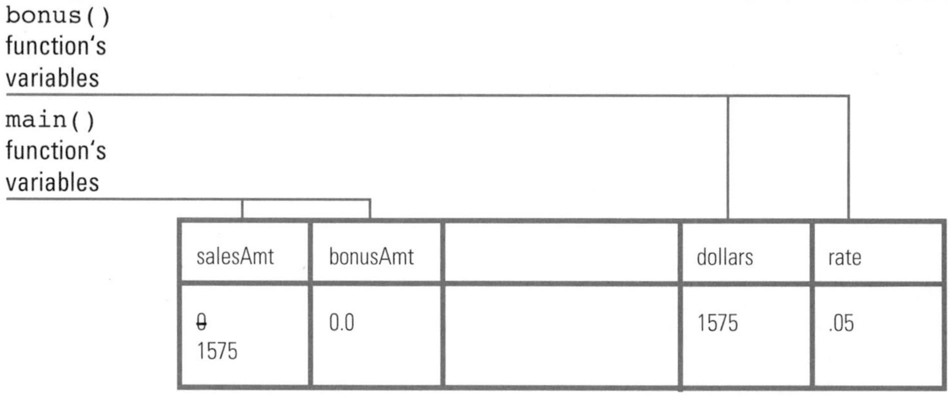

bonus() function's variables

main() function's variables

salesAmt	bonusAmt		dollars	rate
~~0~~ 1575	0.0		1575	.05

The first statement in the **`bonus()`** function body reserves an additional local variable. The variable, named **`bonusAmt`**, has a data type of **`double`**. The second statement in the function body multiplies the contents of the **`dollars`** variable (1575) by the contents of the **`rate`** variable (.05), and assigns the result (78.75) to the **`bonusAmt`** variable, as shown in Figure 4-12.

Figure 4-12: Contents of memory after the bonus is calculated

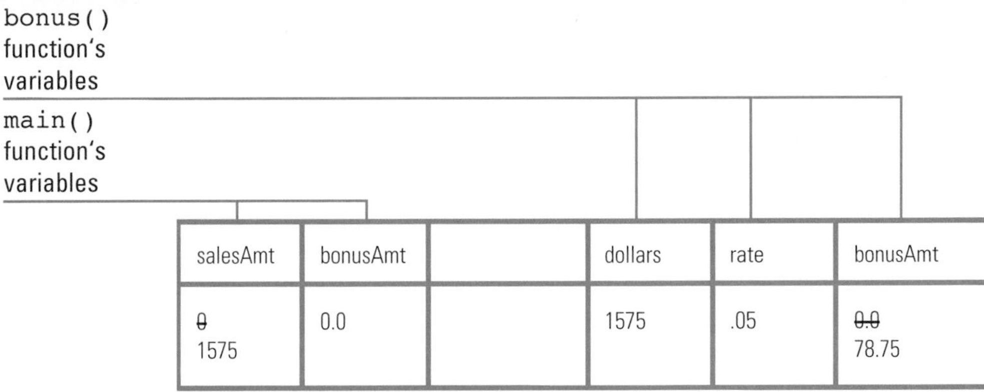

Notice that the computer's memory contains two locations having the same name, `bonusAmt`. When the variable's name appears in a statement, the computer knows which of the two locations to use by the position of the statement in the program. If the program statement appears in the `main()` function, the computer uses the `bonusAmt` variable located in the `main()` function's section in memory. However, if the program statement appears in the `bonus()` function, the computer uses the `bonusAmt` variable located in the `bonus()` function's section of memory.

tip

For clarity, it is recommended that you use unique variable names throughout the program.

Next, the computer processes the `return bonusAmt;` statement, which returns the contents of the `bonus()` function's `bonusAmt` variable (78.75) to the statement that called the function—the `bonusAmt = bonus(salesAmt, .05);` statement in the `main()` function. The `bonusAmt = bonus(salesAmt, .05);` statement assigns the value returned to it to the `main()` function's `bonusAmt` variable. At this point, the computer removes the `bonus()` function's local variables (`dollars`, `rate`, and `bonusAmt`) from memory. Figure 4-13 shows the contents of memory after the `bonus()` function completes its task and returns its value. Notice that only the variables local to the `main()` function are still in memory.

Figure 4-13: Contents of memory after the `bonus()` function completes its task and returns its value

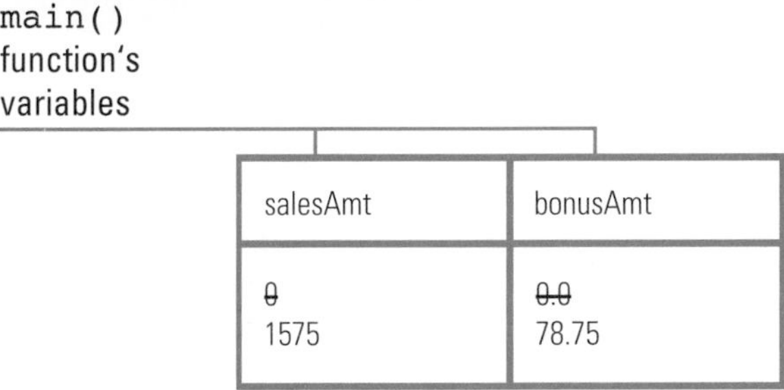

After processing the `bonusAmt = bonus(salesAmt, .05);` statement, the computer processes the `Console::WriteLine(bonusAmt);` statement, which displays the contents of the `main()` function's `bonusAmt` variable (78.75) on the screen. The `return 0;` statement then returns the number 0 to the operating system, indicating that the program ended normally. After processing the `return 0;` statement, the computer removes the `main()` function's local variables (`salesAmt` and `bonusAmt`) from memory, and then the program ends.

MINI-QUIZ

Mini-Quiz 2

1) The data type and name of each formal parameter must match the data type and name of its corresponding actual argument.
   a. True
   b. False
2) Unless specified otherwise, variables in a C++ program are passed ________________, which means that only the contents of the variables are passed.
3) A variable's________________ indicates which portions of a program can use the variable.
4) Assume two functions declare a variable having the same name. How does the computer know which variable to use?

You now have completed Tutorial 4's Concept lesson. You can either take a break or complete the end-of-lesson questions and exercises before moving on to the Application lesson.

SUMMARY

Programmers use functions for two reasons: functions allow the programmer to avoid duplicating code in different parts of a program, and they allow large and complex programs to be broken into small and manageable tasks. You call a function by including its name and actual arguments (if any) in a statement.

All functions are classified as either value-returning functions or void functions. A value-returning function returns a value after completing its assigned task; a void function does not return a value.

A function is composed of a function header and a function body. The function header is the first line in the function definition. The function header specifies the type of data the function returns, as well as the name of the function and an optional *parameterList* enclosed in parentheses. The *parameterList* contains the data type and name of each formal parameter the function uses to store the data passed to it. The number and sequence of formal parameters included in the *parameterList* should agree with the number and sequence of actual arguments passed to the function. Additionally, the data type of each formal parameter must agree with the data type of its corresponding actual argument. The name of each formal parameter typically is different than the name of the actual argument to which it corresponds. Functions that do not require a *parameterList* will have an empty set of parentheses after the function's name. Unless specified otherwise, variables in C++ are passed to a function *by value*, which means that only the contents of the variables are passed.

The function body in a function definition contains the instructions the function must follow to perform its assigned task. The function body begins with an opening brace and ends with a closing brace. The last statement in the function body of a value-returning function typically is one that instructs the function to return its value.

A variable's scope, which can be either local or global, indicates which portions of a program can use the variable. A variable's lifetime, on the other hand, indicates how long the variable remains in the computer's memory. Local variables can be used only by the function in which they are created, and they remain in memory until the function ends. (As you will learn in future tutorials, variables declared in a statement block in a C++ program are local to the statement block, and they remain in memory until the statement block ends.) Global variables, which you should avoid using, can be used anywhere in the program, and they remain in memory until the program ends.

If more than one memory location has the same name, and the name appears in a statement, the computer uses the position of the statement within the program to determine which memory location to use. For clarity, you should use unique variable names within a program.

ANSWERS TO MINI-QUIZZES

Mini-Quiz 1

1) c. `double calcDisc(double sales)`
2) `int calcTotal(int sale1, int sale2)`
3) `double calcGross(int hoursWkd, double payRate)`
4) `return grossPay;`

Mini-Quiz 2

1) b. False
2) *by value*
3) scope
4) By the position of the statement that refers to the variable in the program.

QUESTIONS

1) A function whose function header is `double calcShipping()` is an example of a _____________ function.
   A. value-returning
   B. void
2) Value-returning functions can return _____________.
   A. one value only
   B. one or more values
   C. the number 0 only
   D. none of the above
3) The function header specifies _____________.
   A. the data type of the function's return value
   B. the name of the function
   C. the function's formal parameters
   D. all of the above

4) Which of the following is false?

A. The number of actual arguments should agree with the number of formal parameters.

B. The data type of each actual argument should match the data type of its corresponding formal parameter.

C. The name of each actual argument should be identical to the name of its corresponding formal parameter.

D. When you pass information to a function *by value*, the function stores the value of each item it receives in a separate memory location.

5) Each memory location listed in the *parameterList* in the function header is referred to as ______________.

A. an actual argument

B. an actual parameter

C. a formal argument

D. a formal parameter

6) In a C++ function, the function body ends with the ______________.

A. { (opening brace)

B. } (closing brace)

C. ; (semicolon)

D. `return` statement

7) Assume a program uses the statement `tax = calcTax(sales);` to call the `calcTax()` function. (`sales` is a `float` variable.) The function returns a number having a decimal place. Which of the following is a valid function header for the `calcTax()` function?

A. `calcTax(float sales);`

B. `float calcTax(salesAmount)`

C. `float calcTax(float salesAmount)`

D. `float calcTax(int sales);`

8) Which of the following is a valid function header for a C++ function that receives an integer first and a number with a decimal place second, and then returns a number with a decimal place?

A. `fee(int base, double rate);`

B. `int fee(int base, double rate)`

C. `double fee(double base, int rate)`

D. `double fee(int base, double rate)`

9) Which of the following instructs a function to return the contents of the `stateTax` variable to the `main()` function?

A. `restore stateTax;`

B. `return stateTax`

C. `return to main(stateTax);`

D. none of the above

10) If the statement `netPay = calcNet(gross, taxes);` passes the contents of the `gross` and `taxes` variables to the `calcNet()` function, the variables are said to be passed ______________.

A. *by address*

B. *by content*

C. *by reference*

D. *by value*

11) Assume a program contains a function named `displayGross`. When the computer processes the `displayGross` function's `return` statement, ______________.

A. it removes the function's local variables (if any) from memory, then continues program execution with the statement immediately following the one that called the function

B. it removes the function's local variables (if any) from memory, then continues program execution with the statement that called the function

C. it removes the function's global variables (if any) from memory, then continues program execution with the statement immediately following the one that called the function

D. it removes the function's global variables (if any) from memory, then continues program execution with the statement that called the function

12) A variable's ______________ indicates which portions of a program can use the variable.

A. lifetime

B. range

C. scope

D. span

13) Assume a variable named `beginBalance` appears in a function's *parameterList*. Which of the following statements is true?

A. The `beginBalance` variable remains in memory until the computer processes the function's `return` statement.

B. The `beginBalance` variable is called a functional variable.

C. The `beginBalance` variable can be used anywhere in the program.

D. both a and b

14) Assume a program contains three functions named `main()`, `calcGross()`, and `displayGross()`. Both the `main()` and `calcGross()` functions declare a variable named `pay`. The `pay` variable name also appears in the `displayGross()` function header. When the computer processes the statement `pay = hours * rate;` in the `calcGross()` function, it multiplies the contents of the `hours` variable by the contents of the `rate` variable, and then ______________.

A. stores the result in the `calcGross()` function's `pay` variable

B. stores the result in the `displayGross()` function's `pay` variable

C. stores the result in the `main()` function's `pay` variable

D. displays an error message because you can't have three memory locations with the same name

Look For These Symbols

Debugging

Discovery

EXERCISES

1) Write the C++ code for a function that receives an integer passed to it. The function, named `halveNumber()`, should divide the integer by 2, and then return the result (which may contain a decimal place.)

2) Write the C++ code for a function that prompts the user to enter a character, and then stores the user's response in a `char` variable. The function should return the character entered by the user. (The function will not have any actual arguments passed to it.) Name the function `getChar()`.

3) Write the C++ code for a function that receives four integers. The function should calculate the average of the four integers, and then return the result (which may contain a decimal place). Name the function `calcAverage()`.

4) Write the C++ code for a function that receives two numbers that both have a decimal place. The function should divide the first number by the second number, and then return the result. Name the function `quotient()`.

5) Desk-check the program shown in Figure 4-14. Show the desk-check table after the first four statements in the `main()` function are processed, after the `calcEnd()` function's `return` statement is processed (but before local variables are removed from memory), and after the `calcEnd()` function's local variables are removed from memory.

Figure 4-14

<table>
<tr><th><code>main()</code> function</th><th>Function definition</th></tr>
<tr><td><pre>int main()
{
   int begVal   = 1000;
   int purchase   = 500;
   int sale   = 200;
   int endVal   = 0;

   endVal = calcEnd(begVal,
   purchase, sale);

   Console::WriteLine(endVal);
   return 0;
} //end of main function</pre></td><td><pre>int calcEnd(int b, int p, int sale)
{
    int endValue = 0;
    endValue = b + p – sale;
    return endValue;
}   //end of calcEnd function</pre></td></tr>
</table>

6) In this exercise, you learn how to create a function that returns a string.

A. If necessary, start Visual Studio .NET. Open the T4ConE06 Solution (T4ConE06 Solution.sln) file, which is contained in the CppNet\Tut04\T4ConE06 Solution folder. The `main()` function calls the `getName()` function to get and return a name.

B. Build the solution. The C++ compiler displays several error messages. Read the error messages that pertain to Lines 8 and 20 in the program. These error messages provide a hint on how to fix the errors in the program.

C. Close the Task List and Output windows.

D. Fix the errors, then save and build the solution.

E. Execute the program. When you are prompted to enter a name, type your name and press Enter. The `main()` function displays your name on the computer screen.

F. Close the Command Prompt and Output windows, and then use the File menu to close the solution.

7) In this exercise, you experiment with the concepts of scope and lifetime.

A. If necessary, start Visual Studio .NET. Open the T4ConE07 Solution (T4ConE07 Solution.sln) file, which is contained in the CppNet\Tut04\T4ConE07 Solution folder.

B. Build the solution. The C++ compiler displays an error message indicating that the `calcDoubleNumber()` function does not recognize the `number` variable. This error occurs because the `number` variable is local to the `main()` function. To fix this error, you can either pass the `number` variable's value to the `calcDoubleNumber()` function, or create a global variable named `number`. Passing the variable's value is the preferred way for the `main()` function to communicate with the `calcDoubleNumber()` function. However, to give you an opportunity to see how global variables work in a program, you will fix the program's error by creating a global variable named `number`.

C. Close the Output and Task List windows.

D. Change the `int number = 0;` statement in the `main()` function to a comment by preceding the statement with //.

E. Recall that global variables are declared outside of any functions in the program. In the blank line below the `//declare global variable` comment, type `int number = 0;` and press Enter. Because the `number` variable is now a global variable, both the `main()` and `calcDoubleNumber()` functions have access to it. You can verify that by running the program.

F. Save and then build the solution. Execute the program. When prompted for a number, type 5 and press Enter. The Command Prompt window shows that doubling the number five results in the number `10`.

G. Close the Command Prompt and Output windows, and then use the File menu to close the solution.

8) Assume a C++ function named `calcCommission()` is passed three items of information when it is called by the `main()` function: a `String` variable followed by two `double` variables. (The variables are passed *by value*.) The `calcCommission()` function returns a number with a decimal place. Rewrite the following function header correctly.

```
calcCommission(name, double sales, double rate);
```

Application Lesson

Using Values-Returning Functions in a C++ Program

CASE After weeks of car shopping, David Liu still hasn't decided what car to purchase. Recently, David has noticed that many car dealers, in an effort to boost sales, are offering buyers a choice of either a large cash rebate or an extremely low financing rate, much lower than the rate David would pay by financing the car through his local credit union. David is not sure whether to take the lower financing rate from the dealer, or take the rebate and then finance the car through the credit union. In this tutorial, you create a program that David can use to calculate and display the monthly payments using both options.

Analyzing, Planning, and Desk-checking the Periodic Payment Algorithm

You need to calculate a periodic payment on a loan for David. The formula to calculate the payment is *principal* * *rate* / (1 – (*rate* + 1)$^{-term}$), where *principal* is the amount of the loan, *rate* is the periodic interest rate, and *term* is the number of periodic payments. Figure 4-15 shows two examples of using the periodic payment formula to calculate the periodic payment on a loan.

Figure 4-15: Periodic payment formula and examples

Periodic payment formula: *principal* * *rate* / (1 – (*rate* + 1)$^{-term}$)

Note: When you apply for a loan, the lender typically quotes you an annual interest rate, and the term is expressed in years.

Example 1 – calculate the annual payment for a loan of $9000 for 3 years at 5% interest

Principal:	9000
Annual rate:	.05
Term (years):	3
Formula:	9000 * .05 / (1 – (.05 + 1)$^{-3}$)
Annual payment:	$3304.88 (rounded to two decimal places)

Example 2 – calculate the monthly payment for a loan of $12,000 for 5 years at 6% interest

Principal:	12,000
Monthly rate:	.005 (annual rate of .06 divided by 12)
Term (months):	60 (5 years multiplied by 12)
Formula:	12,000 * .005 / (1 – (.005 + 1)$^{-60}$)
Monthly payment:	$231.99 (rounded to two decimal places)

Example 1 uses the periodic payment formula to calculate the annual payment for a $9000 loan for three years at 5% interest; the annual payment is $3304.88 (rounded to two decimal places). In other words, if you borrow $9000 for three years at 5% interest, you would need to make three annual payments of $3304.88 to pay off the loan.

Example 2 uses the periodic payment formula to calculate the monthly payment for a $12,000 loan for five years at 6% interest. To pay off this loan, you would need to make 60 payments of $231.99. Notice that, before you can calculate the monthly payment, you need to convert the annual interest rate to a monthly interest rate by dividing the annual rate by 12. You also need to convert the term, which is expressed in years, to months by multiplying the number of years by 12.

You will use the periodic payment formula to calculate David Liu's monthly car payment if he accepts the dealer's rebate and finances the car through his credit union. You also will use the formula to calculate David's monthly payment if he chooses the car dealer's lower financing rate instead of the rebate. Figure 4-16 shows the IPO chart for the David Liu problem.

Figure 4-16: IPO chart for the David Liu problem

Input	Processing	Output
car price rebate credit union rate (annual) dealer rate (annual) term (years)	Processing items: monthly credit union rate monthly dealer rate number of months Algorithm: 1. enter the car price, rebate, credit union rate, dealer rate, and term 2. calculate the monthly credit union rate by dividing the credit union rate by 12 3. calculate the monthly dealer rate by dividing the dealer rate by 12 4. calculate the number of months by multiplying the term by 12 5. calculate the credit union payment using the periodic payment formula: (car price - rebate) * monthly credit union rate / (1 - (monthly credit union rate + 1)$^{-\text{number of months}}$) 6. calculate the dealer payment using the periodic payment formula: car price * monthly dealer rate / (1 - (monthly dealer rate + 1)$^{-\text{number of months}}$) 7. display the credit union payment and the dealer payment	credit union payment dealer payment

As Figure 4-16 indicates, the output is the monthly payment to the credit union and the monthly payment to the car dealer. To display the output, the program must know the car price, rebate, credit union rate, dealer rate, and term.

According to the algorithm, the program first will have the user enter the five input items. It then will convert the two annual rates to monthly rates, and the term, which is stated in years, to months. The program then will use the periodic payment formula to calculate the two monthly car payments, and it will display the result of both calculations on the screen.

Notice that the periodic payment formula appears in Steps 5 and 6 in the algorithm. Rather than having to enter the code for such a complex formula two times in the program, it would be more efficient to enter the code once, in a value-returning function, which you will name **`calcPayment()`**. You then can have the program's **`main()`** function call the **`calcPayment()`** function twice: first to calculate and return the monthly payment if David finances the car through the credit union, and again to calculate and return the monthly payment if he finances through the car dealer. Each time the **`main()`** function calls the **`calcPayment()`** function, the **`main()`** function will need to pass the **`calcPayment()`** function the appropriate information. Figure 4-17 shows the revised IPO chart for the program's **`main()`** function, and Figure 4-18 shows the IPO chart for the **`calcPayment()`** function. (Changes made to the original IPO chart are shaded in Figure 4-17.)

Figure 4-17: Revised IPO chart for the program's `main()` function

Input	Processing	Output
car price rebate credit union rate (annual) dealer rate (annual) term (years)	Processing items: monthly credit union rate monthly dealer rate number of months Algorithm: 1. enter the car price, rebate, credit union rate, dealer rate, and term 2. calculate the monthly credit union rate by dividing the credit union rate by 12 3. calculate the monthly dealer rate by dividing the dealer rate by 12 4. calculate the number of months by multiplying the term by 12 5. calculate the credit union payment = calcPayment(car price - rebate, monthly credit union rate, number of months) 6. calculate the dealer payment = calcPayment(car price, monthly dealer rate, number of months) 7. display the credit union payment and the dealer payment	credit union payment dealer payment

the values of the items in parentheses will be passed to the **`calc-Payment`** function

Figure 4-18: IPO chart for the `calcPayment()` function

Input	Processing	Output
principal monthly rate number of months	Processing items: none Algorithm: 1. calculate the monthly payment = principal * monthly rate / (1 - (monthly rate + 1)$^{-number\ of\ months}$) 2. return the monthly payment	monthly payment

Notice that the `calcPayment()` function's output is the monthly payment. Also notice that the function needs to know three items of information to calculate the monthly payment: the principal, monthly rate, and number of months. The values of these items will be passed to the `calcPayment()` function by the `main()` function, as indicated in the shaded steps shown in Figure 4-17. For example, when calling the `calcPayment()` function to calculate the credit union payment, the `main()` function will pass the difference between the car price and the rebate as the principal; it also will pass the monthly credit union rate and the number of months. Likewise, when calling the `calcPayment()` function to calculate the dealer payment, the `main()` function will pass the car price as the principal, and also the monthly dealer rate and the number of months.

Recall that you should desk-check an algorithm several times before you begin coding it. In this case, you will use the following two sets of data to desk-check the algorithms shown in Figures 4-17 and 4-18:

Data for first desk-check		Data for second desk-check	
Principal:	16000	Principal:	18000
Rebate:	3000	Rebate:	2000
Credit union rate:	.08	Credit union rate:	.09
Dealer rate:	.03	Dealer rate:	.02
Term (years):	4	Term (years):	5

Figure 4-19 shows the completed desk-check table. (The payment amounts in the figure are shown rounded to two decimal places.)

Figure 4-19: Completed desk-check table for the algorithms shown in Figures 4-17 and 4-18

`main()` function

car price	rebate	credit union rate	dealer rate	term	monthly credit union rate	monthly dealer rate	number of months	credit union payment	dealer payment
~~16000~~	~~3000~~	~~.08~~	~~.03~~	~~4~~	~~.007~~	~~.0025~~	~~48~~	~~317.37~~	~~354.15~~
18000	2000	.09	.02	5	.0075	.002	60	332.13	315.50

rounded up from .00666

rounded up from .001666

`calcPayment()` function

principal	monthly rate	number of months	monthly payment
~~16000~~	~~.007~~	~~48~~	~~317.37~~
~~16000~~	~~.0025~~	~~48~~	~~354.15~~
~~18000~~	~~.0075~~	~~60~~	~~332.13~~
18000	.002	60	315.50

tip

Although you can calculate the payment amounts using a calculator, it's easier to calculate them using a spreadsheet program, such as Microsoft Excel. For example, you can calculate the dealer payment for the first desk-check by entering the formula =16000*0.0025/(1 -(0.0025+1)^-48) into an Excel spreadsheet.

After desk-checking the algorithm to verify its accuracy, you are ready to translate it into a language the computer can understand. You begin by coding the program's `main()` function.

Coding the `main()` Function

First determine how many memory locations the `main()` function needs to reserve. In this case, the `main()` function requires 10 memory locations to store the values of its input, processing, and output items. You will store the values in variables, because the values will be different each time the program is executed. You will use the `int` data type for the variables that store the car price, rebate, term, and number of months, which are whole numbers. You will use the `double` data type for the variables that store the interest rates and monthly payments, which will contain a decimal place. Figure 4-20 shows the C++ statements that you will use to reserve the 10 variables in the `main()` function.

tip

The variables shown in Figure 4-20 are local to the `main()` function and remain in memory until the `main()` function's `return` statement is processed.

Figure 4-20: C++ statements to reserve variables in the `main()` function

IPO chart information	C++ instructions
Input	
car price	`int carPrice = 0;`
rebate	`int rebate = 0;`
credit union rate (annual)	`double creditRate = 0.0;`
dealer rate (annual)	`double dealerRate = 0.0;`
term (years)	`int term = 0;`
Processing	
monthly credit union rate	`double mthCreditRate = 0.0;`
monthly dealer rate	`double mthDealerRate = 0.0;`
number of months	`int numMonths = 0;`
Output	
credit union payment	`double creditPay = 0.0;`
dealer payment	`double dealerPay = 0.0;`

Now you can begin translating the `main()` function's algorithm into C++ statements. Figure 4-21 shows the C++ statements corresponding to the first four steps in the algorithm.

Figure 4-21: C++ statements corresponding to the first four steps in the main( ) function's algorithm

IPO chart information	C++ instructions
Input	
car price	`int carPrice = 0;`
rebate	`int rebate = 0;`
credit union rate (annual)	`double creditRate = 0.0;`
dealer rate (annual)	`double dealerRate = 0.0;`
term (years)	`int term = 0;`
Processing	
monthly credit union rate	`double mthCreditRate = 0.0;`
monthly dealer rate	`double mthDealerRate = 0.0;`
number of months	`int numMonths = 0;`
Output	
credit union payment	`double creditPay = 0.0;`
dealer payment	`double dealerPay = 0.0;`
Algorithm	

1. enter the car price, rebate, credit union rate, dealer rate, and term	`Console::Write("Enter the car price: ");`
	`carPrice = Convert::ToInt32(Console::ReadLine());`
	`Console::Write("Enter the rebate: ");`
	`rebate = Convert::ToInt32(Console::ReadLine());`
	`Console::Write("Enter the credit union rate: ");`
	`creditRate = Convert::ToDouble (Console::ReadLine());`
	`Console::Write("Enter the dealer rate: ");`
	`dealerRate = Convert::ToDouble (Console::ReadLine());`
	`Console::Write("Enter the term (years): ");`
	`term = Convert::ToInt32(Console::ReadLine());`

2. calculate the monthly credit union rate by dividing the credit union rate by 12	`mthCreditRate = creditRate / 12;`
3. calculate the monthly dealer rate by dividing the dealer rate by 12	`mthDealerRate = dealerRate / 12;`
4. calculate the number of months by multiplying the term by 12	`numMonths = term * 12;`

The appropriate statement to use for the fifth step in the algorithm is `creditPay = calcPayment(carPrice - rebate, mthCreditRate, numMonths);`. The statement calls the `calcPayment()` function, passing it the information needed to calculate the credit union payment. It assigns the value returned by the `calcPayment()` function to the `main()` function's `creditPay` variable.

The sixth step in the algorithm is to call the `calcPayment()` function again—this time passing it the information needed to calculate the dealer payment. The statement should assign the value returned by the function to the `main()` function's `dealerPay` variable. The appropriate statement to use in this case is `dealerPay = calcPayment(carPrice, mthDealerRate, numMonths);`.

tip

Recall that the items of information within parentheses in a function call are called actual arguments.

The last step in the `main()` function's algorithm is to display the monthly payments, which are stored in the `creditPay` and `dealerPay` variables, on the screen; you can use the `Console::WriteLine()` method to do so. Figure 4-22 shows the C++ code corresponding to the `main()` function's algorithm.

Figure 4-22: C++ instructions for the `main()` function

IPO chart information	C++ instructions
Input	
car price	`int carPrice = 0;`
rebate	`int rebate = 0;`
credit union rate (annual)	`double creditRate = 0.0;`
dealer rate (annual)	`double dealerRate = 0.0;`
term (years)	`int term = 0;`
Processing	
monthly credit union rate	`double mthCreditRate = 0.0;`
monthly dealer rate	`double mthDealerRate = 0.0;`
number of months	`int numMonths = 0;`
Output	
credit union payment	`double creditPay = 0.0;`
dealer payment	`double dealerPay = 0.0;`
Algorithm	

1. enter the car price, rebate, credit union rate, dealer rate, and term	`Console::Write("Enter the car price: ");`
	`carPrice = Convert::ToInt32(Console::ReadLine());`
	`Console::Write("Enter the rebate: ");`
	`rebate = Convert::ToInt32(Console::ReadLine());`
	`Console::Write("Enter the credit union rate: ");`
	`creditRate = Convert::ToDouble(Console::ReadLine());`
	`Console::Write("Enter the dealer rate: ");`
	`dealerRate = Convert::ToDouble(Console::ReadLine());`
	`Console::Write("Enter the term (years): ");`
	`term = Convert::ToInt32(Console::ReadLine());`

2. calculate the monthly credit union rate by dividing the credit union rate by 12	`mthCreditRate = creditRate / 12;`
3. calculate the monthly dealer rate by dividing the dealer rate by 12	`mthDealerRate = dealerRate / 12;`
4. calculate the number of months by multiplying the term by 12	`numMonths = term * 12;`
5. calculate the credit union payment = calcPayment(car price – rebate, monthly credit union rate, number of months)	`creditPay = calcPayment(carPrice – rebate,` `mthCreditRate, numMonths);`
6. calculate the dealer payment = calcPayment(car price, monthly dealer rate, number of months)	`dealerPay = calcPayment(carPrice, mthDealerRate,` `numMonths);`

7. display the credit union payment and the dealer payment	`Console::WriteLine("Credit union payment: {0}",`
	`Convert::ToString(creditPay));`
	`Console::WriteLine("Dealer payment: {0}",`
	`Convert::ToString(dealerPay));`

Next, you code the `calcPayment()` function.

Coding the calcPayment() Function

As the IPO chart shown earlier in Figure 4-18 indicates, the **calcPayment()** function requires four memory locations: three for the input items and one for the output item. The values of the input items—principal, monthly rate, and number of months—are passed to the **calcPayment()** function when the function is called by the **main()** function. Recall that when you pass variables to a function *by value*, which is the default way variables are passed in C++, the function stores the value of each item it receives in a separate memory location. The name and data type of the memory locations that a function uses to store the information it receives are listed in the function's *parameterList*, which appears in the function header. In this case, you need to list three variables in the **calcPayment()** function's *parameterList*: an **int** variable to store the principal, a **double** variable to store the monthly rate, and an **int** variable to store the number of months.

tip

Recall that the data type and sequence of the formal parameters in a function's *parameterList* must match the data type and sequence of the actual arguments passed to the function and listed in the *argumentList*.

Unlike the **calcPayment()** function's input items, the value of its output item (monthly payment) is not passed by the **main()** function. Instead, the value is calculated in the **calcPayment()** function itself, and then returned to the **main()** function. You will store the calculated value in a **double** variable, because the value might contain a decimal place and will change each time the function is called.

Figure 4-23 shows the function header and statement that you will use to reserve the four variables required by the **calcPayment()** function. Notice that the IPO chart's input items, which are passed to the **calcPayment()** function, appear in the function header. Also notice that the function's data type is the same as the data type of the value returned by the function: **double**.

Figure 4-23: Function header and C++ statement to reserve variables in the calcPayment() function

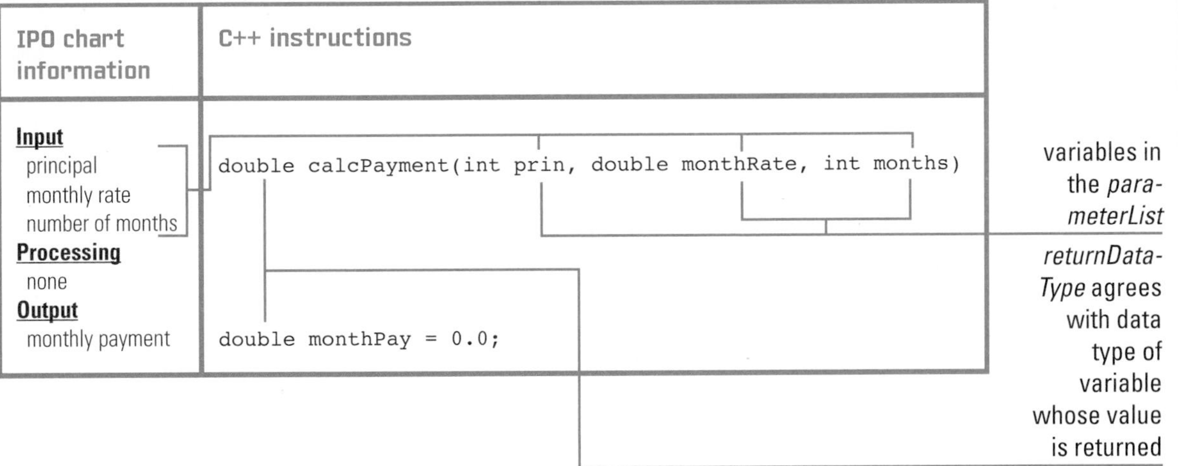

tip

The variables shown in Figure 4-23 are local to the calcPayment() function and remain in memory until the function's return statement is processed.

According to the **calcPayment()** function's algorithm, the function should calculate the monthly payment, and then return the monthly payment to the **main()** function. Before you can complete the **calcPayment()** function, you need to learn about the **Math::Pow()** method, which you will use in the statement that calculates the monthly payment amounts.

The `Math::Pow()` Method

You use the **`Math::Pow()` method** to raise a number to a power—in other words, to perform exponentiation—and then return the result. Figure 4-24 shows the syntax of the `Math::Pow()` method and includes examples of using the method in a C++ statement.

Figure 4-24: Syntax and examples of the `Math::Pow()` method

Syntax	Return value
Math::Pow(*x*, *y*)	*x* raised to the *y* power
C++ statement	**Results**

`cube = Math::Pow(4, 3);`
`Console::Write(Math::Pow(100, .5));`
`Console::Write(10 * Math::Pow(2, 4));`
	the number 64 assigned to the `cube` variable
	the number 10 displayed on the screen
	the number 160 displayed on the screen

tip

As you learned in Tutorial 3, `Math::Pow()` indicates that the `Pow()` method is contained in the `Math` class. The `Math` class comes with Visual C++ .NET.

The `cube = Math::Pow(4, 3);` statement shown in Figure 4-24 first raises the number four to the third power—in other words, it multiplies the number four by itself three times (4 * 4 * 4). The statement assigns the result (64) to the `cube` variable.

The second statement shown in Figure 4-24, `Console::Write(Math::Pow(100, .5));`, raises a number—in this case, 100—to the .5 power, which is the same as finding the square root of the number. The statement will display the number 10 on the computer screen.

The last statement shown in Figure 4-24, `Console::Write(10 * Math::Pow(2, 4));`, raises the number two to the fourth power. It then multiplies the result (16) by 10, and then displays the product (160) on the computer screen.

You will need to use the `Math::Pow()` method in the `calcPayment()` function, because the formula for calculating the monthly payment amounts involves exponentiation. (Recall that the formula, shown earlier in Figure 4-15, requires you to raise a number to the –term power.) The appropriate C++ statement to use for calculating the monthly payment amounts is `monthPay = prin * monthRate / (1 – Math::Pow(monthRate + 1, -months));`.

The last statement in the `calcPayment()` function will be `return monthPay;`. This statement returns the monthly payment amount to the `main()` function. Figure 4-25 shows the C++ instructions for the `calcPayment()` function's code.

Figure 4-25: C++ instructions for the calcPayment() function

IPO chart information	C++ instructions

Input
principal
monthly rate
number of months
Processing
none
Output
monthly payment
	`double calcPayment(int prin, double monthRate, int months)`
	
	`double monthPay = 0.0;`

Algorithm
1. calculate the monthly payment = principal * monthly rate / (1 – (monthly rate + 1)$^{-months}$)
2. return the monthly payment
	`monthPay = prin * monthRate / (1 – Math::Pow (monthRate + 1, -months));`
	
	`return monthPay;`

After coding the algorithm, you then need to desk-check the program, using the same data you used to desk-check the algorithm. Figure 4-26 shows the data and the completed desk-check table for the program. The payment amounts are shown rounded to two decimal places.

Figure 4-26: Data and completed desk-check table for the program

Data for first desk-check		Data for second desk-check	
Principal:	16000	Principal:	18000
Rebate:	3000	Rebate:	2000
Credit union rate:	.08	Credit union rate:	.09
Dealer rate:	.03	Dealer rate:	.02
Term (years):	4	Term (years):	5

Desk-check table
main() function's variables

carPrice	rebate	creditRate	dealerRate	term
~~0~~	~~0~~	~~0.0~~	~~0.0~~	~~0~~
~~16000~~	~~3000~~	~~.08~~	~~.03~~	~~4~~
~~0~~	~~0~~	~~0.0~~	~~0.0~~	~~0~~
18000	2000	.09	.02	5

Figure 4-26: Data and completed desk-check table for the program (continued)

mthCreditRate	mthDealerRate	numMonths	creditPay	dealerPay
~~0.0~~ ~~.007~~ ~~0.0~~ .0075	~~0.0~~ ~~.0025~~ ~~0.0~~ .002	~~0~~ ~~48~~ ~~0~~ 60	~~0.0~~ ~~317.37~~ ~~0.0~~ 332.13	~~0.0~~ ~~354.15~~ ~~0.0~~ 315.50

`calcPayment()` function's variables

prin	monthRate	months	monthPay
~~16000~~ ~~16000~~ ~~18000~~ 18000	~~.007~~ ~~.0025~~ ~~.0075~~ .002	~~48~~ ~~48~~ ~~60~~ 60	~~0.0~~ ~~317.37~~ ~~0.0~~ ~~354.15~~ ~~0.0~~ ~~332.13~~ ~~0.0~~ 315.50

The results obtained when desk-checking the program agree with the results obtained when desk-checking the algorithm. You now are ready to enter the C++ instructions into the computer.

Completing the David Liu Program

On your computer's hard disk is a partially completed C++ program that contains most of the instructions shown in Figure 4-22. You open that program in the next set of steps.

To open the partially completed C++ program:

1. Start Microsoft Visual Studio .NET. If necessary, close the Start Page window.
2. Click **File** on the menu bar, and then click **Open Solution**. The Open Solution dialog box opens.
3. Locate and then open the **CppNet\Tut04\T4App Solution** folder.
4. Click **T4App Solution** (T4App Solution.sln) in the list of filenames, and then click the **Open** button.
5. If the T4App.cpp source file is not displayed, right-click **T4App.cpp** in the Solution Explorer window, and then click **Open**. Figure 4-27 shows the instructions contained in the partially completed T4App.cpp program.

Figure 4-27: Instructions contained in the partially completed T4App.cpp program

```
//T4App.cpp
//displays monthly payments

#using <mscorlib.dll>
using namespace System;

int main()
{
    int carPrice          = 0;
    int rebate            = 0;
    double creditRate     = 0.0;
    double dealerRate     = 0.0;
    int term              = 0;
    double mthCreditRate = 0.0;
    double mthDealerRate = 0.0;
    int numMonths         = 0;
    double creditPay      = 0.0;
    double dealerPay      = 0.0;

    //enter input items
    Console::Write("Enter the car price: ");
    carPrice = Convert::ToInt32(Console::ReadLine());
    Console::Write("Enter the rebate: ");
    rebate = Convert::ToInt32(Console::ReadLine());
    Console::Write("Enter the credit union rate: ");
    creditRate = Convert::ToDouble(Console::ReadLine());
    Console::Write("Enter the dealer rate: ");
    dealerRate = Convert::ToDouble(Console::ReadLine());
    Console::Write("Enter the term (years): ");
    term = Convert::ToInt32(Console::ReadLine());

    //convert annual rates and term to monthly
    mthCreditRate = creditRate /12;
    mthDealerRate = dealerRate /12;
    numMonths = term * 12;

    //calculate monthly payments

    //display monthly payments
    Console::WriteLine("Credit union payment: {0}",
    Convert::ToString(creditPay));
    Console::WriteLine("Dealer payment: {0}",
    Convert::ToString(dealerPay));

    return 0;
}   //end of main function

//*****function definitions*****
```

function calls are missing

function definition is missing

Help? The T4App.cpp file is contained in the Source Files folder in the T4App Project.

Help? You will need to scroll down the T4App.cpp window to view all of its instructions.

Missing from the program are the statements that call the `calcPayment()` function and the `calcPayment()` function definition. You enter the missing instructions in the next set of steps, and then you test the program to verify that it is working correctly.

To enter the missing instructions, then test the program:

1. Position the insertion point in the blank line below the `//calculate monthly payments` comment.

   First enter the two function calls.

2. Press **Tab**, if necessary, then type **creditPay = calcPayment(carPrice - rebate, mthCreditRate, numMonths);** and press **Enter**.
3. Type **dealerPay = calcPayment(carPrice, mthDealerRate, numMonths);** and press **Enter**.

   Next, enter the `calcPayment()` function definition. Most C++ programmers enter the definitions of functions below the `main()` function in the program.

4. Position the insertion point in the blank line below the `//*****function definitions*****` comment.

   First enter the function header.

5. Type **double calcPayment(int prin, double monthRate, int months)** and press **Enter**.

   Next, enter the function body.

6. Type the additional lines of code shaded in Figure 4-28, which shows the completed function definition for the `calcPayment()` function.

tip

To make the program easier to read, use a comment, such as `//***** function definitions *****`, to separate the function definitions from the `main()` function.

tip

Recall that the function header does not end with a semicolon, because it is not considered a statement in C++.

Figure 4-28: Function definition for the `calcPayment()` function

```
//*****function definitions*****
double calcPayment(int prin, double monthRate,
int months)
{
    //calculates and returns a monthly payment
    double monthPay = 0.0;
    monthPay = prin * monthRate /
    (1 - Math::Pow(monthRate + 1, -months));
    return monthPay;
}   //end of calcPayment function
```

enter these six lines of code

7. Save and then build the solution. The Task List window indicates that the compiler found errors in the program.
8. Double-click the first error message. See Figure 4-29.

Figure 4-29: Screen showing that the compiler found errors in the program

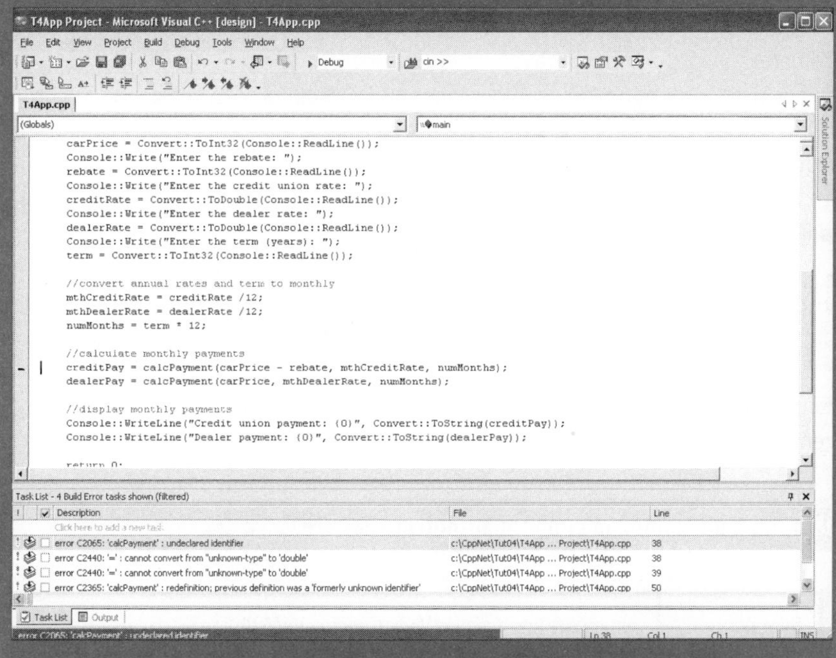

When you double-click an error message in the Task List window, the Visual C++ editor displays an arrow at the location where the error was encountered in the program. In this case, the arrow is pointing to the statement that calculates the credit union payment. The error message indicates that 'calcPayment', which is used in that statement, is an undeclared identifier (name). This means that the compiler does not recognize the function name. Close the Task List and Output windows before learning about this error.

9. Close the Task List and Output windows, and then scroll up the T4App.cpp window to view the beginning of the program.

tip

Do not be overwhelmed by the number of errors that might appear in the Task List window. Begin by correcting the first error, then save and build the solution again. Usually you will find that correcting one error corrects many of the errors that follow it.

Before you can call a function in C++, you first must either define it or declare it. You define a function with a function definition, and you declare it with a function prototype, which you learn about in the next section. One way to fix the undeclared identifier problem in the current program is to move the `calcPayment()` function definition to a location above the `main()` function, so that it appears before the function call in the `creditPay = calcPayment(carPrice - rebate, mthCreditRate, numMonths);` statement. When you enter a function definition above the `main()` function, the computer does not process the statements within the function until the function is called. Instead, the computer merely remembers the function's name and the data type of its formal parameters so that calling the function later in the program will not produce the undeclared identifier error.

Another way to fix the undeclared identifier problem in the current program is to leave the function definition in its current location below the `main()` function, and then declare the function by entering a function prototype above the `main()` function.

tip

Recall that the execution of a C++ program always begins with the `main()` function.

Using a Function Prototype

You declare a function by using a **function prototype**, which is simply a statement that specifies the function's name, the data type of its return value (if any), and the data type of each of its formal parameters. A program will have one function prototype for each function defined below the `main()` function. You usually place the function prototypes at the beginning of the program, after the `#using` and `using` directives.

A function prototype alerts the compiler that the function will be defined later in the program. It may help to think of the function prototypes in a program as being similar to the table of contents in a book. Each prototype, like each entry in a table of contents, is simply a preview of what will be expanded on later in the program (or in the book). In the programs you will create in the tutorials in this book, you will place the function definitions after the `main()` function, and then use function prototypes to declare the functions above the `main()` function.

tip If the function definition appears above the `main()` function in a program, then you do not need to include a function prototype for the function. The function prototype is necessary only when the function is defined after the `main()` function.

Figure 4-30 shows the syntax of a function prototype. It also shows the function prototype for the current program's `calcPayment()` function.

Figure 4-30: Syntax and an example of a function prototype

Syntax:	*returnDataType functionName*(**[***parameterList***]**);
Example:	`double calcPayment(int, double, int);`

only the data types of the formal parameters are necessary

If you compare the function prototype shown in Figure 4-30 to the function header shown in Figure 4-28, you will notice two differences: First, the function prototype ends with a semicolon, whereas the function header does not. Second, the function header contains both the data type and name of each formal parameter, but the function prototype contains only the data type.

tip Some programmers also include the name of each formal parameter in the function prototype, but this is optional.

Now enter the function prototype for the `calcPayment()` function, and then test the program using the same data you used to desk-check the algorithm and program.

To enter the function prototype, and then test the program:

1. In the blank line below the `using namespace System;` directive, press **Enter**, then type **//function prototype** and press **Enter**.
2. Type **double calcPayment(int, double, int);** and press **Enter**. Figure 4-31 shows the completed T4App.cpp program.

Figure 4-31: Completed T4App.cpp program

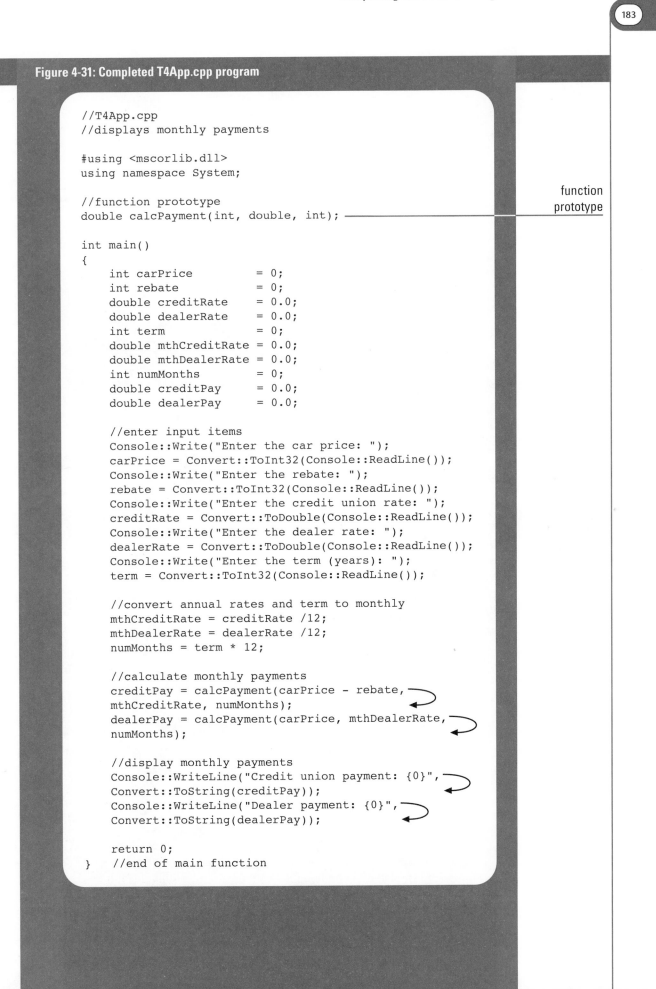

```
//T4App.cpp
//displays monthly payments

#using <mscorlib.dll>
using namespace System;

//function prototype
double calcPayment(int, double, int);

int main()
{
    int carPrice          = 0;
    int rebate            = 0;
    double creditRate     = 0.0;
    double dealerRate     = 0.0;
    int term              = 0;
    double mthCreditRate = 0.0;
    double mthDealerRate = 0.0;
    int numMonths         = 0;
    double creditPay      = 0.0;
    double dealerPay      = 0.0;

    //enter input items
    Console::Write("Enter the car price: ");
    carPrice = Convert::ToInt32(Console::ReadLine());
    Console::Write("Enter the rebate: ");
    rebate = Convert::ToInt32(Console::ReadLine());
    Console::Write("Enter the credit union rate: ");
    creditRate = Convert::ToDouble(Console::ReadLine());
    Console::Write("Enter the dealer rate: ");
    dealerRate = Convert::ToDouble(Console::ReadLine());
    Console::Write("Enter the term (years): ");
    term = Convert::ToInt32(Console::ReadLine());

    //convert annual rates and term to monthly
    mthCreditRate = creditRate /12;
    mthDealerRate = dealerRate /12;
    numMonths = term * 12;

    //calculate monthly payments
    creditPay = calcPayment(carPrice - rebate,
    mthCreditRate, numMonths);
    dealerPay = calcPayment(carPrice, mthDealerRate,
    numMonths);

    //display monthly payments
    Console::WriteLine("Credit union payment: {0}",
    Convert::ToString(creditPay));
    Console::WriteLine("Dealer payment: {0}",
    Convert::ToString(dealerPay));

    return 0;
}   //end of main function
```

function prototype

Figure 4-31: Completed T4App.cpp program (continued)

```
//*****function definitions*****
double calcPayment(int prin, double monthRate,
int months)
{
    //calculates and returns a monthly payment
    double monthPay = 0.0;
    monthPay = prin * monthRate /
    (1 - Math::Pow(monthRate + 1, -months));
    return monthPay;
}   //end of calcPayment function
```

3. Save and then build the solution. This time the undeclared identifier error does not occur, because the function prototype declares the `calcPayment()` function before the function is called in the program.
4. Verify that the program generated no warnings.
5. Close the Output window, then execute the program. The "Enter the car price: " prompt appears in the Command Prompt window. Type **16000** and press **Enter**. When prompted for the rebate, type **3000** and press **Enter**.
6. When prompted for the credit union rate, type **.08** and press **Enter**. When prompted for the dealer rate, type **.03** and press **Enter**.
7. When prompted for the term, type **4** and press **Enter**. The program calculates and displays the two monthly payments, as shown in Figure 4-32.

Figure 4-32: Command Prompt window showing the results of the first test

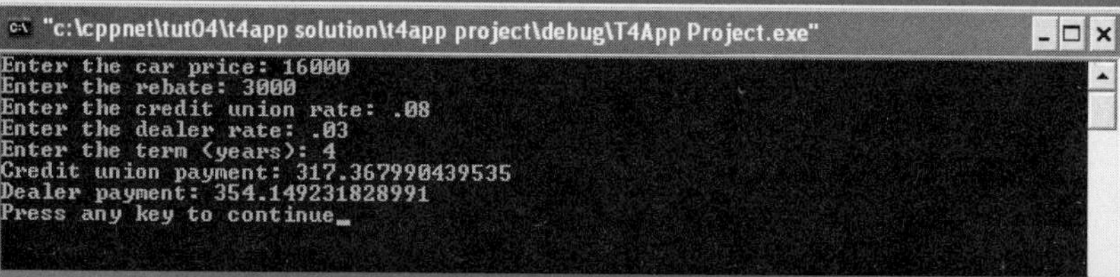

The Command Prompt window shows that the monthly payments are approximately 317.37 and 354.15, which agree with the results shown earlier in the desk-check tables. In this case, it would be better for David to take the dealer's rebate and finance the car through the credit union.

8. Press **Enter** to close the Command Prompt window.
9. Execute the program again. Enter **18000** as the car price, **2000** as the rebate, **.09** as the credit union rate, **.02** as the dealer rate, and **5** as the term.

   The Command Prompt window shows that the monthly payments are approximately 332.13 and 315.50, which agree with the results shown earlier in the desk-check tables. In this case, it would be better for David to finance the car through the dealer.
10. Press **Enter** to close the Command Prompt window, then close the Output window.

Although the current program is working correctly, the message it displays would look more professional if the monthly payment amounts were rounded to two decimal places and included a dollar sign. In the next section, you learn how to format a program's numeric output.

Formatting Numeric Output

Numbers representing monetary amounts typically are displayed with either zero or two decimal places and usually include a dollar sign and a thousand separator. Similarly, numbers representing percentage amounts usually are displayed with zero or more decimal places and a percent sign. Specifying the number of decimal places and the special characters to display in a number is called **formatting**. You format a number using the syntax *variablename*.**ToString(*formatString*)**, where *variablename* is the name of a numeric variable, and *formatString* is a string that specifies the format you want to use. The *formatString* argument, which must be enclosed in double quotation marks, takes the form *Axx*, where *A* is an alphabetic character called the **format specifier**, and *xx* is a sequence of digits called the **precision specifier**. The format specifier must be one of the built-in format characters; the most commonly used format characters are listed in Figure 4-33. The precision specifier controls the number of significant digits or zeros to the right of the decimal point in the formatted number.

Figure 4-33: Most commonly used format specifiers

Format specifier	Name	Description
C or c	Currency	displays a number with a dollar sign; the precision specifier indicates the desired number of decimal places; if appropriate, displays a number with a thousand separator; negative numbers are enclosed in parentheses
D or d	Decimal	formats only integers; the precision specifier indicates the minimum number of digits desired; if required, the number is padded with zeros to its left to produce the number of digits specified by the precision specifier; if appropriate, displays a number with a thousand separator; negative numbers are preceded by a minus sign
F or f	Fixed-point	the precision specifier indicates the desired number of decimal places; negative numbers are preceded by a minus sign
N or n	Number	the precision specifier indicates the desired number of decimal places; if appropriate, displays a number with a thousand separator; negative numbers are preceded by a minus sign
P or p	Percent	the precision specifier indicates the desired number of decimal places; multiplies the number by 100 and displays the number with a percent sign; negative numbers are preceded by a minus sign

Notice that you can use either an uppercase letter or a lowercase letter as the format specifier. Figure 4-34 shows examples of how various *formatString*s format numeric values.

Figure 4-34: Examples of how various *formatStrings* format numeric values

formatString	Value	Result
C	3764	$3,764.00
C0	3764	$3,764
C2	3764	$3,764.00
C2	456.783	$456.78
C2	456.785	$456.79
C2	-75.31	($75.31)
D	3764	3764
D	-53	-53
D3	8	008
D3	15	015
F	3764	3764.00
F0	3764	3764
F2	3764	3764.00
F2	456.783	456.78
F2	456.785	456.79
F2	-75.31	-75.31
N	3764	3,764.00
N0	3764	3,764
N2	3764	3,764.00
N2	456.783	456.78
N2	456.785	456.79
N2	-75.31	-75.31
P	.364	36.40 %
P	-.05	-5.00 %
P1	.3645	36.5 %
P2	1.1	110.00%

tip

To learn how to create custom *formatStrings*, click Help on the menu bar, and then click Index. Click Visual C++ and Related in the Filtered by list box, then type *custom numeric format strings* in the Look for text box, and then press Enter.

tip

You also can use the `Math::Round()` method to round a number to zero or more decimal places. You can experiment with the `Math::Round()` method by completing Discovery Exercise 8 at the end of this lesson.

You will use the "C2" *formatString* to format the monthly payment amounts in the current program to Currency with two decimal places.

To format the monthly payment amounts:

1. In the statement that displays the credit union payment, change `Convert::ToString(creditPay)` to **creditPay.ToString("C2")**.
2. In the statement that displays the car dealer payment, change `Convert::ToString(dealerPay)` to **dealerPay.ToString("C2")**. See Figure 4-35.

Figure 4-35: Program showing modified `Console::WriteLine()` statements

modified code

```
//display monthly payments
Console::WriteLine("Credit union payment: {0}", creditPay.ToString("C2"));
Console::WriteLine("Dealer payment: {0}", dealerPay.ToString("C2"));
```

3. Save and then build the solution. Verify that the program generated no warnings.
4. Execute the program.
5. When the "Enter the car price: " prompt appears in the Command Prompt window, type **16000** and press **Enter**. When prompted for the rebate, type **3000** and press **Enter**.
6. When prompted for the credit union rate, type **.08** and press **Enter**. When prompted for the dealer rate, type **.03** and press **Enter**.
7. When prompted for the term, type **4** and press **Enter**. The program calculates the two monthly payments and displays them using the "C2" format, as shown in Figure 4-36.

Figure 4-36: Command Prompt window showing the formatted monthly payment amounts

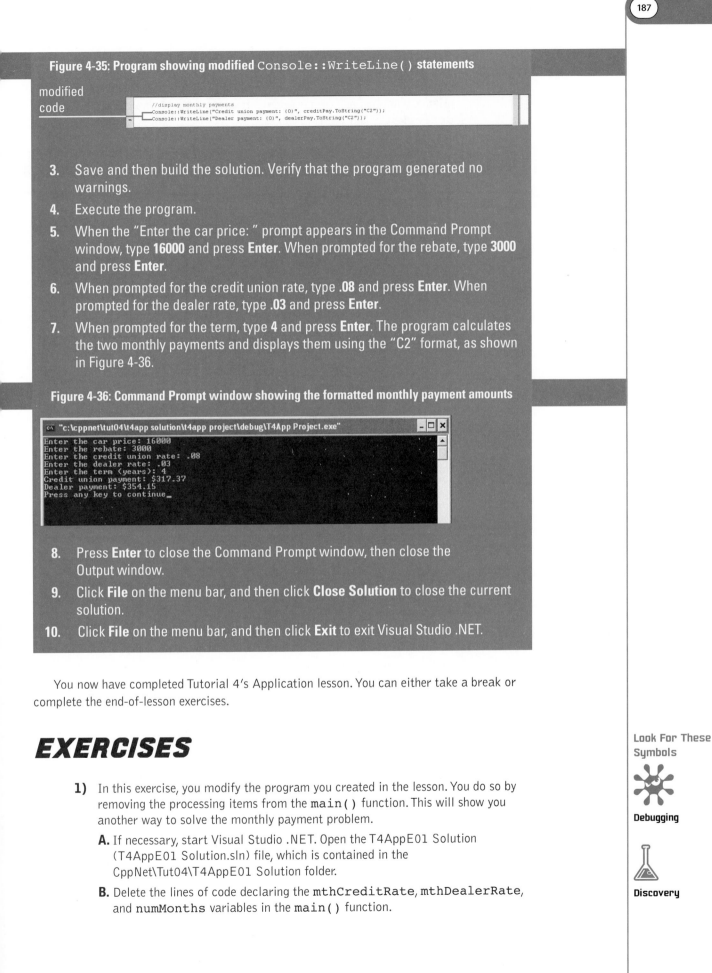

```
"c:\cppnet\tut04\t4app solution\t4app project\debug\T4App Project.exe"
Enter the car price: 16000
Enter the rebate: 3000
Enter the credit union rate: .08
Enter the dealer rate: .03
Enter the term (years): 4
Credit union payment: $317.37
Dealer payment: $354.15
Press any key to continue_
```

8. Press **Enter** to close the Command Prompt window, then close the Output window.
9. Click **File** on the menu bar, and then click **Close Solution** to close the current solution.
10. Click **File** on the menu bar, and then click **Exit** to exit Visual Studio .NET.

You now have completed Tutorial 4's Application lesson. You can either take a break or complete the end-of-lesson exercises.

EXERCISES

Look For These Symbols

Debugging

Discovery

1) In this exercise, you modify the program you created in the lesson. You do so by removing the processing items from the `main()` function. This will show you another way to solve the monthly payment problem.

A. If necessary, start Visual Studio .NET. Open the T4AppE01 Solution (T4AppE01 Solution.sln) file, which is contained in the CppNet\Tut04\T4AppE01 Solution folder.

B. Delete the lines of code declaring the `mthCreditRate`, `mthDealerRate`, and `numMonths` variables in the `main()` function.

C. Modify the `main()` function according to the revised IPO chart shown in Figure 4-37. The revisions are shaded in the figure. (*Hint*: Rather than using processing items for the monthly rates and term, you can perform the appropriate calculation and then assign the result to the `creditRate`, `dealerRate`, and `term` variables.)

Figure 4-37

Input	Processing	Output
car price rebate credit union rate (annual) dealer rate (annual) term (years)	Processing items: none Algorithm: 1. enter the car price, rebate, credit union rate, dealer rate, and term 2. convert the credit union rate to monthly by dividing the rate by 12 3. convert the dealer rate to monthly by dividing the rate by 12 4. convert the term to months by multiplying the term by 12 5. calculate the credit union payment = calcPayment(car price - rebate, credit union rate, term) 6. calculate the dealer payment = calcPayment(car price, dealer rate, term) 7. display the credit union payment and the dealer payment	credit union payment dealer payment

D. Save and then build the solution.

E. Execute the program. Enter 20000 as the car price, 2500 as the rebate, .07 as the credit union rate, .025 as the dealer rate, and 4 as the term. Is it better to finance the car through the credit union or through the car dealer?

F. When the program is working correctly, close the Output window, and then use the File menu to close the solution.

2) In this exercise, you create a program that converts a Fahrenheit temperature to a Celsius temperature.

A. If necessary, start Visual Studio .NET. Open the T4AppE02 Solution (T4AppE02 Solution.sln) file, which is contained in the CppNet\Tut04\T4AppE02 Solution folder.

B. Use the IPO charts shown in Figure 4-38 to complete the program. Notice that the program contains three functions: `main()`, `getFahrenheit()`, and `calcCelsius()`. Display the Celsius temperature as an integer.

C. Complete a desk-check table for the program, using the following Fahrenheit temperatures: 32 F and 212 F.

D. Save and then build the solution.

E. Execute the program. Use the data from Step C to test the program.

F. When the program is working correctly, close the Output window, and then use the File menu to close the solution.

Figure 4-38

`main()` function

Input	Processing	Output
Fahrenheit temperature	Processing items: none Algorithm: 1. Fahrenheit temperature = getFahrenheit() 2. Celsius temperature = calcCelsius(Fahrenheit temperature) 3. display the Celsius temperature	Celsius temperature

`getFahrenheit()` function

Input	Processing	Output
	Processing items: Fahrenheit temperature Algorithm: 1. enter the Fahrenheit temperature 2. return the Fahrenheit temperature	Fahrenheit temperature

`calcCelsius()` function

Input	Processing	Output
Fahrenheit temperature	Processing items: none Algorithm: 1. Celsius temperature = 5.0 / 9.0 * (Fahrenheit temperature - 32) 2. return the Celsius temperature	Celsius temperature

3) In this exercise, you create a program that displays a bonus.

A. If necessary, start Visual Studio .NET. Open the T4AppE03 Solution (T4AppE03 Solution.sln) file, which is contained in the CppNet\Tut04\T4AppE03 Solution folder.

B. Use the IPO charts shown in Figure 4-39 to complete the program. Notice that the program contains three functions: `main()`, `getSales()`, and `calcBonus()`. Display the bonus amount with two decimal places and a dollar sign.

Figure 4-39

`main()` function

Input	Processing	Output
sales	Processing items: none Algorithm: 1. sales = getSales() 2. bonus = calcBonus(sales) 3. display the bonus	bonus

`getSales()` function

Input	Processing	Output
	Processing items: sales Algorithm: 1. enter the sales 2. return the sales	sales

`calcBonus()` function

Input	Processing	Output
sales	Processing items: none Algorithm: 1. bonus = sales * .1 2. return the bonus	bonus

C. Complete a desk-check table for the program, using the following sales amounts: 24,500 and 134,780.

D. Save and then build the solution.

E. Execute the program. Use the data from Step C to test the program.

F. When the program is working correctly, close the Output window, and then use the File menu to close the solution.

4) In this exercise, you modify the program you created in Tutorial 3's Application lesson by adding three additional value-returning functions to the program.

A. If necessary, start Visual Studio .NET. Open the T4AppE04 Solution (T4AppE04 Solution.sln) file, which is contained in the CppNet\Tut04\T4AppE04 Solution folder.

B. Modify the program so that it uses a function to calculate and return the perimeter, a function to calculate and return the area, and a function to calculate and return the number of rolls of wallpaper. Display the number of rolls as an integer.

C. Save and then build the solution.

D. Execute the program. Enter 10 as the room length, 12 as the room width, 8 as the ceiling height, and 30 as the single roll coverage. The number of rolls of wallpaper should be 12.

E. When the program is working correctly, close the Output window, and then use the File menu to close the solution.

5) In this exercise, you create a program that calculates the average of three test scores.

A. Write the IPO charts for a program that contains three value-returning functions: `main()`, `getTestScore()`, and `calcAverage()`. The `main()` function should call the `getTestScore()` function to get and return each of three test scores. The test scores may contain a decimal place. (*Hint*: The `main()` function will need to call the `getTestScore()` function three times.) The `main()` function then should call the `calcAverage()` function to calculate the average of the three test scores. When the `calcAverage()` function has completed its task, the `main()` function should display the average on the screen.

B. If necessary, start Visual Studio .NET. Create a blank solution named T4AppE05 Solution. Save the solution in the CppNet\Tut04 folder.

C. Add a new managed C++ empty project to the solution. Name the project T4AppE05 Project.

D. Add a new C++ source file to the project. Name the source file T4AppE05.

E. Enter the appropriate C++ instructions into the source file. Use the IPO charts you created in Step A to code the program. Display the average with one decimal place.

F. Complete a desk-check table for the program, using the following two groups of test scores:

95, 83, 76
54, 89, 77

G. Save and then build the solution.

H. Execute the program. Use the data from Step F to test the program.

I. When the program is working correctly, close the Output window, and then use the File menu to close the solution.

6) In this exercise, you create a program that displays an employee's gross pay.

A. Write the IPO charts for a program that contains four value-returning functions: `main()`, `getHoursWorked()`, `getPayRate ()`, and `calcGross()`. The `main()` function should call each function, and then display the gross pay on the computer screen. When coding the `calcGross()` function, you do not have to worry about overtime pay. You can assume that everyone works 40 or fewer hours per week. The hours worked and rate of pay may contain a decimal place.

B. If necessary, start Visual Studio .NET. Create a blank solution named T4AppE06 Solution. Save the solution in the CppNet\Tut04 folder.

C. Add a new managed C++ empty project to the solution. Name the project T4AppE06 Project.

D. Add a new C++ source file to the project. Name the source file T4AppE06.

E. Enter the appropriate C++ instructions into the source file. Use the IPO charts you created in Step A to code the program. Display the gross pay with a dollar sign and two decimal places.

F. Complete a desk-check table for the program, using the following two sets of data:

25.5 hours, $12 per hour
40 hours, $11.55 per hour

G. Save and then build the solution.

H. Execute the program. Use the data from Step F to test the program.

I. When the program is working correctly, close the Output window, and then use the File menu to close the solution.

7) In this exercise, you modify the program you created in the lesson so that it uses a function that does not return a value.

A. If necessary, start Visual Studio .NET. Open the T4AppE07 Solution (T4AppE07 Solution.sln) file, which is contained in the CppNet\Tut04\T4AppE07 Solution folder.

B. Create a function named `displayPayment()`. The function should accept a monthly payment, and then display the monthly payment on the screen. Unlike the functions you learned about in the tutorial, the `displayPayment()` function will not return a value. Functions that do not return a value have a *returnDataType* of `void`.

C. Enter the appropriate function prototype for the `displayPayment()` function.

D. Modify the `main()` function so that it calls the `displayPayment()` function to display each monthly payment.

E. Save and then build the solution.

F. Execute the program. Enter 9000 as the car price, 500 as the rebate, .09 as the credit union rate, .03 as the dealer rate, and 2 as the term. Is it better to finance the car through the credit union or through the car dealer?

G. When the program is working correctly, close the Output window, and then use the File menu to close the solution.

8) In this exercise, you modify the program you created in the lesson so that it uses the `Math::Round()` method to round the monthly payment amounts to two decimal places.

A. If necessary, start Visual Studio .NET. Open the T4AppE08 Solution (T4AppE08 Solution.sln) file, which is contained in the CppNet\Tut04\T4AppE08 Solution folder.

B. In the statement that displays the credit union payment, change `creditPay.ToString("C2")` to `Convert::ToString(creditPay)`.

C. In the statement that displays the car dealer payment, change `dealerPay.ToString("C2")` to `Convert::ToString(dealerPay)`.

You can use the `Math::Round()` method to round a numeric value to a specified number of decimal places. The syntax of the `Math::Round()` method is Math::Round(*x*[, *y*]), where *x* is the value you want to round and *y* (which is optional) is the number of decimal places.

D. Modify the program so that it uses the `Math::Round()` method to round the payment amounts to two decimal places.

E. Save and then build the solution.

F. Execute the program. Enter 15000 as the car price, 1500 as the rebate, .08 as the credit union rate, .02 as the dealer rate, and 5 as the term. Is it better to finance the car through the credit union or through the car dealer?

G. When the program is working correctly, close the Output window, and then use the File menu to close the solution.

9) In this exercise, you debug a C++ program.

A. Open the T4AppE09 Solution (T4AppE09 Solution.sln) file, which is contained in the CppNet\Tut04\T4AppE09 Solution folder. The program should calculate and display the miles per gallon, but it is not working correctly. Study the program's code, and then build the solution.

B. Correct any errors in the program, then save and build the solution again.

C. Execute the program. Enter 200 as the number of miles, and 15 as the number of gallons. The miles per gallon should be 13.3.

D. When the program is working correctly, close the Output window, and then use the File menu to close the solution.

Tutorial 5

Void Functions

Objectives

After completing this tutorial, you will be able to:

- Create and invoke a function that does not return a value
- Pass information, *by reference*, to a function
- Pass a `String` variable, *by value* and *by reference*, to a function

Concept Lesson

More About Functions

As you learned in Tutorial 4, programmers use functions for two reasons. First, functions allow the programmer to avoid duplicating code in different parts of a program. If a program needs to perform the same task several times, it is more efficient to enter the appropriate code once, in a function, and then simply call the function to perform its task when needed. Second, functions allow large and complex programs, which typically are written by a team of programmers, to be broken into small and manageable tasks; each member of the team is assigned one of the tasks to code as a function. When writing a payroll program, for example, one team member might code the function that calculates the federal withholding tax, while another might code the function that calculates the state income tax. When each programmer has completed his or her function, all of the functions then are gathered together into one program. The `main()` function in the program typically is responsible for calling each of the other functions when needed.

tip Any function, not just `main()`, can call another function.

tip You can use functions to streamline `main()`. By removing the detail from `main()` and leaving only the function names, which should be descriptive, the `main()` function provides an overview of the program.

Recall that all functions fall into one of two categories: value-returning or void. Value-returning functions return precisely one value to the statement that called the function. You learned how to create and invoke value-returning functions in Tutorial 4. Figure 5-1 shows the syntax and an example of creating a value-returning function in a C++ program.

Figure 5-1: Syntax and an example of creating and invoking a value-returning function in C++

Syntax

function header: *returnDataType functionName*(*[parameterList]*)

function body:
{
 one or more statements ending with a semicolon
 return *expression*;
}

Example

```
int main()
{
    double sales = 0.0;
    double tax   = 0.0;
    Console::Write("Enter the sales amount: ");
    sales = Convert::ToDouble(Console::ReadLine());
    tax = calcTax(sales);
    Console::WriteLine(tax.ToString("C2"));
    return 0;
}   //end of main function

//*****function definitions*****
double calcTax(double dollars)
{
    return dollars * .05;
}   //end of calcTax function
```

(function definition: the `calcTax` function above)

As indicated in the syntax shown in Figure 5-1, the function header for a value-returning function specifies the data type of the return value, as well as the function's name and any formal parameters. The function body contains the instructions necessary for the function to perform its assigned task. Recall that the last instruction in the function body of a value-returning function in C++ typically is **return** *expression*;, where *expression* represents the value the function returns to the statement that called it. In the example shown in Figure 5-1, for instance, the `calcTax()` function returns the tax amount to the `tax = calcTax(sales);` statement in the `main()` function.

Unlike value-returning functions, void functions do not return a value. You learn how to create void functions in this tutorial.

Creating Void Functions

A **void function** is a function that does not return a value after completing its assigned task. You might want to use a void function in a program simply to display information, such as a title and column headings, at the top of each page in a report. Rather than repeat the necessary code several times in the program, you can enter the code once, in a void function, and then call the function whenever the program needs to display the information. A void function is appropriate in this situation because the function does not need to return a value after completing its task.

Figure 5-2 shows the syntax used to create (or define) a void function in a C++ program. It also shows an example of a void function whose task is to display a straight line.

tip

Another advantage of using a function to perform a repetitive task is that, if the task needs to be modified in the future, you need to make the modification in only one place—the function.

Figure 5-2: Syntax and an example of creating and invoking a void function in C++

Syntax

function header:

void *functionName*(**[***parameterList***]**)

function body:

{
one or more statements ending with a semicolon
}

Example

```
int main()
{
     displayLine();            // function call

     Console::WriteLine("ABC Company");

     displayLine();            // function call

     return 0;
}    //end of main function

//*****function definitions*****
void displayLine()             // function definition
{
     Console::WriteLine("-----------");
}    //end of displayLine function
```

tip
Recall that a function header in a C++ program does not end with a semicolon, because it is not considered a statement.

There are two differences between the syntax of a value-returning function (shown earlier in Figure 5-1) and the syntax of a void function. First, the function header in a void function begins with the keyword `void`, rather than with a data type. The keyword `void` indicates that the function does not return a value. Second, the function body in a void function does not contain a **`return`** *expression*; statement, which is required in the function body of a value-returning function. The `return` statement is not necessary in a void function body, because a void function does not return a value.

As you do with a value-returning function, you call a void function by including its name and actual arguments (if any) in a statement. However, unlike a call to a value-returning function, a call to a void function appears as a statement by itself, rather than as part of another statement. For example, compare the function call shown in Figure 5-1 with the two function calls shown in Figure 5-2. Notice that the call to the value-returning `calcTax()` function in Figure 5-1 is included in the `tax = calcTax(sales);` statement, which assigns the function's return value to the `tax` variable. Each call to the void `displayLine()` function in Figure 5-2, on the other hand, is a self-contained statement.

tip
As you learned in Tutorial 4, value-returning functions typically are called from statements that display the function's return value, use the return value in a calculation, or assign the return value to a variable.

When the computer processes a statement that calls a void function, the computer first locates the function's code in the program. If the function call contains an *argumentList*, the computer passes the values of the actual arguments (assuming the variables included in the *argumentList* are passed *by value*) to the called function. The function receives these values and stores them in the formal parameters listed in its *parameterList*. Then the computer processes the function's code and, in the case of a void function, it continues program execution with the statement immediately below the one that called the function. In Figure 5-2's example, for instance, the computer continues program execution with the statement `Console::WriteLine("ABC Company");` after processing the `displayLine()` function's code the first time. It continues with the statement `return 0;` after processing the function's code the second time.

MINI-QUIZ

Mini-Quiz 1

1) A void function header in C++ begins with the keyword ______________.

2) Which of the following C++ statements correctly calls a void function named `displayTaxes()`, passing it two `double` variables named `federal` and `state`?
   a. `Console::WriteLine(displayTaxes(federal, state));`
   b. `taxes = displayTaxes(federal, state);`
   c. `displayTaxes(federal, state);`
   d. all of the above

3) Write the function header for the `displayTaxes()` function in Question 2. Use the names `fedTax` and `stateTax` for the formal parameters.

4) The `return` statement typically is the last statement in a C++ void function.
   a. True
   b. False

In Tutorial 4, you learned that a variable can be passed to a function either *by value* or *by reference*. In the remainder of this lesson, you learn more about passing variables to functions.

Passing Variables

Each variable you create in a program has both a value and a unique address that represents the location of the variable in the computer's internal memory. Most programming languages allow you to pass either the variable's value (referred to as passing *by value*) or its address (referred to as passing *by reference*) to the receiving function. The method you choose—*by value* or *by reference*—depends on whether you want the receiving function to have access to the variable in memory—in other words, whether you want to allow the receiving function to change the contents of the variable.

Although the idea of passing information *by value* and *by reference* may sound confusing at first, it is a concept with which you already are familiar. To illustrate, assume that you have a savings account at a local bank. During a conversation with a friend, you mention the amount of money you have in the account. Telling someone the amount of money in your account is similar to passing a variable *by value*. Knowing the balance in your account doesn't give your friend access to your bank account; it merely gives your friend some information that he or she can use—perhaps to compare to the amount of money he or she has saved.

tip

Recall from the Overview that the internal memory of a computer is like a large post office, where each memory cell, like each post office box, has a unique address.

The savings account example also provides an illustration of passing information *by reference*. To deposit money to or withdraw money from your account, you must provide the bank teller with your account number. The account number represents the location of your account at the bank and allows the teller to change the account balance. Giving the teller your bank account number is similar to passing a variable *by reference*. The account number allows the teller to change the contents of your bank account, just as the variable's address allows the receiving function to change the contents of the variable passed to the function.

Before learning how to pass a variable *by reference*, review passing *by value*.

Passing Variables by Value

As you learned in Tutorial 4, when you pass a variable *by value*, the computer passes only the contents of the variable to the receiving function. When only the contents are passed, the receiving function is not given access to the variable in memory, so it cannot change the value stored inside the variable. You pass a variable *by value* when the receiving function needs to *know* the variable's contents, but the receiving function does not need to *change* the contents. Recall that, unless specified otherwise, variables are automatically passed *by value* in C++.

tip

In the programs you created in Tutorial 4, all of the variables passed to functions were passed *by value*, because none of the programs required the receiving function to change the contents of the variables passed to it.

Figure 5-3 shows a C++ program that calculates and displays a salesperson's total sales and his or her bonus. Notice that the program's `main()` function calls a void function named `calcAndDisplay()`, passing it three variables *by value*.

Figure 5-3: Example of passing variables *by value*

function prototype

function call

function definition

```
//function prototype
void calcAndDisplay(double, double, double);

int main()
{
    double sale1      = 0.0;
    double sale2      = 0.0;
    double bonusRate = 0.0;
    //enter input items
    Console::Write("Enter first sale: ");
    sale1 = Convert::ToDouble(Console::ReadLine());
    Console::Write("Enter second sale: ");
    sale2 = Convert::ToDouble(Console::ReadLine());
    Console::Write("Enter bonus rate: ");
    bonusRate = Convert::ToDouble(Console::ReadLine());
    //calculate and display total sales and bonus
    calcAndDisplay(sale1, sale2, bonusRate);
    return 0;
}   //end of main function

//*****function definitions*****
void calcAndDisplay(double s1, double s2, double rate)
{
    double total = 0.0;
    double bonus = 0.0;
    total = s1 + s2;
    bonus = total * rate;
    Console::WriteLine("Total: {0}", total.ToString("C2"));
    Console::WriteLine("Bonus: {0}", bonus.ToString("C2"));
}   //end of calcAndDisplay function
```

Because the `calcAndDisplay()` function shown in Figure 5-3 is a void function, its function call (which is shaded in the figure) appears as a statement by itself. Notice that the number, data type, and sequence of the actual arguments in the function call match the number, data type, and sequence of the corresponding formal parameters in both the function header and function prototype. Also notice that the names of the formal parameters do not need to be identical to the names of their corresponding actual arguments. In fact, for clarity, it usually is better to use different names for the actual arguments and formal parameters. To review the concept of passing *by value*, you will desk-check the program shown in Figure 5-3.

Desk-checking Figure 5-3's Program

The first three statements in the `main()` function shown in Figure 5-3 create and initialize three `double` variables named `sale1`, `sale2`, and `bonusRate`. These variables are local to the `main()` function, and they remain in memory until the `main()` function's `return 0;` statement is processed.

The next six statements prompt the user to enter two sale amounts and the bonus rate, and store the user's responses in the three `double` variables. Assume that the user enters the numbers 2350.25, 3000.75, and .1. Figure 5-4 shows the contents of memory after the first nine statements in the `main()` function are processed.

Figure 5-4: Contents of memory after the first nine statements in the `main()` function are processed

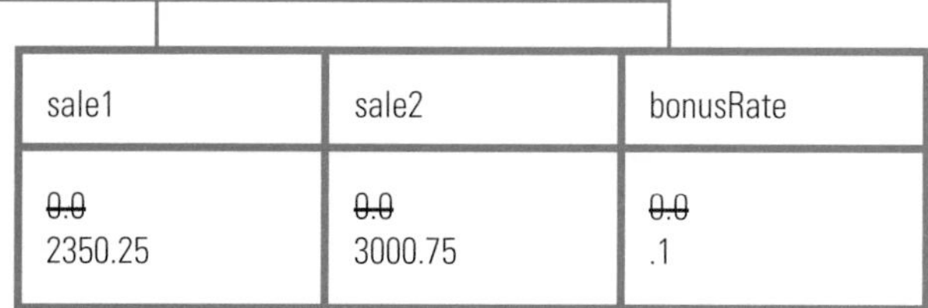

The tenth statement in the `main()` function, `calcAndDisplay(sale1, sale2, bonusRate);`, calls the `calcAndDisplay()` function, passing it three variables *by value*, which means that only the contents of the variables are passed to the function. In this case, the computer passes the numbers 2350.25, 3000.75, and .1 to the `calcAndDisplay()` function.

tip Recall that variables in a C++ program are passed, automatically, *by value*.

At this point, the computer leaves the `main()` function, temporarily, to process the code contained in the `calcAndDisplay()` function. The `calcAndDisplay()` function header indicates that the computer should create three local `double` variables named `s1`, `s2`, and `rate`. The computer stores the values passed to the function in these local variables, as shown in Figure 5-5.

Figure 5-5: Contents of memory after the `calcAndDisplay()` function header is processed

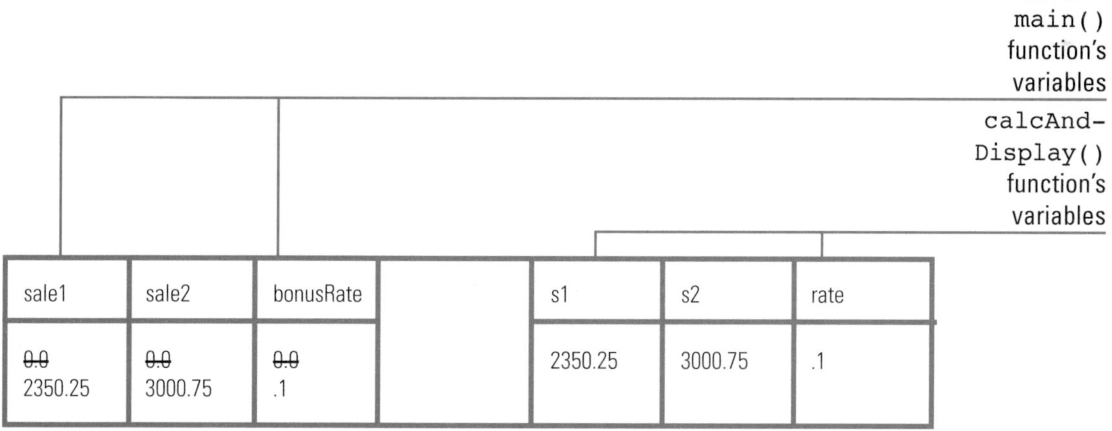

Next, the computer processes the statements contained in the `calcAndDisplay()` function body. The first two statements create and initialize two local `double` variables named `total` and `bonus`. The third statement adds together the contents of the `s1` and `s2` variables, and then assigns the sum (5351.00) to the `total` variable. The fourth statement multiplies the contents of the `total` variable by the contents of the `rate` variable, and then assigns the product (535.10) to the `bonus` variable, as shown in Figure 5-6.

tip Recall that the variables listed in a function header are local to the function, which means they can be used only by the function.

Figure 5-6: Contents of memory after the first four statements in the `calcAndDisplay()` function are processed

`calcAndDisplay()` function's variables: s1, s2, rate, total, bonus

`main()` function's variables: sale1, sale2, bonusRate

sale1	sale2	bonusRate		s1	s2	rate	total	bonus
~~0.0~~ 2350.25	~~0.0~~ 3000.75	~~0.0~~ .1		2350.25	3000.75	.1	~~0.0~~ 5351.00	~~0.0~~ 535.10

tip

A void function's local variables are removed from memory when the computer encounters the function's closing brace. A value-returning function's local variables, on the other hand, are removed from memory after the function's `return` statement is processed.

The last two statements in the **`calcAndDisplay()`** function display the contents of the **`total`** and **`bonus`** variables on the screen. When the computer encounters the **`calcAndDisplay()`** function's closing brace, which marks the end of the function, it removes the function's local variables (**`s1`**, **`s2`**, **`rate`**, **`total`**, and **`bonus`**) from memory. It then continues program execution with the statement immediately following the one that called the **`calcAndDisplay()`** function. In this case, program execution continues with the **`return 0;`** statement in the **`main()`** function. Figure 5-7 shows the contents of memory after the **`calcAndDisplay()`** function has completed its task. Notice that only the **`main()`** function's local variables (**`sale1`**, **`sale2`**, and **`bonusRate`**) remain in the computer's memory.

Figure 5-7: Contents of memory after the `calcAndDisplay()` function ends

`main()` function's variables

sale1	sale2	bonusRate
~~0.0~~ 2350.25	~~0.0~~ 3000.75	~~0.0~~ .1

The **`return 0;`** statement in the **`main()`** function is the next statement processed. The statement returns the number 0 to the operating system to indicate that the program ended normally. The computer then removes the **`main()`** function's local variables (**`sale1`**, **`sale2`**, and **`bonusRate`**) from memory before ending the program.

Next, you learn how to pass variables *by reference*.

Passing Variables by Reference

In addition to passing a variable's value to a function, most programming languages also allow you to pass a variable's address—in other words, its location in the computer's internal memory. Passing a variable's address is referred to as passing *by reference*, and it gives the receiving function access to the variable being passed. You pass a variable *by reference* when you want the receiving function to change the contents of the variable.

To pass a variable *by reference* to a C++ function, you simply include an ampersand (&), called the **address-of operator**, before the name of the corresponding formal parameter in the function header. If the function definition appears below the **main()** function in the program, you also must include the address-of operator in the function prototype. The address-of operator tells the computer to pass the variable's address rather than its contents.

Figure 5-8 shows a C++ program that calculates and displays the average of two test scores. Notice that the program's **main()** function calls a void function named **getScores()**, passing it two variables *by reference*. You can tell that the variables are passed *by reference* because the address-of operator appears in both the function prototype and function header.

Figure 5-8: Example of passing variables *by reference*

```
//function prototype
void getScores(double &, double &);

int main()
{
    double test1 = 0.0;
    double test2 = 0.0;
    double avg   = 0.0;
    //enter input items
    getScores(test1, test2);
    //calculate and display average
    avg = (test1 + test2) / 2;
    Console::WriteLine("Average: {0}", avg.ToString("F1"));
    return 0;
}   //end of main function

//*****function definitions*****
void getScores(double &score1, double &score2)
{
    Console::Write("Enter first test score: ");
    score1 = Convert::ToDouble(Console::ReadLine());
    Console::Write("Enter second test score: ");
    score2 = Convert::ToDouble(Console::ReadLine());
}   //end of getScores function
```

address-of operator

function call

address-of operator

Because the **getScores()** function is a void function, its function call, which is shaded in the figure, appears as a statement by itself. Notice that the number, data type, and sequence of the actual arguments in the function call match the number, data type, and sequence of the corresponding formal parameters in both the function header and function prototype. Also notice that the names of the formal parameters do not need to be identical to the names of their corresponding actual arguments. Additionally, notice that the address-of operator appears before the name of the formal parameter in the function header, and it appears after the data type and a space in the function prototype. Desk-checking the program shown in Figure 5-8 will help you understand the concept of passing *by reference*.

tip
The statement that calls a function does not indicate whether an item is passed *by value* or *by reference*. To determine how an item is passed, you need to examine the *parameterList* in either the function header or function prototype.

Desk-checking Figure 5-8's Program

The first three statements in the `main()` function shown in Figure 5-8 create and initialize three `double` variables named `test1`, `test2`, and `avg`. Figure 5-9 shows the contents of memory after these statements are processed.

Figure 5-9: Contents of memory after the first three statements in the `main()` function are processed

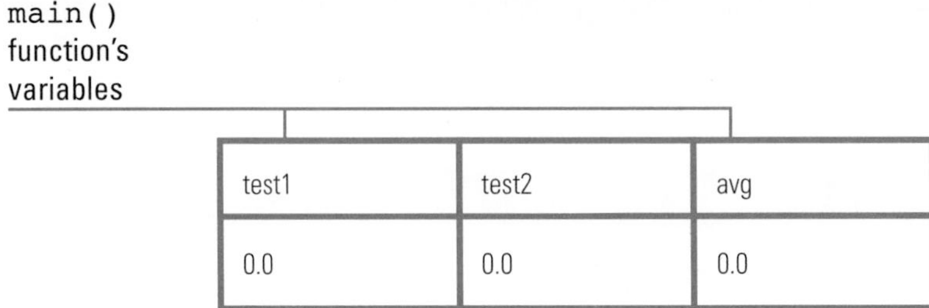

The fourth statement in the `main()` function, `getScores(test1, test2);`, calls the `getScores()` function, passing it two variables. Both variables are passed *by reference*, which means that each variable's address in memory, rather than its contents, are passed. At this point, the computer temporarily leaves the `main()` function to process the code contained in the `getScores()` function.

The `getScores()` function header indicates that the function receives the addresses of two `double` variables. When you pass a variable's address to a function, the computer uses the address to locate the variable in memory; it then assigns the name appearing in the function header to the memory location. In this case, for example, the computer locates the `test1` and `test2` variables in memory, and assigns the names `score1` and `score2`, respectively, to these locations. At this point, each of the two memory locations has two names: one assigned by the `main()` function, and the other assigned by the `getScores()` function, as shown in Figure 5-10.

Figure 5-10: Contents of memory after the `getScores()` function header is processed

variable belonging only to `main()`

variables belonging to both `main()` and `get-Scores()`

test1 [`main()`] score1 [`getScores()`]	test2 [`main()`] score2 [`getScores()`]	avg
0.0	0.0	0.0

As Figure 5-10 indicates, only one of the memory locations shown in the figure—the one named avg—belongs strictly to the main() function. The other two memory locations shown in the figure belong to both the main() and getScores() functions. Although both functions can access these two memory locations, each function uses a different name to do so. The main() function, for example, uses the names test1 and test2 to refer to these memory locations. The getScores() function, on the other hand, uses the names score1 and score2.

After processing the getScores() function header, the computer processes the statements contained in the function body. Those statements prompt the user to enter two test scores, and store the user's responses in the score1 and score2 variables. Assume the user enters the numbers 93 and 84. Figure 5-11 shows the contents of memory after the four statements in the getScores() function are processed.

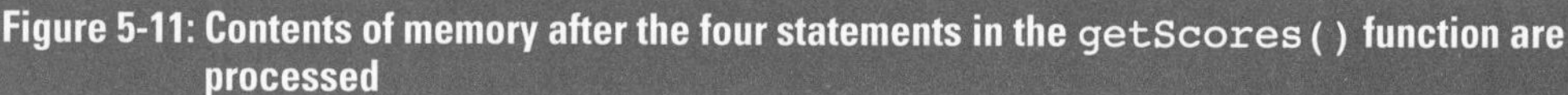

Figure 5-11: Contents of memory after the four statements in the getScores() function are processed

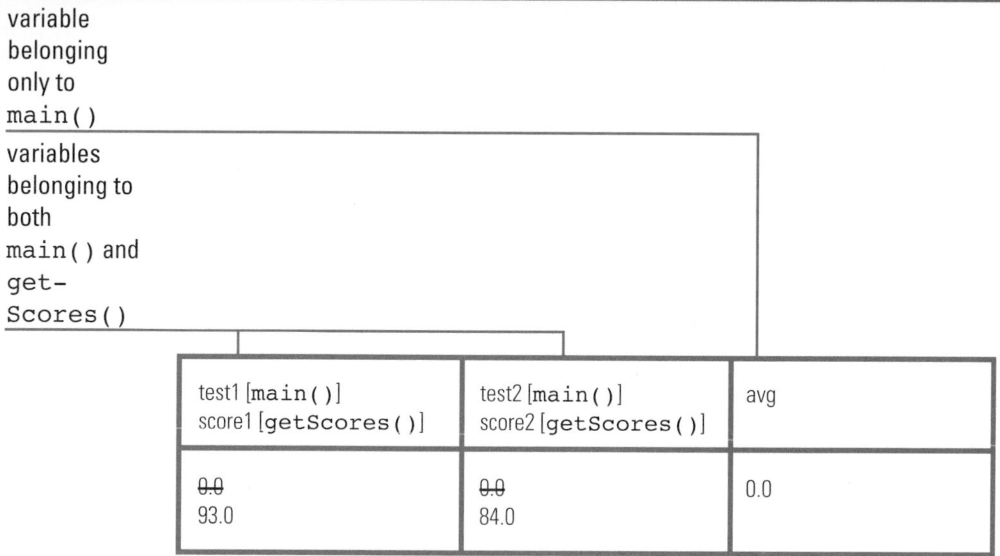

Changing the contents of the score1 and score2 variables also changes the contents of the test1 and test2 variables, respectively. This is because the names refer to the same locations in memory.

When the computer encounters the getScores() function's closing brace, it removes the score1 and score2 names assigned to the main() function's test1 and test2 variables. Program execution then continues with the statement immediately following the one that called the getScores() function. In this case, program execution continues with the avg = (test1 + test2) / 2; statement in the main() function. Figure 5-12 shows the contents of memory after the getScores() function ends. Notice that only the main() function's local variables (test1, test2, and avg) remain in the computer's memory.

tip

A value-returning function uses its return value to send information back to the function that called it. A void function uses variables that are passed *by reference* to send information back to the function that called it.

Figure 5-12: Contents of memory after the `getScores()` function ends

`main()` function's variables

test1	test2	avg
~~0.0~~ 93.0	~~0.0~~ 84.0	0.0

The `avg = (test1 + test2) / 2;` statement in the `main()` function adds the contents of the `test1` variable to the contents of the `test2` variable. It then divides the sum (177) by two and assigns the result (88.5) to the `avg` variable, as shown in Figure 5-13.

Figure 5-13: Contents of memory after the average is calculated

`main()` function's variables

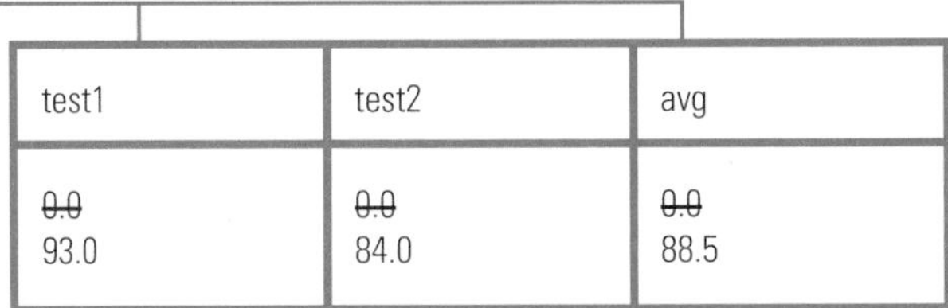

test1	test2	avg
~~0.0~~ 93.0	~~0.0~~ 84.0	~~0.0~~ 88.5

Next, the computer processes the `Console::WriteLine("Average: {0}", avg.ToString("F1"));` statement, which displays the average test score on the screen. When the computer encounters the `return 0;` statement, it removes the `main()` function's local variables (`test1`, `test2`, and `avg`) from memory before ending the program.

MINI-QUIZ

Mini-Quiz 2

1) Write the function header for a C++ void function named `getInput()`. The function is passed the addresses of the `main()` function's `hours` and `rate` variables. The variables are of the `double` data type. Use the names `hoursWkd` and `payRate` for the formal parameters.
2) Write the statement to call the `getInput()` function in Question 1.
3) Write the function prototype for the `getInput()` function in Question 1.
4) A void function's local variables are removed from memory when the computer encounters the function's ______________.

Next, view a program that passes variables both *by value* and *by reference*.

Passing Variables *by Value* and *by Reference*

In the program shown earlier in Figure 5-3, the variables passed to the `calcAndDisplay()` function are passed *by value*. In Figure 5-8's program, on the other hand, the variables are passed to the `getScores()` function *by reference*. You also can mix the way variables are passed when a function is called, passing some *by reference* and others *by value*, as shown in Figure 5-14's program.

Figure 5-14: Example of passing variables *by value* and *by reference*

```
//function prototype
void calc(double, double, double &, double &);

int main()
{
    double salary     = 0.0;
    double raiseRate = 0.0;
    double raise      = 0.0;
    double newSalary = 0.0;
    //enter input items
    Console::Write("Enter current salary: ");
    salary = Convert::ToDouble(Console::ReadLine());
    Console::Write("Enter raise rate: ");
    raiseRate = Convert::ToDouble(Console::ReadLine());
    //calculate raise and new salary
    calc(salary, raiseRate, raise, newSalary);
    //display raise and new salary
    Console::WriteLine("Raise: {0}", raise.ToString("C2"));
    Console::WriteLine("New salary: {0}", newSalary.ToString("C2"));
    return 0;
}   //end of main function

//*****function definitions*****
void calc(double current, double rate, double &increase, double &pay)
{
    increase = current * rate;
    pay = current + increase;
}   //end of calc function
```

passed *by reference*

passed *by value*

function call

The program shown in Figure 5-14 calculates and displays an employee's raise and new salary amounts, given the employee's current salary amount and the raise rate. The first four statements in the `main()` function create and initialize four `double` variables named `salary`, `raiseRate`, `raise`, and `newSalary`. The next four statements prompt the user to enter the current salary amount and the raise rate, and store the user's responses in the `salary` and `raiseRate` variables. Assume that the user enters the numbers 34500 and .06 for the salary and rate, respectively. Figure 5-15 shows the contents of memory after the first eight statements in the `main()` function are processed.

Figure 5-15: Contents of memory after the first eight statements in the `main()` function are processed

main()
function's
variables

salary	raiseRate	raise	newSalary
~~0.0~~ 34500.0	~~0.0~~ .06	0.0	0.0

Next, the computer processes the **`calc(salary, raiseRate, raise, newSalary);`** statement, which calls the **`calc()`** function, passing it four variables. Two of the variables, **`salary`** and **`raiseRate`**, are passed *by value*, because the receiving function needs to *know* the values stored in these variables, but it does not need to change those values. The other two variables, **`raise`** and **`newSalary`**, are passed *by reference*, because it is the receiving function's responsibility to calculate the raise and new salary amounts and then store the results in these memory locations.

tip

Recall that when you pass a variable *by value*, the variable's contents are passed. When you pass a variable *by reference*, on the other hand, the variable's address in memory is passed.

At this point, the computer temporarily leaves the **`main()`** function to process the code contained in the **`calc()`** function. The **`double current, double rate`** portion of the **`calc()`** function header tells the computer to create two **`double`** memory locations named **`current`** and **`rate`**. These memory locations will store the values of the **`salary`** and **`raiseRate`** variables passed to the function. The **`double &increase, double &pay`** portion of the **`calc()`** function header tells the computer to assign the name **`increase`** to the **`main()`** function's **`raise`** variable, and assign the name **`pay`** to the **`main()`** function's **`newSalary`** variable. Figure 5-16 shows the contents of memory after the **`calc()`** function header is processed.

Figure 5-16: Contents of memory after the calc() function header is processed

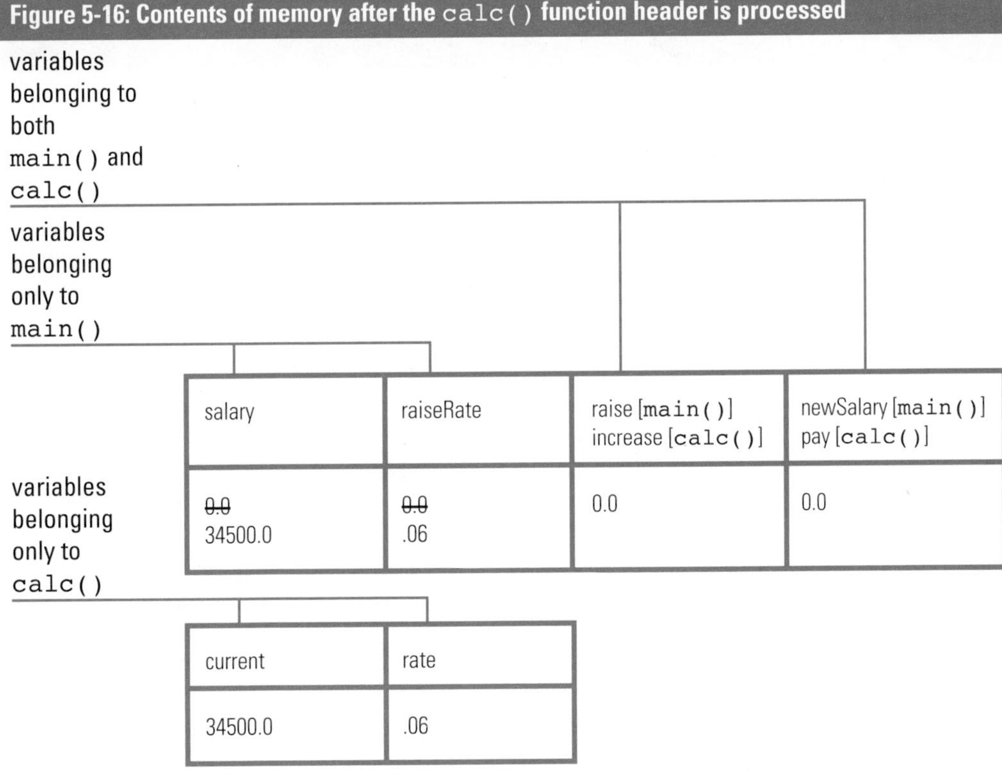

The statements contained in the `calc()` function body are processed next. The first statement multiplies the contents of the `current` variable by the contents of the `rate` variable, and then assigns the result (2070) to the `increase` variable. The second statement adds together the contents of the `current` and `increase` variables, and then assigns the sum (36570) to the `pay` variable, as shown in Figure 5-17.

Figure 5-17: Contents of memory after the two statements in the `calc()` function are processed

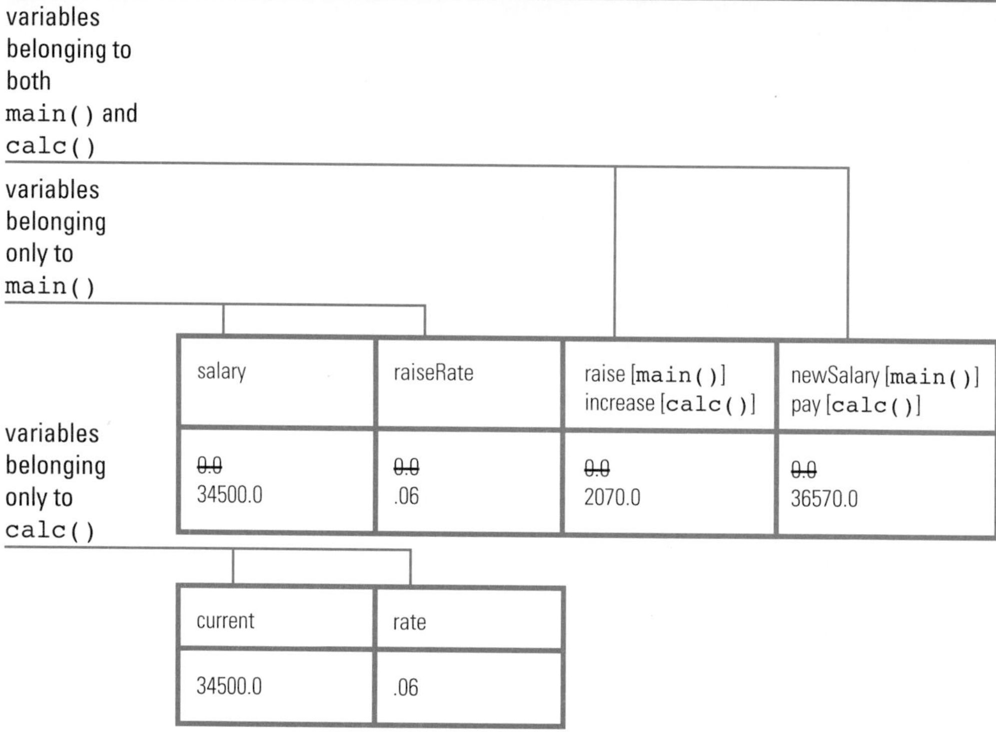

When the computer encounters the `calc()` function's closing brace, it removes the `increase` and `pay` names assigned to the `main()` function's `raise` and `newSalary` variables. It also removes the `calc()` function's `current` and `rate` variables from memory. Program execution then continues with the statement immediately following the one that called the `calc()` function. In this case, program execution continues with the `Console::WriteLine("Raise: {0}", raise.ToString("C2"));` statement in the `main()` function. Figure 5-18 shows the contents of memory after the `calc()` function ends. Notice that only the `main()` function's local variables (`salary`, `raiseRate`, `raise`, and `newSalary`) remain in the computer's memory.

Figure 5-18: Contents of memory after the `calc()` function ends

main() function's variables

salary	raiseRate	raise	newSalary
~~0.0~~ 34500.0	~~0.0~~ .06	~~0.0~~ 2070.0	~~0.0~~ 36570.0

The `Console::WriteLine("Raise: {0}", raise.ToString("C2"));` statement in the `main()` function is the next statement processed and displays the raise amount on the screen. The `Console::WriteLine("New salary: {0}",` `newSalary.ToString("C2"));` statement then displays the new salary amount. When the computer processes the last statement in the `main()` function—`return 0;`—it returns the number 0 to the operating system to indicate that the program ended normally. The computer then removes the `main()` function's local variables (`salary`, `raiseRate`, `raise`, and `newSalary`) from memory before ending the program.

The examples you have viewed so far in this lesson show you how to pass a numeric variable to a function. In the next section, you learn how to pass a String variable to a function.

Passing a String Variable to a Function

As you learned in Tutorial 3, the `String` data type is not a fundamental data type in C++. Rather, it is a data type that is added to the C++ language through the use of a class. Recall that a class is a group of instructions used to create an object. The `String` class (data type), for example, creates a string object.

To pass a String variable *by value* to a C++ function, you use the syntax **String** **variablename* in the function header, and the syntax **String *** in the function prototype. To pass a String variable *by reference* to a C++ function, you use the syntax **String** *&*variablename* in the function header, and the syntax **String *&** in the function prototype.

The program listing shown in Figure 5-19 provides an example of passing a String variable *by value* and *by reference*.

tip

As you may remember from Tutorial 3, the * (asterisk) indicates that a memory location is a pointer.

Figure 5-19: Example of passing a String variable *by value* and *by reference*

```
//function prototype
void displayName(String *);      //pass by value
void getNewName(String *&);      //pass by reference

int main()
{
    //declare a String variable
    String *student = "Chris";
    //display the student name
    displayName(student);
    //get another student name
    getNewName(student);
    //display the student name
    displayName(student);
    return 0;
}   //end of main function

//*****function definitions*****
void displayName(String *name)
{
    Console::WriteLine("Name: {0}", name);
    Console::WriteLine();
}   //end of displayName function

void getNewName(String *&newName)
{
    Console::Write("Enter a different name: ");
    newName = Console::ReadLine();
}   //end of getNewName function
```

The main() function shown in Figure 5-19 first creates a String variable named student and initializes it to the string "Chris". The main() function then calls the displayName() function, passing it the student variable *by value*. You can tell that the student variable is passed *by value* to the displayName() function because no ampersand appears in the function's prototype and header.

The displayName() function stores the string passed to it in its local name variable. It then displays the contents of the name variable, followed by a blank line, on the screen. When the displayName() function ends, the computer removes the name variable from memory. Processing then continues with the getNewName(student); statement in the main() function.

The getNewName(student); statement calls the getNewName() function, passing it the student variable *by reference*. You can tell that the student variable is passed *by reference* to the getNewName() function because an ampersand appears in the function's prototype and header.

The getNewName() function assigns the name newName to the student variable. The function then prompts the user to enter a name, storing the user's response in the newName variable. Because the student variable is passed *by reference*, changing the contents of the newName variable also changes the contents of the student variable. When the getNewName() function ends, the computer removes the newName name from the student variable in memory, and continues processing with the second displayName (student); statement in the main() function.

The displayName(student); statement calls the displayName() function, passing it the student variable *by value*. The displayName() function stores the string passed to it in its local name variable. It then displays the contents of the name variable, followed by a blank line, on the screen. When the displayName() function ends, the computer removes the name variable from memory. Processing then continues with the return 0; statement in the main() function.

The return 0; statement returns the number 0 to the operating system to indicate that the program ended normally. The computer then removes the student variable from memory before ending the program.

MINI-QUIZ

Mini-Quiz 3

1) Write the function header for a C++ void function named calcTaxes(). The function is passed the value of the main() function's gross variable, and the addresses of the main() function's federal and state variables. The variables are of the double data type. Use the names pay, fedTax, and stateTax for the formal parameters.

2) Write the statement to call the calcTaxes() function in Question 1.

3) Write the function prototype for the calcTaxes() function in Question 1.

4) When used in a function prototype, which of the following indicates that the state variable is passed *by reference* to the function?

a. String *&state
b. String &*state
c. String &state
d. String *state

You now have completed Tutorial 5's Concept lesson. You can either take a break or complete the end-of-lesson questions and exercises before moving on to the Application lesson.

SUMMARY

All functions fall into one of two categories: value-returning or void. A value-returning function returns precisely one value to the statement that called the function. A void function, on the other hand, does not return a value after completing its assigned task.

Like a value-returning function, a void function is composed of a function header and a function body. However, unlike a value-returning function, the function header for a void function begins with the keyword `void`, rather than with a data type. Also unlike a value-returning function, the function body for a void function does not contain a `return` statement.

As you do with a value-returning function, you call a void function by including its name and actual arguments (if any) in a statement. However, unlike a call to a value-returning function, a call to a void function appears as a statement by itself, rather than as part of another statement. When the computer finishes processing a void function's code, it continues program execution with the statement immediately below the one that called the function.

Variables can be passed to functions either *by value* or *by reference*. When you pass a variable *by value*, only the value stored inside the variable is passed to the receiving function. The receiving function is not given access to a variable passed *by value*, so it cannot change the variable's contents. When you pass a variable *by reference*, on the other hand, its address in memory is passed to the receiving function, allowing the receiving function to change the variable's contents. Unless specified otherwise, variables in C++ are passed automatically *by value*. To pass a variable *by reference* in a C++ program, you include the address-of operator (&) before the corresponding formal parameter's name in the function header. If the function definition appears below the `main()` function in the program, you also must include the address-of operator in the function prototype. The address-of operator tells the computer to pass the variable's address rather than its contents.

To pass a String variable *by value* to a C++ function, you use the syntax **String** ******variablename* in the function header, and the syntax **String** * in the function prototype. To pass a String variable *by reference* to a C++ function, you use the syntax **String** ***&***variablename* in the function header, and the syntax **String** ***&** in the function prototype.

ANSWERS TO MINI-QUIZZES

Mini-Quiz 1

1) `void`

2) c. `displayTaxes(federal, state);`

3) `void displayTaxes(double fedTax, double stateTax)`

4) b. False

Mini-Quiz 2

1) `void getInput(double &hoursWkd, double &payRate)`

2) `getInput(hours, rate);`

3) `void getInput(double &, double &);`

4) closing brace (})

Mini-Quiz 3

1) `void calcTaxes(double pay, double &fedTax, double &stateTax)`

2) `calcTaxes(gross, federal, state);`

3) `void calcTaxes(double, double &, double &);`

4) a. `String *&state`

QUESTIONS

1) Which of the following is false?

A. A void function does not return a value after completing its assigned task.

B. A void function call typically appears as its own statement in a C++ program.

C. A void function cannot receive any items of information when it is called.

D. A void function header begins with the keyword `void`.

2) Which of the following C++ statements correctly calls a void function named `displayHeading()`, passing it one `String` variable named `companyName`?

A. `Console::Write(displayHeading(String companyName));`

B. `Console::Write(displayHeading(companyName));`

C. `displayHeading(String companyName);`

D. `displayHeading(companyName);`

3) Which of the following function prototypes is correct for a void function named `calcEndingBalance()`? The function is passed the value of two `int` variables.

A. `void calcEndingBalance(int, int);`

B. `void calcEndingBalance(int, int)`

C. `void calcEndingBalance(int &, int &);`

D. `int calcEndingBalance(void);`

4) Assume that a void function named `calcEndingInventory()` receives four `int` variables from the `main()` function: `beginInventory`, `sales`, `purchases`, and `endingInventory`. The function's task is to calculate the ending inventory, based on the beginning inventory, sales, and purchase amounts passed to the function. The function should store the result in the `endingInventory` memory location. Which of the following function headers is correct?

A. `void calcEndingInventory(&int b, &int s, &int p, &int e)`

B. `void calcEndingInventory(int b, int s, int p, int e)`

C. `void calcEndingInventory(int &b, int &s, int &p, int e)`

D. `void calcEndingInventory(int b, int s, int p, int &e)`

5) Which of the following statements calls the `calcEndingInventory()` function described in Question 4?

A. `calcEndingInventory(int, int, int, int);`

B. `calcEndingInventory(beginInventory, sales, purchases, &endingInventory);`

C. `calcEndingInventory(beginInventory, sales, purchases, endingInventory);`

D. `calcEndingInventory(int beginInventory, int sales, int purchases, int &endingInventory);`

6) In C++, variables are passed automatically ______________.

A. *by address*

B. *by number*

C. *by reference*

D. *by value*

7) If you want the receiving function to change the contents of a variable, you must pass the variable ______________.

A. *by address*

B. *by number*

C. *by reference*

D. *by value*

8) To determine whether an item is being passed *by value* or *by reference*, you must examine either the ______________ or the ______________.

A. function call, function header

B. function call, function prototype

C. function header, function prototype

D. function header, function body

9) Which of the following is false?

A. You enclose a function's statements in a set of braces.

B. The function header is considered a C++ statement, so it must end with a semicolon.

C. The keyword `void` tells the computer that the function does not return a value.

D. An empty set of parentheses after the function's name in the function header tells you that the function does not receive any information.

10) Which of the following calls a function named `displayName()`, passing it no actual arguments?

A. `call displayName();`

B. `displayName;`

C. `displayName()`

D. `displayName();`

11) Assume a program contains a void function named `displayName()`. Which of the following is a correct function prototype for this function, assuming that the function requires no formal parameters?

A. `displayName();`

B. `void displayName;`

C. `void displayName();`

D. `void displayName(none);`

12) When the computer encounters a void function's closing brace, it continues program execution with the statement ______________.

A. immediately above the statement that called the function

B. that called the function

C. immediately below the statement that called the function

13) A program will have one function prototype for each function defined in the function definitions section of the program. (Assume that the function definitions section is located below the `main()` function.)

A. True

B. False

14) Variables that can be used only by the function in which they are declared are called ______________ variables.

A. global

B. local

C. separate

D. void

15) Which of the following is false?

A. When you pass a variable *by reference*, the receiving function can change the variable's contents.

B. When you pass a variable *by value*, the receiving function creates a local variable that it uses to store the passed value.

C. Unless specified otherwise, all variables in C++ are passed *by value*.

D. To pass a variable *by reference* in C++, you place an ampersand (&) before the variable's name in the statement that calls the function.

16) Assume a program contains a void function named `calcNewPrice()`. The function receives two `double` variables named `oldPrice` and `newPrice`. The function multiplies the contents of the `oldPrice` variable by `1.1`, and then stores the result in the `newPrice` variable. Which of the following is the best function prototype for this function?

A. `void calcNewPrice(double, double);`

B. `void calcNewPrice(double &, double);`

C. `void calcNewPrice(double, double &);`

D. `void calcNewPrice(double &, double &);`

17) Which of the following can be used to call the `calcNewPrice()` function in Question 16?

A. `calcNewPrice(double oldPrice, double newPrice);`

B. `calcNewPrice(&oldPrice, newPrice);`

C. `calcNewPrice(oldPrice, &newPrice);`

D. `calcNewPrice(oldPrice, newPrice);`

18) Which of the following is false?

A. The names of the formal parameters in the function header must be identical to the names of the actual arguments in the function call.

B. When listing the formal parameters in a function header, you include each parameter's data type and name.

C. The formal parameters should be the same data type as the actual arguments.

D. If a function call passes an `int` variable first and a `char` variable second, the receiving function must receive an `int` variable first and a `char` variable second.

19) To pass a `String` variable *by value* to a function, you must include _______________ before the variable's name in the function header.

A. an ampersand (&)

B. an asterisk(*)

C. an ampersand and an asterisk (&*)

D. an asterisk and an ampersand (*&)

20) To pass a `String` variable *by reference* to a function, you must include _______________ before the variable's name in the function header.

A. an ampersand (&)

B. an asterisk(*)

C. an ampersand and an asterisk (&*)

D. an asterisk and an ampersand (*&)

EXERCISES

Look For These Symbols

Debugging

Discovery

1) Write the C++ code for a void function named `halveNumber()`. The function receives an integer passed to it. It then divides the integer by 2 and displays the result on the computer screen.

2) Write the C++ code for a void function that prompts the user to enter the name of an item, and then stores the user's response in the `String` variable whose address is passed to the function. Name the function `getItemName()`.

3) Write the C++ code for a void function that receives four `int` variables: the first two *by value* and the last two *by reference*. The function should calculate the sum of and the difference between the two variables passed *by value*, and then store the results in the variables passed *by reference*. When calculating the difference, subtract the contents of the second variable from the contents of the first variable. Name the function `calcSumAndDiff()`.

4) Write the C++ code for a void function that receives three `double` variables: the first two *by value* and the last one *by reference*. The function should divide the first variable by the second variable, and then store the result in the third variable. Name the function `quotient()`.

5) Write the C++ code for a void function that receives a `String` variable *by value*. The function should display the string on the computer screen. Name the function `displayName()`.

6) Desk-check the program shown in Figure 5-20. Show the desk-check table after the first four statements in the `main()` function are processed, after the `calcEnd()` function's statement is processed, and after the `calcEnd()` function ends.

Figure 5-20

```
//function prototype
void calcEnd(int, int, int, int &);

int main()
{
    int begVal    = 1000;
    int purchase = 500;
    int sale      = 200;
    int endVal    = 0;
    calcEnd(begVal, purchase, sale, endVal);
    Console::WriteLine(endVal);
    return 0;
}   //end of main function

//*****function definitions*****
void calcEnd(int beg, int pur, int sale, int &ending)
{
    ending = beg + pur - sale;
}   //end of calcEnd function
```

7) In this exercise, you experiment with passing *by value* and *by reference*.

A. If necessary, start Visual Studio .NET. Open the T5ConE07 Solution (T5ConE07 Solution.sln) file, which is contained in the CppNet\Tut05\T5ConE07 Solution folder. Notice that the `main()` function passes the `age` variable *by value* to the `getAge()` function.

B. Build the solution, then execute the program. When prompted to enter your age, type your age and press Enter. Notice that the program displays the number 0, rather than your age, in the message; this is because the `age` variable is passed *by value* to the `getAge()` function.

C. Close the Command Prompt and Output windows.

D. Modify the program so that it passes the `age` variable *by reference* to the `getAge()` function.

E. Save and then build the solution.

F. Execute the program. When prompted to enter your age, type your age and press Enter. Notice that, this time, the program displays your age in the message; this is because the `age` variable is passed *by reference* to the `getAge()` function. Close the Command Prompt window.

G. When the program is working correctly, close the Output window, and then use the File menu to close the solution.

8) In this exercise, you learn about a common error made when using arithmetic expressions in a program.

A. If necessary, start Visual Studio .NET. Open the T5ConE08 Solution (T5ConE08 Solution.sln) file, which is contained in the CppNet\Tut05\T5ConE08 Solution folder.

B. Study the existing code. Although the `calcTax1()` and `calcTax2()` functions use slightly different formulas for calculating the sales tax, both formulas should produce the same result.

C. Build the solution, then execute the program. Notice that the `calcTax1()` function displays $2.63 as the sales tax, which is correct. The `calcTax2()` function, however, displays $1.75 as the sales tax, which is incorrect.

D. Close the Command Prompt and Output windows.

In C++, dividing an integer by an integer results in an integer. In the `calcTax2()` function, for example, dividing the `saleAmt` variable (which is an `int` variable) by the integer 1000 results in the integer 1. Multiplying the integer 1 by the contents of the `taxRate` variable (1.75) results in an incorrect sales tax amount.

E. Modify the formula in the `calcTax2()` function so that it tells the computer to divide the `saleAmt` variable by the `double` value 1000.0.

F. Save and then build the solution.

G. Execute the program. This time, both functions produce the same sales tax amount. Close the Command Prompt window.

H. Change the 1000.0 in the `calcTax2()` function's formula to 1000. Now modify the formula in the `calcTax2()` function so that it tells the computer to divide the `saleAmt` variable, treated as a `double`, by the integer 1000.

I. Save and then build the solution.

J. Execute the program. Here again, both functions produce the same sales tax amount. Close the Command Prompt window.

K. When the program is working correctly, close the Output window, and then use the File menu to close the solution.

9) In this exercise, you debug a C++ program.

A. If necessary, start Visual Studio .NET. Open the T5ConE09 Solution (T5ConE09 Solution.sln) file, which is contained in the CppNet\Tut05\T5ConE09 Solution folder.

B. Build the solution. Correct any errors.

C. Save and then build the solution.

D. Execute the program. When prompted to enter your name, type your name and press Enter. Close the Command Prompt window.

E. When the program is working correctly, close the Output window, and then use the File menu to close the solution.

10) In this exercise, you debug a C++ program.

A. If necessary, start Visual Studio .NET. Open the T5ConE10 Solution (T5ConE10 Solution.sln) file, which is contained in the CppNet\Tut05\T5ConE10 Solution folder.

B. Build the solution. Correct any errors.

C. Save and then build the solution.

D. Execute the program. Test the program using the numbers 10 and 20. The program should display the number 30 as the sum of both numbers. Close the Command Prompt window.

E. When the program is working correctly, close the Output window, and then use the File menu to close the solution.

Application Lesson

Using Void Functions in a C++ Program

CASE Jane Hernandez is employed by the public works office in Allenton, a small rural town with a population of 500. Each month, Jane uses a calculator to calculate each customer's water bill—a time-consuming task and one that is prone to errors. Your task in this lesson is to create a program that makes the appropriate calculations, and then displays the customer's name, gallons of water used, and water charge. Currently, the charge for water is $1.75 per 1000 gallons, or .00175 per gallon.

Analyzing, Planning, and Desk-checking

Figure 5-21 shows the IPO chart for the water bill problem described in this lesson's Case.

Figure 5-21: IPO chart for the water bill problem

Input	Processing	Output
customer name current reading (gallons) previous reading (gallons) rate per gallon (.00175)	Processing items: none Algorithm: 1. enter the customer name, current reading, and previous reading 2. calculate the gallons used by subtracting the previous reading from the current reading 3. calculate the water charge by multiplying the gallons used by the rate per gallon 4. display the customer name, gallons used, and water charge	customer name gallons used water charge

According to the IPO chart, the program's output is the customer name, gallons used, and water charge. To display the output, the program must know the customer name, the current and previous water meter readings (in gallons), and the rate per gallon. According to the algorithm, the program first will have the user enter the customer name and the current and previous readings. It then will calculate both the gallons used and the water charge, and it will display the result of both calculations, along with the customer name, on the screen.

As you learned in Tutorial 2, most algorithms follow a format similar to the one shown in Figure 5-21. That is, they first get the input data, then process that data (typically by performing calculations on it), and then display the output data. For simple algorithms (such as the water bill algorithm), the input, processing, and output tasks can be performed quite easily by the `main()` function itself. As programs become larger and more complex, however, it is helpful to assign these tasks to functions, and then have the `main()` function call each function when needed. Doing this allows the programmer to code and test one small portion of the program at a time. It also allows a team of programmers to work on a program, with each member of the team responsible for coding one or more of the functions.

Although the water bill algorithm is small and very simple, it can be used to demonstrate the concept of assigning major tasks to multiple functions, and then using the `main()` function to call each function at the appropriate time. Toward that end, you will assign the water bill algorithm's four tasks to three void functions named `getInput()`, `calculate()`, and `displayBill()`. The `getInput()` function will be assigned the task of getting the user input (customer name, current reading, and previous reading). A void function is appropriate in this case, because the `getInput()` function needs to get three values for the `main()` function, and a value-returning function can return only one value. The `calculate()` function will be responsible for calculating both the gallons used and the water charge. Here again, a void function is appropriate because the `calculate()` function needs to calculate more than one value for the `main()` function. The `displayBill()` function will be responsible for displaying the output (customer name, gallons used, and water charge) on the screen. The `displayBill()` function also should be a void function, because it will not need to return a value to the `main()` function after completing its task. Figure 5-22 shows the IPO charts for the water bill problem using functions.

tip

In most cases, the processing task for large and complex programs is assigned to more than one function. For example, a payroll program's processing task might be assigned to four functions that calculate the gross pay, calculate the tax deductions, calculate the insurance deductions, and calculate the net pay.

Figure 5-22: Revised IPO charts for the water bill problem

`main()` **function**

Input	Processing	Output
customer name current reading (gallons) previous reading (gallons) rate per gallon (.00175)	Processing items: none Algorithm: 1. getInput(customer name, current reading, previous reading) 2. calculate(current reading, previous reading, rate per gallon, gallons used, water charge) 3. displayBill(customer name, gallons used, water charge)	customer name gallons used water charge

`getInput()` **function**

Input	Processing	Output
address of customer name address of current reading address of previous reading	Processing items: none Algorithm: 1. enter the customer name, current reading, and previous reading	customer name current reading previous reading

tip

Rather than using one void function to get the three input items in the water bill problem, you could use three value-returning functions, one to get each input item. You also could use two value-returning functions, rather than one void function, to calculate and return the gallons used and the water charge.

Figure 5-22: Revised IPO charts for the water bill problem (continued)

`calculate()` **function**

Input	Processing	Output
current reading previous reading rate per gallon address of gallons used address of water charge	Processing items: none Algorithm: 1. calculate the gallons used by subtracting the previous reading from the current reading 2. calculate the water charge by multiplying the gallons used by the rate per gallon	gallons used water charge

`displayBill()` **function**

Input	Processing	Output
customer name gallons used water charge	Processing items: none Algorithm: 1. display the customer name, gallons used, and water charge	customer name gallons used water charge

First compare the `main()` function's IPO chart shown in Figure 5-22 with the IPO chart shown earlier in Figure 5-21. Notice that the `main()` function's input and output items are the same in both charts; the algorithms, however, are different. Figure 5-21's algorithm indicates that the `main()` function will perform the required input, processing, and output tasks, while Figure 5-22's algorithm indicates that the `main()` function will call three functions to perform those tasks.

According to the IPO charts shown in Figure 5-22, the `main()` function first will call the `getInput()` function, whose task is to get the required information from the user. Notice that the `getInput()` function's output is the customer name, current reading, and previous reading. For the function to perform its task, the `main()` function must pass to the `getInput()` function the addresses of the variables where the customer name, current reading, and previous reading should be stored.

After the `getInput()` function performs its task, the `main()` function will call the `calculate()` function to make the appropriate calculations. Notice that the `calculate()` function's output is the gallons used and the water charge. For the function to perform the necessary calculations, the `main()` function must pass it the current reading, the previous reading, the rate per gallon, and the memory addresses of the variables where the gallons used and water charge should be stored.

Finally, the `main()` function will call the `displayBill()` function, whose task is to display the appropriate information on the screen. Notice that the `displayBill()` function's output is the customer name, gallons used, and water charge. For the function to perform its task, it must receive the name, usage, and charge information from the `main()` function.

Recall that you should desk-check an algorithm several times before you begin coding it. In this case, you will use the following two sets of data to desk-check the algorithms shown in Figure 5-22:

Data for first desk-check
Customer name: Joe Smith
Current reading (gallons): 9000
Previous reading (gallons): 8000
Rate per gallon: .00175

Data for second desk-check
Customer name: Suman Patel
Current reading (gallons): 14000
Previous reading (gallons): 7500
Rate per gallon: .00175

Figure 5-23 shows the completed desk-check tables, with the water charge amounts shown rounded to two decimal places.

Figure 5-23: Completed desk-check tables for the algorithms shown in Figure 5-22

`main()` function

customer name	current reading	previous reading	rate per gallon	gallons used	water charge
~~Joe Smith~~ Suman Patel	~~9000~~ 14000	~~8000~~ 7500	~~.00175~~ .00175	~~1000~~ 6500	~~1.75~~ 11.38

`calculate()` function

current reading	previous reading	rate per gallon
~~9000~~ 14000	~~8000~~ 7500	~~.00175~~ .00175

`displayBill()` function

customer name	gallons used	water charge
~~Joe Smith~~ Suman Patel	~~1000~~ 6500	~~1.75~~ 11.38

After desk-checking an algorithm to verify its accuracy, you are ready to translate it into a language the computer can understand. Begin by coding the current program's `main()` function.

tip

The `getInput()` function does not need a separate desk-check table, because it receives the addresses of items appearing in the `main()` function's desk-check table. For the same reason, the `calculate()` function's desk-check table does not include the gallons used and water charge items.

Coding the `main()` Function

According to its IPO chart, the `main()` function requires six memory locations: five variables and one named constant. After reserving the memory locations, the `main()` function will call the `getInput()` function, then the `calculate()` function, and finally the `displayBill()` function. Figure 5-24 shows the C++ statements that correspond to the `main()` function.

Figure 5-24: C++ statements that correspond to the `main()` function

IPO chart information	C++ instructions
Input	
customer name	`String *name = "";`
current reading (gallons)	`int current = 0;`
previous reading (gallons)	`int previous = 0;`
rate per gallon (.00175)	`const double RATE = .00175;`
Processing	
none	
Output	
customer name	
gallons used	`int gallons = 0;`
water charge	`double charge = 0.0;`
Algorithm	
1. getInput(customer name, current reading, previous reading)	`getInput(name, current, previous);`
2. calculate(current reading, previous reading, rate per gallon, gallons used, water charge)	`calculate(current, previous, RATE, gallons, charge);`
3. displayBill(customer name, gallons used, water charge)	`displayBill(name, gallons, charge);`

Now code the `getInput()` function.

Coding the `getInput()` Function

Recall that the `main()` function will pass to the `getInput()` function the memory addresses of its `name`, `current`, and `previous` variables. The `getInput()` function will use the formal parameters `&cust`, `&cur`, and `&prev` to receive the information. As you learned earlier, the address-of operator (&) alerts the computer that what is being passed to the function is a variable's address rather than its value. Figure 5-25 shows the C++ code for the `getInput()` function.

Figure 5-25: C++ code for the getInput() function

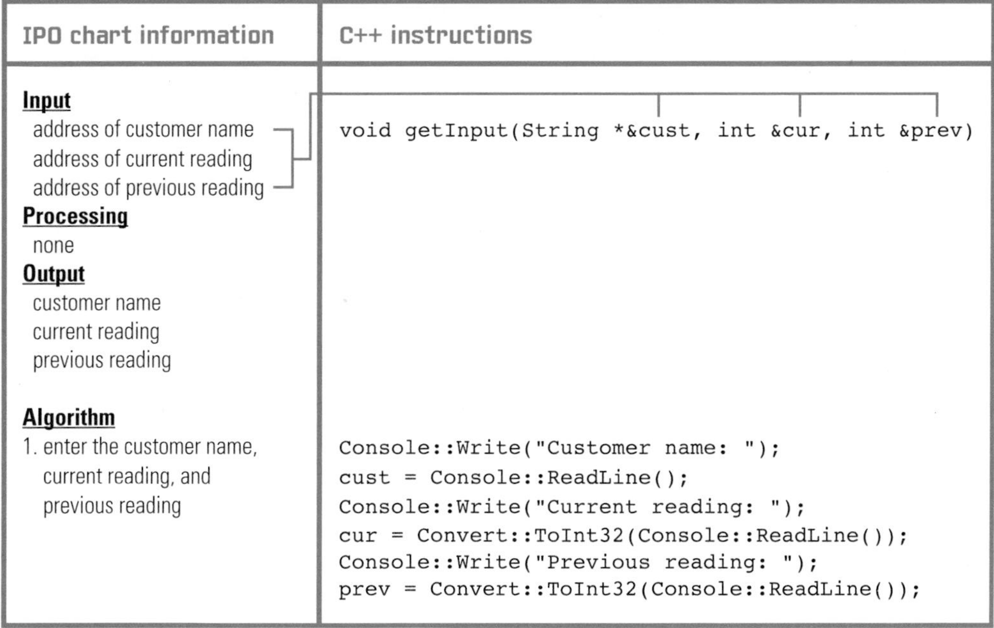

IPO chart information	C++ instructions
Input address of customer name address of current reading address of previous reading **Processing** none **Output** customer name current reading previous reading	`void getInput(String *&cust, int &cur, int &prev)`

Algorithm
1. enter the customer name, current reading, and previous reading
	`Console::Write("Customer name: ");`
	`cust = Console::ReadLine();`
	`Console::Write("Current reading: ");`
	`cur = Convert::ToInt32(Console::ReadLine());`
	`Console::Write("Previous reading: ");`
	`prev = Convert::ToInt32(Console::ReadLine());`

tip

Recall that the number, data type, and sequence of the formal parameters in a function header should match the number, data type, and sequence of the corresponding actual arguments passed to the function.

tip

The variable names cust, cur, and prev are local to the getInput() function and are removed from memory when the computer encounters the function's closing brace.

Next, code the **calculate()** function.

Coding the calculate() Function

The IPO charts shown earlier in Figure 5-22 indicate that the **main()** function will pass to the **calculate()** function the values of three memory locations (**current**, **previous**, and **RATE**) and the addresses of two memory locations (**gallons** and **charge**). The **calculate()** function will use the formal parameters **c**, **p**, **r**, **&gal**, and **&due** to receive the information. Figure 5-26 shows the C++ code for the **calculate()** function.

Figure 5-26: C++ code for the `calculate()` function

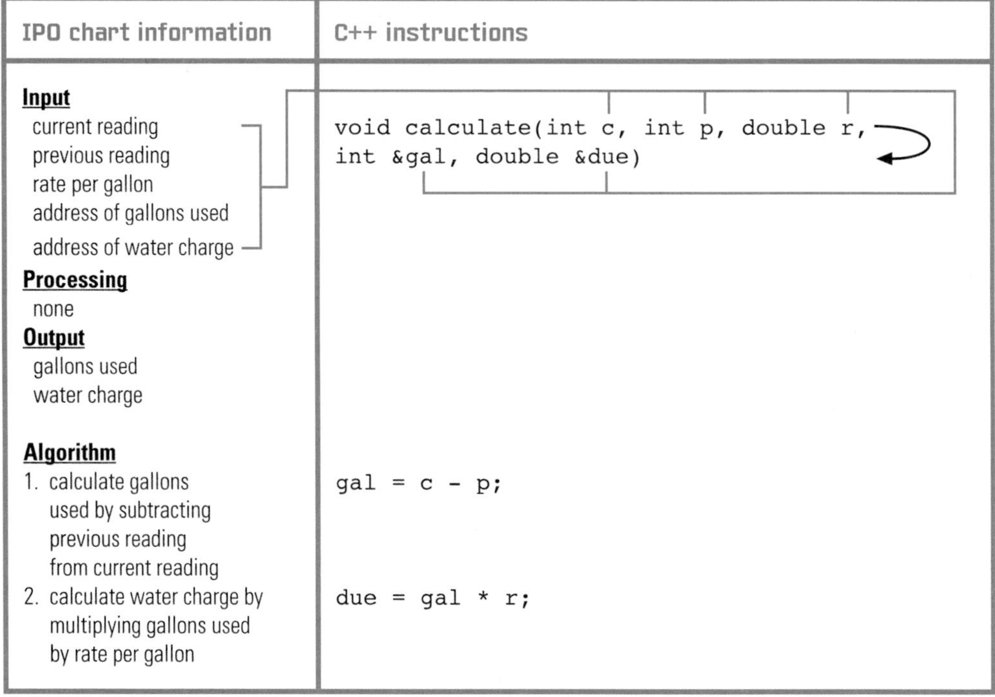

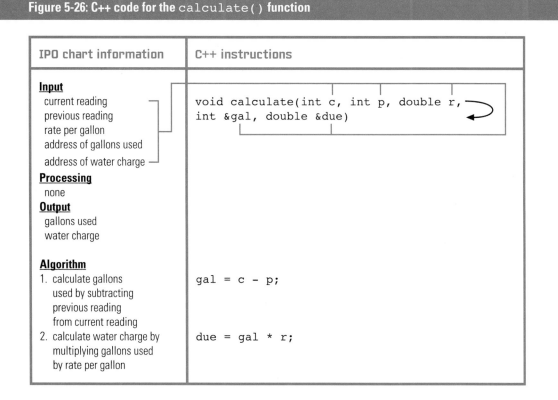

IPO chart information	C++ instructions
Input current reading previous reading rate per gallon address of gallons used address of water charge	`void calculate(int c, int p, double r, int &gal, double &due)`
Processing none	
Output gallons used water charge	
Algorithm 1. calculate gallons used by subtracting previous reading from current reading	`gal = c - p;`
2. calculate water charge by multiplying gallons used by rate per gallon	`due = gal * r;`

tip

The variable names `c`, `p`, `r`, `gal`, and `due` are local to the `calculate()` function and are removed from memory when the computer encounters the function's closing brace.

Finally, code the `displayBill()` function.

Coding the `displayBill()` Function

Recall that the `main()` function will pass the values of its `name`, `gallons`, and `charge` variables to the `displayBill()` function. The `displayBill()` function will use the formal parameters `cust`, `used`, and `amtDue` to receive the information. Figure 5-27 shows the C++ code for the `displayBill()` function.

Figure 5-27: C++ code for the displayBill() function

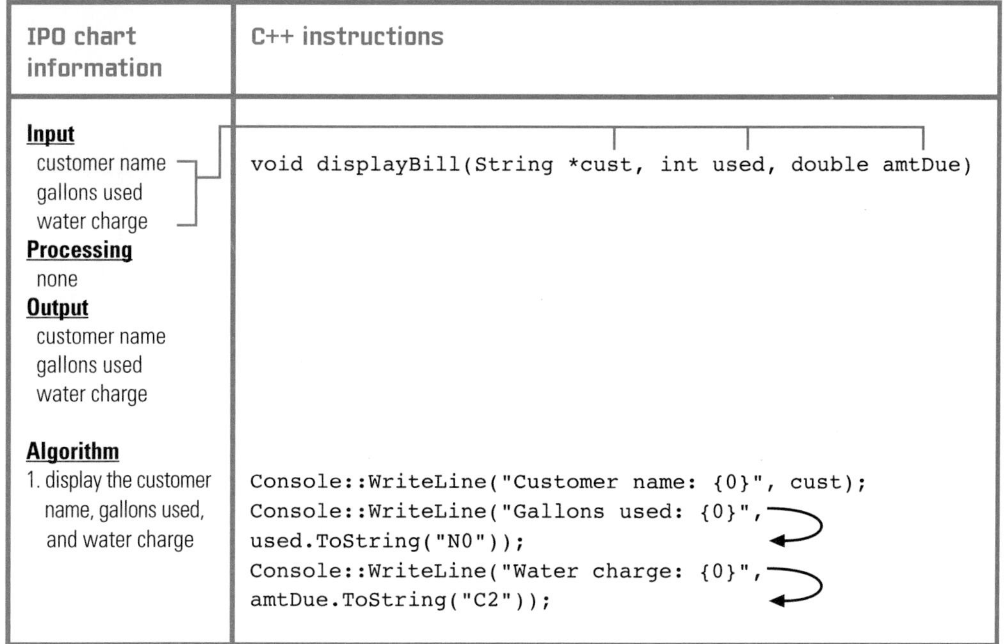

IPO chart information	C++ instructions
Input customer name gallons used water charge **Processing** none **Output** customer name gallons used water charge	`void displayBill(String *cust, int used, double amtDue)`

Algorithm
1. display the customer name, gallons used, and water charge
	`Console::WriteLine("Customer name: {0}", cust);`
	`Console::WriteLine("Gallons used: {0}", used.ToString("N0"));`
	`Console::WriteLine("Water charge: {0}", amtDue.ToString("C2"));`

tip

The variable names cust, used, and amtDue are local to the displayBill() function and are removed from memory when the computer encounters the function's closing brace.

Now that you have finished coding the algorithms, you need to desk-check the program, using the same data you used to desk-check the algorithms. Figure 5-28 shows the data and the completed desk-check tables for the program, with the payment amounts shown rounded to two decimal places.

Figure 5-28: Data and completed desk-check table for the program

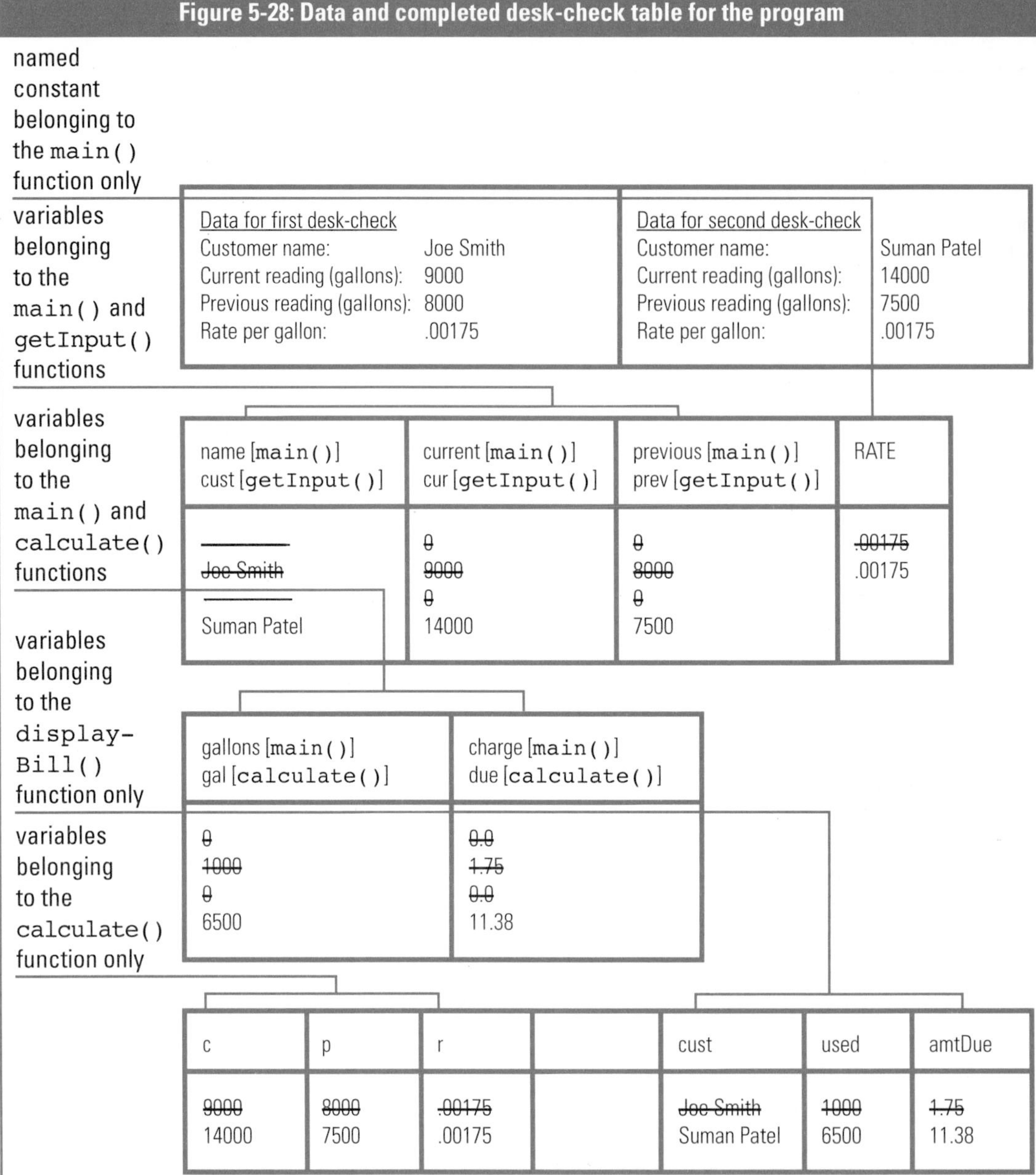

named constant belonging to the main() function only
variables belonging to the main() and getInput() functions
variables belonging to the main() and calculate() functions
variables belonging to the displayBill() function only
variables belonging to the calculate() function only
Data for first desk-check
Customer name: Joe Smith
Current reading (gallons): 9000
Previous reading (gallons): 8000
Rate per gallon: .00175
Data for second desk-check
Customer name: Suman Patel
Current reading (gallons): 14000
Previous reading (gallons): 7500
Rate per gallon: .00175
name [main()] cust [getInput()]
Joe Smith
Suman Patel
current [main()] cur [getInput()]
0
9000
0
14000
previous [main()] prev [getInput()]
0
8000
0
7500
RATE
.00175
.00175
gallons [main()] gal [calculate()]
0
1000
0
6500
charge [main()] due [calculate()]
0.0
1.75
0.0
11.38
c
9000
14000
p
8000
7500
r
.00175
.00175
cust
Joe Smith
Suman Patel
used
1000
6500
amtDue
1.75
11.38

The results obtained when desk-checking the program agree with the results obtained when desk-checking the algorithm. You now are ready to enter the C++ instructions into the computer.

Completing the Water Bill Program

On your computer's hard disk is a partially completed C++ program containing many of the instructions for the water bill program. You open that program in the next set of steps.

To open the partially completed C++ program:

1. Start Microsoft Visual Studio .NET. If necessary, close the Start Page window.
2. Click **File** on the menu bar, and then click **Open Solution**. The Open Solution dialog box opens.

3. Locate and then open the **CppNet\Tut05\T5App Solution** folder.
4. Click **T5App Solution** (T5App Solution.sln) in the list of filenames, and then click the **Open** button.
5. If the T5App.cpp source file is not displayed, right-click **T5App.cpp** in the Solution Explorer window, and then click **Open**. Figure 5-29 shows the instructions contained in the partially completed T5App.cpp program.

Figure 5-29: Instructions contained in the partially completed T5App.cpp program

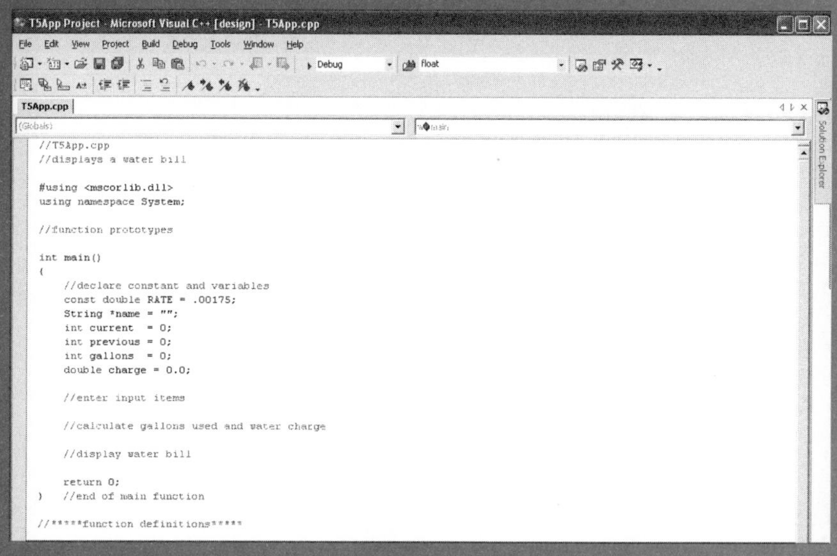

```
//T5App.cpp
//displays a water bill

#using <mscorlib.dll>
using namespace System;

//function prototypes

int main()
{
    //declare constant and variables
    const double RATE = .00175;
    String *name = "";
    int current  = 0;
    int previous = 0;
    int gallons  = 0;
    double charge = 0.0;

    //enter input items

    //calculate gallons used and water charge

    //display water bill

    return 0;
}   //end of main function

//*****function definitions*****
```

Missing from the program are the statements that call the `getInput()`, `calculate()`, and `displayBill()` functions, as well as the prototypes and definitions of those functions.

To enter the missing instructions:

1. Position the insertion point in the blank line below the `//function prototypes` comment.

   First enter the `getInput()` function prototype. Recall that the function prototype is simply the function header (shown earlier in Figure 5-25) without the names of the formal parameters, but with a semicolon at the end.
2. Type **void getInput(String *&, int &, int &);** and press **Enter**.

   Now, enter the `getInput()` function call (shown earlier in Figure 5-24).
3. Position the insertion point in the blank line below the `//enter input items` comment in the `main()` function. Press **Tab**, if necessary, then type **getInput(name, current, previous);**.

   Next, enter the `getInput()` function definition (shown earlier in Figure 5-25).
4. Position the insertion point in the blank line below the `//*****function definitions*****` comment, then type the `getInput()` function definition, which is shaded in Figure 5-30.

Figure 5-30: T5App.cpp program showing the `getInput()` function definition

function prototype

function call

enter this function definition

```
//T5App.cpp
//displays a water bill

#using <mscorlib.dll>
using namespace System;

//function prototypes
void getInput(String *&, int &, int &);

int main()
{
    //declare constant and variables
    const double RATE = .00175;
    String *name = "";
    int current  = 0;
    int previous = 0;
    int gallons  = 0;
    double charge = 0.0;

    //enter input items
    getInput(name, current, previous);
    //calculate gallons used and water charge

    //display water bill

    return 0;
}   //end of main function

//*****function definitions*****
void getInput(String *&cust, int &cur, int &prev)
{
    Console::Write("Customer name: ");
    cust = Console::ReadLine();
    Console::Write("Current reading: ");
    cur = Convert::ToInt32(Console::ReadLine());
    Console::Write("Previous reading: ");
    prev = Convert::ToInt32(Console::ReadLine());
}   //end of getInput function
```

Next, enter the instructions pertaining to the `calculate()` and `displayBill()` functions.

5. Enter the two function prototypes, two function calls, and two function definitions shaded in Figure 5-31, which shows the completed T5App.cpp program.

Figure 5-31: Completed T5App.cpp program

```
//T5App.cpp
//displays a water bill

#using <mscorlib.dll>
using namespace System;

//function prototypes
void getInput(String *&, int &, int &);
void calculate(int, int, double, int &, double &);
void displayBill(String *, int, double);

int main()
{
    //declare constant and variables
    const double RATE = .00175;
    String *name = "";
    int current  = 0;
    int previous = 0;
    int gallons  = 0;
    double charge = 0.0;

    //enter input items
    getInput(name, current, previous);
    //calculate gallons used and water charge
    calculate(current, previous, RATE, gallons, charge);
    //display water bill
    displayBill(name, gallons, charge);
    return 0;
}   //end of main function

//*****function definitions*****
void getInput(String *&cust, int &cur, int &prev)
{
    Console::Write("Customer name: ");
    cust = Console::ReadLine();
    Console::Write("Current reading: ");
    cur = Convert::ToInt32(Console::ReadLine());
    Console::Write("Previous reading: ");
    prev = Convert::ToInt32(Console::ReadLine());
}   //end of getInput function

void calculate(int c, int p, double r, int &gal,
double &due)
{
    gal = c - p;     //calculate gallons used
    due = gal * r;   //calculate water charge
}   //end of calculate function

void displayBill(String *cust, int used, double amtDue)
{
    Console::WriteLine("Customer name: {0}", cust);
    Console::WriteLine("Gallons used: {0}",
    used.ToString("N0"));
    Console::WriteLine("Water charge: {0}",
    amtDue.ToString("C2"));
}   //end of displayBill function
```

enter these function prototypes

enter these function calls

enter these function definitions

6. Verify the accuracy of your code by comparing the code on your screen with the code shown in Figure 5-31. Be sure to enter the letter N followed by the number zero—"N0"—when formatting the `used` variable in the `displayBill()` function.

Now test the program to verify that it works correctly.

To test the program:

1. Save and then build the solution. Verify that the program generated no warnings.
2. Execute the program. When prompted for the customer's name, type **Joe Brown** and press **Enter**.
3. When prompted for the current reading, type **9000** and press **Enter**. When prompted for the previous reading, type **8000** and press **Enter**. The program calculates and displays the water bill, as shown in Figure 5-32.

Figure 5-32: Command Prompt window showing the results of the first test

"c:\CppNet\Tut05\T5App Solution\T5App Project\Debug\T5App Project.exe"
Customer name: Joe Brown
Current reading: 9000
Previous reading: 8000
Customer name: Joe Brown
Gallons used: 1,000
Water charge: $1.75
Press any key to continue_

The Command Prompt window shows that the gallons used and water charge are 1,000 and $1.75, respectively, which agree with the results shown earlier in the desk-check tables.

4. Press **Enter** to close the Command Prompt window, then close the Output window.
5. Execute the program again. Enter **Suman Patel** as the customer name, **14000** as the current reading, and **7500** as the previous reading. The Command Prompt window shows that the gallons used and the water charge are 6,500 and $11.38, respectively, which agree with the results shown earlier in the desk-check tables.
6. Press **Enter** to close the Command Prompt window, then close the Output window.
7. Click **File** on the menu bar, and then click **Close Solution** to close the current solution.
8. Click **File** on the menu bar, and then click **Exit** to exit Visual Studio .NET.

You now have completed Tutorial 5's Application lesson. You can either take a break or complete the end-of-lesson exercises.

Look For These Symbols

Debugging

Discovery

EXERCISES

1) In this exercise, you modify the program you created in the lesson so that it uses two void functions, rather than one void function, to calculate the gallons used and the water charge.

A. If necessary, start Visual Studio .NET. Open the T5AppE01 Solution (T5AppE01 Solution.sln) file, which is contained in the CppNet\Tut05\T5AppE01 Solution folder.

B. Replace the `calculate()` function with two void functions named `calcGallons()` and `calcCharge()`. The `calcGallons()` function should calculate the number of gallons used, and the `calcCharge()` function should calculate the water charge.

C. Save and then build the solution.

D. Execute the program. Enter Sue Jones as the name, 6000 as the current reading, and 3000 as the previous reading.

E. When the program is working correctly, close the Output window, and then use the File menu to close the solution.

2) In this exercise, you create a simple payroll program using a `main()` function and four void functions.

A. Figure 5-33 shows the partially completed IPO charts for the payroll program. Complete the Input and Output columns of the IPO charts for the four void functions named `getInput()`, `calcFedTaxes()`, `calcNetPay()`, and `displayInfo()`. The FWT (Federal Withholding Tax) rate is 20% of the weekly salary, and the FICA (Federal Insurance Contributions Act) rate is 8% of the weekly salary.

Figure 5-33

`main()` **function**

Input	Processing	Output
name weekly salary FWT rate (.2) FICA rate (.08)	Processing items: none Algorithm: 1. getInput(name, weekly salary) 2. calcFedTaxes(weekly salary, FWT rate, FICA rate, FWT, FICA) 3. calcNetPay(weekly salary, FWT, FICA, weekly net pay) 4. displayInfo(name, FWT, FICA, weekly net pay)	name FWT FICA weekly net pay

`getInput()` **function**

Input	Processing	Output
	Processing items: none Algorithm: 1. enter the name and weekly salary	

Figure 5-33 (continued)

`calcFedTaxes()` **function**

Input	Processing	Output
	Processing items: none Algorithm: 1. calculate the FWT by multiplying the weekly salary by the FWT rate 2. calculate the FICA by multiplying the weekly salary by the FICA rate	

`calcNetPay()` **function**

Input	Processing	Output
	Processing items: none Algorithm: 1. calculate the weekly net pay by subtracting the FWT and FICA from the weekly salary	

`displayInfo()` **function**

Input	Processing	Output
	Processing items: none Algorithm: 1. display the name, FWT, FICA, and weekly net pay	

B. If necessary, start Visual Studio .NET. Open the T5AppE02 Solution (T5AppE02 Solution.sln) file, which is contained in the CppNet\Tut05\T5AppE02 Solution folder.

C. Use the IPO charts you completed in Step A to complete the program. Display the taxes and net pay using the "N2" format.

D. Complete a desk-check table for the program, using Samuel Montez as the employee's name and 500 as the weekly salary, and then using Barbara Jacks as the employee's name and 650 as the weekly salary.

E. Save and then build the solution.

F. Execute the program. Use the data from Step D to test the program.

G. When the program is working correctly, close the Output window, and then use the File menu to close the solution.

3) In this exercise, you create a program that converts a Fahrenheit temperature to a Celsius temperature. The program uses a `main()` function and three void functions.

A. Figure 5-34 shows the partially completed IPO charts for the temperature program. Complete the IPO charts for the `main()` function and the three void functions named `getFahrenheit()`, `calcCelsius()`, and `displayCelsius()`.

Figure 5-34

`main()` **function**

Input	Processing	Output
Fahrenheit temperature	Processing items: none Algorithm: 1. getFahrenheit( ) 2. calcCelsius( ) 3. displayCelsius( )	Celsius temperature

`getFahrenheit()` **function**

Input	Processing	Output
	Processing items: none Algorithm: 1. enter the Fahrenheit temperature	

`calcCelsius()` **function**

Input	Processing	Output
	Processing items: none Algorithm: 1. calculate the Celsius temperature as follows: 5.0/9.0 * (Fahrenheit temperature – 32)	

`displayCelsius()` **function**

Input	Processing	Output
	Processing items: none Algorithm: 1. display the Celsius temperature	

B. If necessary, start Visual Studio .NET. Open the T5AppE03 Solution (T5AppE03 Solution.sln) file, which is contained in the CppNet\Tut05\T5AppE03 Solution folder.

C. Use the IPO charts you completed in Step A to complete the program. Display the Celsius temperature using the "F0" format.

D. Complete a desk-check table for the program, using the following Fahrenheit temperatures: 32 F and 212 F.

E. Save and then build the solution.

F. Execute the program. Use the data from Step D to test the program.

G. When the program is working correctly, close the Output window, and then use the File menu to close the solution.

4) In this exercise, you create a program that displays a 10% bonus. The program uses a `main()` function and three void functions.

A. Figure 5-35 shows the partially completed IPO charts for the bonus program. Complete the IPO charts for the `main()` function and the three void functions named `getSales()`, `calcBonus()`, and `displayBonus()`.

Figure 5-35

`main()` **function**

Input	Processing	Output
sales bonus rate (.1)	Processing items: none Algorithm: 1. getSales( ) 2. calcBonus( ) 3. displayBonus( )	bonus

`getSales()` **function**

Input	Processing	Output
	Processing items: Algorithm:	

`calcBonus()` **function**

Input	Processing	Output
	Processing items: Algorithm:	

Figure 5-35 (continued)

`displayBonus()` **function**

Input	Processing	Output
	Processing items: Algorithm:	

B. If necessary, start Visual Studio .NET. Open the T5AppE04 Solution (T5AppE04 Solution.sln) file, which is contained in the CppNet\Tut05\T5AppE04 Solution folder.

C. Use the IPO charts you completed in Step A to complete the program. Display the bonus amount with a dollar sign and two decimal places.

D. Complete a desk-check table for the program, using the following sale amounts: 24,500 and 134,780.

E. Save and then build the solution.

F. Execute the program. Use the data from Step D to test the program.

G. When the program is working correctly, close the Output window, and then use the File menu to close the solution.

5) In this exercise, you modify the program you created in Tutorial 4's Application lesson. The modified program uses a `main()` function and two void functions.

A. If necessary, start Visual Studio .NET. Open the T5AppE05 Solution (T5AppE05 Solution.sln) file, which is contained in the CppNet\Tut05\T5AppE05 Solution folder.

B. Modify the program so that it uses a void function, rather than a value-returning function, to calculate the monthly payments.

C. Save and then build the solution.

D. Execute the program. Enter 16000 as the car price, 3000 as the rebate, .08 as the credit union rate, .03 as the dealer rate, and 4 as the term. The program should display $317.37 as the credit union payment and $354.15 as the dealer payment.

E. When the program is working correctly, close the Output window, and then use the File menu to close the solution.

6) In this exercise, you create a program that calculates the average of three test scores. The program uses two value-returning functions and two void functions.

A. Write the IPO charts for a program that contains four functions: `main()`, `getTestScores()`, `calcAverage()`, and `displayAverage()`. The `main()` function should call the void `getTestScores()` function, whose task is to get three test scores. (The test scores might contain a decimal place.) The `main()` function then should call the value-returning `calcAverage()` function to calculate and return the average of the three test scores. When the `calcAverage()` function has completed its task, the `main()` function should call the void `displayAverage()` function to display the average of the three scores on the screen.

B. If necessary, start Visual Studio .NET. Create a blank solution named T5AppE06 Solution. Save the solution in the CppNet\Tut05 folder.

C. Add a new managed C++ empty project to the solution. Name the project T5AppE06 Project.

D. Add a new C++ source file to the project. Name the source file T5AppE06.

E. Enter the appropriate C++ instructions into the source file. Use the IPO charts you created in Step A to code the program. Display the average with one decimal place.

F. Complete a desk-check table for the program, using the following two groups of test scores:

95.5, 83, 76
54, 89, 77

G. Save and then build the solution.

H. Execute the program. Use the data from Step F to test the program.

I. When the program is working correctly, close the Output window, and then use the File menu to close the solution.

7) In this exercise, you modify the program you created in the lesson so that it uses two value-returning functions, rather than one void function, to calculate the gallons used and the water charge.

A. If necessary, start Visual Studio .NET. Open the T5AppE07 Solution (T5AppE07 Solution.sln) file, which is contained in the CppNet\Tut05\T5AppE07 Solution folder.

B. Replace the `calculate()` function with two value-returning functions named `calcGallons()` and `calcCharge()`. The `calcGallons()` function should calculate and return the number of gallons used. The `calcCharge()` function should calculate and return the water charge.

C. Save and then build the solution.

D. Execute the program. Enter Sue Jones as the name, 6000 as the current reading, and 3000 as the previous reading.

E. When the program is working correctly, close the Output window, and then use the File menu to close the solution.

8) In this exercise, you create a simple payroll program that uses four value-returning functions named `main()`, `calcFwt()`, `calcFica()`, and `calcNetPay()`. The program also uses two void functions named `getInput()` and `displayInfo()`.

A. Figure 5-36 shows the partially completed IPO charts for the payroll program. Complete the IPO charts appropriately. The FWT (Federal Withholding Tax) rate is 20% of the weekly salary, and the FICA (Federal Insurance Contributions Act) rate is 8% of the weekly salary. Remember that only the `getInput()` and `displayInfo()` functions are void functions.

Figure 5-36

`main()` **function**

Input	Processing	Output
name weekly salary FWT rate (.2) FICA rate (.08)	Processing items: none Algorithm: 1. getInput( ) 2. FWT = calcFwt( ) 3. FICA = calcFica( ) 4. weekly net pay = calcNetPay( ) 5. displayInfo( )	name FWT FICA weekly net pay

`getInput()` **function**

Input	Processing	Output
	Processing items: none Algorithm:	

`calcFwt()` **function**

Input	Processing	Output
	Processing items: none Algorithm:	

`calcFica()` **function**

Input	Processing	Output
	Processing items: none Algorithm:	

`calcNetPay()` **function**

Input	Processing	Output
	Processing items: none Algorithm:	

Figure 5-36 (continued)

`displayInfo()` **function**

Input	Processing	Output
	Processing items: none Algorithm:	

B. If necessary, start Visual Studio .NET. Open the T5AppE08 Solution (T5AppE08 Solution.sln) file, which is contained in the CppNet\Tut05\T5AppE08 Solution folder.

C. Use the IPO charts you completed in Step A to complete the program. Display the taxes and net pay with a dollar sign and two decimal places.

D. Complete a desk-check table for the program, using Bonnie James as the employee's name and 350 as the weekly salary, and then using Drew Carlisle as the employee's name and 700 as the weekly salary.

E. Save and then build the solution.

F. Execute the program. Use the data from Step D to test the program.

G. When the program is working correctly, close the Output window, and then use the File menu to close the solution.

9) In this exercise, you learn how to pass a named constant so that the receiving function cannot change the value passed to it.

A. If necessary, start Visual Studio .NET. Open the T5AppE09 Solution (T5AppE09 Solution.sln) file, which is contained in the CppNet\Tut05\T5AppE09 Solution folder.

The water bill program that you created in the lesson passed the value of the RATE named constant to the `calculate()` function. The `calculate()` function stored the value it received (.00175) in the `r` variable. Because the passed value was stored in a variable, the value could be changed by the `calculate()` function. First verify that the `calculate()` function can change the value stored in the `r` variable.

B. Insert a blank line above the `gal = c - p;` statement in the `calculate()` function. In the blank line, type `r = 1.5;`.

C. Save and then build the solution. Execute the program. Enter your name as the customer name, 3000 as the current reading, and 2000 as the previous reading. Rather than displaying $1.75 as the water charge, the program displays $1,500.00.

D. Close the Command Prompt and Output windows.

E. To prevent the `calculate()` function from changing the water rate, you must indicate that the value being passed is a constant. Make the appropriate modifications to the `calculate()` function's prototype and header.

F. Save and then build the solution. The compiler displays an error message indicating that the contents of the `r` variable in the `r = 1.5;` statement is a constant.

G. Delete the `r = 1.5;` statement from the `calculate()` function.

H. Save and then build the solution. Execute the program. Enter your name as the customer name, 3000 as the current reading, and 2000 as the previous reading. The program correctly displays 1,000 and $1.75 as the gallons used and water charge, respectively.

I. When the program is working correctly, close the Output window, and then use the File menu to close the solution.

10) In this exercise, you debug a C++ program.

A. If necessary, start Visual Studio .NET. Open the T5AppE10 Solution (T5AppE10 Solution.sln) file, which is contained in the CppNet\Tut05\T5AppE10 Solution folder.

B. The program should display an employee's gross pay, but it is not working correctly. Study the program's code, then build the solution.

C. Correct any errors in the program, then save and build the solution.

D. Execute the program. Test the program by entering 35 as the hours worked, and 10 as the pay rate. Close the Command Prompt window.

E. When the program is working correctly, close the Output window, and then use the File menu to close the solution.

11) In this exercise, you debug a C++ program.

A. If necessary, start Visual Studio .NET. Open the T5AppE11 Solution (T5AppE11 Solution.sln) file, which is contained in the CppNet\Tut05\T5AppE11 Solution folder.

B. The program should display a bonus amount, but it is not working correctly. Study the program's code, then build the solution.

C. Execute the program. Test the program by entering 10500 as the sales, and .05 as the bonus rate. Notice that the program does not display the correct bonus amount. Close the Command Prompt window.

D. Correct the errors in the program, then save and build the solution. Execute the program again, using the data from Step C to test the program. Close the Command Prompt window.

E. When the program is working correctly, close the Output window, and then use the File menu to close the solution.

Tutorial 6

The Selection Structure

Objectives

After completing this tutorial, you will be able to:

- Use the selection structure in a program
- Write pseudocode for the selection structure
- Create a flowchart for the selection structure
- Code the `if` and `if/else` forms of the selection structure
- Write code that uses comparison operators and logical operators
- Change the contents of a `String` variable to uppercase or lowercase
- Compare strings using the `CompareTo()` method
- Return a floating-point number when dividing two integers

Concept Lesson

Using the Selection Structure

The programs you created in the previous five tutorials used the sequence programming structure only, where the program instructions are processed, one after another, in the order in which each appears in the program. In many programs, however, the next instruction processed depends on the result of a decision or comparison that the program must make. For example, a payroll program typically needs to compare the number of hours the employee worked with the number 40 to determine whether the employee should receive overtime pay in addition to regular pay. Based on the result of that comparison the program then selects either an instruction that computes regular pay only or an instruction that computes regular pay plus overtime pay.

tip
As you may remember from Tutorial 1, the selection structure is one of the three programming structures. The other two programming structures are sequence, which was covered in the previous tutorials, and repetition, which is covered in Tutorials 8 and 9.

You use the **selection structure**, also called the **decision structure**, when you want a program to make a decision or comparison and then select one of two paths, depending on the result of that decision or comparison. Although the idea of using the selection structure in a program is new, the concept of the selection structure is already familiar to you, because you use it each day to make hundreds of decisions. For example, every morning you have to decide whether you are hungry and, if you are, what you are going to eat. Figure 6-1 shows other examples of selection structures you might use today.

Figure 6-1: Selection structures you might use today

	Example 1	Example 2

condition
condition
	if (it is raining)
	  wear a rain coat
	  bring an umbrella
		if (you have a test tomorrow)
		  study tonight
		else
		  watch a movie

In the examples shown in Figure 6-1, the portion in parentheses, called the **condition**, specifies the decision you are making and is phrased so that it results in either a true or false answer only. For example, either it's raining (true) or it's not raining (false); either you have a test tomorrow (true) or you don't have a test tomorrow (false).

If the condition is true, you perform a specific set of tasks. If the condition is false, on the other hand, you might or might not need to perform a different set of tasks. For instance, look at the first example shown in Figure 6-1. If it is raining (a true condition), then you will wear a raincoat and bring an umbrella. Notice that you do not have anything in particular to do if it is not raining (a false condition). Compare this with the second example shown in Figure 6-1. If you have a test tomorrow (a true condition), then you will study tonight. If you do not have a test tomorrow (a false condition), however, then you will watch a movie.

Like you, the computer also can evaluate a condition and then select the appropriate tasks to perform based on that evaluation. When using the selection structure in a program, the programmer must be sure to phrase the condition so that it results in either a true or a false answer only. The programmer also must specify the tasks to be performed when the condition is true and, if necessary, the tasks to be performed when the condition is false.

Most programming languages offer three forms of the selection structure: `if`, `if/else`, and `switch` (also called `case`). You learn about the `if` and `if/else` forms of the selection structure in this tutorial; the switch form is covered in Tutorial 7. Begin by learning how to show the `if` and `if/else` selection structures in pseudocode.

Including the Selection Structure in Pseudocode

Figure 6-2 shows examples of the `if` and `if/else` selection structures written in pseudocode.

Figure 6-2: Examples of the `if` and `if/else` selection structures written in pseudocode

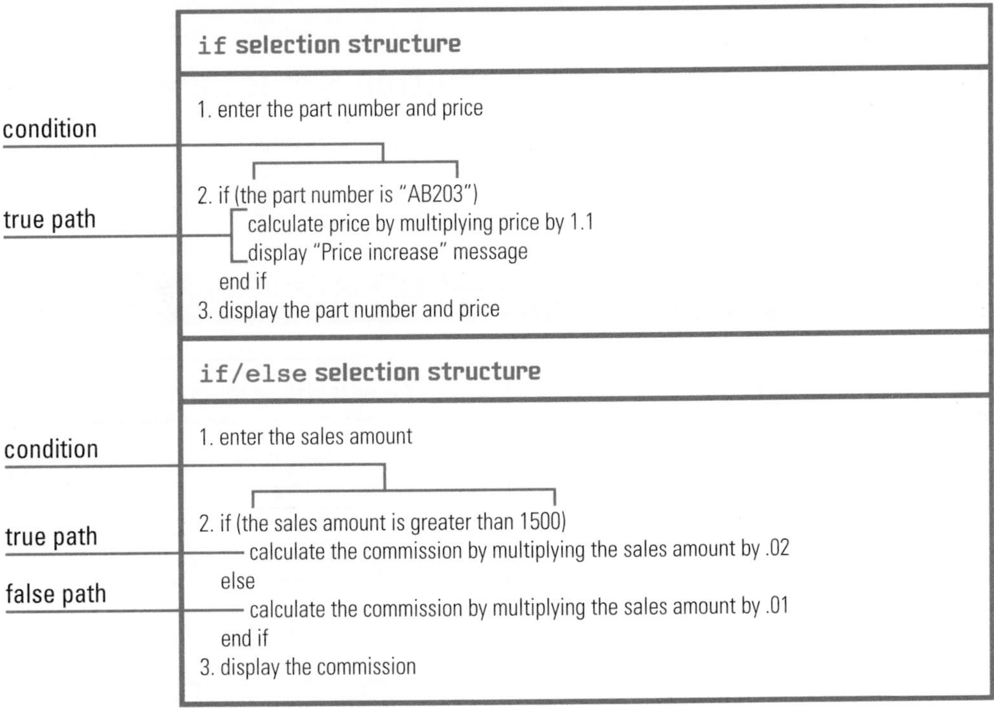

if selection structure
condition
true path
1. enter the part number and price
2. if (the part number is "AB203")
calculate price by multiplying price by 1.1
display "Price increase" message
end if
3. display the part number and price
if/else selection structure
condition
true path
false path
1. enter the sales amount
2. if (the sales amount is greater than 1500)
calculate the commission by multiplying the sales amount by .02
else
calculate the commission by multiplying the sales amount by .01
end if
3. display the commission

Although pseudocode is not standardized—every programmer has his or her own version—you will find some similarities among the various versions. For example, many programmers begin the selection structure with the word `if` and end the structure with the two words **`end if`**. They also use the word **`else`** to designate the instructions to be performed when the condition is false.

In the examples shown in Figure 6-2, the portion within parentheses indicates the condition to be evaluated. Notice that each condition results in either a true or a false answer only. In Example 1, either the part number is "AB203" or it isn't. In Example 2, either the sales amount is greater than the number 1500 or it isn't.

When the condition is true, the set of instructions following the condition is selected for processing. The instructions following the condition are referred to as the **true path**—the path you follow when the condition is true. The true path ends when you come to the `else` or, if there is no `else`, when you come to the end of the selection structure (the `end if`). After the true path instructions are processed, the instruction following the `end if` is processed. In the examples shown in Figure 6-2, the display instructions are processed after the instructions in the true path.

The instructions processed when the `if` structure's condition is false depend on whether the selection structure contains an `else`. When there is no `else`, as in the first example shown in Figure 6-2, the `if` structure ends when its condition is false, and processing continues with the instruction following the `end if`. In the first example, for instance, the "display the part number and price" instruction is processed when the part number is not "AB203." In cases where the selection structure contains an `else`, as in the second example shown in Figure 6-2, the instructions between the `else` and the `end if`—referred to as the **false path**—are processed before the instruction after the `end if` is processed. In the second example, the "calculate the commission by multiplying the sales amount by .01" instruction is processed first, followed by the "display the commission" instruction.

In addition to using pseudocode to plan algorithms, recall from Tutorial 2 that programmers also use flowcharts. In the next section, you learn how to show the selection structure in a flowchart.

Drawing a Flowchart of a Selection Structure

Unlike pseudocode, which consists of short English statements, a flowchart uses standardized symbols to show the steps the computer must take to accomplish the program's goal. Figure 6-3 shows Figure 6-2's examples in flowchart form.

Figure 6-3: Examples of the `if` and `if/else` selection structures drawn in flowchart form

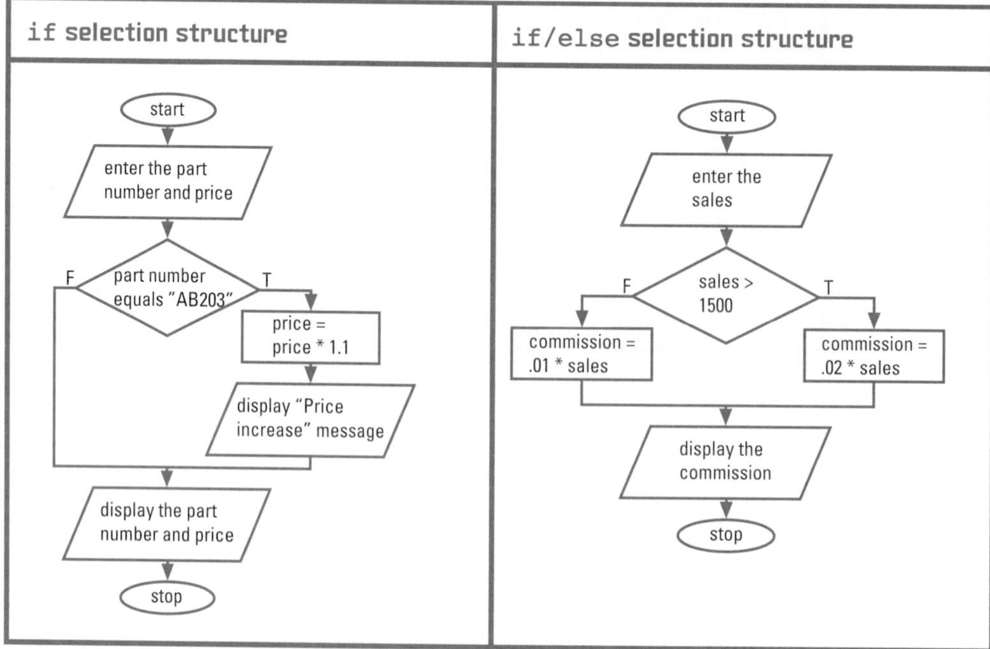

As you learned in Tutorial 2, the oval in the figure is the start/stop symbol, the rectangle is the process symbol, and the parallelogram is the input/output symbol. The new symbol in the flowchart, the diamond, is called the **selection/repetition symbol**, because it is used to represent both selection and repetition. In Figure 6-3's flowcharts, the diamonds represent the selection structure. (You learn how to use the diamond to represent repetition in Tutorial 8.) Notice that inside each diamond is a comparison that evaluates to either true or false only. Each diamond also has one flowline entering the symbol and two flowlines leaving the symbol. The two flowlines leading out of the diamond should be marked so that anyone reading the flowchart can distinguish the true path from the false path. You mark the flowline leading to the true path with a "T" (for true), and you mark the flowline leading to the false path with an "F" (for false).

tip

You also can mark the flowlines leading out of the diamond with a "Y" and an "N" (for yes and no).

Next, you learn how to code the `if` and `if/else` forms of the selection structure.

Coding the Selection Structure

tip

Recall that flowlines are the lines that connect the flowchart symbols.

Figure 6-4 shows the syntax of the `if` statement, which is the statement you use to code the `if` and `if/else` forms of the selection structure in C++.

Figure 6-4: Syntax of the C++ `if` statement

`if` (*condition***)**
  one statement, or a block of statements enclosed in braces, to be processed when the condition is true
[**`else`**
  one statement, or a block of statements enclosed in braces, to be processed when the condition is false]
`//end if`

The items in square brackets ([]) in the syntax are optional. For example, you do not always need to include the `else` portion of the syntax, referred to as the `else` clause, in an `if` statement. Items in **bold**, on the other hand, are essential components of the `if` statement. For example, the keyword `if` and the parentheses that surround the *condition* are required. The keyword `else` must be included only if the statement uses that clause.

tip

Many C++ programmers include the braces even when only one statement needs to be processed. By doing so, the programmer does not need to remember to enter the braces when statements are added to the selection structure in the future. Forgetting to enter the braces is a common error made by C++ programmers.

Items in *italics* in the syntax indicate where the programmer must supply information pertaining to the current program. For instance, the programmer must supply the *condition* to be evaluated. The *condition* must be a Boolean expression, which is an expression that results in a Boolean value (true or false).

In addition to supplying the *condition*, the programmer also must supply the statements to be processed when the *condition* evaluates to true and, optionally, when the *condition* evaluates to false. If more than one statement needs to be processed, the statements must be entered as a statement block. You create a **statement block** by enclosing the statements in a set of braces ({}).

Although it is not required to do so, it is a good programming practice to use a comment, such as `//end if`, to mark the end of the `if` statement in a program. The comment will make your program easier to read and understand. It also will help you keep track of the required `if` and `else` clauses when you nest `if` statements—in other words, when you include one `if` statement inside another `if` statement. You learn how to nest `if` statements in Tutorial 7.

Figure 6-5 shows the different ways of using the C++ `if` statement to code the `if` and `if/else` forms of the selection structure. Notice that, whenever multiple statements are included in a path, the statements are entered as a statement block by enclosing them in braces.

Figure 6-5: Different ways of coding the `if` and `if/else` selection structures in C++

`if` form with one statement	`if` form with multiple statements

if (*condition*)
  one statement
//end if
	if (*condition*)
	{
	  multiple statements
	  require braces
	} //end if

`if/else` form with one statement in each path	`if/else` form with multiple statements in true path and one statement in false path	`if/else` form with multiple statements in false path and one statement in true path	`if/else` form with multiple statements in true and false paths

if (*condition*)
  one statement
else
  one statement
//end if
	if (*condition*)
	{
	  multiple statements
	  require braces
	}
	else
	  one statement
	//end if
		if (*condition*)
		  one statement
		else
		{
		  multiple statements
		  require braces
		} //end if
			if (*condition*)
			{
			  multiple statements
			  require braces
			}
			else
			{
			  multiple statements
			  require braces
			} //end if

As mentioned earlier, the *condition* specified in the `if` statement must be a Boolean expression, which is an expression that evaluates to either true or false. The expression can contain variables, constants, functions, methods, arithmetic operators, comparison operators, and logical operators. You already know about variables, constants, functions, methods, and arithmetic operators. You learn about comparison operators and logical operators in the following sections.

Comparison Operators

Figure 6-6 lists the **comparison operators**, also referred to as **relational operators**, that you can use to make comparisons in a C++ program. The figure also shows the order of precedence for these operators. The precedence numbers indicate the order in which the computer performs the comparisons in a C++ expression. Comparisons with a precedence number of 1 are performed before comparisons with a precedence number of 2. However, you can use parentheses to override the order of precedence.

Notice that you use two equal signs (==) to test for equality in C++. You test for inequality by using an exclamation point, which stands for *not*, followed by an equal sign (`!=`).

It is easy to confuse the equality operator (==), which is used to compare two values, with the assignment operator (=), which is used to assign a value to a memory location. Keep in mind that you use the C++ statement `num = 1;` to assign the number one to the `num` variable. However, you use the C++ *condition* `num == 1` to compare the contents of the `num` variable to the number one.

tip

Entering a space between the symbols in a comparison operator (for example, entering > = instead of >=) is a syntax error. Reversing the symbols in a comparison operator (for example, entering => instead of >=) also is a syntax error.

Figure 6-6: Comparison operators in C++

Operator	Operation	Precedence number
<	less than	1
<=	less than or equal to	1
>	greater than	1
>=	greater than or equal to	1
==	equal to	2
!=	not equal to	2

Important note: Notice that four of the operators contain two symbols. When using these operators, do not include any spaces between the symbols. Also be sure you do not reverse the symbols—in other words, use >=, but don't use =>.

Figure 6-7 shows some examples of using comparison operators in the `if` statement's *condition* in C++.

Figure 6-7: Examples of comparison operators in an `if` statement's *condition*

`if` statement's *condition*	Meaning
`if (quantity < 50)`	Compares the contents of the `quantity` variable to the number 50. The *condition* will evaluate to true if the `quantity` variable contains a number that is less than 50; otherwise, it will evaluate to false.
`if (age >= 25)`	Compares the contents of the `age` variable to the number 25. The *condition* will evaluate to true if the `age` variable contains a number that is greater than or equal to 25; otherwise, it will evaluate to false.
`if (onhand == target)`	Compares the contents of the `onhand` variable to the contents of the `target` variable. The *condition* will evaluate to true if the `onhand` variable contains a number that is equal to the number in the `target` variable; otherwise, it will evaluate to false. (Both variables are `int` variables.)
`if (quantity != 7500)`	Compares the contents of the `quantity` variable to the number 7500. The *condition* will evaluate to true if the `quantity` variable contains a number that is not equal to 7500; otherwise, it will evaluate to false. (The `quantity` variable is an `int` variable.)

tip

Be careful when comparing two floating-point numbers (numbers with a decimal place). Because some floating-point values cannot be stored, precisely, in memory, you should never compare these values for equality or inequality. Rather, test that the difference between the numbers you are comparing is less than some acceptable small value, such as .00001. You can learn how to do this in Discovery Exercise 12 at the end of this lesson.

Notice that the expression contained in each *condition* evaluates to either true or false. All expressions containing a comparison operator result in an answer of either true or false only.

As with arithmetic operators, if an expression contains more than one comparison operator with the same precedence number, the computer evaluates the operators from left to right in the expression. Keep in mind, however, that comparison operators are evaluated after any arithmetic operators in the expression. In other words, in the expression 5 – 2 > 1 + 2, the two arithmetic operators (– and +) are evaluated before the comparison operator (>). The result of the expression is false, as shown in Figure 6-8.

Figure 6-8: Evaluation steps for an expression containing arithmetic and comparison operators

Evaluation steps	Result
Original expression	5 – 2 > 1 + 2
5 – 2 is evaluated first	3 > 1 + 2
1 + 2 is evaluated second	3 > 3
3 > 3 is evaluated last	false

In the next section, you view the pseudocode, flowchart, and C++ code for two programs that contain comparison operators in an `if` statement.

Using Comparison Operators in a Program

Assume you want to swap the values contained in two variables, but only if the first value is greater than the second value. Figure 6-9 shows the pseudocode, flowchart, and C++ code for a program that accomplishes this task.

Figure 6-9: Pseudocode, flowchart, and C++ code showing the `if` form of the selection structure

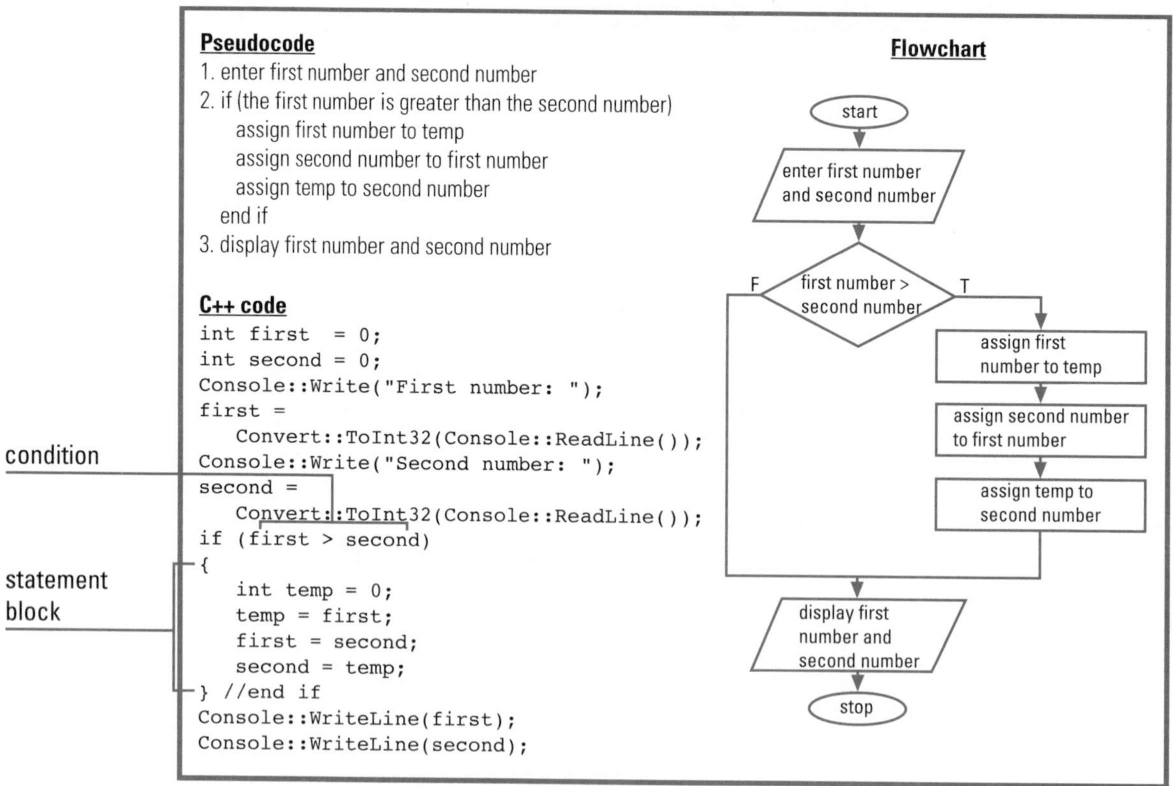

condition
statement block
Pseudocode
1. enter first number and second number
2. if (the first number is greater than the second number)
assign first number to temp
assign second number to first number
assign temp to second number
end if
3. display first number and second number
C++ code
int first = 0;
int second = 0;
Console::Write("First number: ");
first =
Convert::ToInt32(Console::ReadLine());
Console::Write("Second number: ");
second =
Convert::ToInt32(Console::ReadLine());
if (first > second)
{
int temp = 0;
temp = first;
first = second;
second = temp;
} //end if
Console::WriteLine(first);
Console::WriteLine(second);
Flowchart
start
enter first number and second number
first number > second number
F
T
assign first number to temp
assign second number to first number
assign temp to second number
display first number and second number
stop

The `(first > second)` *condition* in the C++ code shown in Figure 6-9 tells the computer to compare the contents of the `first` variable to the contents of the `second` variable. If the *condition* is true, which means that the value in the `first` variable is greater

than the value in the **second** variable, then the four instructions in the **if** statement's true path swap the values contained in those variables. Notice that the four instructions are enclosed in braces, forming a statement block. As you learned earlier, when more than one instruction needs to be processed when the **if** statement's *condition* is true (or false), the C++ syntax requires those instructions to be entered as a statement block.

Study closely the four instructions that swap the two values. The first instruction, **int temp = 0;**, creates and initializes a local variable named **temp**. The **temp** variable is local only to the statement block in which it is declared; in this case, it is local only to the **if** statement's true path. The second instruction, **temp = first;**, assigns the value contained in the **first** variable to the **temp** variable. In other words, it stores a copy of the **first** variable's contents in the **temp** variable. Next, the **first = second;** instruction assigns the value contained in the **second** variable to the **first** variable. Finally, the **second = temp;** instruction assigns the value contained in the **temp** variable to the **second** variable. The **temp** variable is necessary to store the contents of the **first** variable temporarily so that the swap can be made. If you did not store the **first** variable's value in the **temp** variable, the **second** variable's value would write over the value in the **first** variable, and the value in the **first** variable would be lost. Figure 6-10 illustrates the concept of swapping.

Figure 6-10: Illustration of the swapping concept

	temp	first	second
Values stored in the variables after the Console::ReadLine() statements are processed	0	8	4
Result of the temp = first; statement	8	8	4
Result of the first = second; statement	8	4	4
Result of the second = temp; statement (completes the swapping process)	8	4	8

values were swapped

In the next program, assume you want to give the user the option of displaying either the sum of two numbers he or she enters, or the difference between the two numbers. Figure 6-11 shows the pseudocode, flowchart, and C++ code for a program that accomplishes this task.

Figure 6-11: Pseudocode, flowchart, and C++ code showing the `if/else` form of the selection structure

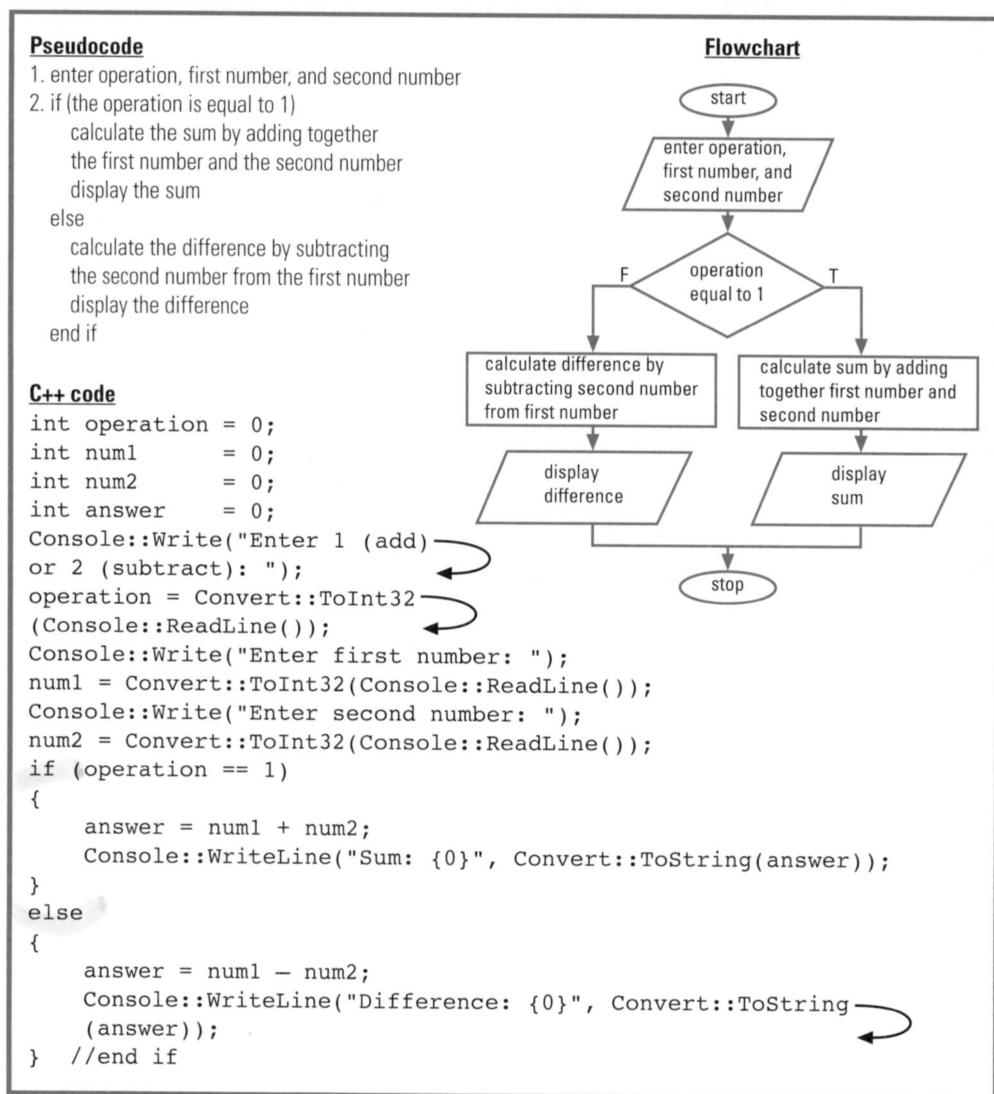

Pseudocode

1. enter operation, first number, and second number
2. if (the operation is equal to 1)
   calculate the sum by adding together the first number and the second number
   display the sum
   else
   calculate the difference by subtracting the second number from the first number
   display the difference
   end if

C++ code

```
int operation = 0;
int num1      = 0;
int num2      = 0;
int answer    = 0;
Console::Write("Enter 1 (add)
or 2 (subtract): ");
operation = Convert::ToInt32
(Console::ReadLine());
Console::Write("Enter first number: ");
num1 = Convert::ToInt32(Console::ReadLine());
Console::Write("Enter second number: ");
num2 = Convert::ToInt32(Console::ReadLine());
if (operation == 1)
{
    answer = num1 + num2;
    Console::WriteLine("Sum: {0}", Convert::ToString(answer));
}
else
{
    answer = num1 – num2;
    Console::WriteLine("Difference: {0}", Convert::ToString
    (answer));
} //end if
```


The `(operation == 1)` *condition* in the C++ code shown in Figure 6-11 tells the computer to compare the contents of the `operation` variable to the number one. If the *condition* is true, then the selection structure calculates and displays the sum of the two numbers entered by the user. If the *condition* is false, however, the selection structure calculates and displays the difference between the two numbers. Here again, because more than one instruction appears in both the true and false paths of the `if` statement, the instructions in each path are entered as a statement block.

MINI-QUIZ

Mini-Quiz 1

1) Assume that a program needs to determine whether a student's score is less than 70. If it is, the program should display the "Fail" message; otherwise, it should display the "Pass" message. Write the pseudocode for this selection structure.

2) Write a C++ `if` statement that corresponds to the pseudocode you wrote in Question 1. The student's score is stored in an `int` variable named `score`.

3) Which of the following C++ `if` clauses determines whether the `quantity` variable, which is of data type `int`, contains the number 100?

a. `if (quantity = 100)`
b. `if (quantity = 100);`
c. `if (quantity == 100)`
d. `if (quantity == 100);`

4) Which of the following C++ statements assigns the number 5 to a variable named `area`?

a. `area = 5`
b. `area = 5;`
c. `area == 5`
d. `area == 5;`

5) Write a C++ `if` clause that determines whether a variable named `area` has the value 5 stored in it.

Recall that you also can use logical operators to form the `if` statement's *condition*. You learn about logical operators next.

Logical Operators

The most commonly used **logical operators**, sometimes referred to as **Boolean operators**, are And and Or. Both of these operators allow you to combine two or more *conditions* into one compound *condition*. When the **And logical operator** is used to create a compound condition, all of the conditions must be true for the compound condition to be true. However, when the **Or logical operator** is used, only one of the conditions must be true for the compound condition to be true.

C++ uses special symbols to represent the And and Or logical operators in a program. The And operator in C++ is two ampersands (`&&`), and the Or operator is two pipe symbols (`||`). The pipe symbol (|) usually is located on the same key as the backslash (\) on the computer's keyboard.

The tables shown in Figure 6-12, called **truth tables**, summarize how the computer evaluates the logical operators in an expression.

tip

You learn about another logical operator, Not (`!`), in a later tutorial.

Figure 6-12: Truth tables for the And and Or logical operators

Truth table for the && (And) operator

Value of *condition1*	Value of *condition2*	Value of *condition1 && condition2*
true	true	true
true	false	false
false	true	false
false	false	false

Truth table for the || (Or) operator

Value of *condition1*	Value of *condition2*	Value of *condition1 || condition2*
true	true	true
true	false	true
false	true	true
false	false	false

tip

If you use the `&&` (And) operator to combine two conditions in a C++ expression, the computer does not evaluate the second condition if the first condition is false. Because both conditions combined with the `&&` operator must be true for the compound condition to be true, there is no need to evaluate the second condition when the first condition is false. If, on the other hand, you use the `||` (Or) operator to combine two conditions in a C++ expression, the computer does not evaluate the second condition if the first condition is true. Because only one of the conditions combined with the `||` operator must be true for the compound condition to be true, there is no need to evaluate the second condition when the first condition is true.

As Figure 6-12 indicates, when you use the And (`&&`) operator to combine two conditions (*condition1* `&&` *condition2*), the resulting compound condition is true only when both conditions are true. If either condition is false, or if both conditions are false, then the compound condition is false. Compare the And operator with the Or operator. When you combine conditions using the Or (`||`) operator, as in *condition1* `||` *condition2*, notice that the compound condition is false only when both conditions are false. If either condition is true, or if both conditions are true, then the compound condition is true. In the next section, you use the truth tables to determine which logical operator is appropriate for the `if` statement's *condition*.

Using the Truth Tables

Assume that you want to pay a bonus to your A-rated salespeople—those whose monthly sales total more than $10,000. To receive a bonus, the salesperson must be rated A and he or she must sell more than $10,000 in product. Assuming the program uses a `char` variable named `rate` and an `int` variable named `sales`, you can phrase *condition1* as `rate == 'A'`, and you can phrase *condition2* as `sales > 10000`. Now the question is, should you use the And operator or the Or operator to combine both conditions into one compound condition? You can use the truth tables shown in Figure 6-12 to answer this question.

For a salesperson to receive a bonus, remember that both *condition1* (`rate == 'A'`) and *condition2* (`sales > 10000`) must be true at the same time. If either condition is false, or if both conditions are false, then the compound condition is false, and the salesperson should not receive a bonus. According to the truth tables, both the And and the Or operators evaluate the compound condition as true when both conditions are true. Only the And operator, however, evaluates the compound condition as false when either one or both of the conditions are false. The Or operator, you will notice, evaluates the compound condition as false only when *both* conditions are false. Therefore, the correct compound condition to use here is `(rate == 'A' && sales > 10000)`.

Now assume that you want to send a letter to all A-rated salespeople and all B-rated salespeople. Assuming the program uses a `char` variable named `rate`, you can phrase *condition1* as `rate == 'A'`, and you can phrase *condition2* as `rate == 'B'`. Now which operator do you use—And or Or?

At first it might appear that the And operator is the correct one to use, because the example says to send the letter to "all A-rated salespeople and all B-rated salespeople." In everyday conversations, people sometimes use the word *and* when what they really mean is *or*. Although both words do not mean the same thing, using *and* instead of *or* generally does not cause a problem because we are able to infer what another person means. Computers, however, cannot infer anything; they simply process the directions you give them, word for word. In this case, you actually want to send a letter to all salespeople with either an A or a B rating, so you need to use the Or operator to combine both conditions. As the truth tables indicate, the Or operator is the only operator that evaluates the compound condition as true if at least one of the conditions is true. The correct compound condition to use here is (rate == 'A' || rate == 'B').

Like expressions containing comparison operators, expressions containing logical operators always result in an answer of either true or false. If an expression contains both an And and an Or logical operator, the And operator is evaluated first, and then the Or operator is evaluated. Figure 6-13 shows the order of precedence for the arithmetic, comparison, and logical operators you have learned so far.

Figure 6-13: Order of precedence for arithmetic, comparison, and logical operators in a C++ expression

Operator	Operation	Precedence number
()	Overrides all other normal precedence rules	1
–	Performs negation	2
*, /, %	Performs multiplication, division, and modulus arithmetic	3
+, –	Performs addition and subtraction	4
<, <=, >, >=	Less than, less than or equal to, greater than, greater than or equal to	5
==, !=	Equal to, not equal to	6
&& (And)	All conditions connected by the And operator must be true for the compound condition to be true	7
|| (Or)	Only one of the conditions connected by the Or operator needs to be true for the compound condition to be true	8

Notice that the And and Or logical operators are evaluated after any arithmetic operators or comparison operators in an expression. In other words, in the expression `12 > 0 && 12 < 10 * 2`, the arithmetic operator (*) is evaluated first, followed by the two comparison operators (> and <), followed by the And logical operator (`&&`). The expression evaluates to true, as shown in Figure 6-14.

Figure 6-14: Evaluation steps for an expression containing arithmetic, comparison, and logical operators

Evaluation steps	Result
Original expression	12 > 0 && 12 < 10 * 2
10 * 2 is evaluated first	12 > 0 && 12 < 20
12 > 0 is evaluated second	true && 12 < 20
12 < 20 is evaluated third	true && true
true && true is evaluated last	true

MINI-QUIZ

Mini-Quiz 2

1) Using the truth tables shown in Figure 6-12, evaluate the following compound condition: `(true || false)`.
2) Using the truth tables shown in Figure 6-12, evaluate the following compound condition: `(7 > 3 && 5 < 2)`.
3) Using the truth tables shown in Figure 6-12, evaluate the following compound condition: `(5 * 4 < 20 || false)`.

In the next section, you view the C++ code for three programs that contain a logical operator in an `if` statement.

Using Logical Operators in a Program

Assume you want to create a program that calculates and displays an employee's gross pay. To keep this example simple, assume that no one at the company works more than 40 hours per week, and everyone earns the same hourly rate, $10.65. Before making the gross pay calculation, the program should verify that the number of hours entered by the user is greater than or equal to zero, but less than or equal to 40. Programmers refer to the process of verifying that the input data is within the expected range as **data validation**. In this case, if the number of hours is valid, the program should calculate and display the gross pay; otherwise, it should display an error message alerting the user that the input data is incorrect. Figure 6-15 shows two ways of writing the C++ code for this program. Notice that the `if` statement in the first example uses the And (`&&`) logical operator, whereas the `if` statement in the second example uses the Or (`||`) logical operator.

Figure 6-15: C++ code showing the And and Or logical operators in the `if` statement's *condition*

Example 1: using the && (And) operator

```
double hours = 0.0;
double gross = 0.0;
Console::Write("Enter hours worked: ");
hours = Convert::ToDouble(Console::ReadLine());
if (hours >= 0 && hours <= 40)
{
   gross = hours * 10.65;
   Console::WriteLine(gross.ToString("C2"));
}
else
   Console::WriteLine("Input error");
//end if
```

Example 2: using the || (Or) operator

```
double hours = 0.0;
double gross = 0.0;
Console::Write("Enter hours worked: ");
hours = Convert::ToDouble(Console::ReadLine());
if (hours < 0 || hours > 40)
   Console::WriteLine("Input error");
else
{
   gross = hours * 10.65;
   Console::WriteLine(gross.ToString("C2"));
}  //end if
```

The `(hours >= 0 && hours <= 40)` *condition* in the first example shown in Figure 6-15 tells the computer to determine whether the value stored in the `hours` variable is greater than or equal to the number 0 and, at the same time, less than or equal to the number 40. If the *condition* is true, then the selection structure calculates and displays the gross pay; otherwise, it displays an error message.

The `(hours < 0 || hours > 40)` *condition* in the second example shown in Figure 6-15 tells the computer to determine whether the value stored in the `hours` variable is less than the number 0 or greater than the number 40. If the *condition* is true, then the selection structure displays an error message; otherwise, it calculates and displays the gross pay. Both `if` statements shown in Figure 6-15 produce the same results, and simply represent two different ways of performing the same task.

In this next program, assume you want to display the word "Pass" if the user enters the letter P, and the word "Fail" if the user enters anything else. Figure 6-16 shows three ways of writing the C++ code for this program.

tip As you learned in Tutorial 3, character literal constants (for example, the letter 'P') are enclosed in single quotation marks, and string literal constants (for example, the word "Pass") are enclosed in double quotation marks.

Figure 6-16: C++ code showing the Or and And logical operators used to compare characters in the `if` statement's *condition*

Example 1: using the || (Or) operator

```
char letter = ' ';
Console::Write("Enter a letter: ");
letter = Console::Read();
if (letter == 'P' || letter == 'p')
   Console::WriteLine("Pass");
else
   Console::WriteLine("Fail");
//end if
```

Example 2: using the && (And) operator

```
char letter = ' ';
Console::Write("Enter a letter: ");
letter = Console::Read();
if (letter != 'P' && letter != 'p')
   Console::WriteLine("Fail");
else
   Console::WriteLine("Pass");
//end if
```

Example 3: correct, but less efficient, solution

```
char letter = ' ';
Console::Write("Enter a letter: ");
letter = Console::Read();
if (letter == 'P' || letter == 'p')
   Console::WriteLine("Pass");
//end if
if (letter != 'P' && letter != 'p')
   Console::WriteLine("Fail");
//end if
```

The first statement in each example shown in Figure 6-16 creates and initializes a `char` variable named `letter`. The second statement prompts the user to enter a letter, and the third statement assigns the user's response to the `letter` variable. Notice that the third statement in each example uses the **`Console::Read()` method** rather than the `Console::ReadLine()` method. Unlike the `Console::ReadLine()` method, which gets a string from the user at the keyboard, the `Console::Read()` method gets one character from the user at the keyboard.

The `(letter == 'P' || letter == 'p')` *condition* in the first example shown in Figure 6-16 tells the computer to determine whether the value stored in the `letter` variable is either the uppercase letter P or the lowercase letter p. If the *condition* is true, which means that the variable contains one of those two letters, then the selection structure displays the word "Pass" on the screen; otherwise, it displays the word "Fail". You may be wondering why you need to tell the computer to compare the contents of the `letter` variable to both the uppercase and lowercase version of the letter P. As is true in many programming languages, character comparisons in C++ are case sensitive. That means that the uppercase version of a letter is not the same as its lowercase counterpart. So, although a human recognizes P and p as being the same letter, a computer does not; to a computer, a P is different from a p. The reason for this differentiation is that each character on the computer's keyboard is stored differently in the computer's internal memory. The uppercase letter P, for example, is stored using the eight bits 01010000 (ASCII code 80), whereas the lowercase letter p is stored using the eight bits 01110000 (ASCII code 112).

The `(letter != 'P' && letter != 'p')` *condition* in the second example shown in Figure 6-16 tells the computer to determine whether the value stored in the `letter` variable is not equal to either the uppercase letter P or the lowercase letter p. If the *condition* is true, which means that the variable does not contain either of those two letters, then the selection structure displays the word "Fail" on the screen; otherwise, it displays the word "Pass".

tip

You learned about the ASCII codes in Tutorial 3's Concept lesson. The full ASCII chart is shown in Appendix A.

Rather than using one `if` statement with an `else` clause, as in Examples 1 and 2, Example 3 in Figure 6-16 uses two `if` statements with no `else` clause in either one. Although the `if` statements in Example 3 produce the same results as the `if` statement in Examples 1 and 2, they do so less efficiently. For example, assume that the user enters the letter P in response to the "Enter a letter: " prompt. The *condition* in the first `if` statement shown in Example 3 determines whether the value stored in the `letter` variable is equal to either P or p. In this case, the *condition* evaluates to true, because the `letter` variable contains the letter P. The first `if` statement's true path displays the word "Pass" on the screen, and then the first `if` statement ends. Although the appropriate word ("Pass") already appears on the screen, the program instructs the computer to evaluate the second `if` statement's *condition* to determine whether to display the "Fail" message. The second evaluation is unnecessary and makes Example 3's code less efficient than the code shown in Examples 1 and 2.

In addition to performing numeric and character comparisons in an `if` statement's *condition*, you also can perform string comparisons.

Comparing Strings

Like character comparisons, string comparisons are case-sensitive, which means that the string "Yes" is not the same as the string "YES" or the string "yes". A problem occurs when you need to include a string, entered by the user, in a comparison, because you cannot control the case in which the user enters the string. Before using a string in a comparison, you should convert it to either uppercase or lowercase, and then use the converted string in the comparison.

You use the **`ToUpper()` method** to convert a string to uppercase, and the **`ToLower()` method** to convert a string to lowercase. The syntax of the `ToUpper()` method is *string*->**ToUpper()**, and the syntax of the `ToLower()` method is *string*->**ToLower()**. In each syntax, *string* is the name of a `String` variable that contains the string you want to convert. Both methods temporarily convert the string to the appropriate case. For example, to temporarily convert the contents of the `state` variable to uppercase, you use `state->ToUpper()`. Similarly, to temporarily convert the contents of the `state` variable to lowercase, you use `state->ToLower()`.

You also can use the `ToUpper()` or `ToLower()` methods to permanently convert the contents of a `String` variable to uppercase or lowercase. To do so, you simply include the appropriate method in an assignment statement. For example, to permanently change the contents of the `state` variable to uppercase, you use the assignment statement `state = state->ToUpper();`. You use the assignment statement `state = state->ToLower();` to convert the `state` variable's contents to lowercase.

tip

You learn about classes and their members in a later tutorial.

The -> that appears in the syntax for the `ToUpper()` and `ToLower()` methods is called the member access operator. You use the **member access operator** (**->**) to access the members of a class. In this case, the member access operator allows you to access the `ToUpper()` and `ToLower()` methods, which are members of the String class.

After converting to the appropriate case the strings involved in a comparison, you then can use the **`CompareTo()` method**, whose syntax is *string1*->**CompareTo(***string2***)**, to compare the strings. The method returns the number 0 if *string1* is equal to *string2*. It returns the number -1 if *string1* is less than *string2*, and the number 1 if *string1* is greater than *string2*. Figure 6-17 shows examples of using the `CompareTo()` method to compare strings.

Figure 6-17: Examples of using the `CompareTo()` method to compare strings

Example	Result
Example 1: assume that the `firstName` variable contains the string "John" `firstName->CompareTo("John")`	the `CompareTo()` method returns the number 0, because "John" is equal to "John"
Example 2: assume that the `name1` variable contains the string "Sue", and the `name2` variable contains the string "Sam" `name1->CompareTo(name2)`	the `CompareTo()` method returns the number 1, because "Sue" is greater than "Sam"
Example 3: assume that the `name1` variable contains the string "Sue", and the `name2` variable contains the string "Sam" `name2->CompareTo(name1)`	the `CompareTo()` method returns the number -1, because "Sam" is less than "Sue"

Look closely at each example shown in Figure 6-17. As Example 1 indicates, if the `firstName` variable contains the string "John", then the `firstName->CompareTo("John")` method returns the number 0 to indicate that both *string1* (the contents of the `firstName` variable) and *string2* ("John") are equal. In Example 2, the `name1->CompareTo(name2)` method returns the number 1 to indicate that *string1* (the contents of the `name1` variable) is greater than *string2* (the contents of the `name2` variable). In Example 3, the `name2->CompareTo(name1)` method returns the number -1 to indicate that *string1* (the contents of the `name2` variable) is less than *string2* (the contents of the `name1` variable).

In the next section, you view two examples that use both the `ToUpper()` and `CompareTo()` methods to compare strings.

Using the ToUpper() and CompareTo() Methods in a Program

Assume you want a program to display the message "We have a store in this state." when the user enters any of the following three state IDs: Il, In, Ky. When the user enters an ID other than these, you want the program to display the message "We don't have a store in this state." Figure 6-18 shows two ways of writing the C++ code for this program. Notice that the `if` statement in the first example uses the Or (`||`) logical operator, whereas the `if` statement in the second example uses the And (`&&`) logical operator.

Figure 6-18: C++ code comparing strings in the `if` statement's *condition*

Example 1: using the `ToUpper()` and `CompareTo()` methods and the || (Or) operator

```
String *state = "";
Console::Write("Enter a state ID: ");
state = Console::ReadLine();
state = state->ToUpper();
if (state->CompareTo("IL") == 0 ||
    state->CompareTo("IN") == 0 ||
    state->CompareTo("KY") == 0)
       Console::WriteLine("We have a store in this state.");
else
       Console::WriteLine("We don't have a store in this state.");
//end if
```

Example 2: using the `ToUpper()` and `CompareTo()` methods and the && (And) operator

```
String *state = "";
Console::Write("Enter a state ID: ");
state = Console::ReadLine();
state = state->ToUpper();
if (state->CompareTo("IL") != 0 &&
    state->CompareTo("IN") != 0 &&
    state->CompareTo("KY") != 0)
       Console::WriteLine("We don't have a store in this state.");
else
       Console::WriteLine("We have a store in this state.");
//end if
```

Notice that the code in both examples creates a `String` variable named `state`. It then prompts the user to enter a state ID, and stores the user's response in the `state` variable. The `state = state->ToUpper();` statement in each example uses the `ToUpper()` method to convert the contents of the `state` variable to uppercase.

The `(state->CompareTo("IL") == 0 || state->CompareTo("IN") == 0 || state->CompareTo("KY") == 0)` *condition* in the first example shown in Figure 6-18 tells the computer to compare the contents of the `state` variable to each of the three state IDs. If one of the three IDs is stored in the `state` variable, the *condition* evaluates to true, and the selection structure displays the message "We have a store in this state." If, on the other hand, neither of the three IDs is stored in the `state` variable, the *condition* evaluates to false, and the selection structure displays the message "We don't have a store in this state."

Similar to the *condition* in the first example, the `(state->CompareTo("IL") != 0 && state->CompareTo("IN") != 0 && state->CompareTo("KY") != 0)` *condition* in Example 2 also compares the contents of the `state` variable to each of the three state IDs. However, Example 2's *condition* compares for inequality, rather than equality. In this case, if neither of the three IDs is stored in the `state` variable, the *condition* evaluates to true, and the selection structure displays the message "We don't have a store in this state." If, however, one of the three IDs is stored in the `state` variable, the *condition* evaluates to false, and the selection structure displays the message "We have a store in this state." Here again, both `if` statements shown in Figure 6-18 produce the same results, and simply represent two different ways of performing the same task.

MINI-QUIZ

Mini-Quiz 3

1) Write a compound condition for a C++ `if` statement that determines whether the value in the `age` variable is between 30 and 40, including 30 and 40.
2) Write a compound condition for a C++ `if` statement that determines whether the `age` variable contains a value that is either less than 30 or greater than 50.
3) Write a condition for an `if` statement that determines whether the `char` variable named `key` contains the letter R (in any case).
4) Write a C++ statement that converts the contents of a `String` variable named `department` to uppercase.
5) Write a condition for an `if` statement that determines whether the `department` variable in Question 4 contains the word "Accounting".

You now have completed Tutorial 6's Concept lesson. You can either take a break or complete the end-of-lesson questions and exercises before moving on to the Application lesson.

SUMMARY

The selection structure, also called the decision structure, is one of the three programming structures; the other two programming structures are sequence and repetition. You use the selection structure when you want a program to make a decision or comparison and then select one of two paths—either the true path or the false path—based on the result of that decision or comparison. Most programming languages offer three forms of the selection structure: `if`, `if/else`, and `switch` (also referred to as `case`).

A diamond, called the selection/repetition symbol, is used in a flowchart to represent the selection structure. The diamond contains a question that has a true or false answer only. Each selection diamond has one flowline entering the symbol and two flowlines leaving the symbol. The two flowlines leading out of the diamond should be marked so it is clear to the reader which path is the true path and which is the false path.

You can use the C++ `if` statement to code both the `if` and `if/else` forms of the selection structure. If either the `if` statement's true path or false path contains more than one statement, you must enclose the statements in a set of braces ({}). Statements enclosed in braces are referred to as a statement block. It is a good programming practice to include an `//end if` comment to identify the end of the `if` statement in a program.

The *condition* in an `if` statement can contain variables, constants, functions, methods, arithmetic operators, comparison operators, and logical operators. The comparison operators in C++ are <, <=, >, >=, ==, and !=. The logical operators—And and Or—are signified in C++ by the symbols `&&` and `||`, respectively. If more than one operator with the same precedence number appears in a C++ expression, the computer evaluates those operators from left to right in the expression. All expressions containing either a relational or logical operator result in an answer of either true or false only.

As is true in many programming languages, character and string comparisons in C++ are case sensitive. You can use the `ToUpper()` method to convert a string to uppercase, and the `ToLower()` method to convert a string to lowercase. The syntax of the `ToUpper()` method is *string*->**ToUpper()**, and the syntax of the `ToLower()` method is *string*->**ToLower()**. Both methods temporarily convert the string to the appropriate case.

You can use the `CompareTo()` method, whose syntax is *string1*->**CompareTo(***string2***)**, to compare two strings. The method returns the number 0 if *string1* is equal to *string2*. It returns the number -1 if *string1* is less than *string2*, and the number 1 if *string1* is greater than *string2*.

ANSWERS TO MINI-QUIZZES

Mini-Quiz 1

1)
```
if (score < 70)
    display "Fail"
else
    display "Pass"
end if
```

2)
```
if (score < 70)
     Console::WriteLine("Fail");
else
     Console::WriteLine("Pass");
//end if
```

3) c. `if (quantity == 100)`

4) b. `area = 5;`

5) `if (area == 5)`

Mini-Quiz 2

1) true

2) false

3) false

Mini-Quiz 3

1) `(age >= 30 && age <= 40)`

2) `(age < 30 || age > 50)`

3) `(key == 'R' || key == 'r')`

4) `department = department->ToUpper();`

5) `(department->CompareTo("ACCOUNTING") == 0)`

QUESTIONS

1) Which of the following symbols is used in a flowchart to represent the selection structure?
   A. diamond
   B. oval
   C. parallelogram
   D. rectangle

2) Which of the following is the equality operator in C++?
   A. !=
   B. =
   C. ==
   D. ->

3) Which of the following is the inequality operator in C++?
   A. !=
   B. ==
   C. ->
   D. <>

4) Assume you want to determine whether the `item` variable contains either the word Chair or the word Desk. Which of the following *conditions* should you use in the `if` statement? You can assume that the `item` variable's contents are uppercase.
   A. `(item->CompareTo("CHAIR") == 0 ||`
   `item->CompareTo("DESK") == 0)`
   B. `(item->CompareTo('CHAIR') == 0 ||`
   `item->CompareTo('DESK') == 0)`
   C. `(item->CompareTo("CHAIR") == 0 &&`
   `item->CompareTo("DESK") == 0)`
   D. `(item->CompareTo("CHAIR" || "DESK") == 0)`

5) Assume you want to compare the character stored in the `initial` variable to the letter A. Which of the following *conditions* should you use in the `if` statement? (Be sure the *condition* will handle the letter A entered in any case.)
   A. `(initial = 'a' or 'A')`
   B. `(initial == 'a' or 'A')`
   C. `(initial == 'A' && initial == 'a')`
   D. `(initial == 'A' || initial == 'a')`

6) The expression 3 > 6 && 7 > 4 evaluates to ______________.
   A. true
   B. false

7) The expression 4 > 6 || 10 < 2 * 6 evaluates to ______________.
   A. true
   B. false

8) The expression 7 >= 3 + 4 || 6 < 4 && 2 < 5 evaluates to ____________.

A. true

B. false

9) The expression 4 * 3 < (6 + 7) && 7 < 6 + 9 evaluates to ____________.

A. true

B. false

10) Assuming the expression does not contain parentheses, which of the following operators is performed first in the expression?

A. arithmetic

B. comparison

C. logical

EXERCISES

Look For These Symbols

Debugging

Discovery

1) Write the C++ `if` statement that compares the contents of the `quantity` variable to the number 10. If the `quantity` variable contains a number that is greater than 10, display the string "Over 10"; otherwise, display the string "Not over 10".

2) Write the C++ statements that correspond to the flowchart shown in Figure 6-19.

Figure 6-19

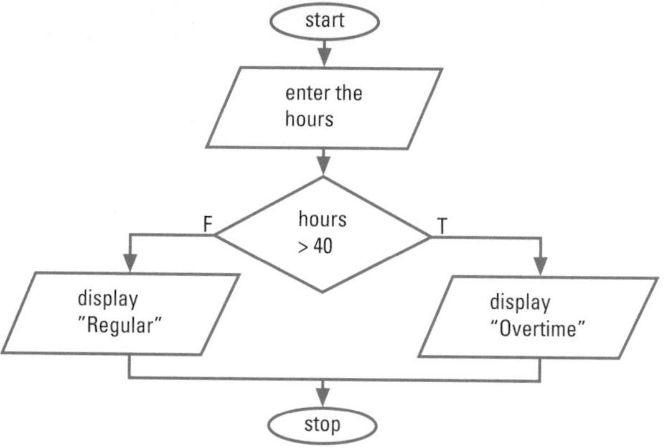

3) In this exercise, you complete a program by writing an `if` statement.

A. If necessary, start Visual Studio .NET. Open the T6ConE03 Solution (T6ConE03 Solution.sln) file, which is contained in the CppNet\Tut06\T6ConE03 Solution folder.

B. Complete the program by writing an `if` statement that displays the string "Firebird" when the user enters the letter F (in any case).

C. Save and then build the solution.

D. Execute the program three times, using the following letters: F, f, and x.

E. When the program is working correctly, close the Output window, and then use the File menu to close the solution.

4) In this exercise, you complete a program by writing an `if` statement.

A. If necessary, start Visual Studio .NET. Open the T6ConE04 Solution (T6ConE04 Solution.sln) file, which is contained in the CppNet\Tut06\T6ConE04 Solution folder.

B. Complete the program by writing an `if` statement that displays the string "Entry error" when the user enters a number that is less than zero; otherwise, display the string "Valid number".

C. Save and then build the solution.

D. Execute the program three times, using the following numbers: 5, 0, and -3.

E. When the program is working correctly, close the Output window, and then use the File menu to close the solution.

5) In this exercise, you complete a program by writing an `if` statement.

A. If necessary, start Visual Studio .NET. Open the T6ConE05 Solution (T6ConE05 Solution.sln) file, which is contained in the CppNet\Tut06\T6ConE05 Solution folder.

B. Complete the program by writing an `if` statement that displays the string "Reorder" when the user enters a number that is less than 10; otherwise, display the string "OK".

C. Save and then build the solution.

D. Execute the program three times, using the following numbers: 5, 10, and 19.

E. When the program is working correctly, close the Output window, and then use the File menu to close the solution.

6) In this exercise, you complete a program by writing an `if` statement.

A. If necessary, start Visual Studio .NET. Open the T6ConE06 Solution (T6ConE06 Solution.sln) file, which is contained in the CppNet\Tut06\T6ConE06 Solution folder.

B. Complete the program by writing an `if` statement that assigns the number 10 to the `bonus` variable when the user enters a sales amount that is less than or equal to $250. When the user enters a sales amount that is greater than $250, prompt the user to enter the bonus rate, and then multiply the user's response by the sales amount and assign the result to the `bonus` variable. After assigning the appropriate bonus amount, display the bonus amount on the screen.

C. Save and then build the solution.

D. Execute the program three times. First, use 240 as the sales amount. Second, use 250 as the sales amount. Third, use 251 as the sales amount and .05 as the bonus rate.

E. When the program is working correctly, close the Output window, and then use the File menu to close the solution.

7) In this exercise, you complete a program by writing an `if` statement.

A. If necessary, start Visual Studio .NET. Open the T6ConE07 Solution (T6ConE07 Solution.sln) file, which is contained in the CppNet\Tut06\T6ConE07 Solution folder.

B. Assume that employees working more than 40 hours receive overtime pay (time and one-half) for the hours over 40. Complete the program by writing an `if` statement that calculates the overtime pay (if any) and the gross pay. Display the overtime pay (if any) and the gross pay.

C. Save and then build the solution.

D. Execute the program two times. First, use 40 as the number of hours worked and 7 as the pay rate. The program should display $0.00 as the overtime pay and $280.00 as the gross pay. Second, use 42 as the number of hours worked and 10 as the pay rate. The program should display $30.00 as the overtime pay and $430.00 as the gross pay.

E. When the program is working correctly, close the Output window, and then use the File menu to close the solution.

8) In this exercise, you complete a program by writing an `if` statement.

A. If necessary, start Visual Studio .NET. Open the T6ConE08 Solution (T6ConE08 Solution.sln) file, which is contained in the CppNet\Tut06\T6ConE08 Solution folder.

B. The program should prompt the user to enter an animal ID, and then store the user's response in a `char` variable named `animal`. The program should display the string "Dog" when the `animal` variable contains the letter D (in any case); otherwise, it should display the string "Cat". Complete the program appropriately.

C. Save and then build the solution.

D. Execute the program three times, using the letters D, d, and h.

E. When the program is working correctly, close the Output window, and then use the File menu to close the solution.

9) In this exercise, you complete a program by writing an `if` statement.

A. If necessary, start Visual Studio .NET. Open the T6ConE09 Solution (T6ConE09 Solution.sln) file, which is contained in the CppNet\Tut06\T6ConE09 Solution folder.

B. Complete the program by writing an `if` statement that displays the string "Valid entry" when the user enters either the integer 1, the integer 2, or the integer 3; otherwise, display the string "Entry error".

C. Save and then build the solution.

D. Execute the program four times, using the integers 1, 2, 3, and 4.

E. When the program is working correctly, close the Output window, and then use the File menu to close the solution.

10) In this exercise, you complete a program by writing an `if` statement.

A. If necessary, start Visual Studio .NET. Open the T6ConE10 Solution (T6ConE10 Solution.sln) file, which is contained in the CppNet\Tut06\T6ConE10 Solution folder.

B. Complete the program by writing an `if` statement that swaps the two numbers entered by the user, but only if the first number is less than the second number.

C. Save and then build the solution.

D. Execute the program two times. First, use the numbers 5 and 3. The program should display "5, 3". Second, use the numbers 3 and 80. The program should display "80, 3".

E. When the program is working correctly, close the Output window, and then use the File menu to close the solution.

11) In this exercise, you complete a program by writing an `if` statement.

A. If necessary, start Visual Studio .NET. Open the T6ConE11 Solution (T6ConE11 Solution.sln) file, which is contained in the CppNet\Tut06\T6ConE11 Solution folder.

B. Complete the program by writing an `if` statement that assigns the appropriate price. The price is based on the item number entered by the user. If the item number is AB123, then the price is $5. All other items are $10.

C. Save and then build the solution.

D. Execute the program three times. First, use item number AB123. The program should display $5. Second, use item number ab123. The program should display $5. Third, use item number XX345. The program should display $10.

E. When the program is working correctly, close the Output window, and then use the File menu to close the solution.

12) Recall that you must be careful when comparing two floating-point values (values with a decimal place) for either equality or inequality. This is because some floating-point values cannot be stored, precisely, in memory. To determine whether two floating-point values are either equal or unequal, you should test that the difference between the values you are comparing is less than some acceptable small value, such as .00001.

A. If necessary, start Visual Studio .NET. Open the T6ConE12 Solution (T6ConE12 Solution.sln) file, which is contained in the CppNet\Tut06\T6ConE12 Solution folder.

B. Study the program's code. Notice that the code divides the contents of the `num1` variable (10.0) by the contents of the `num2` variable (3.0), and then stores the result (approximately 3.33333333333333) in the `quotient` variable. An `if` statement is used to compare the contents of the `quotient` variable to the number 3.33333333333333. The `if` statement then displays an appropriate message, indicating whether the numbers are equal.

C. Build the solution, then execute the program. Although the Command Prompt window indicates that the quotient is 3.33333333333333, the `if` statement displays the message "No, the quotient 3.33333333333333 is not equal to 3.33333333333333." Close the Command Prompt window.

The proper procedure for comparing two floating-point values is first to find the difference between the values, and then compare the absolute value of that difference to a small number, such as .00001. You can use the C++ `Math::Abs()` method to find the absolute value of a number. The absolute value of a number is a positive number that represents how far the number is from zero on the number line. For example, the absolute value of the number 5 is 5; the absolute value of the number –5 also is 5.

D. Modify the program appropriately.

E. Save and then build the solution.

F. Execute the program. The `if` statement displays the message "Yes, the quotient 3.33333333333333 is equal to 3.33333333333333." Close the Command Prompt window.

G. When the program is working correctly, close the Output window, and then use the File menu to close the solution.

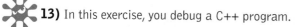

13) In this exercise, you debug a C++ program.

A. If necessary, start Visual Studio .NET. Open the T6ConE13 Solution (T6ConE13 Solution.sln) file, which is contained in the CppNet\Tut06\T6ConE13 Solution folder.

B. The program should display a message based on the sales amount entered by the user. Study the program's code, then build the solution.

C. Correct any errors in the program, then save and build the solution.

D. Execute the program twice. First, use 5000 as the sales amount. Second, use 20000 as the sales amount.

E. When the program is working correctly, close the Output window, and then use the File menu to close the solution.

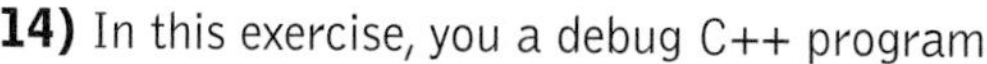

14) In this exercise, you a debug C++ program.

A. If necessary, start Visual Studio .NET. Open the T6ConE14 Solution (T6ConE14 Solution.sln) file, which is contained in the CppNet\Tut06\T6ConE14 Solution folder.

B. The program should display a message based on the age entered by the user. Study the program's code, then build the solution. Correct any errors.

C. Save and then build the solution.

D. Execute the program twice. First, use John as the name and 32 as the age. Second, use Mary as the name and 16 as the age.

E. When the program is working correctly, close the Output window, and then use the File menu to close the solution.

Application Lesson

Using the Selection Structure in a C++ Program

CASE Marshall Cabello is the manager of Willow Springs Health Club. Every other month, Marshall teaches a three-hour seminar titled "Healthy Living." The seminar stresses the importance of daily exercise (at least 20 minutes per day) and eating a low-fat diet (no more than 30 percent of the calories consumed should come from fat). Each time Marshall teaches the seminar, many of the participants ask him how to determine whether a specific food item is considered low-fat. Your task in this lesson is to create a program that allows Marshall to enter the number of calories and grams of fat contained in a specific food. The program then should calculate and display two values: the food's fat calories (the number of calories attributed to fat) and its fat percentage (the ratio of the food's fat calories to its total calories).

Analyzing, Planning, and Desk-checking

You can calculate the number of fat calories in a food by multiplying the number of fat grams contained in the food by the number nine, because each gram of fat contains nine calories. To calculate the fat percentage, which is the percentage of a food's total calories derived from fat, you divide the food's fat calories by its total calories, and then multiply the result by `100`. You use both of these calculations in the health club's algorithm.

Recall that most algorithms follow a similar format: first they get the input data, then they process that data (typically by performing calculations on it), and then they display the output data. For simple algorithms (such as the health club algorithm), the input, processing, and output tasks can be performed by the `main()` function itself. However, to help reinforce the concept of functions, which are important for most real-world programs, you will use one additional function in the health club algorithm. The additional function will calculate the fat calories and fat percentage. Figure 6-20 shows the IPO charts for one possible solution to the health club problem.

As Figure 6-20 indicates, the `main()` function's output is the fat calories and fat percentage, and its input is the total calories and grams of fat. According to its algorithm, the `main()` function first has the user enter the two input values; it then validates both values. If both values are greater than or equal to zero, the `main()` function calls the `calcFatInfo()` function to calculate the fat calories and fat percentage. For the `calcFatInfo()` function to perform its task, the `main()` function needs to pass it the values of the total calories and grams of fat, as well as the addresses of the variables in which to store the fat calories and fat percentage. After the `calcFatInfo()` function completes its task, the `main()` function displays the fat calories and fat percentage on the screen.

Figure 6-20: IPO charts for the health club problem

`main()` **function**

Input	Processing	Output

total calories
grams of fat
	Processing items: none
	
	Algorithm:
	1. enter the total calories and grams of fat
	2. if (the total calories are greater than or equal to zero and the grams of fat are greater than or equal to zero)
	calcFatInfo(total calories, grams of fat, fat calories, fat percentage)
	display fat calories and fat percentage
	else
	display error message
	end if
		fat calories
		fat percentage

`calcFatInfo()` **function**

Input	Processing	Output
total calories grams of fat address of fat calories address of fat percentage	Processing items: none Algorithm: 1. calculate fat calories by multiplying grams of fat by 9 2. calculate fat percentage by dividing fat calories by total calories, then multiplying the result by 100	fat calories fat percentage

Notice, however, that if both input values are not greater than or equal to zero—which means that at least one of the values is less than zero—the `main()` function should not call the `calcFatInfo()` function, nor should it display the fat calories and fat percentage on the screen. Rather, it simply should display an error message to alert the user that one of the values he or she entered is incorrect.

Recall that you should desk-check an algorithm several times, using both valid and invalid data, before you begin coding it. As you learned in Tutorial 2, valid data is data that the programmer is expecting the user to enter. In the health club algorithm, for example, the programmer expects the user to provide positive numbers for the input items (total calories and grams of fat). Invalid data, on the other hand, is data that the programmer is not expecting the user to enter. In this case, the programmer is not expecting the user to enter negative values for the input items. A negative value entered as either the number of calories or grams of fat is obviously an input error. In this case, you will use the following three sets of data to desk-check the algorithms shown in Figure 6-20:

Data for first desk-check
Total calories: 150
Grams of fat: 6

Data for second desk-check
Total calories: 105
Grams of fat: 2

Data for third desk-check
Total calories: 100
Grams of fat: -3

Figure 6-21 shows the completed desk-check tables, with the fat percentage amounts shown rounded to two decimal places.

Figure 6-21: Completed desk-check tables for the algorithms shown in Figure 6-20

`main()` function

total calories	grams of fat	fat calories	fat percentage
~~150~~ ~~105~~ 100	~~6~~ ~~2~~ -3	~~54~~ 18	~~36.00~~ 17.14

`calcFatInfo()` function

total calories	grams of fat
~~150~~ ~~105~~ 100	~~6~~ ~~2~~ -3

tip

Notice that the `calcFatInfo()` function's desk-check table does not include the fat calories and fat percentage items, which are passed to the function *by reference*. As you learned in Tutorial 5, when a function receives the address of an item from the `main()` function, any changes the function makes to the item are recorded in the `main()` function's desk-check table.

After desk-checking an algorithm to verify its accuracy, you are ready to translate it into a language the computer can understand. Begin by coding the program's `main()` function.

Coding the `main()` Function

According to its IPO chart, the `main()` function requires four memory locations to store the values of its input and output items. You will store the values in variables, because the values will be different each time the program is executed. You will use the `int` data type for the variables that store the total calories, grams of fat, and fat calories; this is because these variables need to store whole numbers only. You will use the `double` data type for the variable that stores the fat percentage, which will contain a decimal place.

After reserving the memory locations, the `main()` function will prompt the user to enter the total calories and grams of fat. It will assign the user's responses to the appropriate variables.

Next, the `main()` function will use the `if/else` form of the selection structure to determine whether the user's input is valid, and then take the appropriate action based on the result. As you learned in the Concept lesson, you use the `if` statement to code the `if/else` form of the selection structure in C++. Figure 6-22 shows the C++ code corresponding to the `main()` function.

Figure 6-22: C++ statements corresponding to the main() function

<table>
<tr><th>IPO chart information</th><th>C++ instructions</th></tr>
<tr><td>Input
total calories
grams of fat
Processing
none
Output
fat calories
fat percentage

Algorithm
1. enter the total calories and grams of fat

2. if (the total calories are greater than or equal to zero and the grams of fat are greater than or equal to zero)
calcFatInfo(total calories, grams of fat, fat calories, fat percentage)

display fat calories and fat percentage

else
display error message
end if</td><td><pre>
int totalCal = 0;
int fatGrams = 0;

int fatCal = 0;
double fatPercent = 0.0;

Console::Write("Enter the total calories: ");
totalCal =
  Convert::ToInt32(Console::ReadLine());
Console::Write("Enter the grams of fat: ");
fatGrams =
  Convert::ToInt32(Console::ReadLine());

if (totalCal >= 0 && fatGrams >= 0)
{
    calcFatInfo(totalCal, fatGrams,
        fatCal, fatPercent);

    Console::WriteLine("Fat calories: {0}",
        Convert::ToString(fatCal));
    Console::WriteLine("Fat percentage:{0}%",
        Convert::ToString(fatPercent));
}
else
    Console::WriteLine("Input error");
//end if
</pre></td></tr>
</table>

tip

The four variables declared in the code shown in Figure 6-22 are local to the `main()` function and remain in memory until the function's `return 0;` statement is processed.

You code the `calcFatInfo()` function next.

Coding the calcFatInfo() Function

Recall that the `main()` function passes the values of two of its variables (`totalCal` and `fatGrams`), along with the addresses of two of its variables (`fatCal` and `fatPercent`), to the `calcFatInfo()` function. You will use the formal parameters `tCal`, `grams`, `&fCal`, and `&fPer` to receive the information. Figure 6-23 shows the C++ code for the `calcFatInfo()` function.

tip
Recall that the address-of operator (&) alerts the computer that what is being passed to the function is a variable's address rather than its value.

tip
The four variables appearing in the `calcFatInfo()` function header are local to the `calcFatInfo()` function. When the function's closing brace is encountered, the `tCal` and `grams` variables and the `fCal` and `fPer` variable names are removed from memory.

Figure 6-23: C++ code for the `calcFatInfo()` function

IPO chart information	C++ instructions
Input total calories grams of fat address of fat calories address of fat percentage **Processing** none **Output** fat calories fat percentage	`void calcFatInfo(int tCal, int grams, int &fCal, double &fPer)`
Algorithm 1. calculate fat calories by multiplying grams of fat by 9	`fCal = grams * 9;`
2. calculate fat percentage by dividing fat calories by total calories, then multiplying the result by 100	`fPer = fCal / tCal * 100;`

Now that you have finished coding the algorithms, you need to desk-check the program, using the same data you used to desk-check the algorithms. Figure 6-24 shows the data and the completed desk-check table for the program, with the fat percentage amounts shown rounded to two decimal places.

Figure 6-24: Data and completed desk-check table for the program

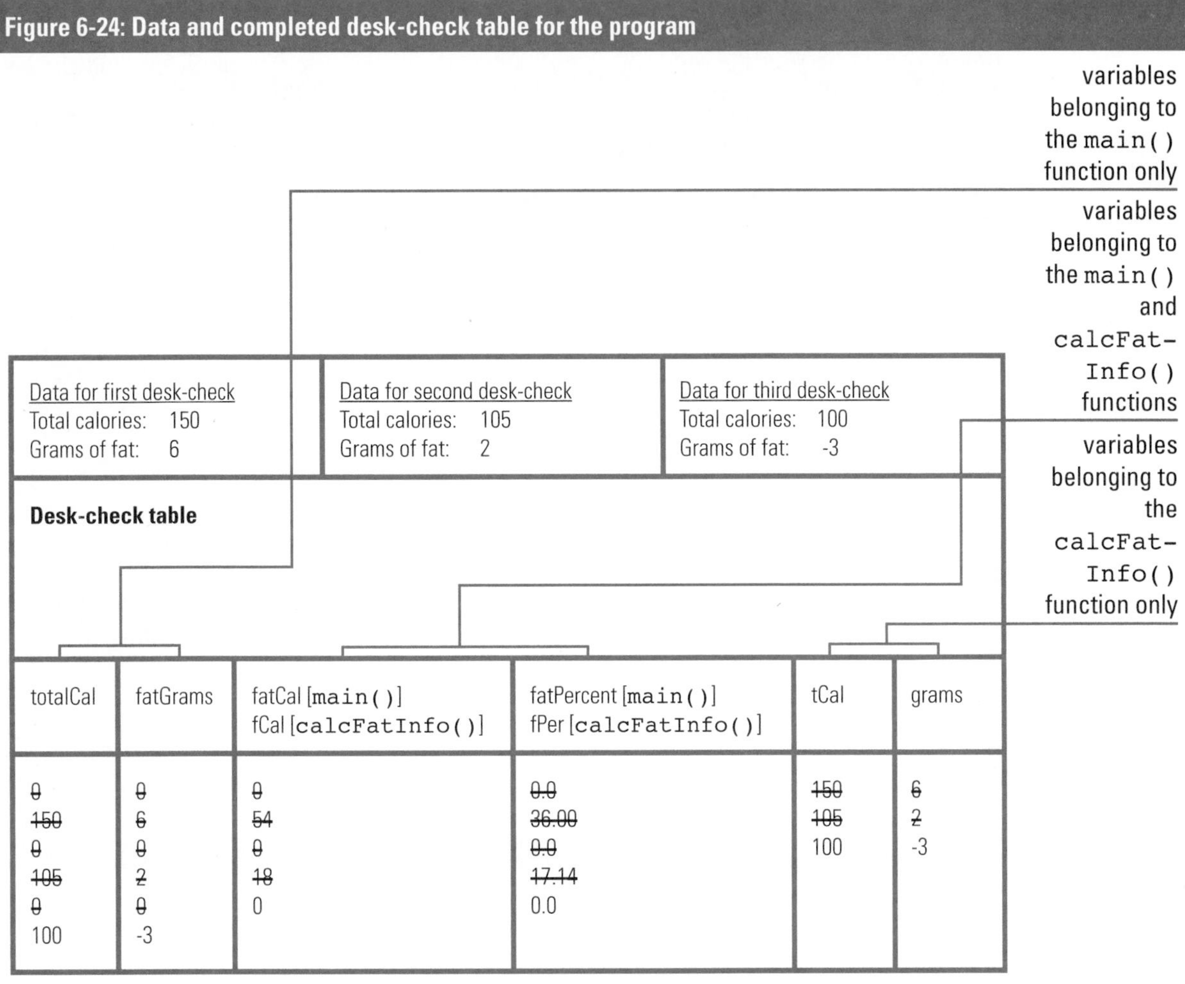

totalCal	fatGrams	fatCal [main()] fCal [calcFatInfo()]	fatPercent [main()] fPer [calcFatInfo()]	tCal	grams
~~0~~ ~~150~~ ~~0~~ ~~105~~ ~~0~~ 100	~~0~~ ~~6~~ ~~0~~ ~~2~~ ~~0~~ -3	~~0~~ ~~54~~ ~~0~~ ~~18~~ 0	~~0.0~~ ~~36.00~~ ~~0.0~~ ~~17.14~~ 0.0	~~150~~ ~~105~~ 100	~~6~~ ~~2~~ -3

The results obtained when desk-checking the program agree with the results obtained when desk-checking the algorithm. You now are ready to enter the C++ instructions into the computer.

Completing the Health Club Program

On your computer's hard disk is a partially completed C++ program containing most of the instructions for the health club program. You open that program in the next set of steps.

To open the partially completed C++ program:

1. Start Microsoft Visual Studio .NET. If necessary, close the Start Page window.
2. Click **File** on the menu bar, and then click **Open Solution**. The Open Solution dialog box opens.
3. Locate and then open the **CppNet\Tut06\T6App Solution** folder.
4. Click **T6App Solution** (T6App Solution.sln) in the list of filenames, and then click the **Open** button.

5. If the T6App.cpp source file is not displayed, right-click **T6App.cpp** in the Solution Explorer window, and then click **Open**. Figure 6-25 shows the instructions contained in the partially completed T6App.cpp program.

Figure 6-25: Instructions contained in the partially completed T6App.cpp program

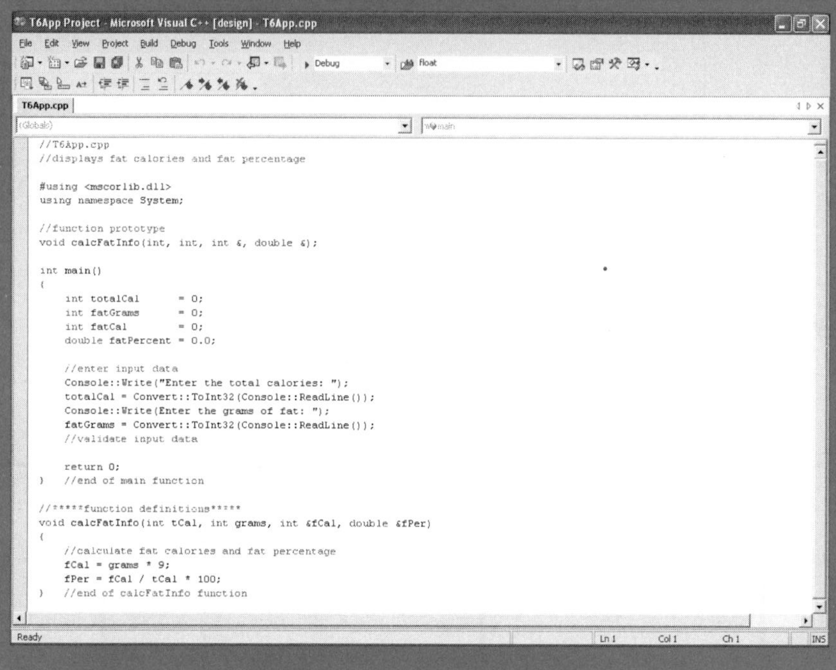
```
//T6App.cpp
//displays fat calories and fat percentage

#using <mscorlib.dll>
using namespace System;

//function prototype
void calcFatInfo(int, int, int &, double &);

int main()
{
    int totalCal      = 0;
    int fatGrams      = 0;
    int fatCal        = 0;
    double fatPercent = 0.0;

    //enter input data
    Console::Write("Enter the total calories: ");
    totalCal = Convert::ToInt32(Console::ReadLine());
    Console::Write(Enter the grams of fat: ");
    fatGrams = Convert::ToInt32(Console::ReadLine());
    //validate input data

    return 0;
}   //end of main function

//*****function definitions*****
void calcFatInfo(int tCal, int grams, int &fCal, double &fPer)
{
    //calculate fat calories and fat percentage
    fCal = grams * 9;
    fPer = fCal / tCal * 100;
}   //end of calcFatInfo function
```

The `if` statement in the `main()` function is missing from the program. You enter the statement in the next set of steps.

To enter the `if` statement, then test the program:

1. Position the insertion point in the blank line below the `//validate input data` comment. Press **Tab**, if necessary, then enter the selection structure shaded in Figure 6-26.

Figure 6-26: Program showing the `if` statement entered in the `main()` function

```
//T6App.cpp
//displays fat calories and fat percentage

#using <mscorlib.dll>
using namespace System;

//function prototype
void calcFatInfo(int, int, int &, double &);

int main()
{
    int totalCal      = 0;
    int fatGrams      = 0;
    int fatCal        = 0;
    double fatPercent = 0.0;
```

Figure 6-26: Program showing the `if` statement entered in the `main()` function (continued)

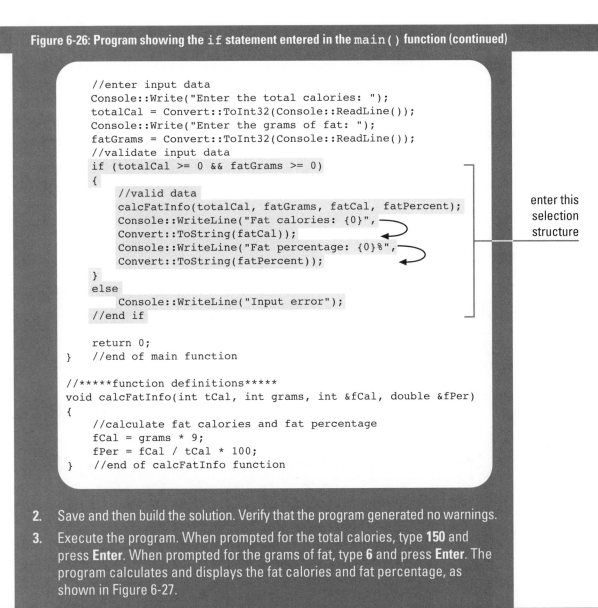

```
    //enter input data
    Console::Write("Enter the total calories: ");
    totalCal = Convert::ToInt32(Console::ReadLine());
    Console::Write("Enter the grams of fat: ");
    fatGrams = Convert::ToInt32(Console::ReadLine());
    //validate input data
    if (totalCal >= 0 && fatGrams >= 0)
    {
        //valid data
        calcFatInfo(totalCal, fatGrams, fatCal, fatPercent);
        Console::WriteLine("Fat calories: {0}",
        Convert::ToString(fatCal));
        Console::WriteLine("Fat percentage: {0}%",
        Convert::ToString(fatPercent));
    }
    else
        Console::WriteLine("Input error");
    //end if

    return 0;
}   //end of main function

//*****function definitions*****
void calcFatInfo(int tCal, int grams, int &fCal, double &fPer)
{
    //calculate fat calories and fat percentage
    fCal = grams * 9;
    fPer = fCal / tCal * 100;
}   //end of calcFatInfo function
```

enter this selection structure

2. Save and then build the solution. Verify that the program generated no warnings.
3. Execute the program. When prompted for the total calories, type **150** and press **Enter**. When prompted for the grams of fat, type **6** and press **Enter**. The program calculates and displays the fat calories and fat percentage, as shown in Figure 6-27.

Figure 6-27: Command Prompt window showing the results of the first test

```
"c:\cppnet\tut06\t6app solution\t6app project\debug\T6App Project.exe"
Enter the total calories: 150
Enter the grams of fat: 6
Fat calories: 54
Fat percentage: 0%
Press any key to continue_
```

The Command Prompt window shows that the fat calories are 54, which agrees with the desk-check tables. However, it shows that the fat percentage is 0%, which is incorrect.

4. Press **Enter** to close the Command Prompt window, then close the Output window.

According to the desk-check tables, the fat percentage for a food with 150 total calories and 6 grams of fat should be 36% (54 fat calories / 150 total calories * 100). Why doesn't the program produce the correct result? The reason for the discrepancy is due to the way that the computer performs division between two integers in a C++ expression. When dividing an integer by another integer in a C++ expression, the computer returns only the integer portion of the quotient. In other words, if the quotient contains a decimal portion, the decimal portion is truncated (dropped from the number). In this case, when dividing the fat calories (the integer 54) by the total calories (the integer 150), the computer returns 0, which is the integer portion of the quotient 0.36. You can fix this problem by type casting the variables involved in the division operation to the `double` data type. When the computer divides two `double` numbers, the result is always a `double` number that contains the entire quotient—both the integer and decimal portions. As you learned in Tutorial 3, you type cast (or explicitly convert) an item of data by using the methods defined in the `Convert` class. In this case, you will use the `Convert::ToDouble()` method.

To type cast the variables involved in calculating the fat percentage, then test the program:

1. Change the `fPer = fCal / tCal * 100;` statement in the `calcFatInfo()` function to **fPer = Convert::ToDouble(fCal) / Convert::ToDouble(tCal) * 100;**.
2. Save and then build the solution. Verify that the program generated no warnings.
3. Execute the program. When prompted for the total calories, type **150** and press **Enter**. When prompted for the grams of fat, type **6** and press **Enter**. The program correctly calculates and displays the fat calories and fat percentage as 54 and 36%, respectively.
4. Press **Enter** to close the Command Prompt window.
5. Execute the program again. When prompted for the total calories, type **105** and press **Enter**. When prompted for the grams of fat, type **2** and press **Enter**. The program correctly calculates and displays the fat calories and fat percentage as 18 and 17.1428571428571%, respectively. (In Exercise 1 at the end of the lesson, you modify the program so that it displays the fat percentage as an integer.)
6. Press **Enter** to close the Command Prompt window.
7. Execute the program again. When prompted for the total calories, type **100** and press **Enter**. When prompted for the grams of fat, type **–3** and press **Enter**. The program displays the message "Input error", which is correct.
8. Press **Enter** to close the Command Prompt window, then close the Output window.
9. Click **File** on the menu bar, and then click **Close Solution** to close the current solution.
10. Click **File** on the menu bar, and then click **Exit** to exit Visual Studio .NET.

You now have completed Tutorial 6's Application lesson. You can either take a break or complete the end-of-lesson exercises.

Look For These Symbols

Debugging

Discovery

EXERCISES

1) In this exercise, you modify the program you created in the lesson so that it displays the fat percentage with zero decimal places.

A. If necessary, start Visual Studio .NET. Open the T6AppE01 Solution (T6AppE01 Solution.sln) file, which is contained in the CppNet\Tut06\T6AppE01 Solution folder.

B. Modify the program so that it displays the fat percentage as an integer.

C. Save and then build the solution.

D. Execute the program. Use 105 as the total calories, and 2 as the grams of fat. The program should display 18 as the fat calories, and 17% as the fat percentage.

E. When the program is working correctly, close the Output window, and then use the File menu to close the solution.

2) In this exercise, you create a program that displays an employee's name and gross pay.

A. Figure 6-28 shows the partially completed IPO chart for the payroll program. Employees working over 40 hours should be paid time and one-half for the hours worked over 40. Complete the IPO chart.

Figure 6-28

Input	Processing	Output
name hours worked pay rate	Processing items: none Algorithm:	name gross pay

B. If necessary, start Visual Studio .NET. Open the T6AppE02 Solution (T6AppE02 Solution.sln) file, which is contained in the CppNet\Tut06\T6AppE02 Solution folder.

C. Use the IPO chart you completed in Step A to complete the program. Display the gross pay amount with a dollar sign and two decimal places.

D. Complete a desk-check table for the program. First, use Jack Henderson as the name, 35 as the hours worked, and 10 as the hourly pay rate. Then, use Mary Matiez as the name, 45 as the hours worked, and 7.50 as the hourly pay rate.

E. Save and then build the solution.

F. Execute the program. Use the data from Step D to test the program.

G. When the program is working correctly, close the Output window, and then use the File menu to close the solution.

3) In this exercise, you create a program that displays a bonus amount.

A. Figure 6-29 shows the partially completed IPO charts for the bonus program. Complete the IPO charts. The `calcBonus()` function should be a value-returning function that calculates and returns the appropriate bonus amount. The bonus rate is 10% on the first $12,000 of sales, and 15% on sales over $12,000. (For example, a salesperson selling $15,000 in product should receive a bonus in the amount of $1,650.)

Figure 6-29

`main()` **function**

Input	Processing	Output
sales	Processing items: none Algorithm:	bonus

`calcBonus()` **function**

Input	Processing	Output
	Processing items: Algorithm:	

B. If necessary, start Visual Studio .NET. Open the T6AppE03 Solution (T6AppE03 Solution.sln) file, which is contained in the CppNet\Tut06\T6AppE03 Solution folder.

C. Use the IPO chart you completed in Step A to complete the program. Display the bonus amount with a dollar sign and zero decimal places.

D. Complete a desk-check table for the program, using the following sale amounts: 5000 and 96000.

E. Save and then build the solution.

F. Execute the program. Use the data from Step D to test the program.

G. When the program is working correctly, close the Output window, and then use the File menu to close the solution.

4) In this exercise, you modify the periodic payment program you created in Tutorial 4's Application lesson. The modified program will allow the user to enter the interest rates as either integers or decimal numbers.

A. If necessary, start Visual Studio .NET. Open the T6AppE04 Solution (T6AppE04 Solution.sln) file, which is contained in the CppNet\Tut06\T6AppE04 Solution folder.

B. The interest rates entered by the user can be entered as either integers or decimal numbers. Modify the program appropriately.

C. Save and then build the solution.

D. Execute the program. Enter 16000 as the car price, 3000 as the rebate, .08 as the credit union rate, .03 as the dealer rate, and 4 as the term. The program should display $317.37 as the credit union payment and $354.15 as the dealer payment. Close the Command Prompt window.

E. Execute the program again. Enter 16000 as the car price, 3000 as the rebate, 8 as the credit union rate, 3 as the dealer rate, and 4 as the term. The program should display $317.37 as the credit union payment and $354.15 as the dealer payment. Close the Command Prompt window.

F. Execute the program again. Enter 16000 as the car price, 3000 as the rebate, .08 as the credit union rate, 3 as the dealer rate, and 4 as the term. The program should display $317.37 as the credit union payment and $354.15 as the dealer payment. Close the Command Prompt window.

G. When the program is working correctly, close the Output window, and then use the File menu to close the solution.

5) In this exercise, you create a program that displays the average of three test scores entered by the user. The program uses a `main()` function and one void function named `calcAverage()`.

A. Write the IPO charts for the average program, which should contain two functions: `main()` and `calcAverage()`. Before calling the `calcAverage()` function to calculate the average, have the `main()` function validate the input data. To be valid, each test score must be greater than or equal to zero. If one or more test scores is not valid, the program should display an appropriate message.

B. If necessary, start Visual Studio .NET. Create a blank solution named T6AppE05 Solution. Save the solution in the CppNet\Tut06 folder.

C. Add a new managed C++ empty project to the solution. Name the project T6AppE05 Project.

D. Add a new C++ source file to the project. Name the source file T6AppE05.

E. Enter the appropriate C++ instructions into the source file. Use the IPO charts you created in Step A to code the program. Display the average with one decimal place.

F. Complete a desk-check table for the program, using the following two groups of test scores:

95.5, 76, and 59

45, –78, and 30 (notice the minus sign before the number 78)

G. Save and then build the solution.

H. Execute the program. Use the data from Step F to test the program.

I. When the program is working correctly, close the Output window, and then use the File menu to close the solution.

6) In this exercise, you modify the water bill program you created in Tutorial 5's Application lesson. The modified program will verify that the two meter readings are greater than zero, and the current reading is greater than or equal to the previous reading.

A. If necessary, start Visual Studio .NET. Open the T6AppE06 Solution (T6AppE06 Solution.sln) file, which is contained in the CppNet\Tut06\T6AppE06 Solution folder.

B. Modify the program so that it calls the `calculate()` and `displayBill()` functions only when the meter readings are valid. To be valid, both meter readings must be greater than zero, and the current meter reading must be greater than or equal to the previous meter reading. If one or both of the meter readings is not valid, display an appropriate message.

C. Save and then build the solution.

D. Execute the program. Enter your name, 9000 as the current reading, and 8000 as the previous reading. The program should display 1,000 as the gallons used and $1.75 as the water charge. Close the Command Prompt window.

E. Execute the program again. Enter your name, 1000 as the current reading, and 1000 as the previous reading. The program should display 0 as the gallons used and $0.00 as the water charge. Close the Command Prompt window.

F. Execute the program again. Enter your name, 6000 as the current reading, and 13000 as the previous reading. The program should display an appropriate message. Close the Command Prompt window.

G. Execute the program again. Enter your name, -5 as the current reading, and 73 as the previous reading. The program should display an appropriate message. Close the Command Prompt window.

H. Execute the program again. Enter your name, 4000 as the current reading, and -1 as the previous reading. The program should display an appropriate message. Close the Command Prompt window.

I. When the program is working correctly, close the Output window, and then use the File menu to close the solution.

7) In this exercise, you create a program that displays the total amount a company owes for a seminar. The seminar charge is $80 per person.

A. Write an IPO chart for the seminar program. The input is the number of seminar registrants, which should be greater than 0, but less than 50. Display an appropriate error message when the number of registrants is invalid.

B. If necessary, start Visual Studio .NET. Open the T6AppE07 Solution (T6AppE07 Solution.sln) file, which is contained in the CppNet\Tut06\T6AppE07 Solution folder.

C. Use the IPO chart you completed in Step A to complete the program. Display the total amount with a dollar sign and zero decimal places.

D. Complete a desk-check table for the program, using the following data: 5 and -20.

E. Save and then build the solution.

F. Execute the program. Use the data from Step D to test the program.

G. When the program is working correctly, close the Output window, and then use the File menu to close the solution.

8) In this exercise, you create a program that displays a shipping charge.

A. Write an IPO chart for the shipping charge program. The shipping charge is based on the state name entered by the user, as shown in the following table:

State	Shipping charge ($)
Hawaii	30
Oregon	30

If the user enters any other state name, the program should display the message "Incorrect state".

B. If necessary, start Visual Studio .NET. Open the T6AppE08 Solution (T6AppE08 Solution.sln) file, which is contained in the CppNet\Tut06\T6AppE08 Solution folder.

C. Use the IPO chart you completed in Step A to complete the program.

D. Complete a desk-check table for the program, using the following state names: Oregon, Hawaii, and Kentucky.

E. Save and then build the solution.

F. Execute the program. Use the data from Step D to test the program.

G. When the program is working correctly, close the Output window, and then use the File menu to close the solution.

9) In this exercise, you complete a program that displays the result of dividing two numbers.

A. If necessary, start Visual Studio .NET. Open the T6AppE09 Solution (T6AppE09 Solution.sln) file, which is contained in the CppNet\Tut06\T6AppE09 Solution folder.

B. Study the existing code. Notice that the code to calculate the quotient is missing from the program. Complete the program by entering the appropriate code. Be sure to always divide the larger number by the smaller number.

C. Save and then build the solution.

D. Execute the program twice. First, use the numbers 40 and 10. Second, use the numbers 9 and 81.

E. When the program is working correctly, close the Output window, and then use the File menu to close the solution.

10) In this exercise, you create a program that displays a shipping charge.

A. Write an IPO chart for the shipping charge program. The shipping charge is based on the state name entered by the user, as shown in the following table:

State	Shipping charge ($)
Alabama	25
Alaska	50

If the user enters any other state name, the shipping charge should be 0 (zero).

(*Hint*: You can nest an `if` statement, which means you can place one `if` statement inside another `if` statement.)

B. If necessary, start Visual Studio .NET. Open the T6AppE10 Solution (T6AppE10 Solution.sln) file, which is contained in the CppNet\Tut06\T6AppE10 Solution folder.

C. Use the IPO chart you completed in Step A to complete the program.

D. Complete a desk-check table for the program, using the following state names: Alabama, Alaska, and Illinois.

E. Save and then build the solution.

F. Execute the program. Use the data from Step D to test the program.

G. When the program is working correctly, close the Output window, and then use the File menu to close the solution.

11) In this exercise, you debug a C++ program.

A. If necessary, start Visual Studio .NET. Open the T6AppE11 Solution (T6AppE11 Solution.sln) file, which is contained in the CppNet\Tut05\T6AppE11 Solution folder.

B. The program should display a message when the sales amount is greater than or equal to zero, but it is not working correctly. Study the program's code, then build the solution.

C. Execute the program. Test the program by entering 21500 as the sales amount. Close the Command Prompt window.

D. Correct any errors in the program, then save and build the solution.

E. Execute the program. Test the program by entering 21500 as the sales amount. Close the Command Prompt window.

F. When the program is working correctly, close the Output window, and then use the File menu to close the solution.

Tutorial 7

More on the Selection Structure

Objectives

After completing this tutorial, you will be able to:

- Include a nested selection structure in pseudocode and in a flowchart
- Code a nested selection structure in C++
- Recognize common logic errors in selection structures
- Include the `switch` form of the selection structure in pseudocode and in a flowchart
- Code the `switch` form of the selection structure in C++

Concept Lesson

Nested Selection Structures

As you learned in Tutorial 6, you use the selection structure when you want a program to make a decision and then select one of two paths—either the true path or the false path—based on the result of that decision. Both paths in a selection structure can include instructions that declare and initialize variables, perform calculations, and so on; both also can include other selection structures. When either a selection structure's true path or its false path contains another selection structure, the inner selection structure is referred to as a **nested selection structure**, because it is contained (nested) within the outer selection structure.

You use a nested selection structure when more than one decision must be made before the appropriate action can be taken. For example, assume you want to create a voter eligibility program that displays one of three messages. The messages and the criteria for displaying each message are shown here:

Message	Criteria
"You are too young to vote."	person is younger than 18 years old
"You can vote."	person is at least 18 years old and is registered to vote
"You need to register before you can vote."	person is at least 18 years old but is not registered to vote

As the chart indicates, the person's age and voter registration status determine the appropriate message to display. If the person is younger than 18 years old, the program should display the message "You are too young to vote." However, if the person is at least 18 years old, the program should display one of two different messages. The correct message to display is determined by the person's voter registration status. If the person is registered, then the appropriate message is "You can vote."; otherwise, it is "You need to register before you can vote." Notice that determining the person's voter registration status is important only *after* his or her age is determined. You can think of the decision regarding the age as being the **primary decision**, and the decision regarding the registration status as being the **secondary decision**, because whether the registration decision needs to be made depends on the result of the age decision. The primary decision is always made by the outer selection structure, while the secondary decision is always made by the inner (nested) selection structure.

Figure 7-1 shows the pseudocode and C++ code for the voter eligibility program, and Figure 7-2 shows the corresponding flowchart. In both figures, the outer selection structure determines the age (the primary decision), and the nested selection structure determines the voter registration status (the secondary decision). Notice that the nested selection structure appears in the outer selection structure's true path in both figures.

Figure 7-1: Pseudocode and C++ code showing the nested selection structure in the true path

Pseudocode

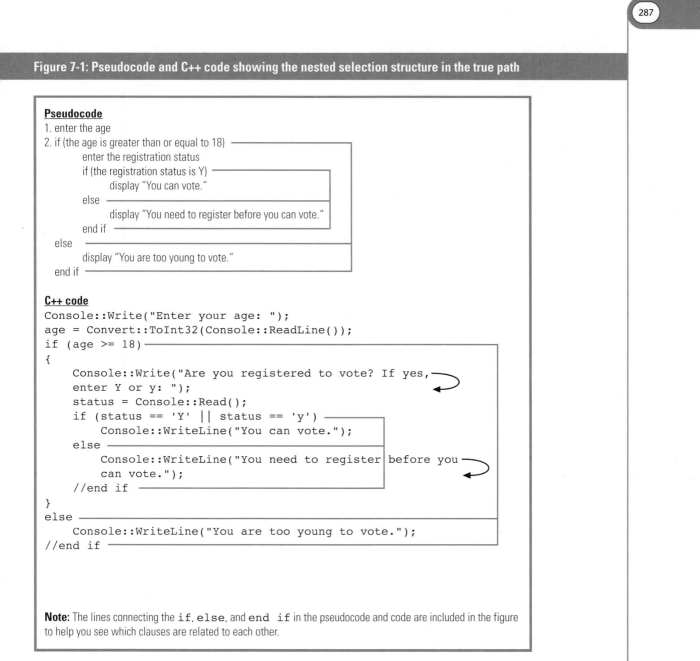

```
1. enter the age
2. if (the age is greater than or equal to 18)
        enter the registration status
        if (the registration status is Y)
            display "You can vote."
        else
            display "You need to register before you can vote."
        end if
   else
        display "You are too young to vote."
   end if
```

C++ code

```
Console::Write("Enter your age: ");
age = Convert::ToInt32(Console::ReadLine());
if (age >= 18)
{
    Console::Write("Are you registered to vote? If yes,
    enter Y or y: ");
    status = Console::Read();
    if (status == 'Y' || status == 'y')
        Console::WriteLine("You can vote.");
    else
        Console::WriteLine("You need to register before you
        can vote.");
    //end if
}
else
    Console::WriteLine("You are too young to vote.");
//end if
```

Note: The lines connecting the `if`, `else`, and `end if` in the pseudocode and code are included in the figure to help you see which clauses are related to each other.

Figure 7-2: Flowchart showing the nested selection structure in the true path

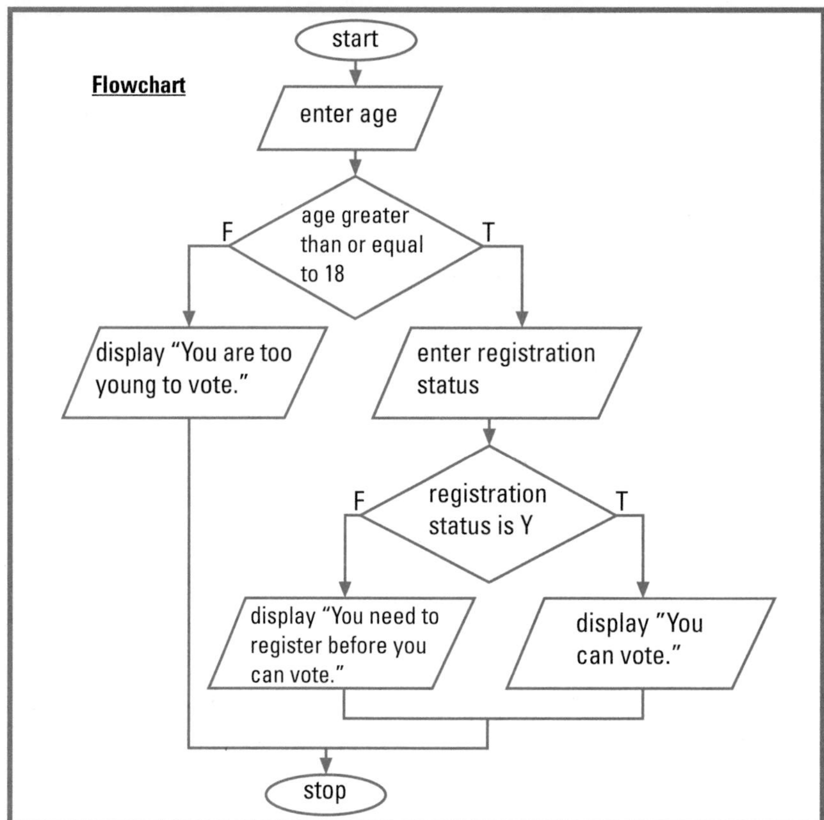

As both figures indicate, the program first gets the age from the user. The condition in the outer selection structure then checks whether the age is greater than or equal to 18. If the condition is false, it means that the person is not old enough to vote. In that case, only one message—the "You are too young to vote." message—is appropriate. After the message is displayed, both the outer selection structure and the program end.

If the outer selection structure's condition is true, on the other hand, it means that the person *is* old enough to vote. Before displaying the appropriate message, the instructions in the outer selection structure's true path first get the registration status from the user. A nested selection structure then is used to determine whether the person is registered. If he or she is registered, the instruction in the nested selection structure's true path displays the message "You can vote."; otherwise, the instruction in the nested selection structure's false path displays the message "You need to register before you can vote." After the appropriate message is displayed, both selection structures and the program end. Notice that the nested selection structure in this program is processed only when the outer selection structure's condition is true.

Figures 7-3 and 7-4 show the pseudocode, C++ code, and flowchart for a different version of the voter eligibility program. As in the previous version, the outer selection structure in this version determines the age (the primary decision), and the nested selection structure determines the voter registration status (the secondary decision). In this version of the program, however, the nested selection structure appears in the false path of the outer selection structure.

Figure 7-3: Pseudocode and C++ code showing the nested selection structure in the false path

Pseudocode

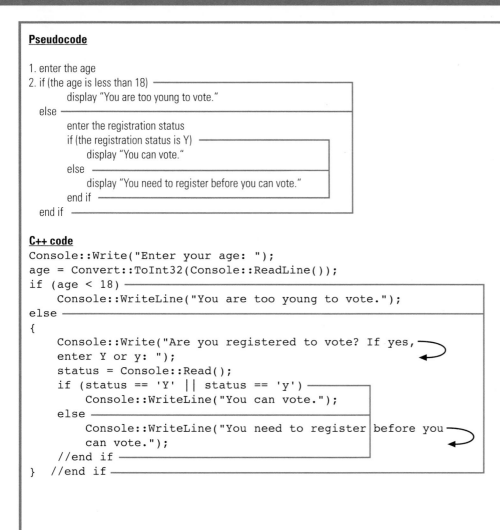

```
1. enter the age
2. if (the age is less than 18)
        display "You are too young to vote."
   else
        enter the registration status
        if (the registration status is Y)
             display "You can vote."
        else
             display "You need to register before you can vote."
        end if
   end if
```

C++ code

```
Console::Write("Enter your age: ");
age = Convert::ToInt32(Console::ReadLine());
if (age < 18)
    Console::WriteLine("You are too young to vote.");
else
{
    Console::Write("Are you registered to vote? If yes,
    enter Y or y: ");
    status = Console::Read();
    if (status == 'Y' || status == 'y')
        Console::WriteLine("You can vote.");
    else
        Console::WriteLine("You need to register before you
        can vote.");
    //end if
}   //end if
```

Note: The lines connecting the `if`, `else`, and `end if` in the pseudocode and code are included in the figure to help you see which clauses are related to each other.

Figure 7-4: Flowchart showing the nested selection structure in the false path

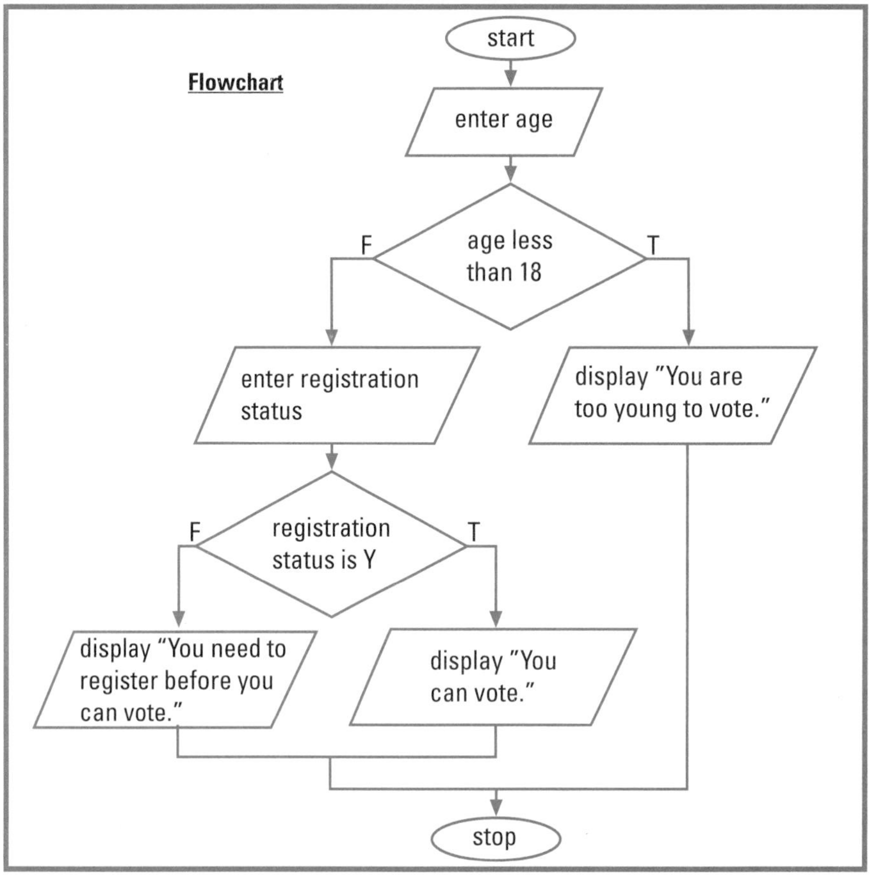

Like the version shown earlier, this version of the voter eligibility program first gets the age from the user. However, rather than checking whether the age is greater than or equal to 18, the outer selection structure in this version checks whether the age is less than 18. If the condition is true, the instruction in the outer selection structure's true path displays the message "You are too young to vote." If the condition is false, the instructions in the outer selection structure's false path first get the registration status from the user, and then use a nested selection structure to determine whether the person is registered. If the person is registered, the instruction in the nested selection structure's true path displays the message "You can vote."; otherwise, the instruction in the nested selection structure's false path displays the message "You need to register before you can vote." Unlike in the previous version, the nested selection structure in this version of the program is processed only when the outer selection structure's condition is false.

Notice that both versions of the voter eligibility program produce the same results. Neither version is better than the other; each simply represents a different way of solving the same problem.

Next, view another example of a nested selection structure.

Another Example of a Nested Selection Structure

In Tutorial 6's Application lesson, you created a program for Marshall Cabello, the manager of Willow Springs Health Club. As you may remember, the program allows Marshall to enter the number of calories and grams of fat contained in a specific food. The program then calculates and displays two values: the food's fat calories (the number of calories attributed to fat) and its fat percentage (the ratio of the food's fat calories to its total calories). Now suppose that

Marshall wants you to modify the program so that it displays the message "This food is high in fat." when a food's fat percentage is greater than 30%; otherwise, the program should display the message "This food is not high in fat." The modified health club program, which uses a nested selection structure, is shown in Figure 7-5.

Figure 7-5: Health club program containing a nested selection structure

```
//Modified T6App.cpp
//displays fat calories, fat percentage, and a message

#using <mscorlib.dll>
using namespace System;

//function prototype
void calcFatInfo(int, int, int &, double &);

int main()
{
    int totalCal      = 0;
    int fatGrams      = 0;
    int fatCal        = 0;
    double fatPercent = 0.0;

    //enter input data
    Console::Write("Enter the total calories: ");
    totalCal = Convert::ToInt32(Console::ReadLine());
    Console::Write("Enter the grams of fat: ");
    fatGrams = Convert::ToInt32(Console::ReadLine());
    //validate input data
    if (totalCal >= 0 && fatGrams >= 0)
    {
        //valid data
        calcFatInfo(totalCal, fatGrams, fatCal, fatPercent);
        Console::WriteLine("Fat calories: {0}", Convert::
        ToString(fatCal));
        Console::WriteLine("Fat percentage: {0}%", Convert::
        ToString(fatPercent));
        if (fatPercent > 30)
            Console::WriteLine("This food is high in fat.");
        else
            Console::WriteLine("This food is not high in fat.");
        //end if
    }
    else
        Console::WriteLine("Input error");
    //end if

    return 0;
}   //end of main function

//*****function definitions*****
void calcFatInfo(int tCal, int grams, int &fCal, double &fPer)
{
    //calculate fat calories and fat percentage
    fCal = grams * 9;
    fPer = Convert::ToDouble(fCal) / Convert::ToDouble(tCal) * 100;
}   //end of calcFatInfo function
```

nested selection structure

outer selection structure

In this case, the outer selection structure's condition, which represents the primary decision, determines whether the user's input (total calories and grams of fat) is valid. If the condition is false, the instruction in the outer selection structure's false path displays an error message on the screen. However, if the condition is true, the instructions in the outer selection structure's true path both calculate and display the fat calories and fat percentage, and then use a nested selection structure to determine whether the secondary decision—which checks whether the fat percentage is greater than 30—is true or false. If the fat percentage is greater than 30, the nested selection structure's true path displays the message "This food is high in fat."; otherwise, the nested selection structure's false path displays the message "This food is not high in fat." As in the voter eligibility program, the result of the primary decision in the health club program determines whether the secondary decision needs to be made.

MINI-QUIZ

Mini-Quiz 1

1) Assume you want to create a program that displays the message "Highest honors" when a student's test score is 90 or above. When the test score is 70 through 89, the program should display the message "Good job". For all other test scores, the program should display the message "Retake the test". Write the pseudocode for this program's selection structure.
2) Write the C++ code that corresponds to the pseudocode you wrote in Question 1. The student's score is stored in an `int` variable named `score`.
3) Assume that the manager of a golf course has asked you to create a program that displays the appropriate fee to charge a golfer. The club uses the following fee schedule:

Fee	Criteria
0	Club members
15	Non-members golfing on Monday through Thursday
25	Non-members golfing on Friday through Sunday

In this program, which is the primary decision and which is the secondary decision? Why?

In the next section, you learn some of the common logic errors made when writing selection structures. Being aware of these errors will help to prevent you from making them.

Logic Errors in Selection Structures

Typically, logic errors commonly made when writing selection structures are a result of one of the following mistakes:

1. Using a logical operator rather than a nested selection structure
2. Reversing the primary and secondary decisions
3. Using an unnecessary nested selection structure

The XYZ Company's vacation program can be used to demonstrate each of these logic errors. Assume that the company employs both full-time and part-time employees. Only full-time employees receive a paid vacation, as shown here:

Vacation weeks	Criteria
0	Part-time employees
2	Full-time employees working at the company for 5 years or fewer
3	Full-time employees working at the company for over 5 years

The company wants you to create a program that allows the user to enter the employee's status—either F for full-time or P for part-time—and the number of years the employee has worked for the company. If the employee is full-time, the program should display the number of vacation weeks the employee has earned, and then the program should end. If the employee is not full-time, the program should simply end without displaying anything.

As the vacation chart indicates, the employee's status—either full-time or part-time—is a factor in determining whether the employee receives any paid vacation. If the employee is entitled to a paid vacation, then the number of years he or she has worked for the company determines the appropriate number of vacation weeks. In this case, the decision regarding the employee's status is the primary decision, and the decision regarding the years employed is the secondary decision, because whether the years employed decision needs to be made depends on the result of the status decision.

Figure 7-6 shows a correct algorithm for the vacation program.

Figure 7-6: A correct algorithm for the vacation program

Correct algorithm for the vacation program

```
1. enter the status and years
2. if (the status is F)
      if (the years are greater than 5)
            display "3-week vacation"
      else
            display "2-week vacation"
      end if
   end if
```

To observe why the algorithm shown in Figure 7-6 is correct, you will desk-check it using the following test data:

Data for first desk-check
Status: F
Years: 4

Data for second desk-check
Status: F
Years: 15

Data for third desk-check
Status: P
Years: 11

The algorithm should display "2-week vacation" for the first set of test data, "3-week vacation" for the second set, and nothing for the third set.

Using the first set of test data, the user enters F as the status and 4 as the years. The outer selection structure's condition determines whether the status is F; it is, so the nested selection structure's condition checks whether the years are greater than 5. The years are not greater than 5, so the nested selection structure's false path displays the message "2-week vacation," which is correct. After doing so, both selection structures and the program end.

tip

You also can write the condition in the nested selection structure shown in Figure 7-6 as follows: *if (the years are less than or equal to 5)*. The nested structure's true path then would contain the instruction *display "2-week vacation"*, and its false path would contain the instruction display *"3-week vacation"*.

Using the second set of test data, the user enters F as the status and 15 as the years. The outer selection structure's condition determines whether the status is F; it is, so the nested selection structure's condition checks whether the years are greater than 5. The years are greater than 5, so the nested selection structure's true path displays the message "3-week vacation," which is correct. After doing so, both selection structures and the program end.

Using the third set of test data, the user enters P as the status and 11 as the years. The outer selection structure's condition determines whether the status is F. The status is not F, so the outer selection structure and the program end. Notice that the nested selection structure is not processed when the outer selection structure's condition is false. Figure 7-7 shows the results of desk-checking the correct algorithm shown in Figure 7-6.

Figure 7-7: Results of desk-checking the correct algorithm shown in Figure 7-6

Desk-check	Result
First: using F as the status and 4 as the years Second: using F as the status and 15 as the years Third: using P as the status and 11 as the years	"2-week vacation" displayed "3-week vacation" displayed Nothing is displayed

In the next section, you view and desk-check another algorithm for the vacation program. You will find that the algorithm does not produce the desired results because it contains a logical operator instead of a nested selection structure.

Using a Logical Operator Rather Than a Nested Selection Structure

One common error made when writing selection structures is to use a logical operator in the outer selection structure's condition when a nested selection structure is needed. Figure 7-8 shows an example of this error in the vacation algorithm. The correct algorithm is included in the figure for comparison.

Figure 7-8: Correct algorithm and an incorrect algorithm containing the first logic error

logical operator used rather than a nested selection structure

Correct algorithm	Incorrect algorithm

1. enter the status and years
2. if (the status is F)
    if (the years are greater than 5)
        display "3-week vacation"
    else
        display "2-week vacation"
    end if
  end if
	1. enter the status and years
	2. if (the status is F and the years are greater than 5)
	      display "3-week vacation"
	  else
	      display "2-week vacation"
	  end if

Notice that the incorrect algorithm uses one selection structure, rather than two selection structures, and the selection structure's condition contains the logical operator *and*. Consider why the selection structure in the incorrect algorithm cannot be used in place of the selection structures in the correct algorithm. In the correct algorithm, the outer and nested selection structures indicate that a hierarchy exists between the status and years employed decisions: the status decision is always made first, followed by the years employed decision (if necessary). In the incorrect algorithm, on the other hand, the logical operator in the selection structure's condition indicates that no hierarchy exists between the status and years employed decisions; each has equal weight and neither is dependent on the other, which is incorrect. To better understand why this algorithm is incorrect, you will desk-check it using the same test data you used to desk-check the correct algorithm.

After the user enters the first set of test data—F as the status and 4 as the years—the selection structure's condition in the incorrect algorithm determines whether the status is F and, at the same time, the years are greater than 5. Only one of these conditions is true, so the compound condition evaluates to false and the selection structure's false path displays the message "2-week vacation" before both the selection structure and the program end. Even though the algorithm's selection structure is phrased incorrectly, notice that the incorrect algorithm produces the same result as the correct algorithm.

After the user enters the second set of test data—F as the status and 15 as the years—the selection structure's condition in the incorrect algorithm determines whether the status is F and, at the same time, the years are greater than 5. Both conditions are true, so the compound condition is true and the selection structure's true path displays the message "3-week vacation" before both the selection structure and the program end. Here again, using the second set of test data, the incorrect algorithm produces the same result as the correct algorithm.

After the user enters the third set of test data—P as the status and 11 as the years—the selection structure's condition in the incorrect algorithm determines whether the status is F and, at the same time, the years are greater than 5. Only one of these conditions is true, so the compound condition is false and the selection structure's false path displays the message "2-week vacation" before both the selection structure and the program end. Notice that the incorrect algorithm produces erroneous results for the third set of test data; according to Figure 7-7, the algorithm should not have displayed anything using this data. As you learned in Tutorial 2, it is important to desk-check an algorithm several times, using different test data. In this case, if you had used only the first two sets of data to desk-check the incorrect algorithm, you would not have discovered the error.

Figure 7-9 shows the results of desk-checking the incorrect algorithm shown in Figure 7-8. As indicated in the figure, the results of the first and second desk-checks are correct, but the result of the third desk-check is not correct.

tip

As you learned in Tutorial 6, when you use the logical operator *and* to combine two conditions in a selection structure, both conditions must be true for the compound condition to be true. If at least one of the conditions is false, then the compound condition is false and the instructions in the selection structure's false path (assuming there is a false path) are processed.

Figure 7-9: Results of desk-checking the incorrect algorithm shown in Figure 7-8

Desk-check	Result
First: using F as the status and 4 as the years	"2-week vacation" displayed
Second: using F as the status and 15 as the years	"3-week vacation" displayed
Third: using P as the status and 11 as the years	"2-week vacation" displayed

correct results (First, Second)

incorrect result (Third)

Next, you view and desk-check another algorithm for the vacation program. You will find that this algorithm also does not produce the desired results; this is because the primary and secondary decisions are reversed in the selection structures.

Reversing the Primary and Secondary Decisions

Another common error made when writing a selection structure that contains a nested selection structure is to reverse the primary and secondary decisions—in other words, put the secondary decision in the outer selection structure, and put the primary decision in the nested selection structure. Figure 7-10 shows an example of this error in the vacation algorithm. The correct algorithm is included in the figure for comparison.

Figure 7-10: Correct algorithm and an incorrect algorithm containing the second logic error

	Correct algorithm	Incorrect algorithm

primary and secondary decisions reversed	1. enter the status and years
	2. if (the status is F)
	    if (the years are greater than 5)
	        display "3-week vacation"
	    else
	        display "2-week vacation"
	    end if
	  end if
		1. enter the status and years
		2. if (the years are greater than 5)
		    if (the status is F)
		        display "3-week vacation"
		    else
		        display "2-week vacation"
		    end if
		  end if

Unlike the selection structures in the correct algorithm, which determine the employment status before determining the number of years employed, the selection structures in the incorrect algorithm determine the number of years employed before determining the employment status. Consider how this difference changes the algorithm. In the correct algorithm, the selection structures indicate that only employees whose status is full-time receive a paid vacation, which is correct. The selection structures in the incorrect algorithm, on the other hand, indicate that all employees who have been with the company for more than 5 years receive a paid vacation, which is not correct. Desk-check the incorrect algorithm to see the results.

After the user enters the first set of test data—F as the status and 4 as the years—the condition in the outer selection structure determines whether the years are greater than 5. The years are not greater than 5, so both the outer selection structure and the program end. Notice that the incorrect algorithm does not display the expected message, "2-week vacation."

After the user enters the second set of test data—F as the status and 15 as the years—the condition in the outer selection structure determines whether the years are greater than 5; they are, so the condition in the nested selection structure determines whether the status is F. The status is F, so the nested selection structure's true path displays the message "3-week vacation," which is correct.

After the user enters the third set of test data—P as the status and 11 as the years—the condition in the outer selection structure determines whether the years are greater than 5; they are, so the condition in the nested selection structure determines whether the status is F. The status is not F, so the nested selection structure's false path displays the message "2-week vacation," which is not correct.

Figure 7-11 shows the results of desk-checking the incorrect algorithm shown in Figure 7-10. As indicated in the figure, only the results of the second desk-check are correct.

Figure 7-11: Results of desk-checking the incorrect algorithm shown in Figure 7-10

Desk-check	Result
First: using F as the status and 4 as the years	Nothing is displayed
Second: using F as the status and 15 as the years	"3-week vacation" displayed
Third: using P as the status and 11 as the years	"2-week vacation" displayed

only this result is correct

Next, you view and desk-check another algorithm for the vacation program. This algorithm contains the third logic error—using an unnecessary nested selection structure. Like the correct algorithm, this algorithm produces the desired results; however, it does so in a less efficient manner than the correct algorithm.

Using an Unnecessary Nested Selection Structure

Another common error made when writing selection structures is to include an unnecessary nested selection structure. In most cases, a selection structure containing this error still produces the correct results. The only problem is that it does so less efficiently than selection structures that are properly structured. Figure 7-12 shows an example of this error in the vacation algorithm. The correct algorithm is included in the figure for comparison.

Figure 7-12: Correct algorithm and an inefficient algorithm containing the third logic error

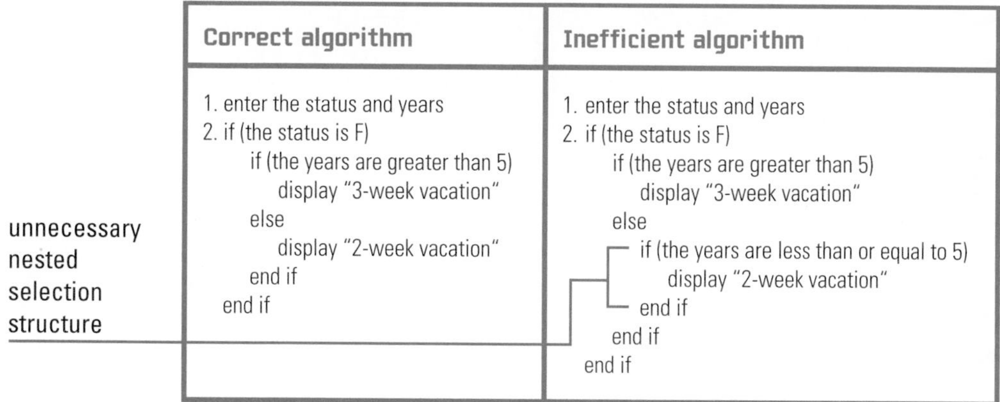

Correct algorithm

```
1. enter the status and years
2. if (the status is F)
       if (the years are greater than 5)
           display "3-week vacation"
       else
           display "2-week vacation"
       end if
   end if
```

Inefficient algorithm

```
1. enter the status and years
2. if (the status is F)
       if (the years are greater than 5)
           display "3-week vacation"
       else
           if (the years are less than or equal to 5)
               display "2-week vacation"
           end if
       end if
   end if
```

unnecessary nested selection structure

Unlike the correct algorithm, which contains two selection structures, the inefficient algorithm contains three selection structures. Notice that the condition in the third selection structure determines whether the years are less than or equal to 5, and is processed only when the condition in the second selection structure is false; in other words, it is processed only when the years are not greater than 5. However, if the years are not greater than 5, then they would have to be either less than or equal to 5, so the third selection structure is unnecessary. To better understand the error in the inefficient algorithm, you will desk-check the algorithm.

After the user enters the first set of test data—F as the status and 4 as the years—the first selection structure's condition determines whether the status is F; it is, so the second selection structure's condition determines whether the years are greater than 5. The years are not greater than 5, so the third selection structure's condition checks whether the years are less than or equal to 5—an unnecessary decision. In this case, 4 is less than 5, so the third selection structure's true path displays the message "2-week vacation," which is correct. After doing so, the three selection structures and the program end.

After the user enters the second set of test data—F as the status and 15 as the years—the first selection structure's condition determines whether the status is F; it is, so the second selection structure's condition determines whether the years are greater than 5. The years are greater than 5, so the second selection structure's true path displays the message "3-week vacation," which is correct. After doing so, the first and second selection structures and the program end.

After the user enters the third set of test data—P as the status and 11 as the years—the condition in the first selection structure determines whether the status is F; it isn't, so the first selection structure and the program end.

Figure 7-13 shows the results of desk-checking the inefficient algorithm shown in Figure 7-12. As indicated in the figure, although the results of the three desk-checks are correct, the result of the first desk-check is obtained in a less efficient manner.

Figure 7-13: Results of desk-checking the inefficient algorithm shown in Figure 7-12

correct result is obtained in a less efficient manner

Desk-check	Result
First: using F as the status and 4 as the years	"2-week vacation" displayed
Second: using F as the status and 15 as the years	"3-week vacation" displayed
Third: using P as the status and 11 as the years	Nothing is displayed

MINI-QUIZ

Mini-Quiz 2

1) List the three errors commonly made when writing selection structures.

2) Which of the errors from Question 1 makes the selection structure inefficient, but still produces the correct results?

Some algorithms require selection structures that are capable of choosing from several alternatives. You can create such selection structures, commonly referred to as multiple-path or extended selection structures, using either the `if/else` or `switch` form of the selection structure. First learn how to use the `if/else` form.

Using the `if/else` Form to Create Multiple-Path Selection Structures

At times, you may need to create a selection structure that can choose from several alternatives. For example, assume you are asked to create a program that displays a message based on a letter grade that the user enters. Figure 7-14 shows the valid letter grades and their corresponding messages.

Figure 7-14: Letter grades and messages

Letter grade	Message
A	Excellent
B	Above Average
C	Average
D	Below Average
F	Below Average

As Figure 7-14 indicates, if the letter grade is an A, then the program should display the message "Excellent." If the letter grade is a B, then the program should display the message "Above Average," and so on. Figure 7-15 shows two versions of the C++ code for the grade problem. Both versions use the `if/else` form of the selection structure to display the appropriate message.

Figure 7-15: Two versions of the C++ code for the grade problem

Version 1

```
Console::Write("Grade: ");
grade = Console::Read();

if (grade == 'A' || grade == 'a')
    Console::WriteLine("Excellent");
else
    if (grade == 'B' || grade == 'b')
        Console::WriteLine("Above Average");
    else
        if (grade == 'C' || grade == 'c')
            Console::WriteLine("Average");
        else
            if (grade == 'D' || grade == 'd' || grade == 'F' ||
            grade == 'f')
                Console::WriteLine("Below Average");
            else
                Console::WriteLine("Error");
            //end if
         //end if
    //end if
//end if
```

Figure 7-15: Two versions of the C++ code for the grade problem (continued)

you can use one comment to mark the end of the entire structure

you can include another statement on the same line as the else

Version 2

```
Console::Write("Grade: ");
grade = Console::Read();
if (grade == 'A' || grade == 'a')
    Console::WriteLine("Excellent");
else if (grade == 'B' || grade == 'b')
    Console::WriteLine("Above Average");
else if (grade == 'C' || grade == 'c')
    Console::WriteLine("Average");
else if (grade == 'D' || grade == 'd' || grade == 'F' || grade
== 'f')
    Console::WriteLine("Below Average");
else Console::WriteLine("Error");
//end ifs
```

Although you can write the `if/else` form of the selection structure using either of the two methods shown in Figure 7-15, the second method provides a much more convenient way of writing this logic.

In addition to using the `if/else` form to create multiple-path selection structures, you also can use the `switch` form.

Using the `switch` Form to Create Multiple-Path Selection Structures

It is often simpler and clearer to use the `switch` form of the selection structure, rather than the `if/else` form, in situations where the selection structure has many paths from which to choose. Figure 7-16 shows the flowchart and pseudocode for the grade problem, using the `switch` form of the selection structure.

Figure 7-16: Flowchart and pseudocode showing the switch form of the selection structure

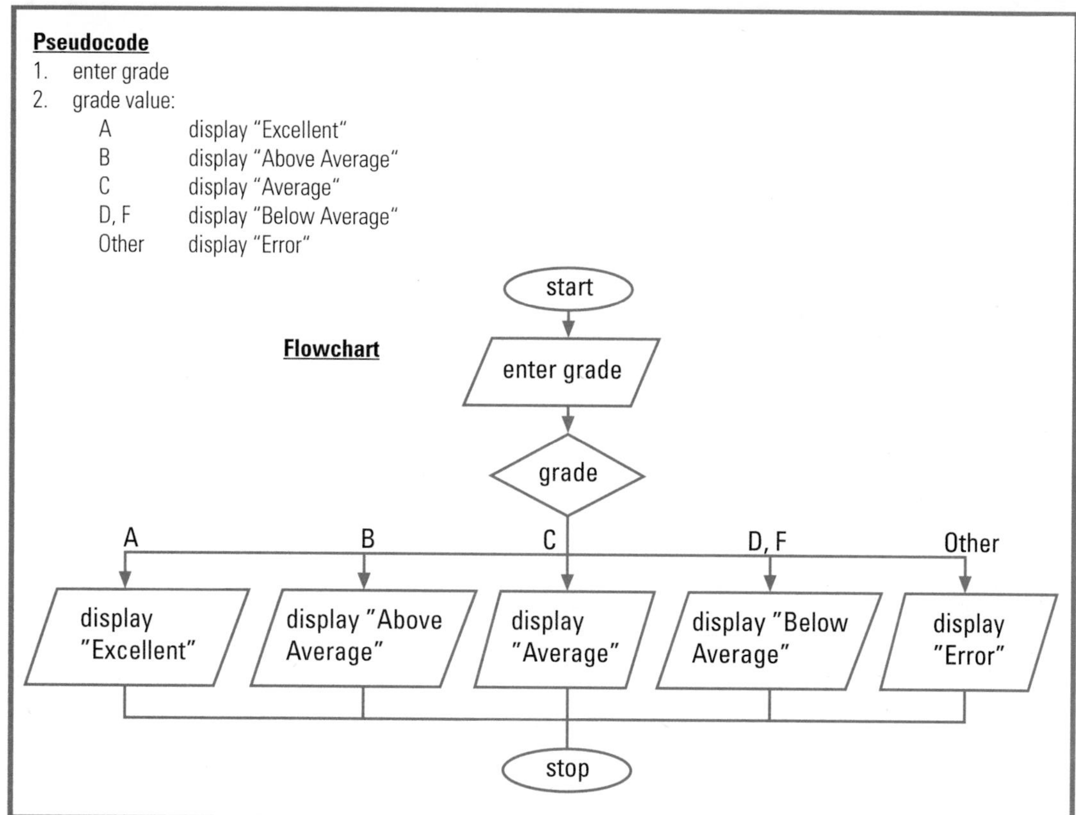

Notice that the flowchart symbol for the **switch** form of the selection structure is the same as the flowchart symbol for the **if** and **if/else** forms—a diamond. However, unlike the **if** and **if/else** diamond, the **switch** diamond does not contain a condition requiring a true or false answer. Instead, the **switch** diamond contains an expression—in this case, grade—whose value determines which path is chosen.

Like the **if** and **if/else** diamond, the **switch** diamond has one flowline leading into the symbol. Unlike the **if** and **if/else** diamond, however, the **switch** diamond has many flowlines leading out of the symbol. Each flowline represents a possible path for the selection structure. The flowlines must be marked appropriately, indicating which value(s) are necessary for each path to be chosen.

Figure 7-17 shows the syntax of the **switch** statement, which is used to code the **switch** form of the selection structure in C++. It also shows how to use the **switch** statement to code the grade problem.

tip

In some programming languages—for example, Visual Basic—the switch form of the selection structure is called the case form.

Figure 7-17: Syntax and an example of the C++ switch statement

Syntax

switch (*selectorExpression*)
{
case *value1*: *one or more statements*
[**case** *value2*: *one or more statements*]
[**case** *valueN*: *one or more statements*]
[**default**: *one or more statements processed when the selectorExpression does not match any of the values*]
} //end switch

Example

```
Console::Write("Enter grade: ");
grade = Console::Read();

switch (grade)
{
case 'A':
case 'a':          Console::WriteLine("Excellent");
                   break;
case 'B':
case 'b':          Console::WriteLine("Above Average");
                   break;
case 'C':
case 'c':          Console::WriteLine("Average");
                   break;
case 'D':
case 'd':
case 'F':
case 'f':          Console::WriteLine("Below Average");
                   break;
default:           Console::WriteLine("Error");
}  //end switch
```

case clause

selector-Expression

a break statement tells the computer to exit the switch statement

default clause

tip

The default clause can appear anywhere within the switch statement. However, for clarity, it is recommended that you place the default clause at the end of the switch statement.

The switch statement begins with the switch clause, followed by an opening brace; the statement ends with a closing brace. It is a good programming practice to document the end of the switch statement with the //end switch comment, as shown in Figure 7-17.

The switch clause is composed of the keyword switch followed by a *selectorExpression* enclosed in parentheses. The *selectorExpression* can contain any combination of variables, constants, functions, methods, and operators, as long as the combination results in a value whose data type is either bool, char, short, int, or long. In the switch statement shown in the example in Figure 7-17, the *selectorExpression* contains a char variable named grade.

Between the switch statement's opening and closing braces are the individual case clauses, each representing a different path that the selection structure can follow. You can have as many case clauses as necessary in a switch statement. If a default clause is included in the switch statement, it usually is the last clause in the statement.

Each of the individual clauses within the **switch** statement (except for the **default** clause) contains a *value*, followed by a colon. The data type of the *value* should be compatible with the data type of the *selectorExpression*. In other words, if the *selectorExpression* is a numeric variable, the *values* in the **case** clauses should be numeric. Likewise, if the *selectorExpression* is a **char** variable, the *values* should be characters. The *values* in the **case** clauses can be literal constants, named constants, or expressions composed of literal and named constants. In the **switch** statement shown in the example in Figure 7-17, the data type of the *values* in the **case** clauses ('A', 'a', 'B', 'b', 'C', 'c', 'D', 'd', 'F', and 'f') is **char** to match the data type of the *selectorExpression* (**grade**).

Following the colon in each **case** clause are one or more statements that are processed when the *selectorExpression* matches that case's *value*. Notice that the statements within a **case** clause are not entered as a statement block—in other words, the statements are not enclosed in braces.

tip

Recall from Tutorial 3 that character literal constants are enclosed in single quotation marks in C++ code.

After the computer processes the instructions in the **case** clause whose *value* matches the *selectorExpression*, you typically want the computer to leave the **switch** statement without processing the remaining instructions in the statement. You do so by including the **break** statement as the last statement in the **case** clause. The **break** statement tells the computer to leave ("break out of") the **switch** statement at that point. If you do not use the **break** statement to leave the **switch** statement, the computer continues processing the remaining instructions in the statement, which may or may not be what you want to happen. After processing the **break** statement, the computer then processes the instruction that follows the **switch** statement's closing brace. To better understand the **switch** statement, you will desk-check the code shown in the example in Figure 7-17 using the grades *a*, *B*, *D*, and *X*.

tip

Complete Exercises 10 and 11 at the end of this lesson to learn what happens when you do not use the break statement to break out of the switch statement.

Desk-Checking the Grade Program

Assume the user enters the letter *a* in response to the "Enter grade:" prompt shown in the example in Figure 7-17. The code stores the user's input in the **grade** variable, which then is used as the *selectorExpression* in the program's **switch** statement. When processing the **switch** statement, the computer compares the value of the *selectorExpression* with the *value* listed in each of the **case** clauses, one **case** clause at a time beginning with the first. If a match is found, the computer processes the instructions contained in that **case** clause until it encounters either a **break** statement or the **switch** statement's closing brace (which marks the end of the selection structure). The computer then skips to the instruction following the **switch** statement's closing brace. In this case, the value of the *selectorExpression*—the letter *a*—does not match the letter contained in the first **case** clause (which is 'A'); however, it does match the letter contained in the second **case** clause. The first statement in the second **case** clause is **Console::WriteLine ("Excellent");**, which displays the message "Excellent" on the screen. The next statement in the second **case** clause is **break;**, which tells the computer to skip the remaining instructions in the **switch** statement, and continue processing with the instruction that follows the **switch** statement's closing brace.

Now assume the user enters the letter *B* in response to the "Enter grade:" prompt shown in the example in Figure 7-17. As before, the code stores the user's input in the **grade** variable, which then is used as the *selectorExpression* in the program's **switch** statement. The computer compares the value of the *selectorExpression*—in this case, the letter *B*—with the *value* listed in each of the **case** clauses, one **case** clause at a time beginning with the first. In this case, the letter *B* matches the letter listed in the third **case** clause. However, notice that there is no statement to the immediate right of the **case 'B':** clause. So, what (if anything) will appear when the grade is *B*?

Recall that, when the *value* of the *selectorExpression* matches the *value* in a **case** clause, the computer processes the instructions contained in that clause until it encounters either a **break** statement or the **switch** statement's closing brace. In this case, not finding any instructions in the **case 'B':** clause, the computer continues processing with the instructions in the next clause—the **case 'b':** clause. The first instruction in the **case 'b':** clause displays the message "Above Average," which is the correct message to display, and the second instruction tells the computer to break out of the **switch** statement. In other words, the **Console::WriteLine("Above Average");** and **break;** statements are processed when the grade is either the letter *B* or the letter *b*. As this example shows, you can process the same instructions for more than one *value* by listing each *value* in a separate **case** clause, as long as the clauses appear together in the **switch** statement. The last clause in the group of related clauses should contain the instructions you want the computer to process when one of the *values* in the group matches the *selectorExpression*. Only the last **case** clause in the group of related clauses should contain the **break** statement.

Next, assume the user enters the letter *D* as the grade. The letter *D* matches the letter listed in the **case 'D':** clause. Not finding any statements in that clause, the computer processes the next statement it encounters. In this case, the computer processes the **Console::WriteLine("Below Average");** statement contained in the **case 'f':** clause, followed by that clause's **break;** statement. The computer then skips to the instruction following the **switch** statement's closing brace.

Finally, assume the user enters the letter *X* as the grade. Notice that the letter *X* does not appear as a *value* in any of the **case** clauses. If the *selectorExpression* does not match any of the *values* listed in the **case** clauses, the computer processes the instructions contained in the **default** clause (if there is one). The instruction in the **default** clause shown in the example in Figure 7-17 displays the message "Error" on the screen. If the **default** clause is the last clause in the **switch** statement, as it is in Figure 7-17, the computer then skips to the instruction following the **switch** statement's closing brace. Figure 7-18 shows the results of desk-checking the code shown in the example in Figure 7-17.

tip

If the `default` clause is not the last clause in the `switch` statement, you will need to include a `break` statement at the end of the clause.

Figure 7-18: Results of desk-checking the grade program example shown in Figure 7-17

Desk-check	Result
First: using a	"Excellent" displayed
Second: using B	"Above Average" displayed
Third: using D	"Below Average" displayed
Fourth: using X	"Error" displayed

MINI-QUIZ

Mini-Quiz 3

1) Assume you want to create a program that displays the message "Highest honors" when a student's test score is 90 or above. When the test score is 70 through 89, the program should display the message "Good job". For all other test scores, the program should display the message "Retake the test". Write the appropriate C++ code, using the shorter version of the `if/else` form of the selection structure.

2) If the *selectorExpression* used in the `switch` statement is a numeric variable, then the values listed in each `case` clause should be ______________.

3) The ______________ statement tells the computer to leave the `switch` statement at that point.

4) If the *selectorExpression* in the `switch` statement is the `int` variable `code`, which of the following `case` clauses is valid?

a. `case "2":`
b. `case 2:`
c. `case 2;`
d. `case == 2`

You now have completed Tutorial 7's Concept lesson. You can either take a break or complete the end-of-lesson questions and exercises before moving on to the Application lesson.

SUMMARY

You can nest a selection structure within either the true path or false path of another selection structure. You use a nested selection structure when more than one decision must be made before the appropriate action can be taken. The outer selection structure always represents the primary decision, while the nested (or inner) selection structure always represents the secondary decision.

Typically, logic errors commonly made when writing selection structures are a result of one of the following mistakes: using a logical operator when a nested selection structure is needed, or reversing the primary and secondary decisions, or using an unnecessary nested selection structure.

Some algorithms require selection structures that are capable of choosing from several alternatives. You can code such selection structures using either the `if/else` or `switch` form of the selection structure.

The flowchart symbol for the `switch` form of the selection structure is a diamond. The diamond should contain an expression; the expression's value controls which alternative is chosen. The `switch` diamond has one flowline leading into the symbol, and many flowlines leading out of the symbol. Each flowline represents a possible path for the selection structure, and should be marked to indicate which value(s) are necessary for each path to be chosen. In C++, you use the `switch` statement, along with the `break` statement, to code the `switch` form of the selection structure.

ANSWERS TO MINI-QUIZZES

Mini-Quiz 1

1)
```
if (score >= 90)
    display "Highest honors"
else
    if (score >= 70)
        display "Good job"
    else
        display "Retake the test"
end if
    end if
```

2)
```
if (score >= 90)
      Console::WriteLine("Highest honors");
else
      if (score >= 70)
            Console::WriteLine("Good job");
      else
            Console::WriteLine("Retake the test");
      //end if
//end if
```

3) The decision regarding the member status is the primary decision. The decision regarding the day of the week is the secondary decision, because whether it needs to be made depends on the result of the member status decision.

Mini-Quiz 2

1) Using a logical operator when a nested selection structure is needed
Reversing the primary and secondary decisions
Using an unnecessary nested selection structure

2) Using an unnecessary nested selection structure

Mini-Quiz 3

1)
```
if (score >= 90)
      Console::WriteLine("Highest honors");
else if (score >= 70)
      Console::WriteLine("Good job");
else Console::WriteLine("Retake the test");
//end ifs
```

2) numeric

3) `break`

4) b. `case 2:`

QUESTIONS

Use the code shown in Figure 7-19 to answer Questions 1 through 3.

Figure 7-19

```
if (number <= 100)
     number = number * 2;
else
     if (number > 500)
          number = number * 3;
     //end if
//end if
```

1) Assume the `number` variable contains the number 90. What value will be in the `number` variable after the code shown in Figure 7-19 is processed?

A. 0

B. 90

C. 180

D. 270

2) Assume the `number` variable contains the number 1000. What value will be in the `number` variable after the code shown in Figure 7-19 is processed?

A. 0

B. 1000

C. 2000

D. 3000

3) Assume the `number` variable contains the number 200. What value will be in the `number` variable after the code shown in Figure 7-19 is processed?

A. 0

B. 200

C. 400

D. 600

Use the code shown in Figure 7-20 to answer Questions 4 through 7.

Figure 7-20

```
if (id == 1)
     Console::WriteLine("Janet");
else if (id == 2 || id == 3)
     Console::WriteLine("Paul");
else if (id == 4)
     Console::WriteLine("Jerry");
else Console::WriteLine("Sue");
//end ifs
```

4) What, if anything, will the code shown in Figure 7-20 display when the `id` variable contains the number 2?

A. Jerry

B. Paul

C. Sue

D. nothing

5) What, if anything, will the code shown in Figure 7-20 display when the `id` variable contains the number 4?

A. Jerry

B. Paul

C. Sue

D. nothing

6) What, if anything, will the code shown in Figure 7-20 display when the `id` variable contains the number 3?

A. Jerry

B. Paul

C. Sue

D. nothing

7) What, if anything, will the code shown in Figure 7-20 display when the `id` variable contains the number 8?

A. Jerry

B. Paul

C. Sue

D. nothing

8) You can use the C++ ______________ statement to code the `switch` form of the selection structure.

A. `case`

B. `case of`

C. `struc`

D. `switch`

9) Which of the following flowchart symbols represents the `switch` form of the selection structure?

A. diamond

B. hexagon

C. parallelogram

D. rectangle

10) If the *selectorExpression* used in the `switch` statement is a `char` variable named `code`, which of the following `case` clauses is valid?

A. `case "3":`

B. `case '3':`

C. `case 3;`

D. `case = 3`

Use the code shown in Figure 7-21 to answer Questions 11 through 13.

Figure 7-21

```
switch (id)
{
case 1:    Console::WriteLine("Janet");
           break;
case 2:    Console::WriteLine("Paul");
           break;
case 3:
case 5:    Console::WriteLine("Jerry");
           break;
default:   Console::WriteLine("Sue");
} //end switch
```

11) What, if anything, will the code shown in Figure 7-21 display when the `id` variable contains the number 2?

A. Jerry

B. Paul

C. Sue

D. nothing

12) What, if anything, will the code shown in Figure 7-21 display when the `id` variable contains the number 4?

A. Jerry

B. Paul

C. Sue

D. nothing

13) What, if anything, will the code shown in Figure 7-21 display when the `id` variable contains the number 3?

A. Jerry

B. Paul

C. Sue

D. nothing

EXERCISES

Look For These Symbols

Debugging

Discovery

1) Write the C++ `if` statement that compares the contents of the `quantity` variable to the number 10. If the `quantity` variable contains a number that is equal to 10, display the string "Equal". If the `quantity` variable contains a number that is greater than 10, display the string "Over 10". If the `quantity` variable contains a number that is less than 10, display the string "Not over 10".

2) Write the C++ code that corresponds to the flowchart shown in Figure 7-22.

Figure 7-22

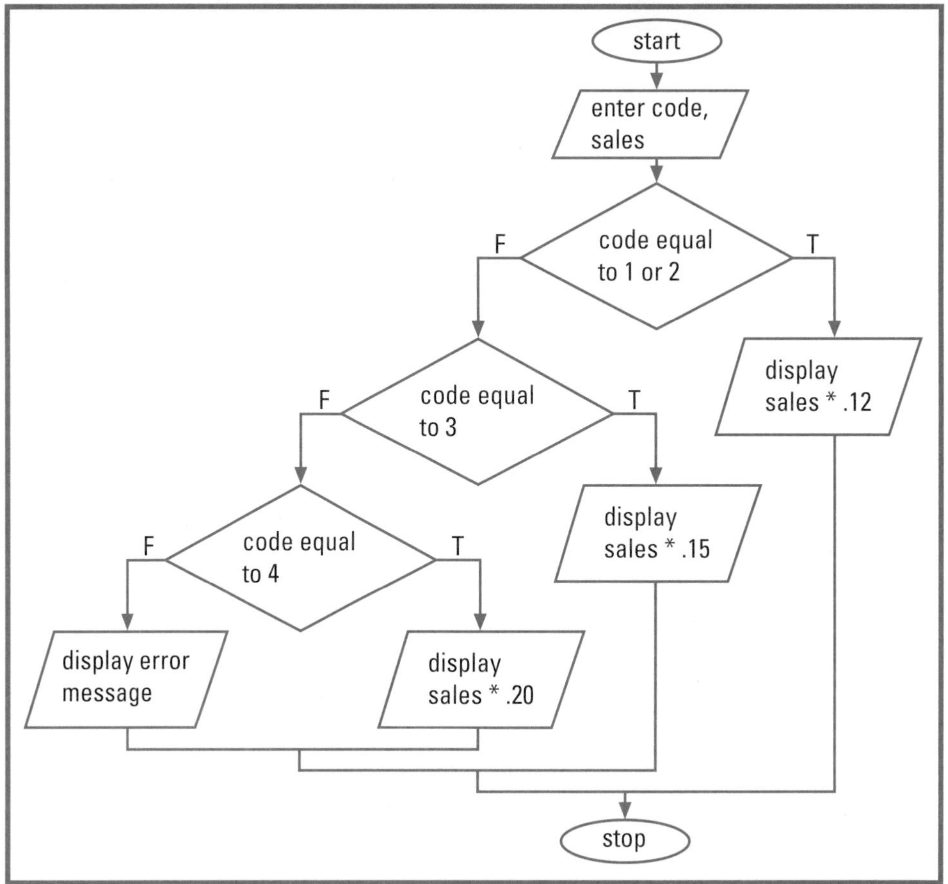

3) Write the C++ code that corresponds to the flowchart shown in Figure 7-23.

Figure 7-23

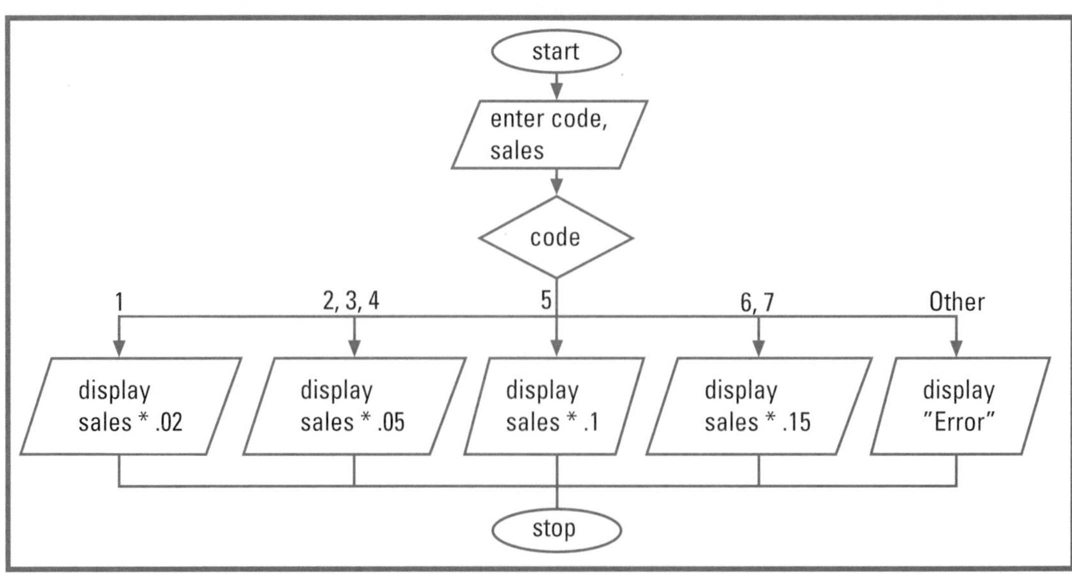

4) In this exercise, you complete a program by writing a selection structure.

A. If necessary, start Visual Studio .NET. Open the T7ConE04 Solution (T7ConE04 Solution.sln) file, which is contained in the CppNet\Tut07\T7ConE04 Solution folder.

B. Complete the program by writing an `if` statement that displays the string "Dog" when the `animal` variable contains the number 1. Display the string "Cat" when the `animal` variable contains the number 2. Display the string "Bird" when the `animal` variable contains anything other than the number 1 or the number 2.

C. Save and then build the solution.

D. Execute the program three times, using the following numbers: 1, 2, and 5.

E. When the program is working correctly, close the Output window, and then use the File menu to close the solution.

5) In this exercise, you complete a program by writing a selection structure.

A. If necessary, start Visual Studio .NET. Open the T7ConE05 Solution (T7ConE05 Solution.sln) file, which is contained in the CppNet\Tut07\T7ConE05 Solution folder.

B. Complete the program by writing a `switch` statement that displays the month corresponding to the number entered by the user. For example, when the user enters the number 1, the program should display the string "January". When the user enters an invalid number (one that is not in the range 1 through 12), the program should display an appropriate error message.

C. Save and then build the solution.

D. Execute the program three times, using the following numbers: 3, 7, and 20.

E. When the program is working correctly, close the Output window, and then use the File menu to close the solution.

6) In this exercise, you complete a program by writing a selection structure.

A. If necessary, start Visual Studio .NET. Open the T7ConE06 Solution (T7ConE06 Solution.sln) file, which is contained in the CppNet\Tut07\T7ConE06 Solution folder.

B. Complete the program by writing an `if` statement that assigns the number 25 to the `bonus` variable when the user enters a sales amount that is greater than or equal to $100, but less than or equal to $250. When the user enters a sales amount that is greater then $250, assign the number 50 to the `bonus` variable. When the user enters a sales amount that is less than $100, assign the number 0 to the `bonus` variable.

C. Save and then build the solution.

D. Execute the program three times, using the following sales amounts: 100, 300, and 40.

E. When the program is working correctly, close the Output window, and then use the File menu to close the solution.

7) In this exercise, you complete a program by writing a selection structure.

A. If necessary, start Visual Studio .NET. Open the T7ConE07 Solution (T7ConE07 Solution.sln) file, which is contained in the CppNet\Tut07\T7ConE07 Solution folder.

B. The program should display the appropriate seminar fee, which is based on the membership status and age entered by the user. Use the following information to complete the program:

Seminar fee	Criteria
10	Club member less than 65 years old
5	Club member at least 65 years old
20	Non-member

C. Save and then build the solution.

D. Execute the program three times. For the first test, use M as the status and 65 as the age. For the second test, use m as the status and 40 as the age. For the third test, use N as the status.

E. When the program is working correctly, close the Output window, and then use the File menu to close the solution.

8) In this exercise, you complete a program by writing a selection structure.

A. If necessary, start Visual Studio .NET. Open the T7ConE08 Solution (T7ConE08 Solution.sln) file, which is contained in the CppNet\Tut07\T7ConE08 Solution folder.

B. The program should display the appropriate grade based on the average of three test scores entered by the user. (Each test is worth 100 points.) Use the following information to complete the program:

Test average	Grade
90-100	A
80-89	B
70-79	C
60-69	D
below 60	F

C. Save and then build the solution.

D. Execute the program three times. For the first test, use scores of 90, 95, and 100. For the second test, use scores of 83, 72, and 65. For the third test, use scores of 40, 30, and 20.

E. When the program is working correctly, close the Output window, and then use the File menu to close the solution.

9) In this exercise, you complete a program by writing a selection structure.

A. If necessary, start Visual Studio .NET. Open the T7ConE09 Solution (T7ConE09 Solution.sln) file, which is contained in the CppNet\Tut07\T7ConE09 Solution folder.

B. The program should display the class rank, which is based on the code entered by the user. Use the information below to complete the program. Be sure to use the `switch` statement.

Code	Rank
1	Freshman
2	Sophomore
3	Junior
4	Senior
other	Error

C. Save and then build the solution.

D. Execute the program three times, using the following codes: 1, 3, and 5.

E. When the program is working correctly, close the Output window, and then use the File menu to close the solution.

10) In this exercise, you experiment with the `switch` statement.

A. If necessary, start Visual Studio .NET. Open the T7ConE10 Solution (T7ConE10 Solution.sln) file, which is contained in the CppNet\Tut07\T7ConE10 Solution folder.

B. Build the solution, then execute the program. When you are prompted to enter a grade, type d and press Enter. What, if anything, did the `switch` statement display on the screen? Close the Command Prompt window.

C. Enter a `break;` statement in the `case 'd':` clause. Save and then build the solution. Execute the program. When you are prompted to enter a grade, type d and press Enter. What, if anything, did the `switch` statement display on the screen? Close the Command Prompt window.

D. Remove the `break;` statement from the `case 'd':` clause. Also remove the `break;` statement from the `case 'f':` clause. Save and then build the solution. Execute the program. When you are prompted to enter a grade, type d and press Enter. What, if anything, did the `switch` statement display on the screen? Close the Command Prompt window.

E. Put the `break;` statement back in the `case 'f':` clause, then save and build the solution. Execute the program. When you are prompted to enter a grade, type d and press Enter. Close the Command Prompt window.

F. Close the Output window, and then use the File menu to close the solution.

11) In this exercise, you experiment with the `switch` statement.

A. If necessary, start Visual Studio .NET. Open the T7ConE11 Solution (T7ConE11 Solution.sln) file, which is contained in the CppNet\Tut07\T7ConE11 Solution folder. The program uses the `switch` statement to display the names of the gifts mentioned in the song "The Twelve Days of Christmas."

B. Build the solution, and then execute the program. When you are prompted to enter the day, type the number 1 and press Enter. You will notice that the names of the gifts for the first through the twelfth day appear in the Command Prompt window. Close the Command Prompt window.

C. Execute the program again. When you are prompted to enter the day, type the number 9 and press Enter. The names of the gifts for the ninth through the twelfth day appear in the Command Prompt window. Close the Command Prompt window.

D. Modify the program so that it displays only the name of the gift corresponding to the day entered by the user. For example, when the user enters the number 4, the program should display the "4 calling birds" message only.

E. Save and then build the solution. Execute the program. When you are prompted to enter the day, type the number 4 and press Enter. The "4 calling birds" message should appear on the screen. Close the Command Prompt window.

F. Close the Output window, and then use the File menu to close the solution.

 **12)** In this exercise, you use both the `if` and `switch` statements.

A. If necessary, start Visual Studio .NET. Open the T7ConE12 Solution (T7ConE12 Solution.sln) file, which is contained in the CppNet\Tut07\T7ConE12 Solution folder. The program should calculate and display the price of an order, based on the number of units ordered and the customer's status (either 1 for wholesaler or 2 for retailer). The price per unit is shown in Figure 7-24.

Figure 7-24

Wholesaler		Retailer	
Number of units	Price per unit ($)	Number of units	Price per unit ($)
1 through 4	10	1 through 3	15
5 and over	9	4 through 8	14
		9 and over	12

B. Complete the program appropriately. Use a `switch` statement to determine the customer's status. If the user enters a status other than 1 or 2, display an appropriate error message. Use an `if` statement to determine the price per unit. If the user enters an invalid number of units (in other words, a negative number or zero), display an appropriate error message.

C. Save and then build the solution. Execute the program. Test the program using the number 1 as the status and 5 as the number of units ordered. The Command Prompt window should show that the price of the order is $45. Close the Command Prompt window.

D. Execute the program again. Test the program using 2 as the status and 2 as the number of units ordered. The Command Prompt window should show that the price of the order is $30. Close the Command Prompt window.

E. Execute the program again. Test the program using 4 as the status and 3 as the number of units ordered. An appropriate error message should appear in the Command Prompt window. Close the Command Prompt window.

F. Execute the program again. Test the program using 2 as the status and –5 as the number of units ordered. An appropriate error message should appear in the Command Prompt window. Close the Command Prompt window.

G. When the program is working correctly, close the Output window, and then use the File menu to close the solution.

13) In this exercise, you debug a C++ program.

A. If necessary, start Visual Studio .NET. Open the T7ConE13 Solution (T7ConE13 Solution.sln) file, which is contained in the CppNet\Tut07\T7ConE13 Solution folder. The program should display "Illinois" when the user enters a state code of 1, "Kentucky" when the user enters a state code of 2, "New Hampshire" when the user enters a state code of 3, "Vermont" when the user enters a state code of 4, and "Massachusetts" when the user enters a state code of 5.

B. Study the program's code, then build the solution.

C. Correct any errors in the program, then save and build the solution.

D. Execute the program. Test the program six times, using state codes of 1, 2, 3, 4, 5, and 6.

E. When the program is working correctly, close the Output window, and then use the File menu to close the solution.

Application Lesson

Using the Selection Structure in a C++ Program

CASE Jennifer Yardley is the owner of Golf Pro, a U.S. company that sells golf equipment both domestically and abroad. Each of Golf Pro's salespeople receives a commission based on the total of his or her domestic and foreign sales. Your task in this lesson is to create a program that Jennifer can use to calculate and display a salesperson's commission.

Analyzing, Planning, and Desk-Checking the Golf Pro Commission Problem

Many companies pay their sales force a commission rather than, or in addition to, a salary or hourly wage. A commission is a percentage of the sales made by the salesperson. Some companies use a fixed rate to calculate the commission, while others—like Golf Pro—use a rate that varies with the amount of sales. Figure 7-25 shows Golf Pro's commission schedule, along with examples of using the schedule to calculate the commission on three different sales amounts.

Figure 7-25: Commission schedule and examples

Sales	Commission
1 – 100,000 100,001 – 400,000 400,001 and over	2% * sales 2,000 + 5% * sales over 100,000 17,000 + 10% * sales over 400,000

Example 1: Sales: 15,000
Commission: 2% * 15,000 = $300

Example 2: Sales: 250,000
Commission: 2000 + 5% * (250,000 – 100,000) = $9500

Example 3: Sales 500,000
Commission: 17,000 + 10% * (500,000 – 400,000) = $27,000

Notice that the commission for each range in the schedule is calculated differently. For instance, the commission for sales in the first range—1 through 100,000—is calculated by multiplying the sales amount by 2%. As Example 1 shows, sales of $15,000 would earn a $300 commission. The commission for sales in the second range—100,001 through 400,000—is calculated by multiplying the amount of sales over 100,000 by 5%, and then adding $2,000 to the result. As Example 2 shows, sales of $250,000 would earn a $9500 commission. The commission for sales starting at 400,001 is calculated by multiplying the amount of sales over 400,000 by 10%, and then adding $17,000 to the result. Example 3 indicates that sales of $500,000 would earn a $27,000 commission.

In addition to the `main()` function, you will use a value-returning function named `calcCommission()` to solve the commission problem. The `calcCommission()` function's task is to calculate and return the commission. Figure 7-26 shows the IPO charts for the commission problem.

Figure 7-26: IPO charts for the commission problem

`main()` function

Input	Processing	Output

sales	Processing items: none
	
	Algorithm:
	1. enter the sales
	2. if (the sales are greater than 0)
	    calculate the commission = calcCommission(sales)
	    display the commission
	  else
	    display "The sales amount must be greater than 0." message
	  end if
		commission

`calcCommission()` function

Input	Processing	Output

sales	Processing items: none
	
	Algorithm:
	1. if (the sales are less than or equal to 100,000)
	    calculate the commission by multiplying the sales by .02
	  else if (the sales are less than or equal to 400,000)
	    calculate the commission using the following
	    expression: 2000 + .05 * (sales – 100,000)
	  else calculate the commission using the following
	    expression: 17,000 + .1 * (sales – 400,000)
	  end ifs
	2. return the commission
		commission

As Figure 7-26 indicates, the `main()` function's output is the commission, and its input is the sales. According to its algorithm, the `main()` function first gets the sales amount from the user. It then validates the user's input; in this case, only numbers that are greater than zero are valid. If the sales amount is greater than zero, the `main()` function calls the `calcCommission()` function to calculate the commission. For the `calcCommission()` function to perform its task, the `main()` function must pass it the value of the sales amount entered by the user. After the `calcCommission()` function completes its task, it returns the commission amount to the `main()` function. The `main()` function then displays the commission amount on the screen.

If, on the other hand, the sales amount is invalid—which means that it is less than or equal to zero—the `main()` function displays a message alerting the user that the sales amount must be greater than zero.

Recall that you should desk-check an algorithm several times before you begin coding it. In this case, you will use the following four sales amounts to desk-check the algorithms shown in Figure 7-26: `15000`, `250000`, `500000`, and `-1`. Figure 7-27 shows the completed desk-check tables.

Figure 7-27: Completed desk-check tables for the algorithms shown in Figure 7-26

`main()` **function**

sales	commission
~~15000~~ ~~250000~~ ~~500000~~ -1	~~300~~ ~~9500~~ 27000

`calcCommission()` **function**

sales	commission
~~15000~~ ~~250000~~ 500000	~~300~~ ~~9500~~ 27000

After desk-checking an algorithm to verify its accuracy, you are ready to translate it into a language the computer can understand. Begin by coding the program's `main()` function.

Coding the `main()` Function

According to its IPO chart, the `main()` function requires two memory locations to store the values of its input and output items. You will store the input value (the sales amount) in an `int` variable named `sales`, and the output value (the commission amount) in a `double` variable named `commission`. After reserving the memory locations, the `main()` function will prompt the user to enter the sales amount, storing the user's response in the `sales` variable.

The next step in the algorithm is to use the `if/else` form of the selection structure to determine whether the user's input is valid, and then take the appropriate action based on the result. As you learned in Tutorial 6, you use the C++ `if` statement to code the `if/else` form of the selection structure. Figure 7-28 shows the C++ code corresponding to the `main()` function.

Figure 7-28: C++ statements for the `main()` function

IPO chart information	C++ instructions
Input sales	`int sales = 0;`
Processing none	
Output commission	`double commission = 0.0;`

Algorithm
1. enter the sales
	`Console::Write("Enter the sales amount: ");`
	`sales =`
	`Convert::ToInt32(Console::ReadLine());`

2. if (the sales are greater than 0)	`if (sales > 0)` `{`
calculate the commission = calcCommission(sales)	`commission = calcCommission(sales);`

display the commission	`Console::WriteLine("Commission: {0}",`
	`commission.ToString("C2"));`
	`}`

else
display "The sales amount must be greater than 0." message
end if
	`else`
	`Console::WriteLine("The sales amount`
	`must be greater than 0.");`
	`//end if`

tip
The two variables declared in the code shown in Figure 7-28 are local to the `main()` function and remain in memory until the `main()` function's `return` statement is processed.

Next, you code the `calcCommission()` function.

Coding the `calcCommission()` Function

As its IPO chart indicates, the `calcCommission()` function requires two memory locations: one for the input item and one for the output item. The value of the input item—sales—is passed to the `calcCommission()` function when the function is called; you will use the formal parameter `amountSold` to receive this information. Within the `calcCommission()` function, you will declare and initialize a variable to store the output item—commission. You will name the variable `commDollars` and declare it as a `double` variable.

According to its algorithm, the `calcCommission()` function needs to use two selection structures to calculate the commission. The outer selection structure's condition determines whether the sales amount falls in the 1 through 100,000 range. If it does, the outer selection structure's true path calculates the commission by multiplying the sales amount by .02. If the sales amount does not fall in the 1 through 100,000 range, the outer selection structure's false path uses a nested selection structure to determine whether the sales amount falls in the 100,001 through 400,000 range. If it does, the nested selection structure's true path calculates the commission using the following expression: 2000 + .05 * (sales – 100,000). Otherwise—which means that the sales amount is over 400,000—the nested selection structure's false path uses the following expression to calculate the commission: 17,000 + .1 * (sales – 400,000). Figure 7-29 shows the C++ code for the `calcCommission()` function.

tip

The `calcCommission()` function does not need to verify that the sales amount is valid (in other words, greater than zero), as this task is handled by the `main()` function.

tip

The `amountSold` and `commDollars` variables are local to the `calcCommission()` function and remain in memory until the `calcCommission()` function's `return` statement is processed.

Figure 7-29: C++ statements for the `calcCommission()` function

IPO chart information	C++ instructions
Input sales	`double calcCommission(int amountSold)`
Processing none	
Output commission	`double commDollars = 0.0;`
Algorithm 1. if (the sales are less than or equal to 100,000)	`if (amountSold <= 100000)`
calculate the commission by multiplying the sales by .02	`commDollars = amountSold * .02;`
else if (the sales are less than or equal to 400,000)	`else if (amountSold <= 400000)`
calculate the commission using the following expression: 2000 + .05 * (sales – 100,000)	`commDollars = 2000 + .05 * (amountSold – 100000);`
else calculate the commission using the following expression: 17,000 + .1 * (sales – 400,000)	`else commDollars = 17000 + .1 * (amountSold - 400000);`
end ifs	`//end ifs`
2. return the commission	`return commDollars;`

Now that the coding for the algorithms is complete, you need to desk-check the program, using the same data you used to desk-check the algorithms. Figure 7-30 shows the data and the completed desk-check table for the commission program.

Figure 7-30: Data and completed desk-check table for the commission program

variables belonging to the calc-Commission() function

variables belonging to the main() function

Data for first desk-check Sales: 15000	Data for second desk-check Sales: 250000	Data for third desk-check Sales: 500000	Data for fourth desk-check Sales: -1

Desk-check tables

sales	commission	amountSold	commDollars
~~0~~ ~~15000~~ ~~0~~ ~~250000~~ ~~0~~ ~~500000~~ ~~0~~ -1	~~0.0~~ ~~300.0~~ ~~0.0~~ ~~9500.0~~ ~~0.0~~ ~~27000.0~~ 0.0	~~15000~~ ~~250000~~ 500000	~~0.0~~ ~~300.0~~ ~~0.0~~ ~~9500.0~~ ~~0.0~~ 27000.0

The results obtained when desk-checking the program agree with the results obtained when desk-checking the algorithm. You now are ready to enter the C++ instructions into the computer.

Completing the Commission Program

On your computer's hard disk is a partially completed C++ program containing most of the instructions for the commission program. You open that program in the next set of steps.

To open the partially completed C++ program:

1. Start Microsoft Visual Studio .NET. If necessary, close the Start Page window.
2. Click **File** on the menu bar, and then click **Open Solution**. The Open Solution dialog box opens.
3. Locate and then open the **CppNet\Tut07\T7App Solution** folder.
4. Click **T7App Solution** (T7App Solution.sln) in the list of filenames, and then click the **Open** button.
5. If the T7App.cpp source file is not displayed, right-click **T7App.cpp** in the Solution Explorer window, and then click **Open**.

Missing from the program is the code for the `calcCommission()` function.

1. Position the insertion point in the blank line below the `//*****function definitions*****` comment, then enter the additional instructions shaded in Figure 7-31.

Figure 7-31: Program showing the code entered in the `calcCommission()` function

```
//T7App.cpp
//displays a commission amount

#using <mscorlib.dll>
using namespace System;

//function prototype
double calcCommission(int);

int main()
{
    int sales          = 0;
    double commission = 0.0;

    //enter input data
    Console::Write("Enter the sales amount: ");
    sales = Convert::ToInt32(Console::ReadLine());
    if (sales > 0)
    {
        //calculate and display commission
        commission = calcCommission(sales);
        Console::WriteLine("Commission: {0}",
        commission.ToString("C2"));
    }
    else
        Console::WriteLine("The sales amount must be
        greater than 0.");
    //end if

    return 0;
}   //end of main function

//*****function definitions*****
double calcCommission(int amountSold)
{
    //calculates and returns the commission
    double commDollars = 0.0;
    if (amountSold <= 100000)
        commDollars = amountSold * .02;
    else if (amountSold <= 400000)
        commDollars = 2000 + .05 * (amountSold - 100000);
    else commDollars = 17000 + .1 * (amountSold - 400000);
    //end ifs
    return commDollars;
}   //end of calcCommission function
```

enter this code

2. Save and then build the solution. Verify that the program generated no warnings.
3. Execute the program. When you are prompted for the sales amount, type

15000 and press **Enter**. The program calculates and displays the commission amount, as shown in Figure 7-32.

Figure 7-32: Command Prompt window showing the result of the first test

"c:\CppNet\Tut07\T7App Solution\T7App Project\Debug\T7App Project.exe"
Enter the sales amount: 15000
Commission: $300.00
Press any key to continue_

The Command Prompt window shows that the commission is $300.00, which agrees with the desk-check tables.

4. Press **Enter** to close the Command Prompt window, then execute the program again. Type **250000** as the sales amount, then press **Enter**. The program correctly calculates and displays the commission as $9,500.00.
5. Close the Command Prompt window, then execute the program again. Type **500000** as the sales amount, then press **Enter**. The program correctly calculates and displays the commission as $27,000.00.
6. Close the Command Prompt window, then execute the program again. Type **–1** as the sales amount, then press **Enter**. The program displays the message "The sales amount must be greater than 0.", which is correct.
7. Close the Command Prompt window, then close the Output window.
8. Click **File** on the menu bar, and then click **Close Solution** to close the current solution.
9. Click **File** on the menu bar, and then click **Exit** to exit Visual Studio .NET.

You now have completed Tutorial 7's Application lesson. You can either take a break or complete the end-of-lesson exercises.

EXERCISES

1) In this exercise, you modify the program you created in the lesson so that it calculates the commission for five sales ranges, rather than three sales ranges.

A. If necessary, start Visual Studio .NET. Open the T7AppE01 Solution (T7AppE01 Solution.sln) file, which is contained in the CppNet\Tut07\T7AppE01 Solution folder. Figure 7-33 shows Golf Pro's new commission rate schedule.

Look For These Symbols

Debugging

Discovery

Figure 7-33

Sales	Commission
1 – 100,000	2% * sales
100,001 – 200,000	4% * sales
200,001 – 300,000	6% * sales
300,001 – 400,000	8% * sales
400,001 and over	10% * sales

B. Modify the `calcCommission()` function to accommodate the new commission rate schedule. Use the shorter version of the `if/else` form of the selection structure.

C. Save and then build the solution.

D. Execute the program four times, using the following sales amounts: 15000, 250000, 500000, and -1. (The Command Prompt window should display the following commission amounts: $300.00, $15,000.00, $50,000.00, and "The sales amount must be greater than 0.", respectively.)

E. When the program is working correctly, close the Output window, and then use the File menu to close the solution.

2) In this exercise, you create a program that displays the total amount of money a company owes for a seminar.

A. Write one or more IPO charts for the problem. The seminar fee per person is based on the number of people the company registers, as shown in the following table. (For example, if the company registers seven people, then the total amount owed by the company is $560.)

Number of registrants	Fee per person
1 – 4	$100
5 – 10	$ 80
11 or more	$ 60

If the user enters the number 0 or a negative number, the program should display an appropriate error message.

B. If necessary, start Visual Studio .NET. Create a blank solution named T7AppE02 Solution. Save the solution in the CppNet\Tut07 folder.

C. Add a new managed C++ empty project to the solution. Name the project T7AppE02 Project.

D. Add a new C++ source file to the project. Name the source file T7AppE02.

E. Enter the appropriate C++ instructions into the source file. Use the IPO charts you created in Step A to code the program. Display the total amount owed with a dollar sign and no decimal places.

F. Complete a desk-check table for the program, using the following data: 4, 8, 12, 0, and –2.

G. Save and then build the solution.

H. Execute the program. Use the data from Step F to test the program.

I. When the program is working correctly, close the Output window, and then use the File menu to close the solution.

3) In this exercise, you create a program that displays a shipping charge.

A. Write one or more IPO charts for the problem. The shipping charge is based on the state code, as shown in the following table. Use the `switch` form of the selection structure to display the appropriate shipping charge.

State code	Shipping charge ($)
1	25
2	30
3	40
4	40
5	30
6	30

If the user enters any other state code, the program should display the message "Incorrect state code".

B. If necessary, start Visual Studio .NET. Open the T7AppE03 Solution (T7AppE03 Solution.sln) file, which is contained in the CppNet\Tut07\T7AppE03 Solution folder.

C. Use the IPO charts you created in Step A to code the program.

D. Complete a desk-check table for the program, using the following data: 1, 2, 3, 4, 5, 6, 7, and -2.

E. Save and then build the solution.

F. Execute the program. Use the data from Step D to test the program.

G. When the program is working correctly, close the Output window, and then use the File menu to close the solution.

4) In this exercise, you create a program that displays the price of a concert ticket.

A. Write one or more IPO charts for the problem. The concert ticket's price is based on the seat location, as shown in the following table. (The user should be able to enter the seat location using either an uppercase or lowercase letter.)

Seat location	Concert ticket price ($)
B (box)	75
P (Pavilion)	30
L (Lawn)	21

If the user enters any other seat location, the program should display the message "Invalid location".

B. If necessary, start Visual Studio .NET. Open the T7AppE04 Solution (T7AppE04 Solution.sln) file, which is contained in the CppNet\Tut07\T7AppE04 Solution folder.

C. Use the IPO charts you created in Step A to code the program.

D. Complete a desk-check table for the program, using the following data: B, p, L, and g.

E. Save and then build the solution.

F. Execute the program. Use the data from Step D to test the program.

G. When the program is working correctly, close the Output window, and then use the File menu to close the solution.

5) In this exercise, you create a program that displays the number of vacation weeks due an employee.

A. Write one or more IPO charts for the problem. The number of vacation weeks is based on the number of years the employee has been with the company, as shown in the following table.

Years with the company	Weeks of vacation
0	0
1 – 5	1
6 – 10	2
11 and over	3

If the user enters a negative number of years, the program should display the message "Invalid years".

B. If necessary, start Visual Studio .NET. Open the T7AppE05 Solution (T7AppE05 Solution.sln) file, which is contained in the CppNet\Tut07\T7AppE05 Solution folder.

C. Use the IPO charts you created in Step A to code the program.

D. Complete a desk-check table for the program, using the following data: 0, 2, 10, 11, and -2.

E. Save and then build the solution.

F. Execute the program. Use the data from Step D to test the program.

G. When the program is working correctly, close the Output window, and then use the File menu to close the solution.

6) In this exercise, you modify the program you created in Tutorial 6's Application lesson so that it displays a message that informs the user whether a food is high in fat.

A. If necessary, start Visual Studio .NET. Open the T7AppE06 Solution (T7AppE06 Solution.sln) file, which is contained in the CppNet\Tut07\T7AppE06 Solution folder.

B. Modify the program so that it displays the message "Low-fat food" when the fat percentage is less than or equal to 30%; otherwise, display the message "High-fat food".

C. Save and then build the solution.

D. Execute the program. Test the program two times. For the first test, use 150 as the total calories and 6 as the grams of fat. For the second test, use 105 as the total calories and 2 as the grams of fat.

E. When the program is working correctly, close the Output window, and then use the File menu to close the solution.

7) In this exercise, you create a program that displays the number of daily calories needed to maintain your current weight.

A. Write one or more IPO charts for the problem, using the information shown in Figure 7-34.

Figure 7-34

Female: *To maintain your current weight: Moderately active: total calories per day = weight multiplied by 12 calories per pound Relatively inactive: total calories per day = weight multiplied by 10 calories per pound
Male: *To maintain your current weight: Moderately active: total calories per day = weight multiplied by 15 calories per pound Relatively inactive: total calories per day = weight multiplied by 13 calories per pound
*Formulas from ViaHealth

B. If necessary, start Visual Studio .NET. Open the T7AppE07 Solution (T7AppE07 Solution.sln) file, which is contained in the CppNet\Tut07\T7AppE07 Solution folder.

C. Use the IPO charts you created in Step A to code the program.

D. Complete a desk-check table for the program, using the following data: (F stands for female, M for male, A for active, and I for inactive.)

- F, I, 150
- F, A, 120
- M, I, 180
- M, A, 200
- Also desk-check the program two additional times: first, using an invalid gender status of G, and then using a valid gender status of F, but an invalid activity status of B.

E. Save and then build the solution.

F. Execute the program. Use the data from Step D to test the program.

G. When the program is working correctly, close the Output window, and then use the File menu to close the solution.

8) In this exercise, you create a program that displays a message indicating whether a student passed or failed a course.

A. Write one or more IPO charts for the problem. The program will need to get two test scores from the user. Both scores should be positive numbers and can include 0. Both numbers also can contain a decimal place. If the first number is negative, the program should not ask the user to enter the second number; rather, it should display an appropriate error message before the program ends. If both numbers are positive, on the other hand, the program should calculate the average of the two numbers. If the average is at least 70, the program should display the message "Pass"; otherwise, it should display the message "Fail".

B. If necessary, start Visual Studio .NET. Open the T7AppE08 Solution (T7AppE08 Solution.sln) file, which is contained in the CppNet\Tut07\T7AppE08 Solution folder.

C. Use the IPO charts you created in Step A to code the program.

D. Complete a desk-check table for the program, using the following data: 95 and 73, 65 and 50, 0 and 100, 80 and -3, and –1.

E. Save and then build the solution.

F. Execute the program. Use the data from Step D to test the program.

G. When the program is working correctly, close the Output window, and then use the File menu to close the solution.

9) In this exercise, you create a program that displays either the sum of or the difference between two integers entered by the user.

A. Write one or more IPO charts for the problem. The program will need to get a letter (either A for addition or S for subtraction) and two integers from the user. If the user enters a letter that is not A, a, S, or s, the program should not ask the user for the two integers; rather, it should display an appropriate error message before the program ends. If the letter is A (or a), the program should calculate and display the sum of both numbers entered by the user. If the letter is S (or s), the program should calculate and display the difference between both numbers (subtracting the second number from the first number), but only if the first number is larger than, or equal to, the second number. If the first number is smaller than the second number, the program should swap both numbers before calculating and displaying the difference.

B. If necessary, start Visual Studio .NET. Open the T7AppE09 Solution (T7AppE09 Solution.sln) file, which is contained in the CppNet\Tut07\T7AppE09 Solution folder.

C. Use the IPO charts you created in Step A to code the program.

D. Complete a desk-check table for the program, using the following five sets of data:

- A, 10, 20
- a, 45, 15
- S, 65, 50
- s, 7, 13
- G

E. Save and then build the solution.

F. Execute the program. Use the data from Step D to test the program.

G. When the program is working correctly, close the Output window, and then use the File menu to close the solution.

10) In this exercise, you modify the program you created in the lesson so that it uses a value returning function to get and validate the sales amount entered by the user. The function should return a value that indicates whether the sales amount is valid.

A. If necessary, start Visual Studio .NET. Open the T7AppE10 Solution (T7AppE10 Solution.sln) file, which is contained in the CppNet\Tut07\T7AppE10 Solution folder.

B. Modify the program so that it uses a value-returning function named `getAndValidateSales()` to get and validate the sales amount.

C. Save and then build the solution.

D. Execute the program. Use the following sales amounts to test the program: 15000 and –10.

E. When the program is working correctly, close the Output window, and then use the File menu to close the solution.

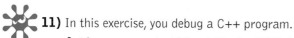

11) In this exercise, you debug a C++ program.

A. If necessary, start Visual Studio .NET. Open the T7AppE11 Solution (T7AppE11 Solution.sln) file, which is contained in the CppNet\Tut07\T7AppE11 Solution folder. The program should display the salary amount corresponding to the code entered by the user. A code of 1 corresponds to a salary amount of $45,000. Codes of 2 and 5 correspond to a salary amount of $33,000. Codes of 3 and 4 correspond to a salary amount of $25,000.

B. Study the program's code, then build the solution.

C. Correct any errors in the program, then save and build the solution. Execute the program. Test the program using a code of 2. $33,000 should appear in the Command Prompt window.

D. When the program is working correctly, close the Output window, and then use the File menu to close the solution.

Tutorial 8

The Repetition Structure

Objectives

After completing this tutorial, you will be able to:

- Include a repetition structure in pseudocode and in a flowchart
- Code a pretest loop using the C++ `while` statement
- Initialize and update counters and accumulators
- Code a pretest loop using the C++ `for` statement

Concept Lesson

Using the Repetition Structure

As you learned in Tutorial 1, the three control structures used in programs are sequence, selection, and repetition. Every program contains the sequence structure, in which the program instructions are processed, one after another, in the order in which each appears in the program. Most programs also contain the selection structure, which you learned about in Tutorials 6 and 7. Recall that programmers use the selection structure when they need the computer to make a decision and then take the appropriate action based on the result of that decision.

In addition to including the sequence and selection structures, most programs also include the repetition structure. Programmers use the **repetition structure**, referred to more simply as a **loop**, when they need the computer to repeatedly process one or more program instructions until some condition is met, at which time the repetition structure ends. For example, you may want to process a set of instructions—such as the instructions to calculate net pay—for each employee in a company. Or, you may want to process a set of instructions until the user enters a negative sales amount, which indicates that he or she has no more sales amounts to enter.

tip As with the sequence and selection structures, you already are familiar with the repetition structure. For example, shampoo bottles typically include a direction that tells you to repeat the "apply shampoo to hair," "lather," and "rinse" steps until your hair is clean.

A repetition structure can be either a pretest loop or a posttest loop. In both types of loops, the condition is evaluated with each repetition, or iteration, of the loop. In a **pretest loop**, the evaluation occurs before the instructions within the loop are processed, while in a **posttest loop**, the evaluation occurs after the instructions within the loop are processed. Depending on the result of the evaluation, the instructions in a pretest loop may never be processed. The instructions in a posttest loop, however, always will be processed at least once. Of the two types of loops, the pretest loop is the most commonly used. You learn about the pretest loop in this tutorial. The posttest loop is covered in Tutorial 9.

tip Pretest and posttest loops also are called top-driven and bottom-driven loops, respectively.

Pretest Loops

As you already know, not all problems require a loop in their solutions. Consider, for example, Acme Hardware's problem description and IPO chart shown in Figure 8-1.

tip As you can with selection structures, you also can nest repetition structures, which means that you can place one repetition structure within another repetition structure. Nested repetition structures are covered in Tutorial 9.

Figure 8-1: Problem description and IPO chart for Acme Hardware

Problem description

At the beginning of each year, the president of Acme Hardware is paid a 10% bonus. The bonus is based on the amount of sales made by the company during the previous year. The payroll clerk wants a program that can be used to calculate and display the amount of the president's bonus.

Input	Processing	Output
bonus rate (10%) sales	Processing items: none Algorithm: 1. enter the sales 2. calculate the bonus by multiplying the sales by the bonus rate 3. display the bonus	bonus

The problem description for Acme Hardware indicates that the bonus for only one employee needs to be displayed. Therefore, the enter, calculate, and display steps contained in the algorithm need to be processed only once. Because no steps in the algorithm need to be repeated, the algorithm does not require a loop.

Now, however, consider the O'Donnell Incorporated problem description and IPO chart shown in Figure 8-2.

Figure 8-2: Problem description and IPO chart for O'Donnell Incorporated

Problem description

In January of each year, O'Donnell Incorporated pays a 10% bonus to each of its salespeople. The bonus is based on the amount of sales made by the salesperson during the previous year. The payroll clerk wants a program that can be used to calculate and display each salesperson's bonus amount.

Input	Processing	Output
bonus rate (10%) sales	Processing items: none Algorithm 1: 1. enter the sales 2. calculate the bonus by multiplying the sales by the bonus rate 3. display the bonus Algorithm 2: 1. enter the sales 2. repeat while (the sales are not equal to -1) calculate the bonus by multiplying the sales by the bonus rate display the bonus enter the sales end repeat while	bonus

displays the bonus for one salesperson only (Algorithm 1)

displays the bonus for as many salespeople as desired (Algorithm 2)

The problem description for O'Donnell Incorporated is similar to the problem description for Acme Hardware, except it indicates that the bonus for more than one employee needs to be calculated and displayed. You could use either of the algorithms shown in Figure 8-2's IPO chart to solve the O'Donnell Incorporated problem; however, as you will learn shortly, the second algorithm is a much better choice.

The first algorithm shown in Figure 8-2 is identical to the Acme Hardware algorithm shown in Figure 8-1; neither algorithm contains a loop. Although the first algorithm shown in Figure 8-2 can be used to solve the O'Donnell Incorporated problem, the algorithm is inefficient for that purpose, because it displays only one bonus amount. A program based on this algorithm would need to be executed once for each salesperson receiving a bonus. In other words, if O'Donnell Incorporated has 100 salespeople, the payroll clerk would need to execute the program 100 times to calculate and display each salesperson's bonus amount.

The second algorithm shown in Figure 8-2 contains a loop and represents a more efficient solution to the O'Donnell Incorporated problem. After executing a program based on the second algorithm, the payroll clerk can calculate and display the bonus amount for as many salespeople as desired. The payroll clerk indicates when he or she is finished calculating and displaying bonus amounts by entering –1 (a negative number one) as the sales amount. Figure 8-3 identifies the important components of the loop shown in the second algorithm.

Figure 8-3: Components of a loop

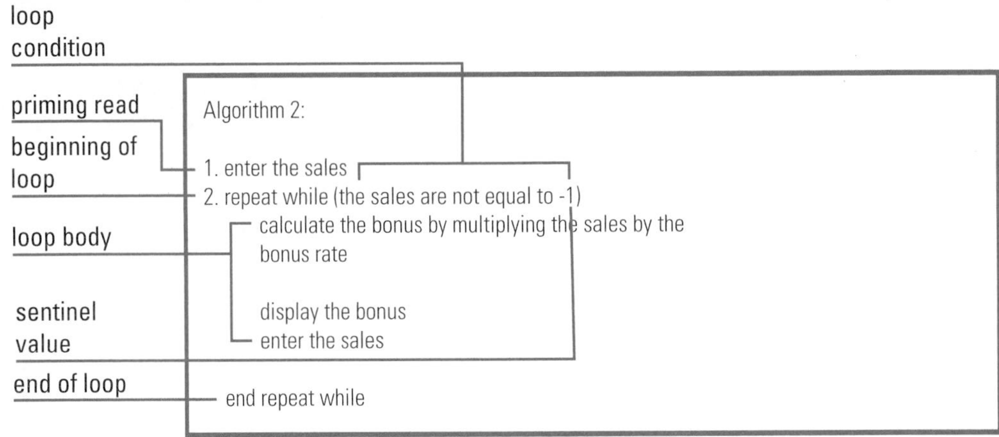
loop condition
priming read
beginning of loop
loop body
sentinel value
end of loop
Algorithm 2:
1. enter the sales
2. repeat while (the sales are not equal to -1)
calculate the bonus by multiplying the sales by the bonus rate
display the bonus
enter the sales
end repeat while

With very rare exceptions, every loop has a loop condition and a loop body. The **loop condition**, which appears at the beginning of a pretest loop, determines the number of times the instructions within the loop, referred to as the **loop body**, are processed. Similar to a selection structure condition, a loop condition must result in either a true or false answer only. In the loop shown in Figure 8-3, for example, if the sales amount entered by the user is not equal to –1, then the loop condition evaluates to true; otherwise, in which case the user entered –1 as the sales amount, the loop condition evaluates to false.

Some loops, such as the one shown in Figure 8-3, require the user to enter a special value to end the loop. Values that are used to end loops are referred to as **sentinel values**. In the loop shown in Figure 8-3, the sentinel value is –1. The sentinel value should be one that is easily distinguishable from the valid data recognized by the program. The number 1000, for example, would not be a good sentinel value for the loop in Figure 8-3's algorithm, because it is possible that a salesperson could have made that amount of sales. The number -1, on the other hand, is a good sentinel value for the loop, because a sales amount cannot be negative.

tip
Values used to end loops also are called trip values or trailer values.

When the loop condition evaluates to true, the one or more instructions listed in the loop body are processed; otherwise, these instructions are skipped over. Because the loop condition in a pretest loop is evaluated before any of the instructions within the loop body are processed, it is possible that the loop body instructions may not be processed at all; this would occur when the loop condition initially evaluates to false. For example, if the payroll clerk at O'Donnell Incorporated enters the number -1 as the first sales amount, the loop condition shown in Figure 8-3 will evaluate to false, and the instructions in the loop body will be skipped over.

After each processing of the loop body instructions, the loop condition is reevaluated to determine whether the instructions should be processed again. The loop's instructions are processed and its condition evaluated until the condition evaluates to false, at which time the loop ends and processing continues with the instruction immediately following the end of the loop.

Notice that the pseudocode shown in Figure 8-3 contains two "enter the sales" instructions: one of the instructions appears in Step 1, which is above the loop, and the other appears as the last instruction in the loop body. The "enter the sales" instruction that appears above the loop is referred to as the **priming read**, because it is used to prime (prepare or set up) the loop. In this case, the priming read gets only the first salesperson's sales from the user. This first value is compared to the sentinel value (–1) and determines whether the loop body instructions are processed at all. If the loop body instructions are processed, the "enter the sales" instruction that appears within the loop body gets the sales amounts for the remaining salespeople (if any) from the user.

It may be easier to visualize a pretest loop by viewing it in a flowchart.

Flowcharting a Pretest Loop

Figure 8-4 shows the O'Donnell Incorporated algorithm in flowchart form.

Figure 8-4: O'Donnell Incorporated algorithm shown in flowchart form

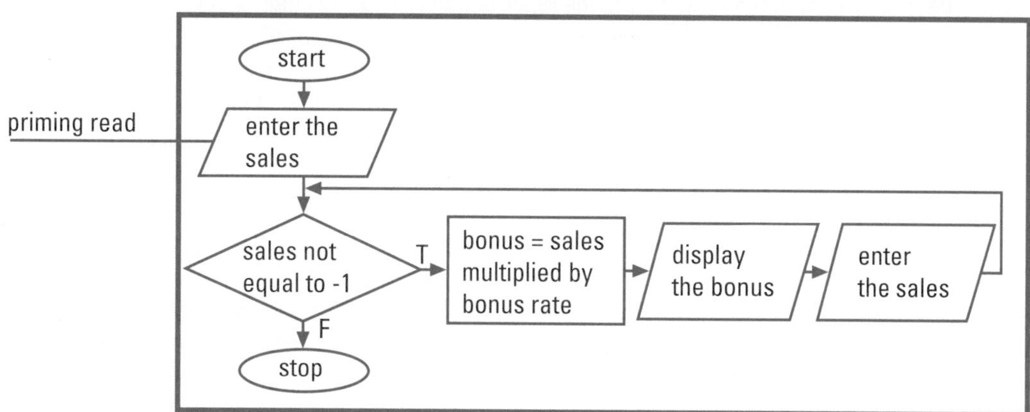

Recall that the oval in a flowchart is the start/stop symbol, the rectangle is the process symbol, the parallelogram is the input/output symbol, and the diamond is the selection/repetition symbol. In Figure 8-4's flowchart, the diamond indicates the beginning of a repetition structure (loop). As with the selection structure diamond, which you learned about in Tutorial 6, the repetition structure diamond contains a comparison that has a true or false answer only. The comparison represents the loop condition, which determines whether the instructions within the loop body are processed.

Like the selection diamond, the repetition diamond has two flowlines leaving the symbol. The flowline marked with a "T" (for true) leads to the loop body—the instructions processed when the loop condition evaluates to true. The flowline marked with an "F" (for false) leads to the instructions that are processed when the loop condition evaluates to false.

Unlike the selection diamond, the repetition diamond has two flowlines leading into the diamond, rather than one. One of the flowlines comes from the symbol located immediately above the diamond. In the flowchart shown in Figure 8-4, this symbol is the parallelogram that represents the priming read, which gets only the first salesperson's sales from the user. Notice that the parallelogram has a flowline that flows into the repetition diamond.

The second flowline leading into the repetition diamond flows from the repetition structure's true path, which contains the loop body instructions. In the flowchart shown in Figure 8-4, for example, the flowline leading out of the "enter the sales" parallelogram in the true path flows back up to the repetition diamond. Notice that the two flowlines leading into the repetition diamond, as well as the symbols and flowlines within the true path, form a circle or loop. It is this loop that distinguishes the repetition structure from the selection structure in a flowchart.

To help you understand how a loop operates in a program, you will desk-check the algorithm shown in Figure 8-4 using the following sales data: 10000, 25000, and –1. The first input parallelogram shown in Figure 8-4's flowchart gets the amount of the first salesperson's sales from the user. Figure 8-5 shows the first salesperson's sales amount—10000—recorded in the desk-check table.

tip

The flowchart shown in Figure 8-4 illustrates why the loop is referred to as a pretest loop. Notice that the repetition diamond, which contains the loop condition, appears *before* the symbols in both the true and false paths.

tip

The symbol located immediately above the repetition diamond represents the instruction processed immediately before the loop condition is evaluated the first time.

tip

The input parallelogram located within the loop in Figure 8-4's flowchart will get the remaining sales amounts (if any) from the user.

Figure 8-5: First salesperson's sales amount recorded in the desk-check table

bonus rate	sales	bonus
.10	10000	

The next symbol in the flowchart is the repetition diamond. This diamond represents the beginning of a pretest loop that repeats its instructions as long as (or while) the user enters a sales amount that is not –1. Before processing the loop instructions, the loop condition, which compares the sales amount entered by the user to the number –1, is evaluated. In this case, the loop condition evaluates to true, because 10000 is not equal to –1. Recall that when the loop condition evaluates to true, the instructions in the loop body are processed. The first two instructions in the loop body shown in Figure 8-4 calculate and then display the bonus amount. Figure 8-6 shows the first salesperson's bonus information recorded in the desk-check table.

Figure 8-6: First salesperson's bonus information recorded in the desk-check table

bonus rate	sales	bonus
.10	10000	1000

The last instruction in the loop body shown in Figure 8-4 is contained in an input parallelogram, and it gets the next salesperson's sales—in this case, 25000—from the user. After getting the sales, the loop condition, which appears in the repetition diamond located at the top of the loop, is reevaluated to determine whether the loop should be processed again (a true condition) or end (a false condition). In this case, the condition evaluates to true, because 25000 is not equal to –1. Because of this, the bonus amount is calculated and then displayed on the screen. Figure 8-7 shows the second salesperson's information recorded in the desk-check table.

Figure 8-7: Second salesperson's information recorded in the desk-check table

bonus rate	sales	bonus
.10	~~10000~~ 25000	~~1000~~ 2500

The input parallelogram that appears as the last flowchart symbol in the loop body then gets the next salesperson's sales from the user. In this case, the user enters the sentinel value (–1) as the sales, as shown in Figure 8-8.

Figure 8-8: Sentinel value recorded in the desk-check table

	bonus rate	sales	bonus
sentinel value	.10	~~10000~~ ~~25000~~ -1	~~1000~~ 2500

Next, the loop condition is reevaluated to determine whether the loop should be processed again (a true condition) or end (a false condition). In this case, the loop condition evaluates to false, because the sales amount entered by the user is equal to `-1`. Recall that when the loop condition evaluates to false, the loop instructions are skipped over and processing continues with the instruction immediately following the end of the loop. In Figure 8-4's flowchart, the stop oval, which marks the end of the algorithm, follows the loop.

You can code the pretest loop in C++ using either the `while` statement or the `for` statement. First, learn how to use the `while` statement.

Using the `while` Statement to Code the Pretest Loop

Figure 8-9 shows the syntax of the `while` statement, which you can use to code a pretest loop in a C++ program.

Figure 8-9: Syntax of the C++ `while` statement

while (*loop condition***)**
    one statement, or a block of statements enclosed in braces, to be processed
    as long as the loop condition evaluates to true
`//end while`

Items in **bold** in the syntax—in this case, the keyword `while` and the parentheses that surround the loop condition—are essential components of the `while` statement. Items in italics indicate where the programmer must supply information pertaining to the current program. In the `while` statement, the programmer must supply the loop condition to be evaluated. The loop condition must be a Boolean expression, which is an expression that evaluates to either true or false. The loop condition can contain variables, constants, functions, methods, arithmetic operators, comparison operators, and logical operators.

In addition to supplying the loop condition, the programmer also must supply the statements to be processed when the loop condition evaluates to true. If more than one statement needs to be processed, the statements must be entered as a statement block. Recall that you create a statement block by enclosing the statements in a set of braces ({}).

Although it is not required to do so, it is a good programming practice to use a comment, such as `//end while`, to mark the end of the `while` statement. The comment will make your program easier to read and understand.

Figure 8-10 shows the C++ code for the O'Donnell Incorporated algorithm, which contains a pretest loop.

tip

Some C++ programmers enclose the loop body in braces even when it contains only one statement, but this is not required by the C++ syntax. However, including the braces in a loop that contains only one statement is convenient, because you will not need to remember to enter the braces if additional statements are added to the loop in the future. Forgetting to enter the braces around a statement block is a common error made by programmers.

Figure 8-10: C++ statements for the O'Donnell Incorporated algorithm

IPO chart information	C++ instructions

Input
bonus rate (10%)
sales
	
	`const double RATE = .1;`
	`double sales = 0.0;`

Processing none	
Output bonus	`double bonus = 0.0;`

Algorithm
1. enter the sales
	
	`Console::Write("Enter the first sales amount: ");`
	`sales = Convert::ToDouble(Console::ReadLine());`

2. repeat while (the sales are not equal to –1)	`while (sales != -1)` `{`
calculate the bonus by multiplying the sales by the bonus rate	`bonus = sales * RATE;`
display the bonus	`Console::WriteLine(bonus.ToString("C2"));`
enter the sales	`Console::Write("Enter the next sales amount: ");` `sales = Convert::ToDouble(Console::ReadLine());`
end repeat while	`} //end while`

Take a closer look at the statements shown in Figure 8-10. The first three statements declare and initialize the RATE named constant and the `sales` and `bonus` variables. The `Console::Write("Enter the first sales amount: ");` statement prompts the user to enter the first sales amount, and the `sales = Convert::ToDouble (Console::ReadLine());` statement stores the user's response in the `sales` variable. The `while (sales != –1)` clause compares the value stored in the `sales` variable to the sentinel value (–1). If the `sales` variable does not contain the sentinel value, the instructions within the loop body are processed. Those instructions calculate and display the bonus, then prompt the user to enter the next sales amount, and store the user's response in the `sales` variable. Each time the user enters a sales amount, the `while` clause compares the sales amount to the sentinel value (–1). When the user enters the sentinel value—in this case, –1—as the sales amount, the loop instructions are skipped over, and processing continues with the line immediately below the end of the loop.

Keep in mind that if you forget to enter the `sales = Convert::ToDouble (Console::ReadLine());` statement within the program's loop, the loop will process its instructions indefinitely, because there will be no way to change the value stored in the `sales` variable. A loop that processes its instructions indefinitely is referred to as either an **endless loop** or an **infinite loop**. Usually, you can stop a program that contains an endless loop by pressing Ctrl+c (press and hold down the Ctrl key as you press the letter c); you also can use the Command Prompt window's Close button.

tip
You can practice stopping a program that contains an endless loop by completing Exercise 17 at the end of this lesson.

MINI-QUIZ

Mini-Quiz 1

1) Write a C++ `while` clause that processes the loop instructions as long as the value in the `quantity` variable is greater than the number 0.
2) Write a C++ `while` clause that stops the loop when the value in the `quantity` variable is less than the number 0.
3) Write a C++ `while` clause that processes the loop instructions as long as the value in the `inStock` variable is greater than the value in the `reorder` variable.
4) Write a C++ `while` clause that processes the loop instructions as long as the value in the `letter` variable is either Y or y. (The `letter` variable is a `char` variable.)
5) Which of the following is a good sentinel value for a program that inputs the number of hours each employee worked this week?
   a. –9
   b. 32
   c. 45.5
   d. 7
6) The input instruction that appears above a pretest loop is called the ______________.

Many times a program will need to display a subtotal, a total, or an average. You calculate this information using a repetition structure that includes a counter, or an accumulator, or both.

Using Counters and Accumulators

Counters and accumulators are used within a repetition structure to calculate subtotals, totals, and averages. A **counter** is a numeric variable used for counting something—such as the number of employees paid in a week. An **accumulator** is a numeric variable used for accumulating (adding together) something—such as the total dollar amount of a week's payroll.

Two tasks are associated with counters and accumulators: initializing and updating. **Initializing** means to assign a beginning value to the counter or accumulator. Typically, counters and accumulators are initialized to zero; however, they can be initialized to any number, depending on the value required by the algorithm. The initialization task is done before the loop is processed, because it needs to be done only once.

Updating, also called **incrementing**, means adding a number to the value stored in the counter or the accumulator. The number can be either positive or negative, integer or noninteger. A counter is always incremented by a constant value—typically the number `1`—whereas an accumulator is incremented by a value that varies. The assignment statement that updates a counter or an accumulator is placed within the loop in a program, because the update task must be performed each time the loop instructions are processed. You use both a counter and an accumulator in the Sales Express program, which you view next.

tip

Counters are used to answer the question, "How many?"—for example, "How many salespeople live in Virginia?" Accumulators are used to answer the question, "How much?"—for example, "How much did the salespeople sell this quarter?"

The Sales Express Program

Assume that Sales Express wants a program that the sales manager can use to display the average amount the company sold during the prior year. The sales manager will enter the amount of each salesperson's sales. The program will use a counter to keep track of the number of sales amounts entered by the sales manager, and an accumulator to total those sales amounts. After all of the sales amounts are entered, the program will calculate the average sales amount by dividing the value stored in the accumulator by the value stored in the counter. It then will display the average sales amount on the screen. Figure 8-11 shows the IPO chart information and C++ code for the Sales Express problem.

Figure 8-11: IPO chart information and C++ code for the Sales Express problem

IPO chart information	C++ instructions
Input sales	`double sales = 0.0;`
Processing number of salespeople (counter) total sales (accumulator)	`int totalPeople = 0;` `double totalSales = 0.0;`
Output average sales	`double average = 0.0;`
Algorithm 1. enter the sales	`Console::Write("Enter the first sales amount: ");` `sales = Convert::ToDouble(Console::ReadLine());`

2. repeat while (the sales are greater than or equal to 0)
add 1 to the number of salespeople
	`while (sales >= 0)`
	`{`
	`totalPeople = totalPeople + 1;`

add the sales to the total sales	`totalSales = totalSales + sales;`
enter the sales	`Console::Write("Enter the next sales amount: ");` `sales = Convert::ToDouble(Console::ReadLine());`
end repeat while	`} //end while`

3. if (the number of salespeople is not equal to 0)
calculate the average sales by dividing the total sales by the number of salespeople
	`if (totalPeople != 0)`
	`{`
	`average = totalSales / totalPeople;`

display the average sales	`Console::WriteLine(average);` `}`
else display an error message	`else` `Console::WriteLine("You didn't enter any sales.");`
end if	`//end if`

Callouts: initialization (points to `int totalPeople = 0;` and `double totalSales = 0.0;`); update (points to `totalPeople = totalPeople + 1;` and `totalSales = totalSales + sales;`); verify that the counter is not 0 before using it as the divisor in an expression (points to `totalPeople != 0`)

tip

The "enter the sales" step located above the loop in the algorithm shown in Figure 8-11 is the priming read.

As Figure 8-11 indicates, the input for the Sales Express problem is each salesperson's sales amount, and the output is the average sales amount. The algorithm uses two processing items: a counter that keeps track of the number of salespeople, and an accumulator that keeps track of the total sales. Notice in the C++ code that the counter (an `int` variable) is initialized to 0, and the accumulator (a `double` variable) is initialized to 0.0.

To better understand counters and accumulators, you will desk-check the Sales Express code using the following sales data: 30000, 40000, and -3. After declaring and initializing the appropriate variables, the program prompts the user to enter the first sales amount, and then stores the user's response in the `sales` variable, as shown in Figure 8-12.

Figure 8-12: First sales amount recorded in the desk-check table

sales	totalPeople	totalSales	average
~~0.0~~ 30000.0	0	0.0	0.0

The `while (sales >= 0)` clause begins a pretest loop that repeats the loop body instructions as long as (or while) the user enters a sales amount that is greater than or equal to zero. The loop stops when the user enters the sentinel value, which, in this program, is any sales amount that is less than zero. Notice that, unlike the loop in the O'Donnell Incorporated algorithm, the loop in the Sales Express algorithm has more than one sentinel value. In the Sales Express algorithm, any number that is less than zero can be used to stop the loop.

If the sales amount entered by the user is greater than or equal to 0, as it is in this case, the instructions in the loop body are processed. The first two instructions update the `totalPeople` counter variable by adding `1` to it, and update the `totalSales` accumulator variable by adding the sales amount to it. The updates are shown in Figure 8-13's desk-check table.

Figure 8-13: Desk-check table showing the first update to the counter and accumulator

sales	totalPeople	totalSales	average
~~0.0~~ 30000.0	~~0~~ 1	~~0.0~~ 30000.0	0.0

The last two instructions in the loop body prompt the user to enter the next sales amount, and then store the user's response—in this case, 40000—in the `sales` variable. The loop condition `while (sales >= 0)` then is reevaluated to determine whether the loop should be processed again (a true condition) or simply end (a false condition). Here again, the loop condition evaluates to true, because 40000 is greater than zero. Because of this, the loop instructions increment the `totalPeople` variable by `1`, and increment the `totalSales` variable by the sales amount, as shown in Figure 8-14.

Figure 8-14: Desk-check table showing the second update to the counter and accumulator

sales	totalPeople	totalSales	average
~~0.0~~ ~~30000.0~~ 40000.0	~~0~~ ~~1~~ 2	~~0.0~~ ~~30000.0~~ 70000.0	0.0

The last two instructions in the loop body prompt the user to enter the next sales amount, and then store the user's response—in this case, -3, which is a sentinel value—in the `sales` variable. The loop condition `while (sales >= 0)` then is reevaluated to determine whether the loop should be processed again or simply end. In this case, the loop condition evaluates to false, because –3 is not greater than or equal to zero. When the loop condition evaluates to false, the loop ends, and processing continues with the statement immediately following the loop.

In the Sales Express program, the statement following the loop is an `if` statement. The `if` statement's condition verifies that the `totalPeople` variable does not contain the number zero. This verification is necessary because the first instruction in the `if` statement's true path uses the `totalPeople` variable as the divisor when calculating the average, and the computer cannot divide by zero. If the `totalPeople` variable contains the number zero, the `if` statement's false path displays an appropriate message. However, if the `totalPeople` variable contains a value other than zero, as it does in this case, the `if` statement's true path calculates and displays the average sales amount (35000) on the screen before the program ends. Figure 8-15 shows the completed desk-check table for the Sales Express program.

Figure 8-15: Completed desk-check table for the Sales Express program

sales	totalPeople	totalSales	average
~~0.0~~ ~~30000.0~~ ~~40000.0~~ -3	~~0~~ ~~1~~ 2	~~0.0~~ ~~30000.0~~ 70000.0	~~0.0~~ 35000.0

sentinel value (→ -3)

MINI-QUIZ

Mini-Quiz 2

1) A(n) ______________ is updated by an amount that varies.
2) Write a C++ assignment statement that updates the `quantity` counter variable by 2.
3) Write a C++ assignment statement that updates the `total` counter variable by –3.
4) Write a C++ assignment statement that updates the `totalPurchases` accumulator variable by the value stored in the `purchases` variable.

In both the O'Donnell Incorporated and Sales Express programs, the termination of the loop is controlled by the user entering a sentinel value. The termination of a loop also can be controlled by the program itself. Typically, this is done using a counter.

Counter-Controlled Pretest Loops

Assume that Jasper Music Company wants a program that allows the sales manager to enter the quarterly sales amount made in each of three regions: Region 1, Region 2, and Region 3. The program should calculate the total quarterly sales and then display the total amount on the screen. Figure 8-16 shows the IPO chart information and C++ code for the Jasper Music Company problem.

Figure 8-16: IPO chart information and C++ code for the Jasper Music Company problem

IPO chart information	C++ instructions
Input region's quarterly sales	`int regionSales = 0;`
Processing counter (1 through 3)	`int numRegion = 1;`
Output total quarterly sales (accumulator)	`int totalSales = 0;`
Algorithm 1. repeat while (the counter is less than or equal to 3)	`while (numRegion <= 3)` `{`
enter the region's quarterly sales	`Console::Write("Enter Region {0}'s quarterly sales:", Convert::ToString(numRegion));` `regionSales = Convert::ToInt32(Console::ReadLine());`
add the region's quarterly sales to the total quarterly sales	`totalSales = totalSales + regionSales;`
add 1 to the counter end repeat while	`numRegion = numRegion + 1;` `} //end while`
2. display the total quarterly sales	`Console::WriteLine(totalSales);`

As Figure 8-16 indicates, the input is each region's quarterly sales amount, and the output is the total quarterly sales amount. The solution uses one processing item: a counter that will keep track of the number of times the loop instructions are repeated. In this case, the loop instructions need to be repeated three times, once for each sales region. Notice in the C++ code that the counter variable, named `numRegion`, is initialized to the number `1`, which corresponds to the first sales region.

To understand how a counter is used to stop a program, you will desk-check the code shown in Figure 8-16. The first three statements in the code create and initialize three variables named `regionSales`, `numRegion`, and `totalSales`. Figure 8-17 shows the desk-check table after these statements are processed.

Figure 8-17: Desk-check table showing initialization of variables

regionSales	numRegion	totalSales
0	1	0

The `while (numRegion <= 3)` clause in the code begins a pretest loop that repeats its instructions as long as (or while) the value in the `numRegion` counter variable is less than or equal to three. The loop stops when the value in the `numRegion` variable is greater than three. At this point in the program, the value stored in the `numRegion` variable is less than three, so the loop condition evaluates to true and the loop instructions are processed. The first statement in the loop body prompts the user to enter Region 1's quarterly sales, and the second statement stores the user's response in the `regionSales` variable. Assume that the user enters the number 2500. The third statement adds Region 1's quarterly sales (2500) to the value stored in the `totalSales` accumulator variable (0), giving 2500. The last statement in the loop body increments the `numRegion` counter variable by one, giving two. Figure 8-18 shows the desk-check table after the loop instructions are processed the first time.

Figure 8-18: Results of processing the loop instructions the first time

regionSales	numRegion	totalSales
~~0~~ 2500	~~1~~ 2	~~0~~ 2500

The loop condition `while (numRegion <= 3)` then is reevaluated to determine whether the loop should be processed again (a true condition) or simply end (a false condition). Here again, the loop condition evaluates to true, because the contents of the `numRegion` counter variable (2) is less than three. Because of this, the loop instructions prompt the user to enter Region 2's quarterly sales, and then store the user's response in the `regionSales` variable. Assume that the user enters the number 6000. The loop instructions add Region 2's quarterly sales (6000) to the value stored in the `totalSales` accumulator (2500), giving 8500. The instructions then increment the `numRegion` counter variable by one, giving three. Figure 8-19 shows the desk-check table after the loop body instructions are processed the second time.

Figure 8-19: Results of processing the loop instructions the second time

regionSales	numRegion	totalSales
~~0~~ ~~2500~~ 6000	~~1~~ ~~2~~ 3	~~0~~ ~~2500~~ 8500

The loop condition `while (numRegion <= 3)` then is reevaluated to determine whether the loop should be processed again or end. Here again, the loop condition evaluates to true, because the contents of the `numRegion` counter variable (3) is equal to three. Because of this, the loop instructions prompt the user to enter Region 3's quarterly sales, and then store the user's response in the `regionSales` variable. Assume that the user enters the number 2000. The loop instructions add Region 3's quarterly sales (2000) to the value stored in the `totalSales` accumulator (8500), giving 10500. The instructions then increment the `numRegion` counter variable by one, giving four. Figure 8-20 shows the desk-check table after the loop body instructions are processed the third (and last) time.

Figure 8-20: Results of processing the loop instructions the third time

regionSales	numRegion	totalSales
~~0~~ ~~2500~~ ~~6000~~ 2000	~~1~~ ~~2~~ ~~3~~ 4	~~0~~ ~~2500~~ ~~8500~~ 10500

The loop condition `while (numRegion <= 3)` then is reevaluated to determine whether the loop should be processed again or end. At this point, the loop condition evaluates to false, because the contents of the `numRegion` counter variable (4) is not less than or equal to three. Because of this, the loop ends and processing continues with the instruction located immediately below the loop; that instruction displays the contents of the `totalSales` variable on the screen. Notice that the quarterly sales program itself, rather than the user, controls the termination of the loop.

Recall that, in addition to using the `while` statement, you also can use the `for` statement to code a pretest loop in C++.

Using the `for` Statement to Code a Pretest Loop

As you can with the `while` statement, you can also use the `for` statement to code any pretest loop. However, the most common use for the `for` statement is to code pretest loops whose processing is controlled by a counter. This is because the `for` statement provides a more compact way of writing that type of loop. Figure 8-21 shows the syntax of the `for` statement in C++.

Figure 8-21: Syntax of the C++ `for` statement

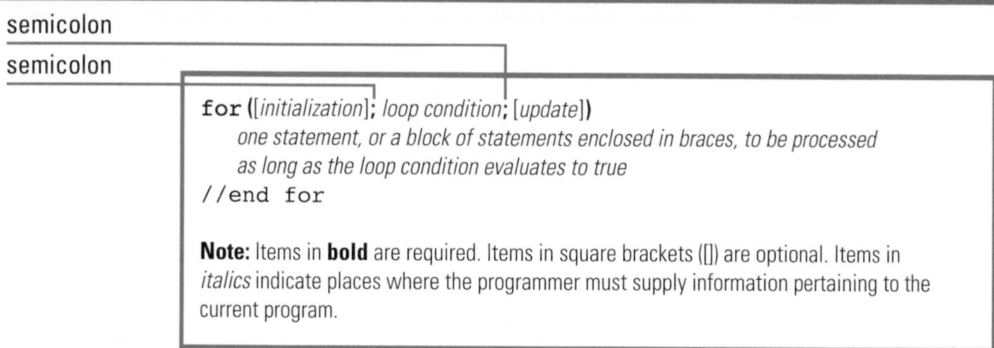

for ([*initialization*]**;** *loop condition***;** [*update*]**)**
one statement, or a block of statements enclosed in braces, to be processed as long as the loop condition evaluates to true
`//end for`

Note: Items in **bold** are required. Items in square brackets ([]) are optional. Items in *italics* indicate places where the programmer must supply information pertaining to the current program.

tip

A common error made by C++ programmers is to separate the three items of information in the `for` clause with two commas rather than with two semicolons.

The `for` statement begins with the `for` clause, followed by the body of the loop, which contains the one or more statements that you want the loop to repeat. If the loop body contains more than one statement, the statements must be entered as a statement block, which means that they must be enclosed in a set of braces ({}). Although it is not required by the C++ syntax, it is helpful to use a comment, such as `//end for`, to document the end of the `for` statement.

As the syntax shown in Figure 8-21 indicates, the `for` clause contains three arguments, separated by two semicolons. In most `for` clauses, the first argument, *initialization*, creates and initializes a counter variable, which is used by the `for` statement to keep track of the number of times the loop instructions are processed. The second argument in the `for` clause, *loop condition*, specifies the condition that must be true for the loop to continue processing the loop body instructions. The loop condition must be a Boolean expression; in other words, it must be an expression that evaluates to either true or false. The loop condition can contain variables, constants, functions, methods, arithmetic operators, comparison operators, and logical operators. The loop stops when the loop condition evaluates to false. The third argument in the `for` clause, *update*, usually contains an expression that updates the counter variable specified in the *initialization* argument.

In the remaining sections in this lesson, you view three examples of the `for` statement.

Example 1 – Displaying the Numbers 1 Through 3

Figure 8-22 shows a `for` statement that displays the numbers 1 through 3 on the screen.

Figure 8-22: `for` statement displays the numbers 1 through 3

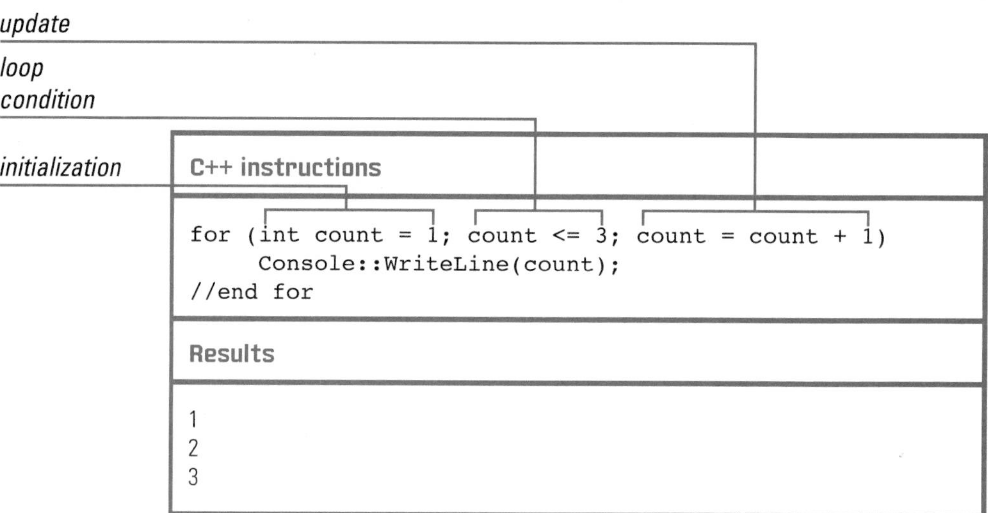

update
loop condition
initialization
C++ instructions
for (int count = 1; count <= 3; count = count + 1)
Console::WriteLine(count);
//end for
Results
1
2
3

Desk-checking the C++ instructions shown in Figure 8-22 will help you to understand how the `for` statement works. When the computer encounters a `for` statement in a program, it first processes the code shown in the `for` clause's *initialization* argument. The code shown in the *initialization* argument is processed only once, at the beginning of the loop. In the case of the `for` statement shown in Figure 8-22, the computer creates an `int` variable named `count` and initializes the variable to the number one, as shown in Figure 8-23.

Figure 8-23: Desk-check table showing the result of processing the *initialization* argument

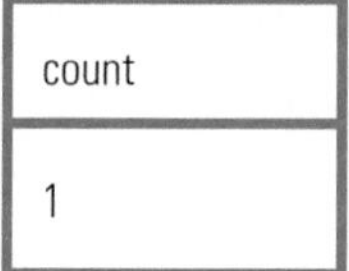

Next, the computer processes the code shown in the `for` clause's *loop condition* argument to determine whether to process the loop body instructions. In the case of the loop condition shown in Figure 8-22, the computer processes the instruction contained in the loop body only when the value stored in the `count` variable is less than or equal to the number three. Currently, the value stored in the `count` variable is the number one, so the loop body instruction is processed and displays the `count` variable's value (1) on the screen. Unlike the *initialization* argument, which is processed only once, the *loop condition* argument is processed with each repetition, or iteration, of the loop.

Next, the computer processes the code shown in the `for` clause's *update* argument. The *update* argument shown in Figure 8-22 instructs the computer to add the number one to the value stored in the `count` variable, giving two. Like the *loop condition* argument, the *update* argument is processed with each repetition of the loop. Figure 8-24 shows the result of processing the *update* argument for the first time.

tip

Like the `while` statement, the `for` statement evaluates the loop condition *before* the loop body instructions are processed.

Figure 8-24: Desk-check table showing the result of processing the *update* argument for the first time

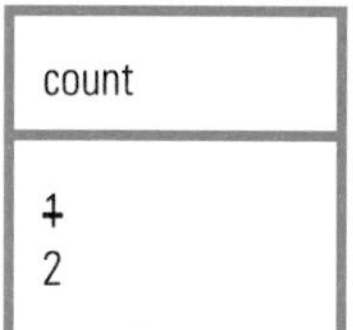

After processing the *update* code for the first time, the computer processes the *loop condition* code again to determine whether to process the loop body instructions once more. In the case of the program shown in Figure 8-22, the `count` variable's value still is less than or equal to three, so the computer displays the `count` variable's value (2) on the screen.

After processing the loop body instructions, the computer processes the *update* argument again. The *update* argument shown in Figure 8-22 increments the `count` variable by one, giving three, as shown in Figure 8-25.

Figure 8-25: Desk-check table showing the result of processing the *update* argument for the second time

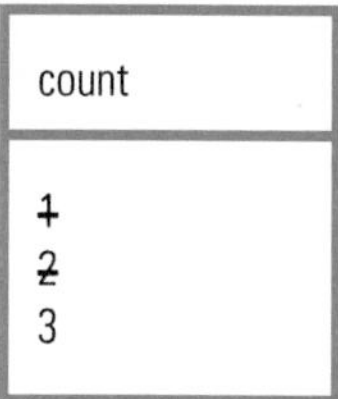

Next, the computer processes the *loop condition* code again to determine whether to process the loop body instructions another time. In this case, the `count` variable's value still is less than or equal to three, so the computer displays the `count` variable's value (3) on the screen.

After processing the loop body instructions, the computer processes the *update* argument again. The *update* argument shown in Figure 8-22 increments the `count` variable by one, giving four, as shown in Figure 8-26.

Figure 8-26: Desk-check table showing the result of processing the *update* argument for the third time

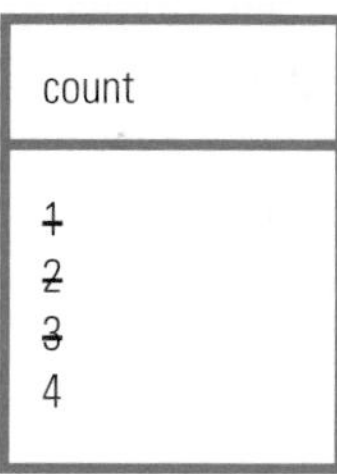

Next, the computer processes the *loop condition* code again to determine whether to process the loop body instructions another time. In this case, the `count` variable's value is not less than or equal to three, so the computer does not process the loop body instruction. Rather, the loop ends (the *update* argument is not processed this time) and the computer processes the instruction following the end of the `for` statement. Notice that the value in the `count` variable is the number four when the loop stops.

Now view an example of a `for` statement that contains more than one instruction in the loop body.

Example 2 - Calculating and Displaying a Commission

Figure 8-27 shows a `for` statement that calculates a commission using commission rates of .1, .15, .2, and .25, and then displays the commission on the screen. Notice that the loop body contains more than one instruction, and the instructions are entered as a statement block by enclosing them in a set of braces ({}).

Figure 8-27: `for` statement calculates and displays a commission

C++ instructions

```
double sales = 0.0;
double comm = 0.0;
Console::Write("Enter the sales: ");
sales = Convert::ToDouble(Console::ReadLine());
for (double rate = .1; rate <= .25; rate = rate + .05)
{
   comm = sales * rate;
   Console::WriteLine("Commission: ${0}",
   Convert::ToString(comm));
}  //end for
```

Results (assuming the user enters 25000 as the sales amount)

Commission: $2500
Commission: $3750
Commission: $5000
Commission: $6250

Figure 8-28 shows the steps the computer follows when processing the code shown in Figure 8-27. Notice that the **for** statement stops when the value stored in the **rate** variable is .3.

Figure 8-28: Processing steps for the code shown in Figure 8-27

Processing steps

1. Computer creates and initializes the **sales** variable to 0.0.
2. Computer creates and initializes the **comm** variable to 0.0.
3. Computer prompts user for sales amount.
4. Computer stores user's response in the **sales** variable.
5. Computer creates the **rate** variable and initializes it to .1 (*initialization* code).
6. Computer determines whether value in **rate** variable is less than or equal to .25 (*loop condition* code). It is.
7. Computer calculates the commission and displays "Commission: $2500" on the screen (loop body instructions).
8. Computer adds .05 to value stored in **rate** variable, giving .15 (*update* code).
9. Computer determines whether value in **rate** variable is less than or equal to .25 (*loop condition* code). It is.
10. Computer calculates the commission and displays "Commission: $3750" on the screen (loop body instructions).
11. Computer adds .05 to value stored in **rate** variable, giving .2 (*update* code).
12. Computer determines whether value in **rate** variable is less than or equal to .25 (*loop condition* code). It is.
13. Computer calculates the commission and displays "Commission: $5000" on the screen (loop body instructions).
14. Computer adds .05 to value stored in **rate** variable, giving .25 (*update* code).
15. Computer determines whether value in **rate** variable is less than or equal to .25 (*loop condition* code). It is.
16. Computer calculates the commission and displays "Commission: $6250" on the screen (loop body instructions).
17. Computer adds .05 to value stored in **rate** variable, giving .3 (*update* code).
18. Computer determines whether value in **rate** variable is less than or equal to .25 (*loop condition* code). It is not.
19. Loop ends and the computer processes the instruction following the end of the **for** statement.

Finally, view an example of a **for** statement that does not use the *initialization* and *update* arguments.

Example 3 - Calculating and Displaying a Bonus

Although the most common use for the **for** statement is to code loops whose processing is controlled by a counter, you actually can use the **for** statement to code any pretest loop. For example, the **for** statement shown in Figure 8-29's code, which calculates and displays a bonus, is controlled by the user rather than by a counter.

Figure 8-29: `for` statement calculates and displays a bonus

tip

You also can omit the *loop condition* argument, which is the second argument in the `for` clause. When doing so, however, you need to include the `break` statement in the loop body to stop the loop. You learned about the `break` statement in Tutorial 7.

C++ instructions

```
const double RATE = .1;
double sales = 0.0;
double bonus = 0.0;
Console::Write("Enter the first sales amount: ");
sales = Convert::ToDouble(Console::ReadLine());
for (; sales > 0;)
{
      bonus = sales * RATE;
      Console::WriteLine("Bonus: ${0}",
      Convert::ToString(bonus));
      Console::Write("Enter the next sales amount: ");
      sales = Convert::ToDouble(Console::ReadLine());
}  //end for
```

semicolon after the *initialization*

loop condition

semicolon after the loop *condition*

Results (assuming the user enters sales amounts of 4000, 3000, and -1)

Bonus: $400
Bonus: $300

tip

Whether you use the `for` statement or the `while` statement to code the loop shown in Figure 8-29 is a matter of personal preference.

Notice that the `for` clause shown in Figure 8-29 contains only the *loop condition* argument. Although the *initialization* and *update* arguments are omitted from the `for` clause, the semicolons after the *initialization* and *loop condition* arguments must be included. Figure 8-30 shows the steps the computer follows when processing the code shown in Figure 8-29.

Figure 8-30: Processing steps for the code shown in Figure 8-29

Processing steps

1. Computer creates and initializes the `RATE` constant to .1.
2. Computer creates and initializes the `sales` variable to 0.0.
3. Computer creates and initializes the `bonus` variable to 0.0.
4. Computer prompts user for sales amount. Assume the user enters the number 4000.
5. Computer stores the user's response (4000) in the `sales` variable.
6. Computer determines whether the value in the `sales` variable is greater than 0 (*loop condition* code). It is.
7. Computer calculates the bonus and displays "Bonus: $400" on the screen. It then prompts the user for another sales amount and stores the user's response in the `sales` variable (loop body instructions). Assume the user enters the number 3000.
8. Computer determines whether the value in the `sales` variable is greater than 0 (*loop condition* code). It is.
9. Computer calculates the bonus and displays "Bonus: $300" on the screen. It then prompts the user for another sales amount and stores the user's response in the `sales` variable (loop body instructions). Assume the user enters the number -1.
10. Computer determines whether the value in the `sales` variable is greater than 0 (*loop condition* code). It is not.
11. Loop ends and the computer processes the instruction following the end of the `for` statement.

As Figure 8-30 indicates, the `for` statement stops when the user enters a sales amount that is less than or equal to zero.

MINI-QUIZ

Mini-Quiz 3

1) Assume a program declares an `int` variable named `evenNum` and initializes it to 2. Write a C++ `while` loop that uses the `evenNum` variable to display the even integers between 1 and 9.

2) Which of the following `for` clauses processes the loop instructions as long as the value stored in the `x` variable is less than or equal to the number 100?
   a. `for (int x = 10; x <= 100; x = x + 10)`
   b. `for (int x = 10, x <= 100, x = x + 10)`
   c. `for (int x == 10; x <= 100; x = x + 10)`
   d. `for (int x = x + 10; x <= 100; x = 10)`

3) What is the value stored in the `x` variable when the loop corresponding to the `for` clause in Question 2 ends?
   a. 100
   b. 110
   c. 101
   d. 110

4) Write a `for` clause that processes the loop instructions as long as the value stored in the `x variable` is greater than 0. The `x` variable should be an `int` variable. Initialize the variable to the number 25 and increment it by -5 with each repetition of the loop.

5) What is the value stored in the `x` variable when the loop corresponding to the `for` clause in Question 4 ends?

6) Write a `for` statement that displays the even integers between 1 and 9 on the screen. Use `num` as the name of the counter variable.

You now have completed Tutorial 8's Concept lesson. You can either take a break or complete the end-of-lesson questions and exercises before moving on to the Application lesson.

SUMMARY

Programmers use the repetition structure, also called a loop, when they need the computer to repeatedly process one or more program instructions until some condition is met, at which time the repetition structure ends. A repetition structure can be either a pretest loop or a posttest loop. In a pretest loop, the loop condition is evaluated before the instructions within the loop are processed, while in a posttest loop, the evaluation occurs after the instructions within the loop are processed. Of the two types of loops, the pretest loop is the most commonly used.

Almost every loop has a loop condition and a loop body. The loop condition appears at the beginning of a pretest loop and determines the number of times the instructions within the loop, referred to as the loop body, are processed. The loop condition must result in either a true or false answer only. When the loop condition evaluates to true, the one or more instructions listed in the loop body are processed; otherwise, these instructions are skipped over.

Some loops require the user to enter a special value, called a sentinel value, to end the loop. You should use a sentinel value that is easily distinguishable from the valid data recognized by the program. Other loops are terminated by the program itself, through the use of a counter.

The input instruction that appears above the pretest loop is referred to as the priming read, because it is used to prime (prepare or set up) the loop. The priming read gets only the first value from the user. The input instruction that appears within the loop gets the remaining values.

The flowchart symbol for the repetition structure (loop) is the repetition/selection diamond. You can use either the `while` statement or the `for` statement to code a pretest loop in C++.

Counters and accumulators are used within a repetition structure to calculate subtotals, totals, and averages. All counters and accumulators must be initialized and updated. Counters are updated by a constant value, whereas accumulators are updated by an amount that varies.

ANSWERS TO MINI-QUIZZES

Mini-Quiz 1

1) `while (quantity > 0)`

2) `while (quantity >= 0)`

3) `while (inStock > reorder)`

4) `while (letter == 'Y' || letter == 'y')`

5) a. –9

6) priming read

Mini-Quiz 2

1) accumulator

2) `quantity = quantity + 2;`

3) `total = total + -3;` (or `total = total – 3;`)

4) `totalPurchases = totalPurchases + purchases;`

Mini-Quiz 3

1) `while (evenNum < 9)` (or `while (evenNum <= 8)`)

```
{
   Console::WriteLine(evenNum);
   evenNum = evenNum + 2;
}  //end while
```

2) a. `for (int x = 10; x <= 100; x = x + 10)`

3) d. 110

4) `for (int x = 25; x > 0; x = x –5)` or
`for (int x = 25; x > 0; x = x + -5)`

5) 0 (zero)

6)

```
for (int num = 2; num <= 8; num = num + 2)
     Console::WriteLine(num);
```

QUESTIONS

1) The `while` loop is referred to as ____________ loop, because the loop condition is tested at the beginning of the loop.

A. a beginning
B. an initial
C. a pretest
D. a priming

2) The loop condition in a flowchart is represented by ____________.

A. a diamond
B. an oval
C. a parallelogram
D. a rectangle

3) A numeric variable used for counting something is called ____________.

A. an accumulator
B. an adder
C. a constant
D. a counter

4) Counters and accumulators must be initialized and ____________.

A. added
B. displayed
C. updated
D. none of the above

5) ____________ are always incremented by a constant amount, whereas ____________ are incremented by an amount that varies.

A. Accumulators, counters
B. Counters, accumulators

6) Which of the following statements correctly updates the counter variable named `numEmployees`?

A. `numEmployees = 0;`
B. `numEmployees = numEmployees + numEmployees;`
C. `numEmployees = numEmployees + sumSalary;`
D. `numEmployees = numEmployees + 1;`

7) Which of the following statements correctly updates the accumulator variable named `total`?

A. `total = 0;`
B. `total = total + total;`
C. `total = total + sales;`
D. `total = total + 1;`

8) Which of the following is a good sentinel value for a program that allows the user to enter a person's age?

A. −4

B. 350

C. 999

D. all of the above

9) Which of the following `while` clauses stops the loop when the value in the `age` variable is less than the number 0?

A. `while (age < 0)`

B. `while age >= 0;`

C. `while (age >= 0);`

D. `while (age >= 0)`

Refer to Figure 8-31 to answer Questions 10 through 13.

Figure 8-31

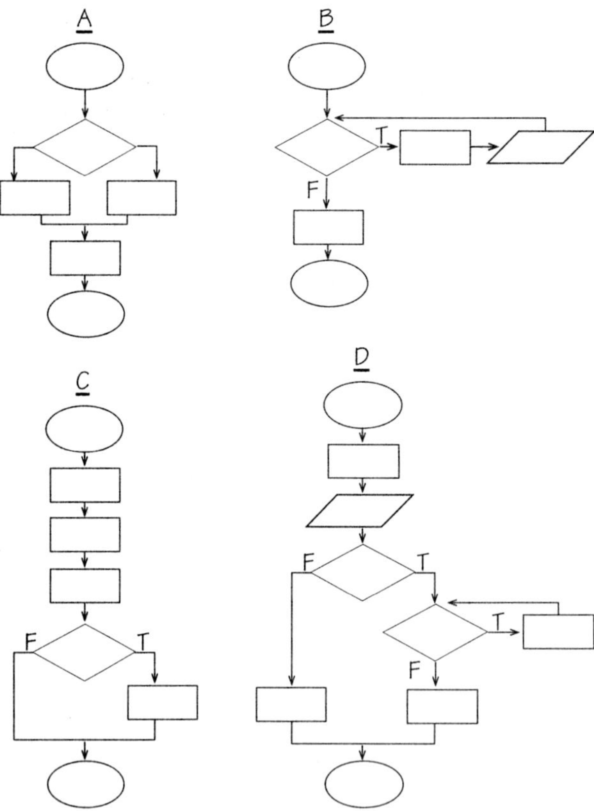

10) Which of the following control structures are used in Figure 8-31's flowchart A? (Select all that apply.)

A. sequence

B. selection

C. repetition

11) Which of the following control structures are used in Figure 8-31's flowchart B? (Select all that apply.)

A. sequence

B. selection

C. repetition

12) Which of the following control structures are used in Figure 8-31's flowchart C? (Select all that apply.)

A. sequence

B. selection

C. repetition

13) Which of the following control structures are used in Figure 8-31's flowchart D? (Select all that apply.)

A. sequence

B. selection

C. repetition

14) Values that are used to end loops are referred to as ______________ values.

A. end

B. finish

C. sentinel

D. stop

15) Assume a program allows the user to enter one or more numbers. The first input instruction will get the first number only and is referred to as the ______________ read.

A. entering

B. initializer

C. priming

D. starter

16) How many times will the `Console::WriteLine(count);` statement in the following loop be processed?

```
for (int count = 1; count < 6; count = count + 1)
        Console::WriteLine(count);
//end for
```

A. 0

B. 1

C. 5

D. 6

17) What is the value stored in the `count` variable when the loop in Question 16 ends?

A. 1

B. 5

C. 6

D. 7

18) How many times will the `Console::WriteLine(count);` statement in the following loop be processed?

```
for (int count = 4; count <= 10; count = count + 2)
        Console::WriteLine(count);
//end for
```

A. 0

B. 3

C. 4

D. 12

19) What is the value stored in the `count` variable when the loop in Question 18 ends?

A. 4

B. 6

C. 10

D. 12

Look For These Symbols

Debugging

Discovery

EXERCISES

1) In this exercise, you complete a program by writing a repetition structure.

A. If necessary, start Visual Studio .NET. Open the T8ConE01 Solution (T8ConE01 Solution.sln) file, which is contained in the CppNet\Tut08\T8ConE01 Solution folder.

B. Complete the program by entering a `while` clause that stops the loop when the user enters a number that is less than zero.

C. Save and then build the solution.

D. Execute the program, using the following numbers: 4, 10, 0, and -3.

E. When the program is working correctly, close the Output window, and then use the File menu to close the solution.

2) In this exercise, you complete a program by writing a repetition structure.

A. If necessary, start Visual Studio .NET. Open the T8ConE02 Solution (T8ConE02 Solution.sln) file, which is contained in the CppNet\Tut08\T8ConE02 Solution folder.

B. Complete the program by entering a `while` clause that stops the loop when the user enters the letter "N" (in any case).

C. Save and then build the solution.

D. Execute the program, using the following data: a, 4, $, and n.

E. When the program is working correctly, close the Output window, and then use the File menu to close the solution.

3) In this exercise, you complete a program by writing a repetition structure.

A. If necessary, start Visual Studio .NET. Open the T8ConE03 Solution (T8ConE03 Solution.sln) file, which is contained in the CppNet\Tut08\T8ConE03 Solution folder.

B. Complete the program by entering a `while` clause that processes the loop instructions as long as the user enters a number that is greater than 0.

C. Save and then build the solution.

D. Execute the program, using the following numbers: 8, 100, and 0.

E. When the program is working correctly, close the Output window, and then use the File menu to close the solution.

4) In this exercise, you complete a program by writing a repetition structure.

A. If necessary, start Visual Studio .NET. Open the T8ConE04 Solution (T8ConE04 Solution.sln) file, which is contained in the CppNet\Tut08\T8ConE04 Solution folder.

B. Complete the program by entering a `while` clause that processes the loop instructions as long as the user enters the letter "Y" (in any case).

C. Save and then build the solution.

D. Execute the program, using the following three sets of data: y and 100, Y and 200, and n. (The total sales should be 300.)

E. Execute the program again. When you are asked if you want to enter a sales amount, type N and press Enter. Notice that you were not asked to enter the sales amount. Explain why.

F. When the program is working correctly, close the Output window, and then use the File menu to close the solution.

5) In this exercise, you complete a program by writing a repetition structure.

A. If necessary, start Visual Studio .NET. Open the T8ConE05 Solution (T8ConE05 Solution.sln) file, which is contained in the CppNet\Tut08\T8ConE05 Solution folder.

B. Complete the program by entering a `while` statement that displays the word "Hello" on the screen 10 times.

C. Save and then build the solution.

D. Execute the program. The word "Hello" (without the quotation marks) should appear on the screen 10 times.

E. When the program is working correctly, close the Output window, and then use the File menu to close the solution.

6) In this exercise, you complete a program by writing a repetition structure.

A. If necessary, start Visual Studio .NET. Open the T8ConE06 Solution (T8ConE06 Solution.sln) file, which is contained in the CppNet\Tut08\T8ConE06 Solution folder.

B. Complete the program by entering a `while` statement that displays the numbers 20, 40, 60, 80, 100, 120, 140, 160, and 180 on the screen. Use the flowchart shown in Figure 8-32 to enter the appropriate code.

Figure 8-32

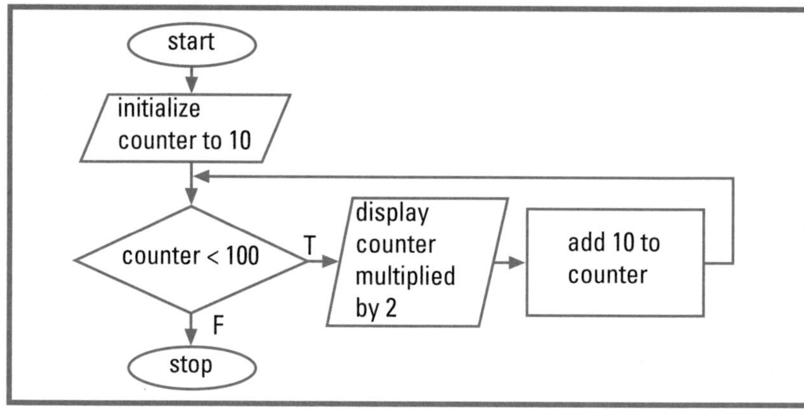

C. Save and then build the solution.

D. Execute the program. The numbers 20, 40, 60, 80, 100, 120, 140, 160, and 180 should appear on the screen.

E. When the program is working correctly, close the Output window, and then use the File menu to close the solution.

7) What will appear on the screen when the code shown in Figure 8-33 is processed, assuming the code is included in a valid C++ program? What is the value in the `temp` variable when the loop stops? Complete a desk-check table for this code.

Figure 8-33

```
int temp = 0;
while (temp < 5)
{
    Console::WriteLine(temp);
    temp = temp + 1;
} //end while
```

8) What will appear on the screen when the code shown in Figure 8-34 is processed, assuming the code is included in a valid C++ program? What is the value in the `totEmp` variable when the loop stops? Complete a desk-check table for this code.

Figure 8-34

```
int totEmp = 0;
while (totEmp <= 5)
{
    Console::WriteLine(totEmp);
    totEmp = totEmp + 2;
}//end while
```

9) Write an assignment statement that updates a counter variable named `numStudents` by 1.

10) Write an assignment statement that updates a counter variable named `quantity` by -5.

11) Write an assignment statement that updates an accumulator variable named `total` by the value in the `sales` variable.

12) Write an assignment statement that updates an accumulator variable named `total` by the value in the `gross` variable.

13) In this exercise, you complete a program by writing a repetition structure.

A. If necessary, start Visual Studio .NET. Open the T8ConE13 Solution (T8ConE13 Solution.sln) file, which is contained in the CppNet\Tut08\T8ConE13 Solution folder.

B. Complete the program by entering a `for` statement that displays the word "Hello" on the screen 10 times.

C. Save and then build the solution.

D. Execute the program. The word "Hello" (without the quotation marks) should appear on the screen 10 times.

E. When the program is working correctly, close the Output window, and then use the File menu to close the solution.

14) In this exercise, you complete a program by writing a repetition structure.

A. If necessary, start Visual Studio .NET. Open the T8ConE14 Solution (T8ConE14 Solution.sln) file, which is contained in the CppNet\Tut08\T8ConE14 Solution folder.

B. Complete the program by entering a `for` statement that displays the numbers 10, 20, 30, 40, 50, 60, 70, 80, 90, and 100 on the screen.

C. Save and then build the solution.

D. Execute the program. The numbers 10, 20, 30, 40, 50, 60, 70, 80, 90, and 100 should appear on the screen.

E. When the program is working correctly, close the Output window, and then use the File menu to close the solution.

15) What will appear on the screen when the code shown in Figure 8-35 is processed, assuming the code is included in a valid C++ program? What is the value in the `temp` variable when the loop stops? Complete a desk-check table for this code.

Figure 8-35

```
for (int temp = 0; temp < 5; temp = temp + 1)
    Console::WriteLine(temp);
//end for
```

16) What will appear on the screen when the code shown in Figure 8-36 is processed, assuming the code is included in a valid C++ program? What is the value in the `totEmp` variable when the loop stops? Complete a desk-check table for this code.

Figure 8-36

```
for (int totEmp = 0; totEmp <= 5; totEmp = totEmp + 1)
    Console::WriteLine(totEmp);
//end for
```

17) In this exercise, you learn two ways to stop a program that is in an endless (infinite) loop.

A. If necessary, start Visual Studio .NET. Open the T8ConE17 Solution (T8ConE17 Solution.sln) file, which is contained in the CppNet\Tut08\T8ConE17 Solution folder.

B. Build the solution, and then execute the program. Notice that the program results in an endless (infinite) loop. (You can tell that the program is in an endless loop because it displays the number 0 over and over again in the Command Prompt window.)

C. On most systems, you can stop a program that is in an endless loop by pressing Ctrl+c (press and hold down the Ctrl key as you press the letter c). Use the Ctrl+c key combination to stop the program. The Command Prompt window closes.

D. Execute the program again. You also can use the Command Prompt window's Close button to stop a program that is in an endless loop. Click the Command Prompt window's Close button. The Command Prompt window closes.

E. Close the Output window, and then use the File menu to close the solution.

18) In this exercise, you learn about the increment and decrement operators in C++.

A. The C++ programming language has an increment operator (++) and a decrement operator (--). What is the purpose of these operators?

B. If necessary, start Visual Studio .NET. Open the T8ConE18 Solution (T8ConE18 Solution.sln) file, which is contained in the CppNet\Tut08\T8ConE18 Solution folder.

C. Complete the program by writing a `for` statement that displays the numbers 10 through 1 on the screen.

D. Save and then build the solution.

E. Execute the program. The numbers 10, 9, 8, 7, 6, 5, 4, 3, 2, and 1 should appear on the screen.

F. When the program is working correctly, close the Output window, and then use the File menu to close the solution.

19) When included in a valid C++ program, the code shown in Figure 8-37 should display the numbers 1, 2, 3, and 4 on the screen. The code is not working properly. Correct the code.

Figure 8-37

```
int num = 1;
while (num < 5)
   Console::WriteLine(num);
//end while
```

20) When included in a valid C++ program, the code shown in Figure 8-38 should print the commission amount for each salesperson. The commission amount is calculated by multiplying the sales amount by .1. The code is not working properly. Correct the code.

Figure 8-38

```
double sales = 0.0;
Console::Write("Enter a sales amount: ");
sales = Convert::ToDouble(Console::ReadLine());
while (sales > 0)
{
    Console::WriteLine(sales * .1);
} //end while
```

Application Lesson

Using the Repetition Structure in a C++ Program

CASE Next Monday is career day at your alma mater. Professor Krelina, one of your computer programming instructors, has asked you to be a guest speaker in her Introduction to Programming class. You gladly accept this speaking engagement and begin planning your presentation. You decide to show the students how to create a program that will calculate their grade in Professor Krelina's class.

Analyzing, Planning, and Desk-Checking the Grade Problem

Professor Krelina assigns four projects and two tests to the students in her Introduction to Programming class. Each project is worth 50 points, and each test is worth 100 points. Figure 8-39 shows the grading scale that Professor Krelina uses to assign a grade to each student in her class.

Figure 8-39: Professor Krelina's grading scale

Total points earned	Grade
360 – 400	A
320 – 359	B
280 – 319	C
240 – 279	D
below 240	F

In addition to using the `main()` function, the grade problem's solution will use two value-returning functions named `getPointsEarned()` and `assignGrade()`. The `getPointsEarned()` function will both get and accumulate the student's project and test scores, and then return the accumulated total to the `main()` function. The `assignGrade()` function will assign the appropriate grade based on the total points earned, and then return the grade to the `main()` function. Figure 8-40 shows the IPO charts for one possible solution to the grade problem.

Figure 8-40: IPO charts for one possible solution to the grade problem

`main()` function

Input	Processing	Output
total points earned grade	Processing items: none Algorithm: 1. total points earned = getPointsEarned() 2. grade = assignGrade(total points earned) 3. display the grade	grade

Figure 8-40: IPO charts for one possible solution to the grade problem (continued)

`getPointsEarned()` **function**

Input	Processing	Output
project or test score	Processing items: none Algorithm: 1. enter the first project or test score 2. repeat while (the project or test score is greater than or equal to 0) add the project or test score to the total points earned enter the next project or test score end repeat while 3. return the total points earned	total points earned

`assignGrade()` **function**

Input	Processing	Output
total points earned	Processing items: none Algorithm: 1. if (the total points earned >= 360) assign A to grade else if (the total points earned >= 320) assign B to grade else if (the total points earned >= 280) assign C to grade else if (the total points earned >= 240) assign D to grade else assign F to grade end ifs 2. return grade	grade

Notice that the `main()` function's output is the student's grade. To display the grade, the `main()` function must know the total number of points the student earned and his or her grade. As the `main()` function's algorithm indicates, the `main()` function will get the total number of points earned by calling the `getPointsEarned()` function, and then assigning the function's return value to a memory location. The `main()` function will get the grade by calling the `assignGrade()` function, passing it the total number of points the student earned. The `main()` function will store the grade returned by the `assignGrade()` function in a memory location. After getting the grade, the `main()` function then will display the grade on the screen.

Next, study the `getPointsEarned()` function's IPO chart. The function's output is the total number of points earned by the student, and its input is the student's score on each project or test. Step 1 in the algorithm is to get the first project or test score from the user. Step 2 is a pretest loop that repeats its instructions as long as (or while) the user enters a score that is greater than or equal to zero. Notice that the instructions within the loop add the score entered by the user to the total points earned (an accumulator) and then get another score from the user. The loop stops when the user enters the sentinel value. In this case, the sentinel value is any number that is less than zero.

Finally, study the `assignGrade()` function's IPO chart. The function's output is the grade, and its input, which it receives from the `main()` function, is the total number of points earned by the student. As its algorithm indicates, the `assignGrade()` function uses a selection structure to assign the appropriate grade, which is based on the total number of points earned.

Recall that you should desk-check an algorithm several times before you begin coding it. In this case, you will use the following scores to desk-check the algorithms shown in Figure 8-40:

Data for first desk-check		Data for second desk-check	
Project 1:	45	Project 1:	35
Project 2:	40	Project 2:	35
Project 3:	45	Project 3:	40
Project 4:	41	Project 4:	43
Test 1:	96	Test 1:	75
Test 2:	89	Test 2:	69
Sentinel:	-1	Sentinel:	-3

Figure 8-41 shows the completed desk-check tables.

Figure 8-41: Completed desk-check tables for the grade problem algorithms shown in Figure 8-40

`main()` function

total points earned	grade
~~356~~ 297	~~B~~ C

`getPointsEarned()` function

project or test score	total points earned
~~45~~ ~~40~~ ~~45~~ ~~41~~ ~~96~~ ~~89~~ ~~-1~~ ~~35~~ ~~35~~ ~~40~~ ~~43~~ ~~75~~ ~~69~~ -3	~~45~~ ~~85~~ ~~130~~ ~~171~~ ~~267~~ ~~356~~ ~~35~~ ~~70~~ ~~110~~ ~~153~~ ~~228~~ 297

`assignGrade()` function

total points earned	grade
~~356~~ 297	~~B~~ C

After desk-checking an algorithm to verify its accuracy, you are ready to translate it into a language the computer can understand. Begin by coding the program's `main()` function.

Coding the `main()` function

According to its IPO chart, the `main()` function requires two memory locations to store the values of its input and output items. You will store the values in variables, because the values will be different each time the program is executed. You will use the `int` data type for the variable that stores the total points earned, and the `String` data type for the variable that stores the grade. Figure 8-42 shows the C++ code corresponding to the `main()` function.

Figure 8-42: C++ statements for the `main()` function

IPO chart information	C++ instructions
Input	
total points earned	`int totalEarned = 0;`
grade	`String *grade = "";`
Processing	
none	
Output	
grade	
Algorithm	
1. total points earned = getPointsEarned()	`totalEarned = getPointsEarned();`
2. grade = assignGrade(total points earned)	`grade = assignGrade(totalEarned);`
3. display the grade	`Console::WriteLine("Grade: {0}", grade);`

Next, you code the `getPointsEarned()` function.

Coding the `getPointsEarned()` Function

As its IPO chart indicates, the `getPointsEarned()` function requires two memory locations to store the values of its input and output items. You will use `int` variables for both items, because the values of both items will be integers and will vary as the program is running. The total points earned variable will be an accumulator, because it will need to accumulate, or add together, the project and test scores entered by the user.

The first step in the `getPointsEarned()` function's algorithm is the priming read, which gets either a project score or a test score from the user. Figure 8-43 shows the C++ code corresponding to the priming read.

Figure 8-43: C++ instructions corresponding to the priming read in the getPointsEarned() function

IPO chart information	C++ instructions
Input project or test score	`int score = 0;`
Processing none	
Output total points earned	`int total = 0;`
Algorithm 1. enter the first project or test score	`Console::Write("First score: ");` `score = Convert::ToInt32(Console::ReadLine());` ← priming read
2. repeat while (the project or test score is greater than or equal to 0) add the project or test score to the total points earned enter the next project or test score end repeat while	
3. return the total points earned	

tip

As you learned in this tutorial's Concept lesson, the priming read primes, or prepares, the loop.

Step 2 in the function's algorithm is a pretest loop that processes its instructions each time the user enters a score that is greater than or equal to zero. The loop ends when the user enters the sentinel value, which is any score that is less than zero. The appropriate clause to begin the loop is `while (score >= 0)`.

The first instruction in the loop updates the total points earned accumulator by adding to the accumulator the score entered by the user. The second instruction in the loop gets the next score from the user.

Step 3 in the `getPointsEarned()` function's algorithm is to return the total number of points earned to the `main()` function. Figure 8-44 shows the C++ instructions for the `getPointsEarned()` function.

Figure 8-44: C++ instructions for the `getPointsEarned()` function

IPO chart information	C++ instructions
Input project or test score	`int score = 0;`
Processing none	
Output total points earned	`int total = 0;`
Algorithm 1. enter the first project or test score	`Console::Write("First score: ");` `score = Convert::ToInt32(Console::ReadLine());`
2. repeat while (the project or test score is greater than or equal to 0)	`while (score >= 0)` `{`
add the project or test score to the total points earned	`total = total + score;`
enter the next project or test score	`Console::Write("Next score: ");` `score = Convert::ToInt32(Console::ReadLine());`
end repeat while	`}  //end while`
3. return the total points earned	`return total;`

Next, you code the **assignGrade()** function.

Coding the assignGrade() Function

As its IPO chart indicates, the **assignGrade()** function requires two memory locations to store the values of its input and output items. The value of the input item—total points earned—is passed to the **assignGrade()** function when the function is called; you will use a formal parameter named **points** to receive this information. Within the **assignGrade()** function, you will declare and initialize a variable to store the output item—grade. You will name the variable **letterGrade** and declare it as a **String** variable.

According to its algorithm, the **assignGrade()** function uses a selection structure to assign the appropriate grade, based on the total number of points earned by the student. The function then returns the grade to the **main()** function. Figure 8-45 shows the C++ instructions for the **assignGrade()** function.

Figure 8-45: C++ instructions for the `assignGrade()` function

IPO chart information	C++ instructions
Input total points earned	`String *assignGrade(int points);`
Processing none	
Output grade	`String *letterGrade = "";`

Algorithm
1. if (the total points earned >= 360)
assign A to grade
else if (the total points earned >= 320)
assign B to grade
else if (the total points earned >= 280)
assign C to grade
else if (the total points earned >= 240)
assign D to grade
else assign F to grade
end ifs
	`if (points >= 360)`
	`letterGrade = "A";`
	`else if (points >= 320)`
	`letterGrade = "B";`
	`else if (points >= 280)`
	`letterGrade = "C";`
	`else if (points >= 240)`
	`letterGrade = "D";`
	`else letterGrade = "F";`
	`//end ifs`

2. return grade	`return letterGrade;`

Now that you have finished coding the algorithms, you need to desk-check the program, using the same data you used to desk-check the algorithms. Figure 8-46 shows the data and the completed desk-check table for the program.

Figure 8-46: Data and completed desk-check table for the program

Data for first desk-check	Data for second desk-check
Project 1: 45 Project 2: 40 Project 3: 45 Project 4: 41 Test 1: 96 Test 2: 89 Sentinel: -1	Project 1: 35 Project 2: 35 Project 3: 40 Project 4: 43 Test 1: 75 Test 2: 69 Sentinel: -3

Desk-check tables

`main()` function's variables

totalEarned	grade
~~0~~ ~~356~~ ~~0~~ 297	- ~~B~~ - C

Figure 8-46: Data and completed desk-check table for the program (continued)

`getPointsEarned()` function's variables

score	total
~~0~~ ~~45~~ ~~40~~ ~~45~~ ~~41~~ ~~96~~ ~~89~~ ~~-1~~ ~~0~~ ~~35~~ ~~35~~ ~~40~~ ~~43~~ ~~75~~ ~~69~~ -3	~~0~~ ~~45~~ ~~85~~ ~~130~~ ~~171~~ ~~267~~ ~~356~~ ~~0~~ ~~35~~ ~~70~~ ~~110~~ ~~153~~ ~~228~~ 297
`assignGrade()` function's variables	
points	letterGrade
~~356~~ 297	– ~~B~~ – C

The results obtained when desk-checking the program agree with the results obtained when desk-checking the algorithm. You now are ready to enter the C++ instructions into the computer.

Completing the Grade Program

On your computer's hard disk is a partially completed C++ program containing most of the instructions for the grade program. You open that program in the next set of steps.

To open the partially completed C++ program:

1. Start Microsoft Visual Studio .NET. If necessary, close the Start Page window.
2. Click **File** on the menu bar, and then click **Open Solution**. The Open Solution dialog box opens.
3. Locate and then open the **CppNet\Tut08\T8App Solution** folder.
4. Click **T8App Solution** (T8App Solution.sln) in the list of filenames, and then click the **Open** button.
5. If the T8App.cpp source file is not displayed, right-click **T8App.cpp** in the Solution Explorer window, and then click **Open**.

Missing from the program is the code for the `getPointsEarned()` function.

To complete the grade program, then test the program:

1. Position the insertion point in the blank line below the `//*****function definitions*****` comment, then enter the instructions shaded in Figure 8-47.

Figure 8-47: Program showing the code for the `getPointsEarned()` function

```
//T8App.cpp
//displays a grade

#using <mscorlib.dll>
using namespace System;

//function prototypes
int getPointsEarned();
String *assignGrade(int);

int main()
{
    //declare variables
    int totalEarned = 0;
    String *grade   = "";

    //get total points earned
    totalEarned = getPointsEarned();
    //assign grade
    grade = assignGrade(totalEarned);
    //display grade
    Console::WriteLine("Grade: {0}", grade);

    return 0;
}   //end of main function

//*****function definitions*****
int getPointsEarned()
{
    //gets and accumulates the scores, then returns the total
    int score = 0;
    int total = 0;

    Console::Write("First score: ");
    score = Convert::ToInt32(Console::ReadLine());
    while (score >= 0)
    {
        total = total + score;
        Console::Write("Next score: ");
        score = Convert::ToInt32(Console::ReadLine());
    }  //end while
    return total;
}   //end of getPointsEarned function
```

enter the function's code

Figure 8-47: Program showing the code for the `getPointsEarned()` function (continued)

```
String *assignGrade(int points)
{
    //assigns and then returns the letter grade
    String *letterGrade = "";

    if (points >= 360)
      letterGrade = "A";
    else if (points >= 320)
      letterGrade = "B";
    else if (points >= 280)
      letterGrade = "C";
    else if (points >= 240)
      letterGrade = "D";
    else letterGrade = "F";
    //end ifs
    return letterGrade;
}   //end of assignGrade function
```

2. Save and then build the solution. Verify that the program generated no warnings.
3. Execute the program. When you are prompted for the first test score, type **45** and press **Enter**. Then enter the following scores, one at a time: **40**, **45**, **41**, **96**, **89**, and **-1**. The program displays a grade of B, as shown in Figure 8-48.

Figure 8-48: Command Prompt window showing the results of the first test

The B grade displayed by the program agrees with the desk-check tables.

4. Press **Enter** to close the Command Prompt window, then execute the program again. When you are prompted for the first score, type **35** and press **Enter**. Then enter the following scores, one at a time: **35**, **40**, **43**, **75**, **69**, and **-3**. The program displays a grade of C, which agrees with the desk-check tables.
5. Close the Command Prompt window, then close the Output window.
6. Click **File** on the menu bar, and then click **Close Solution** to close the current solution.
7. Click **File** on the menu bar, and then click **Exit** to exit Visual Studio .NET.

You now have completed Tutorial 8's Application lesson. You can either take a break or complete the end-of-lesson exercises.

Look For These Symbols

Debugging

Discovery

EXERCISES

1) In this exercise, you modify the program you created in the lesson so that it allows the user to display the grade for any number of students.

A. If necessary, start Visual Studio .NET. Open the T8AppE01 Solution (T8AppE01 Solution.sln) file, which is contained in the CppNet\Tut08\T8AppE01 Solution folder.

B. Modify the program so that it allows the user to display the grade for any number of students. (You will need to add another loop to the program. Be sure to use an appropriate sentinel value.)

C. Save and then build the solution.

D. Execute the program, using the following two sets of data:

45, 40, 45, 41, 96, 89, -1
35, 35, 40, 43, 75, 69, -3

E. When the program is working correctly, close the Output window, and then use the File menu to close the solution.

2) In this exercise, you create a program that displays the sum of the monthly sales amounts made in four regions: North, South, East, and West.

A. Write one or more IPO charts for the problem. Use a `while` loop to allow the user to enter each of the four sales amounts, one at a time.

B. If necessary, start Visual Studio .NET. Open the T8AppE02 Solution (T8AppE02 Solution.sln) file, which is contained in the CppNet\Tut08\T8AppE02 Solution folder.

C. Use the IPO charts you created in Step A to code the program.

D. Complete a desk-check table for the program, using 2000, 3000, 2500, and 1500 as the first set of sales amounts, and 39000, 45000, 25000, and 56000 as the second set of sales amounts.

E. Save and then build the solution.

F. Execute the program. Use the first set of sales amounts from Step D to test the program.

G. Execute the program again. Use the second set of sales amounts from Step D to test the program.

H. When the program is working correctly, close the Output window, and then use the File menu to close the solution.

3) In this exercise, you create a program that displays an employee's name when the employee's ID is entered at the keyboard. The IDs and their corresponding names are as follows:

ID	Name
1234	Sue Nguyen
1345	Janice Blackfeather
3456	Allen Kraus
4567	Margie O'Donnell

If the user enters an ID other than the ones listed above, the program should display the message "Incorrect ID – Please try again".

A. Write one or more IPO charts for the problem. Use a `while` loop to allow the user to enter each ID, one at a time. (Be sure to use an appropriate sentinel value.)

B. If necessary, start Visual Studio .NET. Open the T8AppE03 Solution (T8AppE03 Solution.sln) file, which is contained in the CppNet\Tut08\T8AppE03 Solution folder.

C. Use the IPO charts you created in Step A to code the program.

D. Complete a desk-check table for the program, using 1345 as the first ID, 4567 as the second ID, and your sentinel value as the third ID.

E. Save and then build the solution.

F. Execute the program. Use the data from Step D to test the program.

G. When the program is working correctly, close the Output window, and then use the File menu to close the solution.

4) In this exercise, you create a program that displays the registration information for programming seminars. The price per person depends on the number of people a company registers. (For example, if a company registers four people, then the amount owed by that company is $400.) The following table shows the charges per registrant.

Number of registrants	Charge per person ($)
1–3	150
4–9	100
10 or more	90

A. Write one or more IPO charts for the problem. Use a `while` loop to allow the user to enter the number of people a company registers. The program should allow the user to enter the number registered for as many companies as desired. (Be sure to use an appropriate sentinel value.) The program should display the total number of people registered, the total charge, and the average charge per registrant. (For example, if one company registers four people and a second company registers two people, then the total number of people registered is six, the total charge is $700, and the average charge per registrant is $116.67.)

B. If necessary, start Visual Studio .NET. Open the T8AppE04 Solution (T8AppE04 Solution.sln) file, which is contained in the CppNet\Tut08\T8AppE04 Solution folder.

C. Use the IPO charts you created in Step A to code the program.

D. Complete a desk-check table for the program, using 3 as the number of people registered by the first company, 12 as the number registered by the second company, and 9 as the number registered by the third company; then enter your sentinel value as the number registered.

E. Save and then build the solution.

F. Execute the program. Use the data from Step D to test the program.

G. When the program is working correctly, close the Output window, and then use the File menu to close the solution.

5) In this exercise, you add a loop to an existing program. The program displays a ticket price based on a seat location entered by the user.

A. If necessary, start Visual Studio .NET. Open the T8AppE05 Solution (T8AppE05 Solution.sln) file, which is contained in the CppNet\Tut08\T8AppE05 Solution folder. The program prompts the user to enter a seat location, then displays the ticket price.

B. Modify the program so that it allows the user to enter as many seat locations as desired.

C. Save and then build the solution.

D. Execute the program, using the following seat locations: L, b, p, a, and your sentinel value.

E. When the program is working correctly, close the Output window, and then use the File menu to close the solution.

6) In this exercise, you add a loop and a counter to an existing program. The program displays the number of vacation weeks based on the number of years an employee has been with the company.

A. If necessary, start Visual Studio .NET. Open the T8AppE06 Solution (T8AppE06 Solution.sln) file, which is contained in the CppNet\Tut08\T8AppE06 Solution folder. The program prompts the user to enter the number of years an employee has been with the company, then displays the appropriate number of vacation weeks.

B. Modify the program so that it allows the user to enter the number of years for as many employees as desired. Also add the appropriate code to calculate and display the total number of employees entered.

C. Save and then build the solution.

D. Execute the program, using the following years: 0, 4, 7, 20, and your sentinel value.

E. When the program is working correctly, close the Output window, and then use the File menu to close the solution.

7) In this exercise, you complete a program that displays the product of the odd integers from `1` through `13` (in other words, the result of multiplying `1 * 3 * 5` and so on).

A. If necessary, start Visual Studio .NET. Open the T8AppE07 Solution (T8AppE07 Solution.sln) file, which is contained in the CppNet\Tut08\T8AppE07 Solution folder.

B. Complete the program by entering the appropriate `for` statement.

C. Save and then build the solution.

D. Execute the program.

E. When the program is working correctly, close the Output window, and then use the File menu to close the solution.

8) In this exercise, you complete a program that displays the numbers 0 through `117`, in increments of 9.

A. If necessary, start Visual Studio .NET. Open the T8AppE08 Solution (T8AppE08 Solution.sln) file, which is contained in the CppNet\Tut08\T8AppE08 Solution folder.

B. Complete the program by entering the appropriate `for` statement.

C. Save and then build the solution.

D. Execute the program.

E. When the program is working correctly, close the Output window, and then use the File menu to close the solution.

9) In this exercise, you complete a program that displays the squares of the even numbers from `10` through `25`.

A. If necessary, start Visual Studio .NET. Open the T8AppE09 Solution (T8AppE09 Solution.sln) file, which is contained in the CppNet\Tut08\T8AppE09 Solution folder.

B. Complete the program by entering the appropriate `for` and `while` statements.

C. Save and then build the solution.

D. Execute the program.

E. When the program is working correctly, close the Output window, and then use the File menu to close the solution.

10) In this exercise, you complete a program that displays the first 10 Fibonacci numbers (1, 1, 2, 3, 5, 8, 13, 21, 34, and 55). Notice that, beginning with the third number in the series, each Fibonacci number is the sum of the prior two numbers. In other words, 2 is the sum of 1 plus 1, 3 is the sum of 1 plus 2, 5 is the sum of 2 plus 3, and so on.

A. If necessary, start Visual Studio .NET. Open the T8AppE10 Solution (T8AppE10 Solution.sln) file, which is contained in the CppNet\Tut08\T8AppE10 Solution folder.

B. Complete the program by entering the appropriate `for` statement and code.

C. Save and then build the solution.

D. Execute the program.

E. When the program is working correctly, close the Output window, and then use the File menu to close the solution.

11) In this exercise, you modify the program you created in the lesson so that it uses one value returning function and two void functions, rather than three value-returning functions.

A. If necessary, start Visual Studio .NET. Open the T8AppE11 Solution (T8AppE11 Solution.sln) file, which is contained in the CppNet\Tut08\T8AppE11 Solution folder.

B. Modify the program so that the `getPointsEarned()` and `assignGrade()` functions are void functions rather than value-returning functions.

C. Save and then build the solution.

D. Execute the program, using the following two sets of data:

45, 40, 45, 41, 96, 89, -1
35, 35, 40, 43, 75, 69, -3

E. When the program is working correctly, close the Output window, and then use the File menu to close the solution.

12) In this exercise, you create a program that displays a pattern of asterisks. (*Hint*: You can nest repetition structures.)

A. If necessary, start Visual Studio .NET. Open the T8AppE12 Solution (T8AppE12 Solution.sln) file, which is contained in the CppNet\Tut08\T8AppE12 Solution folder.

B. Enter the C++ instructions to display the following pattern of asterisks (2 asterisks, 4 asterisks, 6 asterisks, 8 asterisks, 10 asterisks, and 12 asterisks).

```
**
****
******
********
**********
************
```

C. Save and then build the solution.

D. Execute the program. When the program is working correctly, close the Output window, and then use the File menu to close the solution.

13) In this exercise, you debug a C++ program.

A. If necessary, start Visual Studio .NET. Open the T8AppE13 Solution (T8AppE13 Solution.sln) file, which is contained in the CppNet\Tut08\T8AppE13 Solution folder. This program should display the squares of the numbers from 1 through 5; in other words, it should display the numbers 1, 4, 9, 16, and 25.

B. Build the solution, then execute the program. Notice that the program results in an endless loop. Stop the program either by pressing Ctrl+c or by clicking the Command Prompt window's Close button.

C. Correct the program's code, then save and build the solution.

D. Execute the program. When the program is working correctly, close the Output window, and then use the File menu to close the solution.

14) In this exercise, you debug a C++ program.

A. If necessary, start Visual Studio .NET. Open the T8AppE14 Solution (T8AppE14 Solution.sln) file, which is contained in the CppNet\Tut08\T8AppE14 Solution folder. This program should display the number of positive integers entered by the user, and the number of negative integers entered by the user. The program should stop when the user enters the number 0.

B. Build the solution, then execute the program. Test the program by entering the following integers: 4, 6, -4, 23, -9, and 0. Notice that the program is not working correctly.

C. Correct the program's code, then save and build the solution.

D. Execute the program. Use the data from Step B to test the program.

E. When the program is working correctly, close the Output window, and then use the File menu to close the solution.

Tutorial 9

More on the Repetition Structure

Objectives

After completing this tutorial, you will be able to:

- Show the posttest repetition structure in pseudocode and in a flowchart
- Code a posttest loop using the C++ do statement
- Nest repetition structures

Concept Lesson

Posttest Loops

As you learned in Tutorial 8, programmers use the repetition structure, referred to more simply as a loop, when they need the computer to repeatedly process one or more program instructions until some condition is met, at which time the repetition structure ends. Recall that a repetition structure can be either a pretest loop or a posttest loop. You learned about the pretest loop in Tutorial 8; you learn about the posttest loop in this tutorial.

As is true of the condition in a pretest loop, the condition in a posttest loop is evaluated with each repetition, or iteration, of the loop. However, unlike the evaluation in a pretest loop, the evaluation in a posttest loop occurs *after* the instructions within the loop are processed, rather than *before* the instructions are processed.

tip Posttest loops also are called bottom-driven loops.

Figure 9-1 shows the problem description and IPO chart for O'Donnell Incorporated. The IPO chart contains two algorithms (written in pseudocode) that could be used to calculate and display a bonus for each of the company's salespeople. Algorithm 1, which you viewed in Tutorial 8's Concept lesson, uses a pretest loop to repeat the appropriate instructions; Algorithm 2 uses a posttest loop to do so.

Figure 9-1: Problem description and IPO chart for O'Donnell Incorporated

Problem description

In January of each year, O'Donnell Incorporated pays a 10% bonus to each of its salespeople. The bonus is based on the amount of sales made by the salesperson during the previous year. The payroll clerk wants a program that can be used to calculate and display each salesperson's bonus amount.

Input	Processing	Output

bonus rate (10%)
sales
	Processing items: none
	
	Algorithm 1:
	1. enter the sales
	2. repeat while (the sales are not equal to -1)
	    calculate the bonus by multiplying the sales by the bonus rate
	    display the bonus
	    enter the sales
	  end repeat while
	
	Algorithm 2:
	1. enter the sales
	2. do
	    calculate the bonus by multiplying the sales by the bonus rate
	    display the bonus
	    enter the sales
	  end repeat while (the sales are not equal to -1)
		bonus

Callouts: loop condition (Algorithm 1, "the sales are not equal to -1"); pretest loop; posttest loop; loop condition (Algorithm 2, "the sales are not equal to -1")

As Figure 9-1 shows, the first step in Algorithm 1 is to enter a sales amount. The second step is a pretest loop whose loop condition compares the sales amount entered by the user with the sentinel value, -1. If the sales amount is not the sentinel value, the loop body instructions calculate and display the bonus amount, and then get another sales amount from the user. The loop condition then compares the sales amount with the sentinel value to determine whether the loop body instructions should be processed again. The loop repeats the loop body instructions as long as (or while) the user does not enter the sentinel value, -1, as the sales amount.

Compare the steps in Algorithm 2 to the steps in Algorithm 1. Like the first step in Algorithm 1, the first step in Algorithm 2 is to enter a sales amount. The second step in Algorithm 2, however, is a posttest loop, rather than a pretest loop. You can tell that Algorithm 2's second step is a posttest loop because it begins with the word **do**, rather than with the words **`repeat while`** followed by the loop condition. In a posttest loop, the words **`repeat while`** and the loop condition appear at the *end* of the loop, which indicates that the loop condition is evaluated only *after* the instructions in the loop body are processed.

Like the loop body instructions in Algorithm 1, the loop body instructions in Algorithm 2 calculate and display the salesperson's bonus, and then get another sales amount from the user. The loop condition, which appears at the bottom of the posttest loop, then compares the sales amount with the sentinel value (-1) to determine whether the instructions in the loop body should be processed again. In a posttest loop, only the second and subsequent sales amounts are compared to the sentinel value; the first sales amount is not compared to the sentinel value, as it is in a pretest loop. While it is possible that the instructions contained in a pretest loop might never be processed, the instructions contained in a posttest loop always are processed at least once. You should use a posttest loop only when you are sure that the loop body instructions can and should be processed at least once.

It may be easier to understand the difference between a pretest loop and a posttest loop by viewing both loops in flowchart form.

tip

As you learned in Tutorial 8, the loop body instructions are not processed if the loop condition in a pretest loop initially evaluates to false.

Flowcharting a Posttest Loop

Figure 9-2 shows the O'Donnell Incorporated algorithms in flowchart form. The flowcharts illustrate why the loops are referred to as pretest and posttest loops. Notice that the repetition diamond, which contains the loop condition, appears at the top of a pretest loop, but it appears at the bottom of a posttest loop.

tip

You often find a posttest loop in programs that allow the user to select from a menu, such as a game program. This type of program uses the posttest loop to control the display of the menu, which must appear on the screen at least once.

Figure 9-2: O'Donnell Incorporated algorithms shown in flowchart form

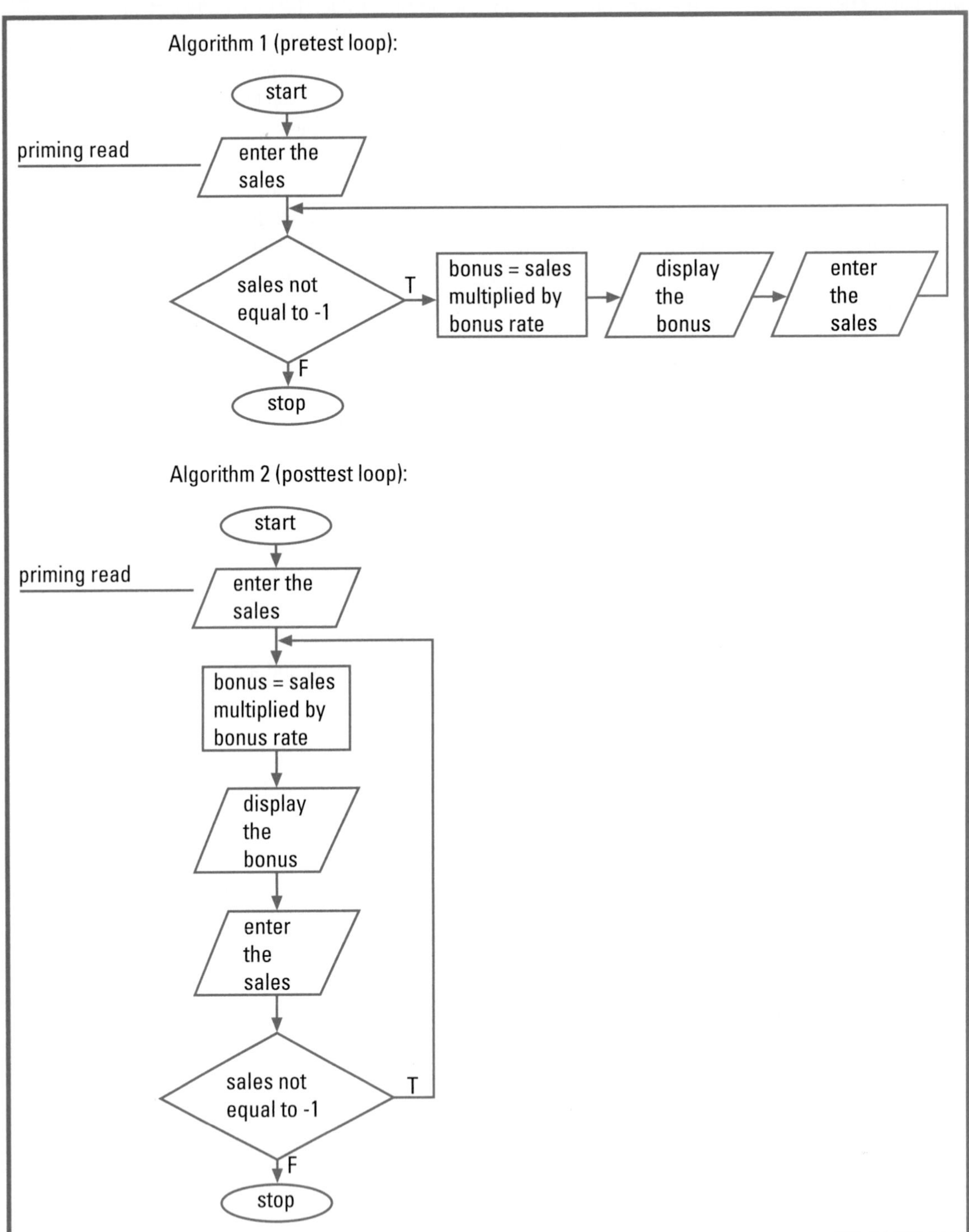

To help you understand how a posttest loop operates in a program, you will desk-check Algorithm 2 shown in Figure 9-2 using the following sales data: 10000, 25000, and –1. The first instruction in the flowchart gets the first sales amount (10000) from the user; recall that this instruction is referred to as the priming read. The next instruction calculates the bonus and is the first instruction in the loop body. Notice that the first sales amount is not compared to the sentinel value in a posttest loop. Figure 9-3 shows the first salesperson's sales and bonus amounts recorded in the desk-check table.

Figure 9-3: First salesperson's sales and bonus amounts recorded in the desk-check table

bonus rate	sales	bonus
.10	10000	1000

The second instruction in the loop body displays the bonus on the screen, and the third instruction gets the next salesperson's sales (25000) from the user. Figure 9-4 shows the second salesperson's sales amount recorded in the desk-check table.

Figure 9-4: Second salesperson's sales amount recorded in the desk-check table

bonus rate	sales	bonus
.10	~~10000~~ 25000	1000

The next symbol in the flowchart is the repetition diamond, which contains the loop condition and marks the end of the posttest loop. The loop condition compares the sales amount entered by the user with the sentinel value, -1, to determine whether the loop should be processed again (a true condition) or end (a false condition). Notice that this is the first time the loop condition is evaluated. In this case, the loop condition evaluates to true, because 25000 is not equal to -1. As is true in a pretest loop, when the loop condition in a posttest loop evaluates to true, the instructions in the loop body are processed. Those instructions calculate and display the bonus for the second salesperson, and then get another sales amount (in this case, the sentinel value) from the user. Figure 9-5 shows the sentinel value recorded in the desk-check table.

Figure 9-5: Sentinel value recorded in the desk-check table

bonus rate	sales	bonus
.10	~~10000~~ ~~25000~~ -1	~~1000~~ 2500

sentinel value (pointing to -1)

The loop condition then is reevaluated to determine whether the loop should be processed again or end. In this case, the loop condition evaluates to false, because the sales amount entered by the user is equal to the sentinel value, -1. As is true in a pretest loop, when the loop condition in a posttest loop evaluates to false, the loop instructions are skipped over and processing continues with the instruction immediately following the end of the loop. In Algorithm 2's flowchart, the stop oval, which marks the end of the algorithm, follows the loop.

MINI-QUIZ

Mini-Quiz 1

1) In a ______________ loop, the loop condition is evaluated *after* the loop instructions are processed, while in a ______________ loop, the evaluation occurs *before* the loop instructions are processed.
   a. pretest, posttest
   b. posttest, pretest

2) The instructions in a ______________ loop always are processed at least once, while the instructions in a ______________ loop might never be processed.
   a. pretest, posttest
   b. posttest, pretest

3) Assume that a program contains a posttest loop that repeats the loop body instructions until the user enters a negative number. How many times will the loop condition be evaluated if the user enters the numbers 5, 8, 9, and –1, respectively?

Next, you learn how to code the posttest loop.

Coding the Posttest Loop

Figure 9-6 shows the syntax of the `do while` statement, which you use to code a posttest loop in a C++ program.

Figure 9-6: Syntax of the C++ `do while` statement

```
do
   one statement, or a block of statements enclosed in braces, to be processed
   one time, and thereafter as long as the loop condition evaluates to true
while (loop condition);
```

notice that the `do while` statement ends with a semicolon

Items in **bold** in the syntax—in this case, the keywords `do` and `while`, the parentheses that surround the loop condition, and the semicolon—are essential components of the `do while` statement. Items in italics indicate where the programmer must supply information pertaining to the current program. In the `do while` statement, the programmer must supply the loop condition to be evaluated. As is true in the C++ `while` statement, the loop condition must be a Boolean expression, which is an expression that evaluates to either true or false. The loop condition can contain variables, constants, functions, methods, arithmetic operators, comparison operators, and logical operators.

tip
As you learned in Tutorial 8, you can use the C++ `while` statement to code a pretest loop.

In addition to supplying the loop condition, the programmer also must supply the statements to be processed when the loop condition evaluates to true. If more than one statement needs to be processed, the statements must be entered as a statement block. Recall that you create a statement block by enclosing the statements in a set of braces ({}).

Figure 9-7 shows how you can use the C++ **do while** statement to code the O'Donnell Incorporated algorithm.

Figure 9-7: C++ `do while` statement included in the code for the O'Donnell Incorporated algorithm

IPO chart information	C++ instructions
Input bonus rate (10%) sales	`const double RATE = .1;` `double sales = 0.0;`
Processing none	
Output bonus	`double bonus = 0.0;`
Algorithm 1. enter the sales	`Console::Write("Enter the first sales amount: ");` `sales = Convert::ToDouble(Console::ReadLine());`
2. do	`do` `{`
calculate the bonus by multiplying the sales by the bonus rate	`bonus = sales * RATE;`
display the bonus	`Console::WriteLine(bonus.ToString("C2"));`
enter the sales	`Console::Write("Enter the next sales amount: ");` `sales = Convert::ToDouble(Console::ReadLine());`
end repeat while (the sales are not equal to -1)	`} while (sales != -1);`

braces mark the start and end of the statement block

do while statement ends with a semicolon

Take a closer look at the instructions shown in Figure 9-7. The first three instructions declare and initialize the **RATE** named constant and the **sales** and **bonus** variables. The **Console::Write("Enter the first sales amount: ");** statement prompts the user to enter the first sales amount, and the **sales = Convert::ToDouble (Console::ReadLine());** statement stores the user's response in the **sales** variable. The **do** clause, which appears next in the program, simply marks the beginning of the posttest loop.

The first instruction in the posttest loop calculates the bonus amount, and the second instruction displays the bonus amount on the screen. The third instruction in the loop prompts the user to enter the next sales amount, and the fourth instruction stores the user's response in the **sales** variable. Notice that the four instructions in the loop body are processed *before* the **while (sales != -1);** clause is evaluated. The **while (sales != -1);** clause compares the value stored in the **sales** variable to the sentinel value (–1). If the **sales** variable does not contain the sentinel value, the instructions within the loop body are processed again; otherwise, the instructions are skipped over, and processing continues with the line immediately below the end of the loop.

tip

Recall that some C++ programmers enclose the loop body in braces even when it contains only one statement, but this is not required by the C++ syntax.

tip

As you learned in Tutorial 8, if you forget to enter the `sales = Convert::ToDouble(Console::ReadLine());` statement within the program's loop, the loop will process its instructions indefinitely. Usually, you can stop a program that contains an infinite (or endless) loop by pressing Ctrl+c; you also can use the Command Prompt window's Close button.

MINI-QUIZ

Mini-Quiz 2

1) The `do while` clause marks the beginning of the C++ `do while` statement.
   a. True
   b. False
2) The `while` clause in the C++ `do while` statement ends with a semicolon.
   a. True
   b. False
3) Write a C++ `while` clause that processes a posttest loop's instructions as long as the value in the `quantity` variable is greater than the number 0.

In Tutorial 7, you learned how to nest selection structures. You also can nest repetition structures, which means you can place one repetition structure inside another repetition structure.

Nested Repetition Structures

In a nested repetition structure, one loop, referred to as the **inner loop**, is placed entirely within another loop, called the **outer loop**. Although the idea of nested loops may sound confusing, you already are familiar with the concept. A clock, for instance, uses nested loops to keep track of the time. For simplicity, consider a clock's second and minute hands only. You can think of the second hand as being the inner loop and the minute hand as being the outer loop. As you know, the second hand on a clock moves one position, clockwise, for every second that has elapsed. Only after the second hand completes its processing—in this case, only after it moves 60 positions—does the minute hand move one position, clockwise; the second hand then begins its journey around the clock again. Figure 9-8 illustrates the logic used by a clock's second and minute hands.

Figure 9-8: Nested loops used by a clock

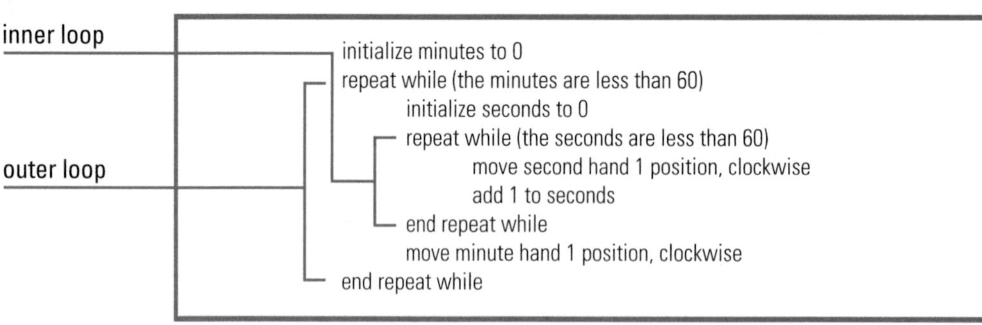
inner loop
outer loop
initialize minutes to 0
repeat while (the minutes are less than 60)
initialize seconds to 0
repeat while (the seconds are less than 60)
move second hand 1 position, clockwise
add 1 to seconds
end repeat while
move minute hand 1 position, clockwise
end repeat while

tip Although both loops in Figure 9-8 are pretest loops, you also could write the logic using two posttest loops or a combination of a pretest and a posttest loop.

As indicated in Figure 9-8, the outer loop corresponds to a clock's minute hand, and the inner loop corresponds to a clock's second hand. Notice that the entire inner loop is contained within the outer loop, which must be true for the loops to be nested and to work correctly.

You will use a nested repetition structure in the Max Beauty Supply program, which you view next.

The Max Beauty Supply Program

Assume that Max Beauty Supply divides its sales territory into two regions: Region 1 and Region 2. The company's sales manager wants a program that allows him to enter each region's sales amounts. The program then should calculate and display the total amount sold in each region. Figure 9-9 shows the IPO chart information and C++ code for the Max Beauty Supply program. Notice that the program contains an outer loop and an inner loop, and that the entire inner loop is contained within the outer loop.

Figure 9-9: IPO chart information and C++ code for Max Beauty Supply

IPO chart information	C++ instructions
Input sales	`double sales = 0.0;`
Processing region counter (1 and 2)	`int region = 1;`
Output region counter total region sales (accumulator)	`double totRegSales = 0.0;`
Algorithm 1. repeat while (the region counter is less than 3)	`while (region < 3)` `{`
enter the sales	`Console::Write("First sales amount for Region {0}: ", Convert::ToString(region));` `sales = Convert::ToDouble(Console::ReadLine());`
repeat while (the sales are greater than 0)	`while (sales > 0)` `{`
add the sales to the total region sales	`totRegSales = totRegSales + sales;`
enter the sales	`Console::Write("Next sales amount for Region {0}: ", Convert::ToString(region));` `sales = Convert::ToDouble(Console::ReadLine());`
end repeat while	`} //end while`
display the region counter and total region sales	`Console::WriteLine("Region {0} sales: {1}", Convert::ToString(region), Convert::ToString(totRegSales));`
add 1 to the region counter	`region = region + 1;`
assign 0 to the total region sales	`totRegSales = 0.0;`
end repeat while	`} //end while`
2. display "End of program"	`Console::WriteLine("End of program");`

As Figure 9-9 indicates, the input for the Max Beauty Supply problem is the sales amounts made in each region, and the output is each region's total sales amount. The problem requires an accumulator to total the sales amounts made in each region. It also requires a counter to keep track of the region numbers (1 and 2). Notice in the C++ code that the `region` counter variable is initialized to the first region number, 1.

After declaring and initializing the appropriate variables, the outer loop's `while (region < 3)` clause begins a pretest loop that repeats its instructions while the value in the `region` variable is less than three. At this point in the program, the value stored in the `region` variable is 1, so the outer loop condition evaluates to true and the outer loop instructions are processed.

The first two instructions in the outer loop prompt the user to enter the first sales amount, and then store the user's response in the `sales` variable. The third instruction in the outer loop is the inner loop's `while (sales > 0)` clause, which begins a pretest loop that repeats its instructions while the sales amount entered by the user is greater than zero.

The first instruction in the inner loop adds the amount stored in the `sales` variable to the contents of the `totRegSales` accumulator variable. The last two instructions in the inner loop prompt the user to enter the next sales amount, and then store the user's response in the `sales` variable. The inner loop condition then is reevaluated to determine whether the inner loop instructions should be processed again. The inner loop continues to process its instructions until the user enters either the number zero or a negative number, at which time the inner loop ends. Figure 9-10 shows the status of the desk-check table, assuming the user enters the following sales amounts for Region 1: 25000, 30000, 10000, -1.

Figure 9-10: Desk-check table after processing Region 1's data

sales	region	totRegSales
~~0.0~~ ~~25000.0~~ ~~30000.0~~ ~~10000.0~~ -1.0	1	~~0.0~~ ~~25000.0~~ ~~55000.0~~ 65000.0

When the inner loop ends, the next statement processed is the one that appears immediately below the inner loop in the program—in this case, the `Console::WriteLine ("Region {0} sales: {1}", Convert::ToString(region), Convert::ToString(totRegSales));` statement. This statement displays the region number (1) along with the total sales made in Region 1 (65000).

Next, the computer processes the `region = region + 1;` statement, which adds 1 to the value stored in the `region` counter variable, giving 2. The `totRegSales = 0.0;` statement then reinitializes the `totRegSales` accumulator variable to zero, as shown in Figure 9-11.

Figure 9-11: Desk-check table after updating the counter and reinitializing the accumulator

sales	region	totRegSales
~~0.0~~ ~~25000.0~~ ~~30000.0~~ ~~10000.0~~ -1.0	~~1~~ 2	~~0.0~~ ~~25000.0~~ ~~55000.0~~ ~~65000.0~~ 0.0

tip

When loops are nested, the outer loop typically reinitializes the counters and accumulators updated within the inner loop. In the Max Beauty Supply program, only the `totRegSales` accumulator is updated within the inner loop, so that is the only variable reinitialized by the outer loop.

The outer loop condition, `while (region < 3)`, then is reevaluated to determine whether the outer loop should be processed again. Here again, the outer loop condition evaluates to true, because the value stored in the `region` variable (2) is less than three. Because of this, the outer loop instructions are processed again.

The first two instructions in the outer loop prompt the user to enter the first sales amount, and then store the user's response in the `sales` variable. The third instruction in the outer loop is the inner loop's `while (sales > 0)` clause, which begins a pretest loop that repeats its instructions while the sales amount entered by the user is greater than zero.

The first instruction in the inner loop adds the sales amount stored in the `sales` variable to the `totRegSales` accumulator variable. The last two instructions in the inner loop prompt the user to enter the next sales amount, and then store the user's response in the `sales` variable. The inner loop condition then is reevaluated to determine whether the inner loop instructions should be processed again. The inner loop continues to process its instructions until the user enters either the number zero or a negative number, at which time the inner loop ends. Figure 9-12 shows the status of the desk-check table, assuming the user enters the following sales amounts for Region 2: `13000`, `10000`, `-1`.

Figure 9-12: Desk-check table after processing Region 2's data

sales	region	totRegSales
~~0.0~~ ~~25000.0~~ ~~30000.0~~ ~~10000.0~~ ~~-1.0~~ ~~13000.0~~ ~~10000.0~~ -1.0	~~1~~ 2	~~0.0~~ ~~25000.0~~ ~~55000.0~~ ~~65000.0~~ ~~0.0~~ ~~13000.0~~ 23000.0

When the inner loop ends, the next statement processed is the one that appears immediately below the inner loop in the program—in this case, the `Console::WriteLine ("Region {0} sales: {1}", Convert::ToString(region), Convert:: ToString(totRegSales));` statement. This statement displays the region number (2) along with the total sales made in Region 2 (23000).

Next, the computer processes the `region = region + 1;` statement, which adds 1 to the value stored in the `region` counter variable, giving 3. The `totRegSales = 0.0;` statement then reinitializes the `totRegSales` accumulator variable to zero, as shown in Figure 9-13.

Figure 9-13: Desk-check table after updating the counter and reinitializing the accumulator

sales	region	totRegSales
~~0.0~~	~~1~~	~~0.0~~
~~25000.0~~	~~2~~	~~25000.0~~
~~30000.0~~	3	~~55000.0~~
~~10000.0~~		~~65000.0~~
-~~1.0~~		~~0.0~~
~~13000.0~~		~~13000.0~~
~~10000.0~~		~~23000.0~~
-1.0		0.0

The outer loop condition, `while (region < 3)`, then is reevaluated to determine whether the outer loop should be processed again. At this point, the outer loop condition evaluates to false, because the value stored in the `region` variable (3) is not less than three. Because of this, the outer loop ends and processing continues with the instruction located immediately below the outer loop. In this case, processing continues with the `Console::WriteLine("End of program");` statement.

Figure 9-14 shows another way of writing the code for the Max Beauty Supply program. This version of the program uses a `for` statement and a `do while` statement, rather than two `while` statements.

Figure 9-14: Another version of the Max Beauty Supply program

IPO chart information	C++ instructions
Input sales	`double sales = 0.0;`
Processing region counter (1 and 2)	(the `region` counter variable is initialized in the `for` statement)
Output region counter total region sales (accumulator)	`double totRegSales = 0.0;`
Algorithm 1. repeat while (the region counter is less than 3)	`for (int region = 1; region < 3; region = region + 1)` `{`
enter the sales	`Console::Write("First sales amount for Region {0}: ", Convert::ToString(region));` `sales = Convert::ToDouble (Console::ReadLine());`
do	`do` `{`
add the sales to the total region sales	`totRegSales = totRegSales + sales;`
enter the sales	`Console::Write("Next sales amount for Region {0}: ", Convert::ToString(region));` `sales = Convert::ToDouble (Console::ReadLine());`
end repeat while (the sales are greater than 0)	`} while (sales > 0);`
display the region counter and total region sales	`Console::WriteLine("Region {0} sales: {1}", Convert::ToString(region), Convert::ToString(totRegSales));`
add 1 to the region counter	(the `region` counter is updated in the `for` statement)
assign 0 to the total region sales	`totRegSales = 0.0;`
end repeat while 2. display "End of program"	`} //end for` `Console::WriteLine("End of program");`

MINI-QUIZ

Mini-Quiz 3

1) For nested loops to work correctly, the entire __________ loop must be contained within the __________ loop.
   a. inner, outer
   b. outer, inner

2) Assume a program declares two `int` variables named `firstLoop` and `secondLoop`. Both variables are initialized to the number 1. Write the C++ code that uses these variables to display the numbers 1 through 3 on four lines, as follows.

```
1   2   3
1   2   3
1   2   3
1   2   3
```

You now have completed Tutorial 9's Concept lesson. You can either take a break or complete the end-of-lesson questions and exercises before moving on to the Application lesson.

SUMMARY

A repetition structure can be either a pretest loop or a posttest loop. In a pretest loop, the loop condition is evaluated *before* the instructions in the loop body are processed. In a posttest loop, on the other hand, the loop condition is evaluated *after* the instructions in the loop body are processed. Depending on the result of the evaluation, the instructions in a pretest loop may never be processed. The instructions in a posttest loop, however, always are processed at least once. As you learned in Tutorial 8, you can use either the `while` statement or the `for` statement to code a pretest loop in C++. You use the `do while` statement to code a posttest loop in C++.

You can nest repetition structures, which means that you can place one repetition structure inside another repetition structure. For repetition structures to be nested and work correctly, the entire inner loop must be contained within the outer loop.

ANSWERS TO MINI-QUIZZES

Mini-Quiz 1

1) b. posttest, pretest

2) b. posttest, pretest

3) three

Mini-Quiz 2

1) b. False

2) a. True

3) `while (quantity > 0);`

Mini-Quiz 3

1) a. inner, outer

2)
```
while (firstLoop <= 4)
{
     while (secondLoop <= 3)
     {
          Console::Write(secondLoop);
          Console::Write(" ");
          secondLoop = secondLoop + 1;
     }  //end while
     Console::WriteLine();
     firstLoop = firstLoop + 1;
     secondLoop = 1;
}  //end while
```

QUESTIONS

1) The condition in the `do while` statement is evaluated ______________ the instructions in the loop body are processed.

A. after

B. before

2) The loop body instructions in the ______________ statement always are processed at least once.

A. `do while`

B. `for`

C. `while`

D. both A and B

3) What numbers appear on the screen when the computer processes the following code?

```
int x = 1;
do
{
       Console::WriteLine(x);
       x = x + 1;
} while (x < 5);
```

A. 0, 1, 2, 3, 4

B. 0, 1, 2, 3, 4, 5

C. 1, 2, 3, 4

D. 1, 2, 3, 4, 5

4) What numbers appear on the screen when the computer processes the following code?

```
int x = 20;
do
{
      Console::WriteLine(x);
      x = x - 4;
} while (x > 10);
```

A. 16, 12, 8

B. 16, 12

C. 20, 16, 12, 8

D. 20, 16, 12

5) What is the value stored in the **x** variable when the loop in Question 4 stops?

A. 0

B. 8

C. 10

D. 12

6) What numbers appear on the screen when the computer processes the following code?

```
int total = 1;
do
{
          Console::WriteLine(total);
          total = total + 2;
} while (total >= 3);
```

A. 1

B. 1, 3

C. 1, 3, 5

D. 0, 1, 3

7) What appears on the screen when the computer processes the following code?

```
for (int x = 1; x < 3; x = x + 1)
{
     for (int y = 1; y < 4; y = y + 1)
            Console::Write("*");
     //end for
     Console::WriteLine();
} //end for
```

A.
```
***
***
```

B.
```
***
***
***
```

C.
```
**
**
**
```

D.
```
***
***
***
***
```

8) What number appears on the screen when the computer processes the following code?

```
int sum = 0;
int y = 0;
do
{
        for (int x = 1; x < 5; x = x + 1)
              sum = sum + x;
        //end for
        y = y + 1;
} while (y < 3);
Console::WriteLine(sum);
```

A. 5

B. 8

C. 15

D. 30

EXERCISES

Look For These Symbols

Debugging

Discovery

1) Write a C++ `while` clause that stops a posttest loop when the value in the `quantity` variable is less than the number 0.

2) Write a C++ `while` clause that processes a posttest loop's instructions as long as the value in the `inStock` variable is greater than the value in the `reorder` variable.

3) Write a C++ `while` clause that processes a posttest loop's instructions as long as the value in the `letter` variable is either Y or y. (The `letter` variable is a `char` variable.)

4) Assume a program declares an `int` variable named `evenNum` and initializes it to 2. Write the C++ code, using the `do while` statement and the `evenNum` variable, to display the even integers between 1 and 9 on the screen.

5) In this exercise, you use a nested loop to display a pattern of asterisks.

A. If necessary, start Visual Studio .NET. Open the T9ConE05 Solution (T9ConE05 Solution.sln) file, which is contained in the CppNet\Tut09\T9ConE05 Solution folder.

B. Complete the program by entering the instructions to display the following pattern of asterisks (2 asterisks, 4 asterisks, 6 asterisks, 8 asterisks, and 10 asterisks).

```
**
****
******
********
**********
```

C. Save and then build the solution.

D. Execute the program.

E. When the program is working correctly, close the Output window, and then use the File menu to close the solution.

6) In this exercise, you use a nested loop to display a pattern of asterisks.

A. If necessary, start Visual Studio .NET. Open the T9ConE06 Solution (T9ConE06 Solution.sln) file, which is contained in the CppNet\Tut09\T9ConE06 Solution folder.

B. Complete the program by entering the instructions to display the following pattern of asterisks (9 asterisks, 8 asterisks, 7 asterisks, 6 asterisks, 5 asterisks, 4 asterisks, 3 asterisks, 2 asterisks, and 1 asterisk).

```
*********
********
*******
******
*****
****
***
**
*
```

C. Save and then build the solution.

D. Execute the program.

E. When the program is working correctly, close the Output window, and then use the File menu to close the solution.

7) In this exercise, you modify the program you created in Exercise 5 so that it allows the user to specify the outer loop's ending value (which determines the largest number of asterisks to display) and its increment value (the number of asterisks to repeat).

A. If necessary, start Visual Studio .NET. Open the T9ConE07 Solution (T9ConE07 Solution.sln) file, which is contained in the CppNet\Tut09\T9ConE07 Solution folder.

B. Click File on the menu bar, point to Open, and then click File. Open the T9ConE05.cpp file, which is contained in the CppNet\Tut09\T9ConE05 Solution\T9ConE05 Project folder. Select all of the `main()` function's code, then copy the code to the clipboard. Close the T9ConE05.cpp window, then paste the code in the T9ConE07.cpp window.

C. Modify the program so that it allows the user to specify the outer loop's ending and increment values.

D. Save and then build the solution.

E. Execute the program. Test the program by entering the number 4 as the maximum number of asterisks, and the number 1 as the increment value. The program should display the following pattern of asterisks (1 asterisk, 2 asterisks, 3 asterisks, and 4 asterisks).

```
*
**
***
****
```

F. Execute the program again. This time, enter the number 9 as the maximum number of asterisks, and the number 3 as the increment value. The program should display the following pattern of asterisks (3 asterisks, 6 asterisks, and 9 asterisks).

```
***
******
*********
```

G. When the program is working correctly, close the Output window, and then use the File menu to close the solution.

8) In this exercise, you modify the program you created in Exercise 6 so that it allows the user to display the asterisks using either of the following two patterns:

Pattern 1 (9 asterisks, 8 asterisks, 7 asterisks, 6 asterisks, 5 asterisks, 4 asterisks, 3 asterisks, 2 asterisks, and 1 asterisk)

```
*********
********
*******
******
*****
****
***
**
*
```

Pattern 2 (1 asterisk, 2 asterisks, 3 asterisks, 4 asterisks, 5 asterisks, 6 asterisks, 7 asterisks, 8 asterisks, and 9 asterisks)

```
*
**
***
****
*****
******
*******
********
*********
```

A. If necessary, start Visual Studio .NET. Open the T9ConE08 Solution (T9ConE08 Solution.sln) file, which is contained in the CppNet\Tut09\T9ConE08 Solution folder.

B. Click File on the menu bar, point to Open, and then click File. Open the T9ConE06.cpp file, which is contained in the CppNet\Tut09\T9ConE06 Solution\T9ConE06 Project folder. Select all of the `main()` function's code, then copy the code to the clipboard. Close the T9ConE06.cpp window, then paste the code in the T9ConE08.cpp window.

C. Modify the program appropriately.

D. Save and then build the solution.

E. Execute the program. Display the asterisks using pattern 1.

F. Execute the program again. Display the asterisks using pattern 2.

G. When the program is working correctly, close the Output window, and then use the File menu to close the solution.

9) In this exercise, you modify the program you created in Exercise 5 so that it allows the user to process the program's code as many times as desired.

A. If necessary, start Visual Studio .NET. Open the T9ConE09 Solution (T9ConE09 Solution.sln) file, which is contained in the CppNet\Tut09\T9ConE09 Solution folder.

B. Click File on the menu bar, point to Open, and then click File. Open the T9ConE05.cpp file, which is contained in the CppNet\Tut09\T9ConE05 Solution\T9ConE05 Project folder. Select all of the `main()` function's code, then copy the code to the clipboard. Close the T9ConE05.cpp window, then paste the code in the T9ConE09.cpp window.

C. Modify the program so that it allows the user to process the code as many times as desired.

D. Save and then build the solution.

E. Execute the program. Test the program by processing its code three times.

F. When the program is working correctly, close the Output window, and then use the File menu to close the solution.

10) In this exercise, you debug a C++ program.

A. If necessary, start Visual Studio .NET. Open the T9ConE10 Solution (T9ConE10 Solution.sln) file, which is contained in the CppNet\Tut09\T9ConE10 Solution folder.

B. Build the solution, then execute the program. The program should display the total sales amount ($11,000) for two departments, but it is not working correctly.

C. Correct the program's code, then save and build the solution.

D. Execute the program. When the program is working correctly, close the Output window, and then use the File menu to close the solution.

Application Lesson

Using a Nested Repetition Structure in a C++ Program

CASE Mrs. Johnson teaches second grade at Allen Primary Center. Last month, Mrs. Johnson began teaching multiplication to the students. Your task in this tutorial is to create a program that Mrs. Johnson can use to display multiplication tables for her students.

Analyzing, Planning, and Desk-Checking the Multiplication Table Problem

Figure 9-15 shows a sample of a multiplication table. In this case, the multiplication table is for the number 6.

Figure 9-15: Sample multiplication table for the number 6

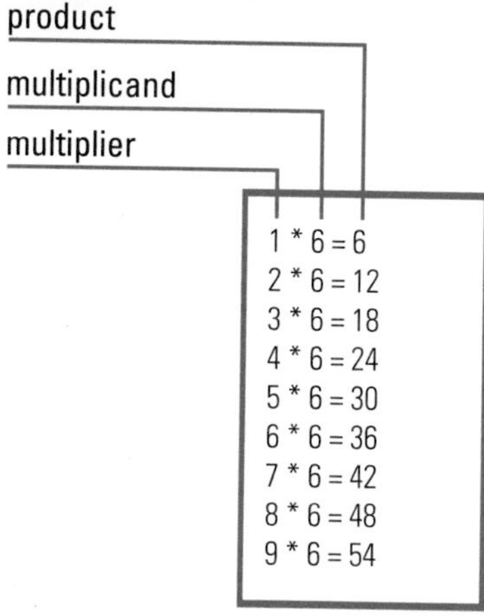

The first column of the multiplication table should always contain the numbers 1 through 9; these numbers represent the multiplier. The number to display in the third column depends on the value entered by the user. For example, if the user enters the number 6, then the number 6 should appear in the third column, as shown in Figure 9-15. However, if the user enters the number 12, then the number 12 should appear in the third column. The number in the third column is called the multiplicand. The last column in the multiplication table is the result of multiplying the multiplier by the multiplicand, and is called the product of the two numbers. Figure 9-16 shows the IPO chart for the multiplication table problem.

Figure 9-16: IPO chart for the multiplication table problem

Input	Processing	Output
multiplicand answer to "another table?" question	Processing items: none Algorithm: 1. do enter the multiplicand assign 1 to the multiplier repeat while (multiplier < 10) calculate product = multiplier * multiplicand display multiplier, multiplicand, and product add 1 to the multiplier end repeat while enter answer to "another table?" question end repeat while (answer to "another table?" question is "Y")	multiplicand multiplier product

Recall that you should desk-check an algorithm several times before you begin coding it. In this case, you will use the following data to desk-check the algorithm shown in Figure 9-16:

<u>Data for first desk-check</u>
Multiplicand: 6
Answer to "another table?" question: Y

<u>Data for second desk-check</u>
Multiplicand: 2
Answer to "another table?" question: N

Figure 9-17 shows the completed desk-check table.

Figure 9-17: Completed desk-check table for the multiplication table algorithm shown in Figure 9-16

multiplicand	multiplier	product	answer to "another table?" question
~~6~~	~~1~~	~~6~~	~~Y~~
2	~~2~~	~~12~~	N
	~~3~~	~~18~~	
	~~4~~	~~24~~	
	~~5~~	~~30~~	
	~~6~~	~~36~~	
	~~7~~	~~42~~	
	~~8~~	~~48~~	
	~~9~~	~~54~~	
	~~10~~	~~2~~	
	~~1~~	~~4~~	
	~~2~~	~~6~~	
	~~3~~	~~8~~	
	~~4~~	~~10~~	
	~~5~~	~~12~~	
	~~6~~	~~14~~	
	~~7~~	~~16~~	
	~~8~~	18	
	~~9~~		
	10		

After desk-checking an algorithm to verify its accuracy, you are ready to translate it into a language the computer can understand.

Coding the Multiplication Table Algorithm

According to its IPO chart, the multiplication table program requires four memory locations to store the values of its input and output items. You will store the values in variables, because the values will be different each time the program is executed. You will use the `int` data type for the variables that store the multiplicand, multiplier, and product, and the `String` data type for the variable that stores the answer to the "another table?" question. Figure 9-18 shows the C++ code corresponding to the `main()` function in the multiplication table program.

Figure 9-18: C++ statements for the `main()` function

IPO chart information	C++ instructions

Input
multiplicand
answer to "another table?" question
	
	`int multiplicand = 0;`
	`String *anotherTable = "";`

Processing none	

Output
multiplicand
multiplier
product
	
	`(the multiplier variable is initialized in the for statement)`
	`int product = 0;`

Algorithm
1. do
	
	`do`
	`{`

enter the multiplicand	`Console::Write("Enter the multiplicand: ");`
assign 1 to the multiplier	`(the multiplier variable is initialized in the for statement)`
repeat while (multiplier < 10)	`for (int multiplier = 1; multiplier < 10; multiplier = multiplier + 1)` `{`
calculate product = multiplier * multiplicand	`product = multiplier * multiplicand;`
display multiplier, multiplicand, and product	`Console::WriteLine("{0} * {1} = {2}", Convert::ToString (multiplier), Convert::ToString (multiplicand), Convert::ToString(product));`
add 1 to the multiplier end repeat while	`(the multiplier variable is updated in the for statement)` `} //end for`

enter answer to "another table?" question	`Console::Write("Do you want to display another multiplication table? (Y/N)");`
	`anotherTable = Console::ReadLine();`
	`anotherTable = anotherTable->ToUpper();`

end repeat while (answer to "another table?" question is "Y")	`} while (anotherTable->CompareTo("Y") == 0);`

Now that you have finished coding the algorithm, you need to desk-check the program, using the same data you used to desk-check the algorithm. Figure 9-19 shows the completed desk-check table for the program.

Figure 9-19: Completed desk-check table for the program

multiplicand	multiplier	product	anotherTable
~~0~~	~~1~~	~~0~~	—
~~6~~	~~2~~	~~6~~	~~Y~~
2	~~3~~	~~12~~	N
	~~4~~	~~18~~	
	~~5~~	~~24~~	
	~~6~~	~~30~~	
	~~7~~	~~36~~	
	~~8~~	~~42~~	
	~~9~~	~~48~~	
	~~10~~	~~54~~	
	~~1~~	~~2~~	
	~~2~~	~~4~~	
	~~3~~	~~6~~	
	~~4~~	~~8~~	
	~~5~~	~~10~~	
	~~6~~	~~12~~	
	~~7~~	~~14~~	
	~~8~~	~~16~~	
	~~9~~	18	
	10		

The results obtained when desk-checking the program agree with the results obtained when desk-checking the algorithm. You now are ready to enter the C++ instructions into the computer.

Completing the Multiplication Table Program

On your computer's hard disk is a partially completed C++ program containing some of the instructions for the multiplication table program. You open the partially completed program in the next set of steps.

To open the partially completed C++ program:

1. Start Microsoft Visual Studio .NET. If necessary, close the Start Page window.
2. Click **File** on the menu bar, and then click **Open Solution**. The Open Solution dialog box opens.
3. Locate and then open the **CppNet\Tut09\T9App Solution** folder.
4. Click **T9App Solution** (T9App Solution.sln) in the list of filenames, and then click the **Open** button.
5. If the T9App.cpp source file is not displayed, right-click **T9App.cpp** in the Solution Explorer window, and then click **Open**.

The inner loop is missing from the program. You complete the program in the next set of steps.

To complete the T9App.cpp program, then test the program:

1. Enter the `for` statement shown in Figure 9-20, which shows the completed T9App.cpp program.

Figure 9-20: Completed T9App.cpp program

enter the `for` statement

```
//T9App.cpp
//displays one or more multiplication tables

#using <mscorlib.dll>
using namespace System;

int main()
{
    //declare variables
    String *anotherTable = "";
    int multiplicand = 0;
    int product = 0;

    do
    {
       //get the multiplicand
       Console::Write("Enter the multiplicand: ");
       multiplicand = Convert::ToInt32(Console::ReadLine());

       //display the multiplication table
       for (int multiplier = 1; multiplier < 10;
       multiplier = multiplier + 1)
       {
           product = multiplier * multiplicand;
           Console::WriteLine("{0} * {1} = {2}",
           Convert::ToString(multiplier),
               Convert::ToString(multiplicand), Convert::
               ToString(product));
       }   //end for

       Console::Write("Do you want to display another
       multiplication table? (Y/N)");
       anotherTable = Console::ReadLine();
       anotherTable = anotherTable->ToUpper();
    } while (anotherTable->CompareTo("Y") == 0);

    return 0;
}   //end of main function
```

2. Save and then build the solution. Verify that the program generated no warnings.
3. Execute the program. When you are prompted to enter the multiplicand, type **6** and press **Enter**. The program displays the multiplication table for the number 6.
4. Type **y** and press **Enter** in response to the "Do you want to display another multiplication table? (Y/N)" prompt.
5. When you are prompted to enter the multiplicand, type **2** and press **Enter**. The program displays the multiplication table for the number 2, as shown in Figure 9-21.

Figure 9-21: Multiplication tables

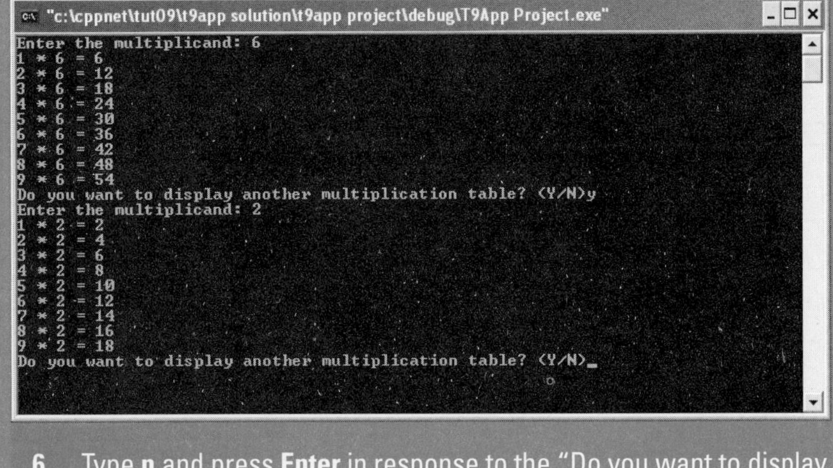

"c:\cppnet\tut09\t9app solution\t9app project\debug\T9App Project.exe"
Enter the multiplicand: 6
1 * 6 = 6
2 * 6 = 12
3 * 6 = 18
4 * 6 = 24
5 * 6 = 30
6 * 6 = 36
7 * 6 = 42
8 * 6 = 48
9 * 6 = 54
Do you want to display another multiplication table? (Y/N)y
Enter the multiplicand: 2
1 * 2 = 2
2 * 2 = 4
3 * 2 = 6
4 * 2 = 8
5 * 2 = 10
6 * 2 = 12
7 * 2 = 14
8 * 2 = 16
9 * 2 = 18
Do you want to display another multiplication table? (Y/N)_

6. Type **n** and press **Enter** in response to the "Do you want to display another multiplication table? (Y/N)" prompt. The multiplication program ends.
7. Close the Command Prompt window, then close the Output window.
8. Click **File** on the menu bar, and then click **Close Solution** to close the current solution.
9. Click **File** on the menu bar, and then click **Exit** to exit Visual Studio .NET.

You now have completed Tutorial 9's Application lesson. You can either take a break or complete the end-of-lesson exercises.

EXERCISES

Look For These Symbols

Debugging

Discovery

1) In this exercise, you modify the program you created in the lesson so that it uses two `while` statements, rather than a `do while` statement and a `for` statement.

A. If necessary, start Visual Studio .NET. Open the T9AppE01 Solution (T9AppE01 Solution.sln) file, which is contained in the CppNet\Tut09\T9AppE01 Solution folder.

B. Replace the `do while` and `for` statements with `while` statements.

C. Save and then build the solution.

D. Execute the program. Display the multiplication tables for the numbers 5 and 3.

E. When the program is working correctly, close the Output window, and then use the File menu to close the solution.

2) In this exercise, you modify the Max Beauty Supply program shown in Figure 9-14 so that it uses a `for` statement instead of a `do while` statement.

A. If necessary, start Visual Studio .NET. Open the T9AppE02 Solution (T9AppE02 Solution.sln) file, which is contained in the CppNet\Tut09\T9AppE02 Solution folder.

B. Replace the `do while` statement with a `for` statement. Assume that each region has four sales amounts.

C. Save and then build the solution.

D. Execute the program. Test the program using the following sales amounts:

Region 1 sales: 400, 200, 500, 600
Region 2 sales: 100, 900, 400, 700

E. When the program is working correctly, close the Output window, and then use the File menu to close the solution.

3) In this exercise, you modify the program you created in Tutorial 8 so that it allows the user to display the grade for as many students as needed.

A. If necessary, start Visual Studio .NET. Open the T9AppE03 Solution (T9AppE03 Solution.sln) file, which is contained in the CppNet\Tut09\T9AppE03 Solution folder.

B. Modify the program appropriately.

C. Save and then build the solution.

D. Execute the program. Test the program using your own sample data for three students.

E. When the program is working correctly, close the Output window, and then use the File menu to close the solution.

4) In this exercise, you create a program that displays the sum of the sales amounts made in each of four regions (North, South, East, and West) during a three-month period. The program also should display the total sales made during the three months.

A. If necessary, start Visual Studio .NET. Open the T9AppE04 Solution (T9AppE04 Solution.sln) file, which is contained in the CppNet\Tut09\T9AppE04 Solution folder.

B. Complete the program by entering the C++ code that allows the user to enter four sets (one set for each region) of three sales amounts (one sales amount for each month). The program should display each region's total sales for the three-month period, and the company's total sales for the three-month period.

C. Save and then build the solution.

D. Execute the program. Use the following four sets of data to test the program:

2000, 4000, 3000
2000, 5000, 5000
3000, 2000, 1000
4000, 1000, 6000

E. When the program is working correctly, close the Output window, and then use the File menu to close the solution.

5) In this exercise, you modify the program you created in Tutorial 6 so that it allows the user to display the fat calories and fat percentage as many times as desired.

A. If necessary, start Visual Studio .NET. Open the T9AppE05 Solution (T9AppE05 Solution.sln) file, which is contained in the CppNet\Tut09\T9AppE05 Solution folder.

B. Modify the program appropriately.

C. Save and then build the solution.

D. Execute the program. Test the program using your own sample data.

E. When the program is working correctly, close the Output window, and then use the File menu to close the solution.

6) In this exercise, you modify the O'Donnell Incorporated program shown in Figure 9-7 so that it uses a `for` statement instead of a `do while` statement.

A. If necessary, start Visual Studio .NET. Open the T9AppE06 Solution (T9AppE06 Solution.sln) file, which is contained in the CppNet\Tut09\T9AppE06 Solution folder.

B. Replace the `do while` statement with a `for` statement. Assume the program needs to calculate the bonus amounts for five salespeople.

C. Save and then build the solution.

D. Execute the program. Test the program using your own sample data.

E. When the program is working correctly, close the Output window, and then use the File menu to close the solution.

7) In this exercise, you modify the program you created in the lesson so that it uses a void function to display the multiplication table.

A. If necessary, start Visual Studio .NET. Open the T9AppE07 Solution (T9AppE07 Solution.sln) file, which is contained in the CppNet\Tut09\T9AppE07 Solution folder.

B. Modify the program appropriately.

C. Save and then build the solution.

D. Execute the program. Test the program using your own sample data.

E. When the program is working correctly, close the Output window, and then use the File menu to close the solution.

8) In this exercise, you modify the program you created in the lesson so that it uses two `for` statements, rather than a `do while` statement and a `for` statement.

A. If necessary, start Visual Studio .NET. Open the T9AppE08 Solution (T9AppE08 Solution.sln) file, which is contained in the CppNet\Tut09\T9AppE08 Solution folder.

B. Replace the `do while` statement with a `for` statement.

C. Save and then build the solution.

D. Execute the program. Display the multiplication tables for the numbers 9 and 12.

E. When the program is working correctly, close the Output window, and then use the File menu to close the solution.

9) In this exercise, you debug a C++ program.

A. If necessary, start Visual Studio .NET. Open the T9AppE09 Solution (T9AppE09 Solution.sln) file, which is contained in the CppNet\Tut09\T9AppE09 Solution folder.

B. Build the solution, then execute the program.

C. Correct the program's code, then save and build the solution.

D. Execute the program. When the program is working correctly, close the Output window, and then use the File menu to close the solution.

Tutorial 10

Classes and Objects

Objectives

After completing this tutorial, you will be able to:

- Differentiate between procedure-oriented and object-oriented programming
- Define the terms used in object-oriented programming
- Create a managed class in C++
- Create a default constructor
- Concatenate strings
- Create an object from a class
- Create and use a header file

Concept Lesson

Programming Methods

Currently, the two most popular methods used to create computer programs are the procedure-oriented method and the object-oriented method. When using the procedure-oriented method to create a program, the programmer concentrates on the major tasks that the program needs to perform. A payroll program, for example, typically performs several major tasks, such as calculating the gross pay, calculating the taxes, and calculating the net pay. A programmer using the procedure-oriented method usually assigns each major task to a function, which is the primary component in a procedure-oriented program. You used the procedure-oriented method to develop the programs that you created in the previous nine tutorials.

Different from the procedure-oriented method, which focuses on the individual tasks the program must perform, the object-oriented method requires the programmer to focus on the objects that a program can use to accomplish its goal. A payroll program, for example, might utilize a time card object, an employee object, and a paycheck object. The primary component in an object-oriented program is an object. In this tutorial, you learn more about object-oriented programming. You also learn how to create simple object-oriented programs.

Object-Oriented Programming

Unlike the procedure-oriented method of programming, the object-oriented method allows the programmer to use familiar objects to solve problems. The ability to use objects that model things found in the real world makes problem solving much easier. For example, assume that the manager of a flower shop asks you to create a program that keeps track of the shop's daily sales revenue. Thinking in terms of the objects used to represent revenue—cash, checks, credit card receipts, and so on—will make the sales revenue problem easier to solve. Additionally, because each object is viewed as an independent unit, an object can be used in more than one program, usually with little or no modification. A check object used in the sales revenue program, for example, also can be used in a payroll program (which issues checks to employees) and an accounts payable program (which issues checks to creditors). The ability to use an object for more than one purpose saves programming time and money—a fact that contributes to the popularity of object-oriented programming.

Although you may have either heard or read that object-oriented programming is difficult to learn, do not be intimidated. Admittedly, creating object-oriented programs does take some practice. However, you already are familiar with many of the concepts upon which object-oriented programming is based. Much of the anxiety of object-oriented programming stems from the terminology used when discussing it. Many of the terms are unfamiliar, because they typically are not used in everyday conversations. The next section will help to familiarize you with the terms used in discussions about object-oriented programming.

Object-Oriented Programming Terminology

When discussing object-oriented programs, you will hear programmers use the term "OOP" (pronounced like *loop*). **OOP** is an acronym for object-oriented programming, which, as you know, is a programming methodology based on objects. An **object** is anything that can be seen, touched, or used; in other words, an object is nearly any *thing*. The objects used in an object-oriented program can take on many different forms. The menus, buttons, and list boxes included in most Windows programs are objects. An object also can represent something encountered in real life—such as a wristwatch, a car, a credit card receipt, and an employee.

Every object has attributes and behaviors. The **attributes** are the characteristics that describe the object. When you tell someone that your wristwatch is a Farentino Model 35A, you are describing the watch (an object) in terms of some of its attributes—in this case, its maker and model number. A watch also has many other attributes, such as a crown, dial, hour hand, minute hand, movement, and so on.

An object's **behaviors**, on the other hand, are the operations (actions) that the object is capable of performing. A watch, for example, can keep track of the time. Some watches also can keep track of the date. Still others can illuminate their dials when a button on the watch is pushed.

You also will hear the term "class" in OOP discussions. Similar to a pattern or blueprint, a **class** is a set of instructions used to create an object. Every object used in an object-oriented program comes from a class. A class contains—or, in OOP terms, it **encapsulates**—all of the attributes and behaviors that describe the object the class creates. The blueprint for the Farentino Model 35A watch, for example, encapsulates all of the watch's attributes and behaviors. Objects created from a class are referred to as **instances** of the class, and are said to be "instantiated" from the class. All Farentino Model 35A watches are instances of the Farentino Model 35A class.

tip

The class itself is not an object; only an instance of the class is an object.

"Abstraction" is another term used in OOP discussions. **Abstraction** refers to the hiding of the internal details of an object from the user. Hiding the internal details helps prevent the user from making inadvertent changes to the object. The internal mechanism of a watch, for example, is enclosed (hidden) in a case to protect the mechanism from damage. Attributes and behaviors that are not **hidden** are said to be **exposed** to the user. Exposed on a Farentino Model 35A watch is the crown used to set the hour and minute hands, and the button used to illuminate the dial. The idea behind abstraction is to expose to the user only those attributes and behaviors that are necessary to use the object, and to hide everything else.

tip

The term "encapsulate" means "to enclose in a capsule." In the context of OOP, the "capsule" is a class.

Another OOP term, **inheritance**, refers to the fact that you can create one class from another class. The new class, called the **derived class**, inherits the attributes and behaviors of the original class, called the **base class**. For example, the Farentino company might create a blueprint of the Model 35B watch from the blueprint of the Model 35A watch. The Model 35B blueprint (the derived class) will inherit all of the attributes and behaviors of the Model 35A blueprint (the base class), but it then can be modified to include an additional feature, such as an alarm.

Finally, you also will hear the term "polymorphism" in OOP discussions. **Polymorphism** is the object-oriented feature that allows the same instruction to be carried out differently depending on the object. For example, you open a door, but you also open an envelope, a jar, and your eyes. You can set the time, date, and alarm on a Farentino watch. Although the meaning of the verbs "open" and "set" are different in each case, you can understand each instruction because the combination of the verb and the object makes the instruction clear. Figure 10-1 uses the wristwatch example to illustrate most of the OOP terms discussed in this section.

Figure 10-1: Illustration of OOP terms

A watch's attributes and behaviors are encapsulated into the blueprint. Some attributes and behaviors are hidden; some are exposed

base class

Blueprint of a Farentino Model 35A

Attributes (Data)	Behaviors
Maker	Track time
Model number	Track date
Crown	Illuminate dial
Dial	
Hour hand	
Minute hand	
Movement	

derived class inherits properties of base class

Blueprint of a Farentino Model 35B

Attributes (Data)	Behaviors
Farentino Model 35A attributes	Farentino Model 35A behaviors
Alarm	Ring alarm

objects—instances of a class

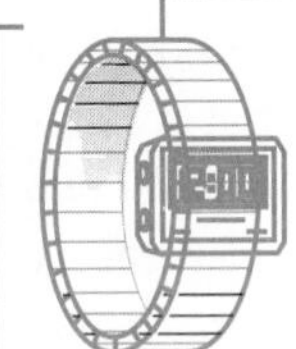
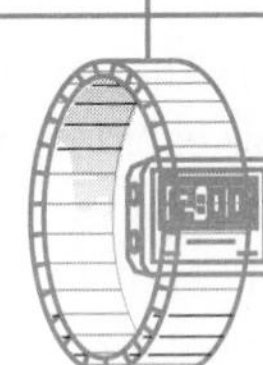
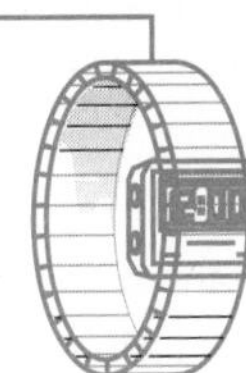

tip

Keep the OOP terms and definitions in mind as you proceed through the remaining sections in this lesson.

MINI-QUIZ

Mini-Quiz 1

1) OOP is an acronym for ______________.

2) A class is an object.
  a. True
  b. False

3) An object created from a class is called ______________.
  a. an attribute
  b. an instance of the class
  c. the base class
  d. the derived class

4) The operations (actions) that an object can perform are called its ______________.

tip

Although you can define and code a C++ class in just a matter of minutes, the objects produced by such a class probably will not be of much use. The creation of a good class—one whose objects can be used in a variety of ways by many different programs—requires a lot of time, patience, and planning.

Now that you are familiar with OOP terminology, you will learn how to define a class in C++.

Defining a Class in C++

Every object used in a program is created from a class. A `String` variable, for example, is an object created from the `String` class. A class defines the attributes and behaviors of the object it creates. The `String` class, for instance, defines the attributes and behaviors of a `String` object.

In addition to using the classes provided by the C++ language, you also can create your own classes. Like the C++ classes, your classes also must specify the attributes and behaviors of the objects they create.

In C++, you create a class using a **class definition**. All class definitions contain two sections: a declaration section and an implementation section. You learn first about the declaration section.

The Declaration Section of the Class Definition

The **declaration section** of the class definition contains the C++ **class** statement, which specifies the name of the class, as well as the attributes and behaviors included in the class. Figure 10-2 shows the syntax of the `class` statement and an example of using the statement to define a simple `Date` class. You can use the `Date` class to create a `Date` object in any program that requires a date—such as a payroll program, a personnel program, or an airline reservation program.

Figure 10-2: Syntax and an example of the C++ `class` statement

public and private keywords end with a colon

class statement ends with a semicolon

Syntax

```
__gc class className
{
public:
      public attributes (data members)
      public behaviors (member methods)
private:
      private attributes (data members)
      private behaviors (member methods)
};
```

Example

method prototypes

variables

```
//declaration section
__gc class Date
{
public:
      //initializes variables
      Date();
      //assigns program values to variables
      void AssignDate(int, int, int);
      //returns formatted date
      String *GetFormattedDate();
private:
      int month;
      int day;
      int year;
};
```

tip

Forgetting to delete an object is a common error made in C++ programs that don't use managed classes and the garbage collector.

The C++ `class` statement begins with the keywords `__gc class`, followed by the name of the class. The name of the class shown in Figure 10-2 is `Date`. Although it is not required by the C++ syntax, most C++ programmers capitalize the first letter in a class name to distinguish it from the name of a variable, which typically begins with a lowercase letter. You will use this naming convention for the classes you create in this book.

The keyword `__gc` (two underscore characters followed by the letters g and c) indicates that the class is a **managed class** whose objects are managed, or controlled, by the .NET Framework's garbage collector. As you may remember from Tutorial 3, the .NET Framework is Microsoft's newest computing platform, and it is the foundation for Visual Studio .NET. The **garbage collector** in .NET is responsible for releasing (freeing up) the memory used by objects that aren't needed any longer by the program. In previous versions of Visual C++, it was the programmer's responsibility to delete the object at the appropriate time, thereby releasing the memory consumed by the object.

As Figure 10-2 indicates, you enclose in braces the attributes and behaviors that define the class, and you end the `class` statement with a semicolon. The attributes, called **data members**, are represented by variables within the `class` statement, and the behaviors, called **member methods**, are represented by method prototypes. The `Date` class shown in Figure 10-2, for example, contains three variables named `month`, `day`, and `year`. Each variable is associated with an attribute of a `Date` object. The `Date` class also contains the prototypes for three methods: `Date()`, `AssignDate()`, and `GetFormattedDate()`. Each prototype represents a task that a `Date` object can perform. Here again, although it is not required by the C++ syntax, the convention is to capitalize the first letter in the method's name and the first letter of each subsequent word in the name. This helps to distinguish a method name from a function name, which typically begins with a lowercase letter.

As Figure 10-2 shows, the members of a class can be either public members or private members. You record the public members below the keyword `public` in the `class` statement, and you record the private members below the keyword `private`. In the `Date` class example shown in Figure 10-2, the method prototypes, which represent the object's behaviors, are listed below the keyword `public` in the `class` statement, while the statements that declare the variables are listed below the keyword `private`. Notice that each variable declaration statement specifies the variable's data type and name, but not its initial value; this is because you cannot initialize variables within the `class` statement. You can, however, use special methods, called constructors, to perform the initialization task when an object is created from the class. The method prototype `Date()`, which appears below the keyword `public` in the `class` statement, is the name of a constructor. You learn more about constructors later in this lesson.

When you use a class to create an object in a program, only the public members of the class are exposed (made available) to the program; the private members are hidden. In most classes, you expose the member methods and you hide the data members. In other words, you list the method prototypes below the keyword `public` in the `class` statement, and you list the variable declarations below the keyword `private`, as shown in Figure 10-2. You expose the member methods to allow the program to use the service each method provides. You hide the data members to protect their contents from being changed incorrectly by the program.

When a program needs to assign data to a private data member, it must use a public member method to do so. It is the public member method's responsibility to validate the data, and then either assign the data to the private data member (if the data is valid), or reject the data (if the data is not valid). Keep in mind that a program does not have direct access to the private members of a class. Rather, it must access the private members indirectly, through a public member method.

tip

As you learned in Tutorial 3, a method is similar to a function in that both are blocks of code that perform a task. The difference between a function and a method is that a method is part of a class, whereas a function is not.

tip

When determining an object's attributes, it is helpful to consider how you would describe the object. A date, for example, typically is described in terms of a month, day, and year. The month, day, and year items, therefore, are the attributes of a `Date` object, and need to be included in the `Date` class.

tip

The private members in a class can be directly accessed only by the member methods in the class.

MINI-QUIZ

Mini-Quiz 2

1) A program cannot access a public member method directly.
   a. True
   b. False

2) In C++, you enter the `class` statement in the ______________ section of a class definition.

3) The data members (attributes) are represented by ______________ in a class definition.
   a. constants
   b. member methods
   c. public data members
   d. variables

4) A private data member can be accessed directly by a public member method.
   a. True
   b. False

Next, you learn about the implementation section of the class definition.

The Implementation Section of the Class Definition

Each method listed in the declaration section must be defined in the **implementation section** of the class definition. The implementation section of the `Date` class definition is shown in Figure 10-3.

Figure 10-3: Implementation section shown in the `Date` class definition

declaration section

implementation section

```
//declaration section
__gc class Date
{
public:
	//initializes variables
	Date();
	//assigns program values to variables
	void AssignDate(int, int, int);
	//returns formatted date
	String *GetFormattedDate();
private:
	int month;
	int day;
	int year;
};

//implementation section
Date::Date()
{
	month = 0;
	day   = 0;
	year  = 0;
} //end of default constructor

void Date::AssignDate(int m, int d, int y)
{
	month = m;
	day = d;
	year = y;
}  //end of AssignDate method

String *Date::GetFormattedDate()
{
	String *separator = "/";
	return String::Concat(Convert::ToString(month), separator,
	Convert::ToString(day), separator, Convert::ToString(year));
}  //end of GetFormattedDate method
```

tip

As you do with functions, you list the data type of the formal parameters, separated by commas, within the parentheses following the method's name in the method prototype. You list both the data type and name of the formal parameters, separated by commas, within the parentheses following the method's name in the method header.

The implementation section shown in Figure 10-3 contains the definitions for three methods. Notice that each definition corresponds to a method prototype listed in the declaration section. The first definition recorded in the implementation section, as well as the first prototype listed in the declaration section, pertains to the default constructor.

The Default Constructor

A **constructor** is a member method whose instructions are processed, automatically, each time you use the class to create—or in OOP terms, **instantiate**—an object. The sole purpose of a constructor is to initialize the class's variables. Every class should have at least one constructor. Each constructor included in a class must have the same name as the class, but its formal parameters (if any) must be different from any other constructor in the class. A constructor that has no formal parameters is called the **default constructor**.

You list each constructor's prototype below the keyword `public` in the declaration section of the class definition; you define each constructor in the implementation section. Unlike other prototypes and definitions, a constructor's prototype and definition do not begin with a data type. Because the sole purpose of a constructor is to initialize the class's variables, a constructor never returns a value, so no data type—not even `void`—is included in the prototype or definition.

The `Date` class shown in Figure 10-3 has one constructor, `Date()`. Because the constructor has no formal parameters, it is the default constructor for the `Date` class. Notice that the default constructor's header contains the name of the class—`Date`—and the name of the constructor—`Date()`. As you learned in Tutorial 3, the two colons (`::`) that appear between the class name and method name are called the scope resolution operator and indicate that the method to the right of the operator is contained in the class whose name appears to the left of the operator. In this case, the scope resolution operator indicates that the `Date()` constructor belongs to the `Date` class.

Recall that a program does not have direct access to the private members of a class. Rather, it must access the private members through a public member method.

Public Member Methods

The public member methods in a class define the tasks that an object can perform. You already have learned about one public member method: a constructor. Recall that a constructor automatically initializes an object's private data members when the object is created in a program.

In addition to one or more constructors, most classes also contain public member methods that programs can use to assign new values to an object's private data members and also view the contents of the private data members. For example, a program can use the `Date` class's `AssignDate()` method to assign new values to a `Date` object's `month`, `day`, and `year` variables. A program can use the `Date` class's `GetFormattedDate()` method, on the other hand, to view the contents of a `Date` object's variables.

As Figure 10-3 indicates, the `AssignDate()` method is a void method, and the `GetFormattedDate()` method is a value-returning method. Notice that the `AssignDate()` method receives three `int` values from the program that calls it. The first value represents the month number, the second value the day number, and the third value the year number. The `AssignDate()` method assigns these values to the three variables listed in the `private` area of the class. Unlike the `AssignDate()` method, the `GetFormattedDate()` method does not receive any information from the program that calls it. The method simply returns the contents of the `month`, `day`, and `year` variables, separated by a slash (/).

Before learning how to use the `Date` class to create an object in a program, you learn about the `String::Concat()` method, which is used in the `Date` class's `GetFormattedDate()` method.

Using the String::Concat() Method

In C++, you use the **String::Concat() method** to connect (or link) together two or more strings, a process referred to as **concatenating**. The syntax of the `String::Concat()` method is **String::Concat(*list*)**, where *list* is a comma-separated list of strings. Figure 10-4 shows examples of using the `String::Concat()` method in a C++ statement.

Figure 10-4: Examples of using the `String::Concat()` method

Examples	Results

Example 1
`String *sentence = "How are you";`
`sentence = String::Concat(sentence, "?");`
	concatenates the contents of the `sentence` variable and a question mark, assigning the result (How are you?) to the `sentence` variable

Example 2
`String *first = "Jerome";`
`String *last = "Jacobs";`
`String *full = "";`
`full = String::Concat(first, " ", last);`
	concatenates the contents of the `first` variable, a space, and the contents of the `last` variable, assigning the result (Jerome Jacobs) to the `full` variable

Example 3
`String *city = "Chicago";`
`String *state = "Illinois";`
`Console::WriteLine(String::Concat`
`(city, ", ", state));`
	concatenates the contents of the `city` variable, a comma, a space, and the contents of the `state` variable, and then displays the result (Chicago, Illinois) on the screen

In Example 1 in Figure 10-4, the statement `sentence = String::Concat(sentence, "?");` concatenates the contents of the `sentence` variable (How are you) and a question mark (?). It assigns the concatenated string (How are you?) to the `sentence` variable.

In Example 2 in Figure 10-4, the statement `full = String::Concat(first, " ", last);` concatenates the contents of the `first` variable (Jerome), a space, and the contents of the `last` variable (Jacobs). It assigns the concatenated string (Jerome Jacobs) to the `full` variable.

In Example 3 in Figure 10-4, the statement `Console::WriteLine(String::Concat(city, ", ", state));` concatenates the contents of the `city` variable (Chicago), a comma and a space, and the contents of the `state` variable (Illinois). It displays the result (Chicago, Illinois) on the screen.

In the definition of the `GetFormattedDate()` method (shown earlier in Figure 10-3), the `String::Concat()` method is used to concatenate the month number, a slash, the day number, a slash, and the year number.

Next, you learn how to use a class to create an object in a program.

Using the Class in a Program

Once a class is defined, you then can create an instance of it—in other words, an object—in a program. You create an object using the syntax *className* **objectName* **= new** *className*;, where *className* is the name of the class, and *objectName* is the name of the object. For example, to create a `Date` object named `hireDate`, you use the statement `Date *hireDate = new Date;`.

You call (invoke) a public member method using the syntax *objectName*->*methodName*, where *objectName* is the name of the object, and *methodName* is the name of the method. For example, to call the `hireDate` object's `GetFormattedDate()` method, you use `hireDate->GetFormattedDate()`. As you learned in Tutorial 6, the -> operator is called the member access operator, and it allows you to access the members of a class. In this case, the member access operator allows you to access the `GetFormattedDate()` method, which is a member of the class used to create the `hireDate` object.

The hire date program shown in Figure 10-5 uses the `Date` class to create a `Date` object. The instruction that creates the `Date` object, as well as the instructions that call the public member methods, are shaded in the figure.

Figure 10-5: Hire date program

```
//displays a formatted hire date

#using <mscorlib.dll>
using namespace System;

//declaration section
__gc class Date
{
public:
      //initializes variables
      Date();
      //assigns program values to variables
      void AssignDate(int, int, int);
      //returns formatted date
      String *GetFormattedDate();
private:
      int month;
      int day;
      int year;
};

//implementation section
Date::Date()
{
      month = 0;
      day   = 0;
      year  = 0;
} //end of default constructor

void Date::AssignDate(int m, int d, int y)
{
      month = m;
      day = d;
      year = y;
}  //end of AssignDate method

String *Date::GetFormattedDate()
{
      String *separator = "/";
      return String::Concat(Convert::ToString(month), separator,
          Convert::ToString(day), separator, Convert::ToString
          (year));
}  //end of GetFormattedDate method
```

Figure 10-5: Hire date program (continued)

```
int main()
{
	//create object
	Date *hireDate = new Date;

	//declare variables
	int hireMonth = 0;
	int hireDay   = 0;
	int hireYear  = 0;

	//get month, day, and year
	Console::Write("Enter the month: ");
	hireMonth = Convert::ToInt32(Console::ReadLine());
	Console::Write("Enter the day: ");
	hireDay = Convert::ToInt32(Console::ReadLine());
	Console::Write("Enter the year: ");
	hireYear = Convert::ToInt32(Console::ReadLine());

	//set the date
	hireDate->AssignDate(hireMonth, hireDay, hireYear);
	//display the date
	Console::WriteLine(hireDate->GetFormattedDate());

	return 0;
} //end of main function
```

tip

Typically, the class definition code is entered in a header file rather than in the program itself. You learn how to enter a class definition in a header file in the Application lesson. In this lesson, you enter the class definition code in the program.

Study closely the `main()` function's code shown in Figure 10-5. When the hire date program is executed, the `Date *hireDate = new Date;` statement creates a `Date` object named `hireDate`. After the object is created, the default constructor is called, automatically, to initialize the private data members—in this case, the `month`, `day`, and `year` variables. The next three statements in the `main()` function create and initialize three `int` variables named `hireMonth`, `hireDay`, and `hireYear`. The user then is prompted to enter the month, day, and year that the employee was hired. The program assigns the user's responses to the `hireMonth`, `hireDay`, and `hireYear` variables.

Next, the program calls the `Date` class's `AssignDate()` method, passing it the hire date information. Recall that the `AssignDate()` method is a public member of the `Date` class. The `AssignDate()` method assigns the hire date information to the private data members of the Date class—the `month`, `day`, and `year` variables. The program then calls the `GetFormattedDate()` method to return the contents of the `month`, `day`, and `year` variables, separated by a slash (/). The program displays the returned information on the screen.

The last statement processed is the `return 0;` statement, which returns the number 0 to the operating system to indicate that the program ended normally.

MINI-QUIZ

Mini-Quiz 3

1) The scope resolution operator is ______________.
2) Write the default constructor's prototype for a class named `Item`.
3) Assume the `Item` class in Question 2 contains two private data members: a `char` variable named `code` and an `int` variable named `price`. Write the definition for the default constructor.
4) Which of the following C++ statements concatenates the opening parenthesis, the contents of the `areaCode` variable, and the closing parenthesis, and then assigns the result to the `fullAreaCode` variable?
   a. `fullAreaCode = Concat("(", areaCode, ")");`
   b. `fullAreaCode = Concat::String("(", areaCode, ")");`
   c. `fullAreaCode = StringConcat("(", areaCode, ")");`
   d. `fullAreaCode = String::Concat("(", areaCode, ")");`

You now have completed Tutorial 10's Concept lesson. You can either take a break or complete the end-of-lesson questions and exercises before moving on to the Application lesson.

SUMMARY

A class is a pattern for creating one or more instances of the class—in other words, one or more objects. A class encapsulates all of an object's attributes and behaviors. An object's attributes are the characteristics that describe the object, and its behaviors are the operations (actions) that the object can perform.

The OOP term "abstraction" refers to the hiding of an object's internal details from the user; this is done to prevent the user from making inadvertent changes to the object. The idea behind abstraction is to expose to the user only the attributes and behaviors that are necessary to use the object, and to hide everything else. In most classes, you expose an object's behaviors (member methods) and you hide its attributes (data members).

Polymorphism is the object-oriented feature that allows the same instruction to be carried out differently depending on the object.

You can use a constructor to initialize the data members in a class when an object is created. A class can have more than one constructor. Each constructor has the same name, but its formal parameters (if any) must be different from any other constructor. A constructor that has no formal parameters is called the default constructor. A constructor does not have a data type; this is because it cannot return a value.

In C++, you use the `String::Concat() method` to connect (or link) together two or more strings, a process referred to as concatenating.

You create an object using the syntax *className* ***objectName* **= new** *className*;, where *className* is the name of the class, and *objectName* is the name of the object. You call (invoke) a public member method using the syntax *objectName*->*methodName*, where *objectName* is the name of the object, and *methodName* is the name of the method.

ANSWERS TO MINI-QUIZZES

Mini-Quiz 1

1) object-oriented programming
2) b. False
3) b. an instance of the class
4) behaviors

Mini-Quiz 2

1) b. False
2) declaration
3) d. variables
4) a. True

Mini-Quiz 3

1) :: (two colons)
2) `Item();`
3)
```
Item::Item()
{
     code = ' ';
     price = 0;
}  //end of default constructor
```
4) d. `fullAreaCode = String::Concat("(", areaCode, ")");`

QUESTIONS

1) A blueprint for creating an object in C++ is called ______________.
   A. a class
   B. an instance
   C. a map
   D. a pattern
2) Which of the following statements is false?
   A. An example of an attribute is the `minutes` variable in a `Time` class.
   B. An example of a behavior is the `SetTime()` method in a `Time` class.
   C. An object created from a class is referred to as an instance of the class.
   D. A class is considered an object.
3) You hide a member of a class by recording the member below the ______________ keyword in the `class` statement.
   A. `confidential`
   B. `hidden`
   C. `private`
   D. `restricted`

4) You expose a member of a class by recording the member below the _______________ keyword in the `class` statement.

A. `common`

B. `exposed`

C. `public`

D. `unrestricted`

5) A program can access the private members of a class _______________.

A. directly

B. only through the public members of the class

C. only through other private members of the class

D. none of the above—the program cannot access the private members of a class in any way

6) In most classes, you expose the _______________ and hide the _______________.

A. attributes, data members

B. data members, member methods

C. member methods, data members

D. variables, member methods

7) The method definitions for a class are entered in the _______________ section in the class definition.

A. declaration

B. implementation

C. method

D. program-defined

8) Which of the following is the scope resolution operator?

A. :: (2 colons)

B. * (asterisk)

C. . (period)

D. -> (hyphen and a greater than symbol)

9) The name of the constructor method for a class named `Animal` is _______________.

A. `Animal()`

B. `AnimalConstructor()`

C. `ConstAnimal()`

D. any of the above could be used as the name of the constructor method

10) Which of the following statements is false?

A. You typically use a public member method to change the value stored in a private data member.

B. Because the constructor does not return a value, you place the keyword `void` before the constructor's name.

C. The public member methods in a class can be accessed by any program that uses an object created from the class.

D. An instance of a class is considered an object.

11) Which of the following creates an `Animal` object named `dog`?

A. `Animal *dog = new Animal;`

B. `Animal dog = new Animal();`

C. `Animal dog = Animal();`

D. `dog Animal();`

12) Which of the following indicates that the `DisplayBreed()` method is a member of the `Animal` class?

A. `Animal::DisplayBreed()`

B. `Animal.DisplayBreed()`

C. `DisplayBreed()::Animal`

D. `DisplayBreed&Animal()`

13) Assume a program creates an `Animal` object named `dog`. Which of the following calls the `DisplayBreed()` method, which is a public member method contained in the `Animal` class?

A. `Animal::DisplayBreed()`

B. `DisplayBreed()`

C. `dog::DisplayBreed()`

D. `dog->DisplayBreed()`

14) Assume that a program creates two `String` variables named `id` and `name`. The `id` variable is initialized to the string "123", and the `name` variable is initialized to the string "John Smith". Which of the following statements will display the string "John Smith's ID is 123" on the screen?

A. `Console::WriteLine(name, "'s ID is ", id);`

B. `Console::WriteLine(Concat(name, "'s ID is ", id));`

C. `Console::WriteLine(String::Concat("name's ID is id"));`

D. `Console::WriteLine(String::Concat(name, "'s ID is ", id));`

Look For These Symbols

Debugging

Discovery

EXERCISES

1) Write the class definition for a class named **Employee**. The class should include data members for an employee object's name and salary. (The salary may contain a decimal place.) The class should contain two member methods: the default constructor and a method that allows a program to assign values to the data members.

2) Add two member methods to the **Employee** class you created in Exercise 1. One member method should allow any program using an **Employee** object to view the contents of the salary data member. The other member method should allow the program to view the contents of the employee name data member. (*Hint*: Have the member method simply return the contents of the appropriate data member.)

3) Add another member method to the **Employee** class you modified in Exercise 2. The member method should calculate an Employee object's new salary, based on a raise percentage provided by the program using the object. Before making the calculation, the member method should verify that the raise percentage is greater than or equal to zero. If the raise percentage is less than zero, the member method should assign the number 0 as the new salary.

4) Write the C++ statement that will display (on the screen) the result of concatenating the string "My dog's name is " with the contents of a `String` variable named `petName`.

5) Write the C++ statement that will display (on the screen) the result of concatenating the string "She is " with the contents of an `int` variable named `age`.

6) In this exercise, you use the `Employee` class from Exercise 3 to create an object in a program.

A. If necessary, start Visual Studio .NET. Open the T10ConE06 Solution (T10ConE06 Solution.sln) file, which is contained in the CppNet\Tut10\T10ConE06 Solution folder.

B. Enter the class definition from Exercise 3.

C. The instructions to create an `Employee` object, assign values to the object, display the name and current salary, calculate the new salary, and display the new salary are missing from the program. Complete the program, using the comments as a guide.

D. Save and then build the solution.

E. Execute the program. Test the program by entering your name, a current salary amount of 54000, and a raise rate of .1. The program should display your name, the number 54000, and the number 59400. Close the Command Prompt window.

F. Modify the program so that it display the salary amounts with a dollar sign and zero decimal places. When displaying the salary amounts, concatenate the message "Current salary: " with the current salary amount, and concatenate the message "New salary: " with the new salary amount.

G. Save and then build the solution.

H. Execute the program. Test the program by entering your name, a current salary amount of 54000, and a raise rate of .1. The program should display your name, the message "Current salary: $54,000", and the message "New salary: $59,400". Close the Command Prompt window.

I. When the program is working correctly, close the Output window, and then use the File menu to close the solution.

7) In this exercise, you modify the `GetFormattedDate()` member method contained in this lesson's `Date` class. The modified method will return the formatted date separated by either slashes (/) or dashes (-).

A. If necessary, start Visual Studio .NET. Open the T10ConE07 Solution (T10ConE07 Solution.sln) file, which is contained in the CppNet\Tut10\T10ConE07 Solution folder.

B. The `GetFormattedDate()` method should receive a string that indicates whether the program wants slashes (/) or dashes (-) in the date. Modify the `GetFormattedDate()` method's code accordingly.

C. Save and then build the solution.

D. Execute the program. Test the program by entering 12 as the month, 5 as the day, 2005 as the year, and a – (dash) as the separator. The formatted date, 12-5-2005, should appear in the Command Prompt window. Close the Command Prompt window.

E. Execute the program again. This time, enter 9 as the month, 30 as the day, 2004 as the year, and a / (slash) as the separator. The formatted date, 9/30/2004, should appear in the Command Prompt window. Close the Command Prompt window.

F. When the program is working correctly, close the Output window, and then use the File menu to close the solution.

8) In this exercise, you modify the `Date` class created in this lesson. The modified class will allow the program to view the contents of the private data members, individually.

A. If necessary, start Visual Studio .NET. Open the T10ConE08 Solution (T10ConE08 Solution.sln) file, which is contained in the CppNet\Tut10\T10ConE08 Solution folder.

B. Add three member methods to the class. Each method should allow a program to view the contents of one of the three private data members.

C. Complete the three statements that display the month, day, and year, using the member methods you created in Step B.

D. Save and then build the solution.

E. Execute the program. Test the program by entering 3 as the month, 7 as the day, and 2005 as the year. The formatted date, month, day, and year should appear on separate lines in the Command Prompt window. Close the Command Prompt window.

F. When the program is working correctly, close the Output window, and then use the File menu to close the solution.

9) In this exercise, you modify the `Date` class created in this lesson. The modified class will validate the month and day values entered by the user.

A. If necessary, start Visual Studio .NET. Open the T10ConE09 Solution (T10ConE09 Solution.sln) file, which is contained in the CppNet\Tut10\T10ConE09 Solution folder.

B. Modify the `AssignDate()` method so that it validates the month and day values passed by the program. Valid month values are the numbers 1 through 12. If the month is 1, then only the numbers 1 through 31 are valid day values. However, if the month is 6, then valid day values are the numbers 1 through 30. If the month is 2, then valid day values are the numbers 1 through 29 if the year is a leap year; otherwise, the valid day values are the numbers 1 through 28.

C. Enter the instruction to display the date, but only if the month and day values are valid. If the month and day values are not valid, display an error message.

D. Save and then build the solution.

E. Execute the program. Test the program by entering 6 as the month, 4 as the day, and 2004 as the year. The date 6/4/2004 should appear in the Command Prompt window. Close the Command Prompt window.

F. Execute the program again. This time enter 6 as the month, 31 as the day, and 2005 as the year. An error message should appear in the Command Prompt window. Close the Command Prompt window.

G. Execute the program again. This time enter 2 as the month, 29 as the day, and 2000 as the year. The date 2/29/2000 should appear in the Command Prompt window. Close the Command Prompt window.

H. Execute the program again. This time enter 2 as the month, 29 as the day, and 2001 as the year. An error message should appear in the Command Prompt window. Close the Command Prompt window.

I. When the program is working correctly, close the Output window, and then use the File menu to close the solution.

10) In this exercise, you modify the `Date` class created in this lesson. The modified class will display the leading zero (if necessary) in the month and day entries.

A. If necessary, start Visual Studio .NET. Open the T10ConE10 Solution (T10ConE10 Solution.sln) file, which is contained in the CppNet\Tut10\T10ConE10 Solution folder.

B. Build the solution, then execute the program. Enter 02 as the month, 06 as the day, and 2004 as the year. Notice that 2/6/2004, rather than 02/06/2004, appears in the Command Prompt window. Close the Command Prompt window.

C. Modify the code so that it displays the leading zero (assuming the user entered the leading zero) in the month and day entries. (*Hint*: Although an `int` variable truncates the leading zero from a number, a `String` variable does not.)

D. Save and then build the solution.

E. Execute the program. Test the program by entering 02 as the month, 06 as the day, and 2004 as the year. The date 02/06/2004 should appear in the Command Prompt window. Close the Command Prompt window.

F. When the program is working correctly, close the Output window, and then use the File menu to close the solution.

11) Correct the errors in the `Item` class shown in Figure 10-6.

Figure 10-6

```
__gc class Item
{
private:
     item();
     void AssignItem(String *, double);
public:
     String *name;
     double price;
}

Item()
{
     name = "";
     price = 0.0;
}  //end of default constructor

void AssignItem(String *n, double p)
{
     name = n;
     price = p;
}  //end of AssignItem method
```

Application Lesson

Using Classes and Objects in a C++ Program

CASE The owners of two small businesses want you to create programs for them. Sharon Terney of Terney Landscaping wants a program that the salespeople can use to estimate the cost of laying sod. Jack Sysmanski, the owner of All-Around Fence Company, wants a program that he can use to calculate the cost of installing a fence. Your task in this lesson is to create these programs.

Analyzing the Problems

While analyzing the Terney Landscaping and All-Around Fence Company problems, you notice that each involves a rectangular shape. For example, in the Terney Landscaping program, you need to find the area of a rectangle on which the sod is to be laid. In the All-Around Fence Company program, on the other hand, you need to find the perimeter of the rectangle around which a fence is to be constructed. To save time, you decide to create a **Rectangle** class that contains the attributes and behaviors of a rectangle. You will use the **Rectangle** class to create a **Rectangle** object in the Terney Landscaping and All-Around Fence Company programs. (You complete the Terney Landscaping program in this lesson. You complete the All-Around Fence Company program in this lesson's Exercise 1.)

Creating the `Rectangle` Class

Before you can create a **Rectangle** object in a program, you first must create a class that specifies a **Rectangle** object's attributes and behaviors. When determining an object's attributes, it is helpful to consider how you would describe the object. Rectangles, for example, typically are described in terms of two dimensions: length and width. The length and width dimensions are the attributes of a **Rectangle** object. You will include both attributes as private data members in the **Rectangle** class, using the **double** variables **length** and **width**.

tip
Recall that a class is a pattern or blueprint for creating an object.

Next, you determine the object's behaviors, which are the tasks that the object can perform. To be useful in both the Terney Landscaping and All-Around Fence Company programs, a **Rectangle** object must be capable of performing the four tasks shown in Figure 10-7.

Figure 10-7: Tasks a `Rectangle` object should be capable of performing

Tasks
1. initialize private data members (default constructor) 2. assign values to the private data members 3. calculate and return the area of the object 4. calculate and return the perimeter of the object

As Figure 10-7 indicates, a **Rectangle** object will need to initialize its private data members; you will include a default constructor in the class for this purpose. A **Rectangle** object also will need to provide a means for the program to assign values to the private data members; this task will be handled by a void member method named **SetDimensions()**.

You will use two value-returning member methods named **CalcArea()** and **CalcPerimeter()** to perform the third and fourth tasks listed in Figure 10-7, which are to calculate and return the area and perimeter of a **Rectangle** object. Figure 10-8 shows the completed declaration section for the **Rectangle** class.

Figure 10-8: Declaration section of the Rectangle class

store the length and width values passed by the program

```
//declaration section
__gc class Rectangle
{
public:
     Rectangle();
     void SetDimensions(double, double);
     double CalcArea();
     double CalcPerimeter();
private:
     double length;
     double width;
};
```

Now that the declaration section of the class is complete, you can move on to the implementation section, which contains the definitions for the member methods.

Completing the Implementation Section of the Rectangle Class

First you will code the **Rectangle** object's default constructor. As you learned in the Concept lesson, the default constructor initializes the data members (variables) in the class. In this case, the data members are **double** variables, so you will initialize each to 0.0, as shown in Figure 10-9.

Figure 10-9: Constructor code shown in the implementation section

```
//implementation section
Rectangle::Rectangle()
{
     length = 0.0;
     width  = 0.0;
}  //end of default constructor
```

Listed second in the declaration section is the prototype for the **SetDimensions()** method. This method will need to receive the length and width values from the program, and then assign those values to the private members of the class. However, the values should be assigned only if both values are greater than zero. Figure 10-10 shows the appropriate code.

Figure 10-10: `SetDimensions()` code included in the implementation section

assign to private data members only if both values are greater than zero

```
//implementation section
Rectangle::Rectangle()
{
     length = 0.0;
     width  = 0.0;
}  //end of default constructor

void Rectangle::SetDimensions(double len, double wid)
{
     //assigns length and width to private data members
     if (len > 0 && wid > 0)
     {
          length = len;
          width = wid;
     }  //end if
}  //end of SetDimensions method
```

The last two prototypes listed in the declaration section are for the `CalcArea()` and `CalcPerimeter()` methods. The `CalcArea()` method will calculate the area by multiplying the contents of the private `length` variable by the contents of the private `width` variable; it then will return the result. The `CalcPerimeter()` method will calculate the perimeter by adding together the contents of the private `length` and `width` variables, and then multiplying the sum by 2; it then will return the result. Figure 10-11 shows both methods in the completed class definition.

Figure 10-11: Completed class definition for the `Rectangle` class

```
//declaration section
__gc class Rectangle
{
public:
     Rectangle();
     void SetDimensions(double, double);
     double CalcArea();
     double CalcPerimeter();
private:
     double length;
     double width;
};

//implementation section
Rectangle::Rectangle()
{
     length = 0.0;
     width  = 0.0;
}  //end of default constructor
```

Figure 10-11: Completed class definition for the Rectangle class (continued)

```
void Rectangle::SetDimensions(double len, double wid)
{
      //assigns length and width to private data members
      if (len > 0 && wid > 0)
      {
            length = len;
            width = wid;
      }  //end if
}  //end of SetDimensions method

double Rectangle::CalcArea()
{
      return length * width;
}  //end of CalcArea method

double Rectangle::CalcPerimeter()
{
      return (length + width) * 2;
}  //end of CalcPerimeter method
```

You typically enter the code for the class definition in a special file, called a **header file**, rather than in the program itself (as you did in the Concept lesson).

To enter the Rectangle class definition in a header file:

1. If necessary, start Visual Studio .NET. Click **File** on the menu bar, point to **New**, and then click **File**. The New File dialog box opens.
2. If necessary, click **Visual C++** in the Categories list box. Click **Header File (.h)** in the Templates list box. See Figure 10-12.

Figure 10-12: New File dialog box

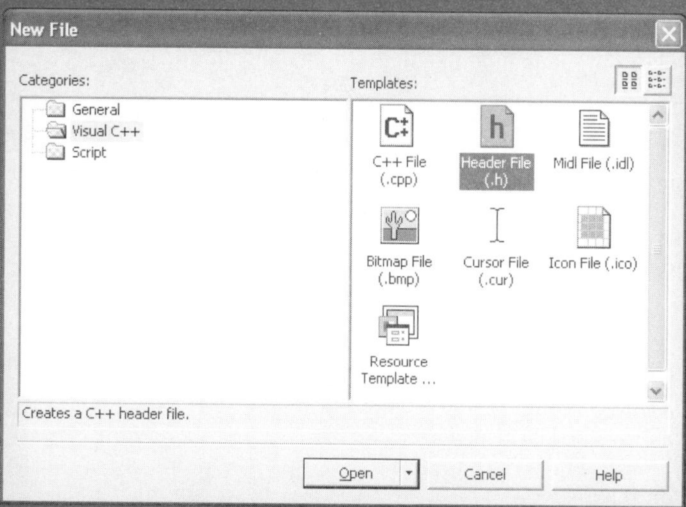

3. Click the Open button. An empty header file appears in the Header1 window.

Before entering any text in the header file, you will save the file, using the name T10App.

4. Click **File** on the menu bar, and then click **Save Header1 As**. The Save File As dialog box opens.

   Typically, header files are saved in a separate folder, because they usually are used in more than one solution. You will save the header files that you create in the MyClasses folder on your computer's hard disk.

5. Locate and then open the **MyClasses** folder, which is contained in the CppNet folder on your computer's hard disk. Type **T10App** in the File name text box, then click the **Save** button. The window tab indicates that the file's name is T10App.h. (The ".h" stands for "header".)

   First enter the declaration section of the `Rectangle` class.

6. Enter the instructions shown in Figure 10-13, then position the insertion point as shown in the figure.

Figure 10-13: Declaration section entered in the T10App.h header file

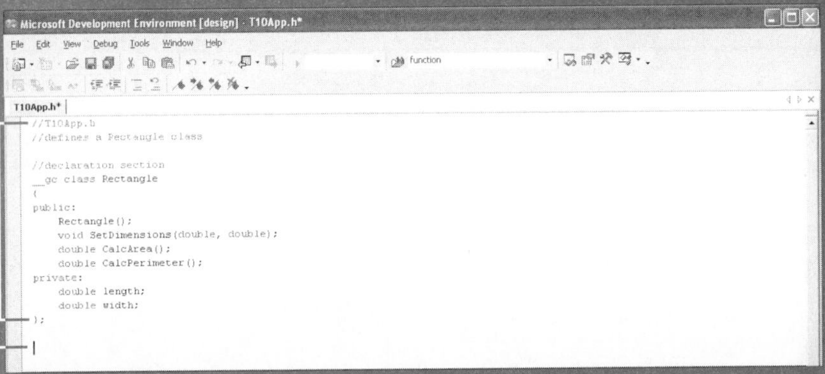

enter these instructions

position the insertion point here

```
//T10App.h
//defines a Rectangle class

//declaration section
__gc class Rectangle
{
public:
    Rectangle();
    void SetDimensions(double, double);
    double CalcArea();
    double CalcPerimeter();
private:
    double length;
    double width;
};
|
```

Next, enter the implementation section of the `Rectangle` class.

7. Enter the instructions shaded in Figure 10-14, which shows the completed `Rectangle` class definition.

Figure 10-14: Completed class definition entered in the T10App.h header file

```
//T10App.h
//defines a Rectangle class

//declaration section
__gc class Rectangle
{
public:
     Rectangle();
     void SetDimensions(double, double);
     double CalcArea();
     double CalcPerimeter();
private:
     double length;
     double width;
};
```

Figure 10-14: Completed class definition entered in the T10App.h header file (continued)

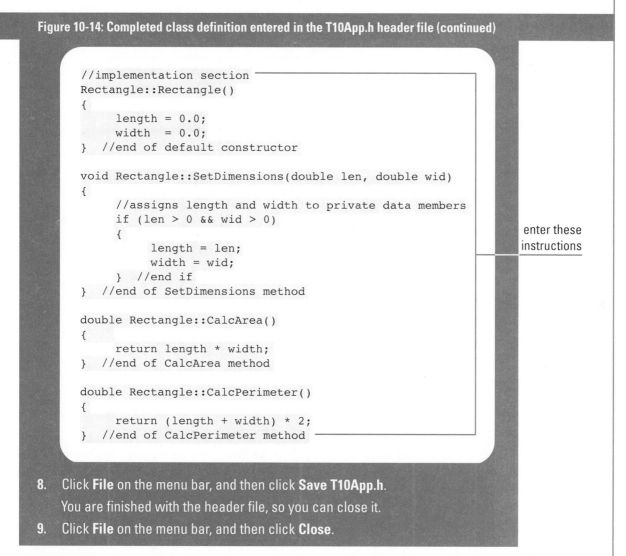

```
//implementation section
Rectangle::Rectangle()
{
     length = 0.0;
     width  = 0.0;
}  //end of default constructor

void Rectangle::SetDimensions(double len, double wid)
{
     //assigns length and width to private data members
     if (len > 0 && wid > 0)
     {
          length = len;
          width = wid;
     }  //end if
}  //end of SetDimensions method

double Rectangle::CalcArea()
{
     return length * width;
}  //end of CalcArea method

double Rectangle::CalcPerimeter()
{
     return (length + width) * 2;
}  //end of CalcPerimeter method
```

enter these instructions

8. Click **File** on the menu bar, and then click **Save T10App.h**.

   You are finished with the header file, so you can close it.

9. Click **File** on the menu bar, and then click **Close**.

Now that you have defined the `Rectangle` class, you can begin creating the Terney Landscaping program, which will use the class to create a `Rectangle` object.

Creating the Terney Landscaping Program

Figure 10-15 shows the IPO chart for the Terney Landscaping program.

Figure 10-15: IPO chart for the Terney Landscaping program

Input	Processing	Output
length in feet width in feet sod price per square yard	Processing items: Rectangle object Algorithm: 1. enter length in feet, width in feet, and sod price per square yard 2. use the Rectangle object's SetDimensions() method to assign the length and width to the Rectangle object 3. use the Rectangle object's CalcArea() method to calculate the area in square feet, then divide the result by 9 to get the area in square yards 4. calculate the total price by multiplying the area in square yards by the sod price per square yard 5. display the area in square yards and the total price	area in square yards total price

The IPO chart shows that the output is the area (in square yards) and the total price. The input is the length and width of the rectangle (both in feet), and the price of a square yard of sod. Notice that a `Rectangle` object is used as a processing item in the program.

As the algorithm shown in Figure 10-15 indicates, the program first gets the length, width, and price information from the user. The program passes the length and width information to the `Rectangle` object's `SetDimensions()` method, which assigns the values (assuming that both are greater than zero) to the `Rectangle` object's private data members.

Step 3 in the algorithm is to calculate the area of the `Rectangle` object in square yards. To do so, the program first calls the `Rectangle` object's `CalcArea()` method to calculate the area in square feet. It then converts the value returned by the `CalcArea()` method from square feet to square yards by dividing the return value by the number 9, which is the number of square feet in a square yard.

Step 4 in the algorithm is to calculate the total price by multiplying the number of square yards by the price per square yard of sod. The last step in the algorithm is to display the area (in square yards) and the total price on the screen. Notice that, although the `Rectangle` object also is capable of calculating its perimeter, the current program does not require the object to perform that task.

tip

You will use the `calcPerimeter()` method in Exercise 1 at the end of this lesson.

Your computer's hard disk contains a partially completed program for Terney Landscaping. You open the program in the next set of steps.

To open the Terney Landscaping program, and then add the header file to the solution:

1. Start Microsoft Visual Studio .NET. If necessary, close the Start Page window.

2. Click **File** on the menu bar, and then click **Open Solution**. The Open Solution dialog box opens.
3. Locate and then open the **CppNet\Tut10\T10App Solution** folder.
4. Click **T10App Solution** (T10App Solution.sln) in the list of filenames, and then click the **Open** button.
5. If the T10App.cpp source file is not displayed, right-click **T10App.cpp** in the Solution Explorer window, and then click **Open**.

   Now add the T10App.h header file to the solution.
6. Click **File** on the menu bar, and then click **Add Existing Item**. The Add Existing Item – T10App Project dialog box opens.
7. Open the CppNet\MyClasses folder, then click **T10App.h** in the list of filenames. Click the **Open** button. The T10App.h header file is added to the current solution. You can verify that fact by displaying the Solution Explorer window, and then opening the Header Files folder.
8. Save the solution.

Recall that the `Rectangle` class is defined in a header file rather than in a program file. For a program to use a class defined in a header file, the program must contain a `#include` directive whose syntax is **#include** *headerFilename*. The `#include` directive tells the C++ compiler to include the contents of another file—in this case, a header file—in the current program. The `#include` directive provides a convenient way to merge the source code from one file with the source code in another file, without having to retype the code.

To complete the Terney Landscaping program:

1. Position the insertion point below the `//include the header file that contains the Rectangle class definition` comment. Type **#include "c:\cppnet\myclasses\t10app.h"** and press **Enter**. (If necessary, change the `#include` directive to reflect the location of the T10App.h header file on your system.)

   Next, enter the instruction to create a `Rectangle` object named `lawnObj`.
2. Position the insertion point below the `//declare Rectangle object` comment. Press **Tab**, if necessary, to indent the line, then type **Rectangle *lawnObj = new Rectangle;** and press **Enter**.

   Now enter the instruction to assign the length and width measurements to the Rectangle object you created in Step 2.
3. Position the insertion point below the `//assign data` comment. Press **Tab**, if necessary, to indent the line, then type **lawnObj->SetDimensions (lawnLength, lawnWidth);** and press **Enter**.

   Finally, enter the instruction to calculate the area in square yards.
4. Position the insertion point below the `//calculate the area in square yards` comment. Press **Tab**, if necessary, to indent the line, then type **lawnArea = lawnObj->CalcArea() / 9;** and press **Enter**. Figure 10-16 shows the completed Terney Landscaping program. The instructions you entered are shaded in the figure.

Figure 10-16: Completed Terney Landscaping program

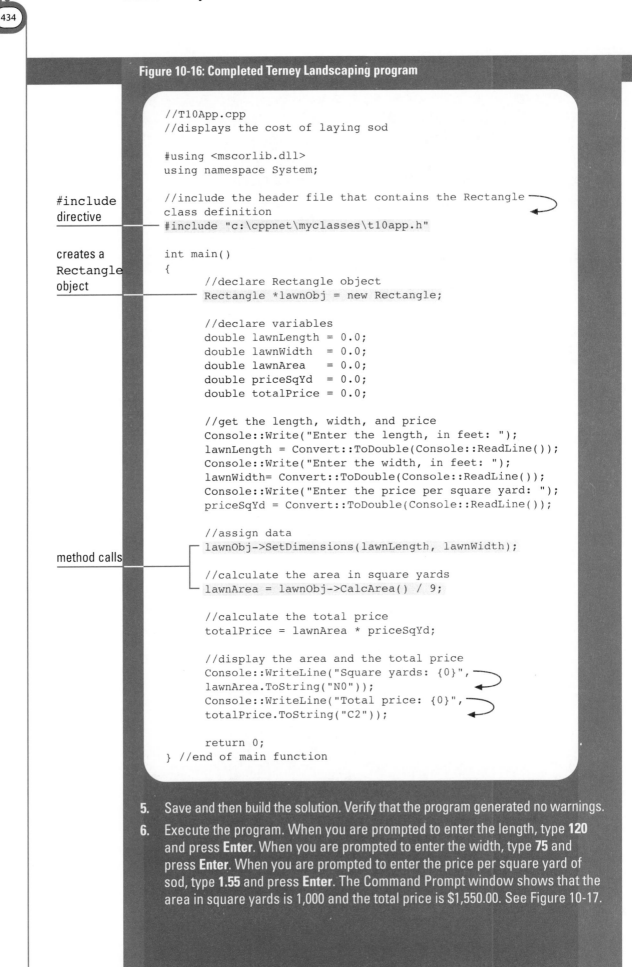

#include directive

creates a Rectangle object

method calls

```
//T10App.cpp
//displays the cost of laying sod

#using <mscorlib.dll>
using namespace System;

//include the header file that contains the Rectangle
class definition
#include "c:\cppnet\myclasses\t10app.h"

int main()
{
      //declare Rectangle object
      Rectangle *lawnObj = new Rectangle;

      //declare variables
      double lawnLength = 0.0;
      double lawnWidth  = 0.0;
      double lawnArea   = 0.0;
      double priceSqYd  = 0.0;
      double totalPrice = 0.0;

      //get the length, width, and price
      Console::Write("Enter the length, in feet: ");
      lawnLength = Convert::ToDouble(Console::ReadLine());
      Console::Write("Enter the width, in feet: ");
      lawnWidth= Convert::ToDouble(Console::ReadLine());
      Console::Write("Enter the price per square yard: ");
      priceSqYd = Convert::ToDouble(Console::ReadLine());

      //assign data
      lawnObj->SetDimensions(lawnLength, lawnWidth);

      //calculate the area in square yards
      lawnArea = lawnObj->CalcArea() / 9;

      //calculate the total price
      totalPrice = lawnArea * priceSqYd;

      //display the area and the total price
      Console::WriteLine("Square yards: {0}",
      lawnArea.ToString("N0"));
      Console::WriteLine("Total price: {0}",
      totalPrice.ToString("C2"));

      return 0;
} //end of main function
```

5. Save and then build the solution. Verify that the program generated no warnings.
6. Execute the program. When you are prompted to enter the length, type **120** and press **Enter**. When you are prompted to enter the width, type **75** and press **Enter**. When you are prompted to enter the price per square yard of sod, type **1.55** and press **Enter**. The Command Prompt window shows that the area in square yards is 1,000 and the total price is $1,550.00. See Figure 10-17.

Figure 10-17: Result of processing the Terney Landscaping program

"c:\cppnet\tut10\t10app solution\t10app project\debug\T10App Project.exe"
Enter the length, in feet: 120
Enter the width, in feet: 75
Enter the price per square yard: 1.55
Square yards: 1,000
Total price: $1,550.00
Press any key to continue_

7. Close the Command Prompt window, then close the Output window.
8. Click **File** on the menu bar, and then click **Close Solution** to close the current solution.
9. Click **File** on the menu bar, and then click **Exit** to exit Visual Studio .NET.

You now have completed Tutorial 10's Application lesson. You can either take a break or complete the end-of-lesson exercises.

EXERCISES

Look For These Symbols

Debugging

Discovery

1) In this exercise, you use the `Rectangle` class that you created in the lesson to declare a `Rectangle` object in the All-Around Fence program. (Recall that the `Rectangle` class is defined in the CppNet\MyClasses\T10App.h file on your computer's hard disk.)

A. If necessary, start Visual Studio .NET. Open the T10AppE01 Solution (T10AppE01 Solution.sln) file, which is contained in the CppNet\Tut10\T10AppE01 Solution folder.

B. Add the T10App.h header file to the solution.

C. Enter the appropriate `#include` directive to include the contents of the T10App.h header file in the program.

D. Jack Sysmanski, the owner of All-Around Fence Company, wants a program that he can use to calculate the cost of installing a fence. Use the IPO chart shown in Figure 10-18 (on the next page) to complete the program. Display the perimeter as an integer. Display the total price with a dollar sign and two decimal places.

E. Save and then build the solution.

F. Execute the program. Test the program using 120 as the length, 75 as the width, and 10 as the cost per linear foot. The program should display 390 as the perimeter and $3,900.00 as the total price.

G. When the program is working correctly, close the Output window, and then use the File menu to close the solution.

Figure 10-18

Input	Processing	Output
length in feet width in feet fence cost per linear foot	Processing items: Rectangle object Algorithm: 1. enter length in feet, width in feet, and fence cost per linear foot 2. use the Rectangle object's SetDimensions() method to assign the length and width to the Rectangle object 3. use the Rectangle object's CalcPerimeter() method to calculate the perimeter 4. calculate the total price by multiplying the perimeter by the fence cost per linear foot 5. display the perimeter and total price	perimeter total price

2) In this exercise, you modify the `Rectangle` class that you created in the lesson so that it allows a program to view the contents of the `length` and `width` data members. You also modify the Terney Landscaping program that you created in the lesson so that it displays the length and width measurements.

A. If necessary, start Visual Studio .NET. Click File on the menu bar, point to Open, and then click File. Open the T10AppE02.h header file, which is contained in the CppNet\MyClasses folder.

B. Add two value-returning methods to the class. Each method should return the value of one of the attributes.

C. Save and then close the header file.

D. Open the T10AppE02 Solution (T10AppE02 Solution.sln) file, which is contained in the CppNet\Tut10\T10AppE02 Solution folder.

E. Add the T10AppE02.h header file to the solution.

F. Enter the appropriate `#include` directive to include the contents of the T10AppE02.h header file in the program.

G. Modify the program so that it displays the length and width of the rectangle, in addition to the area and total price. (Use the methods you created in Step B.)

H. Save and then build the solution.

I. Execute the program. Test the program using 120 feet as the length, 75 feet as the width, and 1.55 as the price. The program should display 120 as the length; 75 as the width; 1,000 as the area in square yards; and $1,550.00 as the total price.

J. When the program is working correctly, close the Output window, and then use the File menu to close the solution.

3) In this exercise, you modify the `Rectangle` class that you created in the lesson so that its `SetDimensions()` method returns a value. You also modify the Terney Landscaping program that you created in the lesson.

A. If necessary, start Visual Studio .NET. Click File on the menu bar, point to Open, and then click File. Open the T10AppE03.h header file, which is contained in the CppNet\MyClasses folder.

B. Modify the `SetDimensions()` method so that it returns a value that indicates whether the length and width dimensions passed to the method are greater than zero.

C. Save and then close the header file.

D. Open the T10AppE03 Solution (T10AppE03 Solution.sln) file, which is contained in the CppNet\Tut10\T10AppE03 Solution folder.

E. Add the T10AppE03.h header file to the solution.

F. Enter the appropriate `#include` directive to include the contents of the T10AppE03.h header file in the program.

G. If the `SetDimensions()` method indicates that the length and width dimensions are greater than zero, the program should calculate and display both the area and the total price; otherwise, it should display an error message. Modify the program appropriately.

H. Save and then build the solution.

I. Execute the program. Test the program using 120 feet as the length, 75 feet as the width, and 1.55 as the price. The program should display 1,000 as the area in square yards, and $1,550.00 as the total price. Close the Command Prompt window.

J. Execute the program again. Enter -5 as the length, 6 as the width, and 3 as the price. The program should display an error message, because the length dimension is less than zero. Close the Command Prompt window.

K. When the program is working correctly, close the Output window, and then use the File menu to close the solution.

4) In this exercise, you create a `Triangle` class. You also complete a program that uses the `Triangle` class to create a `Triangle` object.

A. If necessary, start Visual Studio .NET. Click File on the menu bar, point to Open, and then click File. Open the T10AppE04.h header file, which is contained in the CppNet\MyClasses folder.

B. Create a `Triangle` class. The class should include a void method that allows the program to set the triangle's dimensions. The method should verify that all of the dimensions are greater than zero before assigning the values to the private data members. The class also should include two value-returning methods. One value-returning method should calculate the area of a triangle, and the other should calculate the perimeter of a triangle. (*Hint*: The formula for calculating the area of a triangle is 1/2 * b * h, where b is the base and h is the height. The formula for calculating the perimeter of a triangle is a + b + c, where a, b, and c are the lengths of the sides.) Determine the appropriate variables to include in the class. Be sure to include a default constructor that initializes the variables.

C. Save and then close the header file.

D. Open the T10AppE04 Solution (T10AppE04 Solution.sln) file, which is contained in the CppNet\Tut10\T10AppE04 Solution folder.

E. Add the T10AppE04.h header file to the solution.

F. Enter the appropriate `#include` directive to include the contents of the T10AppE04.h header file in the program.

G. Declare a `Triangle` object. Prompt the user for the triangle's dimensions, then display the triangle's area and perimeter amounts. Display the amounts with zero decimal places.

H. Save and then build the solution.

I. Execute the program. Test the program by entering 10 as the base, 7 as the height, and 7, 10, and 7 as the three side lengths. The program should display 35 as the area and 24 as the perimeter.

J. When the program is working correctly, close the Output window, and then use the File menu to close the solution.

5) In this exercise, you modify an existing header file.

A. If necessary, start Visual Studio .NET. Click File on the menu bar, point to Open, and then click File. Open the T10AppE05.h header file, which is contained in the CppNet\MyClasses folder. The header file defines a class named `Date`. Study the code, then close the header file.

B. Open the T10AppE05 Solution (T10AppE05 Solution.sln) file, which is contained in the CppNet\Tut10\T10AppE05 Solution folder.

C. Add the T10AppE05.h header file to the solution.

D. Enter the appropriate `#include` directive to include the contents of the T10AppE05.h header file in the program.

The program uses the `Date` class to create an object named `today`. Study the code. Notice that the program prompts the user to enter the month, day, and year. It then uses the `Date` class's public methods—`SetDate()` and `DisplayDate()`—to set and display the date entered by the user. The program also uses a public method named `UpdateDate()` to increase the day by 1. It then displays the new date on the screen.

E. Save and then build the solution.

F. Execute the program. Enter 3 as the month, 15 as the day, and 2005 as the year. The Command Prompt window shows that today is 3/15/2005 and tomorrow is 3/16/2005, which is correct. Close the Command Prompt window.

G. Execute the program again. Enter 3 as the month, 31 as the day, and 2004 as the year. The Command Prompt window shows that today is 3/31/2004 and tomorrow is 3/32/2004, which is incorrect. Close the Command Prompt window.

H. Open the Solution Explorer window, then open the Header Files folder. Right-click T10AppE05.h, then click Open. Modify the `UpdateDate()` method so that it updates the date correctly. For example, if today is 3/31/2005, then tomorrow is 4/1/2005. If today is 12/31/2005, then tomorrow is 1/1/2006. You do not have to worry about leap years; treat February as though it always has 28 days.

I. Save and then close the header file.

J. Build the solution, then execute the program. Test the program four times, using the following dates: 3/15/2004, 4/30/2005, 2/28/2004, and 12/31/2005. The Command Prompt window should show that tomorrow's dates are 3/16/2004, 5/1/2005, 3/1/2004, and 1/1/2006.

K. When the program is working correctly, close the Output window, and then use the File menu to close the solution.

6) In this exercise, you modify the Terney Landscaping program that you created in the lesson so that it passes an object to a method.

A. If necessary, start Visual Studio .NET. Open the T10AppE06 Solution (T10AppE06 Solution.sln) file, which is contained in the CppNet\Tut10\T10AppE06 Solution folder.

B. Add the T10AppE06.h header file to the solution.

C. Enter the appropriate `#include` directive to include the contents of the T10AppE06.h header file in the program.

D. Modify the program so that it uses a function named `calcAndDisplay()` to calculate and display the area and the total price. Pass the `Rectangle` object and the price per square yard to the function.

E. Save and then build the solution.

F. Execute the program. Test the program using 120 feet as the length, 75 feet as the width, and 1.55 as the price. The program should display 1,000 as the area in square yards, and $1,550.00 as the total price. Close the Command Prompt window.

G. When the program is working correctly, close the Output window, and then use the File menu to close the solution.

7) In this exercise, you learn how to overload a method.

A. If necessary, start Visual Studio .NET. Click File on the menu bar, point to Open, and then click File. Open the T10AppE07.h header file, which is contained in the CppNet\MyClasses folder.

Pool-Time, which sells in-ground pools, wants a program that its salespeople can use to determine the number of gallons of water required to fill an in-ground pool—a question commonly asked by customers. To calculate the number of gallons, you need to find the volume of the pool. The volume formula is length * width * depth.

B. Modify the `Rectangle` class appropriately. (*Hint*: You will need to include an additional private data member and an additional public method. You also will need to modify the default constructor and the `SetDimensions()` method. Be sure to verify that the depth value is greater than zero before assigning the value to the private data member.)

C. Save and then close the header file.

D. Open the T10AppE07A Solution (T10AppE07A Solution.sln) file, which is contained in the CppNet\Tut10\T10AppE07A Solution folder.

E. Add the T10AppE07.h header file to the solution.

F. Enter the appropriate `#include` directive to include the contents of the T10AppE07.h header file in the program.

G. Complete the program, using the IPO chart shown in Figure 10-19. Display the volume and number of gallons amounts with two decimal places.

Figure 10-19

Input	Processing	Output
length in feet width in feet depth in feet	Processing items: Rectangle object Algorithm: 1. enter length in feet, width in feet, and depth in feet 2. use the Rectangle object's SetDimensions() method to assign the length, width, and depth to the Rectangle object 3. use the Rectangle object's CalcVolume() method to calculate the volume in cubic feet 4. calculate the number of gallons of water by dividing the volume by .13368 5. display the volume in cubic feet and the number of gallons of water	volume in cubic feet number of gallons of water

H. Save and then build the solution.

I. Execute the program. Use 25 feet as the length, 15 feet as the width, and 6.5 feet as the depth. The program should display 2,437.50 as the volume, and 18,233.84 as the number of gallons.

J. When the program is working correctly, close the Output window, and then use the File menu to close the solution.

Now observe what happens when you use the modified `Rectangle` class in the Terney Landscaping program that you created in the lesson.

K. Open the T10AppE07B Solution (T10AppE07B Solution.sln) file, which is contained in the CppNet\Tut10\T10AppE07B Solution folder.

L. Add the T10AppE07.h header file to the solution.

M. Enter the appropriate `#include` directive to include the contents of the T10AppE07.h header file in the program.

N. Study the program's code. Notice that the program passes two actual arguments to the `SetDimensions()` method. Save and then build the solution. The C++ compiler displays an error message indicating that the `SetDimensions()` method does not take two parameters.

In C++, you can assign the same name to more than one method, as long as each method has a different set of formal parameters. To use the `Rectangle` class in both the Terney Landscaping and Pool-Time programs, for example, you will provide two `SetDimensions()` methods in the `Rectangle` class: one having two formal parameters (for the Terney Landscaping program) and the other having three formal parameters (for the Pool-Time program). When two methods have the same name but different parameters, the methods are said to be *overloaded*.

O. Open the Solution Explorer window, then open the Header Files folder. Right-click T10AppE07.h, then click Open. Enter the prototype and definition for a `SetDimensions()` method that first accepts two `double` values, then verifies that the values are greater than zero, and then assigns the values to the private data members.

P. Save and then close the header file.

Q. Save and then build the solution. Execute the program. Enter 120 as the length, 75 as the width, and 1.55 as the price per square yard of sod. The program displays 1,000 as the area in square yards and $1,550.00 as the total price. Close the Command Prompt window.

R. When the program is working correctly, close the Output window, and then use the File menu to close the solution.

8) In this exercise, you debug a C++ program.

A. If necessary, start Visual Studio .NET. Click File on the menu bar, point to Open, and then click File. Open the T10AppE08.h header file, which is contained in the CppNet\MyClasses folder.

B. Study the `Inventory` class code, then close the header file.

C. Open the T10AppE08 Solution (T10AppE08 Solution.sln) file, which is contained in the CppNet\Tut10\T10AppE08 Solution folder. The program prompts the user to enter an item name and the amount of the item in inventory. It then displays the name and amount on the screen.

D. Add the T10AppE08.h header file to the solution.

E. Enter the appropriate `#include` directive to include the contents of the T10AppE08.h header file in the program.

F. Save and then build the solution. Correct any errors in the program and/or header file, then save and build the solution.

G. Execute the program. Enter Chair as the item name and 10 as the amount. The program should display "Name: Chair" and "Amount: 10" in the Command Prompt window.

H. When the program is working correctly, close the Output window, and then use the File menu to close the solution.

Tutorial 11

Sequential Access Files

Objectives

After completing this tutorial, you will be able to:

- Declare `StreamReader` and `StreamWriter` variables
- Open a sequential access file
- Write information to a sequential access file
- Align the text written to a sequential access file
- Read information from a sequential access file
- Test for the end of a sequential access file
- Search a string for one or more characters
- Access characters contained in a string
- Close a sequential access file
- Handle exceptions using a `try/catch` block

Concept Lesson

File Types

In addition to getting information from the keyboard and sending information to the screen, a program also can get information from and send information to a file on a disk. Getting information from a file is referred to as "reading the file," and sending information to a file is referred to as "writing to the file." Files to which information is written are called **output files**, because the files store the output produced by a program. Files that are read by the computer are called **input files**, because a program uses the information in these files as input.

You can create three different types of files in Visual C++ .NET: sequential, random, and binary. The file type refers to how the information in the file is accessed. The information in a sequential access file is always accessed sequentially—in other words, in consecutive order from the beginning of the file through the end of the file. The information stored in a random access file can be accessed either in consecutive order or in random order. The information in a binary access file can be accessed by its byte location in the file. You learn about sequential access files in this tutorial. Random and binary access files are not covered in this book.

Using Sequential Access Files

A **sequential access file** is often referred to as a **text file**, because it is composed of lines of text. The text might represent an employee list, as shown in Example 1 in Figure 11-1. Or, it might be a memo or a report, as shown in Examples 2 and 3 in Figure 11-1.

Figure 11-1: Examples of sequential access files

Examples

Example 1 – employee list

```
Bonnel, Jacob
Carlisle, Donald
Eberg, Jack
Hou, Chang
```

Example 2 – memo

```
To all employees:

Effective January 1, 2004, the cost of dependent
coverage will increase from $35 to $38.50 per month.

Jefferson Williams
Insurance Manager
```

Figure 11-1: Examples of sequential access files (continued)

Examples

Example 3 – report

```
ABC Industries Sales Report

State           Sales
California      15000
Montana         10000
Wyoming          7000
                -----
Total sales:   $32000
```

Sequential access files are similar to cassette tapes in that each line in the file, like each song on a cassette tape, is both stored and retrieved in consecutive order (sequentially). In other words, before you can record (store) the fourth song on a cassette tape, you first must record songs one through three. Likewise, before you can write (store) the fourth line in a sequential access file, you first must write lines one through three. The same holds true for retrieving a song from a cassette tape and a line of text from a sequential access file. To listen to the fourth song on a cassette tape, you must play (or fast-forward through) the first three songs. Likewise, to read the fourth line in a sequential access file, you first must read the three lines that precede it.

Figure 11-2 shows the procedure you follow when using a sequential access file in a program.

Figure 11-2: Procedure for using a sequential access file

Sequential access file procedure

1. declare either a StreamWriter or StreamReader object variable
2. create a StreamWriter or StreamReader object by opening a file; assign the object's address to the object variable declared in Step 1
3. use the StreamWriter object to write one or more lines of text to the file, or use the StreamReader object to read one or more lines of text from the file
4. use the StreamWriter or StreamReader object to close the file

Step 1 in Figure 11-2 is to declare either a `StreamWriter` or `StreamReader` object variable. The appropriate variable to declare depends on whether you want to write information to the file or read information from the file.

Using `StreamWriter` and `StreamReader` Objects

In Visual C++ .NET, you use a **`StreamWriter` object** to write a sequence of characters—referred to as a **stream of characters** or, more simply, a **stream**—to a sequential access file. Similarly, you use a **`StreamReader` object** to read a stream (sequence of characters) from a sequential access file. Before you create the appropriate object, you first must declare a variable to store the address of the object in the computer's internal memory. You use a `StreamWriter` variable to store the address of a `StreamWriter` object, and a `StreamReader` variable to store the address of a `StreamReader` object.

You declare `StreamWriter` and `StreamReader` variables using the syntax *datatype* **variablename*;, where *datatype* is either `IO::StreamWriter` or `IO::StreamReader`, and *variablename* is the name of the variable. The statement `IO::StreamWriter *outFile;`, for example, declares a `StreamWriter` variable named `outFile`. Similarly, the statement `IO::StreamReader *inFile;` declares a `StreamReader` variable named `inFile`.

After you declare the appropriate variable, you then create a `StreamWriter` or `StreamReader` object and assign the object's address to the variable. You create a `StreamWriter` or `StreamReader` object by opening a sequential access file.

tip

The "IO" in `IO::StreamWriter` and `IO::StreamReader` stands for "Input/Output" and indicates that the `StreamWriter` and `StreamReader` classes are contained in the `IO` class.

tip

It is not necessary to include the word "in" at the beginning of a `StreamReader` variable's name, or the word "out" at the beginning of a `StreamWriter` variable's name. However, doing so helps to distinguish the variables associated with input files from those associated with output files.

Opening a Sequential Access File

You use the syntax **IO::File::***method***(***filename***)** to open a sequential access file named *filename*. When you open a sequential access file, the computer creates either a `StreamReader` or `StreamWriter` object, depending on the *method* specified in the syntax. Figure 11-3 lists the *methods* used to open sequential access files and includes a description of each *method*. The figure also indicates the type of object created by each *method*.

Figure 11-3: Methods used to open a sequential access file

Method	Object created	Description
`OpenText()`	`StreamReader`	opens an existing sequential access file for input, which allows the computer to read the information stored in the file; if the file does not exist, an error occurs in the program
`CreateText()`	`StreamWriter`	opens a sequential access file for output, which creates a new, empty file to which data can be written; if the file already exists, its contents are erased before the new data is written
`AppendText()`	`StreamWriter`	opens a sequential access file for append, which allows the computer to write new data to the end of the existing data in the file; if the file does not exist, the file is created before data is written to it

tip

`IO::File::`*method*(*filename*) indicates that the *method* is contained in the `File` class, which is contained in the `IO` class.

The **OpenText() method** opens an existing sequential access file for input and allows the computer to read the information stored in the file. If the file does not exist when the `OpenText()` method is processed, the program results in an error. The `OpenText()` method creates a `StreamReader` object and can be used to open input files only.

You use the **CreateText() method** to create a new, empty sequential access file to which data can be written. If the file already exists, the computer erases the contents of the file before writing any data to it. You use the **AppendText() method** when you want to add data to the end of an existing sequential access file. If the file does not exist, the computer creates the file for you. Unlike the `OpenText()` method, the `CreateText()` and `AppendText()` methods create `StreamWriter` objects and are used to open output files only.

To complete Step 2 in the procedure shown in Figure 11-2, you assign the address of the object created by the `OpenText()`, `CreateText()`, or `AppendText()` method to the variable declared in Step 1. You make the assignment using the syntax *streamvariable* **= IO::File::***method***(***filename***);**, where *streamvariable* is the name of a `StreamReader` or `StreamWriter` variable. Figure 11-4 shows examples of opening sequential access files.

Figure 11-4: Examples of opening sequential access files

Examples and results
Example 1 `inFile = IO::File::OpenText("a:\\reports\\pay.txt");` Result opens for input the pay.txt file contained in the reports folder on the A drive; creates a `StreamReader` object and assigns its address to the `inFile` variable
Example 2 `inFile = IO::File::OpenText("pay.txt");` Result opens the pay.txt file for input; creates a StreamReader object and assigns its address to the `inFile` variable
Example 3 `outFile = IO::File::CreateText("memo.txt");` Result opens the memo.txt file for output; creates a StreamWriter object and assigns its address to the `outFile` variable
Example 4 `outFile = IO::File::AppendText("sales.txt");` Result opens the sales.txt file for append; creates a StreamWriter object and assigns its address to the `outFile` variable

When the computer processes the `inFile = IO::File::OpenText("a:\\reports\\pay.txt");` statement shown in Example 1 in Figure 11-4, it first searches the reports folder on the A drive for a file named pay.txt. If the computer cannot locate the pay.txt file, the program ends with an error; otherwise, the computer opens the file for input, creates a `StreamReader` object, and assigns the object's address to the `inFile` variable. Notice that the `inFile = IO::File::OpenText("pay.txt");` statement shown in Example 2 is identical to the statement shown in Example 1, except the *filename* argument does not specify a folder path. If you do not include a folder path in the *filename* argument, the computer searches for the file in the current project's folder. If the current project is stored in the Payroll Project folder, for example, the computer will search for the pay.txt file in that folder. If you do specify a folder path in the *filename* argument, you must

tip

The backslash followed by one or more characters is called an "escape sequence" in C++. Escape sequences typically are used to specify actions such as carriage returns and tab movements on screens and printers. They also are used to provide literal representations of nonprinting characters and characters that usually have special meanings, such as the double quotation mark (").

tip

You also can both declare a `StreamWriter` or `StreamReader` variable and open a sequential access file in one statement. For example, you can use the statement `IO::StreamReader *inFile = IO::File::OpenText("pay.txt");` to declare the `inFile` variable and open the pay.txt file for input.

use two backslashes (\\), rather than one backslash (\), to separate the names of the folders and the name of the file in the path, as shown in Example 1; this is because the backslash by itself has a special meaning in the C++ language.

When processing the `outFile = IO::File::CreateText("memo.txt");` statement shown in Example 3, the computer searches the current project's folder for a file named memo.txt. If the memo.txt file exists, its contents are erased and the file is opened for output; otherwise, a new, empty file is created and opened for output. In addition to opening the memo.txt file, Example 3's statement also creates a `StreamWriter` object and assigns the object's address to the `outFile` variable.

When the computer processes the `outFile = IO::File::AppendText("sales.txt");` statement shown in Example 4, it searches the current project's folder for a file named sales.txt. If it locates the sales.txt file, the computer opens the file for append, which allows new information to be written to the end of the file. If the computer cannot locate the sales.txt file, it creates a new, empty file and opens the file for append. Example 4's statement also creates a `StreamWriter` object and assigns the object's address to the `outFile` variable.

The computer uses a file pointer to keep track of the next character either to read from or write to a file. When you open a file for input, the computer positions the file pointer at the beginning of the file, immediately before the first character. When you open a file for output, the computer also positions the file pointer at the beginning of the file, but recall that the file is empty. (As you learned earlier, opening a file for output tells the computer to create a new, empty file or erase the contents of an existing file.) However, when you open a file for append, the computer positions the file pointer immediately after the last character in the file. Figure 11-5 illustrates the position of the file pointer when files are opened for input, output, and append.

Figure 11-5: Position of the file pointer when files are opened for input, output, and append

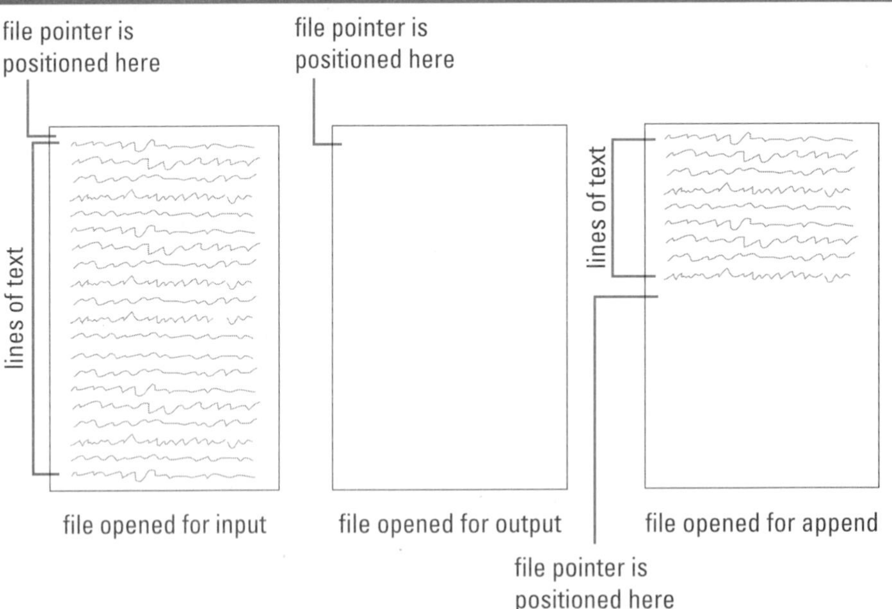

MINI-QUIZ

Mini-Quiz 1

1) In C++, a sequence of characters is referred to as a ____________.
2) Which of the following statements declares a variable that can be used when opening a file for append?
   a. `IO::StreamAppend *outFile;`
   b. `IO::StreamReader *outFile;`
   c. `IO::StreamWriter *outFile;`
   d. `IO::StreamWriter outFile;`
3) If the file opened with the ____________ method already exists, the computer erases the contents of the file before writing any data to it.
   a. `AppendText()`
   b. `CreateText()`
   c. `EraseText()`
   d. `OpenText()`
4) Write the statement to open the employ.txt file for input. Assign the open file to a `StreamReader` variable named `inFile`.

Step 3 in the procedure shown earlier in Figure 11-2 is to use the `StreamWriter` object to write one or more lines of text to the file, or use the `StreamReader` object to read one or more lines of text from the file. First, you learn how to write information to a sequential access file.

Writing Information to a Sequential Access File

Recall that you use the `Console::Write()` and `Console::WriteLine()` methods to write information to the computer screen. When writing information to a sequential access file, you use a different form of the `Write()` and `WriteLine()` methods; more specifically, you use the syntax *streamvariable*->**Write(***data***);** and *streamvariable*->**WriteLine(***data***);**. In each syntax, *streamvariable* is the name of a `StreamWriter` variable, and *data* is the information you want written to the file associated with the variable. The difference between the two methods is the location of the file pointer after the *data* is written to the file. The `Write()` method positions the file pointer at the end of the last character it writes to the file. The `WriteLine()` method, on the other hand, positions the file pointer at the beginning of the next line in the file; it does so by appending a **line terminator character**, which is simply a carriage return followed by a line feed, to the end of the *data*. Figure 11-6 shows examples of using the `Write()` and `WriteLine()` methods to write information to sequential access files. The figure also indicates the placement of the file pointer after the method is processed.

tip

Recall that the difference between the `Console::Write()` and `Console::WriteLine()` methods is the location of the cursor after the data is displayed on the screen.

Figure 11-6: Examples of writing information to a sequential access file

Examples and results

Example 1
```
outFile->Write("Hello");
```

Result
Hello_

file pointer

Figure 11-6: Examples of writing information to a sequential access file (continued)

	Examples and results
file pointer	Example 2 `outFile->WriteLine("Hello");` Result Hello _

file pointer	Example 3
	`outFile->Write("The top salesperson is ");`
	`outFile->WriteLine("{0}.", name);`
	`outFile->WriteLine();`
	`outFile->Write("ABC Sales");`
	
	Result (assuming that the `name` variable contains the string "Jeff")
	The top salesperson is Jeff.
	
	ABC Sales_

file pointer	Example 4 `outFile->WriteLine("Total price: {0}", price.ToString("C2"));` Result (assuming that the `price` variable contains the number 25) Total price: $25.00 _

file pointer	Example 5
	`outFile->WriteLine("{0}#{1}", name,`
	`Convert::ToString(salary));`
	
	Result (assuming that the `name` variable contains the string "Pam" and the `salary` variable contains the number 24500)
	Pam#24500
	_

The `outFile->Write("Hello");` statement in Example 1 writes the string "Hello" to the file and then positions the file pointer immediately after the last letter in the string, as indicated in the example. The `outFile->WriteLine("Hello");` statement in Example 2 writes the string "Hello" and a line terminator character to the file. The line terminator character positions the file pointer at the beginning of the next line in the file, as indicated in the example.

The first statement shown in Example 3, `outFile->Write("The top salesperson is ");`, writes the string "The top salesperson is " to the file and then positions the file pointer after the last character in the string (in this case, after the space character). The next statement, `outFile->WriteLine("{0}.", name);`, writes the contents of the `name` variable followed by a period and a line terminator character to the file. The line terminator character moves the file pointer to the next line in the file. The third statement in Example 3, `outFile->WriteLine();`, writes only a line terminator character to the file; you can use this statement to insert a blank line in a file. The last statement in Example 3, `outFile->Write("ABC Sales");`, writes the string "ABC Sales" to the file, and then positions the file pointer after the last character in the string, as indicated in the example.

In Example 4, the `outFile->WriteLine("Total price: {0}", price.ToString("C2"));` statement writes the string "Total price: " and the contents of the `price` variable (formatted to currency with two decimal places) on the same line in the file. The file pointer is then positioned at the beginning of the next line in the file.

Many times, sequential access files are used to store fields and records. A **field** is a single item of information about a person, place, or thing—for example, a name, a salary, a Social Security number, or a price. A **record** is one or more related fields that contain all of the necessary data about a specific person, place, or thing. The college you are attending keeps a student record on you. Your student record might contain the following fields: your Social Security number, name, address, phone number, credits earned, grades earned, grade point average, and so on. The place where you are employed also keeps a record on you. Your employee record might contain your Social Security number, name, address, phone number, starting date, salary or hourly wage, and so on.

When writing records to a sequential access file, each record should appear on a separate line in the file. If the records contain more than one field, programmers typically separate each field with a special character, such as the # character; this is done to distinguish one field from the next when reading the record later. For example, the `outFile->WriteLine("{0}#{1}", name, Convert::ToString(salary));` statement in Example 5 in Figure 11-6 writes a record that consists of two fields—a name field and a salary field—separated by the # character. The # character indicates where the name field ends in the record and where the salary field begins. The `WriteLine()` method ensures that the record appears on a separate line in the file.

Next, you learn how to use the `PadLeft()` and `PadRight()` methods to control the appearance of the text written to a file.

tip

You can verify that the information was written correctly to a sequential access file by opening the file in the Visual C++ .NET editor. To do so, click File on the menu bar, point to Open, and then click File. When the Open File dialog box opens, click the Files of type list arrow, and then click All Files (*.*).

Using the `PadLeft()` and `PadRight()` Methods

You can use the `PadLeft()` and `PadRight()` methods to pad a string with a character until the string is a specified length. The syntax of the `PadLeft()` method is *string*->**PadLeft(***length*[, *character*]**)**, and the syntax of the `PadRight()` method is *string*->**PadRight(***length*[, *character*]**)**. In each syntax, *string* is the name of the `String` variable that contains the string you want to pad. *Length* is an integer that represents the desired length of the string—in other words, the total number of characters you want the string to contain. The *character* argument, which must be enclosed in single quotation marks, is the character that each method uses to pad the string until it reaches the desired *length*. Notice that the *character* argument is optional in each syntax; if omitted, the default *character* is the space character.

The **PadLeft() method** pads the string on the left—in other words, it inserts the padded characters at the beginning of the string; doing so right-aligns the characters within the string. The **PadRight() method**, on the other hand, pads the string on the right, which inserts the padded characters at the end of the string and left-aligns the characters within the string. Figure 11-7 shows examples of using the `PadLeft()` and `PadRight()` methods to pad strings.

Figure 11-7: Examples of the `PadLeft()` and `PadRight()` methods

Examples and results

Example 1
```
String *name = "Sue";
String *newName = "";
newName = name->PadRight(10);
```

Result
assigns "Sue   " (the string "Sue" and seven spaces) to the **newName** variable

Example 2
```
String *name = "Sue";
name = name->PadRight(10);
```

Result
assigns "Sue   " (the string "Sue" and seven spaces) to the **name** variable

Example 3
```
double netPay = 767.89;
String *netString = "";
netString = netPay.ToString("C2");
netString = netString->PadLeft(15, '*');
```

single quotation marks

Result
assigns "********$767.89" to the **netString** variable

Example 4
```
double netPay = 767.89;
String *netString = "";
netString = netPay.ToString("C2")->PadLeft(15, '*');
```

single quotation marks

Result
assigns "********$767.89" to the **netString** variable

Example 5
```
int num = 42;
String *numString = "";
numString = Convert::ToString(num)->PadLeft(5);
```

Result
assigns "   42" (three spaces and the string "42") to the **numString** variable

When processing the `newName = name->PadRight(10);` statement shown in Example 1, the computer first makes a copy of the string stored in the **name** variable. It then pads the copied string with space characters until the string contains exactly 10 characters. In this case, the computer uses seven space characters, which it inserts at the end of the string. The computer then assigns the resulting string—"Sue   "—to the **newName** variable. Keep in mind that the `newName = name->PadRight(10);` statement does not change the contents of the **name** variable. To assign "Sue   " to the **name** variable, you would need to use the `name = name->PadRight(10);` statement shown in Example 2.

When processing the `netString = netPay.ToString("C2");` statement shown in Example 3 in Figure 11-7, the computer first makes a copy of the number stored in the `netPay` variable. It then converts the copied value to a string and formats it using the "C2" format. The statement assigns the formatted string—$767.89—to the `netString` variable. Next, the computer processes the `netString = netString->PadLeft(15, '*');` statement. When processing the statement, the computer first makes a copy of the string stored in the `netString` variable. It then pads the copied string with asterisks until the string contains exactly 15 characters. In this case, the computer inserts eight asterisks at the beginning of the string. The computer assigns the resulting string ("********$767.89") to the `netString` variable.

The code shown in Example 4 in Figure 11-7 produces the same result as the code shown in Example 3. Notice, however, that Example 4's code combines the `ToString()` and `PadLeft()` methods in one assignment statement, like this: `netString = netPay.ToString("C2")->PadLeft(15, '*');`. When processing the statement, the computer first makes a copy of the number stored in the `netPay` variable; it then converts the copied value to a string and formats it using the "C2" format. Rather than assigning the resulting string ("$767.89") to the `netString` variable, as it does in Example 3's code, the computer pads the "$767.89" string with asterisks before assigning the resulting string "********$767.89" to the `netString` variable. Notice that the computer processes the methods from left to right in the statement; in this case, it processes the `ToString()` method before processing the `PadLeft()` method.

Example 5 in Figure 11-7 shows how you can use the `Convert::ToString()` method to convert a number to a string, and then use the `PadLeft()` method to pad the string with space characters. When processing the `numString = Convert::ToString(num)-> PadLeft(5);` statement, the computer first makes a copy of the number stored in the `num` variable. The `Convert::ToString()` method tells the computer to convert the copied number to a string, and the `PadLeft()` method tells the computer to pad the string with space characters until it contains exactly five characters. The computer assigns the resulting string ("   42") to the `numString` variable. Here again, notice that the computer processes the methods from left to right in the statement; in this case, it processes the `Convert::ToString()` method before processing the `PadLeft()` method. You also could have written Example 5's statement as `numString = num.ToString()-> PadLeft(5);`.

You can use the `PadLeft()` and `PadRight()` methods to align columns of information in a sequential access file, as shown in Figure 11-8.

Figure 11-8: Examples of aligning columns in a sequential access file

Examples and results

Example 1

```
for (int region = 1; region <= 3; region = region + 1)
{
     Console::Write("Enter the sales amount: ");
     sales = Convert::ToDouble(Console::ReadLine());
     salesString = sales.ToString("N2");
     outFile->WriteLine(salesString->PadLeft(8));
} //end for
```

Result (assuming the user enters the following sales amounts: 645.75, 1200, 40.8)

```
  645.75
1,200.00
   40.80
```

Example 2

```
outFile->WriteLine("Name           Age");
Console::Write("Enter the name: ");
name = Console::ReadLine();
while (name->CompareTo("") != 0)
{
     Console::Write("Enter the age: ");
     age = Console::ReadLine();
     outFile->WriteLine("{0}{1}", name->PadRight(15), age);
     Console::Write("Enter the name: ");
     name = Console::ReadLine();
}  //end while
```

Result (assuming the user enters the following names and ages: Janice, 23, Sue, 67)

```
Name           Age
Janice         23
Sue            67
```

Example 1's code shows how you can align a column of numbers by the decimal point. First, you format each number in the column to ensure that each has the same number of digits to the right of the decimal point. You then use the `PadLeft()` method to pad the number with spaces; this right-aligns the number within the column. Because each number has the same number of digits to the right of the decimal point, aligning each number on the right will, in effect, align each by their decimal point.

Example 2's code shows how you can align the second column of information when the first column contains strings whose lengths vary. To do so, you use either the `PadRight()` or `PadLeft()` method to ensure that each string in the first column contains the same number of characters. The code shown in Example 2, for instance, uses the `PadRight()` method to ensure that each name in the first column contains exactly 15 characters before the name is written to the file. Because each name has 15 characters, each age will automatically appear beginning in character position 16 in the file.

MINI-QUIZ

Mini-Quiz 2

1) Which of the following statements writes the contents of the `quantity` variable to a sequential access file?
   a. `outFile->WriteLine(quantity);`
   b. `outFile->quantity.WriteLine();`
   c. `outFile::WriteLine(quantity);`
   d. `WriteLine(quantity);`

2) Which of the following statements writes a record that contains two fields: a city name and a state name?
   a. `outFile->WriteLine(city, state);`
   b. `outFile::WriteLine("city#state");`
   c. `outFile->WriteLine({0 1}, city, state);`
   d. `outFile->WriteLine("{0}#{1}", city, state);`

3) Assume that the `priceString` variable contains the string "5". Which of the following statements assigns the string "5***" to the `priceString` variable?
   a. `priceString = priceString->PadLeft(3, '*');`
   b. `priceString = priceString->PadLeft(4, '*');`
   c. `priceString = priceString->PadRight(3, '*');`
   d. `priceString = priceString->PadRight(4, '*');`

4) The `PadLeft()` method ______________ the characters within a string.
   a. left-aligns
   b. right-aligns

Next, you learn how to read information from a sequential access file.

Reading Information from a Sequential Access File

Similar to the `Console::ReadLine()` method, which you use to read a line of text from the keyboard, you use the **ReadLine() method** to read a line of text from a sequential access file. A **line** is defined as a sequence of characters followed by the line terminator character. The string returned by the `ReadLine()` method contains only the sequence of characters contained in the line; it does not include the line terminator character.

The syntax of the `ReadLine()` method is *streamvariable*-**>ReadLine();**, where *streamvariable* is the name of a `StreamReader` variable. Figure `11-9` shows examples of using the `ReadLine()` method to read lines of text from a sequential access file.

Figure 11-9: Examples of the `ReadLine()` method

Examples and results

Example 1

```
Console::WriteLine(inFile->ReadLine());
```

Result

reads a line from a sequential access file, and then displays the line (excluding the line terminator character) on the computer screen

Figure 11-9: Examples of the `ReadLine()` method (continued)

Examples and results
Example 2 `name = inFile->ReadLine();` Result reads a line from a sequential access file, and then assigns the line (excluding the line terminator character) to the `name` variable
Example 3 `sales = Convert::ToDouble(inFile->ReadLine());` Result reads a line from a sequential access file, converts the line (excluding the line terminator character) to the `double` data type, and then assigns the result to the `sales` variable

Example 4
`while (inFile->Peek() != -1)`
`{`
`      line = inFile->ReadLine();`
`      Console::WriteLine(line);`
`}  //end while`
 	
Result
reads a sequential access file, line by line; assigns each line (excluding the line terminator character) to the `line` variable and displays each line on the computer screen

The `Console::WriteLine(inFile->ReadLine());` statement shown in Example 1 reads a line of text from a sequential access file, and then displays the line, excluding the line terminator character, on the computer screen. The `name = inFile->ReadLine();` statement shown in Example 2 also reads a line of text from a sequential access file; however, it assigns the line, excluding the line terminator character, to the `name` variable.

The `sales = Convert::ToDouble(inFile->ReadLine());` statement shown in Example 3 reads a line of text from a sequential access file. It then converts the line (excluding the line terminator character) to the `double` data type, and then assigns the result to the `sales` variable.

In most cases, a program will need to read each line of text contained in a sequential access file, one line at a time. You can do so using a repetition structure along with the `Peek()` method, as shown in Example 4 in Figure 11-9. The syntax of the `Peek()` method is *streamvariable*->**Peek();**, where *streamvariable* is the name of a `StreamReader` variable. The **Peek() method** "peeks" into the file to see whether it contains another character to read. If the file contains another character, the `Peek()` method returns the character; otherwise, it returns the number -1. The `while (inFile->Peek() != -1)` clause shown in Example 4 tells the computer to process the loop instructions, which read a line of text and then display the line (excluding the line terminator character) on the computer screen, until the `Peek()` method returns the number -1, which indicates that there are no more characters to read.

As you learned earlier, some sequential access files contain records, which are composed of one or more fields. If the records in a sequential access file have only one field, you read a record (and in this case, the field) simply by reading a line of text from the file. For example, assuming each record contains only one field, you can use the statement `name = inFile->ReadLine();` to read a record from the file and assign the contents of the field to the `name` variable. Similarly, you can use the statement `sales = Convert::ToDouble(inFile->ReadLine());` to read a record from the file and assign the contents of its only field, converted to `double`, to the `sales` variable.

You follow a slightly different procedure when the records in a sequential access file have more than one field. First, you read the record by reading a line of text from the file, and you assign the record (line of text) to a `String` variable. You then use the `IndexOf()` method to search for the special character that separates each field in the record, and the `Substring()` method to parse (split or tear apart) the record into fields. You learn about the `IndexOf()` method first, and then you learn about the `Substring()` method.

tip

You also can use the `Split()` method to parse a record into fields. The `Split()` method stores the fields in a one-dimensional array. You can learn about the `Split()` method by completing Discovery Exercise 16 in Tutorial 13's Concept Lesson.

Using the `IndexOf()` Method to Search a String

You can use the **IndexOf() method** to search a string to determine whether it contains a specific sequence of characters. For example, you can use the `IndexOf()` method to determine whether the area code "312" appears in a phone number, or whether the street name "Elm Street" appears in an address.

The syntax of the `IndexOf()` method is *string*->**IndexOf(***value*[, *startIndex*]**)**. In the syntax, *string* is the name of a `String` variable that you want to search, *value* is the sequence of characters for which you are searching, and *startIndex* is the index of the character at which the search should begin—in other words, *startIndex* specifies the starting position for the search. The first character in a string has an index of zero, the second character an index of one, and so on. Notice that the *startIndex* argument is optional in the `IndexOf()` method's syntax. If you omit the *startIndex* argument, the `IndexOf()` method begins the search with the first character in the string.

The `IndexOf()` method searches for *value* within *string*, beginning with the character whose index is *startIndex*. If the `IndexOf()` method does not find the *value*, it returns the number -1; otherwise, it returns the index of the starting position of *value* within *string*. Figure 11-10 shows examples of using the `IndexOf()` method in a C++ statement.

Figure 11-10: Examples of the `IndexOf()` method

Examples and results

Example 1

```
String *message = "Have a nice day";
int index = 0;
index = message->IndexOf("nice", 0);
```

Result

assigns the number 7 to the `index` variable

Example 2

```
String *message = "Have a nice day";
int index = 0;
index = message->IndexOf("nice");
```

Result

assigns the number 7 to the `index` variable

Figure 11-10: Examples of the `IndexOf()` method (continued)

Examples and results

Example 3
```
String *message = "Have a nice day";
int index = 0;
index = message->IndexOf("Nice");
```
Result
assigns the number -1 to the **index** variable

Example 4
```
String *message = "Have a nice day";
int index = 0;
index = message->ToUpper()->IndexOf("NICE");
```
Result
assigns the number 7 to the **index** variable

Example 5
```
String *message = "Have a nice day";
int index = 0;
index = message->IndexOf("nice", 5);
```
Result
assigns the number 7 to the **index** variable

Example 6
```
String *message = "Have a nice day";
int index = 0;
index = message->IndexOf("nice", 8);
```
Result
assigns the number -1 to the **index** variable

You can use either the `index = message->IndexOf("nice", 0);` statement in Example 1 in Figure 11-10, or the `index = message->IndexOf("nice");` statement in Example 2, to search for the word "nice" in the `message` variable, beginning with the first character in the variable. In each case, the word "nice" begins with the eighth character in the `message` variable. The eighth character has an index of seven, so both statements assign the number seven to the `index` variable.

The `IndexOf()` method performs a case-sensitive search, as Example 3 in Figure 11-10 indicates. In this example, the `index = message->IndexOf("Nice");` statement assigns the number -1 to the `index` variable, because the word "Nice" is not contained in the `message` variable.

You can use the `index = message->ToUpper()->IndexOf("NICE");` statement shown in Example 4 to perform a case-insensitive search for the word "nice". The `ToUpper()` method in the statement is processed first and temporarily converts the string stored in the `message` variable to uppercase. The `IndexOf()` method then searches the uppercase string for the word "NICE". The statement assigns the number seven to the `index` variable because, ignoring case, the word "nice" begins with the character whose index is seven.

The `index = message->IndexOf("nice", 5);` statement in Example 5 searches for the word "nice" in the `message` variable, beginning with the character whose index is five; that character is the second letter "a". The statement assigns the number seven to the `index` variable, because the word "nice" begins with the character whose index is seven.

The `index = message->IndexOf("nice", 8);` statement in Example 6 in Figure 11-10 searches for the word "nice" in the `message` variable, beginning with the character whose index is eight; that character is the letter "i". Notice that the word "nice" does not appear anywhere in the "ice day" portion of the string stored in the `message` variable. Therefore, the statement assigns the number -1 to the `index` variable.

Next, you learn how to use the `Substring()` method to access characters contained in a string.

Using the `Substring()` Method to Access Characters Contained in a String

At times, a program may need to access one or more characters contained in a string. For example, a program may need to determine whether the letter K appears as the third character in a string; or, it may need to display only the string's first five characters.

You can use the **Substring() method** to access any number of characters in a string. The syntax of the `Substring()` method is *string*->**Substring(***startIndex*[, *count*]**)**, where *string* is the name of a `String` variable that contains the characters you want to access. In the syntax, *startIndex* is the index of the first character you want to access in the *string*, and *count* (which is optional) specifies the number of characters you want to access. The `Substring()` method returns a string that contains *count* number of characters, beginning with the character whose index is *startIndex*. If you omit the *count* argument, the `Substring()` method returns all characters from the *startIndex* position through the end of the *string*. Figure 11-11 shows examples of using the `Substring()` method in a C++ statement.

Figure 11-11: Examples of the `Substring()` method

Examples and results

Example 1

```
String *name = "Peggy Ryan";
String *first = "";
String *last = "";
first = name->Substring(0, 5);
last = name->Substring(6);
```

Result

assigns "Peggy" to the `first` variable, and assigns "Ryan" to the `last` variable

Example 2

```
String *sales = "";
Console::Write("Enter the sales: ");
sales = Console::ReadLine();
if (sales->Substring(0, 1)->CompareTo("$") == 0)
     sales = sales->Substring(1);
//end if
```

Result

determines whether the string stored in the `sales` variable begins with the dollar sign; if it does, assigns the contents of the variable, excluding the dollar sign, to the `sales` variable

Figure 11-11: Examples of the `Substring()` method (continued)

Examples and results

Example 3

```
String *employee = "Rodney#40500";
String *name = "";
double salary = 0.0;
int position = 0;
position = employee->IndexOf("#");
name = employee->Substring(0, position);
salary = Convert::ToDouble(employee->Substring(position + 1));
```

Result

determines the position of the # character in the **employee** variable; assigns the characters to the left of the # character in the **employee** variable to the **name** variable, and assigns the characters to the right of the # character (converted to **double**) to the **salary** variable

Study closely the three examples shown in Figure 11-11. In Example 1, the `first = name->Substring(0, 5);` statement assigns the first five characters contained in the `name` variable ("Peggy") to the `first` variable. The `last = name->Substring(6);` statement assigns all of the characters contained in the `name` variable, beginning with the character whose index is 6, to the `last` variable. In this case, the statement assigns "Ryan" to the `last` variable.

In Example 2, the condition in the `if (sales->Substring(0, 1)->CompareTo("$") == 0)` clause uses the `Substring()` method to access the first character stored in the `sales` variable. (Recall that the first character has an index of zero.) It then uses the `CompareTo()` method, which you learned about in Tutorial 6, to compare the first character with the dollar sign. In other words, the condition determines whether the string stored in the `sales` variable begins with the dollar sign. If it does, the `sales = sales->Substring(1);` statement assigns all of the characters from the `sales` variable, except the dollar sign, to the `sales` variable.

tip You also can use the `StartsWith()` method to determine whether a specific sequence of characters occurs at the beginning of a string, and the `EndsWith()` method to determine whether a specific sequence of characters occurs at the end of a string. You learn about both methods in Discovery Exercise 28 at the end of this lesson.

The `position = employee->IndexOf("#");` statement in Example 3 in Figure 11-11 uses the `IndexOf()` method to determine the index of the # character within the `employee` variable; the statement assigns the index to the `position` variable. Assuming the `employee` variable contains the string "Rodney#40500", the statement assigns the number 6 to the `position` variable.

The `name = employee->Substring(0, position);` statement in Example 3 assigns `position` characters from the `employee` variable, beginning with the first character in the variable, to the `name` variable. Assuming the `employee` variable contains the string "Rodney#40500", and the `position` variable contains the number 6, the statement assigns the string "Rodney" to the `name` variable.

The `salary = Convert::ToDouble(employee->Substring(position + 1));` statement in Example 3 converts to `double` all of the characters in the `employee` variable, beginning with the character that has an index of `position` + 1; it then assigns the converted value to the `salary` variable. (Recall that the `position` variable contains the index of the # character.) Assuming the `employee` variable contains the string "Rodney#40500", the statement converts the characters "40500" to `double` before assigning the characters to the `salary` variable.

The last step in the sequential access file procedure (shown earlier in Figure 11-2) is to use the `StreamWriter` or `StreamReader` object to close the file.

Closing a Sequential Access File

To prevent the loss of data, you should use the **Close() method** to close a sequential access file as soon as you are finished using it. The syntax of the `Close()` method is *streamvariable*-**>Close();**, where *streamvariable* is the name of either a `StreamReader` or `StreamWriter` variable. Figure 11-12 shows two examples of using the `Close()` method to close sequential access files. The first example closes an input file, and the second example closes an output file.

Figure 11-12: Examples of the `Close()` method

Examples and results
Example 1 `inFile->Close();` Result closes the file associated with the `inFile` object
Example 2 `outFile->Close();` Result closes the file associated with the `outFile` object

tip

Because it is so easy to forget to close the files used in a program, you should enter the statement to close the file as soon as possible after entering the one that opens it.

MINI-QUIZ

Mini-Quiz 3

1) If a sequential access file does not contain another character to read, the `Peek()` method returns ________________.
   a. –1
   b. 0
   c. 1
   d. the last character read

2) Assume that the `name` variable contains the string "Joy Feldon". Which of the following statements assigns the number 8 to the `start` variable?
   a. `start = name->IndexOf("on", 0);`
   b. `start = name->IndexOf("on", 1);`
   c. `start = name->IndexOf("on", 7);`
   d. all of the above

3) Assume that the `state` variable contains the string "North Carolina". Which of the following statements assigns the string "North" to the `temp` variable?
   a. `temp = state->Substring(0);`
   b. `temp = state->Substring(1);`
   c. `temp = state->Substring(0, 5);`
   d. `temp = state->Substring(5);`

4) The string returned by the `ReadLine()` method contains the line terminator character.
   a. true
   b. false

Now view a program that demonstrates most of what you have learned so far about sequential access files.

The Sales Program

Assume that a company wants to record each salesperson's name and quarterly sales in a sequential access file, and then display the contents of the sequential access file on the computer screen. You can use the sales program shown in Figure 11-13 to perform these tasks. (The lines of code pertaining to what you learned in this lesson are shaded in the figure.)

Figure 11-13: The sales program

```
//sales.cpp
//writes records to and reads records from a sequential access file
#using <mscorlib.dll>
using namespace System;

//function prototypes
void addRecords();
void displayRecords();

int main()
{
    addRecords();
    displayRecords();
    return 0;
}   //end of main function

//*****function definitions*****
void addRecords()
{
    //declare variables
    String *name = "";
    int sales    = 0;

    //declare StreamWriter variable and open the file
    IO::StreamWriter *outFile;
    outFile = IO::File::AppendText("sales.txt");

    //get name and quarterly sales
    Console::Write("Enter the name (X to stop): ");
    name = Console::ReadLine();
    while (name->ToUpper()->CompareTo("X") != 0)
    {
        Console::Write("Enter the quarterly sales: ");
        sales = Convert::ToInt32(Console::ReadLine());

        //write record to file
        outFile->WriteLine("{0}#{1}", name,
        Convert::ToString(sales));

        Console::Write("Enter the name (X to stop): ");
        name = Console::ReadLine();
    } //end while
```

Figure 11-13: The sales program (continued)

```
    //close the file
    outFile->Close();
}   //end of addRecords function

void displayRecords()
{
    //declare variables
    String *name   = "";
    int sales      = 0;
    String *record = "";
    int position   = 0;

    //declare StreamReader variable and open the file
    IO::StreamReader *inFile;
    inFile = IO::File::OpenText("sales.txt");

    //read and display records
    while (inFile->Peek() != -1)
    {
        record = inFile->ReadLine();
        position = record->IndexOf("#", 0);
        name = record->Substring(0, position);
        sales = Convert::ToInt32(record->Substring(position + 1));
        Console::WriteLine("{0}{1}", name->PadRight(15),
        sales.ToString("N0")->PadLeft(10));
    } //end while

    //close the file
    inFile->Close();
}   //end of displayRecords function
```

Notice that the `main()` function in the sales program calls two void functions named `addRecords()` and `displayRecords()`. The `addRecords()` function begins by declaring the appropriate variables; it then opens a sequential access file named sales.txt for append. If the sales.txt file does not exist, the computer creates it and positions the file pointer at the beginning of the file; otherwise, it opens the existing file and positions the file pointer after the last record in the file. Next, the `addRecords()` function gets each salesperson's name and quarterly sales amount from the user at the keyboard. Each name and sales amount is written as a record to the sales.txt file. Notice that the program uses the `outFile->WriteLine("{0}#{1}", name, Convert::ToString(sales));` statement to write the record, which contains two fields, on a separate line in the file. In this case, the # character separates the salesperson's name from his or her quarterly sales amount in the record. When the user has finished entering names and sales amounts, the `addRecords()` function closes the sales.txt file, and then the `addRecords()` function ends. The `main()` function calls the `displayRecords()` function next.

The `displayRecords()` function begins by declaring the appropriate variables; it then opens a sequential access file named sales.txt for input. If the sales.txt file does not exist, the program results in an error; otherwise, the computer positions the file pointer at the beginning of the file. Next, the condition in the `while (inFile->Peek() != -1)` clause determines whether the sales.txt file contains a character to read. If the condition evaluates to false, the `displayRecords()` function closes the sales.txt file, and then the `displayRecords()` function ends. However, if the condition evaluates to true, the `displayRecords()` function reads a salesperson's record from the sales.txt file. The `position = record->IndexOf("#", 0);` statement locates the # character in the record, and assigns its index to the `position` variable. The `name = record->Substring(0, position);` statement assigns the name portion of the record to the `name` variable, and the `sales = Convert::ToInt32(record->Substring(position + 1));` statement assigns the sales amount information to the `sales` variable. The `Console::WriteLine("{0}{1}", name->PadRight(15), sales.ToString("N0")->PadLeft(10));` statement then displays the name and sales amount information on the computer screen.

When the computer has finished reading the records stored in the sales.txt file, the `displayRecords()` function closes the file, and then the `displayRecords()` function ends. Processing continues with the `return 0;` statement in the `main()` function. The `return 0;` statement returns the number 0 to the operating system to indicate that the program ended normally, and then the `main()` function ends.

Figure 11-14 shows the Command Prompt window after running the sales program and entering three records.

Figure 11-14: Command Prompt window after running the sales program

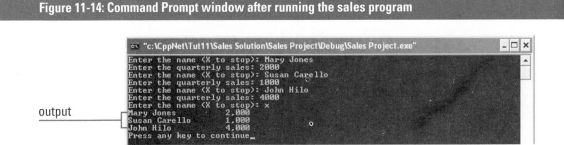

"c:\CppNet\Tut11\Sales Solution\Sales Project\Debug\Sales Project.exe"

```
Enter the name (X to stop): Mary Jones
Enter the quarterly sales: 2000
Enter the name (X to stop): Susan Carello
Enter the quarterly sales: 1000
Enter the name (X to stop): John Hilo
Enter the quarterly sales: 4000
Enter the name (X to stop): x
Mary Jones          2,000
Susan Carello       1,000
John Hilo           4,000
Press any key to continue_
```

output

Figure 11-15 shows the records contained in the sales.txt file. Notice that each record appears on a separate line, and the # character separates the name field from the quarterly sales amount field.

Figure 11-15: Records contained in the sales.txt file

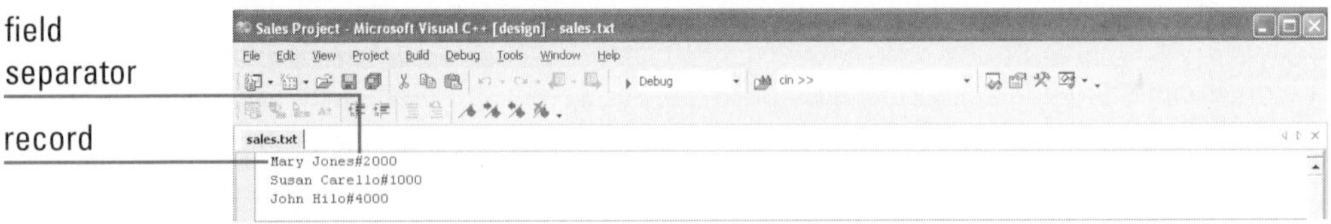

As mentioned earlier, the `OpenText()` method results in an error if the file you are trying to open does not exist. It's also possible for the `CreateText()` and `AppendText()` methods to fail when attempting to open a file. Both methods, for example, fail if the folder path specified in the *filename* argument does not exist. Before attempting either to read data from or write data to a file, you always should verify that the file was opened successfully; you can do so using a C++ `try/catch` block.

Using a `try/catch` Block

In Visual C++ .NET, an error that occurs while a program is running is called an **exception** and typically results in the program ending abruptly. You can use the **try** statement to catch (or trap) an exception when it occurs in a C++ program, and then use a **catch** statement to have the computer take the appropriate action to resolve the problem. A block of code that uses both the `try` and `catch` statements is referred to as a `try/catch` block. Figure 11-16 shows the format of a `try/catch` block in C++. The figure also includes two examples of using a `try/catch` block to catch exceptions.

Figure 11-16: Format of a `try/catch` block in C++

Format

```
try
{
     one or more statements that might generate an exception
}
catch (exceptiontype *variablename)
{
     one or more statements that will execute when an exceptiontype exception occurs
}
[catch (exceptiontype *variablename)
{
     one or more statements that will execute when an exceptiontype exception occurs
}]
```

Examples

Example 1

```
try
{
      average = totalScores / numberOfStudents;
      Console::WriteLine(average);
}
catch (DivideByZeroException *ex)
{
      Console::WriteLine(ex->message);
}
```

Figure 11-16: Format of a try/catch block in C++ (continued)

Examples

Example 2
```
IO::StreamReader *inFile;
bool fileProblem = false;

try
{
      inFile = IO::File::OpenText("sales.txt");
}
catch (IO::IOException *ex)
{
      fileProblem = true;
      Console::WriteLine(ex->message);
}
if (fileProblem == false)
{
      statements to process the records contained in the file
}  //end if
```

tip

You can use any name for the variable in the `catch` statement. In both examples shown in Figure 11-16, the name `ex` (short for "exception") is used.

The `try` statement begins with the keyword `try` and ends with a closing brace. In the `try` statement, you place the code that might generate an exception.

The `catch` statement begins with the keyword `catch`, followed by an exception type and the name of a variable; the `catch` statement ends with a closing brace. A `try/catch` block can contain multiple `catch` statements, with each `catch` statement handling a different type of exception. When an exception occurs in the code shown in the `try` statement, only one of the `catch` statements is processed. The appropriate `catch` statement depends on the exception that occurred.

In Example 1 in Figure 11-16, the `try` portion of the `try/catch` block contains two statements. The first statement, `average = totalScores / numberOfStudents;`, could generate an exception (error)—called the `DivideByZeroException`—if the `numberOfStudents` variable contains the number 0. If the statement does not generate a `DivideByZeroException`, the `catch` statement in the `try/catch` block is not processed. However, if the statement does generate a `DivideByZeroException`, the statement contained in the `catch` portion of the `try/catch` block is processed. That statement displays a message indicating the error that occurred. You display the message using the syntax *variablename*`->`**message**, where *variablename* is the name of the variable used in the **catch (***exceptiontype *variablename***)** clause. In this case, the message *Attempted to divide by zero.* will be displayed.

In Example 2 in Figure 11-16, the `try` portion of the `try/catch` block contains the statement `inFile = IO::File::OpenText("sales.txt");`, which opens a sequential access file for input. The statement will generate an exception—called the `IO::IOException`—if the sales.txt file does not exist. If the `IO::IOException` occurs, the two statements contained in the `catch` portion of the `try/catch` block are processed. The first statement assigns the Boolean value `true` to the `fileProblem` variable to indicate that there was a problem opening the file. The second statement, `Console::WriteLine(ex->message);`, displays a message indicating the error that occurred. In this case, the message *Could not find file "c:\cppnet\tut11\sales solution\sales project\sales.txt".* will be displayed.

Figure 11-17 shows the sales program with a **try/catch** block in both the **addRecords()** and **displayRecords()** functions. The **try/catch** blocks are shaded in the figure.

Figure 11-17: try/catch blocks included in the sales program

```
//sales.cpp
//writes records to and reads records from a sequential access file
#using <mscorlib.dll>
using namespace System;

//function prototypes
void addRecords();
void displayRecords();

int main()
{
    addRecords();
    displayRecords();
    return 0;
}   //end of main function

//*****function definitions*****
void addRecords()
{
    //declare variables
    String *name = "";
    int sales    = 0;
    bool fileProblem = false;

    //declare StreamWriter variable and open the file
    IO::StreamWriter *outFile;
    try
    {
       outFile = IO::File::AppendText("sales.txt");
    }
    catch (IO::IOException *ex)
    {
       Console::WriteLine(ex->Message);
       fileProblem = true;
    }

    if (fileProblem == false)
    {
       //get name and quarterly sales
       Console::Write("Enter the name (X to stop): ");
       name = Console::ReadLine();
       while (name->ToUpper()->CompareTo("X") != 0)
       {
           Console::Write("Enter the quarterly sales: ");
           sales = Convert::ToInt32(Console::ReadLine());

           //write record to file
           outFile->WriteLine("{0}#{1}", name,
           Convert::ToString(sales));

           Console::Write("Enter the name (X to stop): ");
           name = Console::ReadLine();
       } //end while
```

Figure 11-17: try/catch blocks included in the sales program (continued)

```
        //close the file
        outFile->Close();
    } //end if
} //end of addRecords function

void displayRecords()
{
    //declare variables
    String *name    = "";
    int sales       = 0;
    String *record = "";
    int position    = 0;
    bool fileProblem = false;

    //declare StreamReader variable and open the file
    IO::StreamReader *inFile;
    try
    {
        inFile = IO::File::OpenText("sales.txt");
    }
    catch (IO::IOException *ex)
    {
        fileProblem = true;
        Console::WriteLine(ex->Message);
    }
    if (fileProblem == false)
    {
        //read and display records
        while (inFile->Peek() != -1)
        {
            record = inFile->ReadLine();
            position = record->IndexOf("#", 0);
            name = record->Substring(0, position);
            sales = Convert::ToInt32(record->Substring(position + 1));
            Console::WriteLine("{0}{1}", name->PadRight(15),
            sales.ToString("N0")->PadLeft(10));
        } //end while

        //close the file
        inFile->Close();
    } //end if
} //end of displayRecords function
```

You now have completed Tutorial 11's Concept lesson. You can either take a break or complete the end-of-lesson questions and exercises before moving on to the Application lesson.

SUMMARY

Files to which information is written by the computer are called output files, while files that are read by the computer are called input files. The information in a sequential access file is always accessed in consecutive order (sequentially) from the beginning of the file through the end of the file.

In Visual C++ .NET, you use a `StreamWriter` object to write a sequence of characters, referred to as a stream, to a sequential access file. You use a `StreamReader` object to read a stream (sequence of characters) from a sequential access file.

You declare `StreamWriter` and `StreamReader` variables using the syntax *datatype* **variablename*;, where *datatype* is either `IO::StreamWriter` or `IO::StreamReader`, and *variablename* is the name of the variable. You use the syntax *streamvariable* **= IO::File::***method***(***filename***);**, where *streamvariable* is the name of a `StreamWriter` or `StreamReader` variable, to open a sequential access file named *filename*. When you open a sequential access file, the computer creates either a `StreamWriter` or `StreamReader` object, depending on the *method* specified in the syntax. *Method* can be the `CreateText()`, `OpenText()`, or `AppendText()` method.

You use either the `Write()` or `WriteLine()` method to write data to a sequential access file. You use the `ReadLine()` method to read a line of text from a sequential access file. You use the `Peek()` method to determine whether a file contains another character to read. If the file contains another character, the `Peek()` method returns the character; otherwise, it returns the number `-1`.

A field is a single item of information about a person, place, or thing. A record is one or more related fields that contain all of the necessary data about a specific person, place, or thing.

You can use the `PadLeft()` method to right-align the characters in a string, and the `PadRight()` method to left-align the characters in a string. You can use the `IndexOf()` method to search a string to determine whether it contains a specific sequence of characters. You can use the `Substring()` method to access one or more characters from a string.

To prevent the loss of data, you should use the `Close()` method to close a sequential access file as soon as you are finished using it.

You can use a `try/catch` block to catch an exception when it occurs in a C++ program, and then have the computer take the appropriate action to resolve the problem.

ANSWERS TO MINI-QUIZZES

Mini-Quiz 1

1) stream (or stream of characters)
2) c. `IO::StreamWriter *outFile;`
3) b. `CreateText()`
4) `inFile = IO::File::OpenText("employ.txt");`

Mini-Quiz 2

1) a. `outFile->WriteLine(quantity);`
2) d. `outFile->WriteLine("{0}#{1}", city, state);`
3) d. `priceString = priceString->PadRight(4, '*');`
4) b. right-aligns

Mini-Quiz 3

1) a. -1

2) d. all of the above

3) c. `temp = state->Substring(0, 5);`

4) b. false

QUESTIONS

1) Which of the following statements creates a variable that can be used when reading a sequential access file?

A. `IO::CharReader *inFile;`

B. `IO::CharacterReader *inFile;`

C. `IO::FileReader *inFile;`

D. `IO::StreamReader *inFile;`

2) Which of the following methods opens the names.txt file and allows the computer to write information to the end of the existing data in the file?

A. `IO::File::AddText("names.txt")`

B. `IO::File::AppendText("names.txt")`

C. `IO::File::CreateText("names.txt")`

D. `IO::File::OpenText("names.txt")`

3) The `OpenText()` method creates a(n) ______________ object.

A. `OpenStream`

B. `StreamOpen`

C. `StreamReader`

D. `StreamWriter`

4) If the file you want to open exists, the ______________ method erases the file's contents.

A. `AddText()`

B. `AppendText()`

C. `CreateText()`

D. `OpenText()`

5) If the file you want to open does not exist, the ______________ method produces an error.

A. `AddText()`

B. `AppendText()`

C. `CreateText()`

D. `OpenText()`

6) Which of the following writes the string "Your pay is $56" to a sequential access file? (Assume that the `pay` variable is an `int` variable that contains the number 56.)

A.
```
outFile->Write("Your pay is $");
outFile->WriteLine(pay);
```

B.
```
outFile->WriteLine("Your pay is ${0}",
Convert::ToString(pay));
```

C. `outFile->WriteLine("Your pay is {0}",`
`pay.ToString("C0"));`

D. all of the above

7) Assume that the `state` variable contains the string "Florida". Which of the following statements assigns six spaces followed by the contents of the `state` variable to the `state` variable?

A. `state = state->PadLeft(6);`

B. `state = state->PadLeft(13);`

C. `state = state.PadRight(13);`

D. `state = state.Pad(13);`

8) You use the ____________ method to right-align the characters in a string.

A. `AlignLeft()`

B. `PadLeft()`

C. `PadRight()`

D. `StringLeft()`

9) Assume that the `message` variable contains the string "Great job". Which of the following statements assigns the contents of the `message` variable followed by four exclamation points (!) to the `newMessage` variable?

A. `newMessage = message->PadRight(4, '!');`

B. `newMessage = message->PadRight(13, '!');`

C. `newMessage = message->PadRight(4, "!");`

D. `newMessage = message->PadRight(13, "!");`

10) Which of the following statements reads a line of text from a sequential access file, and assigns the line (excluding the line terminator character) to the `textLine` variable?

A. `inFile->ReadLine(textLine);`

B. `textline = Console::ReadLine(inFile);`

C. `textLine = inFile->File::ReadLine();`

D. `textLine = inFile->ReadLine();`

11) You can use the `Close()` method to close files opened for ____________.

A. append

B. input

C. output

D. all of the above

12) The index of the first character in a string is ____________.

A. 0 (zero)

B. 1 (one)

13) Which of the following `if` clauses determines whether the string stored in the `part` variable begins with the letter A?

A. `if (part->Substring(0, 1)->CompareTo("A") == 0)`

B. `if (part->Substring(1, 1)->CompareTo("A") == 0)`

C. `if (part->Substring(0, 1) == "A")`

D. `if (part->Substring(1, "A") == true)`

14) Which of the following statements assigns the first three characters in the `part` variable to the `code` variable?

A. `code = part->Assign(0, 3);`

B. `code = part->Sub(0, 3);`

C. `code = part->Substring(0, 3);`

D. `code = part->Substring(3, 0);`

15) Assuming that the `message` variable contains the string "Happy holidays", the `message->IndexOf("day")` method returns ______________.

A. -1

B. 10

C. 11

D. day

16) Assuming that the `message` variable contains the string "Happy holidays", the `message->ToUpper()->IndexOf("Day")` method returns ______________.

A. -1

B. 10

C. 11

D. day

17) Assuming that the `message` variable contains the string "Happy holidays", the `message->IndexOf("days", 1)` method returns ______________.

A. -1

B. 10

C. 11

D. day

18) A ______________ is a single item of information about a person, place, or thing.

A. data file

B. field

C. program file

D. record

19) Which of the following `while` clauses tells the computer to repeat the loop instructions until the end of the file associated with the `inFile` variable is reached?

A. `while (inFile->Peek() == 0)`

B. `while inFile->Peek() == -1)`

C. `while (inFile->Peek() != 0)`

D. `while (inFile->Peek() != -1)`

20) The ______________ section of a `try/catch` block contains the statements that might generate an exception.

A. `catch`

B. `error`

C. `exception`

D. `try`

Look For These Symbols

Debugging

Discovery

EXERCISES

1) Write the statement to declare a `StreamReader` variable named `inSales`.

2) Write the statement to open a sequential access file named jansales.txt for input. Assign the resulting `StreamReader` object to the `inSales` variable.

3) Write the statement to open a sequential access file named firstQtr.txt for append. Assign the resulting `StreamWriter` object to the `outQtrSales` variable.

4) Write the statement to open a sequential access file named febsales.txt for output. Assign the resulting `StreamWriter` object to the `outFebSales` variable.

5) Assume you want to write the string "Employee" and the string "Name" to the sequential access file associated with the `outFile` variable. Each string should appear on a separate line in the file. Write the code to accomplish this task.

6) Assume you want to write the contents of a `String` variable named `capital` and the line terminator character to the sequential access file associated with the `outFile` variable. Write the code to accomplish this task.

7) Assume that the `sales` variable contains the number 2356.75. Write the statement to assign the contents of the `sales` variable (formatted to "C2") to a `String` variable named `salesString`. The statement also should right-align the contents of the `salesString` variable, which should contain a total of 15 characters. Use the space character to pad the variable.

8) Assume you want a `String` variable named `award` to contain 10 characters, which should be right-aligned in the variable. Write the statement to accomplish this task. Use the asterisk character to pad the variable.

9) Write the statement that will ensure that the `name` variable contains 30 characters, which should be left-aligned in the variable. Use the space character to pad the variable.

10) Write the statement to read a line of text from the sequential access file associated with the `inFile` variable. Assign the line of text (excluding the line terminator character) to the `textLine` variable.

11) Assume you want to read a sequential access file, line by line, and display each line on the computer screen. The file is associated with the `inFile` variable. Write the code to accomplish this task.

12) Write the statement to close the jansales.txt file, which is associated with the `outFile` variable.

13) Assume that the `part` variable contains the string "ABCD34G". Write the statement that assigns the number 34 in the `part` variable to the `code` variable.

14) Write the statement that uses the `IndexOf()` method to determine whether the `address` variable contains the street name "Elm Street" (entered in uppercase, lowercase, or a combination of uppercase and lowercase). Begin the search with the first character in the `address` variable, and assign the method's return value to the `index` variable.

15) In this exercise, you modify the sales program that you viewed in the lesson. The modified program will calculate the total sales amount and then display the amount on the screen.

A. If necessary, start Visual Studio .NET. Open the T11ConE15 Solution (T11ConE15 Solution.sln) file, which is contained in the CppNet\Tut11\T11ConE15 Solution folder.

B. Change the name of the `displayRecords()` function to `displayRecordsAndTotal()`. Modify the `displayRecords-AndTotal()` function so that it calculates the total sales made during the quarter. The function should display the total sales amount after displaying the records in the file. Format the total sales amount using the "C2" format.

C. Save and then build the solution.

D. Execute the program. Test the program by entering the following names and sales amounts:

Karen, 500
Sam, 750
June, 1300
X

E. Each record and the total sales ($2,550.00) should appear on separate lines in the Command Prompt window. Close the Command Prompt window.

F. When the program is working correctly, close the Output window, and then use the File menu to close the solution.

16) Mary Conrad wants a program that allows her to save each letter of the alphabet in a sequential access file. She will enter the letters from the keyboard.

A. If necessary, start Visual Studio .NET. Open the T11ConE16 Solution (T11ConE16 Solution.sln) file, which is contained in the CppNet\Tut11\T11ConE16 Solution folder.

B. Code the program. Name the sequential access file letters.txt. Open the file for output.

C. Save and then build the solution.

D. Execute the program. Enter the 26 letters of the alphabet, one at a time. Close the Command Prompt window.

E. Click File on the menu bar, point to Open, and then click File. Click the Files of type list arrow, then click All Files (*.*) in the list. Open the letters.txt file. The file should contain 26 letters. Each letter should appear on a separate line in the file. Close the letters.txt window.

F. When the program is working correctly, close the Output window, and then use the File menu to close the solution.

17) Cheryl Perry wants a program that saves the squares of the numbers from 1 through 25 in a sequential access file.

A. If necessary, start Visual Studio .NET. Open the T11ConE17 Solution (T11ConE17 Solution.sln) file, which is contained in the CppNet\Tut11\T11ConE17 Solution folder.

B. Code the program. Name the sequential access file squares.txt. Open the file for output.

C. Save and then build the solution.

D. Execute the program. Close the Command Prompt window.

E. Click File on the menu bar, point to Open, and then click File. Click the Files of type list arrow, then click All Files (*.*) in the list. Open the squares.txt file. The file should contain 25 numbers. Each number should appear on a separate line in the file. Close the squares.txt window.

F. When the program is working correctly, close the Output window, and then use the File menu to close the solution.

18) The manager of Checks Inc. wants a program that saves each week's total payroll amount in a sequential access file.

A. If necessary, start Visual Studio .NET. Open the T11ConE18 Solution (T11ConE18 Solution.sln) file, which is contained in the CppNet\Tut11\T11ConE18 Solution folder.

B. Code the program. Name the sequential access file payroll.txt. Open the file for append. Use a negative number as the sentinel value.

C. Save and then build the solution.

D. Execute the program. Enter the following two payroll amounts: 45678.99 and 67000.56. Stop the loop by entering a negative number, then close the Command Prompt window.

E. Execute the program again. Enter the following two payroll amounts: 25000.89 and 35600.55. Stop the loop by entering a negative number, then close the Command Prompt window.

F. Click File on the menu bar, point to Open, and then click File. Click the Files of type list arrow, then click All Files (*.*) in the list. Open the payroll.txt file. The file should contain the four amounts listed in Steps D and E. Each amount should appear on a separate line in the file. Close the payroll.txt window.

G. When the program is working correctly, close the Output window, and then use the File menu to close the solution.

19) The manager of Boggs Inc. wants a program that saves the price of each inventory item in a sequential access file.

A. If necessary, start Visual Studio .NET. Open the T11ConE19 Solution (T11ConE19 Solution.sln) file, which is contained in the CppNet\Tut11\T11ConE19 Solution folder.

B. Code the program. Use a negative number as the sentinel value. Name the sequential access file prices.txt. Open the file for append.

C. Save and then build the solution.

D. Execute the program. Enter the following two prices: 10.50 and 15.99. Stop the loop by entering a negative number, then close the Command Prompt window.

E. Execute the program again. Enter the following three prices: 20, 76.54, and 17.34. Stop the loop by entering a negative number, then close the Command Prompt window.

F. Click File on the menu bar, point to Open, and then click File. Click the Files of type list arrow, then click All Files (*.*) in the list. Open the prices.txt file. The file should contain the five amounts listed in Steps D and E. Each amount should appear on a separate line in the file. Close the prices.txt window.

G. When the program is working correctly, close the Output window, and then use the File menu to close the solution.

20) Mary Conrad wants a program that counts the number of letters stored in the file that you created in Exercise 16.

A. Use Windows to copy the letters.txt file from the CppNet\Tut11\T11ConE16 Solution\T11ConE16 Project folder to the CppNet\Tut11\T11ConE20 Solution\T11ConE20 Project folder.

B. If necessary, start Visual Studio .NET. Open the T11ConE20 Solution (T11ConE20 Solution.sln) file, which is contained in the CppNet\Tut11\T11ConE20 Solution folder.

C. Code the program. Display the count on the computer screen.

D. Save and then build the solution. Execute the program. The program should display the number 26 in the Command Prompt window. Close the Command Prompt window.

E. When the program is working correctly, close the Output window, and then use the File menu to close the solution.

21) Cheryl Perry wants a program that displays the sum of the numbers stored in the file that you created in Exercise 17.

A. Use Windows to copy the squares.txt file from the CppNet\Tut11\T11ConE17 Solution\T11ConE17 Project folder to the CppNet\Tut11\T11ConE21 Solution\T11ConE21 Project folder.

B. If necessary, start Visual Studio .NET. Open the T11ConE21 Solution (T11ConE21 Solution.sln) file, which is contained in the CppNet\Tut11\T11ConE21 Solution folder.

C. Code the program. Display the sum, formatted using the "N0" format, on the computer screen.

D. Save and then build the solution. Execute the program. The program should display the number 5,525 in the Command Prompt window. Close the Command Prompt window.

E. When the program is working correctly, close the Output window, and then use the File menu to close the solution.

22) The manager of Checks Inc. wants a program that calculates and displays the total of the weekly payroll amounts stored in the file that you created in Exercise 18.

A. Use Windows to copy the payroll.txt file from the CppNet\Tut11\T11ConE18 Solution\T11ConE18 Project folder to the CppNet\Tut11\T11ConE22 Solution\T11ConE22 Project folder.

B. If necessary, start Visual Studio .NET. Open the T11ConE22 Solution (T11ConE22 Solution.sln) file, which is contained in the CppNet\Tut11\T11ConE22 Solution folder.

C. Code the program. Display the total amount, formatted using the "C2" format, on the computer screen.

D. Save and then build the solution. Execute the program. The program should display the number $173,280.99 in the Command Prompt window. Close the Command Prompt window.

E. When the program is working correctly, close the Output window, and then use the File menu to close the solution.

23) The manager of Boggs Inc. wants a program that calculates and displays the average price of the company's inventory items. The price of each inventory item is stored in the file that you created in Exercise 19.

A. Use Windows to copy the prices.txt file from the CppNet\Tut11\T11ConE19 Solution\T11ConE19 Project folder to the CppNet\Tut11\T11ConE23 Solution\T11ConE23 Project folder.

B. If necessary, start Visual Studio .NET. Open the T11ConE23 Solution (T11ConE23 Solution.sln) file, which is contained in the CppNet\Tut11\T11ConE23 Solution folder.

C. Code the program. Display the average price, formatted using the "C2" format, on the computer screen.

D. Save and then build the solution. Execute the program. The program should display the number $28.07 in the Command Prompt window. Close the Command Prompt window.

E. When the program is working correctly, close the Output window, and then use the File menu to close the solution.

24) The manager of Stellar Company wants a program that saves the company's payroll codes and corresponding salaries in a sequential access file.

A. If necessary, start Visual Studio .NET. Open the T11ConE24 Solution (T11ConE24 Solution.sln) file, which is contained in the CppNet\Tut11\T11ConE24 Solution folder.

B. Code the program. Name the sequential access file codes.txt. Open the file for output. When writing the records to the file, use the # character to separate one field from another.

C. Save and then build the solution.

D. Execute the program. Enter the following codes and salaries:

Code	Salary
A	27200
B	15000
C	23000
D	12000
E	25500

E. Close the Command Prompt window.

F. Click File on the menu bar, point to Open, and then click File. Click the Files of type list arrow, then click All Files (*.*) in the list. Open the codes.txt file. The file should contain five records, each having two fields separated by the # character. Close the codes.txt window.

G. When the program is working correctly, close the Output window, and then use the File menu to close the solution.

25) The manager of Boggs Inc. wants a program that records, in a sequential access file, the inventory number, quantity, and price of the items in inventory.

A. If necessary, start Visual Studio .NET. Open the T11ConE25 Solution (T11ConE25 Solution.sln) file, which is contained in the CppNet\Tut11\T11ConE25 Solution folder.

B. Code the program. Name the sequential access file inventory.txt. Open the file for output. When writing the records to the file, use the # character to separate one field from another.

C. Save and then build the solution.

D. Execute the program. Enter the following inventory numbers, quantities, and prices:

Inventory number	Quantity	Price ($)
20AB	400	5
30CD	550	9
45XX	600	20

E. Close the Command Prompt window.

F. Click File on the menu bar, point to Open, and then click File. Click the Files of type list arrow, then click All Files (*.*) in the list. Open the inventory.txt file. The file should contain three records, each having three fields separated by the # character. Close the inventory.txt window.

G. When the program is working correctly, close the Output window, and then use the File menu to close the solution.

26) The manager of Stellar Company wants a program that displays the codes and salaries stored in the file that you created in Exercise 24.

A. Use Windows to copy the codes.txt file from the CppNet\Tut11\T11ConE24 Solution\T11ConE24 Project folder to the CppNet\Tut11\T11ConE26 Solution\T11ConE26 Project folder.

B. If necessary, start Visual Studio .NET. Open the T11ConE26 Solution (T11ConE26 Solution.sln) file, which is contained in the CppNet\Tut11\ T11ConE26 Solution folder.

C. Code the program. Display the information in two columns on the computer screen. Display the column headings "Code" and "Salary". Format the salary amounts to "C0".

D. Save and then build the solution. Execute the program. The program should display the fives codes and salaries stored in the codes.txt file. Close the Command Prompt window.

E. When the program is working correctly, close the Output window, and then use the File menu to close the solution.

27) The manager of Boggs Inc. wants a program that calculates and displays the total dollar value of the items in inventory. The inventory numbers, quantities, and prices are stored in the file that you created in Exercise 25.

A. Use Windows to copy the inventory.txt file from the CppNet\Tut11\ T11ConE25 Solution\T11ConE25 Project folder to the CppNet\Tut11\ T11ConE27 Solution\T11ConE27 Project folder.

B. If necessary, start Visual Studio .NET. Open the T11ConE27 Solution (T11ConE27 Solution.sln) file, which is contained in the CppNet\Tut11\ T11ConE27 Solution folder.

C. Code the program. Display the information in three columns on the computer screen. Use the column headings "Number", "Quantity", and "Price". Display the price using the "C2" format, and right-align the numbers.

D. Save and then build the solution. Execute the program. The program should display the three inventory numbers, quantities, and prices stored in the inventory.txt file. Close the Command Prompt window.

E. When the program is working correctly, close the Output window, and then use the File menu to close the solution.

28) In this exercise, you learn about the `StartsWith()` and `EndsWith()` methods.

A. You can use the `StartsWith()` method to determine whether a specific sequence of characters occurs at the beginning of a string. Research the `StartsWith()` method, then write an `if` statement that uses the `StartsWith()` method to determine whether the string stored in a `String` variable named `sales` begins with the dollar sign; if it does, assign the contents of the variable, excluding the dollar sign, to the `sales` variable.

B. You can use the `EndsWith()` method to determine whether a specific sequence of characters occurs at the end of a string. Research the `EndsWith()` method, then write an `if` statement that uses the `EndsWith()` method to determine whether the string stored in a `String` variable named `rate` ends with the percent sign; if it does, assign the contents of the variable, excluding the percent sign, to the `rate` variable.

29) In this exercise, you debug a C++ program.

A. If necessary, start Visual Studio .NET. Open the T11ConE29 Solution (T11ConE29 Solution.sln) file, which is contained in the CppNet\Tut11\T11ConE29 Solution folder.

B. Study the existing code, then build the solution.

C. Execute the program. Enter Chair as the item name and 10 as the quantity, then enter Table as the item name and 20 as the quantity. Enter x as the item name. Close the Command Prompt window.

D. Click File on the menu bar, point to Open, and then click File. Click the Files of type list arrow, then click All Files (*.*) in the list. Open the items.txt file, which is contained in the CppNet\Tut11\T11ConE29 Solution\T11ConE29 Project folder. Notice that the file is empty. Close the items.txt window.

E. Correct any errors in the program, then save and build the program again. Enter Chair as the item name and 10 as the quantity, then enter Table as the item name and 20 as the quantity. Enter x as the item name. Close the Command Prompt window.

F. Open the items.txt file. This time, the file should contain the two records.

G. When the program is working correctly, close the Output window, and then use the File menu to close the solution.

30) In this exercise, you debug a C++ program.

A. If necessary, start Visual Studio .NET. Open the T11ConE30 Solution (T11ConE30 Solution.sln) file, which is contained in the CppNet\Tut11\T11ConE30 Solution folder.

B. Click File on the menu bar, point to Open, and then click File. Click the Files of type list arrow, then click All Files (*.*) in the list. Open the names.txt file, which is contained in the CppNet\Tut11\T11ConE30 Solution\T11ConE30 Project folder. Notice that the file contains six records. Each record contains a last name, a # symbol, and a first name. Close the names.txt window.

C. Study the existing code, then build the solution.

D. Execute the program. The program should display two columns of information, as shown below:

```
First    Last
Joe      Brown
Sue      Jacobs
Jack     Paulson
John     Soo
Muret    Abu
Maurice  Williams
```

E. Close the Command Prompt window. Correct any errors in the program, then save and build the solution. Execute the program.

F. When the program is working correctly, close the Output window, and then use the File menu to close the solution.

Application Lesson

Using a Sequential Access File in a C++ Program

CASE Your nephew John recently completed two C++ courses at a community college, and already has accepted a programming job at a company; he starts in two weeks. Although he performed well in the C++ courses, receiving a grade of A in both, he feels he needs more practice creating classes and objects before he starts his new job. He has asked for your help. You decide to show John the class and programs you created for the owner of Flowers Express, a small flower shop.

Viewing the Salesperson Class

Last month, you created a program for Bob Marquart, the owner of Flowers Express. The program allows Bob to record each salesclerk's name and monthly sales amount in a sequential access file. It also allows him to total the sales amounts contained in the file, and then display the total on the computer screen.

Before creating the Flowers Express program, you defined a `Salesperson` class, which you used to create a `Salesperson` object in the program. Figure 11-18 shows the `Salesperson` class definition.

Figure 11-18: `Salesperson` **class definition**

```
//declaration section
__gc class Salesperson
{
public:
        Salesperson();
        void WriteRecordToFile(String *, int, IO::StreamWriter *);
        void ReadRecordFromFile(IO::StreamReader *);
        String *GetName();
        int GetSales();
private:
        String *name;
        int sales;
};


//implementation section
Salesperson::Salesperson()
{
    name  = "";
    sales = 0;
} //end of default constructor

void Salesperson::WriteRecordToFile(String *n, int s,
IO::StreamWriter *outF)
{
    name = n;
    sales = s;
    outF->WriteLine("{0}#{1}", name, Convert::ToString(sales));
} //end of WriteRecordToFile method
```

Figure 11-18: `Salesperson` class definition (continued)

```
void Salesperson::ReadRecordFromFile(IO::StreamReader *inF)
{
    String *record = "";
    int position   = 0;
    record = inF->ReadLine();
    position = record->IndexOf("#", 0);
    name = record->Substring(0, position);
    sales = Convert::ToInt32(record->Substring(position + 1));
} //end of ReadRecordFromFile method

String *Salesperson::GetName()
{
    return name;
} //end of GetName method

int Salesperson::GetSales()
{
    return sales;
} //end of GetSales method
```

As the declaration section shows, the `Salesperson` class contains two private data members (variables) named `name` and `sales`. The data members represent the attributes of a `Salesperson` object. The class also contains five public member methods. Each member method corresponds to a task that a `Salesperson` object can perform. In this case, a `Salesperson` object can initialize its private data members, write a record to a file, read a record from a file, and return the values stored in its private data members.

The first method listed in the implementation section is the default constructor. As you learned in Tutorial 10, the default constructor's task is to initialize the private data members of the class. In this case, the constructor does so by assigning the empty string and the number 0 to the `name` and `sales` variables, respectively.

The second method, `WriteRecordToFile()`, writes a salesperson's record, which consists of a name and a sales amount, to a sequential access file. The name and sales amount, as well as the `StreamWriter` object associated with the sequential access file, is passed to the `WriteRecordToFile()` method by the program that calls it.

The third method, `ReadRecordFromFile()`, reads a record from a sequential access file, and assigns the field values to the private data members of the class. The `StreamReader` object associated with the sequential access file is passed to the `ReadRecordFromFile()` method by the program that calls it.

The fourth and fifth methods, `GetName()` and `GetSales()`, simply return the values stored in the private data members of the class.

Next, you view the Flowers Express program.

tip

Although the Flowers Express program that you complete in this lesson will not need to view the contents of the `name` data member included in the `Salesperson` class, other programs using the class to create `Salesperson` objects may need to do so. Therefore, you should include the `GetName()` method in the class. Recall from Tutorial 10 that a good class is one whose objects can be used in a variety of ways by many different programs.

The Flowers Express Program

The Flowers Express program contains four functions: `main()`, `displayMenu()`, `addRecords()`, and `displayTotal()`. Figure 11-19 shows the code entered in the program's `main()` and `displayMenu()` functions.

Figure 11-19: Code entered in the `main()` and `displayMenu()` functions

```
int main()
{
    //declare variable
    int menuChoice = 0;
    //display menu and get choice
    menuChoice = displayMenu();
    while (menuChoice != 3)
    {
        if (menuChoice == 1)
            addRecords();
        else if (menuChoice == 2)
            displayTotal();
        else
            Console::WriteLine("Invalid menu choice");
        //end ifs
        menuChoice = displayMenu();
    }   //end while
    return 0;
}     //end of main function

//*****function definitions*****
int displayMenu()
{
    //display menu options and get user's choice
    Console::WriteLine("Options");
    Console::WriteLine("1     Add Records");
    Console::WriteLine("2     Display Total Sales");
    Console::WriteLine("3     Exit Program");
    Console::Write("Enter menu option: ");
    return Convert::ToInt32(Console::ReadLine());
}   //end of displayMenu function
```

The `main()` function begins by declaring and initializing an `int` variable named `menuChoice`. It then calls the `displayMenu()` function to display a menu that contains three options: Add Records, Display Total Sales, and Exit Program. After displaying the menu, the `displayMenu()` function prompts the user to enter his or her menu choice: 1 to add records, 2 to display the total sales, or 3 to exit the program. The user's response is returned to the `main()` function, which assigns the returned value to the `menuChoice` variable.

The `while (menuChoice != 3)` clause in the `main()` function repeats the loop body instructions as long as (or while) the `menuChoice` variable does not contain the number 3. (Recall that menu choice 3 indicates that the user wants to exit the program.) The first instruction in the loop body is a selection structure that compares the contents of the `menuChoice` variable with the number 1. If the `menuChoice` variable contains the number 1, the `main()` function calls the `addRecords()` function to add one or more records to a sequential access file. When the `addRecords()` function completes its processing, the `main()` function calls the `displayMenu()` function to display the menu.

If the `menuChoice` variable does not contain the number 1, the nested selection structure in the loop body compares the contents of the `menuChoice` variable to the number 2. If the `menuChoice` variable contains the number 2, the `main()` function calls the

displayTotal() function to total the sales amounts stored in the sequential access file and then display the total on the screen. When the **displayTotal()** function completes its processing, the **main()** function calls the **displayMenu()** function to display the menu.

If the **menuChoice** variable contains a value other than 1, 2, or 3, the **main()** function displays an appropriate error message before calling the **displayMenu()** function to display the menu.

Next, view the Flowers Express program's **addRecords()** function.

The addRecords() Function

Figure 11-20 shows the code entered in the Flowers Express program's **addRecords()** function. The lines of code pertaining to the **Salesperson** object are shaded in the figure.

Figure 11-20: Code entered in the addRecords() function

```
void addRecords()
{
    //declare variables
    String *name = "";
    int sales     = 0;
    bool fileProblem = false;
    //declare Salesperson object
    Salesperson *salesObj = new Salesperson;

    //declare StreamWriter variable and open the file
    IO::StreamWriter *outFile;
    try
    {
        outFile = IO::File::AppendText("sales.txt");
    }
    catch (IO::IOException *ex)
    {
        Console::WriteLine(ex->Message);
        fileProblem = true;
    }

    if (fileProblem == false)
    {
        //get name and monthly sales
        Console::Write("Enter the name (X to stop): ");
        name = Console::ReadLine();
        while (name->ToUpper()->CompareTo("X") != 0)
        {
            Console::Write("Enter the monthly sales: ");
            sales = Convert::ToInt32(Console::ReadLine());

            //write record to file
            salesObj->WriteRecordToFile(name, sales, outFile);

            Console::Write("Enter the name (X to stop): ");
            name = Console::ReadLine();
        } //end while

        //close the file
        outFile->Close();
    }   //end if
} //end of addRecords function
```

The addRecords() function begins by declaring and initializing the name, sales, and fileProblem variables. The Salesperson *salesObj = new Salesperson; statement then uses the Salesperson class to declare (create) a Salesperson object named salesObj. Recall that the default constructor in the Salesperson class initializes the salesObj object when the object is created.

Next, the IO::StreamWriter *outFile; statement declares a StreamWriter variable named outFile to store the address of a StreamWriter object. A try/catch block then is used to catch and handle any exception generated by the outFile = IO::File::AppendText("sales.txt"); statement. This statement creates a StreamWriter object and assigns its address to the outFile variable; it also opens a sequential access file named sales.txt for append. Notice that, if an exception occurs when opening the file, the catch section of the try/catch block first displays a message indicating the reason for the exception, and then assigns the Boolean value true to the fileProblem variable.

If the fileProblem variable contains the Boolean value true, the addRecords() function ends. Processing continues with the menuChoice = displayMenu(); statement located in the loop body in the main() function.

However, if the fileProblem variable contains the Boolean value false, the addRecords() function prompts the user to enter a name, and then stores the user's response in the name variable. The while (name->ToUpper()->CompareTo("X") != 0) clause indicates that the computer should repeat the loop body instructions as long as the name variable contains a value other than X (in any case).

The first two statements in the loop body prompt the user to enter a sales amount and store the user's response, converted to the int data type, in the sales variable. The salesObj->WriteRecordToFile(name, sales, outFile); statement calls the WriteRecordToFile() method, which is a public member method defined in the Salesperson class, to write the name and sales information to the sequential access file associated with the outFile variable. The last two statements in the loop body prompt the user to enter a name, and then store the user's response in the name variable. When the loop completes its processing, which occurs when the user enters either the letter X or the letter x as the name, the outfile->Close(); statement closes the output file before the addRecords() function ends. Processing continues with the menuChoice = displayMenu(); statement located in the loop body in the main() function.

Next, view the Flowers Express program's displayTotal() function.

The displayTotal() Function

Figure 11-21 shows the code entered in the Flowers Express program's displayTotal() function. The lines of code pertaining to the Salesperson object are shaded in the figure.

Figure 11-21: Code entered in the `displayTotal()` function

```
void displayTotal()
{
    //declare variables
    int total = 0;
    bool fileProblem = false;
    //declare Salesperson object
    Salesperson *salesObj = new Salesperson;

    //declare StreamReader variable and open the file
    IO::StreamReader *inFile;
    try
    {
        inFile = IO::File::OpenText("sales.txt");
    }
    catch (IO::IOException *ex)
    {
        Console::WriteLine(ex->Message);
        fileProblem = true;
    }

    if (fileProblem == false)
    {
        //read record and add sales amount to total sales
        while (inFile->Peek() != -1)
        {
            salesObj->ReadRecordFromFile(inFile);
            total = total + salesObj->GetSales();
        } //end while

        //display the total sales amount
        Console::WriteLine("Total sales: {0}", total.ToString("C2"));

        //close the file
        inFile->Close();
    } //end if
} //end of displayTotal function
```

The `displayTotal()` function begins by declaring and initializing the `total` and `fileProblem` variables. The `Salesperson *salesObj = new Salesperson;` statement then uses the `Salesperson` class to declare (create) a `Salesperson` object named `salesObj`. Recall that the default constructor in the `Salesperson` class initializes the `salesObj` object when the object is created.

Next, the `IO::StreamReader *inFile;` statement declares a `StreamReader` variable named `inFile` to store the address of a `StreamReader` object. A `try/catch` block then is used to catch and handle any exception generated by the `inFile = IO::File::OpenText("sales.txt");` statement. This statement creates a `StreamReader` object and assigns its address to the `inFile` variable; it also opens a sequential access file named sales.txt for input. Notice that, if an exception occurs when opening the file, the `catch` section of the `try/catch` block first displays a message indicating the reason for the exception, and then assigns the Boolean value `true` to the `fileProblem` variable.

If the fileProblem variable contains the Boolean value true, the displayTotal() function ends. Processing continues with the menuChoice = displayMenu(); statement located in the loop body in the main() function.

However, if the fileProblem variable contains the Boolean value false, the computer processes the while (inFile->Peek() != -1) clause in the displayTotal() function. The clause indicates that the computer should process the loop body instructions as long as there are characters to read in the sequential access file associated with the inFile variable.

The first statement in the loop body, salesObj->ReadRecordFromFile (inFile);, calls the ReadRecordFromFile() method, which is a public member method defined in the Salesperson class, to read a record from the sequential access file associated with the inFile variable, and store the field values in the private data members of the Salesperson class. The second statement in the loop, total = total + salesObj->GetSales();, calls the GetSales() method, which is a public member method defined in the Salesperson class, to return the value stored in the sales data member. The statement adds the value returned by the GetSales() method to the accumulator variable, total.

When the loop completes its processing, which occurs when the file pointer is at the end of the sequential access file, the last two statements in the displayTotal() function display the total sales amount on the screen, and then close the sales.txt file before the displayTotal() function ends. Processing continues with the menuChoice = displayMenu(); statement located in the loop body in the main() function.

Next, you complete the Flowers Express program by entering the missing instructions in the program.

Completing the Flowers Express Program

Your computer's hard disk contains a C++ header file that contains the Salesperson class definition. You open the header file and view its contents in the next set of steps.

To open the header file that contains the Salesperson class definition:

1. Start Microsoft Visual Studio .NET. If necessary, close the Start Page window.
2. Click **File** on the menu bar, point to **Open**, and then click **File**.
3. Locate and then open the **CppNet\MyClasses** folder.
4. Click **T11App.h** in the list of filenames, and then click the **Open** button. Figure 11-22 shows the Salesperson class definition contained in the T11App.h file.

Figure 11-22: Salesperson class definition contained in the T11App.h header file

```
//T11App.h
//defines a Salesperson class

//declaration section
__gc class Salesperson
{
```

Figure 11-22: `Salesperson` **class definition contained in the T11App.h header file (continued)**

```
public:
        Salesperson();
        void WriteRecordToFile(String *, int,
        IO::StreamWriter *);
        void ReadRecordFromFile(IO::StreamReader *);
        String *GetName();
        int GetSales();
private:
        String *name;
        int sales;
};

//implementation section
Salesperson::Salesperson()
{
    name  = "";
    sales = 0;
} //end of default constructor

void Salesperson::WriteRecordToFile(String *n, int s,
IO::StreamWriter *outF)
{
    name = n;
    sales = s;
    outF->WriteLine("{0}#{1}", name,
    Convert::ToString(sales));
} //end of WriteRecordToFile method

void Salesperson::ReadRecordFromFile(IO::StreamReader *inF)
{
    String *record = "";
    int position   = 0;
    record = inF->ReadLine();
    position = record->IndexOf("#", 0);
    name = record->Substring(0, position);
    sales = Convert::ToInt32(record->Substring
    (position + 1));
} //end of ReadRecordFromFile method

String *Salesperson::GetName()
{
    return name;
} //end of GetName method

int Salesperson::GetSales()
{
    return sales;
} //end of GetSales method
```

5. Close the T11App.h window.

Your computer's hard disk also contains a partially completed program for Flowers Express. You complete the program in the next set of steps.

To complete the Flowers Express program:

1. Click **File** on the menu bar and then click **Open Solution**. The Open Solution dialog box opens.
2. Locate and then open the **CppNet\Tut11\T11App Solution** folder.
3. Click **T11App Solution** (T11App Solution.sln) in the list of filenames, and then click the **Open** button.
4. If the T11App.cpp source file is not displayed, right-click **T11App.cpp** in the Solution Explorer window, and then click **Open**.

   Now add the T11App.h header file to the solution.
5. Click **File** on the menu bar, and then click **Add Existing Item**. The Add Existing Item – T11App Project dialog box opens.
6. Open the CppNet\MyClasses folder, then click **T11App.h** in the list of filenames. Click the **Open** button. The T11App.h header file is added to the current solution. You can verify that fact by displaying the Solution Explorer window, and then opening the Header Files folder.

   Next, enter the appropriate `#include` directive to include the contents of the T11App.h header file in the program.
7. Position the insertion point below the `//include the header file that contains the Salesperson class definition` comment. Type **#include "c:\cppnet\myclasses\t11app.h"** and press **Enter**. (If necessary, change the `#include` directive to reflect the location of the T11App.h header file on your system.)

   To complete the Flowers Express program, you will need to enter the missing instructions in the `addRecords()` and `displayTotal()` functions.
8. Enter the instructions that are shaded in Figure 11-23, which shows the completed Flowers Express program.

Figure 11-23: Completed Flowers Express program

```
//T11App.cpp
//writes names and monthly sales amounts to a sequential
access file
//calculates and displays the total sales amount
#using <mscorlib.dll>
using namespace System;
//include the header file that contains the Salesperson
class definition
#include "c:\cppnet\myclasses\t11app.h"

//function prototypes
int displayMenu();
void addRecords();
void displayTotal();
```

Figure 11-23: Completed Flowers Express program (continued)

```
int main()
{
    //declare variable
    int menuChoice = 0;
    //display menu and get choice
    menuChoice = displayMenu();
    while (menuChoice != 3)
    {
        if (menuChoice == 1)
            addRecords();
        else if (menuChoice == 2)
            displayTotal();
        else
            Console::WriteLine("Invalid menu choice");
        //end ifs
        menuChoice = displayMenu();
    }   //end while
    return 0;
}   //end of main function

//*****function definitions*****
int displayMenu()
{
    //display menu options and get user's choice
    Console::WriteLine("Options");
    Console::WriteLine("1    Add Records");
    Console::WriteLine("2    Display Total Sales");
    Console::WriteLine("3    Exit Program");
    Console::Write("Enter menu option: ");
    return Convert::ToInt32(Console::ReadLine());
}   //end of displayMenu function

void addRecords()
{
    //declare variables
    String *name = "";
    int sales    = 0;
    bool fileProblem = false;
    //declare Salesperson object
    Salesperson *salesObj = new Salesperson;

    //declare StreamWriter variable and open the file
    IO::StreamWriter *outFile;
    try
    {
        outFile = IO::File::AppendText("sales.txt");
    }
    catch (IO::IOException *ex)
    {
        Console::WriteLine(ex->Message);
        fileProblem = true;
    }
```

Figure 11-23: Completed Flowers Express program (continued)

```
    if (fileProblem == false)
    {
        //get name and monthly sales
        Console::Write("Enter the name (X to stop): ");
        name = Console::ReadLine();
        while (name->ToUpper()->CompareTo("X") != 0)
        {
            Console::Write("Enter the monthly sales: ");
            sales = Convert::ToInt32(Console::ReadLine());

            //write record to file
            salesObj->WriteRecordToFile(name,
            sales, outFile);

            Console::Write("Enter the name (X to stop): ");
            name = Console::ReadLine();
        } //end while

        //close the file
        outFile->Close();
    }   //end if
} //end of addRecords function

void displayTotal()
{
    //declare variables
    int total = 0;
    bool fileProblem = false;
    //declare Salesperson object
    Salesperson *salesObj = new Salesperson;

    //declare StreamReader variable and open the file
    IO::StreamReader *inFile;
    try
    {
        inFile = IO::File::OpenText("sales.txt");
    }
    catch (IO::IOException *ex)
    {
        fileProblem = true;
        Console::WriteLine(ex->Message);
    }

    if (fileProblem == false)
    {
        //read record and add sales amount to total sales
        while (inFile->Peek() != -1)
        {
            salesObj->ReadRecordFromFile(inFile);
            total = total + salesObj->GetSales();
        } //end while
```

Figure 11-23: Completed Flowers Express program (continued)

```
        //display the total sales amount
        Console::WriteLine("Total sales: {0}", 
        total.ToString("C2"));

        //close the file
        inFile->Close();
    }   //end if
} //end of displayTotal function
```

9. Save and then build the solution. Verify that the program generated no warnings.

Now run the Flowers Express program to verify that it is working correctly.

To verify that the Flowers Express program is working correctly:

1. Execute the program. The menu appears in the Command Prompt window. First, add five records to the sales.txt file.
2. Type the number **1** as the menu option and press **Enter**. When you are prompted to enter the name, type **John Hammil** and press **Enter**. When you are prompted to enter the monthly sales amount, type **3000** and press **Enter**.
3. Use the program to enter the following names and monthly sales amounts:

Name	Sales amount
Carol Wren	2000
Sean Junez	1000
Drew Mayer	4500
Jake Treadle	4650
X	

   Now display the total of the sales amounts stored in the sales.txt file.
4. Type **2** as the menu option and press **Enter**. The Command Prompt window indicates that the total sales amount is $15,150.00, as shown in Figure 11-24.

Figure 11-24: Command Prompt window showing the total sales amount

```
"c:\CppNet\Tut11\T11App Solution\T11App Project\Debug\T11App Project.exe"
Options
1    Add Records
2    Display Total Sales
3    Exit Program
Enter menu option: 1
Enter the name (X to stop): John Hammil
Enter the monthly sales: 3000
Enter the name (X to stop): Carol Wren
Enter the monthly sales: 2000
Enter the name (X to stop): Sean Junez
Enter the monthly sales: 1000
Enter the name (X to stop): Drew Mayer
Enter the monthly sales: 4500
Enter the name (X to stop): Jake Treadle
Enter the monthly sales: 4650
Enter the name (X to stop): x
Options
1    Add Records
2    Display Total Sales
3    Exit Program
Enter menu option: 2
Total sales: $15,150.00
Options
1    Add Records
2    Display Total Sales
3    Exit Program
Enter menu option: _
```

total sales amount

Use the menu to exit the program.

5. Type **3** as the menu option and press **Enter**.
6. Close the Command Prompt window, then close the Output window.
7. Click **File** on the menu bar, and then click **Close Solution** to close the current solution.
8. Click **File** on the menu bar, and then click **Exit** to exit Visual Studio .NET.

You now have completed Tutorial 11's Application lesson. You can either take a break or complete the end-of-lesson exercises.

Look For These Symbols

Debugging

Discovery

EXERCISES

1) The manager of Stellar Company wants a program that displays the codes and salaries stored in a sequential access file.

A. If necessary, start Visual Studio .NET. Click File on the menu bar, point to Open, and then click File. Open the codes.txt file, which is contained in the CppNet\Tut11\T11AppE01 Solution\T11AppE01 Project folder. Notice that the file contains five records. Each record contains two fields (code and salary) separated by a # symbol. Close the codes.txt window.

B. Click File on the menu bar, point to Open, and then click File. Open the T11AppE01.h header file, which is contained in the CppNet\MyClasses folder. Create an appropriate class for the codes and salaries. Include a default constructor, as well as methods to read a record, view the code, and view the salary. Save the file, and then close the T11AppE01.h window.

C. Open the T11AppE01 Solution (T11AppE01 Solution.sln) file, which is contained in the CppNet\Tut11\T11AppE01 Solution folder. Add the T11AppE01.h file to the project. Also enter the appropriate `#include` directive.

D. Code the program. Display the information in two columns on the computer screen. Display the column headings "Code" and "Salary". Format the salary amounts to "C0".

E. Save and then build the solution. Execute the program. The program should display the fives codes and salaries stored in the codes.txt file. Close the Command Prompt window.

F. When the program is working correctly, close the Output window, and then use the File menu to close the solution.

2) Consolidated Advertising wants a program that its managers can use to record various cities and their corresponding ZIP codes in a sequential access file. The program also should allow managers to look up a ZIP code in the file and display its corresponding city.

A. If necessary, start Visual Studio .NET. Click File on the menu bar, point to Open, and then click File. Open the T11AppE02.h header file, which is contained in the CppNet\MyClasses folder. Create an appropriate class for the ZIP codes and cities. Include a default constructor, as well as methods to write a record, view the ZIP code, view the city, and search for a ZIP code and return its corresponding city. Save the file, and then close the T11AppE02.h window.

B. Open the T11AppE02 Solution (T11AppE02 Solution.sln) file, which is contained in the CppNet\Tut11\T11AppE02 Solution folder. Add the T11AppE02.h file to the project. Also enter the appropriate `#include` directive.

C. Code the program.

D. Save and then build the solution. Execute the program. First, enter the following ZIP codes and cities:

ZIP code	City
60561	Darien
60544	Hinsdale
60137	Glen Ellyn
60135	Downers Grove
60136	Burr Ridge

E. Next, display the city corresponding to the following ZIP codes: 60135, 60544, and 55555. The program should display Downers Grove, Hinsdale, and an error message.

F. When the program is working correctly, close the Output window, and then use the File menu to close the solution.

3) Each salesperson at BobCat Motors is assigned a code that consists of two characters. The first character is either the letter F for full-time employee, or the letter P for part-time employee. The second character is either a 1 (indicating the salesperson sells new cars) or a 2 (indicating the salesperson sells used cars). The names of BobCat's salespeople, along with their codes, are contained in a sequential access file named T11AppE03.txt.

A. If necessary, start Visual Studio .NET. Click File on the menu bar, point to Open, and then click File. Open the T11AppE03.h header file, which is contained in the CppNet\MyClasses folder. Create an appropriate class for the codes and names. Include a default constructor, as well as methods to view the code, view the name, and search for a code and display the names of the salespeople assigned that code. Save the file, and then close the T11AppE03.h window.

B. Open the T11AppE03 Solution (T11AppE03 Solution.sln) file, which is contained in the CppNet\Tut11\T11AppE03 Solution folder. Add the T11AppE03.h file to the project. Also enter the appropriate `#include` directive.

C. Code the program so that it prompts the user to enter the code (F1, F2, P1, or P2). The program should search the T11AppE03.txt file for that code, and then display only the names of the salespeople assigned that code.

D. Save and then build the solution.

E. Execute the program. Test the program by entering the code F2. The program should display three records: Mary Jones, Joel Adkari, and Janice Paulo.

F. When the program is working correctly, close the Output window, and then use the File menu to close the solution.

4) In this exercise, you update a sequential access file.

A. If necessary, start Visual Studio .NET. Click File on the menu bar, point to Open, and then click File. Open the T11AppE04.txt file, which is contained in the CppNet\Tut11\T11AppE04 Solution\T11AppE04 Project folder. The sequential access file contains one numeric field. Close the T11AppE04.txt window.

B. Open the T11AppE04 Solution (T11AppE04 Solution.sln) file, which is contained in the CppNet\Tut11\T11AppE04 Solution folder.

C. Code the program so that it reads the numbers from the T11AppE04.txt file. The program should add the number 1 to each number, and then write the new value to another sequential file. Name the updated sequential file T11AppE04Updated.txt.

D. Save and then build the solution.

E. Execute the program. Close the Command Prompt window, then open the T11AppE04Updated.txt file. Each number in the file should be one greater than its corresponding number in the T11AppE04.txt file. Close the T11AppE04Updated.txt window.

F. When the program is working correctly, close the Output window, and then use the File menu to close the solution.

5) In this exercise, you read the numbers contained in a sequential access file, and then write only the even numbers to a new sequential access file.

A. If necessary, start Visual Studio .NET. Click File on the menu bar, point to Open, and then click File. Open the T11AppE05.txt file, which is contained in the CppNet\Tut11\T11AppE05 Solution\T11AppE05 Project folder. The sequential access file contains one numeric field. Close the T11AppE05.txt window.

B. Open the T11AppE05 Solution (T11AppE05 Solution.sln) file, which is contained in the CppNet\Tut11\T11AppE05 Solution folder.

C. Code the program so that it reads the numbers from the T11AppE05.txt file. The program should write only the even numbers to a new sequential access file named T11AppE05Even.txt. *Hint*: Use the % (modulus arithmetic) operator, which you learned about in Tutorial 3.

D. Save and then build the solution.

E. Execute the program. Close the Command Prompt window, then open the T11AppE05Even.txt file. Only even numbers should appear in the file. Close the T11AppE05Even.txt window.

F. When the program is working correctly, close the Output window, and then use the File menu to close the solution.

6) In this exercise, you learn how to determine whether a sequential access file exists.

A. Research the IO::File::`Exists()` method. What does the method return if the file exists? What does the method return if the file does not exist?

B. Write an `if` clause that determines whether the sales.txt file exists.

7) In this exercise, you debug a C++ program.

A. If necessary, start Visual Studio .NET. Click File on the menu bar, point to Open, and then click File. Open the T11AppE07.txt file, which is contained in the CppNet\Tut11\T11AppE07 Solution\T11AppE07 Project folder. The sequential access file contains three fields. Close the T11AppE07.txt window.

B. Open the T11AppE07 Solution (T11AppE07 Solution.sln) file, which is contained in the CppNet\Tut11\T11AppE07 Solution folder. The T11AppE07.cpp program should display the records contained in the T11AppE07.txt file.

C. Study the existing code, then build the solution.

D. Execute the program. Correct any errors in the program, then save and build the solution.

E. When the program is working correctly, close the Output window, and then use the File menu to close the solution.

Tutorial 12

Arrays

Objectives

After completing this tutorial, you will be able to:

- Declare an array
- Assign data to an array
- Display the contents of an array
- Access an element in an array
- Search an array
- Compute the average of an array's contents
- Find the highest entry in an array
- Update the contents of an array
- Sort an array
- Pass an array to a function

Concept Lesson

Using Arrays

All of the variables you have used so far have been simple variables. A **simple variable**, also called a **scalar variable**, is one that is unrelated to any other variable in memory. In many programs, however, you may need to reserve a block of variables, referred to as an array.

tip
The variables in an array are stored in consecutive memory locations in the computer's internal memory.

An **array** is a group of variables that have the same name and data type and are related in some way. For example, each variable in the array might contain an inventory quantity, or each might contain a state name, or each might contain an employee record (name, Social Security number, pay rate, and so on). It may be helpful to picture an array as a group of small, adjacent boxes inside the computer's memory. You can write information to the boxes and you can read information from the boxes; you just cannot *see* the boxes.

Programmers use arrays to temporarily store related data in the internal memory of the computer. Examples of data stored in an array would be the federal withholding tax tables in a payroll program, and a price list in an order entry program. Storing data in an array increases the efficiency of a program, because data can be both written to and read from internal memory much faster than it can be written to and read from a file on a disk. Additionally, after the data is entered into an array, which typically is done at the beginning of the program, the program can use the data as many times as desired. A payroll program, for example, can use the federal withholding tax tables stored in an array to calculate the amount of each employee's federal withholding tax.

tip
It takes longer for the computer to access the information stored in a disk file, because the computer must wait for the disk drive to locate the needed information and then read the information into internal memory.

In this tutorial, you learn about arrays declared using one of the C++ fundamental data types. As you learned in Tutorial 3, the fundamental data types are the basic data types built into the C++ language, and they include `char`, `short`, `int`, `float`, `double`, and `bool`. You learn about arrays declared using a data type other than a fundamental data type—for example, the `String` data type—in Tutorial 13.

The most commonly used arrays are one-dimensional and two-dimensional. You learn about one-dimensional arrays first, and then you learn about two-dimensional arrays. Arrays having more than two dimensions, which are used in scientific and engineering programs, are beyond the scope of this book.

One-Dimensional Arrays

You can visualize a **one-dimensional array** as a column of variables. Each variable in a one-dimensional array is identified by a unique number, called a **subscript**, which the computer assigns to the variable when the array is created. The subscript indicates the variable's position in the array. The first variable in a one-dimensional array is assigned a subscript of 0 (zero), the second a subscript of 1 (one), and so on. You refer to each variable in an array by the array's name and the variable's subscript, which is specified in a set of square brackets immediately following the array name. For example, to refer to the first variable in a one-dimensional array named `price`, you use `price[0]`—read "`price` sub zero." Similarly, to refer to the third variable in the `price` array, you use `price[2]`. Figure 12-1 illustrates this naming convention.

Figure 12-1: Names of the variables in a one-dimensional array named `price`

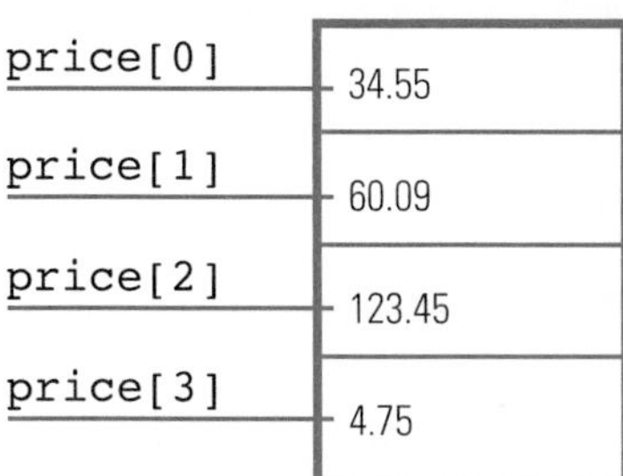

Before you can use an array, you first must declare (create) it. Figure 12-2 shows the syntax for declaring a one-dimensional array using a Visual C++ .NET fundamental data type. The figure also includes several examples of using the syntax to declare one-dimensional arrays.

tip
You also can visualize a one-dimensional array as a row of variables, rather than as a column of variables.

Figure 12-2: Syntax and examples of declaring a one-dimensional array using a fundamental data type

Syntax
datatype arrayname **__gc[] = new** *datatype* **__gc[**elements**];**
Examples and results
Example 1 `double price __gc[] = new double __gc[4];` Result declares a four-element array named `price`; each element is automatically initialized to the number zero
Example 2 `int numbers __gc[] = new int __gc[5];` Result declares a five-element array named `numbers`; each element is automatically initialized to the number zero
Example 3 `char code __gc[] = new char __gc[3];` Result declares a three-element array named `code`; each element is automatically initialized to the number zero
Example 4 `bool insured __gc[] = new bool __gc[6];` Result declares a six-element array named `insured`; each element is automatically initialized to the Boolean value `false`

tip
The __gc in the syntax is two underscore characters followed by the letters g and c. As you learned in Tutorial 10, the __gc indicates that the array will be managed by the .NET Framework's garbage collector.

In the syntax for declaring a one-dimensional array, *datatype* is the type of data the array variables, referred to as **elements**, will store. Recall that each of the elements (variables) in an array has the same data type. *Arrayname* is the name of the array, and *elements* is the number of variables contained in the array.

The statement shown in Example 1 in Figure 12-2, `double price __gc[] = new double __gc[4];`, creates a one-dimensional `double` array named `price`. The `price` array contains four elements with subscripts of 0, 1, 2, and 3. The computer initializes each element in the array to the number zero when the array is created in memory.

The statement shown in Example 2, `int numbers __gc[] = new int __gc[5];`, creates a five-element, one-dimensional `int` array named `numbers`. The array elements have subscripts of 0, 1, 2, 3, and 4, and are initialized to the number zero when the array is created in memory.

The statement shown in Example 3, `char code __gc[] = new char __gc[3];`, creates a three-element, one-dimensional `char` array named `code`. The array elements have subscripts of 0, 1, and 2, and are initialized to the number zero when the array is created in memory.

The statement shown in Example 4 in Figure 12-2, `bool insured __gc[] = new bool __gc[6];`, creates a six-element, one-dimensional `bool` array named `insured`. The array elements have subscripts of 0, 1, 2, 3, 4, and 5, and are initialized to the Boolean value `false` when the array is created in memory.

After declaring the array, you can use various methods to store data in the array.

Storing Data in a One-Dimensional Array

You can use a variety of ways to enter data into an array. The examples shown in Figure 12-3, for instance, can be used to enter data into the arrays declared in Figure 12-2.

Figure 12-3: Examples of entering data into a one-dimensional array

Examples and results

Example 1

```
int sub = 0;
while (inFile->Peek() != -1 && sub < 4)
{
   price[sub] = Convert::ToDouble(inFile->ReadLine());
   sub = sub + 1;
}  //end while
```

Result

reads the numbers from a sequential access file, and stores the numbers in the `price` array, replacing the zeros stored in the array

Example 2

```
price[2] = price[2] * 1.1;
```

Result

increases (by 10%) the price stored in the third element in the `price` array

Figure 12-3: Examples of entering data into a one-dimensional array (continued)

Example 3
```
for (int x = 1; x <= 5; x = x + 1)
     numbers[x - 1] = x * x;
//end for
```

Result
assigns the squares of the numbers from one through five to the `numbers` array, replacing the zeros stored in the array

Example 4
```
code[0] = 'A';
```

Result
assigns the letter A to the first element in the `code` array, replacing the zero stored in the array

Example 5
```
insured[1] = true;
```

Result
assigns the Boolean value `true` to the second element in the `insured` array, replacing the Boolean value `false` stored in the array

Study closely the examples shown in Figure 12-3. The code shown in Example 1 reads the numbers from a sequential access file, and stores the numbers in the `price` array, replacing the zeros stored in the array when the array was created. The assignment statement shown in Example 2 increases (by 10%) the price stored in the third element in the `price` array. Example 3's code assigns the squares of the numbers from one through five to the `numbers` array, writing over the array's initial values. Notice that the number one must be subtracted from the value stored in the `x` variable when assigning the squares to the array; this is because the first array element has a subscript of zero rather than one.

In Example 4, the statement `code[0] = 'A';` assigns the letter A to the first element in the `code` array, replacing the zero that was stored in the element when the array was created. The statement shown in the last example in Figure 12-3, `insured[1] = true;`, assigns the C++ keyword `true` to the second element in the `insured` array, replacing the value `false` that was stored in the array when the array was created.

MINI-QUIZ

Mini-Quiz 1

1) Write a C++ statement that declares a 20-element `int` array named `quantities`.
2) Write a C++ statement that declares a 10-element `bool` array named `hired`.
3) The first subscript in a 25-element array is the number ________________.
4) The last subscript in a 25-element array is the number ________________.
5) Write a C++ statement that assigns the number 7 to the fourth element in the `ages` array.

Now that you know how to declare and enter data into a one-dimensional array, you learn how to manipulate an array in a program.

Manipulating One-Dimensional Arrays

The variables (elements) in an array can be used just like any other variables. For example, you can assign values to them, use them in calculations, display their contents, and so on. In the next several sections, you view sample functions that demonstrate how one-dimensional arrays are used in a program. More specifically, the functions will show you how to perform the following tasks using a one-dimensional array:

1. Display the contents of an array
2. Access an array element using its subscript
3. Search the array
4. Calculate the average of the data stored in a numeric array
5. Find the highest value stored in an array
6. Update the array elements
7. Sort the array elements

Begin by viewing a function that displays the contents of a one-dimensional array.

Displaying the Contents of a One-Dimensional Array

Many times, a function needs simply to display the contents of an array used by the program. The `displayPrices()` function shown in Figure 12-4, for instance, demonstrates how you can display the contents of the `prices` array.

Figure 12-4: `displayPrices()` function

C++ instructions

```
//declare array
double prices __gc[] = new double __gc[4];
//fill array with values
prices[0] = 25.67;
prices[1] = 6.89;
prices[2] = 8.99;
prices[3] = 5.15;
//display contents of array
for (int x = 0; x < 4; x = x + 1)
    Console::WriteLine(prices[x].ToString()->PadLeft(5));
//end for
```

Results (displayed on the screen)

```
25.67
 6.89
 8.99
 5.15
```

tip

In most applications, the values stored in an array come from a file on the computer's disk, and are assigned to the array using a loop. However, so that you can follow the code and its results more easily, most of the functions you view in this lesson use assignment statements to assign values to the array.

The `displayPrices()` function declares a four-element, one-dimensional `double` array named `prices`, and uses four assignment statements to fill the array with data. The function then uses a loop to display the contents of each array element on the screen. The first time the loop is processed, the `x` variable in the `for` statement contains the number zero, and the statement `Console::WriteLine(prices[x].ToString()->PadLeft(5));` displays the contents of the `prices[0]` element—25.67—on the screen. When the loop is processed the second time, the `x` variable contains the number one, and the `Console::WriteLine(prices[x].ToString()->PadLeft(5));` statement displays the contents of the `prices[1]` element—6.89—on the screen, and so on. The computer repeats the loop instructions for each element in the `prices` array, beginning with the element whose subscript is zero and ending with the element whose subscript is three. The computer stops processing the loop when the value contained in the `x` variable is the number four. As Figure 12-4 indicates, the function displays the four prices on the computer screen.

Next, you view a function that uses the array subscript to access the appropriate element in an array.

tip

Notice that the loop in the function shown in Figure 12-4 stops when the x variable contains the number 4, which is one number more than the highest subscript in the array.

Using the Subscript to Access an Element in a One-Dimensional Array

Assume that XYZ Corporation pays its managers based on six different salary codes, 1 through 6. Each code corresponds to a different salary amount. You can use the function shown in Figure 12-5 to display the salary amount corresponding to the code entered by the user.

Figure 12-5: `displaySalary()` procedure

C++ instructions

```
//declare variable and array
int code = 0;
int salaries __gc[] = new int __gc[6];
//fill array with values
salaries[0] = 25000;
salaries[1] = 35000;
salaries[2] = 55000;
salaries[3] = 70000;
salaries[4] = 80200;
salaries[5] = 90500;
//get code, then display corresponding salary
Console::Write("Enter the salary code (1-6): ");
code = Convert::ToInt32(Console::ReadLine());
if (code < 1 || code > 6)
    Console::WriteLine("Invalid code");
else
    Console::WriteLine(salaries[code - 1]);
//end if
```

Results (displayed on the screen)

55000	(assuming the user enters the number 3)
Invalid code	(assuming the user enters the number 8)

tip

Before accessing an array element, a function always should verify that the subscript is valid—in other words, that it is in range. If the function uses a subscript that is not in range, the computer displays an error message and the function ends abruptly.

The `displaySalary()` function declares an `int` variable named `code` and a six-element, one-dimensional `int` array named `salaries`. The function uses six assignment statements to assign values to the elements in the `salaries` array. The salary amount for code 1 is stored in the `salaries[0]` element. Code 2's salary amount is stored in the `salaries[1]` element, and so on. Notice that the code is one number more than its corresponding array subscript.

Next, the **displaySalary()** function prompts the user to enter the salary code, and then stores the user's response in the **code** variable. The selection structure in the function determines whether the code entered by the user is invalid. In this case, invalid codes are numbers that are less than one or greater than six. If the code is not valid, the function displays an appropriate message; otherwise, it displays the corresponding salary from the **salaries** array. Notice that, to access the correct element in the **salaries** array, the number one must be subtracted from the contents of the **code** variable; this is because the code entered by the user is one number more than its associated array subscript. As Figure 12-5 indicates, the function displays the number 55000 when the user enters a code of 3. When the user enters a code of 8, the program displays the message "Invalid code".

In the next section, you learn how to search a one-dimensional array.

Searching a One-Dimensional Array

Assume that the sales manager at Jacobsen Motors wants a function that allows him to determine the number of salespeople selling above a certain amount, which he will enter. To accomplish this task, the function will need to search the array, looking for values that are greater than the amount entered by the sales manager. The function shown in Figure 12-6 shows you how to search an array.

Figure 12-6: searchArray() function

C++ instructions

```
//declare variables and array
int count = 0;       //counter variable
int searchFor = 0;  //number to search for
int sales __gc[] = new int __gc[5];
//fill array with values
sales[0] = 45000;
sales[1] = 35000;
sales[2] = 25000;
sales[3] = 60000;
sales[4] = 23000;
//get number to search for
Console::Write("Enter sales amount: ");
searchFor = Convert::ToInt32(Console::ReadLine());
//search for numbers greater than searchFor value
for (int x = 0; x < 5; x = x + 1)
    if (sales[x] > searchFor)
        count = count + 1;
    //end if
//end for

//display count
Console::WriteLine("Count: {0}", Convert::ToString(count));
```

Results (displayed on the screen)

Count: 2 (assuming the user enters the number 40000)
Count: 0 (assuming the user enters the number 60000)

The `searchArray()` function declares two `int` variables named `count` and `searchFor`. It also declares a five-element, one-dimensional `int` array named `sales`, and uses five assignment statements to store values in the array. Next, the function prompts the user to enter a sales amount, and it stores the user's response in the `searchFor` variable. The loop in the function repeats its instructions for each element in the array, beginning with the element whose subscript is zero and ending with the element whose subscript is four.

The selection structure in the loop compares the contents of the current array element with the contents of the `searchFor` variable. If the array element contains a number that is greater than the number stored in the `searchFor` variable, the selection structure's true path adds the number one to the value stored in the `count` variable. In the `searchArray()` function, the `count` variable is used as a counter to keep track of the number of salespeople selling over the amount entered by the sales manager.

When the loop ends, which is when the `x` variable contains the number five, the `Console::WriteLine("Count: {0}", Convert::ToString(count));` statement displays the contents of the `count` variable on the screen. As Figure 12-6 indicates, the function displays the number two if the sales manager enters 40000 as the sales amount, and it displays the number zero if he enters 60000 as the sales amount.

Next, you learn how to calculate the average of the data stored in a numeric array.

Calculating the Average Amount Stored in a One-Dimensional Numeric Array

Professor Jeremiah wants a function that calculates and displays the average test score earned by his students on the final exam. The `displayAverage()` function shown in Figure 12-7 can be used to accomplish this task.

Figure 12-7: `displayAverage()` function

C++ instructions

```
//declare variables and array
double total = 0.0;     //accumulator variable
double avg = 0.0;       //average score
double scores __gc[] = new double __gc[5];
//fill array with values
scores[0] = 98;
scores[1] = 100;
scores[2] = 56;
scores[3] = 74;
scores[4] = 35;
//accumulate scores
for (int x = 0; x < 5; x = x + 1)
    total = total + scores[x];
//end for

//calculate and display average
avg = total / 5;
Console::WriteLine("Average: {0}", Convert::ToString(avg));
```

Results (displayed on the screen)

Average: 72.6

The `displayAverage()` function declares two `double` variables named `total` and `avg`. It also declares a five-element, one-dimensional `double` array named `scores`, and uses five assignment statements to assign values to the array. The loop in the function adds the score contained in each array element to the `total` variable. In the `displayAverage()` function, the `total` variable is used as an accumulator to add up the test scores. When the loop ends, which is when the `x` variable contains the number five, the `avg = total / 5;` statement calculates the average test score, and the `Console::WriteLine("Average: {0}", Convert::ToString(avg));` statement displays the average test score on the screen. As Figure 12-7 indicates, the program displays the number 72.6.

Figure 12-8 shows another way of writing the `displayAverage()` function. The changes made to the original version of the function, which is shown in Figure 12-7, are shaded in Figure 12-8.

Figure 12-8: `displayAverage()` function using the `GetLength()` method

C++ instructions using the `GetLength()` method

```
//declare variables and array
double total = 0.0;     //accumulator variable
double avg = 0.0;       //average score
double scores __gc[] = new double __gc[5];
//fill array with values
scores[0] = 98;
scores[1] = 100;
scores[2] = 56;
scores[3] = 74;
scores[4] = 35;
//accumulate scores
for (int x = 0; x < scores->GetLength(0); x = x + 1)
    total = total + scores[x];
//end for

//calculate and display average
avg = total / scores->GetLength(0);
Console::WriteLine("Average: {0}", Convert::ToString(avg));
```

Results (displayed on the screen)

Average: 72.6

Notice that this version of the `displayAverage()` function uses the `GetLength()` method, rather than the numeric constant 5, in the `for` clause and in the statement that calculates the average test score. The **GetLength() method**, whose syntax is *arrayname*->**GetLength(***dimension***)**, gets the number of elements in a specified *dimension* of an array. The first dimension in an array has a *dimension* value of zero, the second has a *dimension* value of one, and so on.

All one-dimensional arrays have one *dimension* value: 0. Therefore, you use `scores->GetLength(0)` to determine the number of elements in a one-dimensional array named `scores`. Similarly, you use `letters->GetLength(0)` to determine the number of elements in a one-dimensional array named `letters`. As you will learn later in this lesson, all two-dimensional arrays have two *dimension* values: 0 and 1. Consequently, you use `prices->GetLength(0)` to get the number of elements in the first dimension of a two-dimensional array named `prices`, but `prices->GetLength(1)` to get the number of elements in the second dimension of the `prices` array.

When coding a program, it is better to use the `GetLength()` method rather than a numeric constant to represent the length of (or number of elements in) an array; doing so makes program maintenance easier. For example, assume that the number of elements in the `scores` array needs to be increased to 10. In the `displayAverage()` function shown in Figure 12-7, the programmer would need to change (to 10) the 5 in the array declaration statement, the 5 in the `for` clause, and the 5 in the statement that calculates the average test score. However, in the `displayAverage()` function shown in Figure 12-8, the programmer would need to change (to 10) only the 5 in the array declaration statement. The `GetLength()` method would automatically reflect the new length in the `for` clause and in the statement that calculates the average test score.

MINI-QUIZ

Mini-Quiz 2

1) Which of the following C++ statements displays on the screen the contents of the first element in the `item` array?

a. `Console::WriteLine(item[0]);`
b. `Console::WriteLine(item[1]);`
c. `Console::WriteLine(item(0));`
d. `Console::WriteLine(item(1));`

2) Assume that the `inventory` array is declared using the statement `int inventory __gc[] = new int __gc[20];`. Also assume that the `x` variable, which keeps track of the array subscripts, is initialized to 0. Which of the following C++ `while` clauses tells the computer to process the loop instructions for each element in the array?

a. `while (x > 20)`
b. `while (x < 20)`
c. `while (x >= 20)`
d. `while (x <= 20)`

3) Rewrite the `while` clause from Question 2 using the `GetLength()` method.

4) Assume that the `bonus` array is declared using the statement `double bonus __gc[] = new double __gc[10];`. Also assume that the `x` variable, which keeps track of the array subscripts, is initialized to 0. Write the C++ code to display the contents of the `bonus` array.

In the next section, you learn how to determine the highest value stored in a one-dimensional array.

Determining the Highest Value Stored in a One-Dimensional Array

Sharon Johnson keeps track of the amount of money she spends each week on groceries. She would like a function that displays the highest amount spent in a week. Similar to the `searchArray()` function shown earlier in Figure 12-6, the `displayHighest()` function will need to search the array. However, rather than looking in the array for values that are greater than a specific amount, the function will look for the highest amount in the array, as shown in Figure 12-9.

tip

Notice that the loop shown in Figure 12-9 searches the second through the last element in the `dollars` array. The first element is not included in the search because it is already stored in the `high` variable.

Figure 12-9: `displayHighest()` **function**

C++ instructions

```
//declare array
double dollars __gc[] = new double __gc[5];
//fill array with values
dollars[0] = 25.6;
dollars[1] = 30.25;
dollars[2] = 50.0;
dollars[3] = 20.0;
dollars[4] = 25.45;
//declare variables
int x = 1;                    //begin search with the
                              second element
double high = dollars[0];     //store first array value
                              in the high variable

//search for highest value
while (x < dollars->GetLength(0))
{
     if (dollars[x] > high)
          high = dollars[x];
     //end if
     x = x + 1;
}  //end while

//display highest value
Console::WriteLine("Highest: {0}",
Convert::ToString(high));
```

Results (displayed on the screen)

Highest: 50

The `displayHighest()` function declares a five-element, one-dimensional `double` array named `dollars`, and uses five assignment statements to assign to the array the amounts that Sharon spent on groceries during the last five weeks. The function also declares an `int` variable named `x` and a `double` variable named `high`. The `high` variable is used to keep track of the highest value stored in the `dollars` array, and is initialized using the value stored in the first array element. The `x` variable is used to keep track of the array subscripts. Notice that the function initializes the `x` variable to the number one, which is the subscript corresponding to the second element in the `dollars` array.

The first time the loop in the `displayHighest()` function is processed, the selection structure within the loop compares the value stored in the second array element—`dollars[1]`—with the value stored in the `high` variable. (Recall that the `high` variable contains the same value as the first array element at this point.) If the value stored in the second array element is greater than the value stored in the `high` variable, then the statement `high = dollars[x];` assigns the array element value to the `high` variable. The statement `x = x + 1;` then adds the number one to the `x` variable, giving 2. The next time the loop is processed, the selection structure compares the value stored in the third array element—`dollars[2]`—with the value stored in the `high` variable, and so on.

When the loop ends, which is when the **x** variable contains the number five, the **displayHighest()** function displays the contents of the **high** variable on the screen. As Figure 12-9 indicates, the function displays the number 50.

Next, you learn how to update the values stored in a one-dimensional array.

Updating the Values Stored in a One-Dimensional Array

The sales manager at Jillian Company wants a function that allows her to increase the price of each item the company sells. She also wants the function to display each item's new price on the screen. The **updateArray()** function shown in Figure 12-10 will perform these tasks.

Figure 12-10: updateArray() function

C++ instructions

```
//declare variable and array
double increase = 0.0;  //stores increase amount
double prices __gc[] = new double __gc[4];
//fill array with values
prices[0] = 150.35;
prices[1] = 35.6;
prices[2] = 75.75;
prices[3] = 25.3;

//get increase amount
Console::Write("Enter increase: ");
increase = Convert::ToDouble(Console::ReadLine());

//update each array element
for (int x = 0; x < prices->GetLength(0); x = x + 1)
{
    prices[x] = prices[x] + increase;
    Console::WriteLine("New Price: {0}",
    prices[x].ToString("C2"));
}   //end for
```

Results (displayed on the screen)

New Price: $155.35 (assuming the user enters the number 5)
New Price: $40.60
New Price: $80.75
New Price: $30.30

The **updateArray()** function declares a **double** variable named **increase**. It also declares a four-element, one-dimensional **double** array named **prices**, and uses four assignment statements to assign values to the array. Next, the function prompts the user to enter the amount of the increase, and stores the user's response in the **increase** variable. The loop in the function then repeats its instructions for each element in the **prices** array.

The first instruction in the loop, **prices[x] = prices[x] + increase;**, updates the contents of the current array element by adding the increase amount to it. The **Console::WriteLine("New Price: {0}", prices[x].ToString("C2"));**

statement then displays the updated contents on the screen. The loop ends when the `x` variable contains the number four. Figure 12-10 shows the values displayed by the function when the user enters the number five as the increase amount. Notice that each new price is five dollars more than the corresponding original price.

Next, you learn how to sort the data stored in a one-dimensional array.

Sorting the Data Stored in a One-Dimensional Array

At times, a function might need to arrange the contents of an array in either ascending or descending order. Arranging data in a specific order is called **sorting**. When an array is sorted in ascending order, the first element in the array contains the smallest value, and the last element contains the largest value. When an array is sorted in descending order, on the other hand, the first element contains the largest value, and the last element contains the smallest value.

You can use the **Array::Sort() method** to sort an array in ascending order. The method's syntax is **Array::Sort(*arrayname*)**, where *arrayname* is the name of the array to be sorted. The function shown in Figure 12-11 uses the `Array::Sort()` method to sort the `numbers` array in ascending order.

Figure 12-11: `sortAscending()` **function**

C++ instructions

```
//declare variable and array
int sub = 0;  //keeps track of array subscripts
int numbers __gc[] = new int __gc[6];

//fill array with numbers stored in a sequential access file
IO::StreamReader *inFile;
inFile = IO::File::OpenText("nums.txt");
while (inFile->Peek() != -1 && sub < numbers->GetLength(0))
{
    //read and display the number
    numbers[sub] = Convert::ToInt32(inFile->ReadLine());
    Console::WriteLine(numbers[sub]);
    //update the subscript
    sub = sub + 1;
}  //end while
inFile->Close();

//sort the array in ascending order
Array::Sort(numbers);

//display the sorted array
Console::WriteLine();
for (int x = 0; x < numbers->GetLength(0); x = x + 1)
    Console::WriteLine(numbers[x]);
//end for
```

Figure 12-11: `sortAscending()` function (continued)

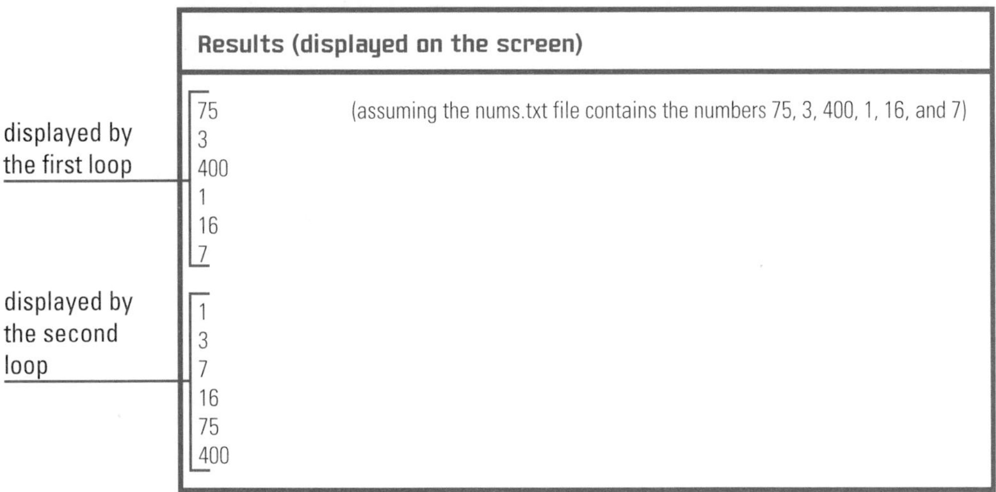

Results (displayed on the screen)
displayed by the first loop
75
3
400
1
16
7
(assuming the nums.txt file contains the numbers 75, 3, 400, 1, 16, and 7)
displayed by the second loop
1
3
7
16
75
400

The **`sortAscending()`** function declares an **`int`** variable named **`sub`** and a six-element, one-dimensional **`int`** array named **`numbers`**. It then opens a sequential access file named nums.txt. The first loop in the function repeats its instructions while the computer has not reached the end of the nums.txt file and, at the same time, the **`sub`** variable contains a value that is less than or equal to the number of elements in the **`numbers`** array. The first statement in the loop reads a number from the nums.txt file and stores the number in the **`numbers`** array, in the element whose subscript is contained in the **`sub`** variable. The second statement in the loop displays the contents of the current array element on the screen. The third statement in the loop increases the value stored in the **`sub`** variable by one. The loop stops either when the computer reaches the end of the nums.txt file or when the value in the **`sub`** variable is six, whichever occurs first. As Figure 12-11 indicates, if the nums.txt file contains the numbers 75, 3, 400, 1, 16, and 7, the first loop displays the numbers 75, 3, 400, 1, 16, and 7 on the screen. When the first loop stops, the statement `inFile->Close();` closes the nums.txt file.

The next statement in the **`sortAscending()`** function, `Array::Sort(numbers);`, sorts the numbers in the **`numbers`** array in ascending order. The second loop in the function then displays the contents of the **`numbers`** array on the screen. As Figure 12-11 indicates, the second loop displays the numbers 1, 3, 7, 16, 75, and 400. Notice that the numbers appear in ascending order.

To sort an array in descending order, you first use the `Array::Sort()` method to sort the array in ascending order, and then use the **Array::Reverse() method** to reverse the array elements. The syntax of the `Array::Reverse()` method is **Array::Reverse(*arrayname*)**, where *arrayname* is the name of the array whose elements you want reversed. The function shown in Figure 12-12 sorts the contents of the **`ages`** array in descending order, and then displays the contents of the array on the screen.

Figure 12-12: `sortDescending()` function

C++ instructions

```
//declare array
int ages __gc[] = new int __gc[6];
//fill array with values
ages[0] = 20;
ages[1] = 15;
ages[2] = 32;
ages[3] = 70;
ages[4] = 45;
ages[5] = 12;

//sort the array in ascending order,
//then reverse the array elements
Array::Sort(ages);
Array::Reverse(ages);

//display the sorted array
for (int x = 0; x < ages->GetLength(0); x = x + 1)
    Console::WriteLine(ages[x]);
//end for
```

Results (displayed on the screen)

```
70
45
32
20
15
12
```

The `sortDescending()` function declares a six-element, one-dimensional `int` array named `ages`, and uses six assignment statements to assign values to the array. It then uses the `Array::Sort()` and `Array::Reverse()` methods to sort the array elements in descending order. The loop in the function displays the contents of the `ages` array on the screen. As Figure 12-12 indicates, the loop displays the numbers 70, 45, 32, 20, 15, and 12. Notice that the numbers appear in descending order.

MINI-QUIZ

Mini-Quiz 3

1) Write an `if` clause that determines whether the value stored in the current array element is less than the value stored in the `low` variable. The name of the array is `price`. Use `x` as the name of the variable that keeps track of the array subscripts.
2) Write a `while` loop that subtracts the number 3 from each of the elements in an array named `numbers`. Use `x` as the name of the variable that keeps track of the array subscripts. You can assume that the `x` variable is initialized to 0.
3) Write the statement to sort the `bonus` array in ascending order.

Recall that, in addition to using one-dimensional arrays, some programs also utilize two-dimensional arrays. You learn how to create and manipulate two-dimensional arrays in the remainder of this lesson.

Two-Dimensional Arrays

Recall that you can visualize a one-dimensional array as a column of variables. A **two-dimensional array**, however, resembles a table in that the variables are in rows and columns. Figure 12-13 illustrates a two-dimensional array.

Figure 12-13: Illustration of a two-dimensional array

75	90
67	55
83	100
66	12

Each variable (element) in a two-dimensional array is identified by a unique combination of two subscripts, which the computer assigns to the variable when the array is created. The subscripts specify the variable's row and column position in the array. Variables located in the first row in a two-dimensional array are assigned a row subscript of 0 (zero). Variables located in the second row are assigned a row subscript of 1 (one), and so on. Similarly, variables located in the first column in a two-dimensional array are assigned a column subscript of 0 (zero). Variables located in the second column are assigned a column subscript of 1 (one), and so on. You refer to each variable in a two-dimensional array by the array's name and the variable's row and column subscripts, which are separated by a comma and specified in a set of square brackets immediately following the array name. For example, to refer to the variable located in the first row, first column in a two-dimensional array named `scores`, you use `scores[0, 0]`—read "`scores` sub zero comma zero." Similarly, to refer to the variable located in the second row, third column in the `scores` array, you use `scores[1, 2]`. Figure 12-14 illustrates this naming convention. Notice that the row subscript is listed first in the square brackets.

Figure 12-14: Names of some of the variables contained in the `scores` array

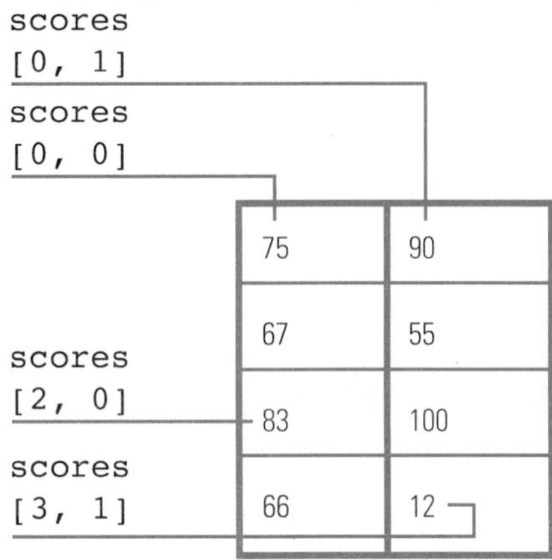

Recall that, before you can use an array, you first must declare (create) it. Figure 12-15 shows the syntax for declaring a two-dimensional array using a Visual C++ .NET fundamental data type. The figure also includes several examples of using the syntax to declare two-dimensional arrays.

Figure 12-15: Syntax and examples of declaring a two-dimensional array using a fundamental data type

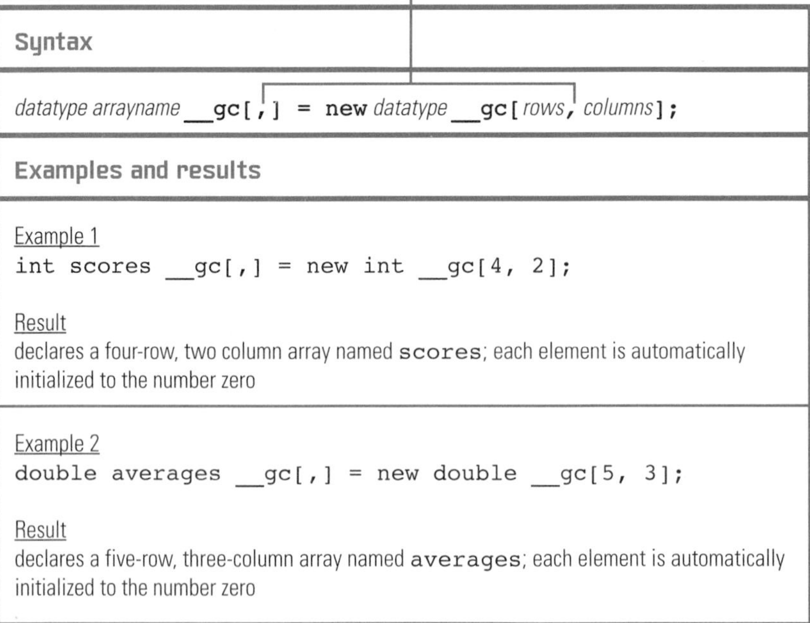

Syntax

datatype arrayname `__gc[,] = new` *datatype* `__gc[`*rows*`,` *columns*`];`

Examples and results

Example 1
```
int scores __gc[,] = new int __gc[4, 2];
```
Result
declares a four-row, two column array named `scores`; each element is automatically initialized to the number zero

Example 2
```
double averages __gc[,] = new double __gc[5, 3];
```
Result
declares a five-row, three-column array named `averages`; each element is automatically initialized to the number zero

In the syntax for declaring a two-dimensional array, *arrayname* is the name of the array, and *datatype* is the type of data the array variables will store. Recall that each of the variables (elements) in an array has the same data type. *Rows* and *columns* in the syntax are integers that specify the number of rows and columns, respectively, in the array. Notice that the syntax requires a comma in both sets of square brackets.

Study closely the two examples shown in Figure 12-15. The `int scores __gc[,] = new int __gc[4, 2];` statement shown in Example 1 creates a two-dimensional `int` array named `scores` that has four rows and two columns. The computer automatically initializes each element in the array to the number zero when the array is created in memory. The statement shown in Example 2, `double averages __gc[,] = new double __gc[5, 3];`, creates a two-dimensional `double` array named `averages` that has five rows and three columns. Here again, the computer automatically initializes each element in the array to the number zero when the array is created in memory.

You can calculate the size of a two-dimensional array—in other words, the total number of elements in the array—by multiplying the number of rows by the number of columns. For example, the `scores` array declared in Figure 12-15 has eight elements (four rows times two columns), and the `averages` array has 15 elements (five rows times three columns). As indicated earlier, you can calculate the number of elements in the first dimension of a two-dimensional array using the syntax *arrayname*->**GetLength(0)**. The first dimension in a two-dimensional array corresponds to the number of rows. Therefore, `scores->GetLength(0)` returns the number four (which is the number of rows in the `scores` array), and `averages->GetLength(0)` returns the number five (which is the number of rows in the `averages` array). Similarly, you can calculate the number of elements in the second dimension of a two-dimensional array using the syntax *arrayname*->**GetLength(1)**. The second dimension in a two-dimensional array corresponds to the number of columns. Therefore, `scores->GetLength(1)` returns the number two, and `averages->GetLength(1)` returns the number three.

After declaring the array, you can use various methods to store data in the array.

Storing Data in a Two-Dimensional Array

You can use a variety of ways to enter data into a two-dimensional array. The examples shown in Figure 12-16, for instance, can be used to enter data into the arrays declared in Figure 12-15.

Figure 12-16: Examples of entering data into a two-dimensional array

Examples and results

Example 1

```
for (int rows = 0; rows < 4; rows = rows + 1)
   for (int cols = 0; cols < 2; cols = cols + 1)
   {
      Console::Write("Enter the score: ");
      scores[rows, cols] = Convert::ToInt32(Console
      ::ReadLine());
   } //end for
//end for
```

Result

assigns to the `scores` array the values entered by the user at the keyboard

Figure 12-16: Examples of entering data into a two-dimensional array (continued)

Example 2
```
int rows = 0;
int cols = 0;
double num1 = 0.0;
double num2 = 0.0;
while (rows < averages->GetLength(0))
{
    while (cols < averages->GetLength(1))
    {
        Console::Write("First number: ");
        num1 = Convert::ToDouble(Console::ReadLine());
        Console::Write("Second number: ");
        num2 = Convert::ToDouble(Console::ReadLine());
        averages[rows, cols] = (num1 + num2) / 2;
        cols = cols + 1;
    }   //end while
    rows = rows + 1;
    cols = 0;
}   //end while
```

Result
assigns to the `averages` array the averages of the numbers entered by the user at the keyboard

The code shown in Example 1 in Figure 12-16 uses two `for` statements to assign values to the two-dimensional `scores` array, which has four rows and two columns. The code shown in Example 2 uses two `while` statements to assign values to the two-dimensional `averages` array, which has five rows and three columns.

Next, view a function that displays the sum of the sales stored in a two-dimensional array.

Calculating the Sum of the Numbers Stored in a Two-Dimensional Array

Conway Enterprises has both domestic and international sales operations. The company's sales manager wants a function that displays the total sales made by the company during a six-month period. The function shown in Figure 12-17 will accomplish this task.

The `displayTotal()` function declares an `int` variable named `total`, which is used as an accumulator to add up the sales amounts. The function also declares a six-row, two-column `int` array named `sales`. The company's domestic sales amounts are stored in the first column in each row in the array, and its international sales amounts are stored in the second column in each row. Notice that two loops are necessary to access each element in a two-dimensional array: one loop to keep track of the row number, and the other to keep track of the column number. According to Figure 12-17, the total sales made during the six months is $412,000.

Figure 12-17: `displayTotal()` function

C++ instructions

```
//declare variable and array
int total = 0;
int sales __gc[,] = new int __gc[6, 2];
//fill array with sales amounts
sales[0, 0] = 12000;
sales[0, 1] = 10000;
sales[1, 0] = 45000;
sales[1, 1] = 56000;
sales[2, 0] = 32000;
sales[2, 1] = 42000;
sales[3, 0] = 67000;
sales[3, 1] = 23000;
sales[4, 0] = 24000;
sales[4, 1] = 12000;
sales[5, 0] = 55000;
sales[5, 1] = 34000;

//accumulate sales amounts
for (int row = 0; row < sales->GetLength(0); row = row + 1)
   for (int col = 0; col < sales->GetLength(1); col = col + 1)
       total = total + sales[row, col];
   //end for
//end for

//display total sales
Console::WriteLine("Total: {0}", total.ToString("C0"));
```

Results (displayed on the screen)
Total: $412,000

MINI-QUIZ

Mini-Quiz 4

1) Write a C++ statement that declares a four-row, two-column `int` array named `quantity`.
2) A five-row, four-column array has a total of ________________ elements.
3) A six-row, three-column array has row subscripts of ________________ through ________________, and column subscripts of ________________ through ________________.
4) Write the statement to display (on the screen) the number of columns in a two-dimensional array named `quantity`.
5) Write a C++ assignment statement that stores the number 5 in the second row, third column of a two-dimensional array named `quantity`.

You now have completed Tutorial 12's Concept lesson. You can either take a break or complete the end-of-lesson questions and exercises before moving on to the Application lesson.

SUMMARY

An array is a group of variables that have the same name and data type and are related in some way. The most commonly used arrays in programs are one-dimensional and two-dimensional. A one-dimensional array is simply a column of variables. A two-dimensional array, on the other hand, resembles a table in that it has rows and columns. Programmers use arrays to temporarily store related data in the internal memory of the computer. By doing so, a programmer can increase the efficiency of a program, because data can be both written to and read from internal memory much faster than it can be written to and read from a file on a disk. Additionally, after the data is entered into an array, which typically is done at the beginning of the program, the program can use the data as many times as desired.

You must declare an array before you can use it. After declaring an array, you can use a variety of ways to enter data into the array. For example, you can enter data from the keyboard or from a file on the computer's disk.

Each of the array elements in memory is assigned a unique number, called a subscript. The first element in a one-dimensional array in C++ is assigned a subscript of 0, the next element in the array is assigned a subscript of 1, and so on. Because the first array subscript is 0, the last subscript in an array is always one less than the number of elements. You refer to each element in the array by the array's name and the element's subscript, which is specified in square brackets immediately following the name.

You can use the `GetLength()` method to determine the number of elements in a specified dimension of an array. You can use the `Array::Sort()` method to sort an array in ascending order, and the `Array::Reverse()` method to reverse the order of the elements included in an array.

The syntax for creating and initializing a two-dimensional array is similar to the syntax for creating and initializing a one-dimensional array. The two-dimensional array syntax, however, requires the programmer to provide both the number of rows and the number of columns in the array, rather than just the number of array elements.

Just as each element in a one-dimensional array is identified by a unique subscript, each element in a two-dimensional array is identified by a unique combination of two subscripts. The first subscript represents the element's row location in the array, and the second represents its column location. The computer assigns the subscripts to the elements when the array is created in memory. The first row subscript in a two-dimensional array is 0. The first column subscript also is 0.

You need to use two loops to access every element in a two-dimensional array. One of the loops keeps track of the row subscript, while the other keeps track of the column subscript.

ANSWERS TO MINI-QUIZZES

Mini-Quiz 1

1) `int quantities __gc[] = new int __gc[20];`

2) `bool hired __gc[] = new bool __gc[10];`

3) `0`

4) `24`

5) `ages[3] = 7;`

Mini-Quiz 2

1) a. `Console::WriteLine(item[0]);`

2) b. `while (x < 20)`

3) `while (x < inventory->GetLength(0))`

4)
```
while (x < bonus->GetLength(0))
{
   Console::WriteLine(bonus[x]);
   x = x + 1;
} //end while
```

Mini-Quiz 3

1) `if (price[x] < low)`

2)
```
while (x < numbers->GetLength(0))
{
    numbers[x] = numbers[x] – 3;
    x = x + 1;
} //end while
```

3) `Array::Sort(bonus);`

Mini-Quiz 4

1) `int quantity __gc[,] = new int __gc[4, 2];`

2) 20

3) 0, 5, 0, 2

4) `Console::WriteLine(quantity->GetLength(1));`

5) `quantity[1, 2] = 5;`

QUESTIONS

1) Which of the following is false?
   A. The elements in an array are related in some way.
   B. All of the elements in an array have the same data type.
   C. All of the elements in a one-dimensional array have the same subscript.
   D. The first element in a one-dimensional array has a subscript of zero.

2) Elements in a one-dimensional array are identified by a unique ______________.
   A. combination of two subscripts
   B. data type
   C. subscript
   D. symbol

3) Which of the following statements declares a five-element array named `population`?
   A. `int population __gc[] = new int __gc[5];`
   B. `int population __gc[] = new int __gc[4];`
   C. `int population __gc[5] = new int __gc[];`
   D. `int population __gc[5] = new int __gc[5];`

Use the **sales** array shown in Figure 12-18 to answer Questions 4 through 8.

Figure 12-18

10000	12000	900	500	20000

4) The `sales[3] = sales[3] + 10;` statement will ______________.

A. replace the 500 amount with 10

B. replace the 500 amount with 510

C. replace the 900 amount with 910

D. result in an error

5) The `sales[4] = sales[4 – 2];` statement will ______________.

A. replace the 20000 amount with 900

B. replace the 20000 amount with 19998

C. replace the 500 amount with 12000

D. result in an error

6) The `Console::WriteLine(sales[0] + sales[1]);` statement will ______________.

A. display 22000

B. display 10000 + 12000

C. display `sales[0] + sales[1]`

D. result in an error

7) Which of the following `if` clauses can be used to verify that the array subscript, named `x`, is valid for the `sales` array?

A. `if (sales[x] >= 0 && sales[x] < 4)`

B. `if (sales[x] >= 0 && sales[x] <= 4)`

C. `if (x >= 0 && x < 4)`

D. `if (x >= 0 && x <= 4)`

8) Which of the following will correctly add 100 to each variable in the `sales` array? (You can assume that the `x` variable is initialized to 0.)

A.
```
while (x <= 4)
      x = x + 100;
//end while
```

B.
```
while (x <= 4)
{
      sales = sales + 100;
      x = x + 1;
} //end while
```

C.
```
while (sales < 5)
{
      sales[x] = sales[x] + 100;
} //end while
```

D.
```
while (x <= 4)
{
     sales[x] = sales[x] + 100;
     x = x + 1;
} //end while
```

Use the **num** array shown in Figure 12-19 to answer Questions 9 through 13. The **x** and **total** variables are **int** variables and are initialized to 0. The **avg** variable is a **double** variable and is initialized to 0.0.

Figure 12-19

10	5	7	2

9) Which of the following correctly calculates and displays the average of the **num** array elements?

A.
```
while (x < 4)
{
     num[x] = total + total;
     x = x + 1;
}    //end while
avg = Convert::ToDouble(total) / x;
Console::WriteLine(avg);
```

B.
```
while (x < 4)
{
     total = total + num[x];
     x = x + 1;
}    //end while
avg = Convert::ToDouble(total) / x;
Console::WriteLine(avg);
```

C.
```
while (x < 4)
{
     total = total + num[x];
     x = x + 1;
}    //end while
avg = Convert::ToDouble(total) / x - 1;
Console::WriteLine(avg);
```

D.
```
while (x < 4)
{
     total = total + num[x];
     x = x + 1;
}    //end while
avg = Convert::ToDouble(total) / (x - 1);
Console::WriteLine(avg);
```

10) The code in Question 9's answer A displays ______________.

A. 0

B. 5

C. 6

D. 8

11) The code in Question 9's answer B displays ______________.

A. 0

B. 5

C. 6

D. 8

12) The code in Question 9's answer C displays ______________.

A. 0

B. 5

C. 6

D. 8

13) The code in Question 9's answer D displays ______________.

A. 0

B. 5

C. 6

D. 8

14) The first element in a two-dimensional array has a row subscript of ______________ and a column subscript of ______________.

A. 0, 0

B. 0, 1

C. 1, 0

D. 1, 1

15) The individual elements in a two-dimensional array are identified by a unique ______________.

A. combination of two subscripts

B. data type

C. order

D. subscript

16) Which of the following statements creates a two-dimensional `int` array named `sales` that contains three rows and four columns?

A. `int sales __gc[] = new int __gc[3, 4];`

B. `int sales __gc[] = new int __gc[4, 3];`

C. `int sales __gc[,] = new int __gc[3, 4];`

D. `int sales __gc[,] = new int __gc[4, 3];`

Use the `sales` array shown in Figure 12-20 to answer Questions 17 through 20.

Figure 12-20

10000	12000	900	500	20000
350	600	700	800	100

17) The statement `sales[1, 3] = sales[1, 3] + 10;` will ______________.

A. replace the 900 amount with 910

B. replace the 500 amount with 510

C. replace the 700 amount with 710

D. replace the 800 amount with 810

18) The statement `sales[0, 4] = sales[0, 4 – 2];` will ______________.

A. replace the 20000 amount with 900

B. replace the 20000 amount with 19998

C. replace the 20000 amount with 19100

D. result in an error

19) The statement `Console::WriteLine(sales[0, 3] + sales[1, 3]);` will ______________.

A. display 1300

B. display 1600

C. display `sales[0, 3] + sales[1, 3]`

D. result in an error

20) Which of the following `if` clauses can be used to verify that the array subscripts named `row` and `column` are valid for the `sales` array?

A. `if (sales[row, column] >= 0 && sales[row, column] < 5)`

B. `if (sales[row, column] >= 0 && sales[row, column] <= 5)`

C. `if (row >= 0 && row < 3 && column >= 0 && column < 6)`

D. `if (row >= 0 && row <= 1 && column >= 0 && column <= 4)`

21) Which of the following statements displays the number of elements contained in a one-dimensional array named `letters`?

A. `Console::WriteLine(letters->GetLength(0));`

B. `Console::WriteLine(letters->GetLength(1));`

C. `Console::WriteLine(letters->GetNumber(0));`

D. `Console::WriteLine(letters->GetNumber(1));`

22) Which of the following statements sorts a one-dimensional array named `letters` in ascending order?

A. `Array::Sort(letters);`

B. `Array::SortAsc(letters);`

C. `Sort::Array(letters);`

D. `Sort::Ascend(letters);`

Look For These Symbols

Debugging

Discovery

EXERCISES

1) Write the C++ statement to declare a one-dimensional `int` array named `numbers`. The array should have 20 elements.

2) Write the C++ statement to store the value 7 in the second element contained in a one-dimensional `int` array named `numbers`.

3) Write the C++ statement to declare a one-dimensional `double` array named `rates` that has five elements. Then write the code to assign the following numbers to the array: 6.5, 8.3, 4, 2, and 10.5.

4) Write the C++ code to display (on the screen) the contents of a one-dimensional `double` array named `rates`. The array has five elements. Use the `for` statement.

5) Rewrite the code from Exercise 4 using the `while` statement.

6) Write the C++ statement to sort in ascending order a one-dimensional array named `rates`.

7) Write the C++ statement to reverse the contents of a one-dimensional array named `rates`.

8) Write the C++ code to calculate the average of the elements included in a one-dimensional `double` array named `rates`. The array has five elements. Display the average on the screen. Use the `for` statement.

9) Rewrite the code from Exercise 8 using the `while` statement.

10) Write the C++ code to display (on the screen) the largest number stored in a one-dimensional `double` array named `rates`. The array has five elements. Use the `while` statement.

11) Rewrite the code from Exercise 10 using the `for` statement.

12) Write the C++ code to subtract the number one from each element in a one-dimensional `double` array named `rates`. The array has five elements. Use the `while` statement.

13) Rewrite the code from Exercise 12 using the `for` statement.

14) Write the C++ code to multiply by two the number stored in the first element included in a one-dimensional `int` array named `num`. Store the result in the `numDoubled` variable.

15) Write the C++ code to add together the numbers stored in the first and second elements included in a one-dimensional `int` array named `num`. Display the sum on the screen.

16) Write the C++ code to declare a two-dimensional `double` array named `balances`. The array should have four rows and six columns.

17) Write the C++ code to store the number 100 in each element in the `balances` array declared in Exercise 16. Use the `for` statement.

18) Rewrite the code from Exercise 17 using the `while` statement.

19) Write the statement to assign the C++ keyword `true` to the variable located in the third row, first column of the `answers` array.

20) Write the C++ code to add together the number stored in the first row, first column of the `num` array, and the number stored in the second row, second column of the `num` array. Display the sum on the screen.

21) In this exercise, you learn how to determine the lowest and highest subscript in an array.

A. Find a method that returns the lowest subscript in an array. Also find a method that returns the highest subscript in an array.

B. Write a C++ statement that displays (on the screen) the lowest subscript included in a one-dimensional array named `price`.

C. Write a C++ statement that displays (on the screen) the highest row subscript included in a two-dimensional array named `quantity`.

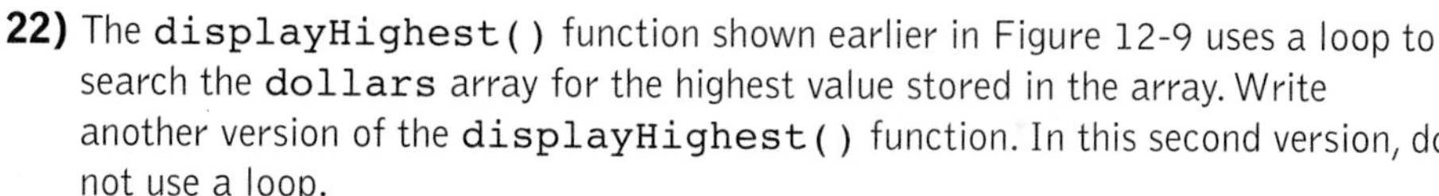

22) The `displayHighest()` function shown earlier in Figure 12-9 uses a loop to search the `dollars` array for the highest value stored in the array. Write another version of the `displayHighest()` function. In this second version, do not use a loop.

23) In this exercise, you debug a C++ program.

A. If necessary, start Visual Studio .NET. Open the T12ConE23 Solution (T12ConE23 Solution.sln) file, which is contained in the CppNet\Tut12\T12ConE23 Solution folder.

B. Study the existing code, then build the solution. Correct any errors in the program, then save and build the solution.

C. Execute the program.

D. When the program is working correctly, close the Output window, and then use the File menu to close the solution.

Application Lesson

Using an Array in a C++ Program

CASE At the beginning of each year, Martha Stenwaldt records the monthly rainfall amounts for the previous year in a sequential access file. Your task in this lesson is to create a program that reads the rainfall amounts from the file, and then calculates and displays the total rainfall amount.

The Rainfall Program

Figure 12-21 shows the contents of a sequential access file named rainfall.txt. Martha uses the rainfall.txt file to record the previous year's rainfall amounts. Notice that the file contains 12 amounts, each corresponding to one of the months in a year.

Figure 12-21: Sample rainfall.txt file

```
2.44
2.36
2.76
1.2
.4
.07
.04
.23
.54
.63
1.54
2.16
```

The program shown in Figure 12-22 represents one possible solution to the rainfall problem. Notice that the program contains two value-returning functions named `main()` and `fillArray()`, and one void function named `displayTotal()`.

Figure 12-22: One possible solution to the rainfall problem

enter the array's datatype followed by __gc[ ] in the function prototype

C++ instructions

```
//function prototypes
bool fillArray(double __gc[]);
void displayTotal(double __gc[]);

int main()
{
    //declare variable and array
    bool problemFillingArray = false;
    double rainfall __gc[] = new double __gc[12];
```

Figure 12-22: One possible solution to the rainfall problem (continued)

```
    //fill array with rainfall amounts
    problemFillingArray = fillArray(rainfall);

    //if there was no problem filling the array,
    //display the total rainfall
    if (problemFillingArray == false)
        displayTotal(rainfall);
    //end if

    return 0;
}   //end of main function

//*****function definitions*****
bool fillArray(double r __gc[])
{
    //declare variables
    bool errorOpeningFile = false;
    int sub = 0;
    IO::StreamReader *inFile;

    //try opening the file
    try
    {
        inFile = IO::File::OpenText("rainfall.txt");
    }
    catch (IO::IOException *ex)
    {
        Console::WriteLine(ex->Message);
        errorOpeningFile = true;
    }
    //if the file was opened successfully
    if (errorOpeningFile == false)
    {
        while (inFile->Peek() != -1 && sub < r->GetLength(0))
        {
            //assign the number to the array
            r[sub] = Convert::ToDouble(inFile->ReadLine());
            //update the subscript
            sub = sub + 1;
        }  //end while
        inFile->Close();
    }   //end if
    return errorOpeningFile;
}   //end of fillArray function

void displayTotal(double r __gc[])
{
    //declare accumulator variable
    double total = 0.0;
    //accumulate rainfall amounts, then display total
    for (int x = 0; x < r->GetLength(0); x = x + 1)
        total = total + r[x];
    //end for
```

enter the array's name in the function call

enter the array's data type and name, followed by __gc[ ], in the function header

enter the array's data type and name, followed by __gc[ ], in the function header

tip

You also could have written the rainfall program shown in Figure 12-22 without using an array. However, in Exercise 1 at the end of this lesson, you will add other functions to the rainfall program, making the array necessary.

tip

It is a good programming practice to use a compound condition, similar to the one shown in the `fillArray()` function in Figure 12-22, in a `while` loop that reads records from a file into an array, even when you know that the file contains the same number of records as there are array elements. Doing so helps to ensure that the program will not end with an error if the file is somehow changed.

tip

Passing an array *by reference* is more efficient than passing it *by value*. Because many arrays are large, passing *by value* would consume a great deal of memory and time since the computer would need to duplicate the array in the receiving function's formal parameter.

Figure 12-22: One possible solution to the rainfall problem (continued)

```
    Console::WriteLine("Total rainfall: {0} inches", ↵
    Convert::ToString(total));
    Console::WriteLine();
}   //end of displayTotal function
```

The `main()` function in the rainfall program declares a `bool` variable named `problemFillingArray` and initializes it using the C++ keyword `false`. The function also declares a one-dimensional `double` array named `rainfall`. The `rainfall` array contains 12 elements—one for each month of the year. After declaring the variable and the array, the `main()` function calls the `fillArray()` function, passing it the `rainfall` array.

Study closely the `fillArray()` function prototype and function header, which are shaded in Figure 12-22. As you know, variables can be passed to functions either *by value* or *by reference*. Recall that, in C++, scalar (simple) variables are passed automatically *by value*. To pass a scalar variable *by reference* in C++, you need to include the address-of (&) operator before the formal parameter's name in the receiving function's header. You also need to include the & operator in the receiving function's prototype.

Unlike scalar variables, arrays in C++ are automatically passed *by reference* rather than *by value*. When you pass an array, the computer passes the address of only the first array element to the receiving function. Because array elements are stored in contiguous locations in memory, the receiving function needs to know only where the first element is located in memory. From there, the function can easily locate the other elements.

Because arrays are automatically passed *by reference*, you do not include the address-of (&) operator before the formal parameter's name in the function header, as you do when passing variables *by reference*. You also do not include the & in the function prototype. To pass an array to a function, you enter the data type and name of the formal parameter, followed by a space and `__gc[]`, in the receiving function's header. You also enter the data type followed by a space and `__gc[]` in the function prototype. As Figure 12-22 shows, you can pass the `rainfall` array to the `fillArray()` function by entering `double r __gc[]` in the `fillArray()` function header, and entering `double __gc[]` in the `fillArray()` function prototype.

The `fillArray()` function begins by declaring the appropriate variables. It then opens a sequential access file named rainfall.txt for input. If a problem occurs when opening the rainfall.txt file, the `catch` statement in the function displays an appropriate error message and also assigns the C++ keyword `true` to the `errorOpeningFile` variable; otherwise, the computer opens the rainfall.txt file and positions the file pointer at the beginning of the file.

Next, the `if (errorOpeningFile == false)` clause is processed. If the `errorOpeningFile` variable contains the value `false`, it means that no errors occurred when opening the rainfall.txt file. In that case, the `while` loop in the `fillArray()` function reads each number from the file, assigning each to an element in the `rainfall` array. Notice that the `while` clause contains two conditions connected by the And (&&) logical operator. The `inFile->Peek() != -1` condition ensures that the loop does not attempt to read past the end of the rainfall.txt file, and the `sub < r->GetLength(0)` condition ensures that the loop does not attempt to access a memory location that is not part of the array. When the loop has completed its processing, the `fillArray()` function closes the rainfall.txt file. Next, the `return errorOpeningFile;` statement is processed and returns the value `false` to the `main()` function, where it is stored in the `problemFillingArray` variable. The `false` value indicates that the `fillArray()` function did not encounter any problems when filling the array.

If, on the other hand, the `errorOpeningFile` variable contains the value `true` when the `if (errorOpeningFile == false)` clause is processed, it indicates that an error occurred when opening the file. In that case, the loop in the `fillArray()` function is skipped over, and processing continues with the `return errorOpeningFile;` statement. The `return errorOpeningFile;` statement returns the value `true` to the `main()` function, where it is stored in the `problemFillingArray` variable. The `true` value indicates that the `fillArray()` function encountered a problem while trying to open the rainfall.txt file; consequently, the array was not filled with data.

Next, the computer processes the `if (problemFillingArray == false)` clause in the `main()` function. If the value stored in the `problemFillingArray` variable does not equal `false`, it indicates that there was a problem filling the array with data. In that case, the computer processes the `return 0;` statement, which returns the number zero to the operating system, and then the program ends.

If, on the other hand, the value stored in the `problemFillingArray` variable is equal to `false`, the program calls the `displayTotal()` function, passing it the `rainfall` array. The `displayTotal()` function accumulates the values stored in the `rainfall` array, and then displays the total rainfall amount on the screen.

Completing the Rainfall Program

On your computer's hard disk is a partially completed C++ program containing most of the instructions for the rainfall program. You open the partially completed program in the next set of steps.

To open the partially completed C++ program:

1. Start Microsoft Visual Studio .NET. If necessary, close the Start Page window.
2. Click **File** on the menu bar, and then click **Open Solution**. The Open Solution dialog box opens.
3. Locate and then open the **CppNet\Tut12\T12App Solution** folder.
4. Click **T12App Solution** (T12App Solution.sln) in the list of filenames, and then click the **Open** button.
5. If the T12App.cpp source file is not displayed, right-click **T12App.cpp** in the Solution Explorer window, and then click **Open**.

The prototype, call, and definition for the `displayTotal()` function are missing from the program. You complete the program in the next set of steps.

To complete the T12App.cpp program, then test the program:

1. Enter the prototype, call, and definition for the `displayTotal()` function. The lines of code you are to enter are shaded in Figure 12-23, which shows the completed T12App.cpp program.

Figure 12-23: Completed T12App.cpp program

```
//T12App.cpp
//reads rainfall amounts from a sequential access file
//calculates and displays the total rainfall amount
#using <mscorlib.dll>
using namespace System;

//function prototypes
bool fillArray(double __gc[]);
void displayTotal(double __gc[]);

int main()
{
    //declare variable and array
    bool problemFillingArray = false;
    double rainfall __gc[] = new double __gc[12];

    //fill array with rainfall amounts
    problemFillingArray = fillArray(rainfall);

    //if there was no problem filling the array,
    //display the total rainfall
    if (problemFillingArray == false)
        displayTotal(rainfall);
    //end if

    return 0;
}   //end of main function

//*****function definitions*****
bool fillArray(double r __gc[])
{
    //declare variables
    bool errorOpeningFile = false;
    int sub = 0;
    IO::StreamReader *inFile;

    //try opening the file
    try
    {
        inFile = IO::File::OpenText("rainfall.txt");
    }
    catch (IO::IOException *ex)
    {
        Console::WriteLine(ex->Message);
        errorOpeningFile = true;
    }
    //if the file was opened successfully
    if (errorOpeningFile == false)
    {
```

Figure 12-23: Completed T12App.cpp program (continued)

```
        while (inFile->Peek() != -1 && sub
        < r->GetLength(0))
        {
            //assign the number to the array
            r[sub] = Convert::ToDouble
            (inFile->ReadLine());
            //update the subscript
            sub = sub + 1;
        }  //end while
        inFile->Close();
    }   //end if
    return errorOpeningFile;
}   //end of fillArray function

void displayTotal(double r __gc[])
{
    //declare accumulator variable
    double total = 0.0;
    //accumulate rainfall amounts, then display total
    for (int x = 0; x < r->GetLength(0); x = x + 1)
        total = total + r[x];
    //end for
    Console::WriteLine("Total rainfall: {0} inches",
    Convert::ToString(total));
    Console::WriteLine();
}   //end of displayTotal function
```

2. Save and then build the solution. Verify that the program generated no warnings.
3. Execute the program. The program displays the message "Total rainfall: 14.37 inches" in the Command Prompt window, as shown in Figure 12-24.

Figure 12-24: Command Prompt window showing the total rainfall amount

"c:\cppnet\tut12\t12app solution\t12app project\debug\T12App Project.exe"
Total rainfall: 14.37 inches
Press any key to continue

4. Close the Command Prompt window, then close the Output window.
5. Click **File** on the menu bar, and then click **Close Solution** to close the current solution.
6. Click **File** on the menu bar, and then click **Exit** to exit Visual Studio .NET.

You now have completed Tutorial 12's Application lesson. You can either take a break or complete the end-of-lesson exercises.

Look For These Symbols

Debugging

Discovery

EXERCISES

1) In this exercise, you modify the program you completed in the lesson so that it includes functions that calculate the following: the average rainfall amount, the highest rainfall amount, and the lowest rainfall amount.

A. If necessary, start Visual Studio .NET. Open the T12AppE01 Solution (T12AppE01 Solution.sln) file, which is contained in the CppNet\Tut12\T12AppE01 Solution folder.

B. Add four additional functions to the program: `displayMenu()`, `displayAvg()`, `displayHigh()`, and `displayLow()`. The `displayMenu()` function should allow the user to choose from four options: Display Average Amount, Display Highest Amount, Display Lowest Amount, and Display Total Amount. The `displayAvg()`, `displayHigh()`, and `displayLow()` functions should display the average rainfall amount, the highest rainfall amount, and the lowest rainfall amount, respectively. Modify the program appropriately.

C. Save and then build the solution.

D. Execute the program. Display the average rainfall amount, the total rainfall amount, the highest rainfall amount, and the lowest rainfall amount.

E. When the program is working correctly, close the Output window, and then use the File menu to close the solution.

2) In this exercise, you complete a program that displays the number of days in a month.

A. If necessary, start Visual Studio .NET. Open the T12AppE02 Solution (T12AppE02 Solution.sln) file, which is contained in the CppNet\Tut12\T12AppE02 Solution folder.

B. Declare a 12-element, one-dimensional `int` array named `days`. Assign the number of days in each month to the array. (Use 28 for February.)

C. Code the program so that it displays (on the screen) the number of days in the month corresponding to the number entered by the user. For example, if the user enters the number one, the program should display 31 on the screen. The program should display an appropriate message if the user enters an invalid number.

D. Save and then build the solution.

E. Execute the program. Use the following numbers to test the program: 20, 1, 2, 3, 4, 5, 6, 7, 8, 9, 10, 11, 12, and -1 (sentinel value).

F. When the program is working correctly, close the Output window, and then use the File menu to close the solution.

3) In this exercise, you complete a program that displays the lowest value stored in an array.

A. If necessary, start Visual Studio .NET. Open the T12AppE03 Solution (T12AppE03 Solution.sln) file, which is contained in the CppNet\Tut12\T12AppE03 Solution folder.

B. Declare a one-dimensional `int` array named `scores`. Assign the 20 numbers contained in the scores.txt file to the array. The scores.txt file is a sequential access file contained in the CppNet\Tut12\T12AppE03 Solution\T12AppE03 Project folder.

C. Code the program so that it displays (on the screen) the lowest score stored in the array.

D. Save and then build the solution.

E. Execute the program. A message containing the lowest score should appear on the screen.

F. When the program is working correctly, close the Output window, and then use the File menu to close the solution.

4) In this exercise, you complete a program that updates the prices stored in a one-dimensional array, and then writes the prices to a sequential access file.

A. If necessary, start Visual Studio .NET. Open the T12AppE04 Solution (T12AppE04 Solution.sln) file, which is contained in the CppNet\Tut12\T12AppE04 Solution folder.

B. Code the program so that it asks the user for a percentage amount by which each price should be increased. The program then should increase each price in the `price` array by that amount, and then save the increased prices (formatted to "C2") to a sequential access file named newprices.txt. (For example, if the user enters the number 15, then each element in the array should be increased by 15%.)

C. Save and then build the solution.

D. Execute the program. Increase each price by 5%. Close the Command Prompt window.

E. Click File on the menu bar, point to Open, and then click File. Click the Files of type list arrow, then click All Files (*.*) in the list. Open the newprices.txt file. The file should contain 10 prices. Each price should be 5% more than the prices originally stored in the array. Close the newprices.txt window.

F. When the program is working correctly, close the Output window, and then use the File menu to close the solution.

5) In this exercise, you modify the program you completed in Exercise 4. The modified program will allow the user to update a specific price.

A. If necessary, start Visual Studio .NET. Open the T12AppE05 Solution (T12AppE05 Solution.sln) file, which is contained in the CppNet\Tut12\T12AppE05 Solution folder.

B. Click File on the menu bar, point to Open, and then click File. Open the T12AppE04.cpp file, which is contained in the CppNet\Tut12\T12AppE04 Solution\T12AppE04 Project folder. Select all of the code, beginning with the `main()` function. Copy the code to the clipboard. Close the T12AppE04.cpp window, then paste the code in the T12AppE05.cpp window.

C. Modify the program so that it also asks the user to enter a number from one through 10. If the user enters the number one, the program should update the first price in the array. If the user enters the number two, the program should update the second price in the array, and so on.

D. Save and then build the solution.

E. Execute the program. Increase the second price by 10%. Then increase the tenth price by 2%. Finally, decrease the first price by 10%. (*Hint*: To decrease a price, enter a negative number.) Stop the program, then close the Command Prompt window.

F. Click File on the menu bar, point to Open, and then click File. Click the Files of type list arrow, then click All Files (*.*) in the list. Open the newprices.txt file. The first price in the file should be 10% less than the original first price. The second price should be 10% more than the original second price, and the tenth price should be 2% more than the original tenth price. Close the newprices.txt window.

G. When the program is working correctly, close the Output window, and then use the File menu to close the solution.

6) In this exercise, you code a program that displays the number of students earning a specific score.

A. If necessary, start Visual Studio .NET. Open the T12AppE06 Solution (T12AppE06 Solution.sln) file, which is contained in the CppNet\Tut12\T12AppE06 Solution folder.

B. Declare a 20-element, one-dimensional `int` array named `scores`. Assign the 20 numbers contained in the scores.txt file to the array. The scores.txt file is a sequential access file located in the CppNet\Tut12\T12AppE06 Solution\T12AppE06 Project folder.

C. Also enter the code that prompts the user to enter a score from zero through 100. The program should display (on the computer screen) the number of students earning that score.

D. Save and then build the solution.

E. Execute the program. Use the program to answer the following questions:

How many students earned a score of 72?

How many students earned a score of 88?

How many students earned a score of 20?

How many students earned a score of 99?

F. Close the Command Prompt window.

G. When the program is working correctly, close the Output window, and then use the File menu to close the solution.

7) In this exercise, you modify the program you completed in Exercise 6. The modified program will allow the user to display the number of students earning a score in a specific range.

A. If necessary, start Visual Studio .NET. Open the T12AppE07 Solution (T12AppE07 Solution.sln) file, which is contained in the CppNet\Tut12\T12AppE07 Solution folder.

B. Click File on the menu bar, point to Open, and then click File. Open the T12AppE06.cpp file, which is contained in the CppNet\Tut12\T12AppE06 Solution\T12AppE06 Project folder. Select all of the code, beginning with the function prototypes. Copy the code to the clipboard. Close the T12AppE06.cpp window, then paste the code in the T12AppE07.cpp window.

C. Modify the program so that it prompts the user to enter a minimum score and a maximum score. The program then should display (on the screen) the number of students who earned a score within that range.

D. Save and then build the solution.

E. Execute the program. Use the program to answer the following questions:

How many students earned a score between 70 and 79, including 70 and 79?

How many students earned a score between 65 and 85, including 65 and 85?

How many students earned a score between 0 and 50, including 0 and 50?

F. Stop the program, then close the Command Prompt window.

G. When the program is working correctly, close the Output window, and then use the File menu to close the solution.

8) In this exercise, you complete a program that sorts the values stored in a sequential access file.

A. If necessary, start Visual Studio .NET. Open the T12AppE08 Solution (T12AppE08 Solution.sln) file, which is contained in the CppNet\Tut12\T12AppE08 Solution folder.

B. Declare a 20-element, one-dimensional `int` array named `numbers`. Assign the 20 numbers contained in the nums.txt file to the array. The nums.txt file is a sequential access file located in the CppNet\Tut12\T12AppE08 Solution\T12AppE08 Project folder.

C. Also enter the code that sorts the contents of the `numbers` array in descending order, and then writes the sorted array to a sequential access file named sortednums.txt.

D. Save and then build the solution.

E. Execute the program. Close the Command Prompt window.

F. Click File on the menu bar, point to Open, and then click File. Open the sortednums.txt file, which is contained in the CppNet\Tut12\T12AppE08 Solution\T12AppE08 Project folder. The numbers should be in descending order. Close the sortednums.txt window.

G. When the program is working correctly, close the Output window, and then use the File menu to close the solution.

9) In this exercise, you complete a program that displays the sum of the numbers stored in a two-dimensional array.

A. If necessary, start Visual Studio .NET. Open the T12AppE09 Solution (T12AppE09 Solution.sln) file, which is contained in the CppNet\Tut12\T12AppE09 Solution folder.

B. Complete the program by entering the code to sum the values stored in the `quantity` array. Also enter the code to display the sum on the screen.

C. Save and then build the solution.

D. Execute the program. The sum of the numbers stored in the array should appear in the Command Prompt window. Close the Command Prompt window.

E. When the program is working correctly, close the Output window, and then use the File menu to close the solution.

10) In this exercise, you create a program that uses a two-dimensional array. Conway Enterprises has both domestic and international sales operations. The company's sales manager wants a program that displays the total sales made by the company during a six-month period. The program also should display the total domestic and total international sales.

A. If necessary, start Visual Studio .NET. Open the T12AppE10 Solution (T12AppE10 Solution.sln) file, which is contained in the CppNet\Tut12\T12AppE10 Solution folder.

B. Complete the program by entering the code to display the total domestic sales, the total international sales, and the total company sales.

C. Save and then build the solution.

D. Execute the program. The three total sales amounts should appear in the Command Prompt window. Close the Command Prompt window.

E. When the program is working correctly, close the Output window, and then use the File menu to close the solution.

11) In this exercise, you create a program that uses a two-dimensional array. The program displays the highest score earned on the midterm and the highest score earned on the final.

A. If necessary, start Visual Studio .NET. Open the T12AppE11 Solution (T12AppE11 Solution.sln) file, which is contained in the CppNet\Tut12\T12AppE11 Solution folder.

B. Click File on the menu bar, point to Open, and then click File. Open the scores.txt file, which is contained in the CppNet\Tut12\T12AppE11 Solution\T12AppE11 Project folder. The first number in each record is the midterm score, and the second number is the final score. Close the scores.txt window.

C. Complete the program by entering the code to display the highest score on the midterm and the highest score on the final.

D. Save and then build the solution.

E. Execute the program. The program should display the highest score earned on the midterm and the highest score earned on the final. Close the Command Prompt window.

F. When the program is working correctly, close the Output window, and then use the File menu to close the solution.

12) In this exercise, you determine the number of times a value appears in a two-dimensional array.

A. If necessary, start Visual Studio .NET. Open the T12AppE12 Solution (T12AppE12 Solution.sln) file, which is contained in the CppNet\Tut12\T12AppE12 Solution folder.

B. Complete the program by entering the code to display the number of times each of the numbers 1 through 9 appears in the two-dimensional `numbers` array. Also enter the code to display the nine counts on the screen. For example, the number 1 appears 2 times in the array, the number 2 appears 4 times, and so on.

C. Save and then build the solution.

D. Execute the program. The nine counts should appear in the Command Prompt window. Close the Command Prompt window.

E. When the program is working correctly, close the Output window, and then use the File menu to close the solution.

13) In this exercise, you learn how to pass a two-dimensional array to a function.

A. If necessary, start Visual Studio .NET. Open the T12AppE13 Solution (T12AppE13 Solution.sln) file, which is contained in the CppNet\Tut12\T12AppE13 Solution folder.

B. Complete the program by entering the code to pass the two-dimensional `sales` array to the `calcTotal()` function.

C. Save and then build the solution.

D. Execute the program. The program should display total sales of $412,000 in the Command Prompt window. Close the Command Prompt window.

E. When the program is working correctly, close the Output window, and then use the File menu to close the solution.

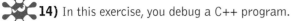

14) In this exercise, you debug a C++ program.

A. If necessary, start Visual Studio .NET. Open the T12AppE14 Solution (T12AppE14 Solution.sln) file, which is contained in the CppNet\Tut12\T12AppE14 Solution folder. After filling the array with the quantities stored in the quantities.txt file, the program prompts the user to enter the amount by which each quantity is to be increased or decreased. It then displays the old and new quantities on the screen.

B. Click File on the menu bar, point to Open, and then click File. Open the quantities.txt file, which is contained in the CppNet\Tut12\T12AppE14 Solution\T12AppE14 Project folder. Print the file, then close the quantities.txt window.

C. Build the solution. Correct any errors in the program, then save and build the solution.

D. Execute the program. When you are prompted to enter a number, type 5 and press Enter. The Command Prompt window should show the old and new quantities. Notice that the program is not working correctly. Close the Command Prompt window.

E. Correct any errors in the program, then save and build the solution.

F. Execute the program. When the program is working correctly, close the Output window, and then use the File menu to close the solution.

Tutorial 13

More on Arrays

Objectives

After completing this tutorial, you will be able to:

- Create and manipulate a `String` array
- Create and manipulate parallel arrays
- Create and manipulate an array of objects created from a class that you define

Concept Lesson

Arrays

As you learned in Tutorial 12, an array is a group of variables that have the same name and data type and are related in some way. Programmers use arrays to temporarily store related data in the internal memory of the computer. Storing data in an array increases the efficiency of a program, because data can be both written to and read from internal memory much faster than it can be written to and read from a file on a disk. Additionally, after the data is entered into an array, which typically is done at the beginning of the program, the program can use the data as many times as desired.

In Tutorial 12, you learned how to create an array using one of the C++ fundamental data types. Recall that the fundamental data types are the basic data types built into the C++ language, and they include `char`, `short`, `int`, `float`, `double`, and `bool`. In this lesson, you learn how to create an array using a data type other than a fundamental data type.

Creating an Array Using a Data Type That Is Not a Fundamental Data Type

Figure 13-1 shows two versions of the syntax for creating a one-dimensional array. As you learned in Tutorial 12, you use Version 1 when the array's *datatype* is one of the C++ fundamental data types. You use Version 2 when the array has a *datatype* that is not a C++ fundamental data type. For example, you use Version 2 to declare a `String` array, and also to declare a `Rectangle` array using the `Rectangle` class that you created in Tutorial 10. Notice that, unlike the syntax shown in Version 1, the syntax shown in Version 2 contains two asterisks: one appears before *arrayname* and the other appears before `__gc[elements]`.

tip

The `__gc` in the syntax is two underscore characters followed by the letters g and c. As you learned in Tutorial 10, the `__gc` indicates that the array will be managed by the .NET Framework's garbage collector.

Figure 13-1: Syntax for declaring a one-dimensional array

Two versions of the syntax for declaring a one-dimensional array
Version 1: use when the *datatype* is a C++ fundamental data type: *datatype arrayname* `__gc[] = new` *datatype* `__gc[`*elements*`];` Version 2: use when the *datatype* is not a C++ fundamental data type: *datatype* `*`*arrayname* `__gc[] = new` *datatype* `*__gc[`*elements*`];`

Figure 13-2 shows several examples of using the syntax shown in Version 2 in Figure 13-1 to create one-dimensional arrays.

Figure 13-2: Examples of creating one-dimensional arrays

Examples and results
Example 1 `String *name __gc[] = new String *__gc[4];` Result declares a four-element `String` array named `name`
Example 2 `Rectangle *shape __gc[] = new Rectangle *__gc[5];` Result declares a five-element `Rectangle` array named `shape`

Example 3
`Salesperson *employee __gc[] = new Salesperson`
`*__gc[50];`
 	
Result
declares a 50-element `Salesperson` array named `employee`

The statement shown in Example 1 in Figure 13-2 creates a one-dimensional `String` array named `name`. The `name` array contains four elements with subscripts of 0, 1, 2, and 3. Each element in the `name` array can store one `String` object.

The statement shown in Example 2 creates a five-element, one-dimensional `Rectangle` array named `shape`. Each element in the `shape` array can store one `Rectangle` object. As you may remember from Tutorial 10, a `Rectangle` object contains two private data members: `length` and `width`. It also contains four public member methods: `Rectangle()`, `SetDimensions()`, `CalcArea()`, and `CalcPerimeter()`.

The statement shown in Example 3 in Figure 13-2 creates a 50-element, one-dimensional `Salesperson` array named `employee`. Each element in the `employee` array can store one `Salesperson` object. As you may remember from Tutorial 11, a `Salesperson` object contains two private data members: `name` and `sales`. It also contains five public member methods: `Salesperson()`, `WriteRecordToFile()`, `ReadRecordFromFile()`, `GetName()`, and `GetSales()`.

In the next section, you view a program that uses a one-dimensional `String` array to sort the names contained in a sequential access file.

The Hansen Inc. Program

Assume that a company named Hansen Inc. wants to display the names of its suppliers in ascending order. The names are stored in a sequential access file named suppliers.txt. The company can use the program shown in Figure 13-3 to perform this task.

Figure 13-3: The Hansen Inc. program

C++ instructions for the Hansen Inc. program

```
//declare variables and array
int x = 0;
bool fileProblem = false;
String *supplier __gc[] = new String *__gc[5];

//declare StreamReader variable and open the file
IO::StreamReader *inFile;
try
{
    inFile = IO::File::OpenText("suppliers.txt");
}
catch (IO::IOException *ex)
{
    fileProblem = true;
    Console::WriteLine(ex->Message);
}
//determine whether the file was opened successfully
if (fileProblem == false)
{
    //read names into array
    while (inFile->Peek() != -1 && x < supplier->GetLength(0))
    {
        supplier[x] = inFile->ReadLine();
        x = x + 1;
    } //end while

    //close the file
    inFile->Close();

    //sort the contents of the array
    Array::Sort(supplier);

    //display the contents of the array
    for (int y = 0; y < supplier->GetLength(0); y = y + 1)
        Console::WriteLine(supplier[y]);
}   //end if
```

Result (assuming the file contains the names XYZ Incorporated, ABC Company, Delta Limited, Sonta Inc., and Trese Company)

ABC Company
Delta Limited
Sonta Inc.
Trese Company
XYZ Incorporated

The Hansen Inc. program declares an `int` variable named `x`, a `bool` variable named `fileProblem`, and a five-element, one-dimensional `String` array named `supplier`. The program uses the `x` variable to keep track of the subscripts in the `supplier` array. It uses the `fileProblem` variable to keep track of whether the suppliers.txt file was opened successfully.

Next, the program declares a `StreamReader` variable and then attempts to open the suppliers.txt file for input. If the file is opened successfully, the `while` loop in the program reads the names from the file and stores them in the `supplier` array. The `while` loop stops either when the computer reaches the end of the suppliers.txt file or when the value in the `x` variable is five, whichever occurs first.

When the `while` loop stops, the program closes the suppliers.txt file. It then sorts the contents of the `supplier` array in ascending order and displays the contents on the computer screen. As Figure 13-3 indicates, the program displays ABC Company, Delta Limited, Sonta Inc., Trese Company, and XYZ Incorporated.

MINI-QUIZ

Mini-Quiz 1

1) Write a C++ statement that declares a 50-element, one-dimensional `String` array named `states`.

2) Assume that a program declares an `int` variable named `x`, and that the `x` variable is initialized to zero. Which of the following `while` clauses tells the computer to process the loop body instructions for each element in the `states` array from Question 1?
   a. `while (x > 50)`
   b. `while (x < 50)`
   c. `while (x >= 50)`
   d. `while (x <= 50)`

3) Write a C++ statement that assigns the string "March" to the third element in a one-dimensional `String` array named `month`.

Next, you learn about parallel one-dimensional arrays.

Using Parallel One-Dimensional Arrays

Takoda Tapahe owns a small gift shop named Takoda Treasures. She has asked you to create a program that displays the price of the item whose product ID she enters. Figure 13-4 shows a portion of the gift shop's price list.

Figure 13-4: A portion of the gift shop's price list

Product ID	Price
BX35	13
CR20	10
FE15	12
KW10	24
MM67	4

Recall that all of the variables in an array have the same data type. So how can you store a price list, which includes a string (the product ID) and a number (the price), in an array?

One way of doing so is to use two one-dimensional arrays: a `String` array to store the product IDs and an `int` array to store the prices. Both arrays are illustrated in Figure 13-5.

Figure 13-5: Illustration of a price list stored in two one-dimensional arrays

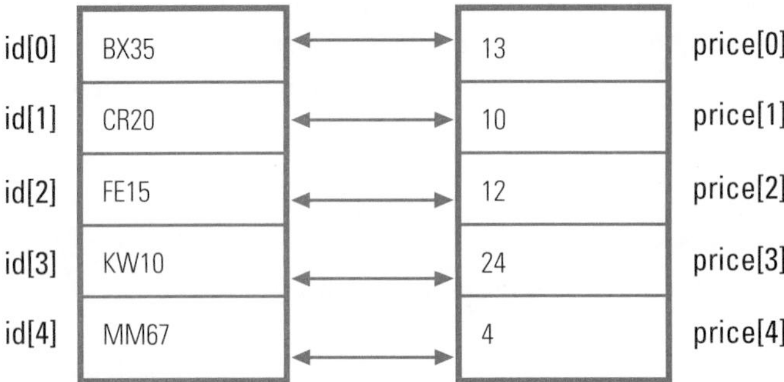

The arrays shown in Figure 13-5 are referred to as parallel arrays. **Parallel arrays** are two or more arrays whose elements are related by their position—in other words, by their subscript—in the arrays. The `id` and `price` arrays shown in Figure 13-5 are parallel arrays because each element in the `id` array corresponds to the element located in the same position in the `price` array. For example, the first element in the `id` array corresponds to the first element in the `price` array. In other words, the item whose product ID is BX35 (`id[0]`) has a price of $13 (`price[0]`). Likewise, the second elements in both arrays—the elements with a subscript of 1—also are related; the item whose product ID is CR20 (`id[1]`) has a price of $10 (`price[1]`). The same relationship is true for the remaining elements in both arrays. If you want to know an item's price, you simply locate the item's ID in the `id` array and then view its corresponding element in the `price` array. Figure 13-6 shows a program that Takoda can use to display the price of an item based on the product ID she enters.

Figure 13-6: Takoda Treasures program using parallel arrays

C++ instructions for the Takoda Treasures program

parallel arrays

```
//declare variable and arrays
String *searchForId = "";
String *id __gc[] = new String *__gc[5];
int price __gc[] = new int __gc[5];

//fill arrays with values
id[0] = "BX35";
id[1] = "CR20";
id[2] = "FE15";
id[3] = "KW10";
id[4] = "MM67";
price[0] = 13;
price[1] = 10;
price[2] = 12;
price[3] = 24;
price[4] = 4;
```

Figure 13-6: Takoda Treasures program using parallel arrays (continued)

```
//get ID to search for, then convert to uppercase
Console::Write("Enter ID (X to exit): ");
searchForId = Console::ReadLine();
searchForId = searchForId->ToUpper();

while (searchForId->CompareTo("X") != 0)
{
    //locate position of product ID in the id array
    int y = 0; //keeps track of array subscripts
    while (y < id->GetLength(0) && id[y]->CompareTo(searchForId) != 0)
        y = y + 1;
    //end while

    //if ID was found, display price from price array
    //otherwise, display error message
    if (y < id->GetLength(0))
        Console::WriteLine("Price: {0}", price[y].ToString("C0"));
    else
        Console::WriteLine("Product ID is not valid.");
    //end if

    //get ID to search for, then convert to uppercase
    Console::Write("Enter ID (X to exit): ");
    searchForId = Console::ReadLine();
    searchForId = searchForId->ToUpper();
} //end while
```

Results

Price: $12 (assuming the user enters FE15 as the product ID)
Product ID is not valid. (assuming the user enters XX89 as the product ID

The Takoda Treasures program shown in Figure 13-6 declares a `String` variable named `searchForId` and two parallel one-dimensional arrays: a five-element `String` array named `id` and a five-element `int` array named `price`. The program stores each item's ID in the `id` array, and stores each item's price in the corresponding location in the `price` array. The program then prompts the user to enter a product ID, and it stores the user's response in the `searchForId` variable. The `ToUpper()` method is used to convert the contents of the `searchForId` variable to uppercase, to match the case of the product IDs stored in the `id` array.

The computer processes the instructions contained in the program's outer `while` loop as long as the user does not enter the letter X (in any case) as the product ID. The first instruction in the body of the outer `while` loop declares and initializes an `int` variable named `y` to keep track of the array subscripts. The second instruction is the beginning of a nested `while` loop.

The nested `while` loop continues to add the number one to the `y` variable as long as the `y` variable contains a value that is less than five and, at the same time, the product ID has not been located in the array. The nested `while` loop stops when either of the following conditions is true: the `y` variable contains the number five (which indicates that the loop reached the end of the array without finding the product ID) or the product ID is located in the array.

After the nested `while` loop completes its processing, the `if` statement in the program compares the number stored in the `y` variable with the number five. If the `y` variable contains a number that is less than five, it indicates that the loop stopped processing because the product ID was located in the `id` array. In that case, the statement `Console::WriteLine("Price: {0}", price[y].ToString("C0"));` displays the corresponding price from the `price` array. However, if the `y` variable contains a number that is not less than 5, it indicates that the loop stopped processing because it reached the end of the `id` array without finding the product ID; in that case, the message "Product ID is not valid." is displayed.

The program then prompts the user to enter another product ID, and it stores the user's response in the `searchForId` variable. The `ToUpper()` method is used to convert the contents of the `searchForId` variable to uppercase, to match the case of the product IDs stored in the `id` array. Processing then continues with the `while (searchForId->CompareTo("X") != 0)` clause. This clause compares the contents of the `searchForId` variable with the letter X to determine whether the instructions in the outer `while` loop should be processed again.

As Figure 13-6 indicates, the Takoda Treasures program displays the message "Price: $12" when the user enters FE15 as the product ID. The program displays the message "Product ID is not valid." when the user enters XX89 as the product ID.

MINI-QUIZ

Mini-Quiz 2

1) Parallel arrays are arrays whose elements are related by their ______________ in the array.
2) Assume that the `employNumber` and `employName` arrays are parallel arrays. If an employee's number is located in `employNumber[3]`, then his or her name is located in ______________.
3) Parallel arrays must have the same data type.
   a. True
   b. False

Using parallel one-dimensional arrays is only one way of solving the Takoda Treasures problem. You also can use a one-dimensional array of objects created from a class that you define. You learn how to do this in the Application lesson.

You now have completed Tutorial 13's Concept lesson. You can either take a break or complete the end-of-lesson questions and exercises before moving on to the Application lesson.

SUMMARY

An array is a group of variables that have the same name and data type and are related in some way. You can declare an array using any of the C++ fundamental data types. To do so, you use the syntax *datatype arrayname* `__gc[] = new` *datatype* `__gc[`*elements*`];`. You also can declare an array using a data type that is not a fundamental data type. You do so using the syntax *datatype *arrayname* `__gc[] = new` *datatype* `*__gc[`*elements*`];`.

Parallel arrays are two or more arrays whose elements are related by their subscript (position) in the arrays.

ANSWERS TO MINI-QUIZZES

Mini-Quiz 1

1) `String *states __gc[] = new String *__gc[50];`
2) b. `while (x < 50)`
3) `month[2] = "March";`

Mini-Quiz 2

1) subscript (or position)
2) `employName[3]`
3) b. False

QUESTIONS

1) Which of the following statements declares a 10-element, one-dimensional `String` array named `artists`?
   A. `String *artists __gc[] = new String *__gc[10];`
   B. `String artists __gc[] = new String __gc[10];`
   C. `String * __gc[] = new String *artists __gc[10];`
   D. `String __gc[] = new String artists __gc[10];`
2) Which of the following statements declares a five-element, one-dimensional `double` array named `price`?
   A. `double *price __gc[] = new double *__gc[5];`
   B. `double price __gc[] = new double __gc[5];`
   C. `double * __gc[] = new double *price __gc[5];`
   D. `double __gc[] = new double price __gc[5];`
3) Which of the following statements declares a 20-element, one-dimensional `Triangle` array named `shapes`?
   A. `Triangle *shapes __gc[] = new Triangle *__gc[20];`
   B. `Triangle shapes __gc[] = new Triangle __gc[20];`
   C. `Triangle * __gc[] = new Triangle *shapes __gc[20];`
   D. `Triangle __gc[] = new Triangle shapes __gc[20];`
4) Assume that the `city` and `zip` arrays are parallel arrays. Which of the following statements displays the city name associated with the zip code stored in `zip[8]`?
   A. `Console::WriteLine(city[zip[8]]);`
   B. `Console::WriteLine(city(zip[8]));`
   C. `Console::WriteLine(city[8]);`
   D. `Console::WriteLine(city(8));`

5) Which of the following is false?

A. An array's data type can be a C++ fundamental data type.

B. An array's data type can be the `String` data type.

C. An array's data type can be a class that you define.

D. A program can have only two parallel arrays.

Look For These Symbols

Debugging

Discovery

EXERCISES

1) Write the C++ statement to declare a 10-element, one-dimensional `String` array named `employees`.

2) Write the C++ statement to store the string "Theodore" in the second element contained in the `employees` array.

3) Write the C++ statement to declare a five-element `String` array named `names`.

4) Write the C++ code to display (on the screen) the contents of a five-element, one-dimensional `String` array named `itemIds`. Use the `for` statement.

5) Rewrite the code from Question 4 using the `while` statement.

6) Write the C++ statement to sort in ascending order a one-dimensional `String` array named `itemIds`.

7) Write the C++ statement to reverse the contents of a one-dimensional `String` array named `itemIds`.

8) In this exercise, you complete a program that uses an array to change the case of the codes stored in a sequential access file.

A. If necessary, start Visual Studio .NET. Open the T13ConE08 Solution (T13ConE08 Solution.sln) file, which is contained in the CppNet\Tut13\T13ConE08 Solution folder.

B. Click File on the menu bar, point to Open, and then click File. Open the codes.txt file, which is contained in the CppNet\Tut13\T13ConE08 Solution\T13ConE08 Project folder. Notice that the case of the codes is not consistent. Close the codes.txt window.

C. Complete the program by declaring a 10-element, one-dimensional `String` array named `codes`. Also enter a loop that reads a code from the file and stores it (in uppercase) in the `codes` array. Also enter the code to save the contents of the array in the codes.txt file.

D. Save and then build the solution.

E. Execute the program. Close the Command Prompt window.

F. Click File on the menu bar, point to Open, and then click File. Open the codes.txt file. The file should contain 10 codes; each code should be uppercase letters. Close the codes.txt window.

G. When the program is working correctly, close the Output window, and then use the File menu to close the solution.

9) In this exercise, you complete a program that uses an array to sort five names entered by the user.

A. If necessary, start Visual Studio .NET. Open the T13ConE09 Solution (T13ConE09 Solution.sln) file, which is contained in the CppNet\Tut13\T13ConE09 Solution folder.

B. Complete the program by declaring a five-element, one-dimensional `String` array named `names`. Also enter the code that allows the user to enter five names, which should be stored in the `names` array. Sort the names in descending order, and then display the names on the screen.

C. Save and then build the solution.

D. Execute the program. Enter the following five names: Karen, Kathleen, Jose, Abby, and Bonnie. The program should display the names Kathleen, Karen, Jose, Bonnie, and Abby in the Command Prompt window. Close the Command Prompt window.

E. When the program is working correctly, close the Output window, and then use the File menu to close the solution.

10) In this exercise, you complete a program that uses an array to sort the fifty state names stored in a sequential access file.

A. If necessary, start Visual Studio .NET. Open the T13ConE10 Solution (T13ConE10 Solution.sln) file, which is contained in the CppNet\Tut13\T13ConE10 Solution folder.

B. Click File on the menu bar, point to Open, and then click File. Open the states.txt file, which is contained in the CppNet\Tut13\T13ConE10 Solution\T13ConE10 Project folder. The file contains the names of the 50 states. Close the states.txt window.

C. Complete the program by declaring a 50-element, one-dimensional `String` array named `state`. Then write a C++ function named `fillArray()` that opens the states.txt sequential access file, reads the contents of the file into the `state` array, and then closes the states.txt file. The `state` array will be passed to the `fillArray()` function by the `main()` function. When the `fillArray()` function has completed its processing, the `main()` function should sort the array in ascending order and then call the `writeToFile()` function. The `writeToFile()` function should write the sorted contents of the `state` array to a sequential access file named sortedstates.txt, and then close the sortedstates.txt file.

D. Save and then build the solution.

E. Execute the program. Close the Command Prompt window.

F. Click File on the menu bar, point to Open, and then click File. Open the sortedstates.txt file, which is contained in the CppNet\Tut13\T13ConE10 Solution\T13ConE10 Project folder. The file contains the names of the 50 states, listed in ascending order. Close the sortedstates.txt window.

G. When the program is working correctly, close the Output window, and then use the File menu to close the solution.

11) In this exercise, you use two parallel arrays. Ms. Jenkins uses the grade table shown in Figure 13-7 for her Introduction to Computers course. She wants a program that displays the grade after she enters the total points earned.

Figure 13-7

Minimum points	Maximum points	Grade
0	299	F
300	349	D
350	399	C
400	449	B
450	500	A

A. If necessary, start Visual Studio .NET. Open the T13ConE11 Solution (T13ConE11 Solution.sln) file, which is contained in the CppNet\Tut13\T13ConE11 Solution folder.

B. Store the minimum points in a one-dimensional `int` array named `minPoints`. Store the grade in a parallel, one-dimensional `String` array named `grade`. The program should display the appropriate grade after Ms. Jenkins enters the number of points earned by a student. Include a loop that allows Ms. Jenkins to enter as many values as desired.

C. Save and then build the solution.

D. Execute the program. Test the program four times, using the following amounts: 455, 210, 400, and 349. The program should display grades of A, F, B, and D.

E. When the program is working correctly, close the Output window, and then use the File menu to close the solution.

12) In this exercise, you use three parallel numeric arrays. You search one of the arrays and then display its corresponding values from the other two arrays.

A. If necessary, start Visual Studio .NET. Open the T13ConE12 Solution (T13ConE12 Solution.sln) file, which is contained in the CppNet\Tut13\T13ConE12 Solution folder.

B. Write a program that uses three numeric arrays. Store the even numbers from 2 through 10 in the first array. Store the square of the even numbers from 2 through 10 in the second array. Store the square root of the even numbers from 2 through 10 in the third array. After filling the arrays, the program should prompt the user to enter a number. The program should then search for the number in the first array, and then use the second and third arrays to display both the square and the square root of the number. Allow the user to display the square and square root for as many numbers as desired without having to execute the program again.

C. Save and then build the solution.

D. Execute the program. Test the program four times, using the following numbers: 5, 10, 8, and 7.

E. When the program is working correctly, close the Output window, and then use the File menu to close the solution.

13) In this exercise, you use two parallel arrays.

A. If necessary, start Visual Studio .NET. Open the T13ConE13 Solution (T13ConE13 Solution.sln) file, which is contained in the CppNet\Tut13\T13ConE13 Solution folder.

B. Click File on the menu bar, point to Open, and then click File. Open the cities.txt file, which is contained in the CppNet\Tut13\T13ConE13 Solution\T13ConE13 Project folder. The file contains 10 city names and their corresponding ZIP codes. Close the cities.txt window.

C. Write a program that uses two parallel arrays. Store the city names in the first array, and store the ZIP codes in the second array.

D. Create two functions named `displayZip()` and `displayName()`. The `displayZip()` function should prompt the user to enter a city name. The function should search for the name in the first array, and then use the second array to display the corresponding ZIP code. Allow the user to display the ZIP code for as many cities as desired without having to execute the program again. The `displayName()` function should prompt the user to enter a ZIP code. The function should search for the ZIP code in the second array, and then use the first array to display the corresponding city name. Allow the user to display the city name for as many ZIP codes as desired without having to execute the program again.

E. Save and then build the solution.

F. Execute the program. Test the program using the following city names: Chicago, Darien, and Glen Ellyn. Also test the program using the following zip codes: 60611, 60561, and 60137.

G. When the program is working correctly, close the Output window, and then use the File menu to close the solution.

14) In this exercise, you use two parallel arrays.

A. If necessary, start Visual Studio .NET. Open the T13ConE14 Solution (T13ConE14 Solution.sln) file, which is contained in the CppNet\Tut13\T13ConE14 Solution folder.

B. Click File on the menu bar, point to Open, and then click File. Open the pricelist.txt file, which is contained in the CppNet\Tut13\T13ConE14 Solution\T13ConE14 Project folder. The file contains 10 item names and their corresponding prices. Close the pricelist.txt window.

C. Write a program that uses two parallel arrays. Store the item names in the first array, and store the prices in the second array.

D. Create two functions named `updatePrice()` and `writeToFile()`. The `updatePrice()` function should prompt the user to enter an item name and the amount by which the item's price should be increased. The function should search for the item name in the first array, and then use the second array to update the item's price. Allow the user to update the price for as many items as desired without having to execute the program again. When the user has finished updating prices, the `main()` function should call the `writeToFile()` function. This function should create a new price list by writing the contents of the two arrays to a sequential access file named newpricelist.txt.

E. Save and then build the solution.

F. Execute the program. Test the program using the following item names and increase amounts:

Printer XL, 25
Laser SP, 50
InkJet KL, 30

G. Click File on the menu bar, point to Open, and then click File. Open the newpricelist.txt file, which is contained in the CppNet\Tut13\T13ConE14 Solution\T13ConE14 Project folder. Verify that the prices of the items listed in Step F were updated correctly. Close the newpricelist.txt window.

H. When the program is working correctly, close the Output window, and then use the File menu to close the solution.

15) In this exercise, you sort the contents of two parallel, one-dimensional arrays.

A. If necessary, start Visual Studio .NET. Open the T13ConE15 Solution (T13ConE15 Solution.sln) file, which is contained in the CppNet\Tut13\T13ConE15 Solution folder.

B. Notice that the program contains a `String` array named `id` and an `int` array named `price`. Complete the program by writing the code to sort the contents of the `id` array. Be sure to keep both arrays parallel. In other words, you may need to change the position of the item's price in the `price` array. Display the contents of both arrays in two columns on the screen.

C. Save and then build the solution.

D. Execute the program. Verify that each item has the correct price. Close the Command Prompt window.

E. When the program is working correctly, close the Output window, and then use the File menu to close the solution.

16) In this exercise, you read into an array the records stored in a sequential access file.

A. If necessary, start Visual Studio .NET. Open the T13ConE16 Solution (T13ConE16 Solution.sln) file, which is contained in the CppNet\Tut13\T13ConE16 Solution folder.

B. Click File on the menu bar, point to Open, and then click File. Open the employees.txt file, which is contained in the CppNet\Tut13\T13ConE16 Solution\T13ConE16 Project folder. The file contains five records. Close the employees.txt window.

C. Study the program's existing code. (You will need to use the C++ Help screens to research many of the lines of code.)

D. Save and then build the solution.

E. Execute the program. Notice the blank line that appears below the name Larue. The blank line appears because the `names[9]` element contains the end of file marker (which you can't see). Close the Command Prompt window.

F. Modify the program so that it removes the character from the `names[9]` element before the array is displayed on the screen.

G. When the program is working correctly, close the Output window, and then use the File menu to close the solution.

17) In this exercise, you debug a C++ program.

A. If necessary, start Visual Studio .NET. Open the T13ConE17 Solution (T13ConE17 Solution.sln) file, which is contained in the CppNet\TuT13\T13ConE17 Solution folder.

B. Study the existing code, then build the solution. Correct any errors in the program, then save and build the solution.

C. Execute the program. If the Just-In-Time Debugging window appears, click the window's Close button. Read the error message that appears in the Command Prompt window, then close the Command Prompt window. Correct any errors in the program, then save and build the solution. Execute the program.

D. When the program is working correctly, close the Output window, and then use the File menu to close the solution.

Application Lesson

Using an Array of Objects in a C++ Program

CASE In the Concept lesson, you viewed a program created for Takoda Tapahe, the owner of a small gift shop named Takoda Treasures. As you may remember, the program allows Takoda to display the price of the item corresponding to the product ID she enters. Recall that the program stores the gift shop's price list in two parallel one-dimensional arrays. In this lesson, you modify the program so that it stores the price list in a one-dimensional array of `Product` objects, rather than in two parallel one-dimensional arrays.

Creating the Product Class

Before you can store objects in an array, you need to create the class from which the objects will be made. Recall that creating a class involves determining the attributes and behaviors of the object you want to create. The attributes describe the object, while the behaviors specify the tasks the object can perform.

To keep the example simple, the `Product` class you will use for the Takoda Treasures price list contains only two attributes (the item's ID and its price) and four behaviors, as indicated in the class definition shown in Figure 13-8.

Figure 13-8: `Product` class definition

```
//declaration section
__gc class Product
{
public:
    Product();
    void AssignData(String *, int);
    String *GetId();
    int GetPrice();
private:
    String *id;
    int price;
};


//implementation section
Product::Product()
{
    id  = "";
    price = 0;
}   //end of default constructor

void Product::AssignData(String *code, int cost)
{
    id = code;
    price = cost;
}   //end of AssignData method
```

behaviors

attributes

Figure 13-8: `Product` class definition (continued)

```
String *Product::GetId()
{
    return id;
}   //end of GetId method

int Product::GetPrice()
{
    return price;
}   //end of GetPrice method
```

Notice that the attributes—the product's ID and its price—are assigned to two variables: a **`String`** variable named **`id`** and an **`int`** variable named **`price`**. As is typical in a class definition, the variables are declared as private data members in the declaration section of the class.

Also notice that the **`Product`** class contains four public member methods, each representing a task that **`Product`** objects can perform. The method prototypes are listed in the declaration section of the class, while the method definitions are entered in the implementation section.

The first member method, **`Product()`**, is the default constructor. Recall that the purpose of the default constructor is to initialize the private data members of an object when the object is created in a program.

The second member method, **`AssignData()`**, allows a program to assign new values to a **`Product`** object's private data members. The remaining two member methods, **`GetId()`** and **`GetPrice()`**, allow a program to view the values stored in a **`Product`** object's private data members.

Your computer's hard disk contains a partially completed header file named T13App.h. The T13App.h file contains the definition of the **`Product`** class. You complete the class definition before modifying the Takoda Treasures program.

To complete the header file that contains the `Product` class definition:

1. Start Microsoft Visual Studio .NET. If necessary, close the Start Page window.
2. Click **File** on the menu bar, point to **Open**, and then click **File**.
3. Locate and then open the **CppNet\MyClasses** folder.
4. Click **T13App.h** in the list of filenames, and then click the **Open** button.
5. Enter the instructions shaded in Figure 13-9, which shows the completed definition for the `Product` class.

Figure 13-9: Completed `Product` class definition contained in the T13App.h header file

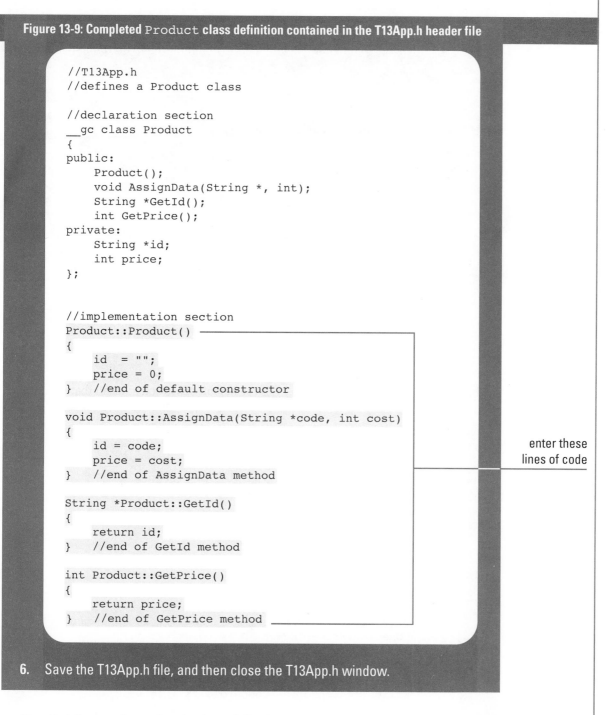

```
//T13App.h
//defines a Product class

//declaration section
__gc class Product
{
public:
    Product();
    void AssignData(String *, int);
    String *GetId();
    int GetPrice();
private:
    String *id;
    int price;
};


//implementation section
Product::Product()
{
    id  = "";
    price = 0;
}   //end of default constructor

void Product::AssignData(String *code, int cost)
{
    id = code;
    price = cost;
}   //end of AssignData method

String *Product::GetId()
{
    return id;
}   //end of GetId method

int Product::GetPrice()
{
    return price;
}   //end of GetPrice method
```

enter these lines of code

6. Save the T13App.h file, and then close the T13App.h window.

Now that the `Product` class has been defined, you can use it to create `Product` objects in the Takoda Treasures program.

Completing the Takoda Treasures Program

Your computer's hard disk contains the Takoda Treasures program that you viewed in Figure 13-6 in the Concept lesson. You open that program in the next set of steps.

To open the Takoda Treasures program:

1. Click **File** on the menu bar, and then click **Open Solution**. The Open Solution dialog box opens.
2. Locate and then open the **CppNet\Tut13\T13App Solution** folder.
3. Click **T13App Solution** (T13App Solution.sln) in the list of filenames, and then click the **Open** button.
4. If the T13App.cpp source file is not displayed, right-click **T13App.cpp** in the Solution Explorer window, and then click **Open**. Figure 13-10 shows the instructions entered in the program.

Figure 13-10: Takoda Treasures program containing two parallel one-dimensional arrays

```
//T13App.cpp
//displays the price corresponding to the ID entered
by the user
#using <mscorlib.dll>
using namespace System;

int main()
{
    //declare variable and arrays
    String *searchForId = "";
    String *id __gc[] = new String *__gc[5];
    int price __gc[] = new int __gc[5];

    //fill arrays with values
    id[0] = "BX35";
    id[1] = "CR20";
    id[2] = "FE15";
    id[3] = "KW10";
    id[4] = "MM67";
    price[0] = 13;
    price[1] = 10;
    price[2] = 12;
    price[3] = 24;
    price[4] = 4;

    //get ID to search for, then convert to uppercase
    Console::Write("Enter ID (X to exit): ");
    searchForId = Console::ReadLine();
    searchForId = searchForId->ToUpper();

    while (searchForId->CompareTo("X") != 0)
    {
       //locate position of product ID in the id array
       int y = 0; //keeps track of array subscripts
       while (y < id->GetLength(0) && id[y]->CompareTo
       (searchForId) != 0)
          y = y + 1;
       //end while
```

Figure 13-10: Takoda Treasures program containing two parallel one-dimensional arrays (continued)

```
        //if ID was found, display price from price array
        //otherwise, display error message
        if (y < 5)
           Console::WriteLine("Price: {0}", price[y].
           ToString("C0"));
        else
           Console::WriteLine("Product ID is not valid.");
        //end if

        //get ID to search for, then convert to uppercase
        Console::Write("Enter ID (X to exit): ");
        searchForId = Console::ReadLine();
        searchForId = searchForId->ToUpper();
     }  //end while

     return 0;
}    //end of main function
```

The Takoda Treasures program shown in Figure 13-10 declares a **String** variable named **searchForId** and two parallel one-dimensional arrays: a **String** array named **id** and an **int** array named **price**. Each array has five elements, one for each item sold by the gift shop. The program stores each item's ID in the **id** array, and stores each item's price in the corresponding location in the **price** array.

tip

As you learned in the Concept lesson, the elements in parallel arrays are related by their position (subscript) in the arrays.

After filling the arrays with data, the program prompts the user to enter a product ID, storing the user's response in the **searchForId** variable. The **ToUpper()** method then converts the contents of the **searchForId** variable to uppercase.

The computer processes the instructions contained in the program's outer **while** loop as long as the user does not enter the letter X (in any case) as the product ID. The first instruction in the body of the outer **while** loop declares and initializes an **int** variable named **y** to keep track of the array subscripts. The second instruction is the beginning of a nested **while** loop that adds the number one to the **y** variable as long as the **y** variable contains a value that is less than five and, at the same time, the product ID has not been located in the array. The nested **while** loop stops when either of the following conditions is true: the **y** variable contains the number five (which indicates that the loop reached the end of the array without finding the product ID) or the product ID is located in the array.

After the nested **while** loop completes its processing, the **if** statement in the program compares the number stored in the **y** variable with the number five. If the **y** variable contains a number that is less than five, it indicates that the loop stopped processing because the product ID was located in the **id** array. In that case, the statement **Console::WriteLine ("Price: {0}", price[y].ToString("C0"));** displays the corresponding price from the **price** array. However, if the **y** variable contains a number that is not less than 5, it indicates that the loop stopped processing because it reached the end of the **id** array without finding the product ID; in that case, the message "Product ID is not valid." is displayed.

The program then prompts the user to enter another product ID, and it stores the user's response in the **searchForId** variable. The **ToUpper()** method is used to convert the contents of the **searchForId** variable to uppercase, to match the case of the product IDs stored in the **id** array. Processing then continues with the **while (searchForId->CompareTo("X") != 0)** clause. This clause compares the contents of the **searchForId** variable with the letter X to determine whether the instructions in the outer `while` loop should be processed again.

You need to make several changes to the current program to store the price list in a one-dimensional array of `Product` objects, rather than in two one-dimensional parallel arrays. First, you will add the T13App.h header file to the solution, and then you will enter the appropriate `#include` directive to include the header file's code in the program.

To include the T13App.h header file in the solution and program:

1. Click **File** on the menu bar, and then click **Add Existing Item**. The Add Existing Item – T13App Project dialog box opens.
2. Open the CppNet\MyClasses folder, then click **T13App.h** in the list of filenames. Click the **Open** button. The T13App.h header file is added to the current solution. You can verify that fact by displaying the Solution Explorer window, and then opening the Header Files folder.
3. Position the insertion point in the blank line below the `using namespace System;` statement. Press **Enter**, then type **//include the header file that contains the Product class definition** and press **Enter**. Type **#include "c:\cppnet\myclasses\T13app.h"** and press **Enter**. (If necessary, change the `#include` directive to reflect the location of the T13App.h header file on your system.)

Next, you will modify several comments in the program.

To modify several of the program comments:

1. Change the `//declare variable and arrays` comment to **//declare variable and array**.
2. Change the `//fill arrays with values` comment to **//fill array with values**.
3. Change the `//locate position of product ID in the id array` comment to **//locate position of product ID in the item array**.
4. Change the `//if ID was found, display price from price array` comment to **//if ID was found, display price from item array**.

Now replace the statements that declare the `String` and `int` arrays with a statement that declares an array of `Product` objects.

To continue modifying the T13App.cpp program:

1. Delete the `String *id __gc[] = new String *__gc[5];` and `int price __gc[] = new int __gc[5];` statements.
2. In the blank line below the `String *searchForId = "";` statement, type **Product *item __gc[] = new Product *__gc[5];** and press **Enter** twice.

Next, enter the code to create five `Product` objects, assigning each object to an element in the `item` array. Then replace the statements that assign values to the `id` and `price` arrays with statements that assign values to the `item` array.

To continue modifying the T13App.cpp program:

1. Type **//create objects, assign to array** and press **Enter**.
2. Type **for (int x = 0; x < item->GetLength(0); x = x + 1)** and press **Enter**.
3. Type **item[x] = new Product;** and press **Enter**.
4. Type **//end for** and press **Enter**.
5. Delete the 10 statements that assign values to the `id` and `price` arrays.
6. In the blank line below the `//fill array with values` comment, type the following five statements:
   item[0]->AssignData("BX35", 13);
   item[1]->AssignData("CR20", 10);
   item[2]->AssignData("FE15", 12);
   item[3]->AssignData("KW10", 24);
   item[4]->AssignData("MM67", 4);

You also must modify the two lines of code that refer to the elements in the parallel arrays. In the `while (y < id->GetLength(0) && id[y]->CompareTo (searchForId) != 0)` clause, for example, you will replace `id->GetLength(0)` with `item->GetLength(0)`, and replace `id[y]` with `item[y]->GetId()`. Recall that the `GetId()` method is a public member of the `Product` class, and it allows a program to view the contents of the `id` data member. Additionally, in the `Console::WriteLine ("Price: {0}", price[y].ToString("C0"));` statement, you will replace `price[y]` with `item[y]->GetPrice()`. The `GetPrice()` method also is a public member of the `Product` class, and it allows a program to view the contents of the `price` data member.

To complete the T13App.cpp program:

1. Modify the two statements shaded in Figure 13-11, which shows the completed Takoda Treasures program.

Figure 13-11: Completed Takoda Treasures program using a one-dimensional array of `Product` objects

```
//T13App.cpp
//displays the price corresponding to the ID entered
by the user
#using <mscorlib.dll>
using namespace System;

//include the header file that contains the Product
class definition
#include "c:\cppnet\myclasses\T13app.h"
```

Figure 13-11: Completed Takoda Treasures program using a one-dimensional array of `Product` objects (continued)

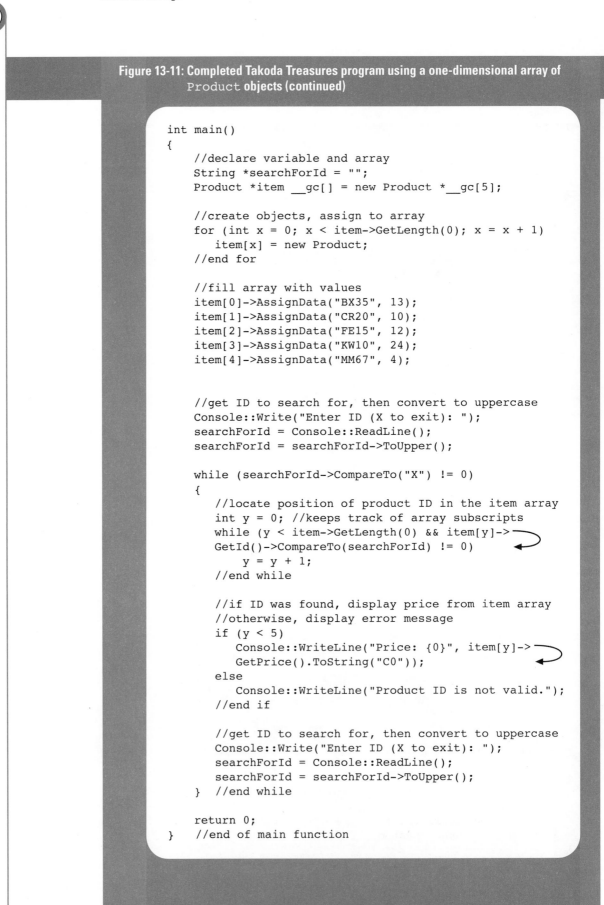

```
int main()
{
    //declare variable and array
    String *searchForId = "";
    Product *item __gc[] = new Product *__gc[5];

    //create objects, assign to array
    for (int x = 0; x < item->GetLength(0); x = x + 1)
       item[x] = new Product;
    //end for

    //fill array with values
    item[0]->AssignData("BX35", 13);
    item[1]->AssignData("CR20", 10);
    item[2]->AssignData("FE15", 12);
    item[3]->AssignData("KW10", 24);
    item[4]->AssignData("MM67", 4);


    //get ID to search for, then convert to uppercase
    Console::Write("Enter ID (X to exit): ");
    searchForId = Console::ReadLine();
    searchForId = searchForId->ToUpper();

    while (searchForId->CompareTo("X") != 0)
    {
       //locate position of product ID in the item array
       int y = 0; //keeps track of array subscripts
       while (y < item->GetLength(0) && item[y]->
       GetId()->CompareTo(searchForId) != 0)
           y = y + 1;
       //end while

       //if ID was found, display price from item array
       //otherwise, display error message
       if (y < 5)
          Console::WriteLine("Price: {0}", item[y]->
          GetPrice().ToString("C0"));
       else
          Console::WriteLine("Product ID is not valid.");
       //end if

       //get ID to search for, then convert to uppercase
       Console::Write("Enter ID (X to exit): ");
       searchForId = Console::ReadLine();
       searchForId = searchForId->ToUpper();
    }  //end while

    return 0;
}   //end of main function
```

2. Verify the accuracy of your code by comparing the code on your screen with the code shown in Figure 13-11.
3. Save and then build the solution. Verify that the program generated no warnings.
4. Execute the program. When you are prompted to enter a product ID, type **cr20** and press **Enter**. The Command Prompt window indicates that the price of this item is $10, as shown in Figure 13-12.

Figure 13-12: Command Prompt window showing the results of the first test

"c:\CppNet\Tut13\Treasures Solution\Treasures Project\Debug\Treasures Project.exe"
Enter ID (X to exit): cr20
Price: $10
Enter ID (X to exit):

5. Next, type **aa22** and press **Enter**. The message "Product ID is not valid." appears in the Command Prompt window.
6. Type **x** and press **Enter** to stop the program.
7. Close the Command Prompt window, then close the Output window.
8. Click **File** on the menu bar, and then click **Close Solution** to close the current solution.
9. Click **File** on the menu bar, and then click **Exit** to exit Visual Studio .NET.

You now have completed Tutorial 13's Application lesson. You can either take a break or complete the end-of-lesson exercises.

EXERCISES

Look For These Symbols

Debugging

Discovery

1) In this exercise, you use an array of objects created from a class that you define. Ms. Jenkins uses the grade table shown in Figure 13-13 for her Introduction to Computers course. She wants a program that displays the grade after she enters the total points earned. (*Hint*: If you completed Exercise 11 in the Concept lesson, you can use that program as a guide when completing this program.)

Figure 13-13

Minimum points	Maximum points	Grade
0	299	F
300	349	D
350	399	C
400	449	B
450	500	A

A. If necessary, start Visual Studio .NET. Click File on the menu bar, point to Open, and then click File. Open the T13AppE01.h header file, which is contained in the CppNet\MyClasses folder. Create a class for the grade table. Include two data members: minimum points and grade. Include a default constructor, as well as methods that allow a program to assign values to the minimum points and grade data members, view the contents of the minimum points data member, and view the contents of the grade data member. Save the T13AppE01.h file, and then close the T13AppE01.h window.

B. Open the T13AppE01 Solution (T13AppE01 Solution.sln) file, which is contained in the CppNet\Tut13\T13AppE01 Solution folder. Add the T13AppE01.h header file to the project.

C. Use the class you created in Step A to declare an array of objects. The program should display the appropriate grade after Ms. Jenkins enters the number of points earned by a student. Include a loop that allows Ms. Jenkins to enter as many values as desired.

D. Save and then build the solution.

E. Execute the program. Test the program four times, using the following amounts: 455, 210, 400, and 349. The program should display grades of A, F, B, and D.

F. When the program is working correctly, close the Output window, and then use the File menu to close the solution.

2) In this exercise, you search an array of objects created from a class that you define. (*Hint*: If you completed Exercise 12 in the Concept lesson, you can use that program as a guide when completing this program.)

A. If necessary, start Visual Studio .NET. Click File on the menu bar, point to Open, and then click File. Open the T13AppE02.h header file, which is contained in the CppNet\MyClasses folder. Create a class that contains two `int` variables (named `num` and `sqNum`) and one `double` variable (named `sqRtNum`) as data members. Include a default constructor, as well as three methods that allow a program to view the contents of the data members, and a method that allows a program to assign values to the data members. Save the T13AppE02.h file, and then close the T13AppE02.h window.

B. Open the T13AppE02 Solution (T13AppE02 Solution.sln) file, which is contained in the CppNet\Tut13\T13AppE02 Solution folder. Add the T13AppE02.h header file to the project.

C. Use the class you created in Step A to declare an array of objects. Store the even numbers from 2 through 10, the square of the even numbers from 2 through 10, and the square root of the even numbers from 2 through 10 in the array.

D. The program should prompt the user to enter a number. The program should search for the number in the array, and then display both the square and the square root of the number. Allow the user to display the square and square root for as many numbers as desired without having to execute the program again. Display an appropriate message if the number is not in the array.

E. Save and then build the solution.

F. Execute the program. Test the program four times, using the following amounts: 2, 8, 6, and 3.

G. When the program is working correctly, close the Output window, and then use the File menu to close the solution.

3) In this exercise, you create a program that uses an array of objects created from a class that you define. Conway Enterprises has both domestic and international sales operations. The company's sales manager wants a program that displays the total sales made by the company during a six-month period. The program also should display the total domestic and total international sales.

A. If necessary, start Visual Studio .NET. Click File on the menu bar, point to Open, and then click File. Open the T13AppE03.h header file, which is contained in the CppNet\MyClasses folder. Create an appropriate class. Include two `int` variables as data members: one variable will represent the domestic sales and the other will represent the international sales. Include a default constructor and methods that allow a program to assign values to the data members and also view the contents of the data members. Save the T13AppE03.h file, and then close the T13AppE03.h window.

B. Open the T13AppE03 Solution (T13AppE03 Solution.sln) file, which is contained in the CppNet\Tut13\T13AppE03 Solution folder. Add the T13AppE03.h header file to the project.

C. Use the class you created in Step A to declare an array of objects. Store the following domestic sales amounts in the array: 12000, 45000, 32000, 67000, 24000, and 55000. Also store the following international sales amounts in the array: 10000, 56000, 42000, 23000, 12000, and 34000.

D. Complete the program by entering the code to display the total domestic sales, the total international sales, and the total company sales.

E. Save and then build the solution.

F. Execute the program. The program should display domestic sales of $235,000; international sales of $177,000; and total sales of $412,000.

G. When the program is working correctly, close the Output window, and then use the File menu to close the solution.

4) In this exercise, you fill an array of objects with the data stored in a sequential access file.

A. If necessary, start Visual Studio .NET. Click File on the menu bar, point to Open, and then click File. Open the T13AppE04.h header file, which is contained in the CppNet\MyClasses folder. Print the T13AppE04.h file, and then close the T13AppE04.h window.

B. Click File on the menu bar, point to Open, and then click File. Open the T13AppE04.txt file, which is contained in the CppNet\Tut13\T13AppE04 Solution\T13AppE04 Project folder. Print the file, and then close the T13AppE04.txt window.

C. Open the T13AppE04 Solution (T13AppE04 Solution.sln) file, which is contained in the CppNet\Tut13\T13AppE04 Solution folder. Add the T13AppE04.h header file to the project.

D. Modify the code so that it reads each record from the T13AppE04.txt sequential access file, and assigns each to the objects in the array.

E. Save and then build the solution.

F. Execute the program. The program should display five IDs and five prices.

G. When the program is working correctly, close the Output window, and then use the File menu to close the solution.

5) In this exercise, you debug a C++ program.

A. If necessary, start Visual Studio .NET. Open the T13AppE05 Solution (T13AppE05 Solution.sln) file, which is contained in the CppNet\TuT13\T13AppE05 Solution folder. Add the T13AppE05.h header file to the project. If necessary, change the `#include` directive to reflect the location of the header file on your system.

B. Study the existing code, then build the solution. Correct any errors in the program, then save and build the solution.

C. Execute the program.

D. When the program is working correctly, close the Output window, and then use the File menu to close the solution.

Tutorial 14

Database Access

Objectives

After completing this tutorial, you will be able to:

- Create a `Connection` object
- Open and close a connection to a database
- Create a `Command` object
- Query a database using the SQL `SELECT` command
- Read database records using a `Reader` object

Concept Lesson

Accessing Data Stored in a Database

To maintain accurate records, most businesses store information about their employees, customers, and inventory in files called databases. In general, a **database** is an organized collection of related information stored in a file on a disk.

tip

You do not have to be a business to make use of a database. Many people use databases to keep track of their medical records, their compact disc collections, and even their golf scores.

Many software packages exist for creating databases; some of the most popular are Microsoft Access, Oracle, and SQL Server. In this tutorial, you learn how to use Visual C++ .NET to access the data stored in a Microsoft Access database.

Databases created by Microsoft Access are relational databases. A **relational database** is one that stores information in tables, which are composed of columns and rows. Each column in a table represents a field, and each row represents a record. As you learned in Tutorial 11, a field is a single item of information about a person, place, or thing—such as a name, address, or phone number—and a record is a group of related fields that contain all of the necessary data about a specific person, place, or thing. A **table** is a group of related records. Each record in the group pertains to the same topic, and each contains the same type of information—in other words, the same fields.

tip

The databases are called relational because the information in the tables can be related in different ways.

A relational database can contain one or more tables. You might use a one-table database to store the information regarding the college courses you have taken. Each record in the table would contain a course ID (department and number), course title, number of credit hours, and grade. You would use a two-table database, on the other hand, to store information about your CD (compact disc) collection: one table to store the general information about each CD (the CD's name and the artist's name) and the other table to store the information about the songs on each CD (their title and track number). You would use a common field—such as a CD number—to relate the records contained in both tables. Figure 14-1 shows an example of both a one-table and a two-table relational database.

tip

The column and row format used in a relational database is similar to the column and row format used in a spreadsheet.

Storing data in a relational database offers many advantages. The computer can retrieve data stored in that format both quickly and easily, and the data can be displayed in any order. For example, the information in the CD database shown in Figure 14-1 can be arranged by artist name, song title, and so on. A relational database also allows you to control how much information you want to view at a time. You can view all of the information in the CD database, or you can view only the information pertaining to a certain artist, or only the names of the songs contained on a specific CD.

You can use a Visual C++ .NET program to access the data stored in a database; you do so using a Connection object.

Figure 14-1: Example of a one-table and a two-table relational database

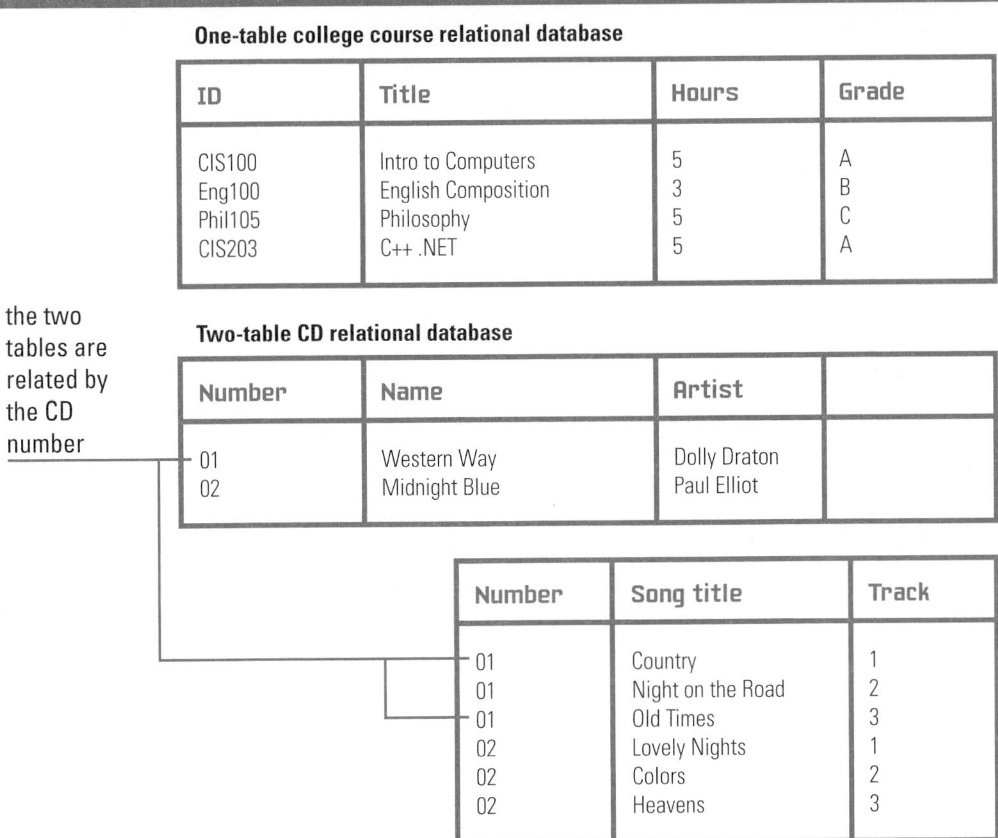

One-table college course relational database
ID
Title
Hours
Grade
CIS100
Eng100
Phil105
CIS203
Intro to Computers
English Composition
Philosophy
C++ .NET
5
3
5
5
A
B
C
A
the two tables are related by the CD number
Two-table CD relational database
Number
Name
Artist
01
02
Western Way
Midnight Blue
Dolly Draton
Paul Elliot
Number
Song title
Track
01
01
01
02
02
02
Country
Night on the Road
Old Times
Lovely Nights
Colors
Heavens
1
2
3
1
2
3

Using a Connection Object

A `Connection` **object** represents the physical connection between a data source—such as a database—and a **data provider**, which is a set of complex interfaces that serves as a bridge between the data source and your C++ program. The data provider is responsible for providing the data in a format that can be utilized by the program. Figure 14-2 illustrates how a data source, `Connection` object, data provider, and C++ program are related.

Figure 14-2: Illustration of a data source, `Connection` object, data provider, and C++ program

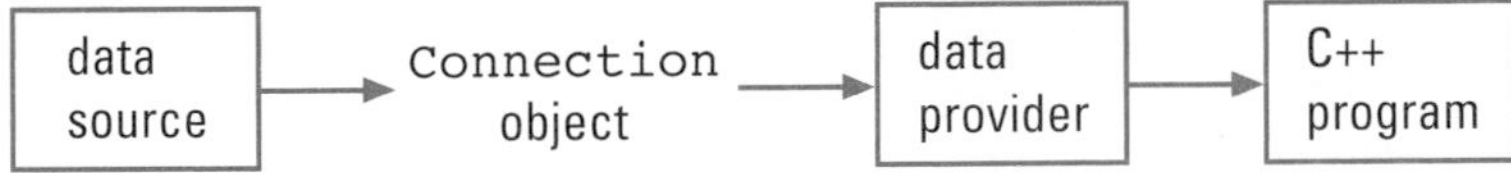

If the data source is a Microsoft Access database, you create a `Connection` object using the syntax **OleDbConnection** **connectionName* **= new OleDbConnection();**, where *connectionName* is the name of the `Connection` object. For example, to create a `Connection` object named `connectInventory`, you use the statement `OleDbConnection *connectInventory = new OleDbConnection();`.

tip
"OleDb" stands for "Object Linking and Embedding for Databases." "Ole" is pronounced *oh-lay*.

tip

The name of the data provider for a Microsoft Access database is Microsoft.Jet.OLEDB.4.0. "Jet" refers to the database engine found in Microsoft Access. Microsoft Access databases have a .mdb filename extension.

tip

If the data source is a Microsoft SQL Server version 7.0 (or later) database, you create a `Connection` object using the syntax **SqlConnection** **connectionName* = **new SqlConnection();**. You then use the syntax *connectionObject*-> **ConnectionString ="Data Source=***sqlserver*; **Initial Catalog=***filename*"; to set the `ConnectionString` property.

As indicated earlier, a `Connection` object connects a data source to a data provider. You specify the data source and data provider in the `Connection` object's `ConnectionString` property. If the data source is a Microsoft Access database, the syntax of the `ConnectionString` property is *connectionObject*->**ConnectionString = "Provider= Microsoft.Jet.OLEDB.4.0; Data Source=***filename*"**;**, where *connectionObject* is the name of the `Connection` object and *filename* is both the location and name of the database. For example, to use the `connectInventory` object to connect to a Microsoft Access database named inventory.mdb, you use the statement `connectInventory->ConnectionString ="Provider=Microsoft.Jet.OLEDB.4.0; Data Source=c:\\cppnet\\databases\\inventory.mdb";`. (As you learned in Tutorial 11, when specifying a folder path in a *filename* argument, you must use two backslashes, rather than one backslash, to separate the names of the folders and the name of the file in the path; this is because the backslash by itself has a special meaning in the C++ language.)

After creating the `Connection` object and setting its `ConnectionString` property, you then use the object's `Open()` method to open a connection to the data source, and its `Close()` method to close the connection.

Opening and Closing a Connection to a Data Source

You use the `Connection` object's **Open() method** to open a connection to the data source specified in the `ConnectionString` property. The syntax of the `Open()` method is *connectionObject*->**Open();**, where *connectionObject* is the name of the `Connection` object. For instance, to open a connection to the inventory.mdb database associated with the `connectInventory` object, you use the statement `connectInventory->Open();`. As you will learn in the next section, when a database is open, you can retrieve information from it.

You always should close a connection to a data source before the program ends; you do so using the `Connection` object's **Close() method**. The syntax of the `Close()` method is *connectionObject*->**Close();**, where *connectionObject* is the name of the `Connection` object. For example, to close the `connectInventory` connection, which is associated with the inventory.mdb database, you use the statement `connectInventory->Close();`.

Figure 14-3 shows an example of using a `Connection` object to connect to a Microsoft Access database in a C++ program. The lines of code associated with the `Connection` object are shaded in the figure.

Figure 14-3: Example of using a `Connection` object in a C++ program

```
#using <mscorlib.dll>
#using <System.dll>
#using <System.Data.dll>
using namespace System;
using namespace System::Data;
using namespace System::Data::OleDb;

int main()
{

    //create Connection object
    OleDbConnection *connectInventory = new OleDbConnection();
    connectInventory->ConnectionString = "Provider=Microsoft
    .Jet.OLEDB.4.0; Data Source=c:\\cppnet\\databases\\
    inventory.mdb";
```

Figure 14-3: Example of using a `Connection` object in a C++ program (continued)

```
    try
    {
        //open connection to database
        connectInventory->Open();

        //code to retrieve information from the database
        .
        .
        .

        //close connection
        connectInventory->Close();

    }

    catch (OleDbException *ex)
    {
        Console::WriteLine(ex->Message);
    }

    return 0;
}   //end of main function
```

the code to retrieve information is missing

For a C++ program to access the data stored in a Microsoft Access database, the program must include the four directives shaded in Figure 14-3. The `#using <System.dll>` and `#using <System.Data.dll>` directives tell the C++ compiler to include in the current program the contents of the two .dll files, which contain the components needed to access a database. The `using namespace System::Data;` and `using namespace System::Data::OleDb;` directives, on the other hand, tell the compiler that the definition of keywords and classes associated with accessing a database can be found in the `System::Data` and `System::Data::OleDb` namespaces. As you may remember from Tutorial 3, a namespace is a special area in the computer's internal memory.

tip

If the data source is a Microsoft SQL Server version 7.0 (or later) database, replace `OleDb` in the `using namespace System::Data::OleDb;` directive with `SqlClient`.

The first statement in the `main()` function creates a `Connection` object named `connectInventory`. The next statement sets the `connectInventory` object's `ConnectionString` property, which connects the Microsoft.Jet.OLEDB.4.0 provider to a Microsoft Access database named inventory.mdb.

Because it is possible for errors to occur when using a database, the code associated with the database should be entered in the `try` section of a `try/catch` block. In the program shown in Figure 14-3, the `connectInventory->Open();` statement, which opens the connection between the Microsoft.Jet.OLEDB.4.0 provider and the inventory.mdb file, appears in the `try` section. Also in the `try` section is the `connectInventory->Close();` statement, which closes the connection. The statements that retrieve information from the database also should be entered in the `try` section. The statements that retrieve information from the inventory.mdb database are missing from the program shown in Figure 14-3. You learn how to retrieve information from a database in the next section.

tip

If the computer has a problem processing a statement associated with a Microsoft SQL Server version 7.0 (or later) database, a `SqlException` occurs.

If the computer has a problem processing a program statement associated with a Microsoft Access database, an `OleDbException` occurs. When an `OleDbException` occurs in the program shown in Figure 14-3, the `Console::WriteLine(ex->Message);` instruction in the `catch` statement displays an appropriate error message.

MINI-QUIZ

Mini-Quiz 1

1) A ________________ is an organized collection of related information stored in a file on a disk.
   a. database
   b. field
   c. record
   d. relational collection

2) Which of the following statements creates a `Connection` object for a Microsoft Access database?
   a. `Connection *connectEmploy = new Connection();`
   b. `Connection *connectEmploy = new OleDbConnection();`
   c. `OleDbConnection *connectEmploy = new Connection();`
   d. `OleDbConnection *connectEmploy = new OleDbConnection();`

3) A group of related fields is called a ________________.

4) You specify the data provider and data source in the `Connection` object's ________________ property.

5) List the four directives associated with accessing a Microsoft Access database in a program.

Next, you learn how to use a `Command` object to retrieve information from a database.

Using a `Command` Object to Retrieve Information From a Database

You use a **`Command` object** to formulate a request for information and pass the request on to the database. The request is called a **query** because it "asks" the database for information. For example, you can create a query that asks the database to retrieve the names of inventory items that need to be reordered. Or, you can create a query that asks the database the question "What is the name of item number ABC11?"

To create a `Command` object that queries a Microsoft Access database, you use the syntax **OleDbCommand** **commandName* **= new OleDbCommand(***query***,** *connectionObject***);**. In the syntax, *commandName* is the name of the `Command` object, and *connectionObject* is the name of the `Connection` object associated with the `Command` object. *Query* is a command that specifies the request and can be either a SQL command enclosed in double quotation marks, or a `String` variable that contains a SQL command.

Using SQL to Query a Database

tip The SQL syntax, which refers to the rules you must follow to use the language, was accepted by the American National Standards Institute (ANSI) in 1986. You can use SQL in many database management systems and programming languages.

SQL, pronounced like the word *sequel*, stands for **Structured Query Language**. **SQL** is a set of commands that allows you to access and manipulate the data stored in many database management systems on computers of all sizes, from large mainframes to small microcomputers. You can use SQL commands to perform database tasks such as storing, retrieving, updating, deleting, and sorting data.

The most commonly used SQL command is the **`SELECT` command**, which allows you to select the fields and records you want to view, as well as control the order in which the fields and records appear when displayed. The basic syntax of the `SELECT` command is **SELECT** *fields* **FROM** *table* [**WHERE** *condition*] [**ORDER BY** *field*]. In the syntax, *fields* is one or more field names (separated by commas), and *table* is the name of the table containing the fields. For example, assume that each record in a table named `tblPatron` contains three fields: a numeric field named `Seat` and two text fields named `Name` and `Phone`. To select all of the fields and records stored in the table, you use the command `SELECT Seat, Name, Phone FROM tblPatron`. However, to select only the `Name` field for each record, you use the command `SELECT Name FROM tblPatron`.

The **`WHERE`** *condition* portion of the `SELECT` command's syntax is referred to as the **`WHERE`** clause and allows you to limit the records selected from the table. For example, to select the name of only the person associated with seat number three in the `tblPatron` table, you use the command `SELECT Name FROM tblPatron WHERE Seat = 3`. Similarly, you use the command `SELECT Seat FROM tblPatron WHERE Name = "Smith, Karen"` to select the seat number associated with the name "Smith, Karen". Notice that the `WHERE` clause is optional in the `SELECT` command.

The **`ORDER BY`** *field* portion of the `SELECT` command's syntax is referred to as the **`ORDER BY` clause** and allows you to control the order in which the records are selected. For example, the command `SELECT Name, Phone FROM tblPatron ORDER BY Name` selects the names and phone numbers in ascending alphabetical order by name. To select the names and phone numbers in descending alphabetical order by name, you use the command `SELECT Name, Phone FROM tblPatron ORDER BY Name DESC`. ("`DESC`" stands for "descending".) Like the `WHERE` clause, the `ORDER BY` clause is optional in the `SELECT` command.

You can use the `WHERE` and `ORDER BY` clauses in the same `SELECT` command. For example, the command `SELECT Seat, Name, Phone FROM tblPatron WHERE Seat > 20 ORDER BY Seat` selects, in seat number order, all records whose seat numbers are greater than 20.

Figure 14-4 shows examples of assigning `SELECT` commands to a `String` variable named `sql`. Notice that, when assigning a `SELECT` command to a `String` variable, you enclose the entire `SELECT` command in double quotation marks. The `tblInventory` table referred to in each example shown in Figure 14-4 contains three fields: `ItemNum`, `Quantity`, and `Price`. The `ItemNum` field contains `String` data. The `Quantity` and `Price` fields contain numeric data: the `Quantity` field contains integers, and the `Price` field contains numbers of the `double` data type.

tip

Although it is not required by the SQL syntax, many programmers capitalize the SQL keywords to distinguish the keywords from the other information in a SQL command. The full syntax of the `SELECT` command contains other clauses and options that are beyond the scope of this book.

Figure 14-4: Examples of `SELECT` commands

Example 1
```
sql = "SELECT ItemNum, Quantity, Price FROM tblInventory";
```
Result
selects all of the fields and records from the `tblInventory` table

Example 2
```
sql = "SELECT ItemNum FROM tblInventory ORDER BY Price";
```
Result
selects (in ascending order by the `Price` field) the `ItemNum` field for all of the records from the `tblInventory` table

Figure 14-4: Examples of SELECT commands (continued)

Example 3
```
sql = "SELECT ItemNum FROM tblInventory WHERE Quantity < 5";
```

Result
selects (from the `tblInventory` table) the `ItemNum` field for only the records whose `Quantity` field contains a value that is less than five

Example 4
```
sql = "SELECT Price FROM tblInventory WHERE ItemNum = 'ABC11'";
```

Result
selects (from the `tblInventory` table) the `Price` field for only the records whose `ItemNum` field contains ABC11

Example 5
```
sql = String::Concat("SELECT Price FROM tblInventory WHERE
ItemNum = '", code, "'");
```

Result
selects (from the `tblInventory` table) the `Price` field for only the records whose `ItemNum` field matches the item number stored in a `String` variable named `code`

Example 6
```
sql = String::Concat("SELECT ItemNum FROM tblInventory WHERE
Quantity > ", Convert::ToString(amt));
```

Result
selects (from the `tblInventory` table) the `ItemNum` field for only the records whose `Quantity` field contains a value that is greater than the value stored in an `int` variable named `amt`

Example 7
```
sql = String::Concat("SELECT Price, Quantity FROM tblInventory
WHERE ItemNum Like 'B%'");
```

Result
selects (from the `tblInventory` table) the `Price` and `Quantity` fields for only the records whose `ItemNum` field contains a value that begins with the letter B

The **SELECT** command shown in Example 1 in Figure 14-4 selects all of the fields and records from the `tblInventory` table. Example 2's **SELECT** command selects only the `ItemNum` field from each record in the `tblInventory` table; it does so in ascending order by the `Price` field. Example 3's **SELECT** command selects the `ItemNum` field from the `tblInventory` table, but only for records whose `Quantity` field contains a value that is less than five. Example 4's **SELECT** command selects the `Price` field from the `tblInventory` table, but only for the ABC11 record. Notice that, because the **SELECT** command is enclosed in double quotation marks, the string within the **SELECT** command—in this case, the string ABC11—must be enclosed in single quotation marks. Unlike in the C++ programming language, `String` comparisons in SQL are not case sensitive.

The statement shown in Example 5 selects the `Price` field from the `tblInventory` table, but only for records whose `ItemNum` field matches the item number stored in a `String` variable named `code`. Notice that the statement uses the `String::Concat()`

method to concatenate the string "SELECT Price FROM tblInventory WHERE ItemNum = '", the code variable, and the string "'".

The statement shown in Example 6 selects the ItemNum field from the tblInventory table, only for records whose Quantity field contains a value that is greater than the value stored in an int variable named amt. Notice that, like the statement shown in Example 5, the statement shown in Example 6 also uses the String::Concat() method. In this case, the method concatenates the string "SELECT ItemNum FROM tblInventory WHERE Quantity > " to the amt variable (converted to a String).

The SELECT command shown in Example 7 in Figure 14-4 uses the **SQL Like operator** along with the % (percent sign) in the WHERE clause. The % is referred to as a **wildcard** because, similar to a wildcard in a game of poker, you can use the % to represent anything you want. The WHERE ItemNum Like 'B%' clause in Example 7 tells the computer to select only records with an item number beginning with the letter B; the % indicates that you don't care which characters (if any) follow the letter B.

After assigning the appropriate SELECT command to a String variable, you can use the String variable as the *query* argument when creating a Command object. For example, assuming a variable named sql contains the appropriate SELECT command, you can use the statement OleDbCommand *commandInventory = new OleDbCommand(sql, connectInventory); to create a Command object named commandInventory.

tip
You learned about the String::Concat() method in Tutorial 10.

MINI-QUIZ

Mini-Quiz 2

1) You use the ______________ clause to limit the records retrieved by the SELECT command.
   a. LIMIT
   b. ORDER
   c. ORDER BY
   d. WHERE
2) Assume the tblInventory table contains three fields named ItemNum, Quantity, and Price. Write a SELECT command that retrieves all of the fields and records in ascending order by the item number. Assign the SELECT command to a String variable named sql.
3) Assume the tblInventory table contains three fields named ItemNum, Quantity, and Price. Write a SELECT command that retrieves the ItemNum field, but only for the records whose price is greater than $15. Assign the SELECT command to a String variable named sql.
4) Assume the tblInventory table contains three fields named ItemNum, Quantity, and Price. Write a SELECT command that retrieves the Quantity field, but only for the records whose item number is XX234. Assign the SELECT command to a String variable named sql.
5) Assume the tblInventory table contains three fields named ItemNum, Quantity, and Price. Write a SELECT command that retrieves the ItemNum field, but only for the records whose price is greater than the value stored in a double variable named cost. Assign the SELECT command to a String variable named sql.

Next, you learn how to use a Reader object to read the records stored in a database.

Using a Reader Object to Read the Database Records

You use a **Reader** object to read the records stored in a database. If the data source is a Microsoft Access database, you can create a **Reader** object using the syntax **OleDbDataReader** **readerName* = *commandObject*->**ExecuteReader();**, where *readerName* is the name of the **Reader** object, and *commandObject* is the name of the **Command** object. Recall that the **Command** object contains the **SELECT** command that specifies the fields and records you want selected from the database. The **Reader** object allows a program to read each record in the database, using the **Command** object to select the appropriate fields and records.

tip

If the data source is a Microsoft SQL Server version 7.0 (or later) database, replace OleDb in the syntax for creating a Reader object with Sql.

You use the **Reader** object's **Read()** method to tell the computer to read a record from the database. The syntax of the **Read()** method is *readerObject*->**Read()**, where *readerObject* is the name of the **Reader** object. The **Read()** method returns the Boolean value **false** when there are no more records to read; otherwise, it returns the Boolean value **true**.

After reading a record, you use the syntax *readerObject*->*methodName*(*fieldNum*) to retrieve the contents of a field in the record. In the syntax, *readerObject* is the name of a **Reader** object. *MethodName* is **GetString** if the field you want to access contains text, **GetInt32** if it contains integers, or **GetDouble** if it contains numbers with a decimal place. *FieldNum* is an integer that indicates the position of the field in the **SELECT** command. The first field listed in the **SELECT** command is in position zero, the second is in position one, and so on. For example, assume that a program creates a **Reader** object named **readerInventory**, and uses the command **SELECT ItemNum, Quantity, Price FROM tblInventory** to retrieve the appropriate records. In that case, you use **readerInventory->GetString(0)** to access the contents of the **ItemNum** field, which contains text and is the first field listed in the **SELECT** command. You use **readerInventory->GetInt32(1)** to access the contents of the **Quantity** field, which contains integers and is the second field listed in the **SELECT** command. Finally, you use **readerInventory->GetDouble(2)** to access the contents of the third field listed in the **SELECT** command—the **Price** field—which contains numbers with a decimal place.

As with the **Connection** object, you should use the **Close()** method to close the **Reader** object as soon as you are finished using it. You close a **Reader** object using the syntax *readerObject*->**Close();**, where *readerObject* is the name of the **Reader** object.

In Figure 14-3, shown earlier in the lesson, you viewed an example of using a **Connection** object to connect to a Microsoft Access database in a C++ program. As you may remember, the code to retrieve the information from the inventory.mdb database was missing from the example. Figure 14-5 shows the completed example, with the missing code shaded.

Figure 14-5: Example of accessing a Microsoft Access database in a C++ program

```
#using <mscorlib.dll>
#using <System.dll>
#using <System.Data.dll>
using namespace System;
using namespace System::Data;
using namespace System::Data::OleDb;

int main()
{
```

Figure 14-5: Example of accessing a Microsoft Access database in a C++ program (continued)

```
    //create Connection object
    OleDbConnection *connectInventory = new OleDbConnection();
    connectInventory->ConnectionString = "Provider=Microsoft.Jet
    .OLEDB.4.0; Data Source=c:\\cppnet\\databases\\
    inventory.mdb";

    try
    {
        //open connection to database
        connectInventory->Open();

        //code to retrieve information from the database
        //create Command object
        sql = "SELECT ItemNum, Quantity, Price FROM tblInventory";
        OleDbCommand *commandInventory = new OleDbCommand(sql,
        connectInventory);
        //create Reader object
        OleDbDataReader *readerInventory = commandInventory->
        ExecuteReader();
        //read records and display fields
        while (readerInventory->Read() == true)
        {
            Console::Write(readerInventory->GetString(0));
            Console::Write(", ");
            Console::Write(readerInventory->GetInt32(1));
            Console::Write(", ");
            Console::WriteLine(readerInventory->GetDouble(2));
        }   //end while

        //close the Reader object
        readerInventory->Close();

        //close connection
        connectInventory->Close();

    }

    catch (OleDbException *ex)
    {
        Console::WriteLine(ex->Message);
    }

    return 0;
}   //end of main function
```

Study closely the statements that are shaded in Figure 14-5. The SELECT command assigned to the sql variable indicates that all of the fields and records in the inventory.mdb database should be selected. Next, the `OleDbCommand *commandInventory = new OleDbCommand(sql, connectInventory);` statement creates a Command object named commandInventory. The statement tells the computer to use the SELECT command stored in the sql variable to retrieve the appropriate records from the inventory.mdb database, which is connected to the program by the connectInventory object.

The `OleDbDataReader *readerInventory = commandInventory->ExecuteReader();` statement creates a `Reader` object named `readerInventory`. The `while (readerInventory->Read() == true)` clause tells the computer to read a record from the database, and process the loop body instructions as long as there was a record to read. The loop body instructions display the contents of each field from the current record, separated by commas. When the `while` loop ends, which is when there are no more records to read, the `readerInventory->Close();` statement closes the `Reader` object.

MINI-QUIZ

Mini-Quiz 3

1) Which of the following creates a `Reader` object that can read a Microsoft Access database?

a. `OleDbDataReader *readerX = commandX->ExecuteReader();`
b. `OleDbReader *readerX = commandX->ExecuteReader();`
c. `OleReader *readerX = commandX->ExecuteReader();`
d. `Reader *readerX = commandX->ExecuteReader();`

2) Write the statement to close the `Reader` object from Question 1.

3) The `Reader` object's `Read()` method returns ______________ when there are no more records to read.

You now have completed Tutorial 14's Concept lesson. You can either take a break or complete the end-of-lesson questions and exercises before moving on to the Application lesson.

SUMMARY

A database is an organized collection of related information stored in a file on a disk. A relational database stores information in tables, which are composed of fields and records. A relational database can contain one or more tables.

A `Connection` object represents the physical connection between a data source and a data provider. You specify the data source and data provider in the `Connection` object's `ConnectionString` property. You use the `Connection` object's `Open()` method to open a connection to the data source, and its `Close()` method to close the connection.

For a C++ program to access the data stored in a Microsoft Access database, the program must include the `#using <System.dll>`, `#using <System.Data.dll>`, `using namespace System::Data;` and `using namespace System::Data::OleDb;` directives.

You use a `Command` object and SQL to query a database. SQL is a set of commands that allows you to perform database tasks such as storing, retrieving, updating, deleting, and sorting data. The most commonly used SQL command is the `SELECT` command, which allows you to select the fields and records you want to view, as well as control the order in which the fields and records appear when displayed.

You use a `Reader` object to read the records stored in a database. You use the `Reader` object's `Read()` method to tell the computer to read a record from the database. You then use various methods—such as `GetString()`, `GetInt32()`, or `GetDouble()`—to retrieve the contents of a field in the record. You use the `Close()` method to close a `Reader` object.

ANSWERS TO MINI-QUIZZES

Mini-Quiz 1

1) a. database
2) d. `OleDbConnection *connectEmploy = new OleDbConnection();`
3) record
4) `ConnectionString`
5) `#using <System.dll>`, `#using <System.Data.dll>`, `using namespace System::Data;`, and `using namespace System::Data::OleDb;`

Mini-Quiz 2

1) d. `WHERE`
2) `sql = "SELECT ItemNum, Quantity, Price FROM tblInventory ORDER BY ItemNum";`
3) `sql = "SELECT ItemNum FROM tblInventory WHERE Price > 15";`
4) `sql = "SELECT Quantity FROM tblInventory WHERE ItemNum = 'XX234'";`
5) `sql = String::Concat("SELECT ItemNum FROM tblInventory WHERE Price > ", Convert::ToString(cost));`

Mini-Quiz 3

1) a. `OleDbDataReader *readerX = commandX->ExecuteReader();`
2) `readerX->Close();`
3) false

QUESTIONS

1) A ______________ database stores information in tables, which are composed of columns and rows.
   A. columnar
   B. relational
   C. sorted
   D. tabular
2) A group of related records in a database is called a ______________.
   A. column
   B. field
   C. row
   D. table

3) Which of the following is true?

A. Data stored in a relational database can be retrieved both quickly and easily by the computer.

B. Data stored in a relational database can be displayed in any order.

C. A relational database stores data in a column and row format.

D. All of the above are true.

4) The ______________ property stores the name of the OLE DB provider and the name of the database.

A. `Connect`

B. `ConnectionString`

C. `DatabaseName`

D. `Names`

5) You use the keyword ______________ to create a `Reader` object that can read the records stored in a Microsoft Access database.

A. `OleDbDataReader`

B. `OleReader`

C. `Reader`

D. `ReaderOleDb`

Use the following database table, named `tblState`, to answer Questions 6 through 9.

Field name	Data type
`State`	`String`
`Capital`	`String`
`Population`	`int`

6) When assigned to the `sql` variable, which of the following `SELECT` commands selects all of the records in the `tblState` table?

A. `"SELECT ALL RECORDS FROM tblState"`

B. `"SELECT Fields FROM tblState"`

C. `"SELECT State, Capital, Population"`

D. `"SELECT State, Capital, Population FROM tblState"`

7) When assigned to the `sql` variable, which of the following `SELECT` commands selects only the record that contains "NY" in its `State` field?

A. `"SELECT the "NY" record FROM tblState"`

B. `"SELECT Fields FROM tblState WHERE State = 'NY'"`

C. `"SELECT State, Capital, Population FROM tblState WHEN State = 'NY'"`

D. `"SELECT State, Capital, Population FROM tblState WHERE State = 'NY'"`

8) When assigned to the `sql` variable, which of the following `SELECT` commands selects all records with a population exceeding 10,000,000?

A. `"SELECT FROM tblState WHERE Population > 10000000"`

B. `"SELECT State, Capital, Population FROM tblState WHERE Population > 10000000"`

C. "SELECT State, Capital, Population FROM tblState WHEN Population > 10000000"

D. "SELECT State, Capital, Population FROM tblState WHERE 'Population > 10000000'"

9) When assigned to the `sql` variable, which of the following `SELECT` commands selects only records whose capital begins with the letter S?

A. "SELECT Capital = 'S' FROM tblState"

B. "SELECT State, Capital, Population FROM tblState WHERE Capital BEGINS WITH 'S'"

C. "SELECT State, Capital, Population FROM tblState WHERE Capital LIKE 'S%'"

D. "SELECT State, Capital, Population FROM tblState WHERE Capital LIKE 'S'"

10) Which of the following statements displays the first field listed in the `SELECT` command?

A. `Console::WriteLine(reader->GetField(0));`

B. `Console::WriteLine(reader->GetField(1));`

C. `Console::WriteLine(reader->GetString(0));`

D. `Console::WriteLine(reader->GetString(1));`

11) A(n) ______________ error occurs when a Microsoft Access database cannot be opened in a C++ program.

A. `DbException`

B. `DbOleException`

C. `Exception`

D. `OleDbException`

12) You use the `Reader` object's ______________ method to read a record.

A. `Get()`

B. `GetString()`

C. `Read()`

D. `ReadRecord()`

EXERCISES

Look For These Symbols

Debugging

Discovery

1) Assume you want to use a Microsoft Access database named states.mdb in a C++ program. Write the statement to create the appropriate `Connection` object. Name the `Connection` object `connectState`.

2) Write the statement to set the `ConnectionString` property for the `Connection` object from Exercise 1. The database is contained in the CppNet\Databases folder.

3) Write the statement to create a `Command` object named `commandState`. The query is stored in the `sql` variable. Use the `Connection` object from Exercise 1.

4) Write the statement to create a `Reader` object named `readerState`. Use the `Command` object from Exercise 3.

5) Assume that two String fields are listed in a SQL **SELECT** statement. Write the statement to display the second field. Use the **Reader** object from Exercise 4.

6) Write the statement to close the **Reader** object from Exercise 4.

7) Write the statement to close the **Connection** object from Exercise 1.

8) In this exercise, you complete a program that displays information stored in a Microsoft Access database.

   A. If necessary, start Visual Studio .NET. Open the T14ConE08 Solution (T14ConE08 Solution.sln) file, which is contained in the CppNet\Tut14\T14ConE08 Solution folder. Figure 14-6 shows the records stored in the **tblFriends** table in the friends.mdb database.

Figure 14-6

First	Last	Age
Janice	Reed	24
Patricia	Qualet	32
Tom	Jacoby	45
Sam	Darwins	33
Chris	Perwon	22
Tom	Rigby	50
Jerry	Duwest	25
Pam	Smith	33
Mike	Smithson	40

   B. If necessary, change the **ConnectionString** property to reflect the location of the friends.mdb database on your system, then save the solution.

   C. Build the solution, then execute the program. The first and last names of all the records contained in the database appear in the Command Prompt window. Close the Command Prompt window.

   D. Insert two slashes at the beginning of the `sql = "SELECT First, Last FROM tblFriends";` statement to make the statement into a comment.

   E. In the blank line below the `//select first and last names for all records, sort in ascending last name order` comment, assign the appropriate **SELECT** command to the **sql** variable.

   F. Save and build the solution. Execute the program. The first and last names appear in ascending order by the last name. Close the Command Prompt window.

   G. Insert two slashes at the beginning of the statement from Step E.

H. In the blank line below the `//select first and last names where first name is Tom` comment, assign the appropriate `SELECT` command to the `sql` variable. Save and build the solution. Execute the program. The names Tom Jacoby and Tom Rigby should appear in the Command Prompt window. Close the Command Prompt window.

I. Insert two slashes at the beginning of the statement from Step H.

J. In the blank line below the `//select first and last names where last name begins with D` comment, assign the appropriate `SELECT` command to the `sql` variable. Save and build the solution. Execute the program. The first and last names of two friends should appear in the Command Prompt window. Close the Command Prompt window.

K. Insert two slashes at the beginning of the statement from Step J.

L. In the blank line below the `//select first and last names where last name begins with Smith` comment, assign the appropriate `SELECT` command to the `sql` variable. Save and build the solution. Execute the program. The first and last names of two friends should appear in the Command Prompt window. Close the Command Prompt window.

M. Insert two slashes at the beginning of the statement from Step L.

N. In the blank line below the `//select first and last names where age is greater than 30` comment, assign the appropriate `SELECT` command to the `sql` variable. Save and build the solution. Execute the program. The first and last names of six friends should appear in the Command Prompt window. Close the Command Prompt window.

O. When the program is working correctly, close the Output window, and then use the File menu to close the solution.

9) Assume that a database contains a Boolean field named `insured`. What is the appropriate `Reader` object method to use to retrieve this information from the current record?

10) In this exercise, you learn how to display the number of records stored in a table in a Microsoft Access database named sales.mdb, and also display the average sales amount stored in the table.

A. If necessary, start Visual Studio .NET. Open the T14ConE10 Solution (T14ConE10 Solution.sln) file, which is contained in the CppNet\Tut14\T14ConE10 Solution folder. If necessary, change the `ConnectionString` property to reflect the location of the sales.mdb file on your system.

B. Complete the program by entering the code to display the number of records stored in the `tblSales` table in the sales.mdb database. Also enter the code to display the average sales amount stored in the table. Figure 14-7 shows the records stored in the `tblSales` table.

Figure 14-7

Salesperson	Sales
Mary Jones	3000
Jose Martinez	5000
Choca Patel	2000
Harry Jones	4000
Shamika Jefferson	6000

C. Save and then build the solution.

D. Execute the program. Close the Command Prompt window.

E. When the program is working correctly, close the Output window, and then use the File menu to close the solution.

11) In this exercise, you debug a C++ program.

A. If necessary, start Visual Studio .NET. Open the T14ConE11 Solution (T14ConE11 Solution.sln) file, which is contained in the CppNet\Tut14\T14ConE11 Solution folder. If necessary, change the `ConnectionString` property to reflect the location of the sales.mdb file on your system. The records contained in the `tblSales` table are listed in Figure 14-7 in Exercise 10.

B. Study the existing code, then build the solution. Correct any errors in the program, then save and build the solution.

C. Execute the program. Enter 3000 as the sales amount. Close the Command Prompt window. Correct any errors in the program, then save and build the solution. Execute the program. Enter 3000 as the sales amount. Three names should appear in the Command Prompt window. Close the Command Prompt window.

D. When the program is working correctly, close the Output window, and then use the File menu to close the solution.

Application Lesson

Using a Database in a C++ Program

CASE ABC Company uses a Microsoft Access database to store information about its employees. The database contains each employee's name, hire date, rate of pay, employment status (full-time or part-time), and job code. Carol Jones, the Personnel Manager, wants a program that she can use to display the names of employees having either a specific employment status or a specific job code.

The ABC Company Program

The CppNet\Databases folder on your computer's hard disk contains a Microsoft Access database named employees.mdb; this is the database that ABC Company uses to record information about its employees. The employees.mdb database contains one table, which is named `tblEmploy`. Figure 14-8 shows the fields and records contained in the `tblEmploy` table.

Figure 14-8: Contents of the `tblEmploy` table in the employees.mdb database

Number	Last	First	Hired	Rate	Status	Code
100	Benton	Jack	3/5/1996	$15.00	F	2
101	Jones	Carol	4/2/1996	$15.00	F	2
102	Ismal	Asaad	1/15/1997	$10.00	P	1
103	Rodriguez	Carl	5/6/1997	$12.00	P	3
104	Iovanelli	Sam	8/15/1997	$20.00	F	1
105	Nyugen	Thomas	10/20/1997	$8.00	P	3
106	Vine	Martha	2/5/1997	$9.50	P	2
107	Smith	Paul	5/14/1998	$17.50	F	2
108	Gerber	Wanda	9/24/1998	$21.00	F	3
109	Zonten	Mary	12/4/1998	$13.50	F	4
110	Sparrow	John	12/4/1998	$9.00	P	4
111	Krutchen	Jerry	12/15/1998	$9.00	P	4

tip
As you learned in the Concept lesson, when including a field in a query, you need to know the data type of the field.

The database contains seven fields. The `Number` and `Code` fields contain integers, and the `Rate` field contains numbers of the `double` data type. The `Last`, `First`, and `Status` fields contain strings, and the `Hired` field contains dates. Notice that employees can have an employment status of either "F" (for full-time) or "P" (for part-time). Also notice that employees can have one of four different job codes (1, 2, 3, or 4).

In addition to containing the employees.mdb database, your computer's hard disk also contains a partially completed program for ABC Company. You open that program in the next set of steps.

To open the partially completed ABC Company program:

1. Click **File** on the menu bar, and then click **Open Solution**. The Open Solution dialog box opens.
2. Locate and then open the **CppNet\Tut14\T14App Solution** folder.
3. Click **T14App Solution** (T14App Solution.sln) in the list of filenames, and then click the **Open** button.
4. If the T14App.cpp source file is not displayed, right-click **T14App.cpp** in the Solution Explorer window, and then click **Open**.

Recall that, to use a Microsoft Access database in a C++ program, the program must contain the following four directives: `#using <System.dll>`, `#using <System.Data.dll>`, `using namespace System::Data;`, and `using namespace System::Data::OleDb;`.

To enter the additional directives in the T14App.cpp program:

1. In the blank line below the `#using <mscorlib.dll>` directive, type **#using <System.dll>** and press **Enter**, then type **#using <System.Data.dll>**.
2. In the blank line below the `using namespace System;` directive, type **using namespace System::Data;** and press **Enter**, then type **using namespace System::Data::OleDb;** and press **Enter**.

The ABC Company program uses four functions: `main()`, `displayMenu()`, `getByCode()`, and `getByStatus()`. First you view the `displayMenu()` function.

Viewing the `displayMenu()` Function

Figure 14-9 shows the code for the `displayMenu()` function.

Figure 14-9: Code for the `displayMenu()` function

```
int displayMenu()
{
    String *choice = "";
    while (choice->CompareTo("1") != 0
        && choice->CompareTo("2") != 0
        && choice->CompareTo("3") != 0)
    {
```

Figure 14-9: Code for the displayMenu( ) function (continued)

```
        Console::WriteLine("*********************************");
        Console::WriteLine("Display employee(s) having this:");
        Console::WriteLine("      1 Job Code");
        Console::WriteLine("      2 Employment Status");
        Console::WriteLine("      3 Exit program");
        Console::Write("Enter choice: ");
        choice = Console::ReadLine();
        Console::WriteLine("*********************************");
        Console::WriteLine();
    }  //end while
    return Convert::ToInt32(choice);
} //end of displayMenu function
```

First, the **displayMenu( )** function declares a **String** variable named **choice**. The next instruction is the beginning of a loop that repeats its instructions while the **choice** variable does not contain a valid choice. In this case, a valid choice is "1", "2", or "3".

The first five instructions in the loop simply display on the computer screen a menu that contains three choices. The first choice is to display the names of employees having a specific job code. The second choice is to display the names of employees having a specific employment status, and the third choice is to exit the program. The next instruction in the loop, **Console::Write("Enter choice: ");**, prompts the user to enter his or her choice, and the **choice = Console::ReadLine();** instruction assigns the user's response to the **choice** variable. The last two instructions in the loop display a row of asterisks followed by a blank line.

When the user enters a valid choice, the loop ends and the computer processes the next instruction, **return Convert::ToInt32(choice);**. This instruction returns the contents of the **choice** variable, converted to an **int**, to the function that called the **displayMenu( )** function. In this case, it returns the value to the **main( )** function. After returning the appropriate value, the **displayMenu( )** function ends.

Next, you will complete the **main( )** function.

tip

Notice that the while loop in the displayMenu( ) function ends only when the user enters a valid choice. Because of this, the displayMenu( ) function always returns a valid value to the function that called it—in this case, the main( ) function.

Completing the main( ) Function

Figure 14-10 (on the next page) shows the pseudocode for the **main( )** function.

According to the pseudocode, the **main( )** function first creates a **Connection** object and then sets the object's **ConnectionString** property. It then tries to open the connection to the employees.mdb database. If the connection cannot be opened, the **main( )** function displays an error message; otherwise, it calls the **displayMenu( )** function to both display the menu and get the user's choice.

Figure 14-10: Pseudocode for the `main()` function

```
1. create a Connection object
2. set the Connection object's ConnectionString property
3. try to open the connection to the employees.mdb database
4. if the connection is successful
     call the displayMenu() function to display the menu and get the user's choice
     repeat while (the user's choice is not 3)
        if (the user's choice is 1)
           call the getByCode() function, passing it the Connection object
        else
           call the getByStatus() function, passing it the Connection object
        //end if
        call the displayMenu() function to display the menu and get the user's choice
     //end while
     close the connection to the database
   else
      display an error message
   //end if
```

The loop in the **`main()`** function repeats its instructions as long as the user does not select the number three from the menu. (Recall that choosing the number three indicates that the user wants to exit the program.) The first instruction in the loop is a selection structure that determines the appropriate function to call based on the user's menu choice. If the user selected choice number one, the **`main()`** function calls the **`getByCode()`** function, passing it the **`Connection`** object. Otherwise, which means that the user selected choice number two, the **`main()`** function calls the **`getByStatus()`** function, passing it the **`Connection`** object. When the appropriate function completes its task, the **`main()`** function calls the **`displayMenu()`** function to display the menu and get another choice from the user.

When the user enters the number three as his or her menu choice, the **`main()`** function closes the connection to the database, and then the **`main()`** function ends.

The instructions to create the **`Connection`** object and set its **`ConnectionString`** property are missing from the **`main()`** function in the T14App.cpp program. Also missing are the instructions to open and close the connection, as well as the **`catch`** statement that will display the appropriate error message if the connection cannot be opened. You complete the **`main()`** function in the next set of steps.

To complete the `main()` function:

1. Position the insertion point in the blank line below the `//create Connection object` comment in the `main()` function.

   First, create the `Connection` object.

2. Type **OleDbConnection *connectEmploy = new OleDbConnection();** and press **Enter**.

   Now set the `Connection` object's `ConnectionString` property. Recall that this property specifies the name of the provider and the name of the database.

3. Type **connectEmploy->ConnectionString = "Provider=Microsoft.Jet. OLEDB.4.0; Data Source=c:\\cppnet\\databases\\employees.mdb";** and press **Enter**. (If necessary, change the Data Source to match the location of the employees.mdb file on your computer system.)

   Next, enter the instruction to open the connection to the database.

4. In the blank line below the `//open connection to database` comment, type **connectEmploy->Open();** and press **Enter**.

   Now enter the instruction to close the connection to the database.

5. In the blank line below the `//close connection` comment, type **connectEmploy->Close();**.

   Finally, enter the `catch` statement that will display an appropriate error message if the database connection cannot be opened.

6. Enter the `catch` statement shaded in Figure 14-11, which shows the completed `main()` function.

Figure 14-11: Completed `main()` function

```
int main()
{
   //declare variable
   int menuChoice = 0;

   //create Connection object
   OleDbConnection *connectEmploy = new
   OleDbConnection();
   connectEmploy->ConnectionString = "Provider=
   Microsoft.Jet.OLEDB.4.0; Data Source=c:\\
   cppnet\\databases\\employees.mdb";

   try
   {
      //open connection to database
      connectEmploy->Open();

      //display menu
      menuChoice = displayMenu();

      while (menuChoice != 3)
      {
          if (menuChoice == 1)
             getByCode(connectEmploy);
          else
             getByStatus(connectEmploy);
          //end if

          //display menu
          menuChoice = displayMenu();
      }  //end while
      //close connection
      connectEmploy->Close();
   }
```

tip

If you enter a string on one line in a C++ program, and then enter another string on the next line, the C++ compiler concatenates both strings automatically. For example, you could enter `connectEmploy->ConnectionString = "Provider=Microsoft.Jet.OLEDB.4.0;"` on one line, and then enter `"Data Source=c:\\cppnet\\databases\\employees.mdb";` on the following line.

Figure 14-11: Completed `main()` function (continued)

```
    catch (OleDbException *ex)
    {
        Console::WriteLine(ex->Message);
    }

    return 0;
}   //end of main function
```

7. Save the solution.

Next, you complete the **`getByCode()`** function.

Completing the `getByCode()` Function

Recall that, if the user selects the number one from the menu, it indicates that he or she wants to display the names of employees having a specific job code. Figure 14-12 shows the pseudocode for the **`getByCode()`** function.

Figure 14-12: Pseudocode for the `getByCode()` function

```
1. repeat while (the job code is not 1, 2, 3, or 4)
     get the job code
   //end while
2. create a Command object, using a SQL command to define the criteria,
   and the Connection object, which is received from the main() function,
   to connect to the database
3. create a Reader object, using the Command object to set the appropriate criteria
4. repeat while (there are records to read)
     display the first and last names of employees matching the
     criteria specified in the Command object
   //end while
5. display a blank line
6. close the Reader object
```

The first loop in the **`getByCode()`** function repeats its instruction until the user enters a valid job code; valid job codes are 1, 2, 3, and 4. When the user enters a valid job code, the **`getByCode()`** function creates a **`Command`** object that uses the job code to define the appropriate criteria. It then creates a **`Reader`** object, using the criteria. The second repetition structure repeats its instruction while there are records to read. The instruction in the loop displays the first and last names of employees matching the criteria. The function then displays a blank line, closes the **`Reader`** object, and then ends.

Several instructions are missing from the **`getByCode()`** function. You complete the function in the next set of steps.

To complete the `getByCode()` function:

1. Position the insertion point in the blank line below the `//create Command object` comment.

First, assign the appropriate SQL command to the `sql` variable.

2. Type **sql = String::Concat("SELECT First, Last FROM tblEmploy WHERE Code = ", jobCode);** and press **Enter**.

   Now use the `Connection` object, which is passed to the function from the `main()` function, and the `sql` variable to create a `Command` object.

3. Type **OleDbCommand *commandEmploy = new OleDbCommand(sql, conObj);** and press **Enter**.

   Next, create a `Reader` object that the program can use to read each record in the database.

4. In the blank line below the `//create Reader object` comment, type **OleDbDataReader *reader = commandEmploy->ExecuteReader();**.

   Now enter the repetition structure to read the records and display the names matching the criteria. Also enter the instruction to close the `Reader` object.

5. Enter the lines of code shaded in Figure 14-13, which shows the completed `getByCode()` function.

Figure 14-13: Completed `getByCode()` function

```
void getByCode(OleDbConnection *conObj)
{
   //declare variables
   String *jobCode = "";
   String *sql = "";

   //get job code
   while (jobCode->CompareTo("1") != 0 && jobCode->CompareTo
   ("2") != 0 && jobCode->CompareTo("3") != 0 &&
   jobCode->CompareTo("4") != 0)
   {
      Console::Write("Enter job code (1, 2, 3, or 4): ");
      jobCode = Console::ReadLine();
   }  //end while

   //create Command object
   sql = String::Concat("SELECT First, Last FROM
   tblEmploy WHERE Code = ", jobCode);
   OleDbCommand *commandEmploy = new OleDbCommand(sql, conObj);

   //create Reader object
   OleDbDataReader *reader = commandEmploy->ExecuteReader();
   //display names
   while (reader->Read() == true)
      Console::WriteLine("{0} {1}", reader->GetString(0),
      reader->GetString(1));
   //end while
   Console::WriteLine();

   //close Reader object
   reader->Close();
}  //end of getByCode function
```

6. Save the solution.

Finally, you will complete the `getByStatus()` function.

Completing the `getByStatus()` Function

Recall that, if the user selects the number two from the menu, it indicates that he or she wants to display the employees matching a specific employment status. Figure 14-14 shows the pseudocode for the `getByStatus()` function.

Figure 14-14: Pseudocode for the `getByStatus()` function

```
1. repeat while (the employment status is not F or P)
     get the employment status
     convert the employment status to uppercase
   //end while
2. create a Command object, using a SQL command to define the criteria, and the
   Connection object, which is received from the main() function, to connect to the database
3. create a Reader object, using the Command object to set the appropriate criteria
4. repeat while (there are records to read)
     display the first and last names of employees matching the
     criteria specified in the Command object
   //end while
5. display a blank line
6. close the Reader object
```

The first repetition structure in the `getByStatus()` function repeats its instructions as long as the user enters an invalid employment status, which is a status that is not the letter F or the letter P. When the user enters a valid employment status, the function creates a `Command` object that uses the status to define the appropriate criteria. It then creates a `Reader` object, using the criteria. The second repetition structure repeats its instruction while there are records to read. The instruction in the loop displays the first and last names of employees matching the criteria. The function then displays a blank line, closes the `Reader` object, and then ends.

Only two instructions are missing from the `getByStatus()` function. You complete the function in the next set of steps.

To complete the `getByStatus()` function:

1. Position the insertion point in the blank line below the `//create Command object` comment.

   First, assign the appropriate SQL command to the `sql` variable.

2. Type **sql = String::Concat("SELECT First, Last FROM tblEmploy WHERE Status = '", status, "'");** and press **Enter**. Be sure to enter a single quotation mark followed by a double quotation mark before the second comma. Also be sure to enter a double quotation mark, a single quotation mark, and a double quotation mark before the closing parantheses.

   Now use the `Connection` object, which is passed to the function from the `main()` function, and the `sql` variable to create a `Command` object.

3. Type **OleDbCommand *commandEmploy = new OleDbCommand(sql, conObj);** and press **Enter**. Figure 14-15 shows the completed `getByStatus()` function.

Figure 14-15: Completed `getByStatus()` function

```
void getByStatus(OleDbConnection *conObj)
{
   //declare variables
   String *status = "";
   String *sql = "";

   //get employment status
   while (status->CompareTo("F") != 0 && status->
   CompareTo("P") != 0)
   {
      Console::Write("Enter the employment status (F or P): ");
      status = Console::ReadLine();
      status = status->ToUpper();
   } //end while

   //create Command object
   sql = String::Concat("SELECT First, Last FROM tblEmploy
   WHERE Status = '", status, "'");
   OleDbCommand *commandEmploy = new OleDbCommand(sql, conObj);

   //create Reader object
   OleDbDataReader *reader = commandEmploy->ExecuteReader();
   //display names
   while (reader->Read() == true)
      Console::WriteLine("{0} {1}", reader->GetString(0),
      reader->GetString(1));
   //end while
   Console::WriteLine();

   //close Reader object
   reader->Close();
} //end of getByStatus function
```

4. Save the solution.

Now that you have finished coding the T14App.cpp program, you can test it to verify that it is working correctly.

To test the T14App.cpp program:

1. Build the solution. Verify that the program generated no warnings.
2. Execute the program. The menu created by the `displayMenu()` function appears in the Command Prompt window.

   First display the names of employees with a job code of 4.
3. Type **1** and press **Enter**. When you are prompted to enter the job code, type **4** and press **Enter**. The names of three employees appear in the Command Prompt window, as shown in Figure 14-16.

Figure 14-16: Command Prompt window showing the names of employees with a job code of 4

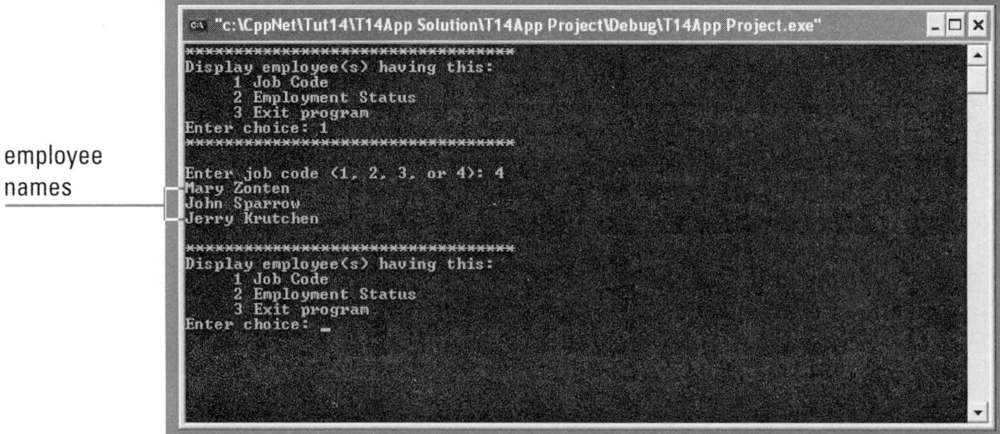

"c:\CppNet\Tut14\T14App Solution\T14App Project\Debug\T14App Project.exe"

```
************************************
Display employee(s) having this:
     1 Job Code
     2 Employment Status
     3 Exit program
Enter choice: 1
************************************

Enter job code (1, 2, 3, or 4): 4
Mary Zonten
John Sparrow
Jerry Krutchen

************************************
Display employee(s) having this:
     1 Job Code
     2 Employment Status
     3 Exit program
Enter choice: _
```

employee names

Now display the names of the full-time employees.

4. Type **2** and press **Enter**. When you are prompted to enter the employment status, type **f** and press **Enter**. The names of the full-time employees appear in the Command Prompt window, as shown in Figure 14-17.

Figure 14-17: Command Prompt window showing the names of the full-time employees

"c:\CppNet\Tut14\T14App Solution\T14App Project\Debug\T14App Project.exe"

```
John Sparrow
Jerry Krutchen

************************************
Display employee(s) having this:
     1 Job Code
     2 Employment Status
     3 Exit program
Enter choice: 2
************************************

Enter the employment status (F or P): f
Jack Benton
Carol Jones
Sam Iovanelli
Paul Smith
Wanda Gerber
Mary Zonten

************************************
Display employee(s) having this:
     1 Job Code
     2 Employment Status
     3 Exit program
Enter choice: _
```

employee names

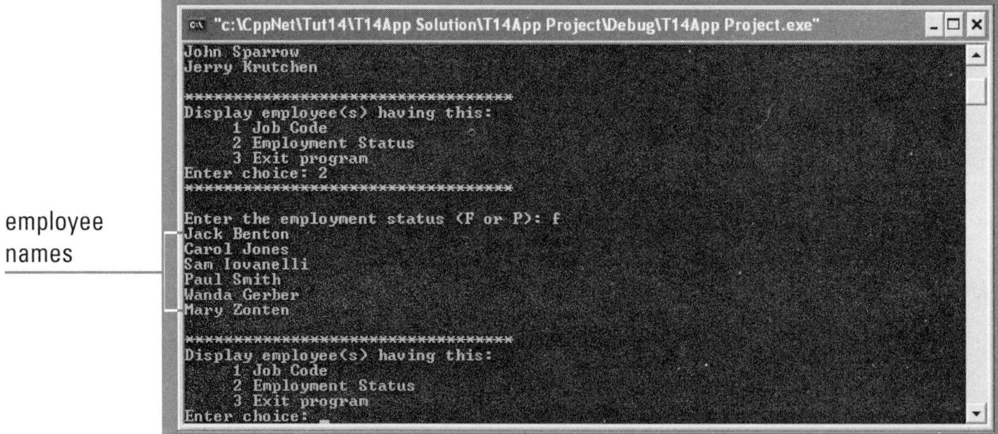

Now stop the program by entering the number three.

5. Type **3** and press **Enter**.
6. Close the Command Prompt window, then close the Output window.
7. Click **File** on the menu bar, and then click **Close Solution** to close the current solution.
8. Click **File** on the menu bar, and then click **Exit** to exit Visual Studio .NET.

You now have completed Tutorial 14's Application lesson. You can either take a break or complete the end-of-lesson exercises.

Look For These Symbols

Debugging

Discovery

EXERCISES

1) In this exercise, you modify the program you completed in the lesson so that it includes a function named `getByNumber()`. The `getByNumber()` function should allow the user to enter an employee number. It then should display the employee's name and pay rate.

   A. If necessary, start Visual Studio .NET. Open the T14AppE01 Solution (T14AppE01 Solution.sln) file, which is contained in the CppNet\Tut14\T14AppE01 Solution folder. If necessary, change the `ConnectionString` property to reflect the location of the employees.mdb file on your system.

   B. Modify the program appropriately. Be sure to add another choice to the menu created in the `displayMenu()` function.

   C. Save and then build the solution.

   D. Execute the program. Display the name and pay rate for employee number 105. The program should display "Thomas Nyugen" and "$8.00".

   E. When the program is working correctly, close the Output window, and then use the File menu to close the solution.

2) In this exercise, you modify the program you completed in the lesson so that it includes a function named `getByRate()`. The `getByRate()` function should allow the user to enter a pay rate. It then should display the employee number and name of employees earning at least that amount.

   A. If necessary, start Visual Studio .NET. Open the T14AppE02 Solution (T14AppE02 Solution.sln) file, which is contained in the CppNet\Tut14\T14AppE02 Solution folder. If necessary, change the `ConnectionString` property to reflect the location of the employees.mdb file on your system.

   B. Modify the program appropriately. Be sure to add another choice to the menu created in the `displayMenu()` function.

   C. Save and then build the solution.

   D. Execute the program. Display the number and name of employees earning $16 or more. The program should display the numbers and names of three employees: 104, Sam Iovanelli, 107, Paul Smith, and 108, Wanda Gerber.

   E. When the program is working correctly, close the Output window, and then use the File menu to close the solution.

3) In this exercise, you modify the program you completed in the lesson so that it includes a function named `getByLastName()`. The `getByLastName()` function should allow the user to enter an employee's last name. It then should display the employee's first name.

   A. If necessary, start Visual Studio .NET. Open the T14AppE03 Solution (T14AppE03 Solution.sln) file, which is contained in the CppNet\Tut14\T14AppE03 Solution folder. If necessary, change the `ConnectionString` property to reflect the location of the employees.mdb file on your system.

   B. Modify the program appropriately. Be sure to add another choice to the menu created in the `displayMenu()` function.

   C. Save and then build the solution.

   D. Execute the program. Display the first name for any employee having a last name of Vine. The program should display "Martha".

   E. When the program is working correctly, close the Output window, and then use the File menu to close the solution.

4) In this exercise, you modify the program you completed in the lesson so that the `getByCode()` function displays the employee's hire date in addition to the employee's name.

A. If necessary, start Visual Studio .NET. Open the T14AppE04 Solution (T14AppE04 Solution.sln) file, which is contained in the CppNet\Tut14\T14AppE04 Solution folder. If necessary, change the `ConnectionString` property to reflect the location of the employees.mdb file on your system.

B. Modify the program appropriately.

C. Save and then build the solution.

D. Execute the program. Display the names and hire dates of employees having a job code of 2. The program should display four names and hire dates.

E. When the program is working correctly, close the Output window, and then use the File menu to close the solution.

5) In this exercise, you modify the program you completed in the lesson so that it includes a function named `getByHireDate()`. The `getByHireDate()` function should allow the user to enter a date. It then should display the names of employees hired on or after that date.

A. If necessary, start Visual Studio .NET. Open the T14AppE05 Solution (T14AppE05 Solution.sln) file, which is contained in the CppNet\Tut14\T14AppE05 Solution folder. If necessary, change the `ConnectionString` property to reflect the location of the employees.mdb file on your system.

B. Modify the program appropriately. Be sure to add another choice to the menu created in the `displayMenu()` function.

C. Save and then build the solution.

D. Execute the program. Display the names of employees hired on or after 12/1/1998. The program should display the names of three employees.

E. When the program is working correctly, close the Output window, and then use the File menu to close the solution.

6) In this exercise, you debug a C++ program.

A. If necessary, start Visual Studio .NET. Open the T14AppE06 Solution (T14AppE06 Solution.sln) file, which is contained in the CppNet\Tut14\T14AppE06 Solution folder. If necessary, change the `ConnectionString` property to reflect the location of the employees.mdb file on your system.

B. Study the existing code, then build the solution. Correct any errors in the program, then save and build the solution.

C. Execute the program. Enter the letter m. Close the Command Prompt window. Correct any errors in the program.

D. Save and build the solution. Execute the program. Enter the letter m. Two names should appear in the Command Prompt window. Close the Command Prompt window.

E. When the program is working correctly, close the Output window, and then use the File menu to close the solution.

Appendix A

ASCII Codes

Character	ASCII	Binary	Character	ASCII	Binary	Character	ASCII	Binary
SPACE	32	00100000	B	66	01000010	d	100	01100100
!	33	00100001	C	67	01000011	e	101	01100101
"	34	00100010	D	68	01000100	f	102	01100110
#	35	00100011	E	69	01000101	g	103	01100111
$	36	00100100	F	70	01000110	h	104	01101000
%	37	00100101	G	71	01000111	i	105	01101001
&	38	00100110	H	72	01001000	j	106	01101010
'	39	00100111	I	73	01001001	k	107	01101011
(	40	00101000	J	74	01001010	l	108	01101100
)	41	00101001	K	75	01001011	m	109	01101101
*	42	00101010	L	76	01001100	n	110	01101110
+	43	00101011	M	77	01001101	o	111	01101111
,	44	00101100	N	78	01001110	p	112	01110000
—	45	00101101	O	79	01001111	q	113	01110001
.	46	00101110	P	80	01010000	r	114	01110010
/	47	00101111	Q	81	01010001	s	115	01110011
0	48	00110000	R	82	01010010	t	116	01110100
1	49	00110001	S	83	01010011	u	117	01110101
2	50	00110010	T	84	01010100	v	118	01110110
3	51	00110011	U	85	01010101	w	119	01110111
4	52	00110100	V	86	01010110	x	120	01111000
5	53	00110101	W	87	01010111	y	121	01111001
6	54	00110110	X	88	01011000	z	122	01111010
7	55	00110111	Y	89	01011001	{	123	01111011
8	56	00111000	Z	90	01011010	|	124	01111100
9	57	00111001	[	91	01011011	}	125	01111101
:	58	00111010	\	92	01011100	~	126	01111110
;	59	00111011	]	93	01011101	DELETE	127	01111111
<	60	00111100	^	94	01011110			
=	61	00111101	_	95	01011111			
>	62	00111110	`	96	01100000			
?	63	00111111	a	97	01100001			
@	64	01000000	b	98	01100010			
A	65	01000001	c	99	01100011			

Appendix B

Built-in Mathematical Methods

Objectives

After completing this appendix, you will be able to:

- Use the `Math::Pow()` and `Math::Sqrt()` methods
- Use the `Math::Cos()`, `Math::Sin()`, and `Math::Tan()` methods
- Use the `Math::Max()`, `Math::Min()`, `Math::Ceiling()`, and `Math::Floor()` methods
- Use the `Math::Sign()` method
- Use the `Math::Round()` method

Using Built-in Mathematical Methods

Certain mathematical tasks—such as raising a number to a power or rounding a numeric value to a specific number of decimal places—are common in programs. Rather than have each programmer start from scratch and create methods to perform these tasks, the C++ programming language includes a set of mathematical methods that any programmer can use in his or her programs. Figure B-1 lists some of the mathematical methods built into the C++ language, along with the purpose of each method. To use the mathematical methods in a program, the program must contain the `#using <mscorlib.dll>` directive, because the definitions of the mathematical methods are contained in the mscorlib.dll file.

Figure B-1: Mathematical methods

Method	Purpose
`Math::Pow()`	raise a number to a power
`Math::Sqrt()`	calculate the square root of a number
`Math::Cos()`	calculate the cosine of an angle expressed in radians
`Math::Sin()`	calculate the sine of an angle expressed in radians
`Math::Tan()`	calculate the tangent of an angle expressed in radians
`Math::Max()`	determine the largest of two numbers
`Math::Min()`	determine the smallest of two numbers
`Math::Ceiling()`	determine the smallest whole number greater than or equal to a specified number
`Math::Floor()`	determine the largest whole number less than or equal to a specified number
`Math::Sign()`	determine the sign of a number
`Math::Round()`	round a number

In the following sections, you are given a brief explanation and several examples of using these methods in a C++ statement.

The `Math::Pow()` and `Math::Sqrt()` Methods

The `Math::Pow()` and `Math::Sqrt()` methods belong to a group commonly referred to as the **exponential methods**. Both methods are value-returning methods, because both return a value after performing their assigned task. The **`Math::Pow()` method**, for example, raises a number to a power, and then returns the result. The **`Math::Sqrt()` method**, on the other hand, returns the square root of a number.

Figure B-2 shows the syntax of the `Math::Pow()` and `Math::Sqrt()` methods and includes examples of using the methods in a C++ statement.

Figure B-2: Syntax and examples of the `Math::Pow()` and `Math::Sqrt()` methods

Syntax	Return value
`Math::Pow(x, y)` `Math::Sqrt(x)`	*x* raised to the *y* power square root of *x*
C++ statement	**Result**
`cube = Math::Pow(4, 3);`	the number 64 assigned to the `cube` variable
`Console::Write(Math::Pow(100, .5));`	the number 10 displayed on the screen
`Console::Write(10 * Math::Pow(2, 4));`	the number 160 displayed on the screen
`sqRoot = Math::Sqrt(16);`	the number 4 assigned to the `sqRoot` variable
`Console::Write(Math::Pow` `(Math::Sqrt(4), 5));`	the number 32 displayed on the screen

The `cube = Math::Pow(4, 3);` statement shown in Figure B-2 first raises the number 4 to the third power—in other words, it multiplies the number 4 by itself three times (4 * 4 * 4). The statement assigns the result (64) to the `cube` variable.

The second statement shown in Figure B-2, `Console::Write(Math::Pow (100, .5));`, raises a number—in this case, 100—to the .5 power, which is the same as finding the square root of the number. The statement will display the number 10 on the screen.

The third statement shown in Figure B-2, `Console::Write(10 * Math::Pow (2, 4));`, raises the number 2 to the fourth power. It then multiplies the result (16) by 10, and then displays the result (160) on the screen. The fourth statement, `sqRoot = Math::Sqrt(16);`, calculates the square root of the number 16, and then assigns the result (4) to the `sqRoot` variable. The last statement shown in Figure B-2, `Console::Write (Math::Pow(Math::Sqrt(4), 5));`, first calculates the square root of 4, which is 2. It then raises the number 2 to the fifth power, and displays the result (32) on the screen.

tip

Recall that items in **bold** in a syntax are required parts of the syntax. Items in *italics* indicate places where the programmer must supply information relative to the program.

tip

As you learned in Tutorial 3, when an assignment statement is encountered in a program, the computer assigns the value of the *expression* appearing on the right side of the assignment operator to the variable whose *variablename* appears on the left side of the assignment operator.

The `Math::Cos()`, `Math::Sin()`, and `Math::Tan()` Methods

The **`Math::Cos()`**, **`Math::Sin()`**, and **`Math::Tan()` methods**, referred to as the **trigonometric methods**, can be used to calculate the cosine, sine, and tangent of *x*, where *x* is an angle expressed in radians. Because angles typically are expressed in degrees, you most times will need to convert the degrees to radians before using these methods. You convert degrees to radians using the equation radians = degrees * pi / 180, where the value of pi is 3.14159265358979323846. For example, using this equation, 30° is approximately .5 radians (30 * 3.14159265358979323846 / 180), and 90° is approximately 1.6 radians (90 * 3.14159265358979323846 / 180). Like the exponential methods, the trigonometric methods are value-returning methods, because they return a value after completing their assigned task. Figure B-3 shows the syntax of the `Math::Cos()`, `Math::Sin()`, and `Math::Tan()` methods and includes examples of using the methods in a C++ statement.

tip

As you may remember from your math courses, one radian is equal to 180 / pi degrees, and one degree is equal to pi / 180 radians.

Figure B-3: Syntax and examples of the `Math::Cos()`, `Math::Sin()`, and `Math::Tan()` methods

Syntax	Return value
`Math::Cos(x)`	cosine of angle *x* (expressed in radians)
`Math::Sin(x)`	sine of angle *x* (expressed in radians)
`Math::Tan(x)`	tangent of angle *x* (expressed in radians)
C++ statement	**Result**
`angleCos = Math::Cos(60 * 3.14159265358979323846 / 180);`	the number .5 assigned to the `angleCos` variable
`Console::WriteLine(Math::Sin(1.57));`	the number 0.999999682931835 displayed on the screen
`Console::Write(Math::Tan(31 * 3.14159265358979323846 / 180));`	the number 0.60086061902756 displayed on the screen
`Console::Write(Math::Tan(31 * Math::PI / 180));`	the number 0.60086061902756 displayed on the screen

The `angleCos = Math::Cos(60 * 3.14159265358979323846 / 180);` statement shown in Figure B-3 first converts 60° into radians by multiplying 60 by pi and then dividing the result by 180. This calculation results in approximately 1.05 radians. The statement then calculates the cosine of an angle that is 1.05 radians and assigns the result (.5) to the `angleCos` variable.

The second statement shown in Figure B-3, `Console::WriteLine(Math::Sin(1.57));`, calculates the sine of an angle that is 1.57 radians, and displays the result (0.999999682931835) on the screen. The third example shown in the figure, `Console::Write(Math::Tan(31 * 3.14159265358979323846 / 180));`, converts 31° into radians, and then finds the tangent of the angle. The statement displays the result (0.60086061902756) on the screen.

Rather than using the literal constant 3.14159265358979323846 as the value of pi in a C++ statement, you can use the intrinsic named constant `Math::PI`, as shown in the last example in Figure B-3. An **intrinsic named constant** is a constant that is built into a programming language. The value of the `Math::PI` constant is the same as the value of pi: 3.14159265358979323846. Unlike the literal constant 3.14159265358979323846, the `Math::PI` constant is much easier to type and makes the program more self-documenting.

MINI-QUIZ

Mini-Quiz 1

1) Write the C++ statement that raises the number 3 to the fifth power, and then stores the result in an `int` variable named `answer`.
2) Write the C++ statement that displays the square root of 25 on the screen.
3) Write the C++ statement that cubes the square root of 16, and then displays the result on the screen.
4) Write the C++ statement that squares the value stored in the `number` variable, and then displays the result on the screen.
5) Write the C++ statement that displays the cosine of a 15° angle.
6) Write the C++ statement that displays the tangent of an angle that is 1.3 radians.

The `Math::Max()`, `Math::Min()`, `Math::Ceiling()`, and `Math::Floor()` Methods

The C++ programming language provides four methods that you can use to determine the smallest and largest number. The **`Math::Max()` method** returns the larger of two numbers, and the **`Math::Min()` method** returns the smaller of two numbers. The **`Math::Ceiling()`** method returns the smallest whole number greater than or equal to a specified number, and the **`Math::Floor()`** method returns the largest whole number less than or equal to a specified number. Figure B-4 shows the syntax of the four methods and includes examples of using each method in a C++ statement.

Figure B-4: Syntax and examples of the `Math::Max()`, `Math::Min()`, `Math::Ceiling()`, and `Math::Floor()` methods

Syntax	Return value
`Math::Max(x, y)`	larger of *x* or *y*
`Math::Min(x, y)`	smaller of *x* or *y*
`Math::Ceiling(x)`	smallest whole number greater than or equal to *x*
`Math::Floor(x)`	largest whole number less than or equal to *x*
C++ statement	**Result**
`largest = Math::Max(35, 78);`	the number 78 assigned to the `largest` variable
`Console::Write(Math::Min(num1, num2));`	assuming the `num1` variable contains the number 3, and the `num2` variable contains the number 7, displays the number 3 on the screen
`Console::Write(Math::Ceiling(3.6));`	the number 4 displayed on the screen
`Console::Write(Math::Floor(85.3));`	the number 85 displayed on the screen

The first statement shown in Figure B-4, **largest = Math::Max(35, 78);**, compares the number 35 to the number 78 to determine the largest number. It then assigns the largest number (78) to the **largest** variable. The second statement, **Console::Write (Math::Min(num1, num2));**, compares the number stored in the **num1** variable to the number stored in the **num2** variable to determine the smallest number. Assuming the **num1** variable contains the number 3, and the **num2** variable contains the number 7, the statement displays the number 3 on the screen.

The third statement shown in Figure B-4, **Console::Write(Math::Ceiling (3.6));**, displays the number 4 on the screen, because the number 4 is the smallest whole number that is greater than or equal to the number 3.6. The last statement, **Console::Write (Math::Floor(85.3));**, displays the number 85 on the screen, because the number 85 is the largest whole number that is less than or equal to the number 85.3.

The Math::Sign() Method

You can use the **Math::Sign()** method to determine the sign of a number—in other words, to determine whether the number is a positive number, a negative number, or zero. Figure B-5 shows the syntax of the **Math::Sign()** method and includes examples of using the method in a C++ statement.

Figure B-5: Syntax and examples of the Math::Sign() method

Syntax	Return value
Math::Sign(*x*)	sign of *x*
C++ statement	**Result**
`Console::Write(Math::Sign(53.2));`	the number 1 displayed on the screen
`Console::Write(Math::Sign(-7));`	the number -1 displayed on the screen
`Console::Write(Math::Sign(0));`	the number 0 displayed on the screen

As the statements shown in Figure B-5 indicate, the **Math::Sign()** method returns the number 1 when the specified number is positive, and returns the number –1 when the specified number is negative. When the specified number is zero, the **Math::Sign()** method returns the number 0.

The Math::Round() Method

You can use the **Math::Round() method** to round a numeric value to a specified number of decimal places. Figure B-6 shows the syntax of the **Math::Round()** method and includes examples of using the method in a C++ statement.

Figure B-6: Syntax and examples of the `Math::Round()` method

Syntax	Return value
`Math::Round(x[, y])`	*x* rounded to *y* decimal places
C++ statement	**Result**
`Console::Write(Math::Round(13.64, 1));`	the number 13.6 displayed on the screen
`Console::Write(Math::Round(13.65, 1));`	the number 13.6 displayed on the screen
`Console::Write(Math::Round(13.651, 1));`	the number 13.7 displayed on the screen
`Console::Write(Math::Round(13.66, 1));`	the number 13.7 displayed on the screen
`Console::Write(Math::Round(6.5836, 2));`	the number 6.58 displayed on the screen
`Console::Write(Math::Round(6.5, 0));`	the number 6 displayed on the screen
`Console::Write(Math::Round(6.6));`	the number 7 displayed on the screen

tip

Recall that items in square brackets ([ ]) in a syntax are optional parts of the syntax.

The first four statements shown in Figure B-6 round a number to one decimal place and then display the result on the screen. Notice that the `Math::Round()` method rounds the numbers 13.64 and 13.65 to 13.6; however, it rounds the numbers 13.651 and 13.66 to 13.7.

The fifth statement shown in Figure B-6, `Console::Write(Math::Round(6.5836, 2));`, rounds the number 6.5836 to two decimal places, resulting in the number 6.58, and then displays the result on the screen. The sixth statement, `Console::Write(Math::Round(6.5, 0));`, rounds the number 6.5 to zero decimal places—in other words, it rounds the number to the nearest integer. In this case, the nearest integer is the number 6. The last statement shown in the figure, `Console::Write(Math::Round(6.6));`, also rounds a number to the nearest integer. (Recall that the *y* argument in the method is optional.) The integer nearest to the number 6.6 is the number 7.

MINI-QUIZ

Mini-Quiz 2

1) You use the ______________ method to determine the larger of two numbers.

a. `Math::Largest()`
b. `Math::Max()`
c. `Math::Maximum()`
d. `Math::Ceiling()`

2) The `Math::Sign(12)` method returns ______________.

a. -1
b. 0
c. 1
d. 12

3) The ______________ method returns the number 45.

a. `Math::Ceiling(45.7)`
b. `Math::Ceiling(44.3)`
c. `Math::Floor(44.4)`
d. both b and c

4) Which of the following returns the number 95.68?

a. `Math::Round(95.6751, 2)`
b. `Math::Round(95.684, 2)`
c. `Math::Round(95.68)`
d. both a and b

You now have completed Appendix B. You can either take a break or complete the end-of-lesson questions and exercises.

SUMMARY

The C++ programming language includes a set of built-in methods for performing common mathematical tasks. The `Math::Pow()` method, for example, raises a number to a power, and then returns the result. The `Math::Sqrt()` method, on the other hand, returns the square root of a number. The `Math::Cos()`, `Math::Sin()`, and `Math::Tan()` methods calculate and return the cosine, sine, and tangent of an angle expressed in radians. The `Math::Max()` and `Math::Min()` methods compare two numbers and then return the largest number and smallest number, respectively. The `Math::Ceiling()` method returns the smallest whole number greater than or equal to a specified number, and the `Math::Floor()` method returns the largest whole number less than or equal to a specified number. You can use the `Math::Sign()` method to determine the sign of a number, and the `Math::Round()` method to round a numeric value to a specific number of decimal places. To use these mathematical methods in a program, the program must contain the `#using <mscorlib.dll>` directive, because the definitions of the mathematical methods are contained in the mscorlib.dll file.

ANSWERS TO MINI-QUIZZES

Mini-Quiz 1

1) `answer = Math::Pow(3, 5);`
2) `Console::Write(Math::Sqrt(25));`
3) `Console::Write(Math::Pow(Math::Sqrt(16), 3));`
4) `Console::Write(Math::Pow(number, 2));`
5) `Console::Write(Math::Cos(15 * Math::PI / 180));`
6) `Console::Write(Math::Tan(1.3));`

Mini-Quiz 2

1) b. `Math::Max()`
2) c. 1
3) b. `Math::Ceiling(44.3)`
4) d. both a and b

QUESTIONS

1) To use one of the mathematical methods built into C++, you must include the ________________ directive in your program.
   A. `#include <mscorlib.dll>;`
   B. `#using <msmathlib.dll>;`
   C. `#using <mathlib.dll>`
   D. none of the above
2) Which of the following C++ methods is equivalent to the mathematical expression 5^3?
   A. `Math::Cube(5)`
   B. `Math::Pow(3, 5)`
   C. `Math::Pow(5, 3)`
   D. `Math::Sqrt(5, 3)`
3) Which of the following C++ methods returns the square root of 100?
   A. `Math::Pow(100, 2)`
   B. `Math::Sqroot(100)`
   C. `Math::Sqrt(100, 2)`
   D. `Math::Sqrt(100)`
4) Which of the following C++ statements displays the sine of a 55° angle?
   A. `Console::Write(Math::Sin(55 * Math::PI / 180));`
   B. `Console::Write(Math::Sin(55 / Math::PI * 180));`
   C. `Console::Write(Math::Sine(55 * Math::PI / 180));`
   D. `Console::Write(Math::Sin(55));`

5) Which of the following C++ methods returns the number 5?

A. `Math::Ceiling(4.7)`

B. `Math::Floor(5)`

C. `Math::Min(7, 5)`

D. all of the above

6) The `Math::Sign(-4)` method returns ______________.

A. –1

B. 0

C. 1

D. –4

7) The ______________ method returns the smallest whole number greater than or equal to a specified number.

A. `Math::Ceiling()`

B. `Math::Floor()`

C. `Math::Min()`

D. `Math::Small()`

8) Which of the following C++ methods returns the number 86?

A. `Math::Round(85.99, 0)`

B. `Math::Round(85.99)`

C. `Math::Round(85.99, -2)`

D. both a and b

9) Which of the following C++ methods returns the number 101.65?

A. `Math::Round(101.6554, 2)`

B. `Math::Round(101.6551, 2)`

C. `Math::Round(101.6495, 2)`

D. all of the above

Look For These Symbols

Debugging

Discovery

EXERCISES

1) Write the C++ statement that adds the square of the number stored in the `num1` variable to the square of the number stored in the `num2` variable, and assigns the result to the `total` variable.

2) Write the C++ statement that displays the square root of the number contained in the `number` variable.

3) Write the C++ statement that displays the square root of the sum of $num1^2$ and $num2^2$.

4) Write the C++ statement that assigns to the `answer` variable the result of the following formula: $x^2 * y^3$.

5) Write the C++ statement that assigns to the `rate` variable the result of the following formula: $(future / present)^{1\text{-}term} - 1$.

6) Write the C++ statement that displays the tangent of a 25° angle.

7) Write the C++ statement that displays the cosine of an angle that is .9 radians.

8) Write the C++ statement that compares the values stored in the `northSales` and `southSales` variables to determine which value is the largest, and then displays the result on the screen.

9) Write the C++ statement that displays the largest whole number that is less than or equal to the number stored in the `sales` variable.

10) Write the C++ statement that rounds the contents of the `bonus` variable to two decimal places, and then displays the result on the screen.

11) Assume you plan to deposit $2000 into your savings account at the end of each year for the next 20 years. Your bank is paying 10% interest, compounded annually and paid on the last day of each year. Your task in this exercise is to create a program that computes the value of your account in 20 years. You will need to use the future value formula in the program. The future value formula is (*payment* * ((1 + *rate*)^{term} – 1)) / *rate*, where *payment* is the periodic payment, *rate* is the periodic interest rate, and *term* is the number of periodic payments.

A. If necessary, start Visual Studio .NET. Create a blank solution named AppBE11 Solution. Save the solution in the CppNet\AppB folder.

B. Add a new managed C++ empty project to the solution. Name the project AppBE11 Project.

C. Add a new C++ source file to the project. Name the source file AppBE11.

D. Enter the appropriate C++ instructions into the source file. Allow the user to enter the periodic payment, interest rate, and term (in years). Display the future value, rounded to an integer, on the screen.

E. Save and then build the solution.

F. Execute the program. Use the program to calculate the future value of $2000 deposited at the end of each year for 20 years at a 10% interest rate. The future value should be $114,550.

G. Execute the program again. What is the future value of $5000 deposited at the end of each year for 10 years at a 6% interest rate?

H. When the program is working correctly, close the Output window, and then use the File menu to close the solution.

12) Assume you are considering taking out a $60000 mortgage for 25 years at an 8% interest rate. Your task in this exercise is to create a program that computes your monthly payment on this loan. You can use the following formula to make the appropriate calculation: *principal* * (*rate* / (1 – (*rate* + 1)$^{-term}$)), where *principal* is the loan amount, *rate* is the monthly interest rate, and *term* is the number of monthly payments.

A. If necessary, start Visual Studio .NET. Create a blank solution named AppBE12 Solution. Save the solution in the CppNet\AppB folder.

B. Add a new managed C++ empty project to the solution. Name the project AppBE12 Project.

C. Add a new C++ source file to the project. Name the source file AppBE12.

D. Enter the appropriate C++ instructions into the source file. Allow the user to enter the principal, annual interest rate, and term (in years). Display the monthly payment, rounded to two decimal places, on the screen.

E. Save and then build the solution.

F. Execute the program. Use the program to calculate the monthly payment for a $60,000 mortgage for 25 years at an 8% interest rate. The monthly payment should be $463.09.

G. Execute the program again. What is the monthly payment for a $120,000 mortgage for 30 years at a 9% interest rate?

H. When the program is working correctly, close the Output window, and then use the File menu to close the solution.

13) In this exercise, you create a program that calculates the sine, cosine, and tangent of an angle.

A. If necessary, start Visual Studio .NET. Create a blank solution named AppBE13 Solution. Save the solution in the CppNet\AppB folder.

B. Add a new managed C++ empty project to the solution. Name the project AppBE13 Project.

C. Add a new C++ source file to the project. Name the source file AppBE13.

D. Enter the appropriate C++ instructions into the source file. Allow the user to enter the angle in degrees, then calculate and display the angle's sine, cosine, and tangent. Display the sine, cosine, and tangent, rounded to two decimal places, on the screen.

E. Save and then build the solution.

F. Execute the program. Use the program to calculate the sine, cosine, and tangent of a 45° angle.

G. When the program is working correctly, close the Output window, and then use the File menu to close the solution.

14) Assume you plan to buy a car, but you don't know how much you can afford to spend on it. You will need to finance all but $2000 of the car price. You would like to pay off the car loan in four years, but the most you can afford to pay each month is $360. Currently, interest rates are in the range of 6% to 8%. Your task in this exercise is to create a program that computes the largest amount you can borrow (the principal) using these constraints. You will need to use the present value formula in the program. The present value formula is *payment* * (1 – (*rate* + 1)$^{-term}$) / *rate*, where *payment* is the periodic payment (usually expressed in whole dollars), *rate* is the periodic interest rate, and *term* is the number of periodic payments.

A. If necessary, start Visual Studio .NET. Create a blank solution named AppBE14 Solution. Save the solution in the CppNet\AppB folder.

B. Add a new managed C++ empty project to the solution. Name the project AppBE14 Project.

C. Add a new C++ source file to the project. Name the source file AppBE14.

D. Enter the appropriate C++ instructions into the source file. Store the payment and term values—$360 and 48, respectively—in named constants. Allow the user to enter the annual interest rate. (*Hint*: The program will need to divide the annual interest rate by 12 to get a monthly rate to use in the present value formula.) Display the principal with a dollar sign and zero decimal places.

E. Save and then build the solution.

F. Execute the program. Use the program to calculate the principal using a 6% interest rate. The program should display $15,329.

G. Execute the program again. What is the principal using an 8% interest rate?

H. When the program is working correctly, close the Output window, and then use the File menu to close the solution.

15) In this exercise, you create a program that displays the largest of three numbers entered by the user.

A. If necessary, start Visual Studio .NET. Open the AppBE15 Solution (AppBE15 Solution.sln) file, which is contained in the CppNet\AppB\AppBE15 Solution folder.

B. Modify the program appropriately.

C. Save and then build the solution.

D. Execute the program. Enter 45, 78, and 6 as the three numbers. The program should display the number 78.

E. When the program is working correctly, close the Output window, and then use the File menu to close the solution.

16) Crossville Industries needs a program that allows the shipping clerk to enter the quantity of an item in inventory, and how many units of the item can be packed in a box for shipping. The program should display the number of full boxes that can be packed from the quantity on hand, and how many of the item are left over.

A. If necessary, start Visual Studio .NET. Open the AppBE16 Solution (AppBE16 Solution.sln) file, which is contained in the CppNet\AppB\AppBE16 Solution folder.

B. Modify the program appropriately. Use the `Math::Ceiling()` method to calculate the number of full boxes.

C. Save and then build the solution.

D. Execute the program. Test the program three times using the following data:

45 in inventory, six can be packed in a box

100 in inventory, three can be packed in a box

78 in inventory, five can be packed in a box

E. When the program is working correctly, close the Output window, and then use the File menu to close the solution.

17) In this exercise, you use the `Math::Sign()` method to display only positive numbers.

A. If necessary, start Visual Studio .NET. Open the AppBE17 Solution (AppBE17 Solution.sln) file, which is contained in the CppNet\AppB\AppBE17 Solution folder.

B. Modify the program appropriately.

C. Save and then build the solution.

D. Execute the program. Enter 7 as the number. The program should display the number 7 on the screen.

E. Execute the program again. This time, enter –13 as the number. The program should display the number 13 on the screen.

F. When the program is working correctly, close the Output window, and then use the File menu to close the solution.

18) You have just won a million dollars in the lottery. You can choose either a single lump sum payment of $450,000, or 20 annual payments of $50,000. If you choose the annual payments of $50,000, you can invest the money at a rate of 10%, compounded annually. Your task in this exercise is to create a program that allows you to determine which option is worth more in present dollars—either the lump sum payment or the annuity.

A. If necessary, start Visual Studio .NET. Open the AppBE18 Solution (AppBE18 Solution.sln) file, which is contained in the CppNet\AppB\AppBE18 Solution folder.

B. Enter the appropriate C++ instructions into the source file. You will need to use the present value formula in the program. The present value formula is *payment* * (1 – (*rate* + 1)$^{-term}$) / *rate*, where *payment* is the periodic payment (usually expressed in whole dollars), *rate* is the periodic interest rate, and *term* is the number of periodic payments.

C. Save and then build the solution.

D. Execute the program. How much is the annuity worth in present dollars? Which option is better—the single lump sum or the annuity?

E. When the program is working correctly, close the Output window, and then use the File menu to close the solution.

19) In this exercise, you determine the number of years it takes to double an investment. The formula to calculate this number is log(2) / log(1 + *rate*), where *rate* is the annual rate of interest.

A. If necessary, start Visual Studio .NET. Open the AppBE19 Solution (AppBE19 Solution.sln) file, which is contained in the CppNet\AppB\AppBE19 Solution folder.

B. Enter the appropriate C++ instructions into the source file. You will need to use the C++ `Math::Log()` method, whose syntax is **Math::Log(*number*)**, in the formula. Allow the user to enter the interest rate as a decimal number. Display the number of years rounded to one decimal place.

C. Save and then build the solution.

D. Execute the program. Enter .08 as the interest rate. The number of years displayed on the screen should be 9.0.

E. Execute the program again. How many years will it take to double an investment using a 6% interest rate?

F. When the program is working correctly, close the Output window, and then use the File menu to close the solution.

20) In this exercise, you debug a C++ program.

A. If necessary, start Visual Studio .NET. Open the AppBE20 Solution (AppBE20 Solution.sln) file, which is contained in the CppNet\AppB\AppBE20 Solution folder. The program should calculate and display the square and square root of the number entered by the user, but it is not working correctly. Study the program's code, then build the solution.

B. Correct any errors in the program, then save and build the solution.

C. Execute the program. Use the program to find the square and square root of the number 9.

D. When the program is working correctly, close the Output window, and then use the File menu to close the solution.

Appendix C

Pointers

Using Pointer Variables

As you learned in Tutorial 3, a variable is a location (within the computer's internal memory) where a program can temporarily store data. The data may be entered by the user at the keyboard, or it may be read from a file, or it may be the result of a calculation made by the computer.

A **pointer variable**, referred to simply as a **pointer**, is a special type of variable. Rather than storing a value, a pointer stores the address of an object in the computer's internal memory. Figure C-1 shows examples of statements that create pointers. In each example, the asterisk (*) designates the variable as a pointer.

Figure C-1: Examples of statements that create pointers

Examples and results
Example 1 String *state = "Arizona"; Result creates a pointer named state that contains the address of the string literal constant "Arizona"
Example 2 Rectangle *lawnObj = new Rectangle; Result creates a pointer named lawnObj that contains the address of a Rectangle object
Example 3 IO::StreamWriter *outFile; Result creates a pointer named outFile that contains the address of a StreamWriter object

tip

You learned about String variables in Tutorial 3. You learned how to create a Rectangle object in Tutorial 10's Application lesson. You learned how to create a StreamWriter object in Tutorial 11's Concept lesson.

In the first example shown in Figure C-1, the statement `String *state = "Arizona";` creates a `String` variable named `state`. The `state` variable is a pointer that contains the address of the string literal constant "Arizona".

The `Rectangle *lawnObj = new Rectangle;` statement in Example 2 creates a pointer named `lawnObj` that contains the address of a `Rectangle` object. The `IO::StreamWriter *outFile;` statement in Example 3 creates a pointer named `outFile` that contains the address of a `StreamWriter` object.

When a pointer appears in a C++ statement, the computer uses the address stored in the pointer to locate the appropriate object in memory. For instance, when processing the statement `Console::WriteLine(state);`, the computer uses the address stored in the `state` pointer to locate the literal constant "Arizona" in memory; it then displays the literal constant on the screen. Similarly, when processing the statement `lawnArea = lawnObj->CalcArea() / 9;`, the computer uses the address stored in the `lawnObj` pointer to locate the appropriate `Rectangle` object in memory. It then uses the `Rectangle` object's `CalcArea()` method to calculate the area of the object. The computer divides the area by nine, and then assigns the result to the `lawnArea` variable. Likewise, when processing the statement `outFile->WriteLine("Paris");`, the computer uses the address stored in the `outFile` pointer to locate the appropriate `StreamWriter` object in memory. It then writes the string "Paris" to the sequential access file associated with the `StreamWriter` object.

tip

You learned about the CPU (Central Processing Unit) in the Overview.

Passing the memory address of an object to the CPU, rather than passing the object itself, makes a program more efficient because it allows the CPU to use the object without having to duplicate it in memory.

You now have completed Appendix C.

Appendix D

Displaying a Web Page

Creating an Application That Displays a Web Page

The purpose of this appendix is to show you how you can integrate the Internet Explorer Web browser into a C++ application. The application you create will simply display a Web page in the browser.

To create a C++ application that displays a Web page:

1. Use Windows to create a folder named AppD in the CppNet folder. If necessary, start Visual Studio .NET. Create a blank solution named AppD Solution. Save the solution in the CppNet\AppD folder.
2. Click **File** on the menu bar, point to **Add Project**, and then click **New Project**. The Add New Project dialog box opens.
3. Click **Visual C++ Projects** in the Project Types list box, then click **MFC Application** in the Templates list box.
4. Change the name entered in the Name text box to **AppD Project**, and then click the **OK** button. The MFC Application Wizard – AppD Project dialog box opens.
5. Click **Application Type** in the dialog box to display the Application Type page, and then click the **Single document** radio button. See Figure D-1.

Figure D-1: Application Type page

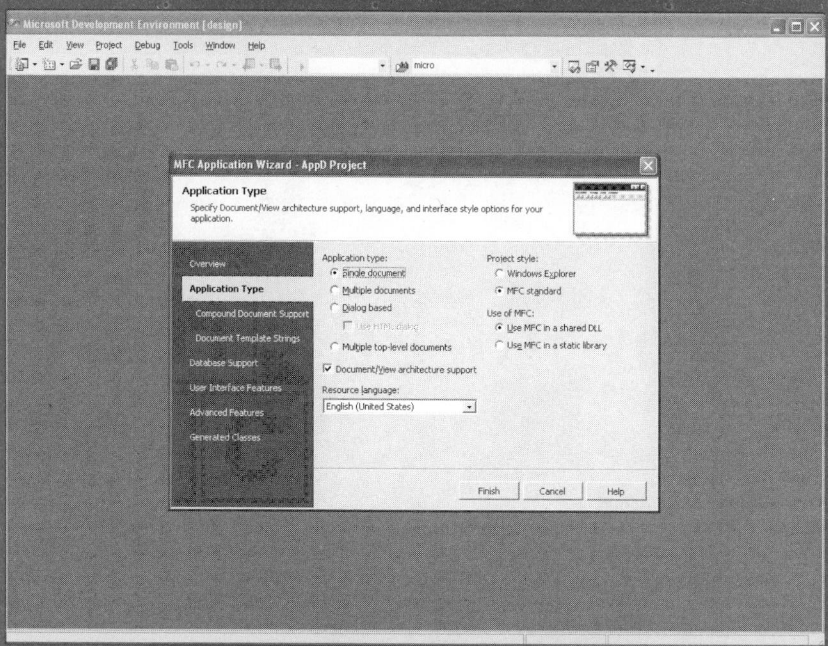

6. Click **User Interface Features** in the dialog box to display the User Interface Features page. If necessary, click the **Standard docking** radio button. Also click the **Browser style** check box to select it. See Figure D-2.

Figure D-2: User Interface Features page

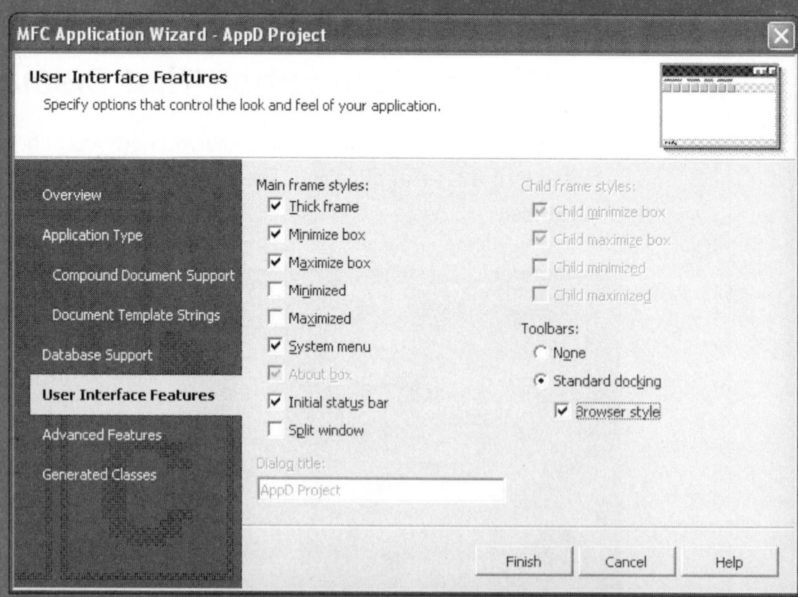

7. Click **Generated Classes** in the dialog box to display the Generated Classes page. Click the **Base class** list arrow, and then click **CHtmlView** in the list. See Figure D-3.

Figure D-3: Generated Classes page

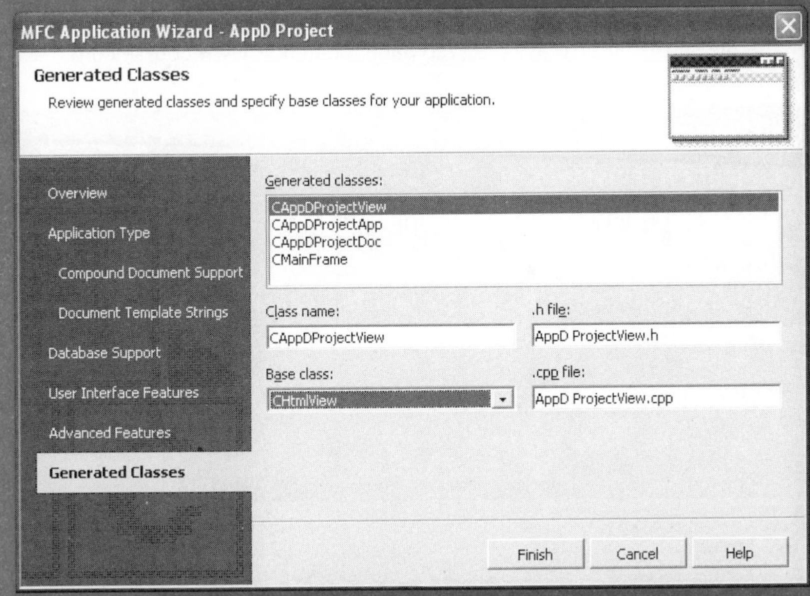

8. Click the **Finish** button. The MFC Application Wizard generates the appropriate files.
9. If necessary, use the View menu to open the Solution Explorer window. If necessary, close the Properties window. See Figure D-4.

Figure D-4: Files generated by the MFC Application Wizard

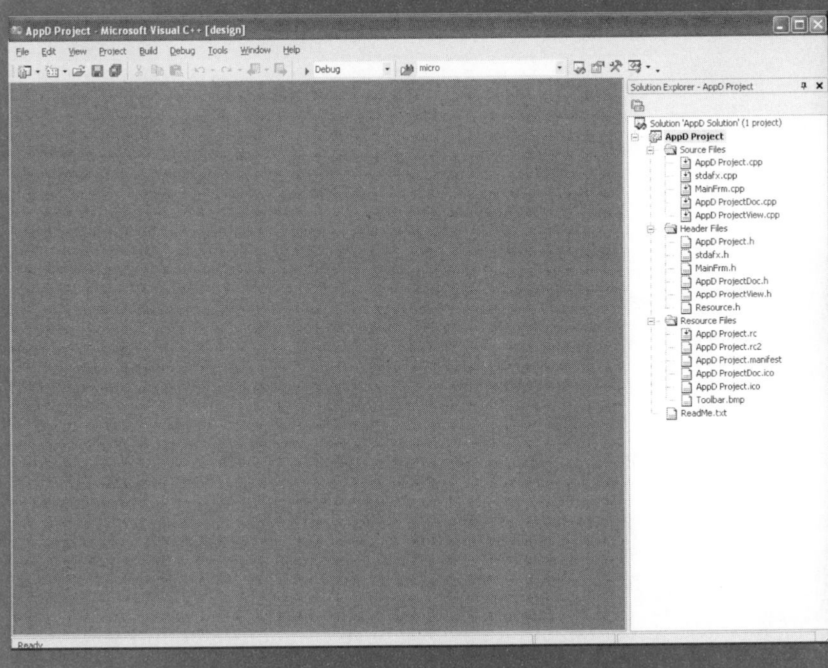

The application created by the MFC Application Wizard will display (in Internet Explorer) the Web page located at www.msdn.microsoft.com/visualc/. You can display a different Web page by modifying the appropriate statement in the AppD ProjectView.cpp file. In the next set of steps, you modify the file so that it displays the Web page located at www.course.com.

To modify the AppD ProjectView.cpp file:

1. Double-click **AppD ProjectView.cpp** in the Source Files folder.
2. Scroll the AppD ProjectView.cpp window until you see the `CAppDProjectView::OnInitialUpdate()` method.
3. Change the URL in the method from http://www.msdn.microsoft.com/visualc/ to **http://www.course.com/**, as shown in Figure D-5.

Figure D-5: Modified URL shown in the `CAppDProjectView::OnInitialUpdate()` method

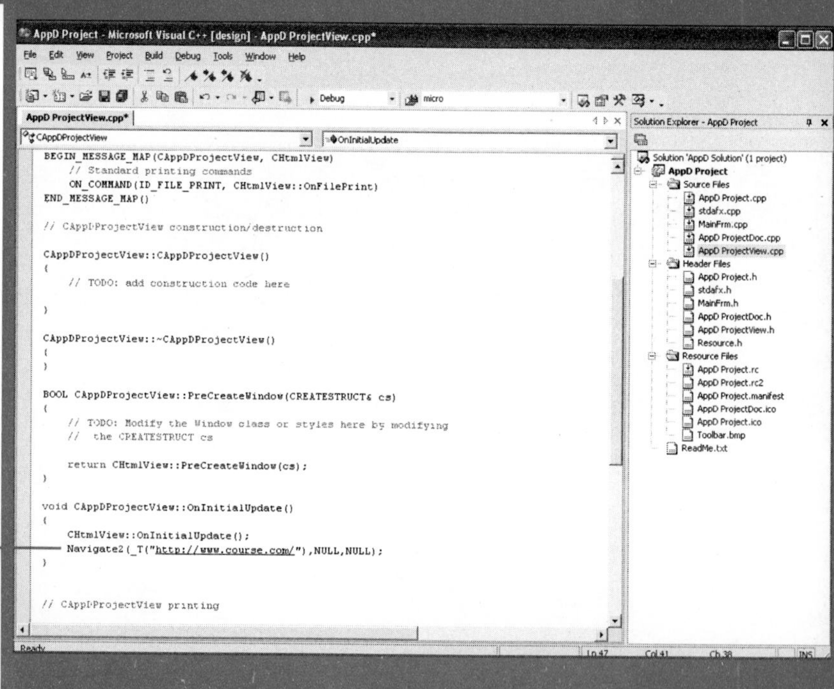

Help? To modify the URL, click to the left of the URL, then use the arrow keys on your keyboard to move the insertion point to the URL.

Now save and build the solution, then run the application.

To save and build the solution, then run the application:

1. Save and then build the solution.
2. Click **Debug** on the menu bar, and then click **Start Without Debugging**. If you are not already connected to the Internet, connect to the Internet now. After a few moments, the Web page located at www.course.com appears in the Internet Explorer window. If necessary, maximize the browser window.

As you know, the content of Web pages changes often. Figure D-6 shows the www.course.com Web page that was current when this book was written. The Web page you are viewing will not be identical to the one shown in Figure D-6.

Figure D-6: Web page located at www.course.com

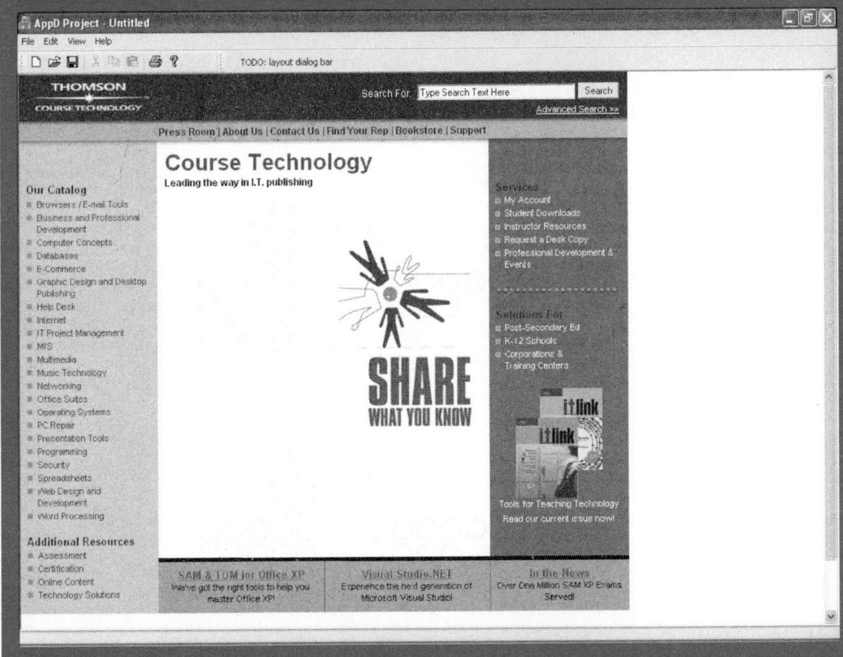

3. Close the browser window.
4. Click **File** on the menu bar, and then click **Close Solution**.
5. Click **File** on the menu bar, and then click **Exit**.

You can modify the application created by the MFC Application Wizard to display an Address box that allows the user to enter a URL in the browser window. You also can modify it to include options that allow the user to navigate to the previous page and to the next page. However, modifications such as these are beyond the scope of this appendix. You now have completed Appendix D.

Index

D

E

F

G

H

I

J

K

L

M

N

O

P

Q

R

S

T

U

V

W

X